R. Gupta's®

POPULAR MASTER GUIDE

SBI

State Bank of India

Clerical Cadre

Junior Associates

(Customer Support & Sales)

Phase-I : Preliminary Exam

by

RPH Editorial Board

2027
EDITION

RAMESH PUBLISHING HOUSE, NEW DELHI

Published by

O.P. Gupta *for* Ramesh Publishing House

Admin. Office

12-H, New Daryaganj Road, Opp. Officers' Mess,
New Delhi-110002 ✆ 23275224, 23245124

E-mail: info@rameshpublishinghouse.com
For Online Shopping: www.rameshpublishinghouse.com

Showroom

- Balaji Market, Nai Sarak, Delhi-110006 ✆ 23282525 📱 9354373464
- 4457, Nai Sarak, Delhi-110006

Book Code: R-1814

ISBN: 978-93-87604-34-6

Price: ₹ 445

Printed at: Deepak Offset, Delhi

CONTENTS

❒❒❒❒❒

SELECTION PROCEDURE

PHASE-I : PRELIMINARY EXAMINATION

Preliminary Exam consisting of Objective Tests for 100 marks will be conducted online. This test would be of 1 hour duration consisting of 3 Sections as follows:

S.No.	Name of Test	No. of Questions	Max. Marks	Duration
1.	English Language	30	30	20 Minutes
2.	Numerical Ability	35	35	20 Minutes
3.	Reasoning Ability	35	35	20 Minutes
	Total	**100**	**100**	**1 Hour**

- Each test will have a separate timing as mentioned above.
- There will be negative marks for wrong answers in the Objective tests. 1/4th of mark assigned for question will be deducted for each wrong answer.
- No minimum qualifying marks are prescribed for individual test OR for aggregate score. Section wise marks will not be maintained.
- Adequate number of candidates in each category as decided by the Bank (approximately 10 times the numbers of vacancies, subject to availability) will be shortlisted for the Main Exam from the list of all candidates arranged in descending order of aggregate marks scored.

State Bank of India (SBI)

CLERICAL CADRE – JUNIOR ASSOCIATES

Phase-I : Preliminary Exam-2025*

(Exam held on 20-09-2025)

ENGLISH LANGUAGE

Directions (Qs. No. 1-5): *The given sentence is divided into four parts: A, B, C, and D. Choose the part that contains an error as your answer. If the sentence is error-free, mark E, i.e., No error as your answer.*

1. She has visited (A)/ more countries in (B)/ a year than (C)/ I have did in my lifetime. (D)/ No error (E)

1. A
2. B
3. C
4. D
5. E

2. Scarcely had they entered (A)/ the building when (B)/ the fire alarm (C)/ started ringing. (D)/ No error (E)

1. A
2. B
3. C
4. D
5. E

3. The teacher, along with (A)/ her students, were waiting (B)/ for the class to (C)/ begin with enthusiasm. (D)/ No error (E)

1. A
2. B
3. C
4. D
5. E

4. Despite of her (A)/ many years of experience, (B)/ she still struggled (C)/ with the new software. (D)/ No error (E)

1. A
2. B
3. C
4. D
5. E

5. The information on (A)/ the website as well as (B)/ in the brochures need to (C)/ be updated immediately. (D)/ No error (E)

1. A
2. B
3. C
4. D
5. E

Directions (Qs. No. 6-13): *Read the given passage carefully to answer the following questions. Each question will have five alternatives as its answer. Choose the correct option as your answer.*

Once upon a time, in the bustling coastal village of Luminara, the sea was the lifeblood of the community. Fishermen set sail each dawn on the azure waters, returning with bountiful catches that sustained their families. Children built sandcastles on the shore, while tourists from far and wide marvelled at the pristine beauty of the beaches. But beneath the shimmering surface, trouble brewed **deep** in the heart of the ocean, as the menace of marine pollution grew day by day. In recent years, the problem of sea pollution had garnered global attention. Streams of polythene and other waste materials had begun to infiltrate the serene waters, causing distress among the marine life and tarnishing the once-immaculate shores of Luminara. The villagers watched in ________ as dead fish and turtles, their stomachs filled with plastic, washed ashore. The impact on their livelihood and the natural beauty of their home was profound, as they feared for the future of their beloved sea. Realising the urgency of the situation, world leaders, activists, and businessmen gathered for an imperative meeting in Rio de Janeiro, Brazil. The International Summit on Marine Pollution drew big people from all corners of the globe, united by a common objective: to combat the escalating crisis of sea pollution. The atmosphere was charged with a blend of anxiety and hope as delegates from over sixty countries convened to share their perspectives and formulate a global strategy. Amelia, a renowned marine biologist and environmental activist from Australia, took to the podium first. Her deep knowledge of marine ecosystems painted a grim picture of the current scenario, detailing how polythene and other pollutants were causing irrevocable

1. 4	**2.** 5	**3.** 2	**4.** 1	**5.** 3

* Based on Memory

damage to marine life. She called for a drastic reduction in plastic production and stronger regulatory frameworks to manage waste disposal.

Following Amelia, Richard Kane, an influential businessman from the United States, shared an innovative **approach** his company had undertaken to tackle the problem. They had developed biodegradable alternatives to conventional plastics and were investing in recycling technologies that showed promising results. Richard emphasised the necessity of public-private collaborations to drive meaningful change, urging his fellow businessmen to contribute to sustainable solutions. Representatives from different countries then provided updates on their national initiatives. India highlighted their recent ban on certain single-use plastics and the aggressive cleanup drives conducted along its extensive coastline. Norway spoke about their success in implementing stringent waste management policies and investing in marine research. Kenya showcased community-led programmes that educated citizens about the dangers of plastic pollution and how to reduce their consumption. The summit concluded with a strong sense of unity and determination. A comprehensive action plan was put forward, emphasising the roles of policy changes, technological advancements, and global cooperation. The representatives pledged to return to their countries with renewed vigour, ready to implement the strategies discussed. Back in Luminara, the villagers felt a glimmer of hope as news of the summit reached them. They understood that change would take time, but knowing that the world was now committed to protecting their precious sea gave them the strength to persevere. With the world finally coming together, there was a deep sense of optimism that the tide of marine pollution could, indeed, be reversed.

6. According to the passage, who was the first speaker at the International Summit on Marine Pollution?
1. Richard Kane
2. A delegate from India
3. Amelia
4. A representative from Norway
5. The President of Brazil

7. Which country highlighted their recent ban on single-use plastics at the International Summit on Marine Pollution?
1. Australia 2. Kenya
3. India 4. Norway
5. Brazil

8. What innovative approach did Richard Kane's company develop to tackle marine pollution?
1. Stringent waste management policies
2. Recycling technologies
3. Biodegradable alternatives to conventional plastics
4. Community-led programmes
5. Cleanup drives along coastlines

9. Which initiative was showcased by Kenya at the summit?
1. Development of biodegradable plastics
2. National ban on single-use plastics
3. Investment in marine research
4. Community-led programs to educate citizens about plastic pollution
5. Stringent waste management policies

10. According to the passage, which of the given statements is correct?
A. The summit concluded with anxiety rather than hope.
B. The villagers of Luminara felt a glimmer of hope after the summit.
C. Amelia is a renowned marine biologist from Brazil.
1. Only A 2. Only B
3. Only C 4. A and B
5. B and C

11. The villagers watched in ________ as dead fish and turtles, their stomachs filled with plastic, washed ashore.
1. curiosity 2. apathy
3. amazement 4. dismay
5. indifference

12. Which of the following words is similar in meaning to "approach" as used in the passage?
1. Retreat 2. Method
3. Avoidance 4. Refusal
5. Deter

13. Which of the following words is the opposite in meaning to "deep" as used in the passage?
1. Shallow 2. Vast
3. Murky 4. Profound
5. Complex

14. Evaluate the following word, accompanied by three sentences containing it. Determine the sentence(s) that accurately convey the meaning of the given word.
Sow
A. In the spring, farmers **sow** seeds in the fields to grow crops.
B. He decided to **sow** his wild oats before settling down.
C. She wanted to **sew** a new dress for the party.
1. Only A 2. Both A & B
3. Only C 4. All A, B & C
5. None of these

6. 3	**7.** 3	**8.** 3	**9.** 4	**10.** 2	**11.** 4	**12.** 2	**13.** 1	**14.** 2

Directions (Qs. No. 15-19): *In the following question, a sentence is given with four words marked as (A), (B), (C), and (D). These words may or may not be placed in the correct order. Four options with different arrangements of these words have been provided. Mark the option with the correct arrangement as the answer. If no rearrangement is required, mark option (5) as your answer.*

15. If the **drought (A)** doesn't end soon, it will **depend (B)** the lives of people who **harm (C)** upon agriculture as their **livelihood (D)**.

1. B-C
2. B-D
3. A-C
4. A-B
5. No change required

16. Even though computers can **calculate (A)** profits and losses very quickly, **bastion (B)** accountants tend to **stick (C)** with the **veteran (D)** of the accounting world, ledgers, and pencils.

1. A-B
2. B-C
3. C-D
4. D-B
5. No change required

17. After the plane **crashed (A)**, each of the **survivors (B)** received free airfare for life as a **suffering (C)** for their **consolation (D)**.

1. A-B
2. C-D
3. B-D
4. C-B
5. No change required

18. The **exhausted (A)** mother asked **experienced (B)** friends and family to **deal (C)** ways to **recommend (D)** with a colicky baby.

1. A-D
2. B-C
3. D-C
4. A-B
5. No change required

19. Without **innovation (A)**, humanity would never gain **prosper (B)** to new technologies to **help (C)** us advance and **access (D)**.

1. A-B
2. B-C
3. C-A
4. D-B
5. No change required

Directions (Qs. No. 20-25): *Select the most appropriate word to fill in the blank.*

20. A peace negotiation has been in _____ for the last 25 years, and the hope is that this would culminate in a lasting settlement.

1. Progress
2. Congress
3. Distress
4. Regress
5. Suppress

21. This year's super-hot summer should be a _____, even if we have not yet learnt from earlier events of extreme temperatures, erratic rainfall, cloudbursts, and cyclones.

1. Entertaining
2. Caning
3. Warning
4. Banning
5. Earning

22. Socialism is a political _____ that continues to cause much ideological and political confusion in India.

1. Legacy
2. Estate
3. Device
4. Capital
5. Fortune

23. The Sanskrit prayer song Sri Venkatesa Suprabhatham is the _____ of most middle-class religious Hindu households of southern India.

1. curability
2. hallmark
3. originality
4. medallion
5. stamp

24. Gopinath is a Brahmin but didn't express any_____ with the portrayal of being anti-caste.

1. emergence
2. manifestation
3. issue
4. development
5. materialising

25. Her first _____ was not to believe any of it, to reject it all.

1. instinct
2. abstain
3. inability
4. attitude
5. distaste

Directions (Qs. No. 26-30): *In the question, six sentences (A), (B), (C), (D), (E) and (F) are given, rearrange these given sentences in a particular sequence to form a meaningful paragraph and answer the questions given.*

(A) "We should extend our visit, father," the young girl insisted, completely enchanted by the rustic charm of the village.

(B) Her father, who had originally planned a brief visit, found himself trying to convince his daughter that it was time to return home.

(C) It had all started when her father mentioned that he was undertaking a trip to the village, invoking in his daughter an enthusiastic wish to accompany him.

(D) He agreed, and they embarked on their village journey together, not realizing the impact it would have on the little girl.

15. 1	**16.** 4	**17.** 2	**18.** 3	**19.** 4	**20.** 1
21. 3	**22.** 1	**23.** 2	**24.** 3	**25.** 1	

(E) Much to her father's surprise, she fell in love with the village at first glance and expressed a desire to spend more time there.

(F) Posing a gentle smile, the father promised his persistent daughter that they would revisit the village, thus finally persuading her to head home.

26. Which of the following is the **FIRST** sentence after rearrangement?

1. A
2. B
3. C
4. D
5. F

27. Which of the following is the **SECOND** sentence after rearrangement?

1. A
2. B
3. C
4. D
5. E

28. Which of the following is the **THIRD** sentence after rearrangement?

1. A
2. C
3. D
4. E
5. B

29. Which of the following is the **FOURTH** sentence after rearrangement?

1. A
2. B
3. C
4. D
5. E

30. Which of the following is the **LAST** sentence after rearrangement?

1. C
2. D
3. E
4. A
5. F

NUMERICAL ABILITY

31. The ratio of the present ages of Gauravi and Gitika is 5 : 3 respectively. If the sum of their ages seven years ago was 66 years, then find the present age of Gitika.

1. 27 years
2. 24 years
3. 36 years
4. 33 years
5. 30 years

32. Raman started business with ₹ 8000 and after 3 months Lakhan joined the business with some amount. After a year, the profit is divided in the ratio 32 : 21. Find the contribution of Lakhan in the business.

1. ₹ 6000
2. ₹ 9000
3. ₹ 7500
4. ₹ 7000
5. ₹ 8500

33. Two cars are running at the speed of 60 km/hr and 35 km/hr respectively and the distance between them is 50 km. Find the time taken by fast car to catch the slow car, if both cars are running in the same direction.

1. 2.5 hours
2. 2 hours
3. 1.5 hours
4. 3 hours
5. 1 hour

Directions (Qs. No. 34-38): *There are two teams X and Y. The bar graph shows the score of two teams in five different years [2019, 2020, 2021, 2022 and 2023]*

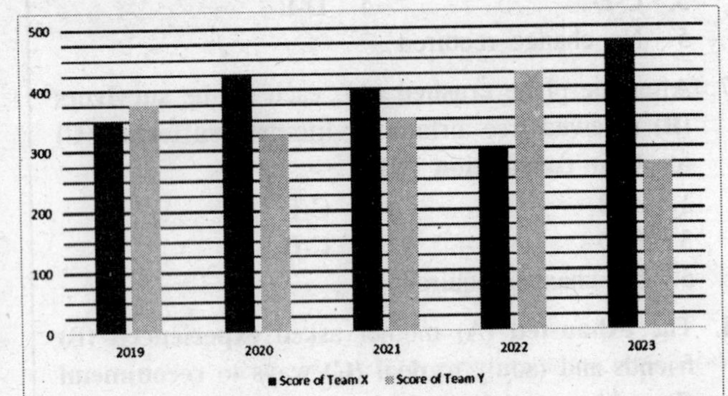

34. Find the ratio of the combined score of Team X (2020 + 2021) to the combined score of Team Y (2020 + 2021)?

1. 6 :
2. 5 2
3. 4 : 5
4. 11 9
5. 12 : 7

35. Find the difference between Team Y's score and Team X's score in 2022 and 2023 together?

1. 72
2. 77
3. 75
4. 25
5. 76

36. What percentage of the total combined score (Team X + Team Y) for 2021 was contributed by Team X.

1. 55%
2. 53.33%
3. 66%
4. 22%
5. 33.33

26. 3	**27.** 4	**28.** 4	**29.** 1	**30.** 5	**31.** 5
32. 4	**33.** 2	**34.** 4	**35.** 3	**36.** 2	

37. What percentage Team Y's score in 2019 was greater than Team X's score?

1. 7.14%   2. 12.5%
3. 22.5%   4. 20%
5. 6%

38. Suppose that in 2024 Team X's score increases by 20% over its 2023 score, while Team Y's score decreases by 10% compared to its 2021 score. Find the difference between score of team X and Y in 2024?

1. 245   2. 255
3. 355   4. 455
5. 625

39. The average marks of A, B and C is 45 while the average marks of B, C and D is 40. If the sum of marks of A and D is 75, find the marks A got in the examination.

1. 45 marks   2. 30 marks
3. 40 marks   4. 35 marks
5. 50 marks

40. A and B together can do a piece of work in 18 days, B and C in 24 days, and A and C in 36 days. The number of days, all of them working together take to complete the work, is:

1. 18   2. 16
3. 17   4. 15
5. 20

41. A container contains a mixture of water and milk in the ratio 3 : 2. When 5 liters of mixture is removed and replaced by pure milk then the ratio becomes 1 : 2. Find the initial quantity of milk in the container.

1. 4.5 liters
2. 3.5 liters
3. 6.25 liters
4. 5.25 liters
5. 2.25 liters

Directions (Qs. No. 42-46): *What will come in place of question mark '?' in the following question?*

42. 987 + 23% of 1500 = ? + 21% of 700

1. 1275   2. 1180
3. 1185   4. 1075
5. 1285

43. 271 + 85 × 3 − 122 = ? + 36 × 9

1. 102   2. 120
3. 162   4. 150
5. 80

44. $3 - [19 + \{14 - (16 - 3 - 21)\}] = ?$

1. −41   2. −38
3. 38   4. 40
5. −40

45. $(42 - 23) \times 6 - 5 \times (4^2 + 5) = ?$

1. 2   2. 5
3. 10   4. 0
5. 9

46. $599 - 339 + 459 - 319 = ?^2$

1. 30   2. 20
3. 900   4. 400
5. 25

47. Find the value of $3^{-2} \times 27^{2/3} \div (729)^{-1/3}$

1. 9   2. 18
3. 8   4. 6
5. 15

Directions (Qs. No. 48-53): *What will come in the place of the question mark '?' in the following question?*

48. $[90 \div 6 \times (24 - 8 \div 4) \div 3] - 90 \div 5 + 34 = ?$

1. 181   2. 154
3. 135   4. 126
5. 142

49. 2487 + 4876 − 5645 + 222 = ?

1. 1940   2. 2160
3. 2040   4. 1870
5. 1904

50. $(27)^2 - (13)^2 + (12)^3 + (23)^2 = ?$

1. 2817   2. 2957
3. 2500   4. 2653
5. 2845

51. $[(-251) \times 21 \times (-12)] \div ? = 63$

1. 2501
2. 1004
3. 3005
4. 1503
5. 1808

52. $(36 + ? + 121)^{1/2} + 26 = 39$

1. 10   2. 11
3. 12   4. 13
5. 14

53. $[(130)^2 \div 25 \times 15] \div 30 = ?$

1. 352   2. 314
3. 326   4. 338
5. 426

37. 1	**38.** 2	**39.** 1	**40.** 2	**41.** 1	**42.** 3	**43.** 5	**44.** 2	**45.** 5
46. 2	**47.** 1	**48.** 4	**49.** 1	**50.** 1	**51.** 2	**52.** 3	**53.** 4	

Directions (Qs. No. 54-56): *Read the data carefully and answer the questions given below.*

There are 3 individuals A, B and C. Salary of A is ₹ 10,000. He spent 10% of his salary. B's salary is ₹ 2000 more than A's salary. Saving of C is ₹ 3000 which is (1/3)rd of his salary. B's saving is the difference of A's and C's saving

54. If the income of A is increased by 20%, then find his saving, if expenses remained the same.
1. ₹ 11,000 2. ₹ 12,000
3. ₹ 13,000 4. ₹ 14,000
5. ₹ 15,000

55. Expenses of C is what per cent of his saving?
1. 150% 2. 30%
3. 300% 4. 200%
5. 20%

56. Saving of B is what per cent of B's income?
1. 20% 2. 30%
3. 40% 4. 50%
5. 10%

57. Find the time in which ₹ 25000 will become ₹ 51840 at 20% per annum compound interest.
1. 5 years 2. 6 years
3. 4 years 4. 3 years
5. 2 years

58. Speed of a boat in still water and speed of current is in ratio 9 : 2. If the difference between distance covered by boat in 2 hours upstream and in 5 hours downstream is 123 km. Speed of boat in still water?
1. 18 2. 24
3. 21 4. 27
5. None of these

59. A man sells 20 bananas at ₹ 600, there is loss equal to cost price of 5 bananas. Find the cost price of a banana.
1. ₹ 40 2. ₹ 45
3. ₹ 35 4. ₹ 30
5. ₹ 60

60. Buses start from a bus terminal with a speed of 40 km/hr at intervals of 20 minutes. What is the speed of a man coming from the opposite direction towards the bus terminal if he meets the bus at intervals of 16 minutes?
1. 12 km/hr 2. 5 km/hr
3. 10 km/hr 4. 20 km/hr
5. 15 km/hr

Directions (Qs. No. 61-65): *The given table shows the total number of books [Fiction + Non-fiction] and number of fictions books sold in five different months [January, February, March, April and May]*

Month	Total number of books sold [Fiction + Non-Fiction]	Number of fiction Books sold
January	175	85
February	280	120
March	225	115
April	320	180
May	260	150

61. Find the ratio of total books sold in February and April together to the total books sold in March and May together?
1. 12 : 17
2. 118 : 129
3. 121 : 123
4. 120 : 97
5. 11 : 17

62. What is the difference between the number of fiction books sold in April and January?
1. 55 2. 95
3. 74 4. 85
5. 35

63. By what percentage is the number of Non-Fiction books sold in February more than that in March?
1. 55%
2. 62.5%
3. 45.5%
4. 36.5%
5. 37.5%

64. The number of Non-Fiction books sold in April what per cent more or less than that in February?
1. 22.5% 2. 62.5%
3. 10% 4. 27.5%
5. 12.5%

65. In June, the total books sold were 300, out of which 40% were Fiction books. Find the difference between number of Non-Fiction books sold in June and Non-Fiction books sold in May?
1. 55 2. 70
3. 75 4. 36
5. 35

54. 1	**55.** 4	**56.** 4	**57.** 3	**58.** 4	**59.** 1
60. 3	**61.** 4	**62.** 2	**63.** 3	**64.** 5	**65.** 2

REASONING ABILITY

Directions (Qs. No. 66-70): *Read the following information carefully and answer the questions based on given information.*

Eight persons A, B, C, D, E, F, G and H live on an eight storey apartment but not necessarily in same order. The bottom most floor is floor 1 just above floor 1 is floor 2 and so on up to floor 8 which is the top most floor. A lives two floors above C. Three persons live between E and F. H lives below the floor of C. One person lives between B and G. F lives on the odd number floor below the fifth floor. G lives just below the floor of E. No two persons whose names start with consecutive letters live adjacent floors.

66. Who among the following person lives two floors above the floor of D?

1. B 2. G
3. E 4. F
5. No one

67. On which floor does A lives?

1. 6th floor 2. 5th floor
3. 3rd floor 4. 4th floor
5. 8th floor

68. Which of the following statement(s) is/are correct?

1. B lives on seventh floor
2. Only one person lives between A and H
3. G lives just below the floor of D
4. H lives on second floor
5. None of these

69. How many persons live between E and A?

1. As many persons live between G and B
2. As many persons live below the floor of F
3. As many persons live above the floor of B
4. As many persons lives above the floor of D

70. Which of the following statement(s) is/are not correct?

A. No lives above B
B. E lives just above the floor of B
C. D and B lives on adjacent floors

1. Only A 2. Only B
3. Only C 4. Both A and B
5. Both B and C

Directions (Qs. No. 71-73): *In the following question assuming the given statements to be true, find which of the conclusion among given conclusions is/are definitely true and then give your answers accordingly.*

71. Statements : $M > C < D = R \leq E < A \geq V > Y$

Conclusions : I. $R < A$ II. $M < E$ III. $D \leq E$

1. Only III is True
2. Both conclusions I and III are True
3. Only II is True
4. Both conclusions I and II are True
5. None is True

72. Statements : $A \geq B > C$; $C \leq D \leq E < F$

Conclusions : I. $A \geq E$ II. $C < F$

1. Only I is True
2. Only II is True
3. Either I or II is true
4. Both conclusions I and II are True
5. None is True

73. Statements : $C \geq F$; $B < C > D < H = I$

Conclusions : I. $I > F$ II. $H > C$

1. Either conclusion I or II is true
2. Only conclusion II is true
3. Only conclusion I is true
4. Both conclusions I and II are true
5. None of the conclusions is true

Directions (Qs. No. 74-78): *Read the following information carefully and answer the questions based on given information.*

Eight persons B, F, H, K, O, R, V and X purchased a gift one after another but not necessarily in same order. At least three persons purchased gift between K and X. O purchased a gift two persons before H. Three persons purchased gift between V and F. K purchased gift before X and neither of them is the first or last person. Only two persons purchased gift between V and O who purchased gift after V. H purchased gift before B. R does not purchase a gift adjacent to X and V.

74. Who among the following person is the first person who purchased a gift?

1. R 2. V
3. O 4. H
5. F

75. How many persons purchased gift between R and F?

1. Three 2. One
3. Two 4. None
5. More than three

66. 3	67. 4	68. 5	69. 2	70. 5	71. 2	72. 2	73. 5	74. 2	75. 2

76. Which of the following statement(s) is/are incorrect?
1. B is the last person who purchased a gift
2. H purchased a gift just before X
3. K purchased a gift just after V
4. More than three persons purchased gift after H
5. None of these

77. As many persons purchased gift before O as many persons after whom?
1. F 2. R
3. X 4. B
5. H

78. Which of the following statement(s) is/are correct regarding R?
A. As many persons purchased gift before R as many persons after H.
B. O purchased gift just after R.
C. F purchased gift before R.
1. Only B 2. Only C
3. Both A and B 4. Only A
5. Both B and C

79. If in a certain code language, SECOND is coded as QLFUCE, then how the word PAUSED would be coded in that language?
1. UCFRYW 2. QBVTFE
3. UCSYW 4. QBVUFE
5. QBSTFE

Directions (Qs. No. 80-84): *Read the information and answer the given questions.*

Eight persons, namely, S, T, U, V, W, X, Y, and Z, have their visits on different dates, either on the 7th or the 20th of the months January, March, May, and September, but not necessarily in the same order. Exactly three people have their visits between X's visit and V's visit. Y's visit takes place immediately before X's visit, and X's visit is on 7th March. U's visit is scheduled immediately after W's visit. T's visit is in a month that has 31 days. Z's visit is scheduled after S's visit. There are more than two people whose visits fall between T's visit and S's visit. Not more than two people visit between T and Z.

80. Who among the following person has a visit immediately before W's visit?
1. Y
2. The one whose visit is on 20th May
3. V
4. The one whose visit is on 7th March
5. S

81. Z has a visit on which date?
1. 20th May 2. 20th September
3. 20th March 4. 7th May
5. 7th September

82. How many persons have a visit between Z and W?
1. Two 2. Three
3. Four 4. One
5. None

83. Find the odd one out.
1. S 2. X
3. U 4. Z
5. T

84. How many persons have visit before T's visit?
1. Three 2. Four
3. Five 4. Two
5. More than five

Directions (Qs. No. 85-88): *In the question below are given two statements followed by three conclusions numbered I, II and III. You have to take the given statements to be true even if they seem to be at variance with commonly known facts. Read all the conclusions and then decide which of the given conclusions logically follows from the given statements disregarding commonly known facts.*

85. Statements : Only few pen are pencils.
No pencil is eraser.

Conclusions : I. No pen is eraser.
II. Some erasers are pencil.
III. All pen being pencils is a possibility.

1. None follows 2. Either I or II follows
3. Only III follows 4. Only I follows
5. Both I and II follow

86. Statements : Some lemons are fruits.
Only fruits are orange.

Conclusions : I. Some lemons are orange.
II. All lemons being fruits is a possibility.
III. Some fruits are lemons.

1. None follows 2. Either I or III follows
3. Only III follows 4. Only I follows
5. Both II and III follow

87. Statements : Some mobiles are charger.
All chargers are laptop.

Conclusions : I. No laptop is charger.
II. Some mobiles are laptop.

1. None follows 2. Either I or II follows
3. Only II follows 4. Only I follows
5. Both I and II follow

76. 4 **77.** 1 **78.** 3 **79.** 1 **80.** 4 **81.** 2 **82.** 2 **83.** 4 **84.** 3 **85.** 1 **86.** 5 **87.** 3

88. Statements : Some sweets are pens.
All pens are clocks.

Conclusions : I. Some clocks are sweets.
II. All sweets are clocks.

1. Only I follows 2. Only II follows
3. Either I or II follows 4. Neither I nor II follows
5. Both I and II follow

Directions (Qs. No. 89-91): *Read the information and answer the given questions.*

A certain number of persons are standing in a straight line, all facing north. There is only one person between R and K. R is positioned at one end of the row. The number of individuals between M and T is the same as that between K and M. Exactly six persons are standing between K and J. J is placed third from one of the ends. P stands fifth to the right of M. There are more than six people standing between R and T. T doesn't stand immediately left of P. Not more than five people stand between J and P.

89. How many persons are sitting in a row?
1. 10 2. 11 3. 12 4. 13 5. 14

90. What is the position of M with respect to J?
1. Third to the left 2. Second to the right
3. Fourth to the left 4. Sixth to the right
5. Immediately left

91. Who among the following is standing immediately right of J?
1. K 2. R 3. P 4. M 5. T

92. How many letters remain unchanged after arranging the letters in ascending order of a given word "IMPACTFUL"?
1. One 2. Two
3. Three 4. None
5. More than three

Directions (Qs. No. 93-97): *The following questions are based on the five three-letter words given below.*

NFG UIZ KGH LTZ OPF

93. If the first letter of all the words is changed to its previous letter of the English alphabetical series, then how many words will have more than two consonants? (Same or different consonant)
1. One 2. Zero
3. Three 4. Two
5. Four

94. If all the letters in each of the words are arranged alphabetically (within the word), how many words will remain unchanged?
1. Two 2. Zero
3. Three 4. One
5. Four

95. If the first and second letter of each word is changed to its next letter according to the alphabetical series, then how many words are there which contains **one or more than one vowels?**
1. Three 2. One
3. Two 4. Four
5. Zero

96. If each vowel of each word is changed to its previous letter according to the alphabetical series, then how many meaningful words will be formed?
1. Two 2. Zero
3. Three 4. One
5. Four

97. If words are arranged according to the alphabetical series from left to right, then which is second from the left end?
1. LTZ 2. NFG
3. OPF 4. KGH
5. UIZ

Directions (Qs. No. 98-100): *Study the information given below carefully and answer the questions that follow.*

Rashmi planned a treasure hunt for her sister Riya. According to the directions given to her, Riya starts from the position O. She walks 10 m to the east and finds first clue A. Then she takes a right turn and walks 5 m where she gets clue B. Then she takes another right turn and walks 5 m to find clue C. Then she turns left and walks 3 m to reach a point where clue D is kept. She finally takes a left turn and walks 10 m to reach the point where the treasure is kept.

98. What is the shortest distance between clue A and clue C?
1. $5\sqrt{2}$ m 2. 5 m
3. 10 m 4. 2 m
5. $10\sqrt{2}$ m

99. In which direction is the starting point with respect to the end point of the treasure hunt?
1. North-east 2. North-west
3. South-east 4. South-west
5. North

100. How far and in which direction is clue B from clue D?
1. $\sqrt{34}$ m, North 2. $\sqrt{34}$ m, North-east
3. $\sqrt{34}$ m, South-east 4. $\sqrt{34}$ m, South-west
5. $\sqrt{34}$ m, South

88. 1	**89.** 3	**90.** 3	**91.** 3	**92.** 4	**93.** 5	**94.** 4
95. 3	**96.** 2	**97.** 1	**98.** 1	**99.** 2	**100.** 2	

EXPLANATORY ANSWERS

1. The error lies in part D because the present perfect tense requires "have" followed by the past participle form of the verb. The past participle of "do" is "done", whereas "did" is its simple past form. Therefore, the correct expression is "I have done in my lifetime".

2. The sentence correctly follows the structure "Scarcely had + subject + past participle + when + simple past". The inverted form "Scarcely had they entered" is grammatically correct, and "when" is the appropriate conjunction used with "scarcely". Therefore, the sentence is completely error-free.

3. The main subject of the sentence is the singular noun "teacher", while the phrase "along with her students" does not affect the number of the subject. Therefore, the singular verb "was" must be used instead of the plural verb "were". The correct expression is "The teacher, along with her students, was waiting".

4. "Despite" is a preposition and is used directly before a noun or noun phrase without the preposition "of". Therefore, "despite of her" is grammatically incorrect and should be replaced with "despite her". Alternatively, the expression "in spite of her" would also be correct.

5. The subject of the sentence is the uncountable singular noun "information", and the phrase introduced by "as well as" does not make the subject plural. Therefore, the singular verb "needs" must be used instead of "need". The correct expression is "The information on the website as well as in the brochures needs to be updated immediately".

6. Amelia was the first person to address the International Summit on Marine Pollution. The passage explicitly states that she took to the podium first and described the severe damage caused by polythene and other pollutants. She also called for reduced plastic production and stronger waste-disposal regulations.

7. India highlighted its recent ban on certain single-use plastics during the International Summit on Marine Pollution. It also informed the delegates about the aggressive cleanup drives conducted along the country's extensive coastline. These initiatives formed part of India's efforts to control marine pollution.

8. Richard Kane stated that his company had developed biodegradable alternatives to conventional plastics. These alternatives were intended to reduce the accumulation of persistent plastic waste in the oceans. His company was also investing in recycling technologies, but the specifically developed innovation was biodegradable plastic alternatives.

9. Kenya showcased community-led programmes aimed at educating citizens about the dangers of plastic pollution. These programmes also taught people how to reduce their consumption of plastic materials. The initiative emphasised public awareness and community participation in controlling marine pollution.

10. Statement B is correct because the villagers of Luminara felt a glimmer of hope after receiving news of the summit. Statement A is incorrect because the summit concluded with unity and determination, not anxiety rather than hope. Statement C is also incorrect because Amelia was a marine biologist and environmental activist from Australia, not Brazil.

11. "Dismay" means a feeling of distress, shock or great disappointment caused by an unpleasant event. The sight of dead fish and turtles with plastic-filled stomachs washing ashore would naturally cause sorrow and alarm among the villagers. Therefore, "dismay" fits the emotional context of the sentence perfectly.

12. In the passage, "approach" refers to the particular method adopted by Richard Kane's company to tackle marine pollution. The company developed biodegradable alternatives and invested in recycling technologies as ways of addressing the problem. Therefore, "method" is the word most similar in meaning to "approach" in this context.

13. The word "deep" is used in the expression "a deep sense of optimism", where it means intense, profound or strongly felt. "Shallow" conveys the opposite sense because it refers to something lacking depth or intensity. Therefore, "shallow" is the correct antonym of "deep" as used in the passage.

14. Sentence A correctly uses "sow" to mean planting seeds in the soil so that crops may grow. Sentence B also uses it correctly in the idiomatic expression "sow one's wild oats", meaning to behave adventurously or irresponsibly during youth. Sentence C uses "sew", meaning to join fabric with stitches, which is a different word despite having a similar pronunciation.

15. The words "depend" and "harm" must exchange their positions to make the sentence grammatically and logically correct. The corrected sentence is: "If the drought doesn't end soon, it will harm the lives of people who depend upon agriculture as their livelihood". A drought harms people, while people depend upon agriculture for their livelihood.

16. The words "veteran" and "bastion" must be interchanged because "veteran accountants" correctly refers to experienced accountants, while "bastion of the accounting world" refers to a traditional stronghold of accounting practices. The corrected sentence states that veteran accountants tend to stick with the bastion of the accounting world—ledgers and pencils. This arrangement gives both words their appropriate grammatical and contextual positions.

17. The words "suffering" and "consolation" must exchange their positions to form the meaningful expression "as a consolation for their suffering". "Consolation" refers to something given to comfort a person after pain or loss, whereas "suffering" refers to the hardship experienced by the survivors. The corrected sentence is: "After the plane crashed, each of the survivors received free airfare for life as a consolation for their suffering".

18. The words "recommend" and "deal" must be interchanged so that the sentence reads "asked experienced friends and family to recommend ways to deal with a colicky baby". The verb "recommend" correctly precedes "ways", while the expression "deal with" means to manage or handle a difficult situation. Therefore, exchanging D and C produces the correct grammatical and logical arrangement.

19. The words "access" and "prosper" must exchange their positions to produce the correct expressions "gain access to" and "advance and prosper". The corrected sentence is: "Without innovation, humanity would never gain access to new technologies to help us advance and prosper". One gains access to technologies, and those technologies help humanity advance and prosper.

20. The fixed expression "in progress" means that an activity or process has begun and is continuing. The sentence states that peace negotiations have continued for the last twenty-five years with the hope of reaching a permanent settlement. Therefore, "progress" is the only word that fits both grammatically and contextually.

21. The unusually hot summer is presented as a sign alerting people to the dangers of extreme climatic events. Earlier incidents involving erratic rainfall, cloudbursts and cyclones should already have made people aware of this threat. Therefore, "warning" appropriately conveys a caution about the serious consequences of climate change.

22. A "legacy" is something inherited from the past that continues to influence the present. In the sentence, socialism is described as a political inheritance that still creates ideological and political confusion in India. The other options do not convey the idea of a continuing influence inherited from an earlier period.

23. A "hallmark" is a distinctive or characteristic feature by which something is commonly recognised. The prayer song *Sri Venkatesa Suprabhatham* is presented as a familiar and defining feature of many middle-class religious Hindu households in southern India. Therefore, "hallmark" fits the intended meaning most precisely.

24. The expression "express any issue with" means to show an objection, concern or disagreement regarding something. The sentence indicates that Gopinath did not object to or express concern about the anti-caste portrayal despite being a Brahmin. Therefore, "issue" is the only option that produces a meaningful and grammatically acceptable sentence.

25. "Instinct" refers to an immediate and natural reaction that occurs without deliberate thought. Her first spontaneous response was to disbelieve and reject everything she had heard. Therefore, "instinct" correctly describes her initial reaction, whereas the other options do not fit the grammatical structure or intended meaning.

26. Sentence C is the first sentence because it introduces the beginning of the entire incident by explaining how the village trip was first proposed. The phrase "It had all started" clearly signals the opening of the narrative. It also introduces both the father's planned journey and the daughter's wish to accompany him.

27. Sentence D follows sentence C because "He agreed" directly refers to the father accepting his daughter's request to accompany him. It then describes the beginning of their journey to the village. Thus, it naturally continues the event introduced in the first sentence and forms the second sentence of the paragraph.

28. Sentence E is the third sentence because it describes the daughter's reaction after arriving in the village. The phrase "Much to her father's surprise" logically follows their journey and explains that she immediately became attracted to village life. Her desire to stay longer also prepares the ground for the later disagreement about returning home.

29. Sentence A is the fourth sentence because it directly continues the daughter's desire to spend more time in the village mentioned in sentence E. Her statement, "We should extend our visit, father", expresses that desire as a direct request. Sentence B follows afterward because the father then tries to persuade her that it is time to return home.

30. Sentence F is the concluding sentence because it resolves the disagreement between the father and daughter. The father promises that they will visit the village again, and this assurance finally persuades her to return home. It provides a complete and satisfactory ending to the sequence of events.

31. Present ages of Gauravi and Gitika = $5x$ and $3x$

$$(5x - 7) + (3x - 7) = 66$$
$$8x - 14 = 66$$
$$8x = 80 \Rightarrow x = 10$$

Present age of Gitika = $3x = 3 \times 10 = 30$ years.

32. Raman's investment ratio = 8000×12

Lakhan's investment ratio = $x \times 9$

$$8000 \times 12 : 9x = 32 : 21$$
$$96000 \times 21 = 32 \times 9x$$
$$x = \frac{96000 \times 21}{32 \times 9} = ₹\ 7000.$$

33. Relative speed = $60 - 35 = 25$ km/hr

$$\text{Time taken} = \frac{\text{Distance}}{\text{Relative Speed}}$$
$$= \frac{50}{25} = 2 \text{ hours.}$$

For Qs. No. 34–38.

- Team X scores:

2019 = 350,
2020 = 425,
2021 = 400,
2022 = 300,
2023 = 475

- Team Y scores:

2019 = 375,
2020 = 325,
2021 = 350,
2022 = 425,
2023 = 275

34. Team X's combined score = 425 + 400 = 825

Team Y's combined score = 325 + 350 = 675

Required ratio = 825 : 675 = 11 : 9.

35. Team X's total score = 300 + 475 = 775

Team Y's total score = 425 + 275 = 700

Required difference = 775 − 700 = 75.

36. Total combined score in 2021 = 400 + 350 = 750

$$\text{Required percentage} = \frac{400}{750}\times 100$$

$$= 53.33\%.$$

37. Difference in scores = 375 − 350 = 25

$$\text{Required percentage} = \frac{25}{350}\times 100$$

$$= 7.14\%.$$

38. $\text{Team X's score in 2024} = 475\times\frac{120}{100} = 570$

$\text{Team Y's score in 2024} = 350\times\frac{90}{100} = 315$

Required difference = 570 − 315 = 255.

39.

$$A + B + C = 45 \times 3 = 135$$
$$B + C + D = 40 \times 3 = 120$$
$$A - D = 135 - 120 = 15$$
$$A + D = 75$$
$$2A = 90$$
$$A = 45 \text{ marks.}$$

40.

$$A + B = \frac{1}{18}$$
$$B + C = \frac{1}{24}$$
$$A + C = \frac{1}{36}$$
$$2(A + B + C) = \frac{1}{18}+\frac{1}{24}+\frac{1}{36}$$
$$= \frac{4}{72}+\frac{3}{72}+\frac{2}{72}$$
$$= \frac{9}{72}=\frac{1}{8}$$
$$A + B + C = \frac{1}{16}$$

Required time = 16 days.

41. Let the initial quantity of mixture = x litres.

$$\text{Initial water} = \frac{3x}{5},$$

$$\text{Initial milk} = \frac{2x}{5}$$

Water removed in 5 litres = 3 litres;

milk removed = 2 litres

$$\text{New water} = \frac{3x}{5} - 3$$

$$\text{New milk} = \frac{2x}{5} - 2 + 5 = \frac{2x}{5} + 3$$

$$\frac{\left(\frac{3x}{5} - 3\right)}{\left(\frac{2x}{5} + 3\right)} = \frac{1}{2}$$

$$\frac{6x}{5} - 6 = \frac{2x}{5} + 3$$

$$\frac{4x}{5} = 9$$

$$\Rightarrow \quad x = 11.25 \text{ litres}$$

$$\text{Initial milk} = \frac{2}{5}\times 11.25 = 4.5 \text{ litres.}$$

42. 987 + 23% of 1500 = ? + 21% of 700

987 + 345 = ? + 147

? = 1332 − 147

? = 1185.

43. 271 + 85 × 3 − 122 = ? + 36 × 9

271 + 255 − 122 = ? + 324

404 = ? + 324

? = 80.

44. 3 − [19 + {14 − (16 − 3 − 21)}]

= 3 − [19 + {14 − (−8)}]

= 3 − [19 + 22]

= 3 − 41 = −38.

45. $(42 - 23) \times 6 - 5 \times (4^2 + 5)$

= 19 × 6 − 5 × (16 + 5)

= 114 − 105 = 9.

46. $599 - 339 + 459 - 319 = ?^2$

$$260 + 140 = ?^2$$
$$400 = ?^2$$
$$? = \sqrt{400} = 20.$$

47. $3^{-2} \times 27^{2/3} \div 729^{-1/3}$

$$= \left(\frac{1}{9}\right)\times\left(\sqrt[3]{27}\right)^2 \div \frac{1}{\sqrt[3]{729}}$$

$$= \left(\frac{1}{9}\right)\times 9 \div \left(\frac{1}{9}\right) = 9.$$

48. $[90 \div 6 \times (24 - 8 \div 4) \div 3] - 90 \div 5 + 34$

$= [15 \times (24 - 2) \div 3] - 18 + 34$

$= 15 \times 22 \div 3 - 18 + 34$

$= 110 - 18 + 34 = 126.$

49. $2487 + 4876 - 5645 + 222$

$= 7363 - 5645 + 222$

$= 1718 + 222$

$= 1940.$

50. $(27)^2 - (13)^2 + (12)^3 + (23)^2$

$= 729 - 169 + 1728 + 529$

$= 560 + 1728 + 529$

$= 2817.$

51. $[(-251) \times 21 \times (-12)] \div ? = 63$

$63252 \div ? = 63$

$? = 63252 \div 63$

$? = 1004.$

52. $\sqrt{(36+?+121)} + 26 = 39$

$\sqrt{(157+?)} = 13$

$157 + ? = 169$

$? = 12.$

53. $[(130)^2 \div 25 \times 15] \div 30$

$= [16900 \div 25 \times 15] \div 30$

$= 676 \times 15 \div 30$

$= 338.$

For Qs. No. 54–56:

A's salary = ₹ 10,000

A's expenses = 10% of ₹ 10,000 = ₹ 1,000

A's saving = ₹ 10,000 – ₹ 1,000 = ₹ 9,000

B's salary = ₹ 10,000 + ₹ 2,000

= ₹ 12,000

C's salary = ₹ 3,000 × 3 = ₹ 9,000

C's expenses = ₹ 9,000 – ₹ 3,000 = ₹ 6,000

B's saving = ₹ 9,000 – ₹ 3,000 = ₹ 6,000

54. Increased income of A = ₹ 10,000 × $\frac{120}{100}$ = ₹ 12,000

Expenses remain unchanged = ₹ 1,000

New saving = ₹ 12,000 – ₹ 1,000

= ₹ 11,000.

55. C's expenses = ₹ 6,000

C's saving = ₹ 3,000

Required percentage = $\frac{6,000}{3,000} \times 100 = 200\%.$

56. B's saving = ₹ 6,000

B's income = ₹ 12,000

Required percentage = $\frac{6,000}{12,000} \times 100 = 50\%$

57. ₹ 51,840 = $25,000\left(1+\frac{20}{100}\right)^n$

$\frac{51,840}{25,000} = \left(\frac{6}{5}\right)^n$

$n = 4$ years.

58. Speed of boat in still water = $9x$ km/hr

Speed of current = $2x$ km/hr

Upstream speed = $9x - 2x = 7x$ km/hr

Downstream speed = $9x + 2x = 11x$ km/hr

$5(11x) - 2(7x) = 123$

$55x - 14x = 123$

$41x = 123 \Rightarrow x = 3$

Speed of boat = 9 × 3 = 27 km/hr.

59. Let the cost price of one banana = ₹ x

Cost price of 20 bananas = ₹ $20x$

Loss = cost price of 5 bananas

= ₹ $5x$

₹ $20x$ – ₹ $5x$ = ₹ 600

₹ $15x$ = ₹ 600 ⇒ x = ₹ 40.

60. Distance between two consecutive buses

$= 40 \times \frac{20}{60} = \frac{40}{3}$ km

Let the speed of the man = x km/hr.

Relative speed = $40 + x$

$(40+x) \times \frac{16}{60} = \frac{40}{3}$

$40 + x = 50$

$x = 10$ km/hr.

For Qs. No. 61–65:

January:

Non-Fiction books = 175 – 85 = 90

February:

Non-Fiction books = 280 – 120 = 160

March:

Non-Fiction books = 225 – 115 = 110

April:

Non-Fiction books = 320 – 180 = 140

May:

Non-Fiction books = 260 – 150 = 110.

61. Total books sold in February and April

= 280 + 320 = 600

Total books sold in March and May

= 225 + 260 = 485

Required ratio = 600 : 485

= 120 : 97.

62. Fiction books sold in April = 180

Fiction books sold in January = 85

Required difference = 180 – 85 = 95.

63. Non-Fiction books sold in February

$= 280 - 120$

$= 160$

Non-Fiction books sold in March

$= 225 - 115$

$= 110$

$$\text{Required percentage} = \frac{160-110}{110}\times 100$$

$$= \frac{50}{110}\times 100 = 45.5\%.$$

64. Non-Fiction books sold in April

$= 320 - 180 = 140$

Non-Fiction books sold in February

$= 280 - 120 = 160$

$$\text{Required percentage} = \frac{160-140}{160}\times 100$$

$$= \frac{20}{160}\times 100$$

$= 12.5\%$ less.

65. Fiction books sold in June $= 40\%$ of $300 = 120$

Non-Fiction books sold in June $= 300 - 120 = 180$

Non-Fiction books sold in May $= 260 - 150 = 110$

Required difference $= 180 - 110 = 70$.

For Qs. No. 66–70:

- F lives on the 3rd floor; therefore, E lives on the 7th floor because three persons live between E and F.
- G lives immediately below E on the 6th floor, and B lives on the 8th floor because one person lives between B and G.
- A lives on the 4th floor and C on the 2nd floor. H lives on the 1st floor, while D occupies the 5th floor.

Floor	Person
8	B
7	E
6	G
5	D
4	A
3	F
2	C
1	H

66. D lives on the 5th floor, and the floor situated two floors above it is the 7th floor. E occupies the 7th floor according to the final arrangement. Therefore, E lives two floors above D.

67. A lives two floors above C, and C occupies the 2nd floor in the final arrangement. Hence, A occupies the 4th floor. Therefore, A lives on the 4th floor.

68. Statement 1—Incorrect: B does not live on the 7th floor. B lives on the 8th floor, whereas E occupies the 7th floor.

Statement 2—Incorrect: A lives on the 4th floor and H lives on the 1st floor.

Two persons, C and F, live between A and H, not one person.

Statement 3—Incorrect: G lives on the 6th floor and D lives on the 5th floor.

Thus, G lives immediately above D, not immediately below D.

Statement 4—Incorrect: H does not live on the 2nd floor. H lives on the 1st floor, while C occupies the 2nd floor.

Therefore, none of the given statements is correct.

69. E lives on the 7th floor and A lives on the 4th floor, so two persons—D and G—live between them. F lives on the 3rd floor, and two persons—H and C—live below F.

Therefore, the two numbers are equal.

70. Statement A—Correct: B lives on the 8th floor, which is the topmost floor.

Therefore, no person lives above B.

Statement B—Incorrect: E lives on the 7th floor, while B lives on the 8th floor.

Thus, E lives immediately below B, not immediately above B.

Statement C—Incorrect: D occupies the 5th floor and B occupies the 8th floor.

They do not live on adjacent floors because the 6th and 7th floors lie between them.

Therefore, statements B and C are not correct.

71. Conclusion I—True: $D = R \leq E < A$.

Since R is either equal to or less than E and E is less than A, $R < A$ is definitely true.

Conclusion II—False: $M > C$ and $C < D = R \leq E$.

Both M and E are greater than C, but no definite relationship between M and E can be established.

Conclusion III—True: $D = R$ and $R \leq E$.

Therefore, $D \leq E$ is definitely true.

72. Conclusion I—False: $A \geq B > C$, while $C \leq D \leq E$.

The given relationships do not establish any definite comparison between A and E.

Conclusion II—True: $C \leq D \leq E < F$.

Therefore, C is definitely less than F.

73. Conclusion I—False: $C \geq F$ and $D < H = I$, but no definite relationship exists between I and F.

Therefore, $I > F$ cannot be established.

Conclusion II—False: $C > D$ and $H > D$ show that both C and H are greater than D.

However, no definite relationship between H and C can be determined.

Qs. No. 74–78:

1st	V
2nd	K
3rd	R
4th	O
5th	F
6th	H
7th	X
8th	B

74. V is the first person to purchase a gift in the final sequence. K purchases immediately after V, while O purchases three positions after V. Therefore, V is the first person who purchased a gift.

75. R purchases the gift in the third position, whereas F purchases it in the fifth position. Only O, who purchases in the fourth position, is placed between R and F. Hence, exactly one person purchased a gift between them.

76. Statement 1—Correct: B is placed in the eighth and last position.
Therefore, B is the last person who purchased a gift.
Statement 2—Correct: H purchases in the sixth position and X in the seventh position.
Therefore, H purchased the gift immediately before X.
Statement 3—Correct: V purchases first and K purchases second.
Therefore, K purchased the gift immediately after V.
Statement 4—Incorrect: H purchases in the sixth position, so only X and B purchase after H.
Thus, only two persons, not more than three persons, purchased gifts after H.

77. Three persons—V, K and R—purchase gifts before O, who occupies the fourth position. F occupies the fifth position, and three persons—H, X and B—purchase gifts after F. Therefore, as many persons purchase before O as purchase after F.

78. Statement A—Correct: Two persons, V and K, purchase gifts before R.
Two persons, X and B, also purchase gifts after H.
Statement B—Correct: R occupies the third position, while O occupies the fourth position.
Therefore, O purchases the gift immediately after R.
Statement C—Incorrect: F occupies the fifth position, whereas R occupies the third position.
Therefore, F purchases the gift after R, not before R.

79. SECOND is divided as SEC | OND,
and the two groups are interchanged as OND | SEC
Applying the pattern +2, −2 and +2 gives OND → QLF and SEC → UCE.
Similarly, PAUSED becomes SED | PAU,
and applying the same pattern gives
UCF | RYW = UCFRYW.

For Qs. No. 80–84:

7th January	S
20th January	Y
7th March	X
20th March	W
7th May	U
20th May	T
7th September	V
20th September	Z

80. W's visit is scheduled for 20th March. The visit immediately preceding W's visit is X's visit, which is scheduled for 7th March. Therefore, the person whose visit is on 7th March visits immediately before W.

81. Z's visit takes place after S's visit and remains within two intervening visits of T. The only position satisfying all the given conditions is the eighth position. Therefore, Z's visit is scheduled for 20th September.

82. W's visit is on 20th March in the fourth position, while Z's visit is on 20th September in the eighth position. U, T and V occupy the fifth, sixth and seventh positions respectively. Therefore, three persons have their visits between W and Z.

83. S visits in January, X in March, and U and T in May; all these months have thirty-one days. Z visits in September, which has only thirty days. Therefore, Z is different from the other four persons and is the odd one out.

84. T's visit is scheduled for 20th May, which is the sixth position in the chronological arrangement. S, Y, X, W and U have their visits before T. Therefore, five persons have visits before T's visit.

85. Conclusion I—Does not follow: "No pencil is an eraser" establishes separation only between pencils and erasers. Since only a few pens are pencils, the remaining pens may or may not be erasers. Therefore, it cannot be concluded that no pen is an eraser.
Conclusion II—Does not follow: The statement explicitly says that no pencil is an eraser. Hence, the conclusion that some erasers are pencils directly contradicts the given relationship and cannot follow.
Conclusion III—Does not follow: "Only a few pens are pencils" means that some pens are pencils and some pens are not pencils.
Therefore, the possibility that all pens are pencils is ruled out.

86. Conclusion I does not follow because no definite relationship between lemons and oranges is established. Conclusion II follows because nothing prevents all lemons from being fruits. Conclusion III follows directly from "Some lemons are fruits", because a particular affirmative statement can be validly converted to "Some fruits are lemons".

87. Conclusion I—Does not follow: All chargers are laptops, and some mobiles are chargers; therefore, chargers cannot be completely separated from laptops. Hence, the

4. Select the word that is most similar in meaning to "impulse" as used in the passage.

A. Instinct B. Calculation
C. Caution D. Delay
E. Indifference

5. Choose the most appropriate word for the given blank.

A. involve B. provide
C. requires D. consisting
E. demanding

6. According to the passage, why did Tyson initially struggle with leadership?

A. He was overly confident and took unnecessary risks, leading to frequent failures.
B. He hesitated to make decisions and avoided risks, believing that safety ensured success.
C. He lacked technical business knowledge and struggled to manage financial resources.
D. He prioritized family responsibilities over business, which led to instability in both areas.
E. He was unable to communicate effectively with his team, causing inefficiencies.

7. What lesson did Tyson learn regarding leadership in both business and family life?

A. The same leadership style should be applied in all situations for consistency.
B. Leadership is only about professional success, as family matters are secondary.
C. Leadership in business requires strategic thinking, while family leadership demands emotional presence.
D. Avoiding risks in business and family life ensures long-term stability.
E. Business and family leadership require entirely different skill sets that do not overlap.

8. Why did Tyson find organizational skills essential for leadership?

A. They allowed him to handle every task personally without delegating responsibilities.
B. They encouraged him to focus on long-term goals instead of daily operations.
C. They helped him focus entirely on business success without worrying about personal commitments.
D. They enabled him to manage his business efficiently while maintaining a work-life balance.
E. They taught him that rigid scheduling is the only way to manage leadership challenges.

Directions (Qs. No. 9-14): *In the following passage there are blanks, each of which has been denoted by a letter. For each blank, five options are given. Choose the most appropriate word from the options that fits the blank appropriately.*

Obesity has become a major health ____(*a*)____ in many countries. Over the past few decades, the number of obese people has increased ____(*b*)____. Poor eating habits, lack of physical activity, and unhealthy lifestyles are some of the main causes of obesity. This condition leads to several serious diseases, including diabetes, heart disease, and high blood pressure.

Governments and health organizations are working to raise ____(*c*)____ about the dangers of obesity. They encourage people to eat a balanced diet and exercise regularly. Schools are also taking steps to promote healthy habits among children. However, despite these efforts, the problem continues to ____(*d*)____. If obesity rates keep rising, it could become an even bigger burden on healthcare systems. To fight obesity, individuals must take responsibility for their health. Simple changes, such as avoiding junk food and staying active, can make a big ____(*e*)____. In addition, the government should implement strict policies to reduce the consumption of sugary drinks and processed foods. Only through collective efforts can we ____(*f*)____ this growing crisis.

9. Which of the following word best fits in blank (*a*)?

A. issue B. solution
C. victory D. policy
E. happiness

10. Which of the following word best fits in blank (*b*)?

A. scarcely B. gradually
C. partially D. carelessly
E. poorly

11. Which of the following word best fits in blank (*c*)?

A. ignorance B. confusion
C. awareness D. hesitation
E. disturbance

12. Which of the following word best fits in blank (*d*)?

A. disappear B. improve
C. recover D. worsen
E. vanish

13. Which of the following word best fits in blank (*e*)?

A. mistake B. difference
C. trouble D. damage
E. loss

4. A	**5.** C	**6.** B	**7.** C	**8.** D	**9.** A	**10.** B	**11.** C	**12.** D	**13.** B

14. Which of the following word best fits in blank (*f*)?

A. invite B. welcome
C. increase D. create
E. control

Directions (Qs. No. 15-19): *Read the sentence to find out whether there is any grammatical or idiomatic error in it. The error, if any, will be in one part of the sentence. The letter of that part is the answer. If the given sentence is grammatically and contextually correct, then choose option "No error" as your answer response. (Ignore errors of punctuation, if any).*

15. The doctor careful (*a*)/ examined the patient (*b*)/ and prescribed the necessary (*c*)/ medication for a speedy recovery. (*d*)

A. (*a*) B. (*b*)
C. (*c*) D. (*d*)
E. No error

16. She decided (*a*)/ to join the gym (*b*)/ in order too (*c*)/ improve her fitness. (*d*)

A. (*a*) B. (*b*)
C. (*c*) D. (*d*)
E. No error

17. The cat escaped (*a*)/ though the open (*b*)/ window before (*c*)/ anyone could catch it. (*d*)

A. (*a*) B. (*b*)
C. (*c*) D. (*d*)
E. No error

18. He carry the (*a*)/ heavy suitcase (*b*)/ up the stairs (*c*)/ without any help. (*d*)

A. (*a*) B. (*b*)
C. (*c*) D. (*d*)
E. No error

19. Please bring (*a*)/ your notebook (*b*)/ to the meeting so (*c*)/ you can took notes. (*d*)

A. (*a*) B. (*b*)
C. (*c*) D. (*d*)
E. No error

Directions (Qs. No. 20-23): *In the sentence given below, three words are highlighted in bold. Rearrange these words to form a meaningful and grammatically correct sentence. If the words are already in the correct order, select "No rearrangement required" as the answer.*

20. The **clock** (*a*) inside feels solemn, with a high wall **silently** (*b*) ticking almost **ambiance** (*c*).

A. (*b*)(*a*)(*c*) B. (*c*)(*a*)(*b*)
C. (*a*)(*c*)(*b*) D. (*c*)(*b*)(*a*)
E. No rearrangement required

21. Their **enduring** (*a*) represented **meeting** (*b*) and goodwill, inspiring an **devotion** (*c*) spirit even today.

A. (*b*)(*c*)(*a*) B. (*b*)(*a*)(*c*)
C. (*c*)(*a*)(*b*) D. (*a*)(*c*)(*b*)
E. No rearrangement required

22. Mini **feeling** (*a*), seeing half her bowl **still** (*b*) full, already **sighed** (*c*) completely satisfied.

A. (*c*)(*a*)(*b*) B. (*b*)(*a*)(*c*)
C. (*a*)(*c*)(*b*) D. (*c*)(*b*)(*a*)
E. No rearrangement required

23. That afternoon, the **snooping** (*a*) visited the **brothers** (*b*) site, curiously **theft** (*c*) around for clues.

A. (*b*)(*a*)(*c*) B. (*c*)(*b*)(*a*)
C. (*b*)(*c*)(*a*) D. (*a*)(*c*)(*b*)
E. No rearrangement required

Directions (Qs. No. 24-28): *In each of the following questions, a sentence contains a highlighted phrase that may be grammatically incorrect. Choose the most appropriate option from the given alternatives to replace the highlighted phrase and correct the sentence. If the highlighted phrase is correct as it is, then choose "No replacement required" as the correct answer.*

24. She **put up** her scarf carefully, enjoying the warmth it provided her.

A. kept B. bought
C. adjusted D. made
E. No replacement required

25. She carefully **book into** the antique vase on the wooden shelf, ensuring it wouldn't tip over.

A. refused B. placed
C. misplaced D. returned
E. No replacement required

26. Tanusha felt **driven away,** as if struck by an unexpected earthquake.

A. adored B. elated
C. fenced D. shaken
E. No replacement required

27. Sun set behind hills, air chilled, and children **look after** for comfort and company.

A. huddled B. packed
C. flowed D. spiced
E. No replacement required

14. E	**15.** A	**16.** C	**17.** B	**18.** A	**19.** D	**20.** B
21. A	**22.** D	**23.** C	**24.** C	**25.** B	**26.** D	**27.** A

28. Many arrive to **take in** royalty, but few can truly prove their lineage.

A. stealing B. fulfilling
C. taking D. claiming
E. No replacement required

Directions (Qs. No. 29-30): *In the question, one word is given in bold and correspondence to that, three sentences are given each containing that word. Choose the option depicting the sentence(s) that have/ has the correct usage of the word.*

29. HOARDING

(I) The government launched a campaign to discourage **hoarding** of essential supplies during the crisis.
(II) His habit of **hoarding** old newspapers and magazines made his house extremely cluttered.
(III) The supermarket imposed a limit on certain items to prevent people from **hoarding** and creating shortages.

A. Only (I) B. Both (I) and (III)
C. Only (III) D. All (I), (II) and (III)
E. Only (II)

30. ALIGHT

(I) The passengers waited for the train to stop before they began to **alight** from the compartments.
(II) He was so tired that he just wanted to **alight** on the bed and **sleep.**
(III) The campfire suddenly caught **alight**, illuminating the dark forest around them.

A. Only (III) B. Only (II)
C. Both (I) and (III) D. Both (I) and (II)
E. All (I), (II) and (III)

NUMERICAL ABILITY

Directions (Qs. No. 31-35): *The table given below shows the number of students (Girls + Boys) in four different classes (A, B, C & D).*

Classes	Girls	Boys
A	24	45
B	60	90
C	12	36
D	84	72

31. Find the average number of boys in C and B is what percent less than girls in D.

A. 25 B. 30
C. 15 D. 40
E. 35

32. Find the ratio of girls in B and C together to boys in D.

A. 2 : 5 B. 1 : 1
C. 1 : 5 D. 4 : 3
E. 5 : 3

33. In class F, the number of boys is 20% more than that in B and number of girls is 5/6 of girls in C. Find the total number of students in F.

A. 125 B. 118
C. 115 D. 114
E. 113

34. 25% students are present in class C. Find the absent students in class C.

A. 12 B. 36
C. 30 D. 40
E. 35

35. Total student in B and A together is what percentage of total girls in D (approx.).

A. 225 B. 230
C. 260 D. 240
E. 235

Directions (Qs. No. 36-40): *The line graph given below shows the products sold in the month of January, February, March and April.*

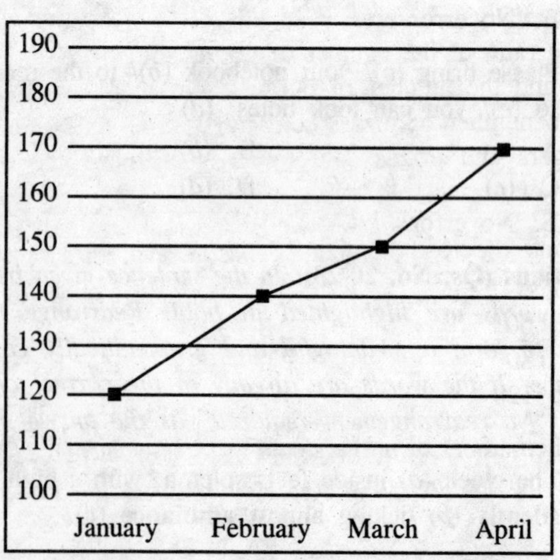

28. D **29.** D **30.** C **31.** A **32.** B **33.** B **34.** B **35.** C

36. The cost of product sold in January is ₹ 20. If the cost of the product sold in the month of February is 20% more than that of January, then find the revenue (in ₹) generated in February.

A. 3325 B. 3360
C. 3315 D. 3340
E. 3335

37. In June, the product sold is the average number of products sold in January and February. If 20% of product are sold in June, then find the unsold product in June.

A. 525 B. 530
C. 104 D. 540
E. 535

38. Find the average number of products sold in the given months.

A. 147.5 B. 130
C. 115.5 D. 140.5
E. 135.5

39. Find the ratio of products sold in January and February together to products sold in April.

A. 1 : 25 B. 13 : 9
C. 12 : 5 D. 1 : 4
E. 9 : 13

40. The product sold in the month of March is what percentage of product sold in January?

A. 125 B. 130
C. 115 D. 140
E. 135

Directions (Qs. No. 41-43): *Read the following information carefully and answer the questions given below.*

The ratio of the number of pizzas sold by A to B is 4 : 7, and the number of burgers sold by A is 20 less than the number of pizzas sold by B. The total number of burgers and pizzas sold by B is 150 and the total number of pizzas sold by A is 40.

41. Find the total number of pizzas and burgers sold by A.

A. 60 B. 90
C. 80 D. 100
E. 120

42. The number of burgers sold by A is what percentage of the number of pizzas sold by B?

A. $29\frac{3}{7}\%$ B. 14.28%
C. 66.67% D. 54.33%
E. $71\frac{3}{7}\%$

43. The number of burgers sold by C is 25% more than pizzas sold by A, then find the difference between the number of burgers sold by C and the number of pizzas sold by A.

A. 5 B. 10
C. 15 D. 20
E. 30

Directions (Qs. No. 44-45): *Read the following information carefully and answer the questions given below.*

Total males planted trees on Saturday is 400, and the total males planted trees on Sunday is 60% more than that of those on Saturday. The ratio of total males to total females who planted trees on Sunday is 8 : 3. Total females who planted trees on Saturday is 40 less than that on Sunday.

44. Find the sum of the total females who planted trees on Saturday and the total males who planted trees on Sunday.

A. 800 B. 840
C. 980 D. 910
E. 750

45. Find the difference between the total males and total females who planted trees on Sunday.

A. 400 B. 450
C. 420 D. 230
E. 320

46. The average weight of 40 students in class is 35 kg. The weights of two students were wrongly entered as 44 kg and 40 kg instead of 42 kg and 38 kg, respectively. Find the correct average weight of the class.

A. 31.9 kg B. 34.4 kg
C. 31.2 kg D. 30.9 kg
E. 34.9 kg

47. The perimeter of a circle is 88 meter and the radius of the circle is 2 meter more than the breadth of a rectangle. If the area of the rectangle is 180 sq meter, then find the length of the rectangle (in meter).

A. 15 B. 20
C. 12 D. 16
E. 24

36. B	**37.** C	**38.** A	**39.** B	**40.** A	**41.** B
42. E	**43.** B	**44.** B	**45.** A	**46.** E	**47.** A

48. The selling price of the article is 270, when it is sold at 10% loss. If the article sold at the profit of 35%, then find the profit (in ₹).

A. 115 B. 105
C. 112 D. 106
E. 124

49. Pipe A and pipe B can fill a tank in 9 hours and 6 hours respectively. Pipe C takes 7.5 hours to empty the tank. If pipe A and pipe B together open for three hours and after that pipe C is open, then find time taken by pipe C to empty the tank.

A. 6.25 B. 5.05
C. 5.12 D. 4.23
E. 6.24

50. In a factory 40% are females and out of total males 65% are above the age of 50 years. If total males under the age of 50 years or equal to 50 years are 4200, then find the number of females in the factory?

A. 5000 B. 8000
C. 1200 D. 1600
E. 6400

Directions (Qs. No. 51-60): *What will come in the place of question (?) mark in following the question:*

51. $140 \times \sqrt{64} \times ? = 560$

A. 0.25 B. 6
C. 0.28 D. 25
E. 12

52. $(10 + 7)^3 = 8.5 \times (? - 12)$

A. 520 B. 525
C. 590 D. 500
E. 490

53. $544 \div 8.5 \times 4 = 2^?$

A. 7 B. 3
C. 1 D. 8
E. 9

54. $?^2 = (10 + 3)^2 - (3 \times 2)^2 - 11 \times 3$

A. 12 B. 10
C. 13 D. 14
E. 16

55. $?^2 \times (2^6 + 6^2) = 60^2$

A. 5 B. 4
C. 8 D. 6
E. 2

56. $?^3 + 2^9 = 32^2$

A. 6 B. 4
C. 8 D. 2
E. 10

57. $2844.8 \times 5 - 2844.8 = ?$

A. 1129.2
B. 113789
C. 11379.2
D. 11223.4
E. None of these

58. $1640 \div 4.1 - 32 \times 50 = ?$

A. 500 B. 490
C. 400 D. 450
E. None of these

59. $1800 \times \frac{4}{9} \times \frac{12}{864} \times \frac{90}{10} = ?$

A. 2 B. 0.10
C. 10 D. 0.01
E. 100

60. $\frac{14}{19}$ of $380 - \frac{11}{2}$ of $1440 = ?$

A. 7770 B. −7640
C. −7550 D. 7550
E. 7610

61. Y is 75% of the P and the average of both the numbers is 30 less than the P, then find value of 20% of Y?

A. 52 B. 36
C. 12 D. 180
E. 64

62. A vessel contains 80 liters of milk and water in the ratio of 3 : 5. If X liters of water are added to the vessel, then the ratio of water to milk becomes 2 : 1, respectively. Find X.

A. 5 B. 10
C. 15 D. 20
E. 25

63. The ratio of the present ages of A to B is 5 : 9, respectively. After four years, the ratio of the ages of A to B is 7 : 11, respectively. Find the age of B two years ago (in years).

A. 9 B. 10
C. 13 D. 22
E. 16

48. B	**49.** A	**50.** B	**51.** A	**52.** C	**53.** D	**54.** B	**55.** D
56. C	**57.** C	**58.** E	**59.** E	**60.** B	**61.** B	**62.** B	**63.** E

64. A man invested ₹ X in simple interest at 20% p.a. for three years and received interest of ₹ 2400. If he invested the same amount in compound interest at 10% p.a. for two years, then find the interest received by him (in ₹).

A. 840 B. 660
C. 1130 D. 820
E. 750

65. A X-meter-long train can cross a pole in 16 seconds, and the speed of the train is 25 m/sec. If the length of a bridge is X + 150 meters, then find the time taken by the train to cross the bridge (in seconds).

A. 40 B. 60
C. 30 D. 20
E. 38

REASONING ABILITY

Directions (Qs. No. 66-70): *Study the following letter-number-symbol sequence and answer the questions given below:*

2 U H # K 7 % M ! R O @ 2 I B 9 8 % P 5 $ 1 * A

66. Which of the following element is 4th to the left of 9th element from the right end?

A. B B. 9
C. % D. @
E. 8

67. How many letters are immediately succeeded by a number and immediately preceded by a symbol?

A. One B. Four
C. Two D. Five
E. None of these

68. How many symbols are immediately preceded as well as immediately succeeded by consonants?

A. One B. Four
C. Five D. Two
E. Three

69. Four of the following five are alike in a certain way and hence form a group. Who among the following does not belong to that group?

A. UK# B. 7P1
C. B%8 D. MOR
E. $A*

70. How many even numbers are between 7th element from left and 3th element from right in the given series?

A. One B. Three
C. Four D. Two
E. None

71. In a certain code language, "POWER" is coded as "OPWRE", and "GREAT" is coded as "RGETA". Following the same pattern, what is the code for "WAVES"?

A. AWVSE B. AWSVE
C. WAVSE D. AWEVS
E. None of these

Directions (Qs. No. 72-76): *In these questions, the relationship between different elements is shown in the statements. The statements are followed by conclusions. Study the conclusions based on the given statements and select the appropriate answer:*

72. Statements:

$S \geq G > K = E > B < J > P$

Conclusions:

I. $B \leq S$ II. $S > E$

A. If only conclusion I is true
B. If only conclusion II is true
C. If either conclusion I or II is true
D. If both conclusions I and II are true
E. If neither conclusion I nor II is true

73. Statements:

$F < Y \leq J \leq Q = L > V < A$

Conclusions:

I. $L = Y$ II. $L > Y$

A. If only conclusion I is true
B. If only conclusion II is true
C. If either conclusion I or II is true
D. If both conclusions I and II are true
E. If neither conclusion I nor II is true

74. Statements:

$G > U = C \geq Z > R > I < W \leq T$

Conclusions:

I. $G > I$ II. $C > T$

A. If only conclusion I is true
B. If only conclusion II is true
C. If either conclusion I or II is true
D. If both conclusions I and II are true
E. If neither conclusion I nor II is true

64. A **65.** E **66.** D **67.** C **68.** D **69.** B **70.** D **71.** A **72.** B **73.** C **74.** A

75. Statements:

Y < W < J ≥ N; W < P ≤ Z

Conclusions:

I. W < Z   II. P > Y

A. If only conclusion I is true
B. If only conclusion II is true
C. If either conclusion I or II is true
D. If both conclusions I and II are true
E. If neither conclusion I nor II is true

76. Statements:

B < K = F ≥ J; N ≤ D > K

Conclusions:

I. J < D   II. D ≥ F

A. If only conclusion I is true
B. If only conclusion II is true
C. If either conclusion I or II is true
D. If both conclusions I and II are true
E. If neither conclusion I nor II is true

77. How many pairs of letters are in the word "DAUGHTER" in both forward and backward directions, each of which has as many letters between them as in the English alphabetical series?

A. Four   B. Two
C. Three   D. One
E. More than four

78. How many such digits are there in the number '74215398' which will remain at the same position when arranged in ascending order from left to right?

A. Four
B. One
C. Three
D. Two
E. None of these

Directions (Qs. No. 79-81): *Study the following information carefully and answer the questions given below:*

Six persons are comparing their weights in decreasing order from left to right. B is just heavier than A. Three persons are lighter than A. C is heavier than J. J is not the lightest person. H is heavier than C. One person is M.

79. How many persons weigh between B and J?

A. One
B. Two
C. Three
D. Four
E. None

80. If H is related to A and in the same way C is related to M, then B is related to who among the following person?

A. C   B. A
C. J   D. M
E. None of these

81. Who among the following is the heaviest person?

A. B   B. M
C. H   D. A
E. None of these

82. If it is possible to make a meaningful word using 1st, 3rd, 5th, and 6th letters (From left end) of the word "MENTORS", then what will be the 2nd letter from left end of that meaningful word? If no such meaningful word can be formed, mark the answer as 'X', if more than one words can be formed, mark the answer as 'Y'?

A. R   B. O
C. M   D. X
E. Y

Directions (Qs. No. 83-85): *Read the given information carefully and answer the relates questions:*

A certain number of persons sit in a row facing north. Three persons sit between A and B. C sits sixth to the left of B. D sits exactly between C and A. E sits fourth to the right of D. Five persons sit between E and F. C sits to the right of F. Number of persons sit between F and B is twice the number of persons to the left of F. Four persons sit between E and G. No one sits to the right of G.

83. How many persons sit in the row?

A. 11   B. 12
C. 13   D. 14
E. 15

84. What is the position of B with respect to G?

A. Second to the right
B. Fourth to the left
C. Seventh to the left
D. Fifth to the right
E. Immediate left

85. How many persons sit to the left of A?

A. Eleven
B. Nine
C. Six
D. Eight
E. Twelve

75. D	76. A	77. A	78. B	79. B	80. A	81. C	82. B	83. E	84. B	85. C

Directions (Qs. No. 86-90): *Study the following information carefully and answer the questions given below:*

Eight boxes – A, B, C, D, E, F, G, and H are placed one above another in a stack but not necessarily in the same order.

Box G is placed three boxes above Box H. Two boxes are placed between box F and box B which is placed immediately above Box H. Box F is placed below Box H. Box F is not placed at either topmost or bottom-most position. Box E is placed above box B. As many boxes are placed above Box E as below Box A. Box C is placed above Box D. Box C is placed above Box H but not at the topmost position.

86. How many boxes are placed between Box E and the box which is placed just below Box H?

A. One B. Two
C. Three D. Four
E. None

87. Which box is placed exactly between Box B and Box A?

A. Box E B. Box C
C. Box H D. Box G
E. Box D

88. Which box is placed at the fourth position from the top?

A. Box G B. Box B
C. Box H D. Box D
E. None of these

89. If all the boxes are arranged in alphabetical order from top to bottom, how many boxes will remain in their original position?

A. None B. One
C. Two D. Three
E. Four

90. How many boxes are placed between box C and box H?

A. One B. Two
C. Three D. Four
E. None

Directions (Qs. No. 91-95): *Read the given information carefully and answer the related questions:*

Eight persons sit around a circular table facing inside. R sits third to the left of M. One person sits between R and S. T sits immediate left of S. G sits opposite to T. K sits immediate left of G. F sits immediate right of O.

91. Who among the following sits second to the right of F?

A. T B. S
C. M D. R
E. K

92. What is the position of O with respect to M?

A. Immediate right
B. Second to the right
C. Third to the right
D. Immediate left
E. Second to the left

93. How many persons sit between S and F when counted from the left of S?

A. None B. One
C. Two D. Three
E. Four

94. Which of the following statement is correct?

A. O and G does not sit adjacent to each other
B. F sits opposite to M
C. None is correct
D. S sits second to the right of O
E. One person sits between M and K

95. Four of the following five are similar in a certain manner, which among the following is dissimilar to others?

A. F-M B. R-K
C. T-G D. S-O
E. R-G

Directions (Qs. No. 96-100): *Study the following information carefully and answer the question given below:*

Nine people A, B, C, D, E, F, G, H and I were born in different months March, April, May, June, July, August, September, October and November of the same year. (But not necessarily in the same order) Three people were born between F and the one who was born in July, and B was born before H but on a month having 30 days. No one was born between F and A. Three people were born between A and H. Three people were born between I and C. Not more than two persons were born between D and E who were born after D. I was born before B. G is not the youngest person and was born after E.

96. Who was born in March?

A. F B. I
C. E D. A
E. B

86. D **87.** E **88.** B **89.** B **90.** A **91.** A **92.** C **93.** C **94.** B **95.** E **96.** B

97. How many people were born between H and F?

A. One B. Two
C. Three D. Four
E. Six

98. Which of the following statement(s) is/are true?

I. B was born on April
II. One person is born between D and C.
III. G was born after F

A. Only I B. Both II and III
C. Both I and II D. Only II
E. All I, II and III

99. Four of the following five are alike in a certain way and hence from a group. Which one does not belong to the group?

A. G B. C
C. D D. E
E. A

100. Which of the following represents the people who were born in September and October respectively?

A. A, F B. G, A
C. C, E D. A, I
E. None of these

EXPLANATORY ANSWERS

1. The passage highlights that Tyson needed strategic, assertive skills for business and emotional presence and time management for family. This implies the need for both strategic (business-related) and emotional (family-related) intelligence.

Option A is incorrect because leadership isn't just about authority or quick decisions. Option B is incorrect because Tyson learned to delegate, showing that even skilled leaders must share responsibilities.

2. Statement A is correct as the passage emphasizes balancing personal (family) and professional (business) life. Statement B is also true—Tyson realized that indecisiveness led to missed opportunities and that making timely decisions was vital. Statement C is wrong because the passage emphasizes informed decisions, not impulsive ones.

3. The word "key" in the passage is used in the sense of an important or essential lesson Tyson learned. "Crucial" is the closest in meaning. The other options suggest lesser importance or irrelevance.

4. "Impulse" in the context of the passage refers to sudden urges or instinctual reactions that need to be managed. "Instinct" is closest in meaning. The other options (e.g., caution, delay) do not align with the context.

5. The sentence reads, "One of the key lessons Tyson learned was that leadership in business and family life ___ different but complementary skills."

The singular subject "leadership" needs a singular verb, and "requires" fits both grammatically and contextually.

It correctly conveys that leadership demands certain skills in both domains. Other options either don't agree in number or don't fit the structure of the sentence.

6. The passage states Tyson feared making the wrong choices and avoided risks. This aligns exactly with option B. The other options are not supported by the passage.

7. The passage makes a direct contrast: strategic, assertive thinking in business vs. being present and making time for loved ones at home. This aligns precisely with option C.

8. Tyson used organizational skills to structure work, delegate, focus on long-term growth, and also make time for family—clearly reflecting work-life balance. The other options misrepresent or narrow this role.

9. The sentence says, "Obesity has become a major health ___ in many countries." The word "issue" correctly fits the context, referring to a serious problem or concern. Words like "solution", "victory", or "happiness" do not reflect the seriousness or negative impact of obesity.

10. The sentence states, "the number of obese people has increased ___." The word "gradually" fits because it refers to a steady increase over time. Options like "scarcely" or "carelessly" don't make logical sense in the context of describing the rate of increase.

11. The sentence says, "working to raise ___ about the dangers of obesity." The correct word is "awareness", which means spreading knowledge or information. Other words like "ignorance" or "confusion" are opposite in meaning.

12. The sentence is, "the problem continues to ___." The correct word is "worsen", meaning to get more severe. The passage implies that despite efforts, obesity is still increasing, which fits with "worsen".

13. The sentence says, "can make a big ___." The right word is "difference", which conveys that even small actions can have a significant positive effect. Other options like "mistake" or "damage" are negative and do not fit the optimistic tone.

14. The sentence is, "Only through collective efforts can we ___ this growing crisis". The most suitable word is "control", indicating efforts to manage or reduce the problem. Words like "invite" or "create" are completely opposite in meaning.

97. D	**98.** C	**99.** A	**100.** B

15. The phrase "The doctor careful examined the patient" is incorrect. The word "careful" should be the adverb "carefully" to modify the verb "examined". So, the correct phrase is "The doctor carefully examined..."

16. The phrase "in order too improve" is incorrect. The correct word is "to", not "too". "Too" means "also" or "excessively", which doesn't fit here. The phrase should be "in order to improve".

17. The phrase "though the open window" is incorrect. It should be "through the open window". "Though" means "although", while "through" indicates movement across an opening, which is required here.

18. The phrase "He carry the heavy suitcase" is incorrect. The verb "carry" should be in past tense: "carried." So, it should be "He carried the heavy suitcase..."

19. The phrase "you can took notes" is incorrect. After "can", the base form of the verb is used. So it should be "you can take notes".

20. The correct rearrangement is (*c*)(*a*)(*b*).

"The ambiance inside feels solemn, with a high wall clock ticking almost silently".

This arrangement logically describes the ambiance and connects the clock's action to its placement.

- ambiance (वातावरण) - the character or atmosphere of a place
- silently (चुपचाप) - without making a sound
- clock (घड़ी) - a device showing time.

21. The correct rearrangement is (*b*)(*c*)(*a*).

"Their meeting represented devotion and goodwill, inspiring an enduring spirit even today".

This arrangement maintains the logical sequence of events and the cause-effect relationship.

- meeting (मुलाकात) - an assembly of people
- devotion (समर्पण) - love, loyalty, or enthusiasm
- enduring (सदा रहने वाला) - lasting or continuing.

22. The correct rearrangement is (*c*)(*b*)(*a*).

"Mini sighed, seeing half her bowl still full, already feeling completely satisfied".

This arrangement appropriately places the action (sighed) at the beginning and the cause (feeling satisfied) at the end.

- sighed (आह भरी) - exhaled audibly due to relief or tiredness
- still (अब भी) - remaining in a specified condition
- feeling (महसूस करना) - experiencing an emotional state.

23. The correct rearrangement is (*b*)(*c*)(*a*).

"That afternoon, the brothers visited the theft site, curiously snooping around for clues".

This arrangement logically connects the visitors (brothers) to the location (theft site) and their action (snooping).

- brothers (भाई) - male siblings
- theft (चोरी) - the act of stealing
- snooping (जासूसी करना) - investigating secretly.

24. The sentence "She put up her scarf carefully..." is awkward. "Put up" is not the correct verb here. The intended meaning is that she positioned or arranged her scarf properly. "Adjusted" fits both the context and grammar, meaning she made sure the scarf was sitting right while enjoying its warmth.

25. The sentence "She carefully book into the antique vase..." is incorrect because "book" is not a verb that fits this context. The logical meaning here is that she set or arranged something carefully into the vase. The correct word is "placed", which fits the sentence meaningfully and grammatically.

26. The sentence "Tanusha felt driven away, as if struck by an unexpected earthquake" is incorrect because "driven away" doesn't logically fit the comparison with an earthquake. The phrase that best matches the feeling of being hit by an earthquake is "shaken", which implies emotional or physical disturbance.

27. The phrase "children look after for comfort and company" is incorrect. The correct verb should describe how children behave in a chilly evening. "Huddled" is the best fit here, meaning they gathered closely together for warmth and companionship. "Look after" is also grammatically incorrect in this context.

28. The phrase "Many arrive to take in royalty..." is incorrect and unclear. The intended idea is that many people claim to have royal descent. "Claiming royalty" clearly expresses the idea of asserting noble lineage. Hence, "claiming" is the best replacement.

29. The word "hoarding" means accumulating and storing large quantities of something, often unnecessarily or selfishly, especially during shortages.

I. "Hoarding of essential supplies" – Correct usage.

II. "Hoarding old newspapers and magazines" – Correct; refers to excessive collecting.

III. "Prevent people from hoarding and creating shortages" – Correct and logical.

All three sentences use "hoarding" accurately.

30. The word "alight" has two common usages:

As a verb, meaning to get down from a vehicle (e.g., bus, train) – as in (I).

As an adjective, "alight" means on fire or lit up – as in (III).

I. "Alight from the compartments" – Correct usage as a verb.

II. "Alight on the bed" – Incorrect; "alight" does not mean "lie down."

III. "Caught alight" – Correct usage meaning "caught fire."

So, only (I) and (III) are correct.

For Qs. No. 31-35: From given table:

31. The average number of boys in C and B

$$= \frac{36+90}{2} = \frac{126}{2} = 63$$

and the number of girls in D = 84

$$\therefore \text{Required per cent} = \frac{84-63}{84} \times 100$$

$$= \frac{21}{84} \times 100$$

$$= \frac{1}{4} \times 100 = 25\%.$$

32. The number of girls in B and C

$$= 60 + 12$$

$$= 72$$

and Boys in D = 72

∴ Required ratio = 72 : 72 = 1 : 1.

33. The total number of students in F

$$= 90 \times \frac{120}{100} + 12 \times \frac{5}{6}$$

$$= 108 + 10$$

$$= 118.$$

34. Students in class C = 12 + 36 = 48

∴ 25% students are present in Class C

$$= 48 \times \frac{25}{100} = 12$$

∴ The absent students in class C

$$= 48 - 12 = 36.$$

35. Total students in B and A together

$$= 60 + 90 + 24 + 45$$

$$= 150 + 69$$

$$= 219$$

and Total girls in D = 84

$$\therefore \text{Required per cent} = \frac{219}{84} \times 100$$

$$= \frac{73}{28} \times 100 = \frac{73 \times 25}{7}$$

$$= \frac{1825}{7} = 260.71$$

= 260% (Approx.)

For Qs. No. 36-40: From given line-graph:

36. The cost of the product sold in the month of February

$$= 20 \times \frac{120}{100} = ₹\ 24$$

∴ Required revenue generated in February

$$= 140 \times 24$$

$$= ₹\ 3360.$$

37. Product sold in June $= \frac{120+140}{2} = 130$

∴ The unsold product in June

$$= 130 \times \frac{(100-20)}{100}$$

$$= \frac{130 \times 80}{100} = 104.$$

38. Required average $= \frac{120+140+150+180}{4}$

$$= \frac{590}{4} = 147.5$$

39. Required ratio = (120 + 140) : 180

= 260 : 180 = 13 : 9.

40. Required percentage

$$= \frac{150}{120} \times 100 = \frac{15}{3} \times 25 = 125\%.$$

For Qs. No. 41-43.

Let the number of pizzas sold by A and B are $4x$ and $7x$

Then, $4x = 40 \Rightarrow x = 10$

and the number of burgers sold by A

$$= 7x - 20$$

$$= 7 \times 10 - 20 = 50$$

and burgers sold by B = 150 − 70 = 80

	Pizzas sold	Burgers sold
A	40	50
B	70	80

41. The total number of pizzas and burgers sold by A = 40 + 50 = 90.

42. Required percentage $= \frac{50}{70} \times 100 = 71\frac{3}{7}\%$.

43. The number of burgers sold by C

$$= 40 \times \frac{125}{100} = 50$$

∴ Required difference = 50 − 40 = 10.

For Qs. No. 44-45. From given information:

Total males planted trees on Saturday = 400

and total males planted trees on Sunday

$$= 400 \times \frac{160}{100} = 640$$

and the ratio of total males to total females who planted trees on Sunday = 8 : 3

∴ Total females who planted tree on Sunday

$$= 640 \times \frac{3}{8} = 240$$

∴ Total females who planted trees on Saturday

$$= 240 - 40 = 200.$$

44. Required sum = 200 + 640 = 840.

45. Required difference = Total males on Sunday – Total females on Sunday
= 640 – 240 = 400.

46. Total weight of 40 students
= 40 × 35 = 1400 kg

∴ Correct weight = 1400 – (44 + 40) + (42 + 38)
= 1400 – 84 + 80
= 1396 kg

∴ Correct average weight = $\frac{1396}{40}$ = 34.9 kg.

47. Given, The perimeter of a circle = 88 m

$$\therefore \quad 2\pi r = 88$$
$$\Rightarrow \quad 2\times\frac{22}{7}r = 88$$
$$\Rightarrow \quad r = 88\times\frac{7}{44} = 14 \text{ m}$$

∴ Breadth of the rectangle = 14 – 2 = 12 m

Area of the rectangle = 180

$$\therefore \quad l \times b = 180$$
$$\Rightarrow \quad l \times 16 = 180$$
$$\Rightarrow \quad l = \frac{180}{12} = 15$$

∴ The length of the rectangle = 15 m.

48. C.P. of the article = $270\times\frac{100}{100-10}$

$= 270\times\frac{100}{90}$ = ₹ 300

∴ Now, S.P. of the article

$= 300\times\frac{135}{100}$ = ₹ 405

∴ The profit = S.P. – C.P.
= 405 – 300 = ₹ 105.

49. Part filled by (A + B) in 3 hours

$$= 3\left(\frac{1}{9}+\frac{1}{6}\right) = 3\left(\frac{2+3}{18}\right) = \frac{5}{6}$$

and part emptied by C in 1 hour

$$= \frac{1}{7.5} = \frac{2}{15}$$

∴ Time taken by pipe C to empty the tank

$$= \frac{5/6}{2/15} = \frac{5}{6}\times\frac{15}{2}$$
$$= \frac{5}{2}\times\frac{5}{2} = \frac{25}{6} = 6\frac{1}{4} \text{ hours}$$

= 6.25 hours.

50. Let the total males and females are 100*x*

Then, Total males = 60*x*

$$\therefore \quad 60x\times\frac{100-65}{100} = 4200$$
$$\Rightarrow \quad 60x\times\frac{35}{100} = 4200$$
$$\Rightarrow \quad x = \frac{4200\times100}{60\times35} = 200$$

∴ The number of females in the factory = 40*x*
= 40 × 200
= 8000.

51.
$$140\times\sqrt{64\times?} = 560$$
$$\Rightarrow \quad \sqrt{64\times?} = \frac{560}{140} = 4$$
$$\Rightarrow \quad 8\sqrt{?} = 4$$
$$\Rightarrow \quad \sqrt{?} = \frac{4}{8} = \frac{1}{2}$$
$$\Rightarrow \quad \sqrt{?} = \frac{1}{2} \Rightarrow ? = \frac{1}{4}$$
$$\Rightarrow \quad ? = 0.25.$$

52.
$$(10 + 7)^3 = 8.5 \times (? - 12)$$
$$\Rightarrow \quad (17)^3 = 8.5 \times (? - 12)$$
$$\Rightarrow \quad (? - 12) = \frac{17\times(17)^2}{8.5} = \frac{189}{.5}$$
$$= 289 \times 2 = 578$$
$$\Rightarrow \quad ? = 578 + 12 = 590.$$

53. $544 \div 8.5 \times 4 = 2^?$
$$\Rightarrow \quad \frac{544}{8.5}\times4 = 2^?$$
$$\Rightarrow \quad 64 \times 4 = 2^?$$
$$\Rightarrow \quad 2^6 \times 2^2 = 2^?$$
$$\Rightarrow \quad 2^8 = 2^?$$
$$\Rightarrow \quad ? = 8.$$

54.
$$?^2 = (10 + 3)^2 - (3 \times 2)^2 - 11 \times 3$$
$$\Rightarrow ?^2 = (13)^2 - (6)^2 - 33$$
$$\Rightarrow ?^2 = 169 - 36 - 33$$
$$\Rightarrow ?^2 = 169 - 69$$
$$\Rightarrow ?^2 = 100$$
$$\Rightarrow ?^2 = 10^2$$
$$\Rightarrow ?^2 = 10.$$

55.
$$?^2 \times (2^6 + 6^2) = 60^2$$
$$\Rightarrow \quad ?^2 \times (64 + 36) = 3600$$
$$\Rightarrow \quad ?^2 \times (100) = 3600$$
$$\Rightarrow \quad ?^2 = 36$$
$$\Rightarrow \quad ?^2 = 6^2$$
$$\Rightarrow \quad ? = 6.$$

56. $?^3 + 2^9 = 32^2$

$\Rightarrow$ $?^3 + 2^9 = (2^5)^2$

$\Rightarrow$ $?^3 + 2^9 = 2^{10}$

$\Rightarrow$ $?^3 = 2^{10} - 2^9$

$\Rightarrow$ $?^3 = 2^9 (2 - 1)$

$\Rightarrow$ $?^3 = 2^9$

$\Rightarrow$ $?^3 = (2^3)^3$

$\Rightarrow$ $?^3 = 8^3$

$\Rightarrow$ $? = 8.$

57. $2844.8 \times 5 - 2844.8 = ?$

$\Rightarrow$ $2844.8 (5 - 1) = ?$

$\Rightarrow$ $2844.8 \times 4 = ?$

$\Rightarrow$ $? = 11379.2.$

58. $1640 \div 4.1 - 32 \times 50 = ?$

$\Rightarrow$ $400 - 32 \times 50 = ?$

$\Rightarrow$ $400 - 1600 = ?$

$\Rightarrow$ $? = -1200.$

59. $1800 \times \frac{4}{9} \times \frac{12}{864} \times \frac{90}{10} = ?$

$\Rightarrow$ $200 \times \frac{12}{216} \times 9 = ?$

$\Rightarrow$ $? = 200 \times \frac{12}{24}$

$\Rightarrow$ $? = 100.$

60. $\frac{14}{19}$ of $380 - \frac{11}{2}$ of $1440 = ?$

$\Rightarrow$ $380 \times \frac{14}{19} - 1440 \times \frac{11}{2} = ?$

$\Rightarrow$ $20 \times 14 - 720 \times 11 = ?$

$\Rightarrow$ $280 - 7920 = ?$

$\Rightarrow$ $? = -7640.$

61. Given, $y = 75\%$ of P

$\Rightarrow$ $y = p \times \frac{75}{100}$

$\Rightarrow$ $y = \frac{3}{4} p$ ...(*i*)

and $\frac{y+p}{2} + 30 = p$

$\Rightarrow$ $p - \frac{y+p}{2} = 30$

$\Rightarrow$ $2p - y - p = 60$

$\Rightarrow$ $p - y = 60$ ...(*ii*)

From (*i*) and (*ii*),

$p - \frac{3}{4} p = 60$

$\Rightarrow$ $\frac{1}{4} p = 60$

$\Rightarrow$ $p = 240$

From (*i*), $y = \frac{3}{4} \times 240 = 180$

$\therefore$ 20% of $y = 180 \times \frac{20}{100} = 36$

$\therefore$ Required answer = 36.

62. Given, A vessel contains milk and water = 80 litre

Quantity of milk $= 80 \times \frac{3}{3+5} = 30$ litres

and Quantity of water $= 80 \times \frac{5}{8} = 50$ litres

According to question,

$\frac{30}{50+x} = \frac{1}{2}$

$\Rightarrow$ $60 = 50 + x \Rightarrow x = 10.$

63. Let the present ages of A and B be $5x$ and $9x$

Then, $(5x + 4) : (9x + 4) = 7 : 11$

$\Rightarrow$ $(5x + 4) \times 11 = (9x + 4) \times 7$

$\Rightarrow$ $55x + 44 = 63x + 28$

$\Rightarrow$ $63x - 55x = 44 - 28$

$\Rightarrow$ $8x = 16 \Rightarrow x = 2$

$\therefore$ The present age of B $= 9x$

$= 9 \times 2 = 18$ years

$\therefore$ The age of B two years ago

$= 18 - 2 = 16$ years.

64. $\because$ Simple interest $= \frac{prt}{100}$

$\therefore$ $2400 = x \times \frac{20}{100} \times 3$

$\Rightarrow$ $x = 2400 \times \frac{5}{3}$

$\Rightarrow$ $x = 4000$

Now, Compound Interest $= P\left(1 + \frac{r}{100}\right)^n - P$

$= P\left[\left(1 + \frac{r}{100}\right)^n - 1\right]$

$= P\left[\left(1 + \frac{10}{100}\right)^2 - 1\right]$

$= 4000\left[\left(\frac{11}{10}\right)^2 - 1\right]$

$= 4000\left[\frac{121}{100} - 1\right] = 4000\left[\frac{21}{100}\right]$

$= 40 \times 21 =$ ₹ 840.

65. The length of a train = Speed × Time

$= 25 \times 16$

$= 400$ m

$\Rightarrow \quad x = 400$ m

∴ The length of a bridge

$= x + 150$

$= 400 + 150 = 550$ m

∴ The time taken by the train to cross the bridge

$= \dfrac{550 + 400}{25}$

$= \dfrac{950}{25}$

$= 38$ seconds.

66. 9th element from the right end = 9

∴ 4th element to the left of 9th element from the right end = @.

67. # k 7, % p 5

∴ Required number of letter = two.

68. H # K, M ! R

∴ Required number of symbols = two.

69. Option (B) 7 P 1 does not belong to that group.

70. Even numbers are between % and 1

= Two (2, 8).

71. Given,

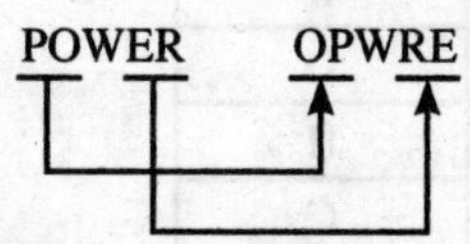

and

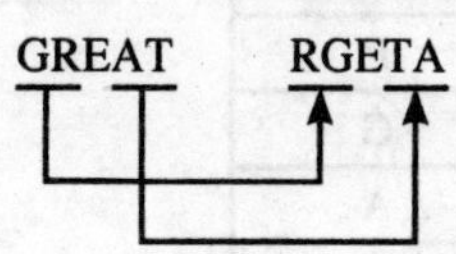

Similarly,

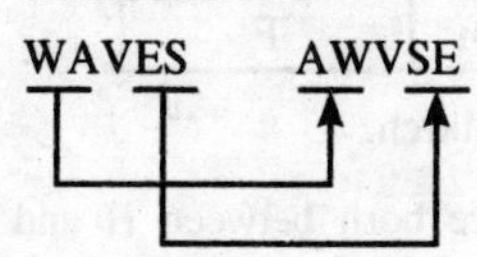

∴ 'WAVES' is coded as 'AWVSE'.

72. Given Statements:

S ≥ G > K = E > B < J > P

⇒ S ≥ G > K = E > B

⇒ S > E, S > B

Conclusions:

I. B ≤ S (False)   II. S > E (True)

Here, Only conclusion II is true.

73. Given Statements:

F < Y ≤ J ≤ Q = L > V < A

⇒ Y ≤ J ≤ Q = L ⇒ Y ≤ L

⇒ Y = L, Y < L

Conclusions:

I. L = Y (True)   II. L > Y (True)

Here, either conclusion I or II is true.

74. Given Statements:

G > U = C ≥ Z > R > I < W ≤ T

⇒ G > U = C ≥ Z > R > I

⇒ G > I

and C ≥ Z > R > I < W ≤ T

⇒ C > I < W ≤ T

Conclusions:

I. G > I (True)   II. C > T (False)

∴ Only conclusion I is true.

75. Given Statements:

Y < W < J ≥ N; W < P ≤ Z

⇒ Y < W < P ≤ Z

⇒ W < Z, Y < P

Conclusions:

I. W < Z (True)   II. P > Y (True)

Here, Both conclusions I and II are true.

76. Given Statements:

B < K = F ≥ J; N ≤ D > K

⇒ N ≤ D > K = F ≥ J

⇒ D > J

Conclusions:

I. J < D (True)   II. D ≥ F (False)

Here, Only conclusion I is true.

77. Given word:

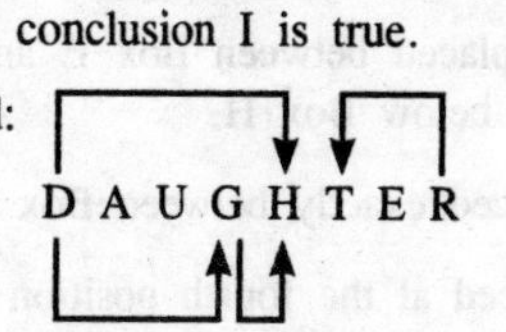

Here, there are four pairs of letters in the given word.

78. Given number = 7 4 2 1 5 3 9 8

After arranging, ↓

in ascending order = 1 2 3 4 5 7 8 9

Here, Only one digit (5) will remain at the same position.

For Qs. No. 79-81:

Given, 6 persons are comparing their weight in decreasing order from Left to Right.

H > B > A > C > J > M.

79. Two persons weight between B and J.

80. Given, H is related to A

⇒ Weight of one person between A and C is related to M

⇒ Weight of one person between C and M

Similarly, B is related to C.

81. H is the heaviest person among them.

82. Given, word : 'MENTORS'

1st, 3rd, 5th and 6th letters are M, N, O and R

Meaningful word can be formed: NORM

Now, 2nd letter from left end of meaningful word = O.

For Qs. No. 83-85:

From given information,

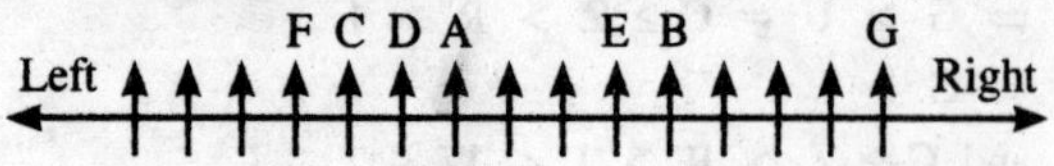

83. 15 persons sit in the row.

84. Fourth to the left position of B with respect to G.

85. Six persons sit to the left of A.

For Qs. No. 86-90:

From given information:

8 boxes are placed one above another in a stack.

Boxes
E
G
C
B
H
D
F
A

86. 4 boxes are placed between Box E and the box which is placed just below Box H.

87. Box D is placed exactly between Box B and Box A.

88. Box B is placed at the fourth position from the top.

89. Given,

Boxes	Alphabetical order
E	A
G	B
C	C
B	D
H	E
D	F
F	G
A	H

Here, only one box C will remain in their original position.

90. One box is placed between box C and box H.

From Qs. No. 91-95:

From given information:

8 persons sit around a circular table facing inside:

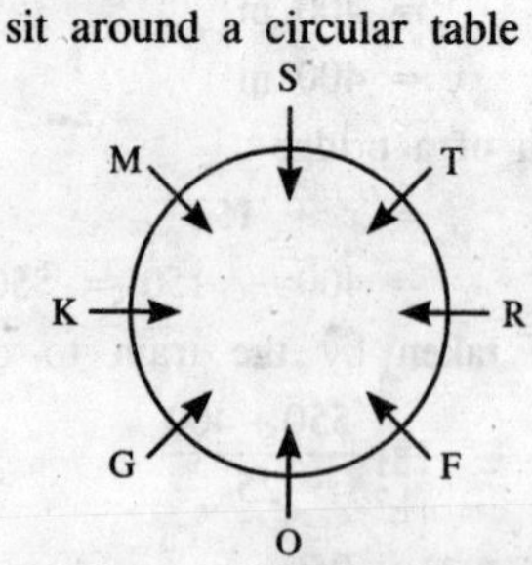

91. T sits second to the right of F.

92. Third to the right is the position of O with respect to M.

93. Two persons sit between S and F when counted from the left of S.

94. Correct statement: F sits opposite to M.

95. R-G, R does not sit opposite to G

$\therefore$ Option (E) is dissimilar to others.

From Qs. No. 96-100:

From given information:

Months	Person
March (31)	I
April (30)	B
May (31)	D
June (30)	H
July (31)	C
August (31)	E
September (30)	G
October (31)	A
November (30)	F

96. I was born in March.

97. Four People were born between H and F.

98. Both I and II are true.

99. Person Days

(A) G $\Rightarrow$ 30

(B) C $\Rightarrow$ 31

(C) D $\Rightarrow$ 31

(D) E $\Rightarrow$ 31

(E) A $\Rightarrow$ 31

$\therefore$ Option (A) does not belong to the group.

100. G, A were born in September and October respectively.

Previous Years' Paper

State Bank of India (SBI)

CLERICAL CADRE – JUNIOR ASSOCIATES

Phase-I : Preliminary Exam, 2023*

ENGLISH LANGUAGE

Directions (Qs. No. 1-8): *Read the given passage carefully to answer the following questions. Each question will have five alternatives as its answer. Choose the correct option as your answer.*

Fishing is a significant industry in Korea, particularly in coastal areas like Jeju Island. The waters around these regions are abundant with various marine life, making them ideal for fishing activities. Local fishermen primarily target species like mackerel, squid, and the Jeju hairtail, which are highly valued in Korean cuisine.

The life of a fisherman involves starting their day early, often before sunrise, to take advantage of the best fishing conditions. They use a combination of traditional and modern techniques to maximize their catch. This includes using nets and lines that are designed to be effective for specific types of fish.

The fishing process is closely tied to the seasons and weather. Spring usually offers the richest haul due to favorable ocean conditions and the life cycle of fish. However, winter fishing can be **challenging** due to rough seas and cold weather, which test the resilience and skill of the fishermen.

On the boat, teamwork is crucial. Fishermen must work together ______ operate the equipment, haul in their catch, and manage their vessel safely. The term **"bloster,"** often used among fishermen, refers to someone exceptionally skilled at handling the most challenging conditions at sea.

After a day at sea, the catch is brought back to shore and sold at local markets. This not only provides income for the fishermen but also supports the local economy by supplying fresh seafood.

Overall, fishing is more than just an occupation in Korea; it is a **heritage** that embodies the relationship between humans and the sea. It demands knowledge, patience, and respect for nature, contributing to the cultural fabric of coastal communities.

1. Find a synonym for **'heritage'** in the passage's context.
A. Legacy
B. Burden
C. Novelty
D. Decline
E. Hindrance

2. According to the passage, what is the impact of fishing on the local economy?
A. It leads to overfishing and depletion of resources
B. It has no significant impact on the local economy
C. It primarily supports international trade
D. It supplies fresh seafood and provides income for fishermen
E. It increases pollution in coastal areas

3. According to the passage, what is the term **"bloster"** used to describe among fishermen?
A. A type of boat used for fishing
B. A special kind of fishing net
C. A fisherman skilled at handling challenging sea conditions
D. A traditional fishing technique
E. A local fish market

4. According to the passage, which of the following statements is/are correct?
(*a*) The local economy benefits from the fishing industry.
(*b*) The primary fish caught are tuna and bass.
(*c*) The fishing industry contributes to pollution as its main impact.
A. Only (*c*)
B. Only (*a*)
C. Only (*b*)
D. Both (*a*) and (*c*)
E. Both (*a*) and (*b*)

1. A	2. D	3. C	4. B

* *Based on Memory.*

5. What does the passage suggest about the role of weather and seasons in fishing?
A. They primarily affect the type of fish caught.
B. They have no significant impact on fishing activities.
C. They are crucial factors affecting the success of fishing.
D. They determine the pricing of fish in markets.
E. They influence the migration patterns of fish but not the fishing itself.

6. According to the passage, which of the following statements is/are incorrect?
(*a*) Fishermen start their day early to use the best fishing conditions.
(*b*) Fishermen in Korea use only modern techniques to fish.
(*c*) Fishermen are not affected by weather conditions.
A. Only (*a*) B. Only (*b*)
C. Only (*c*) D. Both (*b*) and (*c*)
E. Both (*a*) and (*c*)

7. Find an antonym for the word **'challenging'** as used in the context of the passage
A. Difficult B. Easy
C. Complex D. Hard
E. Complicated

8. **Fill in the blank in the passage:**
"Fishermen must work together _______ operate the equipment, haul in their catch, and manage their vessel safely."
A. to B. and
C. but D. as
E. with

Directions (Qs. No. 9-12): *Given below are five scattered segments of a sentence. Indicate the correct sequence which correctly assembles the segments and completes the sentence.*

9. (*a*) may slightly increase the risk of premature death,
(*b*) while insomnia's impact on physical health,
(*c*) like obesity, diabetes, and high blood pressure,
(*d*) potentially linked to underlying diseases,
(*e*) is debated, research suggests only daytime symptoms
A. (*d*), (*e*), (*b*), (*c*), (*a*)
B. (*d*), (*a*), (*b*), (*c*), (*e*)
C. (*b*), (*c*), (*e*), (*a*), (*d*)
D. (*c*), (*a*), (*e*), (*b*), (*d*)
E. (*b*), (*a*), (*e*), (*c*), (*d*)

10. (*a*) Japanese techniques such as Pomodoro and Ikigai
(*b*) resulting from a lack of discipline
(*c*) boosting happiness and productivity through
(*d*) within the framework of capitalism
(*e*) is a key means of overcoming unhappiness
A. (*d*), (*e*), (*b*), (*c*), (*a*)
B. (*e*), (*d*), (*a*), (*b*), (*c*)
C. (*a*), (*b*), (*c*), (*e*), (*d*)
D. (*d*), (*e*), (*c*), (*b*), (*a*)
E. (*c*), (*a*), (*e*), (*b*), (*d*)

11. (*a*) a preventable issue rooted in complex circumstances
(*b*) Society must embrace addiction as
(*c*) to combat its damaging effects
(*d*) on individuals and the economy
(*e*) promoting ethical treatment and collective efforts
A. (*c*), (*e*), (*b*), (*a*), (*d*)
B. (*c*), (*a*), (*d*), (*b*), (*e*)
C. (*b*), (*a*), (*e*), (*c*), (*d*)
D. (*a*), (*b*), (*c*), (*e*), (*d*)
E. (*d*), (*e*), (*c*), (*b*), (*a*)

12. (*a*) as employees worldwide adapted to
(*b*) during the pandemic years,
(*c*) work-from-home or hybrid work patterns,
(*d*) apps and services for work-related reasons
(*e*) a number of them began using personal messaging
A. (*c*), (*e*), (*b*), (*a*), (*d*)
B. (*b*), (*a*), (*c*), (*e*), (*d*)
C. (*e*), (*d*), (*b*), (*c*), (*a*)
D. (*b*), (*a*), (*d*), (*e*), (*c*)
E. (*e*), (*a*), (*d*), (*b*), (*c*)

Directions (Qs. No. 13-17): *Below, a passage is given with five blanks labelled (a)-(e). Below the passage, five options are given for each blank. Choose the word that fits each blank most appropriately in the context of the passage, and mark the corresponding answer.*

Our lives have been simplified by the __**(*a*)**__ of computer and internet, but these benefits which have been ushered in by the technology revolution have had an __**(*b*)**__ affect on the core of our interpersonal-relationships. Communication is no longer __**(*c*)**__ postal mail or face-to-face contact, but via electronic mail, personal internet message boards, and by virtue of hand-held personal electronic assistants. __**(*d*)**__ computer technology has brought us to within a mouse click of any sought-after piece of information, this technology boom has __**(*e*)**__ us to the confines of our computer desks and has taken us away from the traditional settings where personal and communication skills were developed.

5. C	6. D	7. B	8. A	9. C	10. E	11. C	12. B

13. Which of the following words most appropriately fits the blank labelled **(*a*)**?

A. Arrival B. Surfacing
C. Materialisation D. Advent
E. Onset

14. Which of the following words most appropriately fits the blank labelled **(*b*)**?

A. Adverse B. Averse
C. Unpropitious D. Unscrupulous
E. Unlucky

15. Which of the following words most appropriately fits the blank labelled **(*c*)**?

A. Vis-a-vis B. Via
C. En route D. Albeit
E. Sans

16. Which of the following words most appropriately fits the blank labelled **(*d*)**?

A. Since B. Therefore
C. Because D. Although
E. As

17. Which of the following words most appropriately fits the blank labelled **(*e*)**?

A. Unfrequented B. Conceals
C. Concealed D. Sequesters
E. Sequestered

Directions (Qs. No. 18-22): *The given sentence is divided into four parts: (A), (B), (C), and (D). Choose the part that contains an error as your answer. If the sentence is error-free, mark (E) i.e. No error as your answer.*

18. The number of foreign tourists (A)/ visiting India are increasing (B)/ day by day during (C)/ this tourist season. (D)/ No error (E).

19. Chief Minister of the state has announced (A)/ five lakhs rupees compensation (B)/ for the family of those (C)/ killed in the flood and rain (D)/ No error (D)

20. The company has decided to (A)/ layoff a few employees (B)/due to the recent (C)/financial downturn (D)/No error (E)

21. The company is (A)/ in debt and has been (B)/ unable to pay their creditors (C)/ for the past six months (D)/ No error (E).

22. Everybody know (A)/ that his failure can (B)/ be attributed only (C)/ to his lack of practice. (E)/ No error (E).

Directions (Qs. No. 23-26): *In the following sentences, four words given in bold are marked as (a), (b), (c) and (d), which are possible pairs to be interchanged. Choose the pair(s) of words that need to be interchanged to make the sentence grammatically correct and meaningful. If no interchange is required, mark option E i.e., "No interchange required" as your answer.*

23. India's **ecosystem (*a*)** in healthcare AI is **commendable (*b*)**, yet **sustaining (*c*)** growth requires ongoing investments in research, academia-industry collaborations, and innovation-friendly **progress (*d*)**.

A. (*a*)–(*b*) B. (*b*)–(*c*)
C. (*c*)–(*d*) D. (*d*)–(*a*)
E. No interchange required

24. A policy **framework (*a*)** is needed to ensure **equitable (*b*)** contributions from major OTT service providers to **subscriber (*c*)** operators, determined by factors such as **telecom (*d*)** count and data usage.

A. (*c*)–(*d*) B. (*a*)–(*b*)
C. (*b*)–(*c*), (*a*)–(*d*) D. (*d*)–(*a*), (*b*)–(*c*)
E. No interchange required

25. In this era of **professional (*a*)** change, the growing presence of **embracing (*b*)** AI in the workplace presents challenges, but people are **generative (*c*)** the positive impact it can have on their **transformative (*d*)** lives.

A. (*a*)–(*b*), (*c*)–(*d*) B. (*a*)–(*b*)
C. (*a*)–(*d*) D. (*b*)–(*c*), (*d*)–(*a*)
E. No interchange required

26. The Earth, our **unique (*a*)** home in the vast universe, faces **peril (*b*)** due to human actions, and **merely (*c*)** addressing climate change isn't enough; accountability across all boundaries is **essential (*d*)** to protect it.

A. (*b*)–(*c*) B. (*a*)–(*d*), (*b*)–(*c*)
C. (*b*)–(*d*) D. (*c*)–(*a*)
E. No interchange required

Directions (Qs. No. 27-29): *Which of the following phrases (A), (B), (C), (D) given below in the statement should replace the phrase printed in bold in the sentence to make it grammatically correct? If the sentence is correct as it is given and 'No Correction is required', mark (E) as the answer.*

27. They were woken up by someone hammering **below the door.**

A. at the door B. in the door
C. on the door. D. besides the door.
E. No Correction is required

13. D	14. A	15. B	16. D	17. E	18. B	19. B	20. E
21. C	22. A	23. D	24. A	25. D	26. E	27. C	

28. I was very **impressed above how** she made such a powerful and accurate representation of the place.
A. impressed at how
B. impressed on how
C. impressed in how
D. No correction required
E. impressed for how

29. The oil tanker ran aground **below a mud bank** in thick fog.
A. in a mud bank
B. at a mud bank
C. on a mud bank
D. beside a mud bank
E. No Correction required

30. In its report, The State of the World's Children 2019, UNICEF said that every second child in that age group **is affected** by some form of malnutrition
A. are affected B. is effected
C. are effected D. is effect
E. No improvement required

NUMERICAL ABILITY

Directions (Qs. No. 31-35): *What will come in place of the question mark (?) in the following number series?*

31. 1, 3, 8, 19, 39, 71, ?
A. 128 B. 228
C. 118 D. 108
E. None of these

32. 10, 15, 25, 40, ?, 85
A. 55 B. 65
C. 50 D. 70
E. 60

33. 12, 13, 28, ?, 352, 1765
A. 102 B. 81
C. 91 D. 87
E. 105

34. 10, 11, 15, 24, ?, 65
A. 42 B. 45
C. 48 D. 35
E. 40

35. 27, 38, 51, 68, 87, ?
A. 100 B. 120
C. 115 D. 110
E. None of these

36. Speed of Suraj is 16 km/h in still water. Current is flowing at the rate of 4 km/hour, what will be the average speed (in km/h) of Suraj in the journey comprising of an upstream and a downstream journey.
A. 15 B. 20
C. 25 D. 22
E. 18

37. Pavan is 12 years older than Raghav and the respective ratio of Raghav's age 8 years hence and Shreya's present age is 17 : 7. If at present Pavan's age is thrice the age of Shreya. What will be Pavan's age 3 years hence?
A. 21 years B. 24 years
C. 27 years D. 25 years
E. 22 years

38. The compound interest on a certain sum of money for 2 years is ₹ 2,781 and the simple interest for the same time at the same rate is ₹ 2,700. Find the rate of interest.
A. 12% B. 8%
C. 6% D. 3%
E. 10%

39. Ram, Lakhan and Bharat started a business with capital ₹ 85000, ₹ 68000 and ₹ 34000 respectively. At the end of 5 years, the total Profit is ₹ 13,310. What is the difference of profit share between Ram and Bharat?
A. ₹ 3,630 B. ₹ 3,600
C. ₹ 3,500 D. ₹ 2,420
E. None of these

Directions (Qs. No. 40-45): *The following line graph shows the number of projects completed in six different months by a company.*

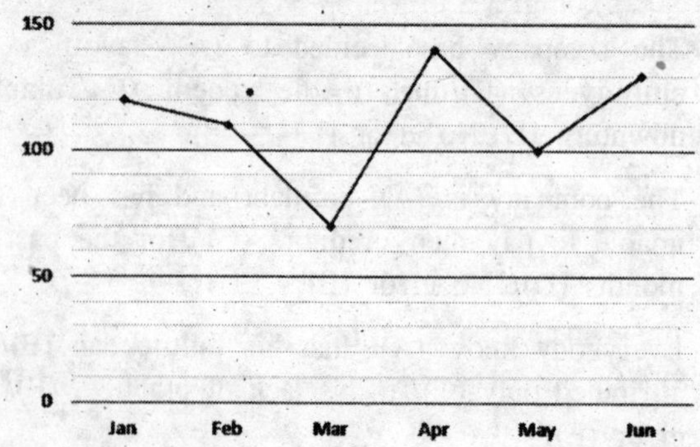

28. A	29. C	30. E	31. C	32. E	33. D
34. E	35. D	36. A	37. B	38. C	39. A

40. The total number of projects completed in January is approximately what percentage more/less than the total number of projects completed in March?
A. 68% B. 77%
C. 76% D. 71%
E. 73%

41. If the total number of projects completed by company B in February is 50% more than that of company A in January and the sum of the total number of projects completed by company B in February and March is 255, then find the difference between the total number of projects completed by company B in February and March.
A. 135 B. 125
C. 105 D. 110
E. 115

42. Find the ratio of the total number of projects completed in May to the total number of projects completed in January and June together.
A. 3 : 7 B. 2 : 3
C. 4 : 5 D. 2 : 5
E. 3 : 5

43. If the average number of projects completed in January, May and December is 115, then the total number of projects completed in February is what percentage of the total number of projects completed in December?
A. 82% B. 84%
C. 88% D. 92%
E. 86%

44. If the total number of projects completed in August is twice the difference between the total number of projects completed in March and June, and the ratio of the total number of projects completed in April to July is 7 : 5, then find the sum of the total number of projects completed in July and August.
A. 265 B. 350
C. 220 D. 240
E. 250

45. If the principal of ₹ 10,000 amounts to ₹ 19,600 with 40% p.a. rate of interest compounded annually. Calculate the time for which it was invested.
A. 10 years B. 5 years
C. 2 years D. 4 years
E. 3 years

46. Ramesh purchased a land for ₹ 45000 and sold (3/5) part at a loss of 5%. How much per cent of profit should be sold the remaining part so that he made 15% profit on the whole?
A. 45% B. 35%
C. 50% D. 55%
E. 40%

Directions (Qs. No. 47-61): *What will come in the place of the question mark '?' in the following question?*

47. $2\frac{1}{4} + 3\frac{1}{6} - 1\frac{2}{8} = ? + 1\frac{1}{12}$
A. $4\frac{3}{12}$ B. $3\frac{4}{24}$
C. $3\frac{1}{12}$ D. $3\frac{5}{12}$
E. $3\frac{4}{12}$

48. $1\frac{1}{6} + \frac{1}{8} + 2\frac{5}{8} - 3\frac{2}{3} = ?$
A. $\frac{1}{5}$ B. $\frac{2}{3}$
C. $\frac{1}{6}$ D. $\frac{1}{4}$
E. $\frac{1}{2}$

49. $58 + (222 \div 3) \div 37 + 2^2 = ?^2$
A. 9 B. 4
C. 8 D. 6
D. 7

50. 250 ÷ 5 × 2/350 + 26/7 = ?
A. 5 B. 6
C. 7 D. 4
D. None of these

51. 115% of 4880 – 85% of 1640 = ?
A. 4218 B. 4368
C. 4448 D. 46228
E. None of these

52. ?% of 590 + 36% of 170 = 150
A. 14.6 B. 16.4
C. 17.8 D. 15.05
E. None of these

40. D	41. C	42. D	43. C	44. C	45. C	46. A
47. C	48. D	49. C	50. D	51. A	52. D	

53. $(102 - 68) + 46 = ? \times 10$
A. 6 B. 5
C. 3 D. 2
E. 8

54. $852 - 13 \times 8 - 102 \times 3 - 1 = ?^2$
A. 21 B. 23
C. 24 D. 20
E. 19

55. $60 - 38 \div 19 \times 26 = ?$
A. 8 B. 6
C. 5 D. 4
E. 9

56. $163 + 7 \times 11 - 9 = ? \times 11$
A. 11 B. 21
C. 35 D. 25
D. 43

57. $31^2 - 928 - 5^2 = 2 \times ? \div 11$
A. 22 B. 34
C. 45 D. 44
E. 76

58. 39% of $700 + 12 = 5 \times ?$
A. 43 B. 57
C. 54 D. 55
E. 66

59. $\sqrt{676} \times \sqrt{576} - ? \times 18 = 300$
A. 14 B. 16
C. 18 D. 20
E. 22

60. $24 + \sqrt{81} \div 3 \times ? = 30$
A. 1 B. 2
C. 3 D. 4
E. 5

61. $4 \times (?/100) \times 210 + 225 = 351$
A. 15 B. 21
C. 25 D. 12
E. 18

62. Two trains cross each other in 16 seconds coming from opposite directions. If the sum of their speeds is 25 m/s and train B is 60 m shorter than train A, then find the length of train A.
A. 235 m B. 240 m
C. 250 m D. 230 m
E. 210 m

63. If each side of a wooden job which is rectangular in shape is increased by 40%, then the percentage increase in the area of a rectangle wooden job is:
A. 70% B. 65%
C. 80% D. 96%
E. None of these

64. If A can fill 2/3 of a tank in 6 hours while B can fill 4/9th of the tank in 8 hours, find the time to fill 1/3 of the tank when both A and B work. (in hours).
A. 1 B. 1.5
C. 2 D. 2.5
E. None of the above/More than one of the above

65. There are two vessels- A and B containing milk and water in the ratio 8 : 7 and 4 : 5 respectively. In what ratio should they be mixed so that the ratio of milk and water in the resultant solution is 1 : 1?
A. 3 : 5 B. 4 : 3
C. 5 : 3 D. 2 : 1
E. 1 : 1

REASONING ABILITY

Directions (Qs. No. 66-70): *Study the following information carefully and answer the questions given below:*

Eight persons A, B, C, D, E, F, G, and H are sitting around a square table in such a way that four of them sit at four corners facing toward the center, and the other four sit at the middle of the sides facing outside. G does not sit at the corner. D sits second to the left of A who sits third left of G. C sits third to the left of B who is not a neighbour of G. Only two persons sit between F and H who sits opposite to E.

66. Who among the following person sits second to the right of E?
A. G B. B
C. A D. C
E. Cannot be determined

67. How many persons sit between F and A when counted from the right of F?
A. Two B. One
C. Three D. Five
E. Four

53. E	**54.** A	**55.** A	**56.** B	**57.** D	**58.** B	**59.** C	**60.** B
61. A	**62.** D	**63.** D	**64.** C	**65.** C	**66.** B	**67.** D	

68. Who among the following person faces C?
A. A B. D
C. F D. G
E. None of these

69. What is the position of D with respect to B?
A. Fourth to the right B. Third to the right
C. Fourth to the left D. Third to the left
E. None of these

70. Find the odd one out:
A. A B. C
C. E D. D
E. F

Directions (Qs. No. 71-73): *Study the following information carefully and answer the questions that follow.*

In a family, there are eight persons. T is the sister of D. D is married to P, who is son of M. T is mother of J. Y is the father of U. Y has only one son and one daughter. U is the daughter of T. Q is son of D. M is a male.

71. How is D related to M?
A. Daughter-in-law B. Grand-daughter
C. Mother D. Sister-in-law
E. None of these

72. How is J related to Y?
A. Son B. Father
C. Uncle D. Nephew
E. None of these

73. How is U related to D?
A. Niece B. Aunt
C. Mother D. Sister
E. None of these

74. How many such pairs of letters are there in the word "HABITABLE" which has as many letters between them as in the English alphabetical order (both forward and backward)?
A. Three B. One
C. Two D. Four
E. None of these

Directions (Qs. No. 75-79): *Study the following information carefully and answer the question below.*

Eight boxes were kept one above the other in the form of a stack such that the box kept at the bottom-most position is numbered as 1, box just above it is numbered as 2 and so on till the box at top-most position is numbered as 8. Box A was kept two places below of box B. Only one box was kept between box C and Box B. Box D kept below box E but above box A. Box E neither kept at odd-numbered stack nor at the topmost position. At most one box was kept between box F and D. Box F kept below of box G but above box H.

75. How many boxes were kept below box D?
A. Two B. Three
C. Four D. Five
E. None of these

76. Which among the following boxes is kept at the topmost position?
A. G B. C
C. D D. Either G or C
E. None of these

77. Box A kept ______ to the ______ of box H?
A. 3rd, above B. 4th, below
C. 3rd, below D. 2nd, above
E. 5th, above

78. What is the position of box C with respect to box F?
A. 7th above B. 4th below
C. 5th above D. 6th above
E. None of these

79. Four from the following are related in a certain way and hence form group. Find the one which doesn't belong to that group?
A. B B. E
C. D D. G
E. F

Directions (Qs. No. 80-84): *The following questions are based on the given numbers. Study the information carefully and answer the questions.*

992 986 867 756 886

80. If the digits are arranged in ascending order from left to right within the numbers, then which among the following numbers will be the second lowest?
A. 992 B. 986
C. 867 D. 756
E. 886

81. If 2 is subtracted from the odd digits within the numbers, then which among the following will be the third highest number?
A. 992 B. 986
C. 867 D. 756
E. 886

68. A	**69.** B	**70.** C	**71.** A	**72.** A	**73.** A	**74.** A
75. B	**76.** A	**77.** D	**78.** C	**79.** A	**80.** D	**81.** B

82. If the digits are arranged in descending order from left to right within the numbers, then how many numbers thus formed are divisible by 2?

A. Four B. Three
C. Two D. Five
E. One

83. If the numbers are arranged in ascending order from right to left, then, which is the third digit of the number that is placed second to the left of the number which is third from the left end in the new arrangement?

A. 9 B. 6
C. 2 D. 5
E. None of the above

84. If the first and the second digits are interchanged within the numbers, then which among the following will be the second highest number?

A. 886 B. 756
C. 867 D. 992
E. 986

Directions (Qs. No. 85-89): *Study the following information carefully and answer based on it.*

Eight people E, F, G, H, I, J, K and L are sitting in a row such that four of them are facing north and four of them are facing south. No two people who are immediate neighbours of each other faces in the same direction. Four people sit between F and G, but none of them sits at an extreme ends. E sits third to the left of F. E is an immediate neighbour of J, who sits third from the right end. I is sitting adjacent to F. More than three people sit between L and K, who does not sit at an extreme end.

85. Who sits at the left end of the row?

A. L B. H
C. I D. J
E. None of these.

86. How many people are sitting between K and G?

A. One B. Three
C. None D. Two
E. More than three

87. Who sits second to the left of the one who is third to the left of H?

A. E B. L
C. K D. F
E. None of these

88. Four of the following options are related to each other in some manner. Find the odd one out.

A. I B. E
C. K D. L
E. G

89. Which of the following statement/s is/are false according to the final arrangement?

I. F sits second to the right of H.
II. Two people are between L and E.
III. K sits fourth to the right of J.

A. Only I and II B. Only II and III
C. Only III D. Only I and III
E. Only II

Directions (Qs. No. 90-92): *In the questions below are given three statements followed by two conclusions numbered I and II. You have to take the given statements to be true even if they seem to be at variance with commonly known facts. Read all the conclusions and then decide which of the given conclusions logically follows from the given statements disregarding the commonly known facts.*

90. Statements:

Only a few Camels are Tables.
No Tables are Beds.
Some Beds are Camels.

Conclusions:

I. All Beds are Tables.
II. All Beds being Camels is a possibility.

A. Only conclusion I follow
B. Only conclusion II follow
C. Either conclusion I or II follows
D. Neither conclusion I nor II follows
E. Both conclusion I and II follow

91. Statements:

Only a few games are sports.
Some adventure is games.

Conclusions:

I. No adventure is a sport.
II. Some adventure is sports.

A. Only I follows
B. Only II follows
C. Either I or II follows
D. Neither I nor II follows
E. Both I and II follows

92. Statements:

Only a few spectacles are transparent
No spectacle is a sunglass.

Conclusions:

I. Some transparent are spectacles.
II. Some sunglasses are definitely not transparent.

A. Only I follows B. Only II follows
C. Both follows D. None follows
E. Either I or II follows

82. A	83. C	84. E	85. C	86. B	87. A	88. D	89. C	90. B	91. C	92. A

Directions (Qs. No. 93-96): *Read the given information carefully and answer the questions asked below.*

A certain number of persons sit in a linear row facing towards North. Five persons are sitting between N and R. X sits fourth to the right of R and third to the left of M. Number of persons sit between N and P is equal to the number of persons sit between P and X. N sits fourth from one of the extreme ends. Number of persons sits between N and A is one more than the persons sit between A and P. Q sits seventh to the left of P. As many persons sit to the right of M is one less than the total number of persons sit to the left of Q. Total number of persons are sitting between N and X is more than four.

93. How many persons are sitting in a row?

A. 15 B. 16
C. 17 D. 10
E. 12

94. Who sits fourth to the left of X?

A. R B. N
C. M D. P
E. Q

95. How many persons are sitting between N and X?

A. Six B. Seven
C. Eight D. Nine
E. Ten

96. How many persons sit to the left of A?

A. One B. Two
C. Three D. Six
E. Five

Directions (Qs. No. 97-99): *In the following questions assuming the given statements to be true, find which of the conclusion(s) among the given conclusions is/are definitely true and then give your answers accordingly.*

97. Statement:

$W \leq H \leq N \leq E \leq P; P > Q \geq B < O > I$

Conclusions:

I. $P > W$ II. $W = P$

A. Only I follows
B. Only II follows
C. Both I and II follow
D. Either I or II follows
E. Neither I nor II follows

98. Statements:

$K < L < M \geq N; M = A < X \leq P$

Conclusion:

I. $K \geq P$ II. $K \geq N$

A. Only I follows
B. Only II follows
C. Both I and II follow
D. Either I or II follows
E. Neither I nor II follows

99. Statements:

$F \geq L \geq M < N = P \geq A \geq B > C$

Conclusions:

I. $F \geq C$ II. $F < C$

A. Only II follows
B. Either I or II follows
C. Neither I nor II follows
D. Only I follows
E. Both I and II follow

100. If it is possible to make a meaningful word with the 1st, 4th, 7th and 8th letter of the word FESTIVAL, which of the following will be the third letter of that word, if more than one such word can be formed, give 'X' as the answer and if no such word can be formed, give 'Y' as the answer?

A. F B. E
C. A D. Y
E. X

EXPLANATORY ANSWERS

1. **(A):** This term means traditions and practices passed down through generations, which aligns with "heritage" in the context of the passage.

2. **(D):** The passage states that the catch is brought back to shore and sold at local markets, providing income for the fishermen and supporting the local economy by supplying fresh seafood.

3. **(C):** The term "bloster" is used among fishermen to describe someone exceptionally skilled at handling the most challenging conditions at sea.

4. **(B):** Statement (*a*) is correct as the passage mentions that the local economy benefits from the fishing industry. The other statements are incorrect as they do not align with the passage.

93. C	94. A	95. D	96. D	97. D	98. E	99. B	100. C

5. **(C):** The passage highlights that weather and seasons are crucial factors affecting the success of fishing, influencing when and how fishing activities are conducted.

6. **(D):** Statements (*b*) and (*c*) are incorrect because the passage mentions that fishermen use both traditional and modern techniques and are affected by weather conditions.

7. **(B):** "Easy" is the opposite of "challenging," which means difficult or requiring effort.

8. **(A):** The correct phrase is "work together to operate," meaning that teamwork is necessary to effectively manage the equipment and tasks on the fishing vessel.

9. **(C):** (*b*) starts with "while insomnia's impact on physical health,"
   (*c*) continues with examples "like obesity, diabetes, and high blood pressure,"
   (*e*) adds "is debated, research suggests only daytime symptoms"
   (*a*) specifies the impact "may slightly increase the risk of premature death,"
   (*d*) concludes with "potentially linked to underlying diseases."

   This sequence logically explains the debated impact of insomnia on health and its potential risks.

10. **(E):** (*c*) starts with "boosting happiness and productivity through,"
   (*a*) introduces the techniques "Japanese techniques such as Pomodoro and Ikigai,"
   (*e*) states "is a key means of overcoming unhappiness,"
   (*b*) explains the cause "resulting from a lack of discipline"
   (*d*) concludes with "within the framework of capitalism."

   This sequence presents a logical flow of using Japanese techniques to boost productivity and happiness within a capitalist context.

11. **(C):** (*b*) starts with "Society must embrace addiction as"
   (*a*) describes it "a preventable issue rooted in complex circumstances"
   (*e*) suggests the solution "promoting ethical treatment and collective efforts"
   (*c*) continues with the action "to combat its damaging effects"
   (*d*) ends with the impact "on individuals and the economy."

   This sequence logically frames addiction as a complex issue requiring collective and ethical efforts to mitigate its effects.

12. **(B):** (*b*) starts with "During the pandemic years,"
   (*a*) describes the adaptation "as employees worldwide adapted to"
   (*c*) specifies the patterns "work-from-home or hybrid work patterns,"
   (*e*) adds the change "a number of them began using personal messaging"
   (*d*) concludes with "apps and services for work-related reasons."

   This sequence logically describes the shift in work patterns during the pandemic and the resulting use of personal messaging apps for work.

13. **(D):** The word "advent" means the arrival or beginning of something significant. It fits well in the context of the passage, indicating the start of the computer and internet era.

14. **(A):** The word "adverse" means harmful or unfavorable. It fits the context as the passage talks about the negative impact of technology on interpersonal relationships.

15. **(B):** The word "via" means through or by way of. It is appropriate here, indicating the means of communication shifting to electronic forms.

16. **(D):** The word "although" is used to introduce a contrast. It fits well in the context, contrasting the benefits of computer technology with its drawbacks.

17. **(E):** The word "sequestered" means isolated or hidden away. It fits the context, indicating that technology has confined people to their computer desks, away from traditional social settings.

18. **(B):** The phrase "The number of foreign tourists visiting India are increasing" is incorrect because "The number" is a singular subject. The correct phrase should be "The number of foreign tourists visiting India is increasing."

19. **(B):** The phrase "five lakhs rupees compensation" is incorrect because in Indian English, when referring to multiples of 100,000, "lakh" is used in the singular form. The correct phrase should be "five lakh rupees compensation."

20. **(E):** The sentence "The company has decided to layoff a few employees due to the recent financial downturn" is correct and error-free.

21. **(C):** The phrase "unable to pay their creditors" is incorrect because "The company" is a singular subject. The correct phrase should be "unable to pay its creditors."

22. **(A):** The phrase "Everybody know" is incorrect because "Everybody" is a singular subject and requires a singular verb. The correct phrase should be "Everybody knows."

23. **(D):** The sentence should read: "India's progress in healthcare AI is commendable, yet sustaining growth requires ongoing investments in research, academia-industry collaborations, and innovation-friendly ecosystem." Here, "progress" and "ecosystem" should be swapped.

24. **(A):** The sentence should read: "A policy framework is needed to ensure equitable contributions from major OTT service providers to telecom operators, determined by factors such as subscriber count and data usage." Here, "subscriber" and "telecom" should be swapped.

25. **(D):** The sentence should read: "In this era of transformative change, the growing presence of generative AI in the workplace presents challenges, but people are embracing the positive impact it can have on their professional lives." Here, "embracing" and "generative" should be swapped, as well as "professional" and "transformative."

26. **(E):** The sentence is correct as is: "The Earth, our unique home in the vast universe, faces peril due to human actions, and merely addressing climate change isn't enough; accountability across all boundaries is essential to protect it." No words need to be swapped.

27. **(C):** The correct phrase is "hammering on the door" because "on" indicates the surface being hammered. The phrase "below the door" is incorrect as it implies a location underneath, not the door itself.

28. **(A):** The correct phrase is "impressed at how," which is used to express admiration for someone's actions. "Impressed above how" is incorrect as "above" is not used in this context.

29. **(C):** The correct phrase is "ran aground on a mud bank." "On" is used to indicate that the oil tanker is resting upon or in contact with the mud bank, rather than being in or beside it.

30. **(E):** The sentence "every second child in that age group is affected by some form of malnutrition" is grammatically correct as it stands. The singular subject "every second child" correctly matches with the singular verb "is affected."

31. **(C):** 1 3 8 19 39 71 [118]

+2 +5 +11 +20 +32 +47

+3 +6 +9 +12 +15

+3 +3 +3 +3

Hence, 118 will come at the place of question mark.

32. **(E):** 10 15 25 40 [60] 85

+5 +10 +15 +20 +25

+5 +5 +5 +5

Hence, 60 will come at the place of question mark.

33. **(D):** 12 13 28 [87] 352 1765

× 1 + 1 × 2 + 2 × 3 + 3 × 4 + 4 × 5 + 5

Hence, 87 will come at the place of question mark.

34. **(E):** 10 11 15 24 [40] 65

+ 1 + 4 + 9 + 16 + 25

1^2 2^2 3^2 4^2 5^2

Hence, 40 will come at the place of question mark.

35. **(D):** 27 38 51 68 87 [110]

+11 + 13 +17 +19 +23

All are prime numbers in increasing order

Hence, 110 will come at the place of question mark.

36. **(A):** Upstream = (16 − 4) = 12 km/hr

Downstream = (16 + 4) = 20 km/hr

$$\text{Average Speed} = \frac{2xy}{x+y} = \frac{2 \times 12 \times 20}{12 + 20}$$

$$= \frac{2 \times 12 \times 20}{32}$$

$$= 15 \text{ km/hr}$$

37. **(B):** Let present age of Raghav = x years.

Pavan's present age = $(x + 12)$ years

Present age of Shreya = y years

According to the question,

$$\frac{x+8}{y} = \frac{17}{7}$$

$\Rightarrow 7x - 17y = -56$ ...(*i*)

Again,

$x + 12 = 3y$

$\Rightarrow x - 3y = -12$ ...(*ii*)

From (*i*) and (*ii*) $x = 9$ and $y = 7$

∴ Pavan's present age = 21 years

After 3 years pavan's age will be 24 years.

38. (C): Here, Simple interest for 1 year

$= \frac{2700}{2}$

$= ₹\ 1350$

Since, Simple interest of ₹ 1350 for 1 year

$= 2781 - 2700$

$= ₹\ 81$

Hence, required rate of interest

$= \frac{81 \times 100}{1350 \times 1}$

$= 6\%.$

39. (A): 5 years = 5 × 12 = 60 months

Ram	Lakhan	Bharat
85000 × 60	68000 × 60	34000 × 60

Ratio of their capitals = 85 : 68 : 34

= 5 : 4 : 2

Ram's share $= \frac{5}{11} \times 13310 = ₹\ 6050$

Lakhan's share $= \frac{4}{11} \times 13310 = ₹\ 4840$

Bharat's share $= \frac{2}{11} \times 13310 = ₹\ 2420$

Required difference = 6050 − 2420 = ₹ 3630

40. (D): January = 120

March = 70

Difference = 120 − 70 = 50

Required% $= \frac{50}{70} \times 100$

$= \frac{500}{7}$

$= 71.4\%$

$= 71\%$ (approx)

41. (C): Total no. of projects completed by company B in February

$= 120 + \frac{50}{100} \times 120$

$= 120 + 60$

$= 180$

According to the question,

$180 + y = 255$

$\Rightarrow \quad y = 255 - 180 = 75$

Required difference = 180 − 75 = 105

42. (D): Required ratio $= \frac{100}{120 + 130}$

$= \frac{100}{250}$

$= \frac{2}{5}$

$= 2:5$

43. (C): Total no. of projects completed in January, May and December = 115 × 3 = 345

According to the question,

$110 = \frac{x}{100} \times (345 - 200)$

$\Rightarrow 110 = \frac{x}{100} \times 125$

$\Rightarrow 110 = \frac{5x}{4}$

$\Rightarrow x = \frac{110 \times 4}{5}$

$\Rightarrow x = 22 \times 4$

$\Rightarrow x = 88\%$

44. (C): Total no. of projects completed in August

$= 2\ (130 - 70) = 2 \times 60 = 120$

$\frac{140}{x} = \frac{7}{5} \Rightarrow 7x = 140 \times 5$

$\Rightarrow x = 100$

Hence, total no. of projects completed in July and August = 100 + 120 = 220

45. (C): $A = P\left(1 + \frac{r}{100}\right)^t$

$\Rightarrow \quad 19600 = 10000\left(1 + \frac{40}{100}\right)^t$

$\Rightarrow \quad \frac{19600}{10000} = \left(\frac{14}{10}\right)^t$

$\Rightarrow \quad \left(\frac{14}{10}\right)^2 = \left(\frac{14}{10}\right)^t$

$\Rightarrow \quad t = 2$ years.

46. (A): C.P. = ₹ 45,000

S.P. $= \frac{115}{100} \times 45000 = ₹\ 51750$

Again S.P. of $\frac{3}{5}$ of 45000 $= \frac{95}{100} \times 27000 = 25650$

C.P. of remaining $\frac{2}{5}$ land = 45000 – 27000 = 18000

S.P. of remaining land = 51750 – 25650 = 26100

Required gain % = $\frac{(26100 - 18000)}{18000} \times 100$

$= \frac{8100}{18000} \times 100$

= 45%

47. (C): $2\frac{1}{4} + 3\frac{1}{6} - 1\frac{2}{8} = x + 1\frac{1}{12}$

$\Rightarrow \frac{9}{4} + \frac{19}{6} - \frac{5}{4} = x + \frac{13}{12}$

$\Rightarrow 1 + \frac{19}{6} - \frac{13}{12} = x$

$\Rightarrow \frac{12 + 38 - 13}{12} = x$

$\Rightarrow \frac{37}{12} = x$

$\Rightarrow x = 3\frac{1}{12}$

Hence, $3\frac{1}{12}$ will come at the place of question mark.

48. (D): $1\frac{1}{6} + \frac{1}{8} + 2\frac{5}{8} - 3\frac{2}{3} = x$

$\Rightarrow \frac{7}{6} + \frac{1}{8} + \frac{21}{8} - \frac{11}{3} = x$

$\Rightarrow \frac{7}{6} + \frac{22}{8} - \frac{11}{3} = x$

$\Rightarrow \frac{7}{6} + \frac{11}{4} - \frac{11}{3} = x$

$\Rightarrow \frac{14 + 33 - 44}{12} = x$

$\Rightarrow \frac{47 - 44}{12} = x$

$\Rightarrow \frac{3}{12} = x$

$\Rightarrow x = \frac{1}{4}$

Hence, $\frac{1}{4}$ will come at the place of question mark.

49. (C): $58 + (222 \div 3) \div 37 + 2^2 = x^2$

$\Rightarrow 58 + 74 \div 37 + 4 = x^2$

$\Rightarrow 58 + 2 + 4 = x^2$

$\Rightarrow 64 = x^2$

$\Rightarrow 8 = x$

Hence, 8 will come at the place of question mark.

50. (D): $250 \div 5 \times \frac{2}{350} + \frac{26}{7} = x$

$\Rightarrow 50 \times \frac{2}{350} + \frac{26}{7} = x$

$\Rightarrow \frac{2}{7} + \frac{26}{7} = x$

$\Rightarrow \frac{28}{7} = x$

$\Rightarrow x = 4$

Hence, 4 will come at the place of question mark.

51. (A): 115% of 4880 – 85% of 1640 = x

$\Rightarrow \frac{115}{100} \times 4880 - \frac{85}{100} \times 1640 = x$

$\Rightarrow 23 \times 244 - 17 \times 82 = x$

$\Rightarrow 5612 - 1394 = x$

$\Rightarrow 4218 = x$

Hence, 4218 will come at the place of question mark.

52. (D): x% of 590 + 36% of 170 = 150

$\Rightarrow \frac{x}{100} \times 590 + \frac{36}{100} \times 170 = 150$

$\Rightarrow \frac{59x}{10} + \frac{612}{10} = 150$

$\Rightarrow 59x + 612 = 1500$

$\Rightarrow 59x = 1500 - 612 = 888$

$\Rightarrow x = \frac{888}{59} = 15.05$

Hence, 15.05 will come at the place of question mark.

53. (E): $(102 - 68) + 46 = x \times 10$

$\Rightarrow 34 + 46 = 10x$

$\Rightarrow 80 = 10x$

$\Rightarrow x = 8$

Hence, 8 will come at the place of question mark.

54. (A): $852 - 13 \times 8 - 102 \times 3 - 1 = x^2$

$\Rightarrow 852 - 104 - 306 - 1 = x^2$

$\Rightarrow 852 - 410 - 1 = x^2$

$\Rightarrow 852 - 411 = x^2$

$\Rightarrow 441 = x^2$

$\Rightarrow x = 21$

Hence, 21 will come at the place of question mark.

55. (A): $60 - 38 \div 19 \times 26 = x$

$\Rightarrow 60 - 2 \times 26 = x$

$\Rightarrow 60 - 52 = x$

$\Rightarrow x = 8$

Hence, 8 will come at the place of question mark.

56. (B): $163 + 7 \times 11 - 9 = x \times 11$

$\Rightarrow 163 + 77 - 9 = 11x$

$\Rightarrow 240 - 9 = 11x$

$\Rightarrow 231 = 11x \Rightarrow x = 21$

Hence, 21 will come at the place of question mark.

57. (D): $31^2 - 928 - 5^2 = 2 \times x \div 11$

$$\Rightarrow 961 - 928 - 25 = \frac{2x}{11}$$

$$\Rightarrow 961 - 953 = \frac{2x}{11}$$

$$\Rightarrow \frac{8 \times 11}{2} = x$$

$\Rightarrow x = 44$

Hence, 44 will come at the place of question mark.

58. (B): 39% of $700 + 12 = 5 \times x$

$$\Rightarrow \frac{39}{100} \times 700 + 12 = 5x$$

$\Rightarrow 273 + 12 = 5x$

$$\Rightarrow \frac{285}{5} = x$$

$\Rightarrow x = 57$

Hence, 57 will come at the place of question mark.

59. (C): $\sqrt{676} \times \sqrt{576} - x \times 18 = 300$

$\Rightarrow 26 \times 24 - 18x = 300$

$\Rightarrow 624 - 300 = 18x$

$\Rightarrow 324 = 18x$

$\Rightarrow x = 18$

Hence, 18 will come at the place of question mark.

60. (B): $24 + \sqrt{81} \div 3 \times x = 30$

$\Rightarrow 24 + 9 \div 3x = 30$

$\Rightarrow 3x = 30 - 24 = 6$

$\Rightarrow x = 2$

Hence, 2 will come at the place of question mark.

61. (A): $4 \times \left(\frac{x}{100}\right) \times 210 + 225 = 351$

$$\Rightarrow \frac{4x}{100} \times 210 = 351 - 225$$

$$\Rightarrow \frac{84\,x}{10} = 126$$

$$\Rightarrow x = \frac{126 \times 10}{84} = 3 \times 5 = 15$$

Hence, 15 will come at the place of question mark.

62. (D): Let length of train A = x m

$\therefore$ Length of train B = $(x - 60)$ m

$$\because t = \frac{\text{distance}}{\text{speed}}$$

$$\Rightarrow 16 = \frac{2x - 60}{25}$$

$\Rightarrow 2x - 60 = 400$

$\Rightarrow 2x = 400 + 60 = 460$

$\Rightarrow x = 230$

Hence, length of train A = 230 m.

63. (D): Area of rectangle = xy

Area of rectangle after increasing each side

Area = $1.4x \times 1.4y = 1.96xy$

Increase in area = $1.96\,xy - xy = 0.96\,xy$.

$$\text{Required \%} = \frac{0.96xy}{xy} \times 100$$

$$= \frac{96}{100} \times 100$$

$= 96\%$

64. (C): A's 1 hr. work = $\frac{1}{6} \times \frac{2}{3} = \frac{1}{9}$

B's 1 hr. work = $\frac{1}{8} \times \frac{4}{9} = \frac{1}{18}$

$$(A + B)\text{'s 1 hr work} = \frac{1}{9} + \frac{1}{18} = \frac{2+1}{18}$$

$$= \frac{3}{18}$$

$$= \frac{1}{6}$$

$$\frac{1}{6}\text{ Part} = 1 \text{ hr.}$$

$$\frac{1}{3}\text{ Part} = \frac{1}{\frac{1}{6}} \times \frac{1}{3} \text{ hr}$$

$$= 6 \times \frac{1}{3} \text{ hr}$$

$$= 2 \text{ hrs.}$$

65. (C): First of all we write the fraction of milk present in three mixtures.

In A : $\frac{8}{15}$, In B : $\frac{4}{9}$

In combination A and B : $\frac{1}{2}$

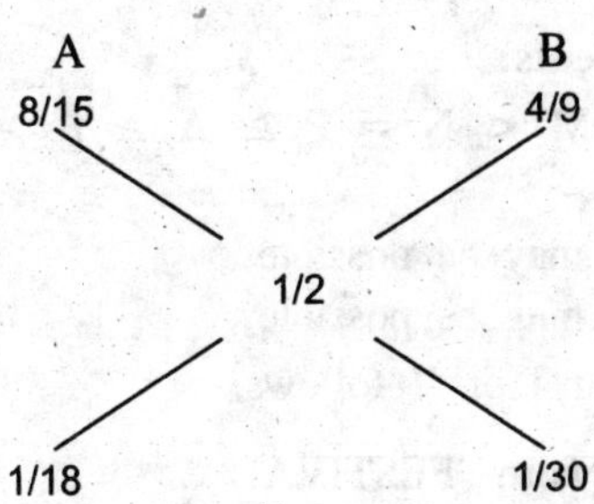

$$\text{Required ratio} = \frac{\frac{1}{18}}{\frac{1}{30}} = \frac{1}{18} \times \frac{30}{1} = 5 : 3$$

For (66-70)

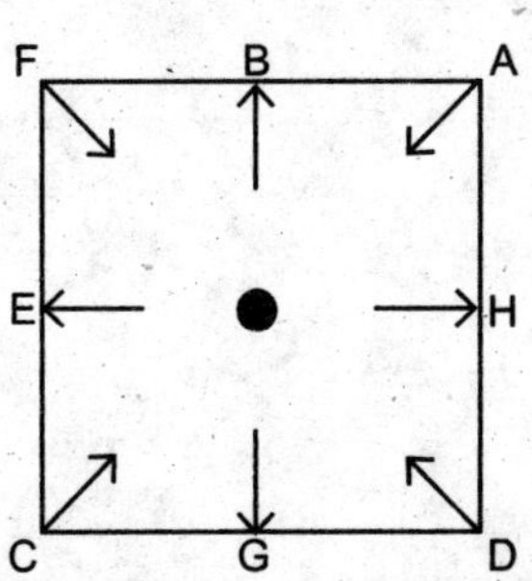

66. (B): B sits second to the right of E.

67. (D): There are five persons that sit between F and A.

68. (A): A faces C.

69. (B): The position of D with respect to B is third to the right.

70. (C): Clearly E is odd one out because E is not sitting on any corner of the table.

For (71-73)

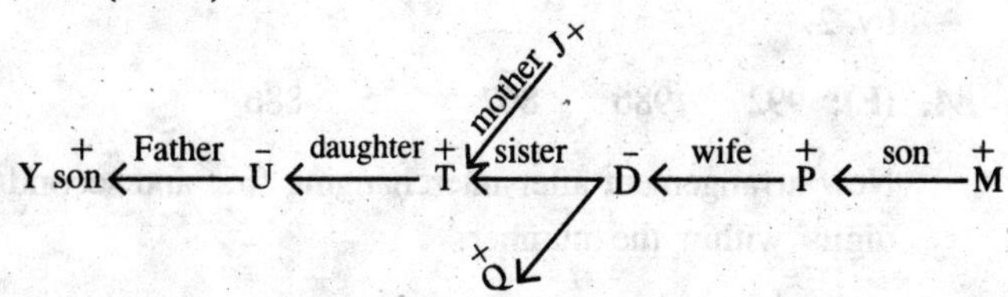

71. (A): Clearly, D is related to M as daughter-in-law.

72. (A): J is related to Y as son.

73. (A): Clearly, U is related to D as niece.

74. (A): "H A B I T A B L E"

$\frac{HB}{1}, \frac{AB}{2}, \frac{AB}{3}$

Required no. of pairs = 3 (three)

For (75 – 79)

Position	Boxes
8th	G
7th	C
6th	E
5th	B
4th	D
3rd	A
2nd	F
1st	H

75. (B): There are three boxes kept below box D.

76. (A): Box G is kept at the top most position.

77. (D): Box A is kept 2nd to the above of box H.

78. (C): The position of box C with respect to box F is above 5th.

79. (A): E, D, G, F boxes are kept at even position but box B is kept at odd position.

Hence, Box B does not belong to that group.

For (80 – 84)

80. (D): 992 986 867 756 886

299 567 678 688 689

Hence, the 2nd lowest will be 756.

81. (B): 992 986 867 756 886

772 786 865 536 886

886 865 786 772 536

Hence, 986 is the third highest number.

82. (A): 992 986 876 765 886

Four numbers (992, 986, 876 and 886) are divisible by 2.

84. (E): 992 986 867 756 886

New arrangement after interchanging first and second digits within the number.

992 896 687 576 886

It is clear that no. 896 is second highest number after new arrangement and the original number for this arranged number is 986.

For (85 - 89)

Eight People are sitting in a row

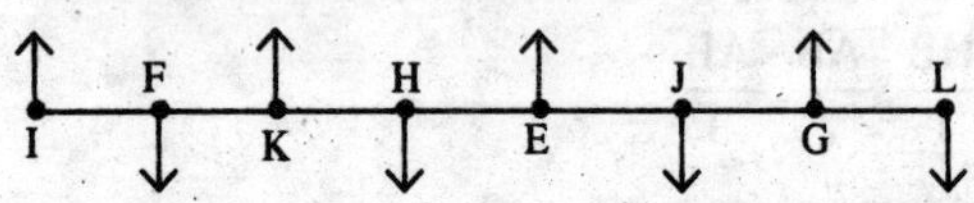

85. (C): Clearly, I sits at the left end of the row.

86. (B): There are three people sitting between G and K.

87. (A): E sits second to the left of the G who is third to the left of H.

88. (D): I, K, E and G are facing in north direction. But L is facing in South direction

Hence, L is odd one out.

89. (C): I. F sits second to the right of H. (True)

II. Two people are sitting between L and E (True).

III. K sits fourth to the right of J. (False)

For (93 - 96)

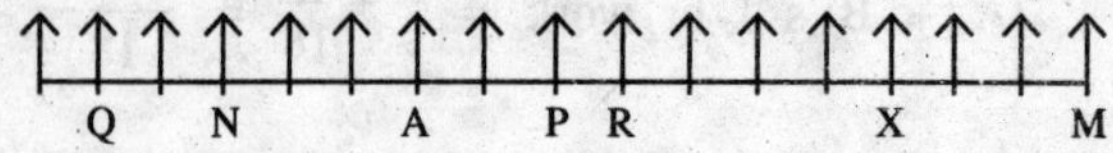

93. (C): 17 persons are sitting in the row.

94. (A): R sits fourth to the left of X.

95. (D): There are nine persons sitting between N and X.

96. (D): There are six persons sitting to the left of A.

For (97 - 99)

97. (D): Statement:

$W \le H \le N \le P;\ P > Q \ge B < O > I$

Conclusions:

I. $P > W$ may be possible.

II. $W = P$ may be possible.

Hence, either I or II follow.

98. (E): Statements:

$K < L < M \ge N;\ M = A < X \le P$

Conclusion:

I. $K \ge P$ not follow

II. $K \ge N$ not follow

Hence, Neither I nor II follows:

99. (B): Statements:

$F \ge L \ge M < N = P \ge A \ge B > C$

Conclusion:

I. $F \ge C$ may be possible

II. $F < C$ may be possible.

Hence, either I or II follows.

100. (C): Given word: FESTIVAL

1st, 4th, 7th and 8th letter of the word = FTAL

Meaningful word formed by using letters FTAL = FLAT

Third letter of the new word = A.

Previous Paper (Solved)

State Bank of India (SBI)

CLERICAL CADRE – JUNIOR ASSOCIATES

Phase-I : Preliminary Exam, 2022*

REASONING ABILITY

Directions (Qs. No. 1-5): *Read the following information carefully and answer the questions given below:*

Eight girls: Dia, Gia, Mia, Nia, Pia, Tia, Sia, and Ria going on a Science Excavation trip from their school on two different dates of the month 16th and the 27th of the months: January, February, September, and October. All information is not necessary in the same order.

Gia goes on the trip in the months which have neither a maximum number of days or a minimum number of days. Only two girls are going on the trip between Gia and Mia. Dia goes on the trip after Gia but not on an odd date. Only three girls are going on the trip between Nia and Sia, who goes on the trip before Tia. Pia goes on the trip before Tia but neither of them will go on the trip on an even number of dates nor in October. Ria goes on the trip after Tia.

1. Who will go on the trip on 16th of any month?

A. Pia B. Tia
C. Gia D. Nia
E. Ria

2. Who goes on the trip exactly before last?

A. Ria B. Dia
C. Gia D. Nia
E. Tia

3. Four of the following five are alike in a certain way and hence they form a group. Which one of the following does not belongs to that group?

A. Pia - Sia B. Tia - Mia
C. Ria - Dia D. Mia - Pia
E. Gia - Nia

4. Who goes on the trip after Gia?

A. Tia B. Pia
C. Nia D. Sia
E. None of these

5. Who goes on the trip on 27th February?

A. Gia
B. Pia
C. Tia
D. Mia
E. Ria

Directions (Qs. No. 6-8): *In the question below are given three statements followed by two conclusions I and II. You have to take the given statements to be true even if they seem to be at variance from commonly known facts. Read all the conclusions and then decide which of the given conclusions logically follows from the given statements disregarding commonly known facts.*

6. **Statements** : All balls are dolls.
All dolls are mobiles.
All mobiles are tablets.

Conclusions : I. All balls are tablets.
II. Some mobiles are dolls.

A. Only conclusion I follows
B. Only conclusion II follows
C. Conclusion I and II both follow
D. Neither conclusion I nor conclusion II follows
E. Either conclusion I or conclusion II follows

7. **Statements** : All apples are oranges.
No orange is lime.
All potatoes are limes.

Conclusions : I. No potato is orange.
II. Some apples are limes.

A. Only conclusion I follows
B. Only conclusion II follows
C. Conclusion I and II both follow
D. Neither conclusion I nor conclusion II follows
E. Either conclusion I or conclusion II follows

1. D	2. B	3. D	4. E	5. C	6. C	7. A

* *Based on memory.*

8. Statements : Only captain is america.
Only a few captain are hydra.
Few hydra are bucky.

Conclusions : I. No bucky is captain.
II. Some america is bucky.

A. Only I follows
B. Only II follows
C. Both I and II follow
D. Neither I nor II follows
E. None of these

Directions (Qs. No. 9-13): *Study the following information carefully to answer the given questions:*

Y 5 @ N 2 # U 9 B E 6 % S © 3 Q A & 7 W I ¥ Z 8 £

9. How many such consonants are there in the above arrangement each of which is immediately preceded by a symbol and immediately followed by a number?
A. Three
B. Two
C. One
D. More than three
E. None

10. What should come in place of question mark on the basis of the above arrangement?

@ 2 U B 6 S ? I Z £

A. 3 A & B. © Q &
C. A 7 I D. 3 A 7
E. None of these

11. If all the vowels in the above arrangement are dropped, then which of the following will be the 8th from the right end?
A. 3 B. &
C. Q D. A
E. None of these

12. If the order of the last 12 elements is reversed, which of the following will be 6th to the left of 21st from the left end?
A. Z B. 8
C. 3 D. Q
E. None of these

13. Four of following five are alike in a certain way based on their positions in the above arrangement and so form a group. Which one does not belong to that group?
A. # 9 N B. 6 S 3
C. 7 I A D. ¥ 8 W
E. @ 2 Y

Directions (Qs. No. 14-16): *In the following questions assuming the given statements to be True, find which of the conclusion among given conclusions is/are definitely true and then give your answers accordingly.*

14. Statements : $T = V < U \geq X; V \leq S; H > U$

Conclusions : I. $S \geq T$ II. $X < H$
A. Only I is True
B. Only II is True
C. Either I or II is True
D. Neither I nor II is True
E. Both I and II are True

15. Statements : $L < O < M; Q > N \geq P > M$

Conclusions : I. $P > L$ II. $M > N$
A. Only I is True
B. Only II is True
C. Both I and II are True
D. Either I or II is True
E. Neither I nor II is True

16. Statements : $X \leq U < V > T; U < S; H > V$

Conclusions : I. $X < H$ II. $T \leq S$
A. Only I is True
B. Only II is True
C. Either I or II is True
D. Neither I nor II is True
E. Both I and II are True

Directions (Qs. No. 17-21): *Study the following information carefully and answer the questions given below.*

Seven boxes—P, Q, R, S, T, U, and V are stacked one above the other but not necessarily in the same order. At most two boxes are placed below box Q. Box U is placed one of the places above box T, but not exactly above. Two boxes are placed between box R and box S, where box S is above box R. Box R is placed exactly above box Q. Box P is placed at one of the places below box S. Number of boxes above box P is the same as the number of boxes below box V. At least five boxes are placed below box S. Box T is placed near Box V.

17. How many boxes are placed above box U?
A. One B. Two
C. Three D. Four
E. Five

18. Which box is placed second from the bottom?
A. R B. S
C. T D. U
E. V

8. D	9. B	10. D	11. C	12. B	13. B	14. E	15. A	16. A	17. B	18. E

19. How many boxes are placed between box T and box S?
A. One
B. Three
C. Four
D. Five
E. None

20. If box S is related to box P and box R is related to box Q in the same way box V is related to which box?
A. T
B. Q
C. R
D. U
E. P

21. If we rearrange all the boxes in alphabetical order from bottom to top, then the position of how many boxes remains unchanged?
A. One
B. Three
C. Four
D. Five
E. None

22. How many such pairs of letters are there in the word 'MISUNDERSTANDING', each of which has as many letters between them in the word (both forward and backward direction) as they have between them in the English Alphabet?
A. One
B. Two
C. Three
D. Four
E. More then four

Directions (Qs. No. 23-25): *Study the information given below carefully and answer the questions that follow.*

Point R is 6 km to the south of point J. Point S is 4 km to the north of point M. Point H is 10 km to the east of point S. Point M is 7 km to the west of point R. Point P is 6 km to the north of point F. Point D is 4 km to the east of point S. Point F is 4 km to the south of point D. Point N is 3 km to the west of point H. Point U is 6 km to the south of point D.

23. What is the distance between points J and P?
A. 4 km
B. 5 km
C. 10 km
D. 6 km
E. 3 km

24. Four of the following five are alike in a certain way based on their position and thus form a group. Which of the following does not belong to the group?
A. S
B. U
C. D
D. N
E. H

25. What is the direction of point S from point U?
A. South-East
B. West
C. East
D. North-West
E. South-West

26. In the word "DOORLOCK" if all the vowels are replaced with the letter immediate next to it in the English alphabet series and all the consonants are replaced with the letter immediately before it in the English alphabet series, then how many vowels are there in the new word so formed?
A. One
B. Two
C. Three
D. None
E. None of these

Directions (Qs. No. 27-32): *Study the following information carefully and answer the questions given below:*

Seven persons A, B, C, D, E, F and G got appointment letter from IBPS in seven different days from Monday to Sunday of a week but not necessarily in the same order. G does not get appointment letter on Sunday. B got appointment letter before E. Only one person got appointment letter between A and D. F got appointment letter in one of the day after D. A got appointment letter on Wednesday. C got appointment letter before D and after B Two people got appointment between B and E.

27. Which of the following is not true?
A. B got appointment letter on Monday
B. E got appointment letter immediately after A
C. Three persons got appointment letter after D
D. Both (A) and (B) are not true
E. All are not true

28. Which of the following combination is correct?
A. B – Monday
B. C – Sunday
C. D – Saturday
D. E – Friday
E. F – Tuesday

29. Who got appointment letter on Friday?
A. B
B. C
C. D
D. E
E. G

30. How many persons got appointment letter between B and F?
A. Three
B. Two
C. None
D. One
E. More than three

31. E got appointment letter in which of the following days?
A. Monday
B. Wednesday
C. Thursday
D. Saturday
E. Tuesday

19. D	20. A	21. E	22. E	23. E	24. B	25. D	26. D	27. C	28. A	29. C	30. E	31. C

32. Select the one which different from other four alternatives.
A. CBD B. GFH
C. MNO D. RQS
E. VUW

Directions (Qs. No. 33-35): *These questions are based on the following information.*

Eight persons P, Q, R, S, T, V, W and X are in a family with three different generations. W is the son of T, who is the only daughter of P. P is the brother-in-law of V and does not has any siblings. Not more than three and not less than two members in the same generation. X is the niece of Q, who is the sibling of T. R is the brother-in-law of Q. V is not a female. Less than four female members are there in the family.

33. How is Q related to S?
A. Nephew B. Cousin
C. Son D. Daughter
E. Father

34. Who among the following is the Maternal uncle of W?
A. Q B. R
C. S D. V
E. Cannot be determined

35. How many females are there in the family?
A. One
B. Four
C. Two
D. Three
E. Cannot be determined

NUMERICAL ABILITY

Directions (Qs. No. 36-47): *What should come in the place of the question mark (?) in the following questions?*

36. $[(27 \times 10) \div 30 + 10500 \div 500] = ? \times 15$
A. 1 B. 4
C. 2.65 D. 0.90
E. 2

37. $999 \div 3 - 165 = 75 + 111 - ?$
A. 20 B. 28
C. 18 D. 22
E. 24

38. $(71 \times 8) + 90 = 132 \times 4 + ?$
A. 160 B. 140
C. 132 D. 130
E. 135

39. $\frac{26}{24}$ of $408 + \frac{25}{48}\%$ of $43200 = ?$
A. 547 B. 447
C. 467 D. 647
E. 667

40. $(8 + 6 \times 7) \div 10 \times 3 = ?$
A. 18 B. 20
C. 30 D. 15
E. 45

41. $5 \times \sqrt{25} + 300 - 100 = ?^2$
A. 12 B. 20
C. 15 D. 25
E. 30

42. $18 - ? + 19 + (11)^2 = 120$
A. 38 B. 48
C. 42 D. 34
E. 24

43. 2.5% of $40 + 4.5\%$ of $80 = ?\%$ of 10
A. 36 B. 24
C. 46 D. 52
E. 38

44. 450% of $? \div 90 + 350\%$ of $200 \div 70 = 20$
A. 180 B. 190
C. 200 D. 210
E. 220

45. $935.5 + 555.4 + 64.5 + 1444.6 = 600\%$ of ?
A. 200 B. 250
C. 300 D. 350
E. None of these

46. $256 \times 2^{-5} \times ? = 2/25$ of 50×75
A. 25 B. 37.5
C. 22.5 D. 50
E. 16

47. $23^2 - 413 \div 59 = ? \times 18$
A. 24 B. 34
C. 29 D. 39
E. None of these

32. C	33. C	34. A	35. D	36. E	37. C	38. D	39. E	40. D	41. C	42. A	43. C
44. C	45. E	46. B	47. C								

48. The present ages of A and B are in the ratio 3 : 4 and ratio of B and C is 1 : 2 and ratio of C and D is 4 : 3. If the age of D is 72 years, then find the age of the oldest of the four.

A. 86 years B. 80 years
C. 78 years D. 82 years
E. 96 years

49. A train crosses a platform in 10 seconds while running at a speed of 45 km/h and it takes 15 seconds to pass a man walking at 5 m/s in the same direction of the train. Find the difference in the length of the train and length of the platform.

A. 200 m B. 145 m
C. 100 m D. 125 m
E. 156 m

50. If the ratio of the radius of two circles is 3 : 5. The perimeter of the smaller circle is 10% more than that of the perimeter of the square. If the side of the square is 30 cm, then, find the area of the larger circle?

A. 3220 cm^2 B. 4250 cm^2
C. 3550 cm^2 D. 3850 cm^2
E. 3250 cm^2

Directions (Qs. No. 51-53): *Read the information carefully and answer the given questions:*

1000 students enrolled for 'NEET EXAM'. 75% of the students appeared in an exam. 30% of the students who appeared in an exam attempts Physics in the exam and remaining attempts only Chemistry and Biology section. The number of students attempts Chemistry section is 75 more than the number of students attempts in Biology section. Ratio of girls and boys appeared in an exam is 2 : 3. Number of girl's attempt in each section are equal. 30% of the girls cleared the exam and the number of boys who cleared the exam is two times the number of girls who cleared the exam.

51. Students who cleared the exam is what% of the students who appeared in the exam?

A. 12% B. 24%
C. 56% D. 36%
E. 46%

52. The total number of boys who attempts the Chemistry section is what percent of total number of students who appeared in Chemistry section?

A. 12.66% B. 13.66%
C. 66.66% D. 68.56%
E. 67.56%

53. The total number of boys who cleared the NEET exam, is what percent of total number of students who appeared in the exam?

A. 12% B. 24%
C. 14% D. 16%
E. 15%

54. Two varieties of milk with different prices is mixed in the ratio 2 : 3. The price of 1st type of milk is ₹ 10 per litre while the price of 2nd type of milk is ₹ 15 per litre. The average price of the mixture.

A. ₹ 11 per litre
B. ₹ 12 per litre
C. ₹ 13 per litre
D. ₹ 14 per litre
E. ₹ 15 per litre

55. Sachin's batting average for 50 innings is 60 runs. His highest score exceeds his lowest score by 182 runs. If these two innings are excluded, the average of the remaining 48 innings is 58 runs. The lowest score made by Sachin in his inning is:

A. 16 B. 17
C. 18 D. 29
E. None of these

56. A boat travels 30 km upstream and 30 km downstream in 8 hours. Time taken for the same boat to travel 50 km downstream if its speed against the stream is 6 km/h.

A. 10 hours
B. 6 hours
C. 8 hours
D. 4 hours
E. 5 hours

57. A seller mixes 26 kg rice of a price of ₹ 20/kg, with 30 kg of different variety rice of a price of ₹ 36/kg. He sells both the mixed rices at ₹ 30/kg. What will be the profit in percentage?

A. 25% B. 10%
C. 15% D. 20%
E. 5%

58. Raj lends an amount of ₹ 50,000 to Sumesh at a rate of 12% for five years. But after two years Raj decided to increase the rate to 20%. Find the extra amount Sumesh has to pay due to this hike in interest.

A. ₹ 8,000
B. ₹ 10,000
C. ₹ 12,000
D. ₹ 14,000
E. ₹ 16,000

48. E	**49.** C	**50.** D	**51.** D	**52.** C	**53.** B	**54.** C	**55.** B	**56.** E	**57.** E	**58.** C

59. In a mixture, the ratio between milk and water is 8 : 1. If 18 litres of mixtures is removed and 4 litres of water is added, then the quantity of milk is 24 litres more than that of water. Find the initial quantity of milk in the mixture.
A. 56 litres
B. 48 litres
C. 40 litres
D. 42 litres
E. 64 litres

60. A and B started a business with ₹ 95000 and ₹ 57000 respectively. But B was a business partner they decided to share their profit in the ratio of 4 : 3. If C joins with a condition that they will share profit and loss in the ratio of 2 : 1 : 3. Find the sacrifice ratio of A and B.
A. 10 : 11 B. 11 : 10
C. 5 : 7 D. 13 : 19
E. 21 : 17

Directions (Qs. No. 61-65): *What should come in place of the question mark '?' in the following number series?*

61. 38, 39, 35, 44, 28, ?
A. 43 B. 53
C. 48 D. 58
E. 63

62. 12, 23, 45, ?, 177, 353
A. 93 B. 97
C. 101 D. 83
E. 89

63. 11.5, 12.5, 27, ?, 340, 1705
A. 84 B. 96
C. 74 D. 114
E. 106

64. 50, 54, 45, 61, ?, 72
A. 46 B. 36
C. 106 D. 56
E. 96

65. 14, 18, 26, ?, 74, 138
A. 32 B. 42
C. 52 D. 22
E. 62

Directions (Qs. No. 66-70): *Read the following graph carefully and answer the following questions:*

The Bar Graph given below shows the number of icecreams and chocolates sold by four different companies.

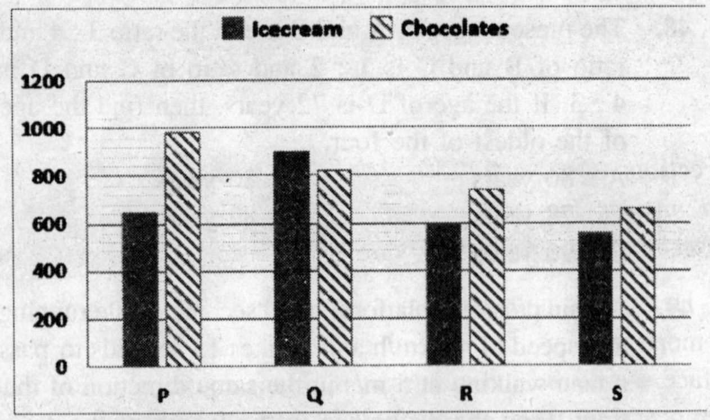

66. The number of chocolates sold by company P and Q together is what percentage more than the number of icecreams sold by company Q and R together?
A. 5% B. 15%
C. 30% D. 40%
E. 20%

67. The number of chocolates sold by company U is 25% more than the number of icecreams sold by company Q. Find the average of the number of chocolates sold by all the five companies together.
A. 865 B. 825
C. 805 D. 860
E. 820

68. What is the difference between the total number of Icecreams and chocolates sold by company P and Q and the total number of chocolates sold by company R and S?
A. 1955 B. 1950
C. 1900 D. 1850
E. 1940

69. If the ratio of Icecreams to Chocolates sold by another company T is 6 : 7 and the number of both items i.e., Icecreams and Chocolates sold by company T increased by same number to company S, then by what per cent number of Icecreams and Chocolates respectively increased with repsect to company S?
A. 40%, 16.66%
B. 20%, 16.66%
C. 25%, 16.66%
D. 24%, 16%
E. 18%, 6.66%

70. What is the ratio of the total number of Icecreams and Chocolates sold by the four companies?
A. 27 : 32 B. 29 : 31
C. 26 : 33 D. 23 : 32
E. None of these

59. B **60.** A **61.** B **62.** E **63.** A **64.** B **65.** B **66.** E **67.** A **68.** E **69.** B **70.** A

ENGLISH LANGUAGE

Directions (Qs. No. 71-80): *Read the passage given below and answer the questions that follow by choosing the correct/most appropriate options:*

Heatwaves unfolding on the bottom of the ocean can be more **intense** and last longer than those on the sea surface, new research suggests, but such extremes in the deep ocean are often **overlooked**. A team of scientists with the U.S. National Oceanic and Atmospheric Administration has conducted the first ________ of marine heatwaves along North America's continental shelves. They found that these bottom heatwaves ranged from 0.5°C to 3°C warmer than normal temperatures and could ________ more than six months—much longer than heatwaves at the surface. "We simply don't have a ton of instruments on the ocean bottom along continental shelves," said study co-author Dillon Amaya, an NOAA climate scientist. The ocean is a powerful thing. It destroys instruments that we have in the water for too long. Surface heatwaves can be picked up by satellites and can result in huge algal blooms. But, Amaya said, often no one knows a bottom marine heatwave is happening until the impacts show up in commercial bottom-dwelling species like lobsters and crabs.

The assessment, published in the journal Nature Communications, used computer models of the ocean and observations to analyze seafloor heatwaves. It found that while sometimes a marine heatwave can hit both the sea surface and ocean bottom at the same time, bottom heatwaves can also occur on their own. The ocean has absorbed about 90% of the excess heat from global warming, with the ocean's average temperature increasing by about 1.5°C over the last century. Marine heatwaves have become about 50% more frequent over the past decade. "It's a little less clear if climate change is strongly impacting bottom marine heatwaves in the same way it would at the surface," Amaya said, saying changes to ocean circulation patterns could also play a role. Past bottom marine heatwaves have **decimated** Pacific cod and snow crab populations. "Pacific cod in the Gulf of Alaska is an important fishery and ... that population has declined by 75% following the big marine heatwave in 2015," said Michael Jacox, a scientist at NOAA's Southwest Fisheries Science Center. Warmer water, he said, can increase the energy needs of species at the same time that there's less prey available for them to eat, leading to more deaths and fewer births.

71. According to the passage, for what purpose does computer models of the ocean and observations are used?

A. To more deaths and fewer births.
B. To hit both the sea surface and ocean bottom at the same time.
C. To decimate Pacific cod and snow crab populations.
D. To increase the energy needs of species.
E. To analyze seafloor heatwaves.

72. When does one get to know a bottom marine heatwave is happening?

A. When a marine heatwave hit both the sea surface and ocean bottom at the same time.
B. When heatwaves unfolding on the bottom of the ocean is more intense.
C. When the impacts show up in commercial bottom-dwelling species like lobsters and crabs.
D. When the bottom heatwaves ranged from 0.5°C to 3°C warmer than normal temperatures.
E. When the ocean's average temperature increases by about 1.5°C.

73. How does less availability of prey affect marine species?

A. It leads to more deaths and fewer births of marine species.
B. It destroys instruments that we have in the water for too long.
C. It strongly impacts bottom marine heatwaves in the same way it would at the surface.
D. It absorbs about 90% of the excess heat from global warming.
E. It leads to less fewer and more births of marine species.

74. Which of the following is/are incorrect according to the given passage?

(*a*) The ocean's average temperature is decreasing by about 1.5°C over the last century.
(*b*) The ocean has absorbed only 10% of the excess heat from global warming.
(*c*) The ocean destroys instruments that are inside the water for too long.

A. Only (*a*)
B. Both (*a*) and (*b*)
C. Only (*b*)
D. Both (*b*) and (*c*)
E. Only (*c*)

71. E	72. C	73. A	74. B

75. Which of the following is/are correct according to the given passage?

(*a*) It is found that a marine heatwave can never hit both the sea surface and ocean bottom at the same time.

(*b*) Surface heatwaves can't be picked up by satellites and can't result in huge algal blooms.

(*c*) Heatwaves unfolding on the bottom of the ocean are often ignored.

A. Only (*a*) B. Both (*a*) and (*b*)
C. Only (*b*) D. Both (*b*) and (*c*)
E. Only (*c*)

76. What will fit in the blank taken from the passage:

"They found that these bottom heatwaves ranged from 0.5°C to 3°C warmer than normal temperatures and could _______ more than six months — much longer than heatwaves at the surface."

A. Last B. Conclusion
C. Termination D. Begin
E. Prior

77. What will fit in the blank taken from the passage:

"A team of scientists with the U.S. National Oceanic and Atmospheric Administration has conducted the first _______ of marine heatwaves along North America's continental shelves."

A. Disappointment B. Contentment
C. Adamant D. Assessment
E. Amusement

78. Choose the antonym of the word **'Decimated'**.

A. Ruined B. Raised
C. Wrecked D. Devastated
E. Shattered

79. Choose the synonym of the word **'Overlooked'**.

A. Regarded B. Valued
C. Discerned D. Noticed
E. Ignored

80. Choose the antonym of the word **'Intense'**.

A. Fierce B. Acute
C. Moderate D. Severe
E. Ferocious

Directions (Qs. No. 81-84): *In the given sentences, three words are marked as (a), (b), and (c). These words may or may not be placed in their right places. Four options with different arrangements of these words are given below, mark the option with the correct arrangement as your answer. If no change is required mark 'No rearrangement required' as your answer.*

81. Many **mechanism** (*a*) banks are over-cautious about using this **restrictions** (*b*) so that it would not invite any secondary **Indian** (*c*) from the U.S.

A. (*b*)(*a*)(*c*) B. (*c*)(*a*)(*b*)
C. (*a*)(*c*)(*b*) D. (*c*)(*b*)(*a*)
E. No rearrangement required

82. He was hired for the job because he was **persuade** (*a*) at speaking and able to **eloquent** (*b*) people and these are the skills that the **company** (*c*) was looking for.

A. (*b*)(*a*)(*c*) B. (*c*)(*a*)(*b*)
C. (*a*)(*c*)(*b*) D. (*c*)(*b*)(*a*)
E. No rearrangement required

83. "The **company** (*a*) announced a new **partnership** (*b*) with a leading technology **firm** (*c*)".

A. (*b*)(*a*)(*c*) B. (*a*)(*b*)(*c*)
C. (*c*)(*a*)(*b*) D. (*c*)(*b*)(*a*)
E. None of the above

84. "The **ahead** (*a*) successfully completed the project **team** (*b*) of the **deadline** (*c*)".

A. (*b*)(*a*)(*c*) B. (*a*)(*b*)(*c*)
C. (*c*)(*a*)(*b*) D. (*c*)(*b*)(*a*)
E. No rearrangement required

Directions (Qs. No. 85-87): *Select the part of the sentence which has an error from the given options. Select 'No error' if all are correct.*

85. Mary speaks more highlier of the iTouch than the iPod. (*a*)/ The price variation between multiple (*b*)/ variants is a staggering ten thousand rupees, so please do consider (*c*)/ other brands rather than following the shepherd. (*d*)

A. (*a*) B. (*b*)
C. (*c*) D. (*d*)
E. No error

86. Justin is the most fastest runner on the track team. (*a*)/ He has won the nationals (*b*)/ twice, but there has been a (*c*)/ deterioration in his form over the years. (*d*)

A. (*d*) B. (*b*)
C. (*a*) D. (*c*)
E. No error

87. Mussolini may be said to have done more (*a*)/ for the unity of Italy than other man. (*b*)/ His methods were inhuman (*c*)/ and probably controversial. (*d*)

A. (*a*) B. (*b*)
C. (*c*) D. (*d*)
E. No error

75. E	76. A	77. D	78. B	79. E	80. C	81. B	82. A	83. B	84. A	85. A	86. C	87. B

Directions (Qs. No. 88 and 89): *Identify the segment of the sentence which contains the grammatical error. If there is no error mark 'No error' as your answer.*

88. If Stefan had studied well (*a*)/ during his board exams, (*b*)/ he will have secured a rank (*c*)/ among the top ten rank holders of his school. (*d*)/ No error

A. (*a*) B. (*b*)
C. (*c*) D. (*d*)
E. No error

89. We need more psychiatrists (*a*)/ who specializes in (*b*)/ treating mentally (*c*)/ ill people in crisis. (*d*)/ No error.

A. (*a*) B. (*b*)
C. (*c*) D. (*d*)
E. No error

Directions (Qs. No. 90-94): *A passage is given below with five blanks labelled (a)-(e). Below the passage, five options are given for each blank. Choose the word that fits each blank most appropriately in the context of the passage, and mark the corresponding answer.*

Graphic art and design ___(*a*)___ the history of humankind from cave paintings to the dazzling neon signs of the modern era. In both its history and in the relatively recent ___(*b*)___ of visual communication in the twentyfirst century, there is sometimes a blurring distinction and overlapping relation of advertising art, graphic design and fine art. They ___(*c*)___ many of the common elements, theories, principles, practices and language. The ___(*d*)___ of graphic design lies in representing information, providing form to ideas, expression and feeling and giving shapes to artefacts that ___(*e*)___ the human experience.

90. Which of the following words would most appropriately fit in the blank (*a*)?

A. Surmount B. Leap
C. Travel D. Slide
E. Span

91. Which of the following words would most appropriately fit in the blank (*b*)?

A. Expansion B. Exhilaration
C. Jubilation D. Supervision
E. Illusion

92. Which of the following words would most appropriately fit in the blank (*c*)?

A. Differ B. Share
C. Penetrate D. Predict
E. Preserve

93. Which of the following words would most appropriately fit in the blank (*d*)?

A. Correspondence B. Precariousness
C. Acceptance D. Essence
E. None of the above

94. Which of the following words would most appropriately fit in the blank (*e*)?

A. Deliberate B. Personify
C. Document D. Demolish
E. Brag

Directions (Qs. No. 95-98): *In a question given below an incomplete sentence that must be filled/completed with one of the sentences/phrases given below i.e. one of the sentences/phrases can be fit into the given blanks. Choose the correct option and complete the given sentence.*

95. It must be remembered that the Galwan clash, ______ after an agreement to disengage

A. in which India lost 20 soldiers, occur immediately
B. in which India lost 20 soldiers, occurred immediately
C. in which India loss 20 soldiers, occurred immediately
D. in which India lost 20 soldiers, occurred immediate
E. India in which lost 20 soldiers, occurred immediately

96. Modi's attempt to convey personal ______ contentious is a good step.

A. warmth so show that politics need not just be
B. warmth and show that politics need not just is
C. warmth and show the politics need not just be
D. warmth and showed that politics need not just be
E. warmth and show that politics need not just be

97. Some countries ______ their citizens to monitor if quarantine laws are being followed, or even welding some residents in their homes to stop the spread of the virus.

A. are annoying B. are analyzing
C. are depending on D. are spying on
E. None of these

98. Our willingness ______ leaves us vulnerable to the insidious threat of creeping authoritarianism.

A. to determine sacrifice
B. to increase sacrifice
C. to accept sacrifice
D. to answer sacrifice
E. None of these

88. C	89. B	90. E	91. A	92. B	93. D	94. C	95. B	96. E	97. D	98. C

Directions (Qs. No. 99 and 100): *The questions below contain five scattered segments of a sentence. Indicate the sequence which correctly assembles the segments and completes the sentence.*

99. (*a*) formation of the stars
(*b*) is gravitational instability
(*c*) one simple
(*d*) physical concept which
(*e*) lies behind the
A. (*c*)(*d*)(*e*)(*a*)(*b*) B. (*b*)(*c*)(*e*)(*a*)(*d*)
C. (*c*)(*d*)(*b*)(*e*)(*a*) D. (*d*)(*b*)(*e*)(*a*)(*c*)
E. (*a*)(*d*)(*e*)(*b*)(*c*)

100. (*a*) after waking
(*b*) people are
(*c*) more susceptible
(*d*) to heart attacks
(*e*) in the first few hours
A. (*c*)(*a*)(*b*)(*d*)(*e*) B. (*b*)(*c*)(*d*)(*e*)(*a*)
C. (*d*)(*e*)(*a*)(*c*)(*b*) D. (*a*)(*e*)(*b*)(*c*)(*d*)
E. (*b*)(*a*)(*c*)(*d*)(*e*)

EXPLANATORY ANSWERS

6. (C): Statements: All balls are dolls.
All dolls are mobiles
All mobiles are tablets

Conclusions:

I. All balls are table

∵ All balls are dolls, mobiles and tablets

Hence, all balls are tablets. It is true.

II. Some mobiles are dolls.

∵ All dolls are mobiles

∴ Some mobiles are dolls. It is true.

Hence, conclusions I and II both follow.

7. (A): Statemetns: All apples are oranges
No orange is lime
All potatoes are limes

Conclusions:

I. No potato is orange

II. Some apples are limes

Clearly, No potato is orange (follow)

But some apples are limes (not follow)

Hence, only I conclusion follows.

8. (D): Statements: Only Captain is america
Only a few captain are hydra
Few hydra are bucky

Conclusions: I. No bucky is captain
II. Some america is bucky

Clearly, neither I nor II follows.

14. (E): Statements: $T = V < U \geq X$; $V \leq S$; $H > U$

Conclusions: I. $S \geq T$

∵ $T = V$ and $V \leq S$

Clearly, $S \geq T$ (True)

II. $X < H$

∵ $U \geq X$ and $H > U$

Clearly $H > U$ (True)

Hence, Both I and II are true.

15. (A): Statements: $L < O < M$; $Q > N \geq P > M$

Conclusions: I. $P > L$

∵ $P > M$ and $M > L$

Hence, $P > L$ (True)

II. $M > N$

∵ $N \geq P > M$

Clearly M is not greater than N, it is not true.

Hence, Only I is true.

16. (A): Statements: $X \leq U < V > T$; $U < S$; $H > V$

Conclusions:

I. $X < H$

∵ $X < V$ and $H > V$

Clearly $X < H$. It is true.

II. $T \leq S$

∵ $U < S$ and $U < V > T$

$T \leq S$ is not true

Hence, Only I is true.

From Qs. No. 17 to 20:

S
P
U
R
Q
V
T

17. (B): Two boxes are placed above U box.

99. A **100.** B

18. **(E):** V box is placed second from the bottom.

19. **(D):** There are 5 boxes placed between box T and S.

20. **(A):** Clearly box V is related to box T.

21. **(E):** If we arrange all the boxes in alphabetical order from bottom to top, then the position of none boxes remains unchanged.

22. **(E):** MISUNDERSTANDING

I – 2

S – 2

N – 3

D – 2

Clearly, more than four letters between them in the word (both forward and backward direction).

From Qs. No. 23 to 25:

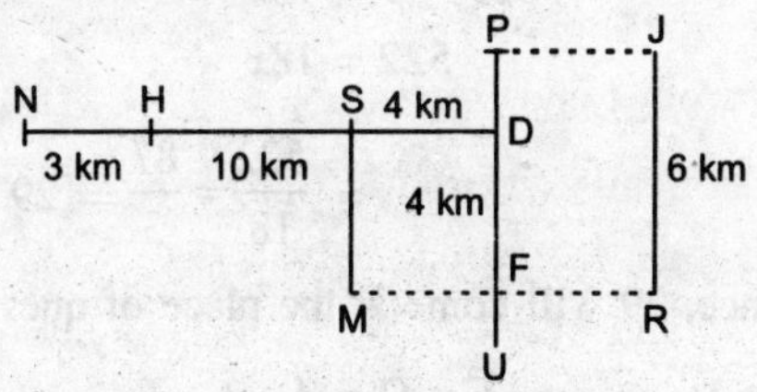

PF = 6 km, MR = 7 km, SD = 4 km

23. **(E):** Distance between J and P = 7 – 4 = 3 km.

24. **(B):** N, H, S, D are in a straight line so they are like. Clearly U does not in the group.

25. **(D):** Clearly, The direction of point S from point U is North-West.

26. **(D):** DOORLOCK

After replacing vowels and consonents letters

CPPQKPBJ

Hence, None vowels are in the new word so formed.

From Qs. No. 27 to 31:

Persons	Days
B	Monday
C	Tuesday
A	Wednesday
E	Thursday
D	Friday
G	Staurday
F	Sunday

27. **(C):** Three persons got appointment letter after D is not correct.

28. **(A):** B–Monday combination is correct.

29. **(C):** D got appointment letter on Friday.

30. **(E):** 5 persons got appointment letter between B and F which is more than 3.

31. **(C):** E got appointment letter on Thursday.

32. **(C):**

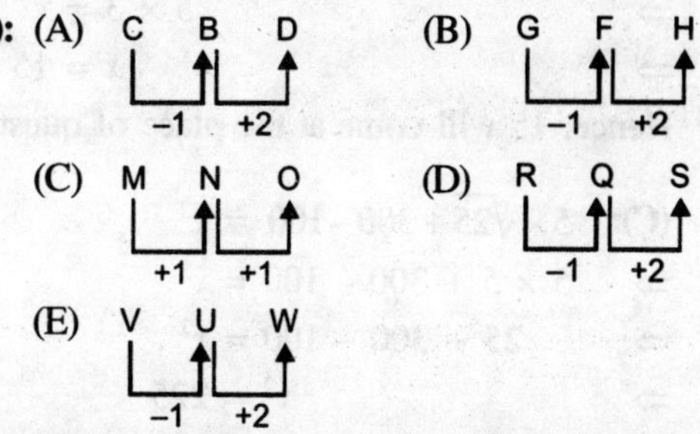

Hence, (C) MNO is different from other four alternatives.

From Qs. No. 33 to 35:

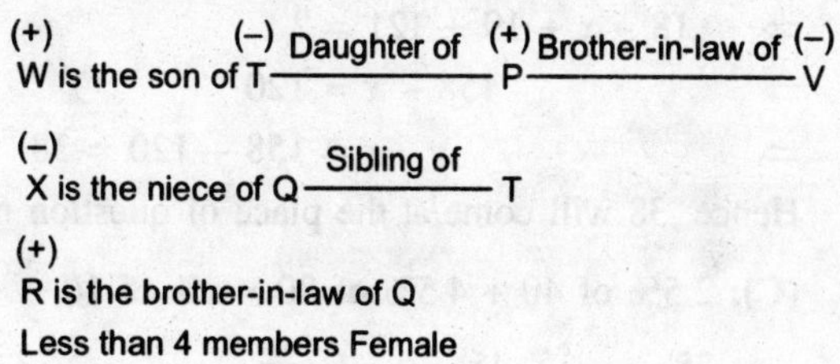

33. **(C):** Clearly, Q related to S as son.

34. **(A):** Clearly Q is the maternal uncle of W.

35. **(D):** X, T and V are females in the family.

36. **(E):** $[(27 \times 10) \div 30 + 10500 \div 500] = ? \times 15$

$\Rightarrow \quad 270 \div 30 + 10500 \div 500 = 15x$

$\Rightarrow \quad 9 + 21 = 15x$

$\Rightarrow \quad 30 = 15x \Rightarrow x = 2$

Hence, 2 will come at the place of question mark.

37. **(C):** $999 \div 3 - 165 = 75 + 111 - x$

$\Rightarrow \quad 333 - 165 = 186 - x$

$\Rightarrow \quad 168 = 186 - x$

$\Rightarrow \quad x = 186 - 168 = 18$

Hence, 18 will come at the place of question mark.

38. **(D):** $(71 \times 8) + 90 = 132 \times 4 + x$

$\Rightarrow \quad 568 + 90 = 528 + x$

$\Rightarrow \quad 658 = 528 + x$

$\Rightarrow \quad x = 658 - 528 = 130$

Hence, 130 will come at the place of question mark.

39. **(E):** $\frac{26}{24} \times 408 + \frac{25}{48 \times 100} \times 43200 = x$

$\Rightarrow \quad 26 \times 17 + 25 \times 9 = x$

$\Rightarrow \quad 442 + 225 = x$

$\Rightarrow \quad x = 667$

Hence, 667 will come at the place of question mark.

40. (D): $(8 + 6 \times 7) \div 10 \times 3 = x$

$\Rightarrow (8 + 42) \div 10 \times 3 = x$

$\Rightarrow 50 \div 10 \times 3 = x$

$\Rightarrow 5 \times 3 = x$

$\Rightarrow x = 15$

Hence, 15 will come at the place of question mark.

41. (C): $5\times\sqrt{25}+300-100 = x^2$

$\Rightarrow 5 \times 5 + 300 - 100 = x^2$

$\Rightarrow 25 + 300 - 100 = x^2$

$\Rightarrow x^2 = 225$

$\Rightarrow x = 15$

Hence, 15 will come at the place of question mark.

42. (A): $18 - x + 19 + (11)^2 = 120$

$\Rightarrow 18 - x + 19 + 121 = ?$

$\Rightarrow 158 - x = 120$

$\Rightarrow x = 158 - 120 = 38$

Hence, 38 will come at the place of question mark.

43. (C): 2.5% of $40 + 4.5\%$ of $80 = x\%$ of 10

$\Rightarrow \frac{25}{1000}\times 40+\frac{45}{1000}\times 80 = \frac{x}{100}\times 10$

$\Rightarrow 1+\frac{36}{10} = \frac{x}{10}$

$\Rightarrow \frac{46}{10} = \frac{x}{10}$

$\Rightarrow x = 46$

Hence, 46 will come at the place of question mark.

44. (C): 450% of $x \div 90 + 350\%$ of $200 \div 70 = 20$

$\Rightarrow \frac{450}{100}\times x\div 90+\frac{350}{100}\times 200\div 70 = 20$

$\Rightarrow \frac{9x}{2}\times\frac{1}{90}+700\div 70 = 20$

$\Rightarrow \frac{x}{20}+10 = 20$

$\Rightarrow \frac{x}{20} = 10$

$\Rightarrow x = 200$

Hence, 200 will come at the place of question mark.

45. (E): $935.5 + 555.4 + 64.5 + 1444.6 = 600\%$ of x

$\Rightarrow 3000 = \frac{600}{100}\times x$

$\Rightarrow 6x = 3000$

$\Rightarrow x = 500$

Hence, 500 will come at the place of question mark.

46. (B): $256 \times 2^{-5} \times x = \frac{2}{25}$ of 50×75

$\Rightarrow \frac{256}{2^5}\times x = \frac{2}{25}\times 50\times 75$

$\Rightarrow \frac{256x}{16\times 2} = 300$

$\Rightarrow 8x = 300$

$\Rightarrow x = \frac{300}{8} = \frac{75}{2} = 37.5$

Hence, 37.5 will come at the place of question mark.

47. (C): $23^2 - 413 \div 59 = x \times 18$

$\Rightarrow 529 - 413 \div 59 = x \times 18$

$\Rightarrow 529 - 7 = 18x$

$\Rightarrow 522 = 18x$

$\Rightarrow x = \frac{522}{18} = \frac{87}{3} = 29$

Hence, 29 will come at the place of question mark.

48. (E): $\because$ C : D = 4 : 3

$\because$ D = 72 years

$\therefore 3x = 72$

$\Rightarrow x = 24$

$\therefore$ Age of C = $24 \times 4 = 96$ years

B : C = 1 : 2

$\Rightarrow 2x = 96$

$\Rightarrow x = 48$

$\therefore$ Age of B = 48 years

Again, A : B = 3 : 4

$4x = 48$

$\Rightarrow x = 12$

$\therefore$ Age of A = $12 \times 3 = 36$ years

Hence, oldest of the four is C whose age = 96 years.

49. (C): Speed of the train = 45 km/hr

$= 45\times\frac{5}{18}$ m/s $= \frac{25}{2}$ m/s

Distance = Speed × Time

$= \frac{25}{2}\times 10 = 125$ m

Relative speed $= \frac{25}{2}-5=\frac{15}{2}$ m/s

$\therefore$ Length of the train = Speed × Time

$= \frac{15}{2}\times 15 = \frac{225}{2}$ m

$\therefore$ Length of the platform $= 125 - \frac{225}{2}$

$$= \frac{250-225}{2} = \frac{25}{2} \text{ m}$$

Required difference $= \left(\frac{225}{2} - \frac{25}{2}\right)$ m

$$= \frac{200}{2} = 100 \text{ m.}$$

50. (D): Perimeter of square = 30 × 4 = 120 cm

$$2\pi r = 120 + \frac{10}{100} \times 120$$

$$= 120 + 12 = 132 \text{ cm}$$

$\Rightarrow \quad 2 \times \frac{22}{7} \times r = 132$

$\Rightarrow \quad r = \frac{132 \times 7}{2 \times 22} = 3 \times 7 = 21$ cm

$\because \quad \frac{r}{R} = 3 : 5$

$$\frac{21}{R} = \frac{3}{5}$$

$\Rightarrow \quad R = \frac{21 \times 5}{3} = 35$ cm

Area of the larger circle $= \pi R^2$

$$= \frac{22}{7} \times 35 \times 35$$

$$= 110 \times 35 = 3850 \text{ cm}^2.$$

51. (D): Total number of students appeared

$$= \frac{75}{100} \times 1000 = 750$$

Numbers of girls + numbers of boys = 750

$$2x + 3x = 750$$

$\Rightarrow \quad 5x = 750$

$\Rightarrow \quad x = 150$

$\therefore \quad$ Number of girls = 2 × 150 = 300

Number of boys = 450

Number of girls clear exam $= \frac{30}{100} \times 300 = 90$

Number of boys clear the exam = 2 × 90 = 180

Total = 90 + 180 = 270

Required % $= \frac{270}{750} \times 100 = 36\%.$

53. (B): Required % $= \frac{180}{750} \times 100$

$$= 6 \times 4 = 24\%.$$

54. (C): Let average price of the mix = ₹ x/litre

By the rule of alligation,

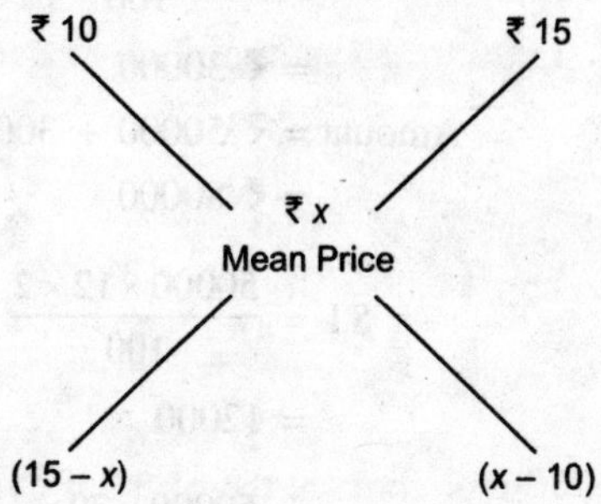

Now, $\quad \frac{15-x}{x-10} = \frac{2}{3}$

$\Rightarrow \quad 2x - 20 = 45 - 3x$

$\Rightarrow \quad 5x = 65$

$\Rightarrow \quad x =$ ₹ 13

Hence, the average price of the mix = ₹ 13/litre

55. (B): Scores in the two excluded innings

$$= 50 \times 60 - 48 \times 58$$

$$= 3000 - 2784 = 216 \text{ runs}$$

Let the lowest score $= x$

$$x + (x + 182) = 216$$

$\Rightarrow \quad 2x = 216 - 182 = 34$

Hence, the lowest score $= \frac{34}{2} = 17.$

56. (E): Let speed of boat = 8 km/hr

and speed of current = 2 km/hr

According to the question,

Time taken upstream and downstream = 8 hours

$$\frac{30}{8+2} + \frac{30}{8-2} = \frac{30}{10} + \frac{30}{6}$$

= 3 hours + 5 hours

= 8 hours

Hence, time taken $= \frac{50}{10} = 5$ hours.

57. (E): C.P. of 26 kg of rice = 26 × 20 = ₹ 520

C.P. of 30 kg of rice = 30 × 36

= ₹ 1080

Total C.P. = 520 + 1080

= ₹ 1600

Total S.P. = 56 × 30

= ₹ 1680

$$\text{Profit} = 1680 - 1600 = ₹\ 80$$

$$\text{Profit}\ \% = \frac{80}{1600} \times 100 = 5\%.$$

58. **(C):**

$$\text{S.I.} = \frac{50000 \times 12 \times 5}{100}$$

$$= ₹\ 30000$$

$$\text{Amount} = ₹\ 50000 + 30000$$

$$= ₹\ 80000$$

$$\text{S.I.} = \frac{50000 \times 12 \times 2}{100}$$

$$= 12000$$

$$\text{S.I.} = \frac{50000 \times 20 \times 3}{100}$$

$$= 30000$$

$$\text{Total interest} = 12000 + 30000$$

$$= ₹\ 42000$$

$$\text{Total amount} = 50000 + 42000$$

$$= ₹\ 92000$$

$$\therefore \text{ Extra amount paid} = 92000 - 80000$$

$$= ₹\ 12000.$$

59. **(B):** Let 54 litre mixture of milk and water

Ratio of milk and water = 8 : 1

$$\therefore \quad \text{Amount of milk} = \frac{8}{9} \times 54$$

$$= 48 \text{ litre}$$

$$\text{Amount of water} = \frac{1}{9} \times 54$$

$$= 6 \text{ litre}$$

Removed 18 litre mixture

Now, (54 – 18) litre = 36 litre of mixture

Now amount of milk = 32 litre

and amount of water = 4 litre

4 litre water added

$\therefore$ Milk = 32 litre

Water = (4 + 4) litre

= 8 litre

32 litre = (24 + 8) litre

Hence, initial quantity of milk in the mixture = 48 litre.

61. **(B):** 38 39 35 44 28 **[53]**

$+1^2$ $-(2)^2$ $+(3)^2$ $-(4)^2$ $+(5)^2$

Hence, 53 will come at the place of question mark.

62. **(E):** 12 23 45 **[89]** 177 353

× 2 – 1 × 2 – 1 × 2 – 1 × 2 – 1 × 2 – 1

Hence, 89 will come at the place of question mark.

63. **(A):** 11.5 12.5 27 **[84]** 340 1705

×1+1 ×2+2 ×3+3 ×4+4 ×5+5

Hence, 84 will come at the place of question mark.

64. **(B):** 50 54 45 61 **[36]** 72

–(5 + 0) –(4 + 5)

+7 +11

Hence, 36 will come at the place of question mark.

65. **(B):** 14 18 26 **[42]** 74 138

4 8 16 32 64

×2 ×2 ×2 ×2

Hence, 42 will come at the place of question mark.

For Qs. No. 66 to 70.

	P	Q	R	S	Total
Chocolate	980	820	740	660	3200
Icecream	640	900	600	560	2700

66. **(E):** Chocolate,

$$P + Q = 980 + 820$$

$$= 1800$$

Icecream, $Q + R = 900 + 600 = 1500$

$$\text{Difference} = 1800 - 1500 = 300$$

$$\text{Required}\ \% = \frac{300}{1500} \times 100 = 20\%.$$

67. **(A):**

$$U = 900 + \frac{25}{100} \times 900$$

$$= 900 + 225 = 1125$$

$$\text{Average} = \frac{P + Q + R + S + U}{5}$$

$$= \frac{980 + 820 + 740 + 660 + 1125}{5}$$

$$= \frac{3200 + 1125}{5}$$

$$= \frac{4325}{5} = 865.$$

68. **(E):** Total Chocolate and Icecream sold by P and Q

$= 980 + 820 + 640 + 900$

$= 3340$

Total Chocolates sold by R and S

$= 740 + 660$

$= 1400$

Required difference $= 3340 - 1400$

$= 1940.$

70. **(A):** Total number of Chocolates sold by four companies = 3200

Total number of icecreams sold by four companies

$= 2700$

$$\text{Required ratio} = \frac{2700}{3200}$$

$= 27 : 32.$

71. **(E):** In the passage, the sentence mentioning the use of computer models of the ocean and observations states: "The assessment published in the journal Nature Communications, used computer models of the ocean and observations to analyze seafloor heatwaves." This indicates that the purpose of using computer models and observations is to analyze seafloor heatwaves. The research conducted by the scientists with the U.S. National Oceanic and Atmospheric Administration involves studying marine heatwaves along North America's continental shelves, specifically focusing on bottom heatwaves that occur on the ocean floor. The computer models and observations help in understanding the characteristics, intensity, and duration of these bottom marine heatwaves.

72. **(C):** According to the passage, it mentions: "But, Amaya said, often no one knows a bottom marine heatwave is happening until the impacts show up in commercial bottom-dwelling species like lobsters and crabs." This implies that the awareness of a bottom marine heatwave typically occurs when its effects become visible in the behavior or conditions of commercial bottom-dwelling species.

73. **(A):** The passage mentions, "Warmer water, he said, can increase the energy needs of species at the same time that there's less prey available for them to eat, leading to more deaths and fewer births." This indicates that when there is less prey available for marine species to eat, it can result in increased mortality and decreased reproduction, ultimately affecting the population dynamics of these species.

74. **(B):**

(*a*) The ocean's average temperature is increasing, not decreasing, by about 1.5°C over the last century. Therefore, statement (*a*) is incorrect.

(*b*) The ocean has absorbed about 90%, not 10%, of the excess heat from global warming. Therefore, statement (*b*) is incorrect.

75. **(E):** This statement aligns with the information provided in the passage. The passage emphasizes that heatwaves occurring on the ocean floor, specifically referred to as bottom marine heatwaves, are often overlooked or ignored. The reason for this is explained in the passage - there are fewer instruments on the ocean bottom along continental shelves compared to the sea surface, and the ocean environment poses challenges for maintaining instruments for extended periods. As a result, these bottom marine heatwaves might not be detected or monitored until their impacts become evident in commercial bottom-dwelling species, such as lobsters and crabs. The statement accurately reflects the passage's emphasis on the under recognition of heatwaves in the deep ocean.

76. **(A):** The complete sentence would be: "They found that these bottom heatwaves ranged from 0.5°C to 3°C warmer than normal temperatures and could last more than six months - much longer than heatwaves at the surface."

77. **(D):** The complete sentence would be: "A team of scientists with the U.S. National Oceanic and Atmospheric Administration has conducted the first assessment of marine heatwaves along North America's continental shelves."

78. **(B):** The word 'decimated' originally refers to the act of killing or destroying a large proportion of something, typically a population. Therefore, the antonym would be a word that implies preserving, increasing, or raising rather than destroying.

79. **(E):** The word "Overlooked" means to fail to notice or consider something, or to neglect to pay attention to it. In this context, if something is overlooked, it means it is not noticed or regarded. The synonym for "Overlooked" among the options provided is "Ignored." If something is ignored, it is also not given attention or consideration.

80. **(C):** The word "Intense" typically describes something that is strong, extreme, or showing a high degree of intensity or concentration. The antonym, "Moderate," suggests something that is not extreme or excessive but rather mild or within reasonable limits.

81. (B): The sentence should read: "Many Indian banks are over-cautious about using this mechanism so that it would not invite any secondary restrictions from the U.S."

82. (A): The corrected sentence would be: "He was hired for the job because he was eloquent at speaking and able to persuade people, and these are the skills that the company was looking for."

83. (B): The correct sentence is: "The company announced a new partnership with a leading technology firm."

84. (A): The corrected sentence would be: "The team successfully completed the project ahead of the deadline."

85. (A): The corrected sentence would be: "Mary speaks more highly of the iTouch than the iPod." The word "highlier" should be corrected to "more highly" to form the comparative degree correctly.

86. (C): The corrected sentence would be: "Justin is the fastest runner on the track team." The use of "most" is redundant when "fastest" is already a superlative form, so "most" should be omitted.

87. (B): The corrected sentence would be: "Mussolini may be said to have done more for the unity of Italy than any other man." The word "other" should be changed to "any other" for proper comparison.

88. (C): The corrected sentence would be: "If Stefan had studied well during his board exams, he would have secured a rank among the top ten rank holders of his school."

The verb "will" should be changed to "would" to maintain the correct sequence of tenses in conditional sentences.

89. (B): The corrected sentence would be: "We need more psychiatrists who specialize in treating mentally ill people in crisis." The verb "specialize" should be used instead of "specializes" to agree with the plural noun "psychiatrists."

90. (E): Span - This conveys the idea that graphic design encompasses the entirety of human history.

91. (A): Expansion - This refers to the recent growth of visual communication in the 21st century.

92. (B): Share - This accurately describes the commonality of elements among the different visual mediums.

93. (D): Essence - This captures the core purpose and meaning of graphic design.

94. (C): Document - This aligns with the idea of graphic design preserving and recording human experience.

95. (B): This option provides a complete and grammatically correct sentence that accurately describes the Galwan clash. The corrected sentence is: "It must be remembered that the Galwan clash, in which India lost 20 soldiers, occurred immediately after an agreement to disengage."

96. (E): The corrected sentence is: "Modi's attempt to convey personal warmth and show that politics need not just be contentious is a good step." This phrase effectively captures the essence of Prime Minister Modi's efforts to convey personal warmth and challenge the perception that politics is solely about power and strategy. It suggests that politics can be infused with genuine human connection and empathy.

97. (D): The corrected sentence is: "Some countries are spying on their citizens to monitor if quarantine laws are being followed, or even welding some residents in their homes to stop the spread of the virus."

98. (C): The corrected sentence is: "Our willingness to accept sacrifice leaves us vulnerable to the insidious threat of creeping authoritarianism."

99. (A): The completed sentence is: "One simple physical concept which lies behind the formation of the stars is gravitational instability."

100. (B): The completed sentence is: people are more susceptible to heart attacks in the first few hours after waking.

Previous Paper (Solved)

State Bank of India (SBI)

CLERICAL CADRE (Junior Associates)

Phase-I : Preliminary Exam 2021*

GENERAL ENGLISH

Directions (Qs. No. 1-8): *Read the passage carefully and answer the given questions.*

The World Economic Forum predicts that by 2023 there will be a staggering 9.1 billion mobile subscriptions. According to telecom-focused technology company Cisco Systems, by 2020, connected mobile devices will produce 30.6 exabytes per month and annual global mobile data traffic will reach 366.8 exabytes (one exabyte is one quintillion bytes). 5G is designed to meet this demand. It not only represents a generational leap in connectivity speeds, the new network standard will also introduce lower latency (for improved response) and the ability to connect more devices at once.

So, after much 5G hype and excitement, we are finally seeing progress — proof of concepts, field trials, buildouts and early deployments, and 5G is on the cusp of becoming a reality. The question is, what will it deliver? With traditional telecom revenues in decline, connectivity fast becoming a commodity and customer-trust **diminishing**, much of the focus (and hope) is on delivering new revenues for mobile network operators. Despite the many recognized advantages of 5G, mobile network operators are still looking for concrete evidence of Return on Investment (RoI). The investment isn't a small one. In fact, it will likely amount to a collective investment of billions of dollars in new network equipment, licences and deployment. So what difference will 5G actually make?

Avoiding the obvious temptation to simply say "Internet of Things" (IoT), here are five 5G-powered use cases — Industry 4.0, mixed reality (MR) applications, which is augmented reality (AR) plus virtual reality (VR), sports and entertainment, fixed wireless access, and autonomous vehicles — that mobile network operators must prepare for.

Like many others, the manufacturing industry is going through a digital revolution. Within the context of Industry 4.0, manufacturers are becoming more efficient through the application of automation and data exchange to their existing factory processes to enable better integrated workflows and smarter manufacturing.

Industrial IoT technologies are streamlining and simplifying many manufacturing processes in revolutionary ways. For instance, production robots now have sensors or software that send information to remote teams; some apps can gather real-time feedback and send alerts on defects or damaged goods; and other apps can help track working schedules of factory workers. 5G plays a vital role in this transformative process, especially as the use of AR and VR applications continues to grow in manufacturing to support the realization of manufacturers' Industry 4.0 goals.

This is followed by MR applications that are likely to be a key driver for 5G. Beyond the consumer market (think *Pokémon Go*), interesting applications are also likely to be found in industrial and medical contexts. Remote medical procedures, engineering, public safety and field-service applications are all strong use case opportunities for the application of low latency 5G services. 5G will also deliver a significantly enhanced experience for audiences at sporting and entertainment events. A combination of VR and AR with ultra high-fidelity enabled by 5G could transform the way fans interact in these events. Motorsports is ideal for VR in particular: equipped with their mobile device or headset, fans could be served information like lap or technical information about cars as they race on the track in a sport like Formula One. The opportunity lies in more than just providing connectivity. Mobile network operators can create partnerships with broadcasters and sports organizations to deliver entertainment services directly to customers through their self-service applications.

1. Which is/are be the probable key driver(s) for 5G as per the passage?

A. Virtual Reality applications
B. Entertainment applications
C. Mixed Reality applications
D. Augmented Reality applications
E. All of the above

2. Choose the antonym of 'diminishing'.

A. Declining B. Impacting
C. Growing D. Reducing
E. Sharpening

* *Based on Memory*

3. Which of the following is true about digital revolution in manufacturing industry as per the passage?
   I. They use automation and data exchange for better workflow.
   II. There is a big role for IoT in simplifying the manufacturing processes.
   III. 5G gives enhanced experience at sporting and entertainment events.
   A. Only I B. Only II
   C. Only III D. Both I and II
   E. Both II and III

4. Apart from improving connectivity speed, what are the other factors that 5G provides?
   A. Improved response
   B. Increased bandwidth
   C. Connecting more devices at once
   D. Both (A) and (B)
   E. Both (A) and (C)

5. Choose a suitable title for the passage from the given options.
   A. Impact of 5G in future
   B. 5G vs Industry 4.0
   C. The jump from 4G
   D. 5G – the significant need
   E. Changing world

6. When it comes to investment in 5G, what do mobile network operators look for?
   A. Millions of users to make profit
   B. Funds from their sources
   C. Investment in infrastructure for production
   D. Evidence on the return on investment
   E. Not mentioned in the passage

7. What is the demand that 5G is designed to meet?
   A. Global mobile data traffic
   B. Mobile subscriptions
   C. Hardware
   D. Communication
   E. None of the above

8. Which of the following use cases of 5G is/are not mentioned in the passage?
   I. Sports and entertainment
   II. Agriculture
   III. Public safety
   IV. Space research
   V. Medical procedures
   A. Only I, II and IV B. Only I, III and V
   C. Only I, II and III D. Only II, III and IV
   E. All of the above use cases are mentioned

Directions (Qs. No. 9-13): *Each sentence is divided into four parts. Rearrange them to make a meaningful sentence. If no rearrangement is required, then choose option (E) as the answer.*

9. As tech companies become (*a*) / a key part of the (*b*) / looking more like giant computers on wheels (*c*) / auto industry, cars are (*d*)
   A. (*a, b, d, c*) B. (*a, c, b, d*)
   C. (*d, b, c, a*) D. (*b, a, c, d*)
   E. No interchange required

10. Its Internet Explorer browser, adding to (*a*) / the digital scrap heap a product once (*b*) / Microsoft Corp is planning to largely retire (*c*) / at the center of one of the tech industry's biggest battles (*d*)
   A. (*b, a, c, d*) B. (*a, d, b, c*)
   C. (*d, b, c, a*) D. (*c, a, b, d*)
   E. No interchange required

11. Efficient at home and work, has raised complex questions about the growing (*a*) / the technology, which handles tasks once (*b*) / the exclusive domain of humans, making life more (*c*) / influence of computer algorithms in a wide range of public and private life (*d*)
   A. (*b, c, a, d*) B. (*b, d, a, c*)
   C. (*d, b, c, a*) D. (*b, a, d, c*)
   E. No interchange required

12. Were the logistical hurdles of evacuating people (*a*) / shifted to safer areas, there (*b*) / while keeping them safe from fresh infections (*c*) / covid patients in hospitals along the cyclone's path had to be. (*d*)
   A. (*a, d, c, b*) B. (*b, d, c, a*)
   C. (*d, b, a, c*) D. (*b, c, d, a*)
   E. No rearrangement required

13. And the Andaman & Nicobar Islands, its first pit-stop in (*a*) / precursor to its entry over mainland India (*b*) / the onset of monsoon over the Southeast Bay (*c*) / Indian waters, is around the normal time and is a. (*d*)
   A. (*b, c, d, a*) B. (*c, a, d, b*)
   C. (*a, b, c, d*) D. (*d, c, a, b*)
   E. No rearrangement required

Directions (Qs. No. 14 and 15): *Find the word which is misspelt or contextually incorrect among the bolded words. If all the words are correct, choose option (E) as your answer.*

14. As human beings, we often **harbour judgments** about ourselves deep down, which exist as self-doubt about our worth, **compitence**, or **appearance**.
   A. harbour B. judgments
   C. appearance D. compitence
   E. All are correct

15. The only way to **overcome** this **defensivness** is to work on **becoming** more self-**validating**.
   A. defensivness B. overcome
   C. becoming D. validating
   E. All are correct

Directions (Qs. No. 16-20): *A sentence is divided into four parts. One of the parts may have an error. Identify the part that has the error and choose from the given options. If there is no error in the given sentence, then choose option (E) as the answer.*

16. Innovations like using solar energy (A) / to heat salt and use that (B) / trapped heat to boil water (C) / but generate steam must be explored. (D) / No Error (E)

17. Thinking about all the things that (A) / you wish never happened to you is (B) / actually preventing all the things you want (C) / to happen from entering into your life. (D) / No Error (E)

18. Confusion is always giving rise to clarity (A) / over time and a moment does come when (B) / all the new learning becomes wonderfully (C) / integrated within your understanding. (D) / No Error (E)

19. Life is a growth school, ideally (A) / created to give us opportunities to learn each of (B) / the lesson we need to learn over the (C) / course of our lives on the planet. (D) / No Error (E)

20. Every person, to live truly and (A) / greatly, must define how he (B) / wants to live and what (C) / his biggest life will looking like. (D) / No Error (E)

Directions: (Qs. No. 21-25) : *Read the passage carefully and fill the blanks with appropriate words from the given options.*

As infants, we really are perfect. We are still connected to the force that created the world. But as we begin to age, we ....**(21)**........ fears from the world around us. We want our parents to love and ....**(22)**........ us. So, we model them and take on their fears, limiting beliefs and false assumptions so we can be more like them. It's all done because we ....**(23)**........ love. Who you are in this moment is not who you truly are. Rather, it's someone you've become as a result of being in this world. To clear all those fears that you have assumed from the world around you, you will need to go back and ....**(24)**........ the source of all your fears. Then you'll have to work through them until they are no longer part of your ....**(25)**........ .

21. A. evolve B. manifest C. practice D. involve E. adopt

22. A. scare B. threaten C. smash D. adore E. frighten

23. A. crave B. create C. manipulate D. design E. exaggerate

24. A. travel B. practice C. explore D. repeat E. assume

25. A. possession B. mental C. physique D. realm E. psyche

Directions (Qs. No. 26-28): *In a sentence four words are given in bold. They may or may not be appropriate contextually. Interchange those words in order to make the sentence meaningful. If no interchange is required, choose option 'E' as the answer.*

26. The messaging platform WhatsApp has **consistently** (*a*) refused to **tracing** (*b*) with the government's demand, saying that **comply** (*c*) the origin of fake/ unlawful messages for over two years will **undermine** (*d*) the privacy of WhatsApp users.

A. (*a-c*) B. (*b-d*) C. (*a-d*) D. (*b-c*) E. No interchange required

27. Internet **restrictions** (*a*) refer to intentional **disruptions** (*b*) on **connectivity** (*c*) that limit people's ability to **access** (*d*) the internet or specific websites and apps.

A. (*a-b*) B. (*a-c*) C. (*c-d*) D. Both (*a*) and (*c*) E. No interchange required

28. While more research is needed to measure the emissions **coming** (*a*) from permafrost, the researchers **thawing** (*b*) that fires along with abrupt **estimate** (*c*) events could increase carbon emissions unless the fossil fuel emission are **drastically** (*d*) reduced.

A. (*a-b*) B. (*b-d*) C. (*b-c*) D. (*c-d*) E. No interchange required

Directions (Qs. No. 29 and 30): *In questions given below, a part of the sentence is bold. Below are given alternatives to the bold part which may improve the sentence. Choose the correct alternative. In case no improvement is needed, choose option 'E' as the answer.*

29. As automakers' investments in electric vehicles (EVs) ramp up, pickup trucks **is fast become** a new front in the electrification wars.

A. are fast becoming
B. becoming fast
C. fast became
D. would become fast
E. No improvement needed

30. Facebook founder and CEO Mark Zuckerberg is telling everyone **whom will listened** that it is time to regulate the internet.

A. for listening
B. whom listens
C. to listen to him
D. who will listen
E. No improvement needed

QUANTITATIVE APTITUDE

Directions (Qs. No. 31-35): *Find the missing numbers (?) in the given series:*

31. 54, 65, 78, ? , 114, 137
A. 92 B. 97
C. 104 D. 100
E. 95

32. ?, 20, 36, 56, 80, 108
A. 10 B. 9
C. 14 D. 8
E. 6

33. 22, 30, 41, 56, ?, 102
A. 100 B. 94
C. 81 D. 76
E. 68

34. 2, 5, 16, 65, ?
A. 326 B. 302
C. 295 D. 329
E. 291

35. ?, 105, 112, 122, 137, 159
A. 97 B. 99
C. 95 D. 102
E. 94

36. $1528 + 525 \div 25 - 840 = 510 + ?$
A. 199 B. 299
C. 159 D. 189
E. 165

37. 45% of $\left(\sqrt{6561} \times 5\right)$ = ? ÷ 124
A. 23599 B. 22599
C. 22579 D. 22753
E. None of these

38. $672 \div 24 \times 18 + 153 - 345 = X$
A. 318 B. 324
C. 305 D. 314
E. None of these

39. 35% of $760 - 13 \div 17 \times 289 + 224 = x^2 - 55$
A. 22 B. 26
C. 18 D. 30
E. 28

40. $11 \times 14 + 221 = \sqrt[3]{x} + 370$
A. 125 B. 140
C. 175 D. 180
E. 150

41. $25 \times 45 + 3^2 \times 44$ – 35% of 440 = x
A. 1388 B. 1356
C. 1367 D. 1300
E. 1320

42. $32 \div 64 \times 16 + 17 \times 13 - 4 = x^2$
A. 15 B. 225
C. 18 D. 324
E. 350

43. 12.5 % of 1584 – $11\sqrt{2} \times 10\sqrt{2} + 221 = x$
A. 199 B. 179
C. 132 D. 145
E. 135

44. 15×98 + 120% of 350 – 20% of 350 = $x - 14 \times 11$
A. 1988 B. 1974
C. 1924 D. 1900
E. 1950

45. 56% of 250 – $19 \times 68 \div 17 + 450 = x$
A. 584 B. 525
C. 514 D. 550
E. 600

Directions (Qs. No. 46-50) : *Study the bar chart given below and answer the following questions.*

The below bar chart shows the total number of fruits and number of rotten fruits in five different shops A, B, C, D & E, respectively.

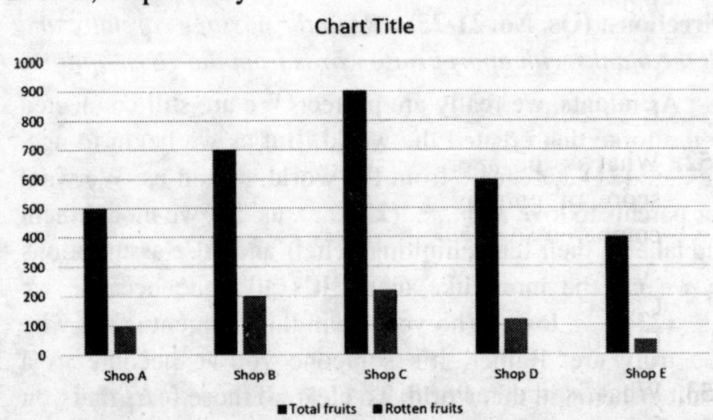

Note : The number of fruits sold = Total fruits – Rotten fruits.

46. Find average number of fruits sold by shops A, C and shop D.
A. 640 B. 420
C. 520 D. 620
E. 560

47. Find the ratio of number of fruits sold by B & C together to the number of fruits sold by A & D together.
A. 51 : 66 B. 59 : 44
C. 49 : 55 D. 48 : 77
E. 51 : 33

48. The number of fruits sold by D is what percentage of the number of fruits sold by A.
A. 120% B. 166.66%
C. 150% D. 133.33%
E. 183.33%

49. The number fruits sold by A & C are how much more or less than the number of fruits sold by B & D together?

A. 200 B. 100
C. 300 D. 150
E. 280

50. The fruits sold by B & C together are what per cent of fruits sold by B?

A. 140% B. 136%
C. 236% D. 240%
E. 156%

Directions (Qs. No. 51-55) : *Read the given information carefully and answer the following questions.*

Following information gives the data regarding employees' performance scores obtained by five employees (A, B, C, D and E) in the month of April and May 2021.

April: Scores obtained by A is 30% of scores obtained by B who got 25 more than C. D and E together got the score of 148. D alone got 56 and the respective ratio of scores obtained by A and D is 9 : 14.

May: A got 25% more score than E and 24 more than C. B and E together got 116. Scores obtained by B and D are in the ratio 4 : 5 respectively and E got score 4 less than B.

51. How much score did employee D got in both the months together?

A. 121 B. 131
C. 144 D. 151
E. 129

52. What is the approximate percentage increase in the score of employee A in the month of May when compared to previous month?

A. 84% B. 72%
C. 94% D. 98%
E. 90%

53. What is the respective ratio of scores obtained by employee C in April month to that employee D in May month?

A. 17 : 18 B. 19 : 25
C. 95 : 17 D. 19 : 15
E. 17 : 15

54. The difference between the average scores obtained by all the given employees in April and the average scores obtained by all the given employees in May?

A. 21 B. 18.4
C. 19.4 D. 15
E. 12.4

55. The scores obtained by employee B in April is what percentage more/less than the scores obtained by employee D in May?

A. 30% more B. 60% less
C. 30% less D. 50% more
E. 60% more

56. Quantity I: A and B can do a piece of work in $22\frac{1}{2}$ days and the ratio of time taken by A and B is 3 : 5. Find the difference between the time taken by A and B alone to complete the whole work?

Quantity II: 25 days.

A. Quantity I > Quantity II
B. Quantity I < Quantity II
C. Quantity I ≥ Quantity II
D. Quantity I ≤ Quantity II
E. Quantity I = Quantity II or Relation cannot be established

Directions (Qs. No. 57-60): *In the Questions given below, two equations numbered I and II are given. You have to solve both the equations and choose the correct option.*

57. I. $x^2 - 25x + 136 = 0$
II. $y^2 - 24y + 143 = 0$

A. $x > y$ B. $x < y$
C. $x \geq y$ D. $x \leq y$
E. $x = y$ (or) can't be determined

58. I. $x^2 = 169$
II. $y = 3\sqrt{2197}$

A. $x > y$ B. $x < y$
C. $x \geq y$ D. $x \leq y$
E. $x = y$ (or) can't be determined

59. I. $x^2 + 3x - 208 = 0$
II. $y^2 - 25y + 156 = 0$

A. $x > y$ B. $x < y$
C. $x \geq y$ D. $x \leq y$
E. $x = y$ (or) can't be determined

60. I. $x^2 - 18x + 45 = 0$
II. $y^2 - 22y + 105 = 0$

A. $x > y$ B. $x < y$
C. $x \geq y$ D. $x \leq y$
E. $x = y$ (or) can't be determined

61. A shopkeeper bought 36 kg of pulses at ₹ 28 per kg. He mixed it with 60 kg of pulses costing ₹ 32 per kg. In order to make a profit of 20%, at what price should he sell per kg of the mixture?

A. ₹ 36.60 B. ₹ 32.60
C. ₹ 32.75 D. ₹ 36.75
E. None of these

62. Raja sold his cycle for ₹ 3600, hence gained a certain amount. Had he sold the cycle for ₹ 2700, he would have suffered a loss equal to 25% of the gain in the first case. Find the cost price of the cycle.

A. ₹ 2800 B. ₹ 2880
C. ₹ 2920 D. ₹ 2980
E. ₹ 2820

63. The speed of the current is 5 km/hr and the speed of the boat in still water is 50% more than speed of the boat in upstream. What is the downstream distance travelled by boat in 2 hours?

A. 60 km B. 80 km
C. 25 km D. 40 km
E. 50 km

64. The ages of father and son before 8 years is in the ratio of 8 : 5 and the ages of father and son after 12 years is in the ratio 13 : 10. What is the age of the father after 4 years?
A. 54 years B. 64 years
C. 44 years D. 35 years
E. 40 years

65. A batsman has a certain average in 9 innings. In the tenth innings, he scores 100 runs, so his average increases by 8 runs. What is the new average of the batsman?
A. 36 B. 28
C. 48 D. 32
E. 24

REASONING ABILITY

Directions (Qs. No. 66-68): *Read the information carefully and answer the questions given below.*

A is the son of B. C has only two children – A and D. E is the sister of F. D is married to G. C has only two sons. H is the father of B. E is married to A. H is married to I. C is the daughter of J.

66. Who among the following is the father of B?
A. H B. J
C. C D. I
E. None of these

67. Who among the following is the brother-in-law of F?
A. D B. A
C. B D. H
E. J

68. How is C related to E?
A. Father-in-law B. Mother-in-law
C. Father D. Mother
E. Brother

69. How many such pairs of letters are there in the 'CONDITION' each of which has as many letters between them in the word as in the English Alphabet?
A. None B. One
C. Two D. Three
E. More than three

70. Point A is 20 m west of point B. Point B is 40 m south of point C. Point D is 30 m west of point C. Point E is 20 m south of point D. Point F is 50 m north of point A. If point G is to the south of A, then G is in which direction with respect to C?
A. South B. North
C. South-west D. North-east
E. None of the above

Directions (Qs. No. 71-75): *Study the following information carefully and answer the given questions.*

Seven persons J, K, L, M, N, O and P are working in a same office. Each person takes a week off on seven different days of the week. Only one person takes week off on one day. The week starts from Sunday. Two persons take week off between J and O. P is not the last person takes week off. N takes week off on immediately after J who takes week off on before Wednesday. K takes week off two days before L. M takes week off immediately before P.

71. Who among the following persons takes week off on Tuesday?
A. J B. N
C. K D. P
E. M

72. Which of the following day P takes week off?
A. Monday B. Tuesday
C. Wednesday D. Thursday
E. Friday

73. How many persons take week off between J and L?
A. None B. One
C. Two D. Three
E. More than three

74. Which of the following combination is true?
A. Sunday - P B. Tuesday - N
C. Thursday - L D. Friday - O
E. Saturday - M

75. Which of the following statement is true?
(*i*) K takes week off last day of week
(*ii*) P takes week off immediately after O
(*iii*) Two persons take week off between L and N
A. Only (*i*) is true B. Only (*ii*) is true
C. Only (*iii*) is true D. Only (*i*) and (*ii*) are true
E. All statements are true

Directions (Qs. No. 76-80): *Study the following arrangement carefully and answer the question given below:*

326 576 627 513 894

76. If the first digit of each number is decreased by two and then the digits in each number are arranged in descending order from left to right. Then, which of the following number is the second smallest number after the rearrangement?
A. 326 B. 576
C. 627 D. 513
E. 894

77. If the odd digits in each number are decreased by one and the even digits are increased by 2 and then the numbers thus formed are arranged in descending order from left to right. Which is the second number from the right end after the rearrangement?

A. 326 B. 576
C. 627 D. 513
E. 894

78. If the first and the last digits of the number are interchanged, then how many numbers thus formed are divisible by 4?

A. 1 B. 2
C. 3 D. 0
E. None of these

79. If the digits in each number are written in descending order and the numbers thus formed are arranged in ascending order from right to left, then which of the following corresponds to the fourth-smallest number after the rearrangement?

A. 326 B. 576
C. 627 D. 513
E. 894

80. If the digits in odd position are decreased by one, and the numbers are arranged in ascending order from right to left, then which of the following number will be the second from the left end?

A. 326 B. 576
C. 627 D. 513
E. 894

Directions (Qs. No. 81-85): *Study the following information carefully and answer the given questions.*

Eight persons S, T, U, V, W, X, Y and Z sit in a circular table and all of them facing center. The distances between the friends are equal. All the above information is not necessarily in the same order. W sits third to the right of X who is not immediate neighbour of T. Y sits third to the left of U. Only two persons sit between V and Z. One person sits between Z and Y. T is not an immediate neighbour of S. Y and T are facing each other. S and X are immediate neighbours.

81. Who among the following person sits opposite to W?

A. S B. T
C. U D. V
E. None of these

82. What is the position of S with respect to T?

A. Second to the right
B. Fourth to the left
C. Fifth to the left
D. Third to the right
E. Both (C) and (D)

83. If Y is related to W in a certain way and in a same way T is related to V then which of the following person is related to S?

A. T B. V
C. U D. X
E. None of these

84. Who sits second to the right of Z?

A. V B. X
C. U D. S
E. T

85. From the above question which of the following persons are odd numbered persons?

A. V, S, T and U B. V, S, W and Y
C. Y, S, Z and U D. V, S, W and U
E. V, S, X and U

Directions (Qs. No. 86-90): *Study the following information carefully and answer the questions given below.*

Eight persons K, M, O, Q, S, U, W, and Z attend the seminar on three different months viz., February, May, August, and November on three different dates 18, 21 of the month but not necessarily in the same order. Only three persons attend the seminar between K and U. Z and M attend the seminar on same month but not in February. O attends the seminar after Q. S attends the seminar immediately after K. Not more than two persons attend the seminar between Z and O. M and Q are attend the seminar on same date but not in same month.

86. Who among the following persons attend the seminar after M?

A. Only U B. Only U and O
C. Only Z and O D. Only O
E. None of these

87. Which of the following statements is true?

A. More than one person attend the seminar between Z and U
B. More than one person attend the seminar between W and K
C. More than one person attend the seminar between K and M
D. More than one person attend the seminar between Q and S
E. None is true

88. Which of the following statement is true about Q?

A. Attends the seminar on 18
B. Attends the seminar on November
C. Attends the seminar on 21
D. Attends the seminar on August
E. Attends the seminar on May

89. Four of the following five are alike in a certain way based on the arrangement and hence form a group. Which one of the following does not belong to that group?

A. WQ B. KS
C. ZM D. SZ
E. UO

90. Who among the following persons are attend the seminar on November?

A. M, U B. Q, W
C. S, Z D. Q, K
E. U, O

Directions (Qs. No. 91-95): *In each question, relationship between different elements is shown in the statements. The statements are followed by conclusions. Study the conclusions based on the given statements and select the appropriate answer.*

91. Statement : $A \geq B > C = D \leq E = F \leq G$

Conclusions : I. $C > A$ II. $G \geq D$

A. Only conclusion I follows
B. Only conclusion II follows
C. Either conclusion I or II follows
D. Both conclusion I and II follow
E. Neither conclusion I nor II follows

92. Statement : $P = Q < R > S > T \geq U = V$

Conclusions : I. $S > V$ II. $S \geq U$

A. Only conclusion I follows
B. Only conclusion II follows
C. Either conclusion I or II follows
D. Both conclusion I and II follow
E. Neither conclusion I nor II follows

93. Statement : $K > L \geq M = N > O < P \leq Q$

Conclusions : I. $O < Q$ II. $K > O$

A. Only conclusion I follows
B. Only conclusion II follows
C. Either conclusion I or II follows
D. Both conclusion I and II follow
E. Neither conclusion I nor II follows

94. Statements : Only few tasks are bore.
No bore is discuss.
All discuss are noted.

Conclusions : (*i*) All task being bore is a possibility.
(*ii*) Some noted being bore is a possibility.

A. Only I follows B. Only II follows
C. Either I or II follows D. Neither I or II follows
E. Both I and II follow

95. Statements : Only few legs are ribs.
All legs are mouths.
All mouths are faces.

Conclusions : (*i*) All face being ribs is a possibility.
(*ii*) Some ribs are not legs.

A. Only conclusion I follows
B. Only conclusion II follows
C. Both conclusion I and II follow
D. Neither conclusion I nor conclusion II follows
E. None of the above

Directions (Qs. No. 96-100): *Study the following information carefully and answer the questions given below:*

Certain numbers of persons are sitting in a row. Five persons sit between C and D. N sits third to the left of S. Three persons sit between S and D. D and C is not an immediate neighbour of N. I is fifth from the right end. I sits fourth to the right of D. Three persons sit between O and T. The number of person sit between T and O is same the number of person sit between T and C. I sits to the left of C.

96. How many persons sit between T and S?
A. Two B. Three
C. Five D. Four
E. One

97. How many persons sit in a row?
A. 15 B. 14
C. 17 D. 16
E. 18

98. If Z sits third to the left of C then, who among the following persons is an immediate neighbour of Z?
A. T B. D
C. O D. S
E. N

99. How many persons sit between N and O?
A. Two B. Three
C. Five D. Four
E. One

100. Who sits sixth from the left end of the row?
A. O B. S
C. N D. D
E. E

ANSWERS

1. (C)	**2. (C)**	**3. (D)**
4. (E)	**5. (A)**	**6. (D)**
7. (A)	**8. (B)**	**9. (A)**
10. (D)	**11. (A)**	**12. (C)**
13. (B)	**14. (D)**	**15. (A)**
16. (D)	**17. (E)**	**18. (A)**
19. (C)	**20. (B)**	**21. (E)**
22. (D)	**23. (A)**	**24. (C)**
25. (E)	**26. (D)**	**27. (A)**
28. (C)	**29. (A)**	**30. (D)**

31. (E): 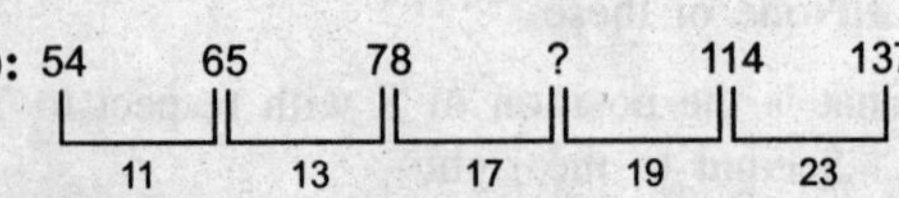

Hence, ? = 95.

32. (D): 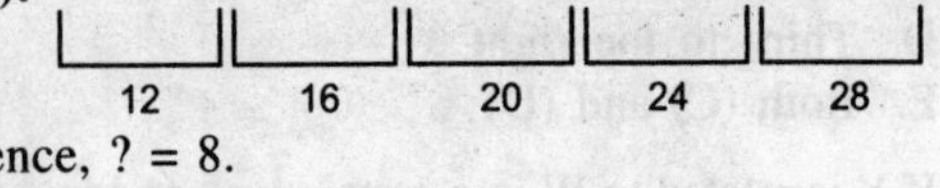

Hence, ? = 8.

33. (D): 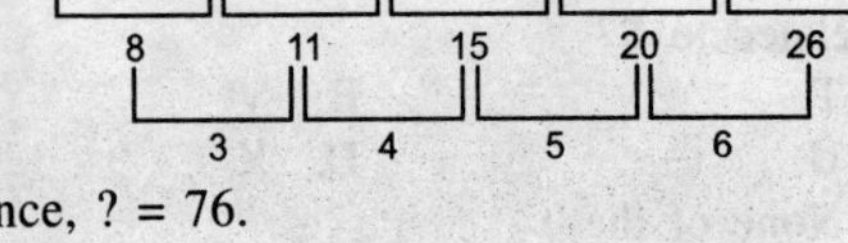

Hence, ? = 76.

34. (A): 2 5 16 65 ?

×2+1 ×3+1 ×4+1 ×5+1

Hence, ? = 326.

35. (B): ? 105 112 122 137 159

6 7 10 15 22

1 3 5 7

Hence, ? = 99.

36. (A): 1528 + 21 − 840 − 510 = ?

? = 1549 − 1350

? = 199

37. (B): $45\%\text{ of }\left(\sqrt{6561}\times 5\right) = ? \div 124$

45% of 81 × 5 = ? ÷ 124

45% of 405 = ? ÷ 124

$? \div 124 = \frac{729}{4} \Rightarrow ? = 22599.$

38. (E): $\Rightarrow 672\times\frac{1}{24}\times 18+153-345 = x$

$\Rightarrow 28 \times 18 + 153 - 345 = x$

$\Rightarrow 504 + 153 - 345 = x$

$\Rightarrow 657 - 345 = x \Rightarrow x = 312$

39. (C): $\Rightarrow \left(760\times\frac{35}{100}\right)-13\div 17\times 289+224 = x^2 - 55$

$\Rightarrow \left(38\times\frac{35}{5}\right)-13\div 17\times 289+224 = x^2 - 55$

$\Rightarrow 266-\frac{13}{17}\times 289+224 = x^2 - 55$

$\Rightarrow 266 - 13 \times 17 + 224 = x^2 - 55$

$\Rightarrow 266 - 221 + 224 = x^2 - 55$

$\Rightarrow 490 - 221 = x^2 - 55$

$\Rightarrow 269 + 55 = x^2$

$\Rightarrow x^2 = 324 = (18)^2$

$\Rightarrow x = 18$

40. (A): $154 + 221 - 370 = \sqrt[3]{x}$

$\sqrt[3]{x} = 5;\ x = 125$

41. (C): $\Rightarrow 25\times 45+3^2\times 44-\left(440\times\frac{35}{100}\right) = x$

$\Rightarrow 25 \times 45 + 3^2 \times 44 - 154 = x$

$\Rightarrow 1125 + 396 - 154 = x$

$\Rightarrow 1521 - 154 = x \Rightarrow x = 1367$

42. (A): $32\times\frac{1}{64}\times 16+221-4 = x^2$

$4 + 221 = x^2$

$x^2 = 225 \Rightarrow x = 15$

43. (A): $\Rightarrow \left(1584\times\frac{12.5}{100}\right)-11\sqrt{2}\times 10\sqrt{2}+221 = x$

$\Rightarrow 1584\times\frac{5}{40}-11\sqrt{2}\times 10\sqrt{2}+221 = x$

$\Rightarrow 198 - 110 \times 2 + 221 = x$

$\Rightarrow 198 - 220 + 221 = x$

$\Rightarrow 419 - 220 = x \Rightarrow x = 199.$

44. (B): $\Rightarrow 15\times 98+\left(350\times\frac{120}{100}\right)-\left(350\times\frac{20}{100}\right) = x-154$

$\Rightarrow 15\times 98+\left(350\times\frac{6}{5}\right)-\left(350\times\frac{1}{5}\right) = x - 154$

$\Rightarrow 15 \times 98 + 420 - 70 = x - 154$

$\Rightarrow 1470 + 420 - 70 = x - 154$

$\Rightarrow 1890 - 70 = x - 154$

$1820 = x - 154$

$\Rightarrow x = 1820 + 154$

$x = 1974.$

45. (C): $\Rightarrow \left(250\times\frac{56}{100}\right)-19\times 68\div 17+450 = x$

$\Rightarrow \left(5\times\frac{56}{2}\right)-19\times 68\times\frac{1}{17}+450 = x$

$\Rightarrow 140 - 19 \times 4 + 450 = x$

$140 - 76 + 450 = x$

$\Rightarrow 590 - 76 = x$

$\Rightarrow x = 514.$

46. (C): Total number of fruits in shops A, C and D = 500 + 900 + 600 = 2000

Total number of rotten fruits in shops A, C and D = 100 + 220 + 120 = 440

The number of fruits sold by shops A, C and D is 2000 − 440 = 1560

Required average $= \frac{1560}{3} = 520.$

47. (B): The number of fruits sold by B & C together is (700 − 200) + (900 − 220) = 500 + 680 = 1180.

The number of fruits sold by A & D together is (500 − 100) + (600 − 120) = 400 + 480 = 880.

Required ratio = 118 : 88 = 59 : 44.

48. (A): The number of fruits sold by D is 480.

The number of fruits sold by A is 400.

Required percentage $= \frac{480}{400}\times 100 = 120\%$.

49. (B): The number fruits sold by A & C together is 400 + 680 = 1080.

The number of fruits sold by B & D together is 500 + 480 = 980

Required difference = 1080 − 980 = 100

50. (C): The fruits sold by B & C together is
500 + 680 = 1180
The fruits sold by B is 500.

Required percentage = $\frac{1180}{500} \times 100 = 236\%$.

(Qs. No. 51-55) According to given information:

Employees	April	May
A	36	70
B	120	60
C	95	46
D	56	75
E	92	56

51. (B): The score that employee D got in both the months together is 56 + 75 = 131.

52. (C): The score of employee A in the month of April is 35.
The score of employee A in the month of May is 70.

Required percentage $\frac{70-36}{36} \times 100 = 94.44 \sim 94\%$.

53. (D): The scores obtained by employee C in April is 95.
The scores obtained by employee D in May is 75.
Required ratio is 19 : 15.

54. (B): The average scores obtained by all the given employees in April is $\frac{36+120+95+56+92}{5} = \frac{399}{5}$.
The average scores obtained by all the given employees in May is

$\frac{70+60+46+75+56}{5} = \frac{307}{5}$.

Required difference $\frac{399-307}{5} = \frac{92}{5} = 18.4$.

55. (E): The scores obtained by employee B in April is 120.
The scores obtained by employee D in May is 75.

Required percentage = $\frac{45}{75} \times 100 = 60\%$ more.

56. (B): Quantity I:

(A + B)'s 1 day's work = $\frac{2}{45}$

$\Rightarrow \frac{1}{3x} + \frac{1}{5x} = \frac{2}{45} \Rightarrow \frac{5+3}{15x} = \frac{2}{45}$

$\Rightarrow \frac{8}{15x} = \frac{2}{45} \Rightarrow x = \frac{8 \times 45}{x \times 15} \Rightarrow x = 12$

Number of days taken by A = 3x = 36 and number of days taken by B = 5x = 60
Difference in days = 60 − 36 = 24 days
Quantity I < Quantity II.

57. (E): I. $x^2 - 25x + 136 = 0$
$\Rightarrow x^2 - 8x - 17x + 136 = 0$
$\Rightarrow x(x-8) - 17(x-8) = 0$
$\Rightarrow (x-8)(x-17) = 0 \Rightarrow x = 8, 17$
II. $y^2 - 24y + 143 = 0$
$y^2 - 11y - 13y + 143 = 0$
$\Rightarrow y(y-11) - 13(y-11) = 0$
$\Rightarrow (y-11)(y-13) = 0 \Rightarrow y = 11, 13$

58. (D): I. $x^2 = 169$
$x = +13, -13$
II. $y = \sqrt[3]{2197}$
$y = +13$
Hence, $y \geq x \Rightarrow x \leq y$

59. (D): I. $x^2 + 3x - 208 = 0$
$\Rightarrow x^2 + 16x - 13x - 208 = 0$
$\Rightarrow x(x+16) - 13(x+16) = 0$
$\Rightarrow (x-13)(x+16) = 0 \Rightarrow x = 13, -16$
II. $y^2 - 25y + 156 = 0$
$\Rightarrow y^2 - 12y - 13y + 156 = 0$
$\Rightarrow y(y-12) - 13(y-12) = 0$
$\Rightarrow (y-12)(y-13) = 0 \Rightarrow y = 12, 13$
Hence, $y \geq x \Rightarrow x \leq y$

60. (D): I. $x^2 - 18x + 45 = 0$
$\Rightarrow x^2 - 3x - 15x - 45 = 0$
$\Rightarrow x(x-3) - 15(x-3) = 0$
$\Rightarrow (x-3)(x-15) = 0$
$\Rightarrow x = 3, 15$
II. $y^2 - 22y + 105 = 0$
$\Rightarrow y^2 - 7y - 15y + 105 = 0$
$\Rightarrow y(y-7) - 15(y-7) = 0$
$\Rightarrow (y-7)(y-15) = 0$
$\Rightarrow y = 7, 15$
Hence, $x \leq y$

61. (A): Total cost price of the pulses
= (36 × 28) + (60 × 32) = 2928
Required selling price per kg of the mixture

$= \frac{2928}{96 \times 5} \times 6 =$ ₹ 36.60

62. (B): Let the gain in the 1st case be 4x and the loss in 2nd case be x. Difference between two selling prices
$= 4x - (-x) =$ ₹ 5x
Actual difference between two selling prices
= 3600 − 2700 = ₹ 900
$5x = 900 \Rightarrow x = 180$
Cost price of the cycle = ₹ 3600 − 4x = 3600 − 720
= ₹ 2880.

63. (D): Let the speed of the boat be B. The speed of the current is 5 km/hr. The speed of the boat in still water is 50% more than speed of the boat in upstream.

$$B = \frac{3}{2}(B-5)$$

$$B = 15 \text{ km/hr}$$

Downstream speed = (15 + 5) = 20 km/hr

Total downstream distance = 20 × 2 = 40 km

64. (C): The ages of father and son before 8 years are in the ratio $8x : 5x$.

The ages of father and son after 12 years

$$\Rightarrow \quad \frac{8x+8+12}{5x+8+12} = \frac{13}{10}$$

$$\Rightarrow \quad 10(8x + 20) = 13(5x + 20)$$

$$\Rightarrow \quad 80x + 200 = 65x + 260 \Rightarrow x = 4$$

Hence, The age of father after 4 years = $8x + 8 + 4$ = (8 × 4) + 12 = 44 years.

65. (B): Let the initial average be x. Total score be $9x$.

$$9x + 100 = 10(x + 8) \Rightarrow x = 20$$

Hence, New average = 20 + 8 = 28

(Qs. No. 66-68):

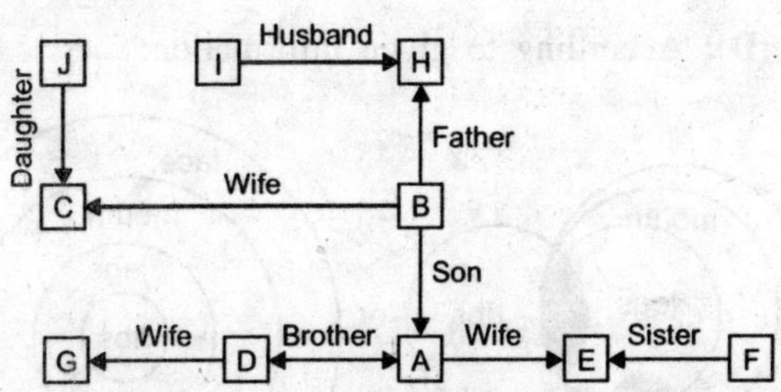

66. (A): Hence, H is the father of B.

67. (B): Hence, A is the brother-in-law of F.

68. (B): C is the Mother-in-law of E.

69. (D):

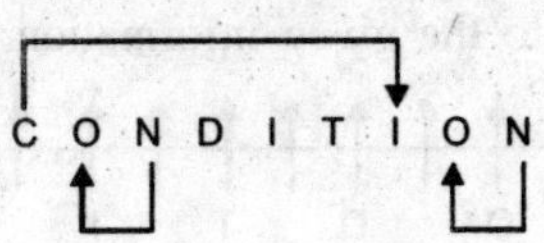

70. (C):

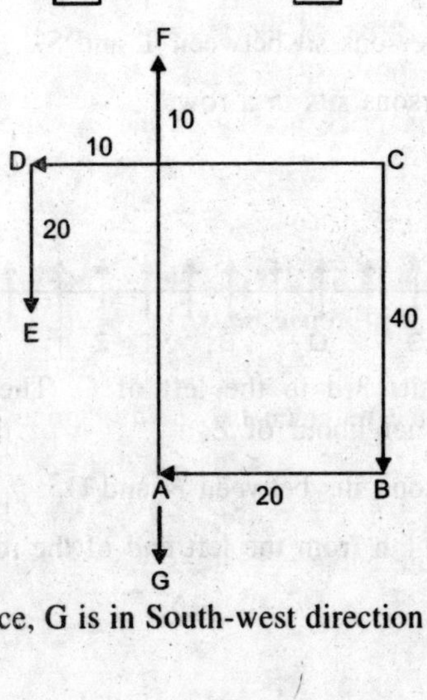

Hence, G is in South-west direction with respect to C.

(Qs. No. 71-75): According to given information.

	Case
Sunday	M
Monday	P
Tuesday	J
Wednesday	N
Thursday	K
Friday	O
Saturday	L

71. (A): J takes week off on Tuesday.

72. (A): P takes week off on Monday.

73. (D): Three persons take week off between J and L.

74. (D): O take week off on Friday.

75. (C): Two persons (K, O) take off between L and N.

76. (A): The given number series is,

326 576 627 513 894

(*i*) The first digit of each number is decreased by two,

126 376 427 313 694

(*ii*) The digits in each number are arranged in descending order from left to right,

621 763 742 331 964

Then, the second smallest number after the rearrangement is 621, and its corresponding number will be 326.

77. (D): The given number series is,

326 576 627 513 894

(*i*) If the odd digits in each number are decreased by one and the even digits are increased by 2,

248 468 846 402 1086

(*ii*) The numbers thus formed are arranged in descending order from left to right.

1086 846 468 402 248

Then, the second number from the right end after the rearrangement is 402, and its corresponding number will be 513.

78. (D): The given number series is,

326 576 627 513 894

If the first and the last digits of the number are interchanged:

623 675 726 315 498

79. (B): The given number series is,

326 576 627 513 894

(*i*) If the digits in each number are written in descending order:

632 765 762 531 984

(*ii*) The numbers formed are arranged in ascending order from right to left : 984 765 762 632 531

Then, the fourth-smallest number after the rearrangement is 765, and its corresponding number is 576.

80. (C): The given number series is,
326 576 627 513 894

(*i*) If the digits in odd position are decreased by one, we get : 225 475 526 412 793

(*ii*) Then the numbers are arranged in ascending order from right to left : 793 526 475 412 225

Then, the number which is the second from the left end is 526, and its corresponding number will be 627.

(Qs. No. 81-85) : According to the given information.

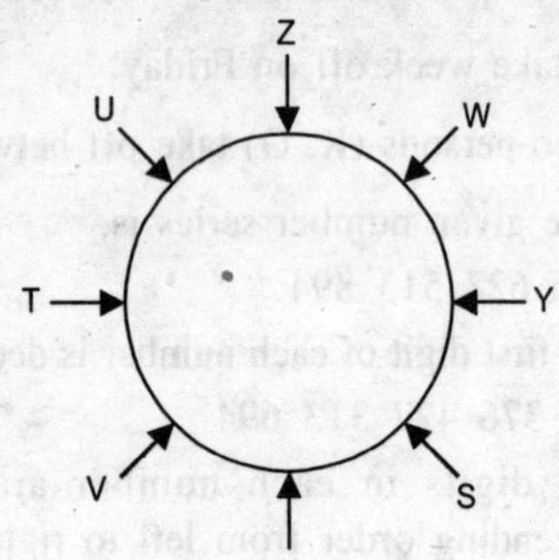

81. (B): V sites opposite to W.

82. (E): Hence, S is 5th to the left of T and S is 3rd to the right of T.

83. (D): Similarly, X is related to S.

84. (E): T sits second to the right of Z.

85. (D): It is alternate right to left (V – S – W – U).

(Qs. 86-90) : According to the given information.

Month	Date	Persons
February	18	W
	21	Q
May	18	K
	21	S
August	18	Z
	21	M
November	18	U
	21	O

86. (B): Only U and O attend the seminar after M.

87. (C): 2 persons attend the seminar between K and M.

88. (C): Q attends the seminar on 21 February.

89. (D): SZ does not belong to that group.

90. (E): U and O attend the seminar in November.

91. (B): $A \geq B > C = D \leq E = F \leq G$

I. $C > A$ (False)

II. $G \geq D$ (True)

92. (A): $P = Q < R > S > T \geq U = V$

I. $S > V$ (True)

II. $S \geq U$ (False)

93. (D): $K > L \geq M = N > O < P \leq Q$

I. $O < Q$ (True)

II. $K > O$ (True)

94. (D): According to given statements.

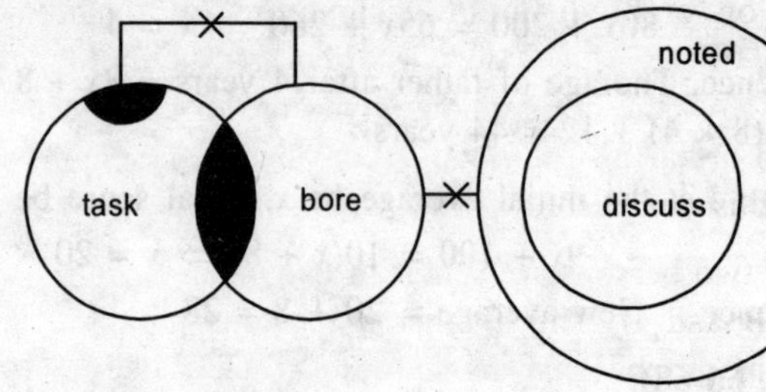

95. (D): According to given information:

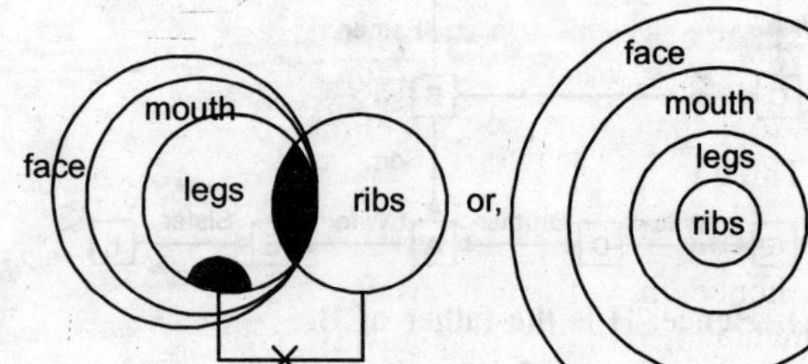

96. (C): According to the given information

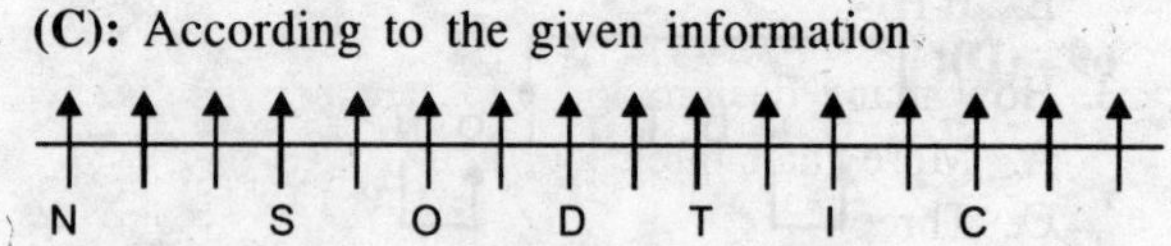

Hence, 5 persons sit between T and S.

97. (D): 16 persons sits in a row.

98. (A):

Case D

Given, Z sits 3rd to the left of C. Then, T is an immediate neighbour of Z.

99. (D): 4 persons sits between N and O.

100. (A): O sits 6th from the left end of the row.

Previous Paper (Solved)

State Bank of India (SBI)
CLERICAL CADRE (Junior Associates)
Phase-I : Preliminary Exam 2020*

REASONING ABILITY

Directions (Qs. No. 1-5): *Study the following information carefully and answer the questions given below:*

There are eight employees of a company and all of them are working on eight different designation of a bank viz. Chairman, CFO, GM, DGM, AGM, Manager, Junior Manager and Clerk. All the designations given are to be considered in a given order (as Chairman is considered as Senior-most and Clerk is considered as the Junior-most).

Only two persons are senior to B. One designation lies between B and G. The number of persons junior to G is same as the number of persons senior to C. H is just senior to E, but junior to C. More than four designations lie between H and F. D is junior to A.

1. How many persons are junior to H?
A. None B. One
C. More than four D. Four
E. Three

2. Four of the following five are alike in a certain way and hence they form a group. Which one of the following does not belong to that group?
A. A-F B. B-A
C. H-D D. G-A
E. E-H

3. How many designation gaps are between A and D?
A. More than three B. Two
C. Three D. One
E. None of these

4. Who among the following is just senior to B?
A. A B. D
C. C D. E
E. None of these

5. Who among the following is AGM?
A. F B. B
C. G D. D
E. None of these

Directions (Qs. No. 6-8): *In each of the questions below are given some statements followed by some conclusions. You have to take the given statements to be true even if they seem to be at variance with commonly known facts. Read all the conclusions and then decide which of the given conclusions logically follows from the given statements disregarding commonly known facts.*

A. If only conclusion I follows.
B. If only conclusion II follows.
C. If either conclusion I or II follows.
D. If neither conclusion I nor II follows.
E. If both conclusions I and II follow.

6. Statements: Some Banana are Orange.
All Orange are Apple.
Conclusions: I. Some Banana are not Apple.
II. Some Orange are Banana.

7. Statements: Only a few East are North.
Few North are South.
All South are West.
Conclusions: I. All East being North is a possibility.
II. Some East are West.

8. Statements: Only a few Song are Melody.
Only a few Melody are Film.
No Film is Award.
Conclusions: I. All Song being Film is a possibility.
II. Some Melody are not Award.

Directions (Qs. No. 9-12): *Study the following information carefully and answer the questions given below:*

In a certain code language:
"Club house near located" is coded as "ol gp ox ot"
"both club view near" is coded as "mt ox sq ot"
"make located house view" is coded as "nk ol gp sq"
"near club view area" is coded as "ot ox sq tm"

9. What is the code for "both" in the given code language?
A. ox B. sq
C. mt D. ot
E. Either B or C

10. What is the code for "house" in the given code language?
A. ol B. ox

* *Based on Memory*

C. gp D. Either A or C
E. None of these

11. The code "nk" is stands for?
A. make B. both
C. area D. club
E. None of these

12. What may be the possible code for "both house" in the given code language?
A. gp mt B. mt nk
C. mt sq D. ox mt
E. gp sq

Directions (Qs. No. 13-17): *Study the following information carefully and answer the questions given below:*

There are eight persons A, B, C, D, E, F, G and H sitting around a circular table facing towards the centre of the table but not necessarily in the same order.

B sits third to the right of A. Only one person sits between B and D. E faces C who is not an immediate neighbour of B. G sits third to the left of F. A is not an immediate neighbour of F.

13. Who among the following sits to the immediate left of C?
A. G B. D
C. F D. H
E. None of these

14. Who among the following sits to the opposite of A?
A. H B. G
C. F D. D
E. None of these

15. How many persons sit between H and G when counted from the left of G?
A. Two B. One
C. Three D. Four
E. None of these

16. If all the persons sit around the circle in clockwise direction by their names according to English alphabetical order starting from A, then how many persons remain unchanged except A?
A. Four B. One
C. Three D. Two
E. None of these

17. What is the position of B with respect to H?
A. Fourth to the left B. Fourth to the right
C. Third to the right D. Both A and C
E. Both A and B

Directions (Qs. No. 18-20): *Study the following information carefully and answer the questions given below:*

Point E is in 15m north of Point D. Point F is in 20m north of Point C. Point A is in 35m east of Point F. Point P is in 25m south of Point A. Point E is in 20m east of Point P.

18. What is the direction of point F with respect to point P?
A. North-west B. North-east
C. South-west D. South-east
E. North

19. Four of the following five are alike in a certain way and hence they form a group. Which one of the following does not belong to that group?
A. C-P B. A-E
C. A-C D. P-D
E. F-E

20. If point X is 20m south of point C, then what is the total distance between point X and point D?
A. 40m B. 35m
C. 55m D. 65m
E. 85m

Directions (Qs. No. 21-25): *Following questions are based on the five numbers given below, Study the given information and answer the following questions.*

625 427 189 258 469

21. What is the sum of the 3rd digit of second number from left and 2nd digit of third number from right?
A. 10 B. 15
C. 14 D. 12
E. None of these

22. If the position of first and third digits of each of the numbers are interchanged, then which among the following is the highest number?
A. 258 B. 469
C. 189 D. 427
E. 625

23. If all the digits in the number are arranged in the descending order within the number from left to right, then which among the following will be the lowest number after rearrangement?
A. 427 B. 189
C. 258 D. 625
E. 469

24. What is the product of 3rd digit of 2nd lowest number and 1st digit of 2nd highest number?
A. 32 B. 72
C. 24 D. 36
E. None of these

25. If 2 is subtracted from each number then how many numbers thus formed are odd numbers?
A. One B. Two
C. Three D. More than three
E. None of these

26. How many such numerals are there in the number '645903287' which will remain at the same position when arranged in ascending order from left to right?

A. Three
B. Two
C. One
D. Four
E. None of these

27. If it is possible to make only one meaningful word with the 1st, 3rd, 5th and 11th letters of the word 'INHERITENCE', which would be the third letter of the word from the left? If more than one such word can be formed give 'Y' as the answer. If no such word can be formed, give 'Z' as your answer.
A. Y
B. R
C. I
D. E
E. Z

Directions (Qs. No. 28-32): *Study the following information carefully and answer the questions given below:*

Eight persons A, B, C, D, E, F, G and H are buying some products one after another but not necessarily in the same order.

At most two persons are buying products before F. Only one person is buying between D and F. C is buying just before H. One person is buying between C and D. A is buying just before E. B is buying before G and after E.

28. How many persons are buying their products after D?
A. Four
B. Two
C. More than three
D. One
E. None of these

29. Who among the following is buying just after G?
A. E
B. F
C. B
D. C
E. None of these

30. If all the persons are arranged in alphabetical order from left to right starting from A, then find how many persons remains at the same position (excluding A)?
A. One
B. None of these
C. Two
D. Four
E. More than Four

31. Who among the following is buying exactly between D and F?
A. E
B. B
C. A
D. H
E. None of these

32. How many persons are buying between E and C?
A. Five
B. Four
C. Three
D. None
E. Two

Directions (Qs. No. 33-35): *In each of the question, relationships between some elements are shown in the statements. These statements are followed by conclusions numbered I and II. Read the statements and give the answer.*
A. If only conclusion I follows.
B. If only conclusion II follows.
C. If either conclusion I or II follows.
D. If neither conclusion I nor II follows.
E. If both conclusion I and II follows.

33. Statements: $P > Q \geq R = S < T = U$
Conclusions: I. $Q > S$ II. $S = Q$

34. Statements: $J < D = L \leq K \leq Q \geq R$
Conclusions: I. $J < Q$ II. $L \leq R$

35. Statements: $O > P = G > B \geq X = M \leq H$
Conclusions: I. $G > X$ II. $O > M$

QUANTITATIVE APTITUDE

Directions (Qs. No. 36-40): *Table given below shows the number of male and female participated in an event from five different schools (A, B, C, D & E). Study the table carefully and answer the following questions.*

Schools	Male	Female
A	650	450
B	540	420
C	720	500
D	560	450
E	680	320

36. Find average number of female participated from school – A, B & D.
A. 400
B. 380
C. 350
D. 440
E. 450

37. Total male participated from school – B & D together are how much more or less than total female participated from school – A & C together?
A. 150
B. 110
C. 170
D. 120
E. 240

38. Total male participated from school – B & C together are what per cent more or less than total female participated from school – A & D together?
A. 20%
B. 60%
C. 50%
D. 40%
E. 30%

39. If total male participated from school – F are 40% more than that of from school – A and ratio of female participated from school – B to that of from school – F is 21:32, then find total students participated from school – F.

A. 1420 B. 1550
C. 1580 D. 1460
E. 1490

40. Find total number of male students participated from all the five schools together.

A. 2860 B. 3150
C. 2940 D. 3200
E. 3020

Directions (Qs. No. 41–45): *What will come in the place of question (?) mark in following number series:*

41. ?, 100, 150, 375, 1312.5

A. 100 B. 200
C. 150 D. 400
E. 50

42. 104, ?, 96, 120, 88, 128

A. 112 B. 110
C. 114 D. 118
E. 108

43. 15, 8, 9, 15, 32, ?

A. 66 B. 99
C. 80 D. 82.5
E. 80.5

44. 6, 8, 14, 26, 46, ?

A. 72 B. 84
C. 96 D. 80
E. 76

45. 72000, 36000, 12000, 3000, 600, ?

A. 120 B. 200
C. 300 D. 150
E. 100

46. 12 men can do a work in 10 days while 10 women can do the same work in 18 days. In how many days 4 men & 6 women together can do the same work?

A. $\frac{120}{7}$ days B. 24 days
C. $\frac{180}{13}$ days D. 15 days
E. 18 days

47. A car can cover a distance in 4 hour at speed 60 kmph then by what per cent should the speed of car be increased to cover the same distance in 2.5 hr?

A. 60% B. 40%
C. 50% D. 100%
E. 75%

48. The ratio of the ages of Ram and Rahim 10 years ago was 1 : 3. The ratio of their ages five years hence will be 2 : 3. Then, the ratio of their present ages is:

A. 1 : 2 B. 3 : 5
C. 3 : 4 D. 2 : 5
E. None of these

49. Two trains of length 140 m & 120 m are running in same direction on parallel tracks with speeds 132 kmph & 80 kmph respectively. How much time will they take to cross each other?

A. 7.09 sec B. 18 sec
C. 11.7 sec D. 4.42 sec
E. Cannot be determined

50. A person sold a book at 20% profit. If he had bought it at 10% less cost and sold for ₹ 90 more then he would have gained 40% profit. Find cost price of book.

A. ₹ 800 B. ₹ 1600
C. ₹ 1500 D. None of these
E. ₹ 1200

Directions (Qs. No. 51–55): *In each question two equations numbered (I) and (II) are given. You have to solve both the equations and mark appropriate answer.*

A. If $x = y$ or no relation can be established
B. If $x > y$
C. If $x < y$
D. If $x \geq y$
E. If $x \leq y$

51. **I.** $x = \sqrt{25}$ **II.** $y^3 = 125$

52. **I.** $x^2 + 2x - 35 = 0$ **II.** $y^2 + 15y + 56 = 0$

53. **I.** $x^2 = 81$ **II.** $y^2 = 64$

54. **I.** $17x^2 - 14x - 83 = -80$ **II.** $y^2 = 2y + 35$

55. **I.** $x^2 + 4x - 45 = 0$ **II.** $y^2 - 13y + 40 = 0$

56. A container contains mixture of milk & water in ratio 5 : 3 respectively. If 8 lit milk is added in it then ratio of milk to water becomes 11 : 5. Find difference between initial quantity of milk & that of water.

A. 5 lit B. 38 lit
C. 18 lit D. 30 lit
E. 10 lit

57. ₹ 6000 when invested at a certain rate at SI for 2 years, it fetches ₹ 1200. If same sum is invested at same rate for a year compounded half – yearly then find compound interest.

A. ₹ 615 B. ₹ 600
C. ₹ 1200 D. ₹ 585
E. ₹ 1260

58. A boat can cover 28 km downstream in 42 min. ratio of speed of boat in still water to speed of stream is 7 : 3. Find difference between time taken by boat to cover 60 km downstream & 40 km upstream.

A. 2.25 hr B. 1 hr
C. 1.5 hr D. 0.4 hr
E. 0.9 hr

59. A & B entered into a business by investing total capital of ₹ 17000. B withdraws ₹ 1500 after 6 months and gets ₹ 8100 as profit out of total profit of ₹ 19500 at the end of year. Find capital of B after 6 months from starting.

A. ₹ 7000 B. ₹ 9500
C. ₹ 7500 D. ₹ 6000
E. ₹ 6500

60. If length of a rectangle increases by 40% while keeping breadth constant then area of rectangle increased by 24 m^2 and perimeter of original rectangle is 32 m. find breadth of rectangle.

A. 8.4 m B. 10 m
C. 6 m D. 14 m
E. 8 m

Directions (Qs. No. 61–70): *What will come in the place of (?) mark in following question.*

61. 280 ÷ 4 ÷ 2 = 170 – ?

A. 105 B. 115
C. 125 D. 135
E. 145

62. $(\sqrt{144}+\sqrt{169})\times 3=\frac{?}{5}$

A. 375 B. 325
C. 350 D. 275
E. 475

63. (12 × 5 ÷ 4) × 8 = ?

A. 100 B. 140
C. 120 D. 80
E. 90

64. (120% of 750) ÷ ? = 25

A. 30 B. 36
C. 24 D. 18
E. 48

65. $8\frac{1}{2}-4\frac{5}{6}=?-3\frac{7}{12}$

A. $3\frac{1}{4}$ B. $3\frac{5}{12}$
C. $2\frac{7}{12}$ D. $7\frac{1}{4}$
E. $5\frac{2}{3}$

66. 275 + 64% of 750 = 750 + ?

A. 25 B. 8
C. 10 D. 15
E. 5

67. $\sqrt{225}+\sqrt{81}$ + 122 = ?

A. 146 B. 164
C. 162 D. 172
E. 182

68. $\frac{510}{?}=\sqrt{324}+3.25$ + 3.25

A. 12 B. 48
C. 24 D. 6
E. 18

69. 12.5% of (120 + ?) = 45

A. 160 B. 180
C. 360 D. 240
E. 120

70. 572 ÷ 13 × 12 – 16 = $(8)^?$

A. 4 B. 2
C. 3 D. 5
E. None of these

ENGLISH LANGUAGE

Directions (Qs. No. 71-77): *Read the given passage carefully and answer the following questions. Certain parts have been highlighted to help answer the questions.*

Every year, around one million people die of mosquito-borne diseases according to the World Health Organization (WHO). This is why mosquitoes are considered one of the **deadliest** living creatures on the planet — not because they are lethal themselves, but because many of the viruses and parasites they transmit are.

In the absence of an effective vaccine for dengue fever, Zika fever, chikungunya and other mosquito-borne diseases, researchers have developed genetic strategies to reduce mosquito populations. One such strategy involves the release into the wild of genetically modified (GM) mosquitoes that express a lethal gene — a strategy believed to have little impact on the overall DNA of wild populations of mosquitoes.

The transfer of new genes from GM organisms to wild or domesticated non-GM populations is a key criticism of GM crops like soybean and corn. There are concerns that the introduction of GM genes into non-target species could have negative consequences for both human and environmental health.

Oxitec, a company that spun out of research at Oxford University in the early 2000s, developed and trademarked GM Friendly™ mosquitoes (also known as strain OX513A of Aedes aegypti). These male GM mosquitoes have what the company describes as a "self-limiting" gene, which means that when these so-called friendly mosquitoes' mate, their offspring inherit the self-limiting gene which is supposed to prevent them surviving into adulthood.

In theory, when these mosquitoes are released in high numbers, a dramatic reduction in the mosquito population should follow. According to research published by Oxitec researchers in 2015, field trials involving recurring releases of Friendly™ mosquitoes demonstrated a reduction of nearly 95 per cent of target populations in Brazil. In these field trials, experiments were not performed to assess whether GM mosquitoes might persist in the wild.

A recent study from the Powell lab at Yale University has since confirmed that some of the offspring of the GM mosquitoes didn't succumb to the self-limiting lethal gene and **survived** to adulthood. They were able to breed with native mosquitoes and thereby introduce some of their genes into the wild population.

Meanwhile, the impact of mosquitoes carrying these new genes remains largely unknown. One significant worry is that a new breed of mosquito might emerge that is more difficult to control. These new genes could also potentially alter evolutionary pressures on viruses carried by mosquitoes, like dengue fever, in unpredictable ways. This includes potentially increasing their virulence or changing their host-insect interactions. These are hypothetical risks that have been raised by scientists, and reflect the need for further study.

71. Why are mosquitoes considered as one of the deadliest living creatures on earth?
A. Capability to transmit life threatening diseases.
B. Mosquito bites cause fatal reactions in human beings
C. Mosquitoes cannot be killed easily
D. Both A and C
E. None of the above

72. What is one of the methods being developed to control population of mosquitoes?
A. Spraying of pesticides using established procedures.
B. Introduction of a lethal gene into wild populations of mosquitoes using genetically modified ones.
C. Not letting any stagnant water build-up near homes
D. Both A and B
E. None of the above

73. What can be the potential side effect(s) of genetically modified mosquito-offspring?
A. Evolution of a breed of mosquitoes which are more difficult to control
B. Increase in the severity of diseases being currently transmitted by mosquitoes
C. Change in host-insect interactions
D. Loss of natural populations of mosquitoes
E. A, B and C

74. Which of the statements can be considered as true with respect to the passage given?
A. Field trials on Genetically modified mosquitoes showed reduction of 96% target populations
B. Oxitec trademarked the GM Friendly mosquitoes in 2015
C. The female GM mosquito has a self-limiting gene
D. Both A and B
E. None of the above

75. What is the desired effect of releasing GM mosquitoes containing the 'Self-limiting Gene'?
A. A substantial reduction in the population of mosquitoes
B. Birth of mosquitoes without a biting mechanism
C. Decrease in the number of diseases caused due to mosquitoes
D. Increase in the number of male mosquitoes
E. Both B and C

76. Which of the following word is similar to **deadliest** as mentioned in the passage given?
A. fatal
B. demeaning
C. fulfil
D. harmless
E. None of the above

77. Which of the statements can be considered as true with respect to the passage given?
A. GM mosquitoes are able to introduce some of their genes into the wild population
B. Mosquitoes having GM genes have been thoroughly researched upon
C. Oxitec released its friendly mosquitoes in Brazil
D. A and C
E. All of the above

Directions (Qs. No. 78-80): *A word has been given in each question and has been used in the sentences given below. Identify the statements where the word has been used in a contextually and grammatically correct manner. If the word has been used correctly in all the statements, mark (E), "All of these", as your answer.*

78. HOSTILE
(*i*) He made **hostile** efficiency a key part of his budget plan.
(*ii*) There has been a **hostile** reaction to the government's proposed tax increase.
(*iii*) The security forces exercised great restraint by not responding to **hostile** attacks and threats.
A. Only (*i*)
B. Both (*i*) and (*ii*)
C. Both (*ii*) and (*iii*)
D. Only (*iii*)
E. All of these

79. VAGUE

(*i*) The judges determined that the law was too **vague** to be fairly enforced.

(*ii*) The merger of these two companies would **vague** the world's biggest accounting firm

(*iii*) The president had a **vague** reception in Ohio this morning.

A. Only (*i*)
B. Both (*i*) and (*ii*)
C. Both (*ii*) and (*iii*)
D. Only (*iii*)
E. All of these

80. ESCALATE

(*i*) The pedestrian was jaywalking when he **escalate** the busy street, walking straight into the path of an oncoming vehicle.

(*ii*) We've tried to **escalate** the most likely problems, but it's impossible to be prepared for every eventuality.

(*iii*) The decision to **escalate** UN involvement has been made in the hopes of a swift end to the hostilities.

A. Only (*i*)
B. Both (*i*) and (*ii*)
C. Both (*ii*) and (*iii*)
D. Only (*iii*)
E. All of these

Directions (Qs. No. 81-85): *In the following question, four sentences are given which may be grammatically and contextually incorrect. You need to find the one which has no error and mark that as your answer. If all the given sentences are incorrect then mark option (E) i.e. 'all are incorrect' as your answer.*

81. A. India's chocolate market is pegged at ₹ 11,000 crore, of which premium chocolates can be sized anywhere among 10% and 15%.
B. South Korea reported 52 new case of coronavirus.
C. ITC has plans to work with cocoa farmers directly in future.
D. The company initially invested ₹ 100 crore to set up a greenfield chocolate manufacture facility in Haridwar.
E. All are incorrect

82. A. Ratnakar Bank was rename as RBL Bank by the government.
B. The government expects all the mergers of public sector banks, which were announced in 2019, to become effective from April 1.
C. Analysts believe that lower gas prices would be bad with exploration
D. The Central Drugs Standard Control Organisation will be regulate the medical devices now.
E. All are incorrect

83. A. Mahindra Renewables will sell its entire stake in 3 subsidiaries to CLP India, a part of Hong Kong-based CLP Group, as nearly ₹ 340 crore.
B. The agreement will be signed to Doha city between Taliban representatives and U.S. special envoy Zalmay Khalilzad.
C. The U.S. intelligence community publicly concluded that Russia intervened in there security matters.
D. The injured animal was nursed back to health by the zookeeper and then released back into the wild
E. All are incorrect

84. A. English language have the potential to connect the world without any barriers
B. P.K. Sinha was appointed in the PMO when Nripendra Misra, the then Principal Secretary, resigns.
C. She drink the caramel liquid too fast and was soon too dizzy to stand.
D. You're coming to the party, isn't you?
E. All are incorrect

85. A. Tamil Nadu is likely to get three textile parks and a technology research centre under schemes that the Union Ministry of Textiles is formulating.
B. What is the uses of a house if you haven't got a tolerable planet to put it on?
C. You have brushed your teeth today?
D. Rahul had barely nothing to help the poor children.
E. All are incorrect

Directions (Qs. No. 86-90): *In the following questions, a sentence is divided into four parts consisting of a highlighted word in each part. Choose the option reflecting the word which is either misspelt or grammatically incorrect. If all the highlighted words are correct, choose option (E) i.e. "all are correct" as your answer choice.*

86. The manager **balanced (A)** the **strength (B)** of his team against that of their **opponent** (C) and **sighed**. (D)

A. balanced B. strength
C. opponent D. sighed
E. All are correct

87. One evening Rohan **pripared (A)** a nice **supper (B)** and put it on low heat in the oven to keep it **tepid (C)** while his wife **dressed**. (D)

A. prepared B. supper
C. tepid D. dressed
E. All are correct

88. She was able to **breathe (A)** easier when she stood outside the **massive(B) fortress (C)** that sat on a clearing the size of two **footbal** (D) fields.

A. breathe
B. massive
C. fortress
D. football
E. All are correct

89. From time to time Jack would **looking over (A)** Mungo's shoulder, **suggesting (B) tactics (C)** which invariably proved **disastrous**. (D)

A. looking over
B. suggesting
C. tactics
D. disastrous
E. All are correct

90. Horrified (A) passengers saw Olive **stumble (B)** and **fall of (C)** a platform as an express **roared (D)** in.

A. Horrified
B. stumble
C. fall of
D. roared
E. All are correct

Directions (Qs. No. 91-95): *In the following questions, a grammatically correct and meaningful sentence is given which is divided into five parts, where the first part is fixed and highlighted , in the remaining parts of the sentence namely (a), (b), (c) and (d) You have to arrange the four parts to make a contextually and grammatically meaningful sentence. If no such rearrangement is possible mark (E) as your answer i.e. 'No rearrangement required'.*

91. (*a*) the merger of Bharti Infratel
(*b*) the world's second largest
(*c*) and Indus Towers will create
(*d*) tower company

A. (*b*), (*c*), (*d*), (*a*)
B. (*c*), (*b*), (*d*), (*a*)
C. (*a*), (*c*), (*b*), (*d*)
D. (*d*), (*c*), (*a*), (*b*)
E. No rearrangement is required

92. (*a*) upcoming visit to India
(*b*) the long-awaited trade agreement
(*c*) during US President Donald Trump's
(*d*) appears to be off the table

A. (*d*), (*a*), (*b*), (*c*)
B. (*b*), (*d*), (*c*), (*a*)
C. (*c*), (*d*), (*a*), (*b*)
D. (*a*), (*d*), (*c*), (*b*)
E. No rearrangement required

93. (*a*) Leaders of the Railway Employees Organization
(*b*) alleged that the government wants to
(*c*) hand over the rail infrastructure
(*d*) to the private operators for financial benefit

A. (*a*), (*d*), (*c*), (*b*)
B. (*c*), (*b*), (*d*), (*a*)
C. (*c*), (*d*), (*b*), (*a*)
D. (*d*), (*a*), (*b*), (*c*)
E. No rearrangement required

94. (*a*) China has not yet given
(*b*) India the go-ahead to send an
(*c*) to coronavirus hit Wuhan
(*d*) aircraft with medical supplies

A. (*d*), (*a*), (*c*), (*b*)
B. (*a*), (*b*), (*d*), (*c*)
C. (*c*), (*b*), (*d*), (*a*)
D. (*b*), (*c*), (*d*), (*a*)
E. No rearrangement is required

95. (*a*) mammals and birds move from
(*b*) with a change in season, many
(*c*) one country to another in search of food
(*d*) and shelter, and for breeding

A. (*a*), (*c*), (*b*), (*d*)
B. (*c*), (*a*), (*d*), (*b*)
C. (*d*), (*a*), (*b*), (*c*)
D. (*b*), (*a*), (*c*), (*d*)
E. No rearrangement is required

Directions (Qs. No. 96-100): *In the following passage there are blanks, each of which has been numbered. These numbers are printed below the passage and against each, five options are given. Find out the appropriate word which fits the blank appropriately.*

Bumblebees, among the most important pollinators, are in **(96)** ________. Fuzzy and buzzy, they excel at spreading pollen and fertilizing many types of wild flora, as well as crucial agricultural crops like tomatoes, blueberries, and squash. But their numbers are **(97)** ________. New research using a massive dataset found that the insects are far less common than they used to be; in North America, you are nearly 50 per cent less likely to see a bumblebee in any given area than you were prior to 1974. Moreover, several once-common species have **(98)** ________ from many areas they were once found, becoming locally extinct in those places. For example, the rusty patched bumblebee, which used to flourish in Ontario, is no longer found in all of Canada—in the U.S., it's endangered. In a new paper published this week in the journal Science, researchers used a complex modeling process to **(99)** ________ that their **(100)** ________ is driven in large part by climate change. Specifically, the scientists found that in areas that have become hotter in the last generation, or have experienced more extreme temperature swings, bumblebees are less abundant. In Europe, they are 17 per cent less plentiful than they were in the early 20th century. The scientists examined the abundance of 66 species across the two continents.

96. A. extinct
B. trouble
C. dropped
D. growth
E. difficult

97. A. increasing
B. dripped
C. removing
D. dropping
E. generating

98. A. multiplied
B. concerning
C. disappeared
D. certain
E. vanish

99. A. proposed
B. recommending
C. implying
D. expresses
E. suggest

100. A. decline
B. deteriorate
C. rejection
D. lessen
E. reduced

ANSWERS

1	2	3	4	5	6	7	8	9	10
B	D	C	A	C	B	D	E	C	D
11	**12**	**13**	**14**	**15**	**16**	**17**	**18**	**19**	**20**
A	A	B	C	B	D	E	A	C	C
21	**22**	**23**	**24**	**25**	**26**	**27**	**28**	**29**	**30**
B	C	D	A	D	C	A	E	D	A
31	**32**	**33**	**34**	**35**	**36**	**37**	**38**	**39**	**40**
B	B	C	A	E	D	A	D	B	B
41	**42**	**43**	**44**	**45**	**46**	**47**	**48**	**49**	**50**
B	A	D	E	E	D	A	B	B	C
51	**52**	**53**	**54**	**55**	**56**	**57**	**58**	**59**	**60**
A	D	A	A	E	E	A	B	D	C
61	**62**	**63**	**64**	**65**	**66**	**67**	**68**	**69**	**70**
D	A	C	B	D	E	A	C	D	C
71	**72**	**73**	**74**	**75**	**76**	**77**	**78**	**79**	**80**
A	B	E	E	A	A	D	C	A	D
81	**82**	**83**	**84**	**85**	**86**	**87**	**88**	**89**	**90**
C	B	D	E	A	A	A	D	A	C
91	**92**	**93**	**94**	**95**	**96**	**97**	**98**	**99**	**100**
C	B	E	B	D	B	D	C	E	A

EXPLANATORY ANSWERS

For Qs. No. 1-5.

Designation	Persons
Chairman	F
CFO	A
GM	B
DGM	C
AGM	G
Manager	D
Junior manager	H
Clerk	E

6.

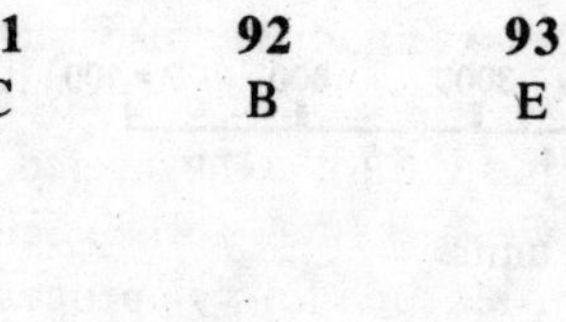

7.

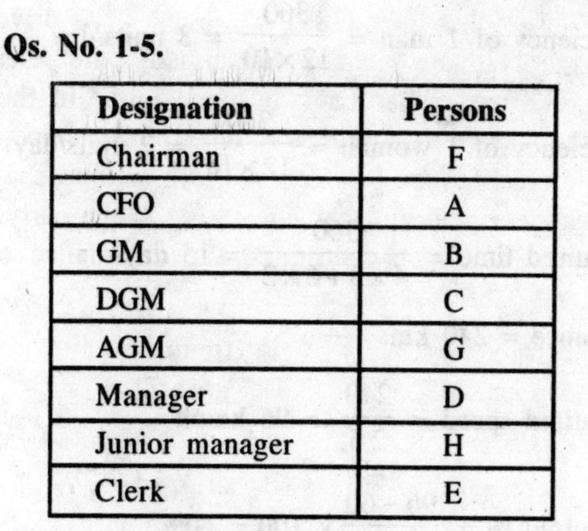

8.

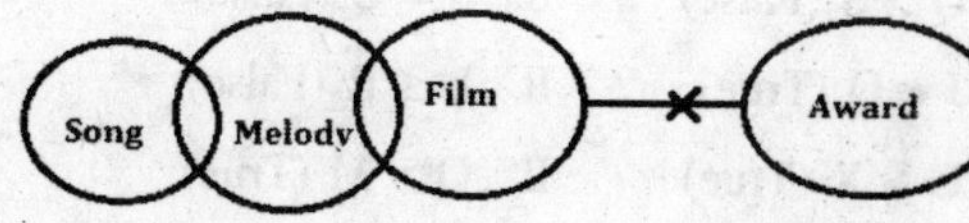

For Qs. No. 9-12.

Word	Code
Club	Ox
Near	Ot
House/Located	Ol/gp
Both	Mt
Make	Nk
Area	Tm
View	Sq

For Qs. No. 13-17.

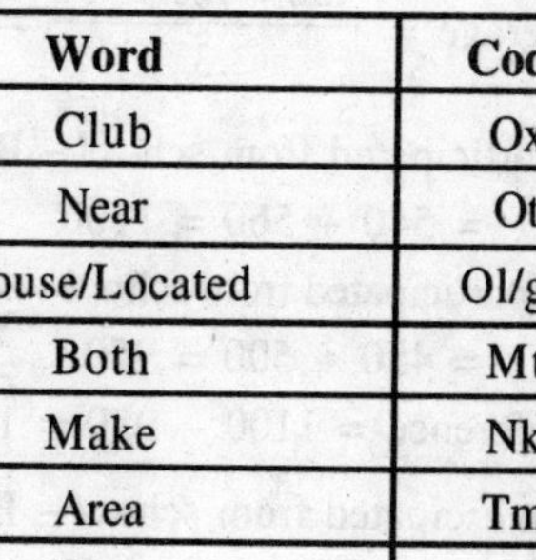

For Qs. No. 18-19.

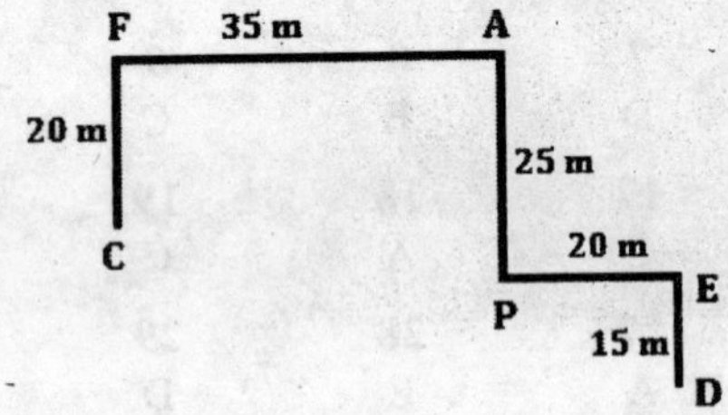

Qs. No. 20.

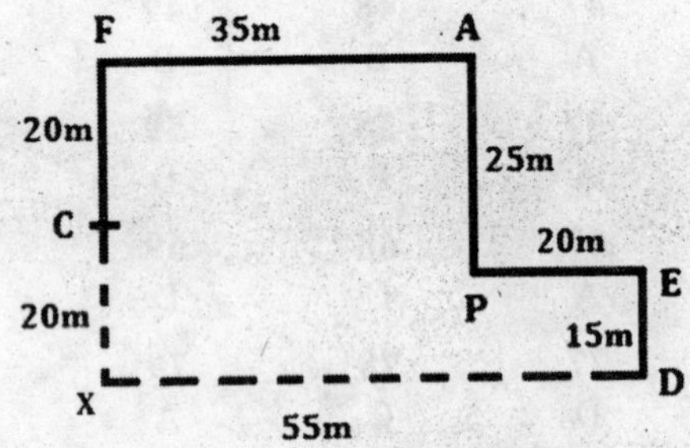

26. 6 4 5 9 0 3 2 8 7
0 2 3 4 5 6 7 8 9

27. Hire, Heir

For Qs. No. 28-32.

A > E > F > B > D > G > C > H

33. I. Q > S (False) II. S = Q (False)

34. I. J < Q (True) II. L ≤ R (False)

35. I. G > X (True) II. O > M (True)

36. Required average = $\frac{450+420+450}{3} = 440$

37. Total male participated from school – B & D together
= 540 + 560 = 1100

Total female participated from school – A & C together
= 450 + 500 = 950

Required difference = 1100 – 950 = 150

38. Total male participated from school – B & C together
= 540 + 720 = 1260

Total female participated from school – A & D together
= 450+450 = 900

Required % = $\frac{1260-900}{900} \times 100 = 40\%$

39. Total students participated from school F

$= \frac{140}{100} \times 650 + 420 \times \frac{32}{21}$

= 910 + 640 = 1550

40. Total number of male students participated from all the five schools

= (650 + 540 + 720 + 560 + 680) = 3150

41. Pattern of series:

? = 200 ×0.5 100 ×1.5 150 ×2.5 375 ×3.5 1312.5

42. Pattern of series:

104 +8 ? = 112 −16 96 + 24 120 −32 88 + 40 128

43. Pattern of series:

15 (×0.5+0.5) 8 (×1+1) 9 (×1.5+1.5) 15 (×2+2) 32 (×2.5+2.5) ? = 82.5

44. Pattern of series:

6 +2 8 +6 14 +12 26 +20 46 +30 ? = 76

+4 +6 +8 +10

45. Pattern of series:

72000 ÷2 36000 ÷3 12000 ÷4 3000 ÷5 600 ÷6 ? = 100

46. Let total work be 360 units

Efficiency of 1 man = $\frac{360}{12 \times 10}$ = 3 units/day

Efficiency of 1 woman = $\frac{360}{12 \times 18}$ = 2 units/day

Required time = $\frac{360}{4 \times 3 + 6 \times 2}$ = 15 days

47. Distance = 240 kms

Required speed = $\frac{240}{2.5}$ = 96 kmph

Required % = $\frac{96-60}{60} \times 100 = 60\%$

48. Let 10 years ago, ages of Ram and Rahim were x years and $3x$ years, respectively.

Then, present age of Ram = $(x + 10)$

and present age of Rahim = $(3x + 10)$

According to the question,

$$\frac{x+10+5}{3x+10+5} = \frac{2}{3}$$

$\Rightarrow$ $3x + 45 = 6x + 30$

$\Rightarrow$ $3x = 15$

$\therefore \quad x = 5$

Hence, required ratio $= \frac{5+10}{3\times5+10}$

$= \frac{15}{25} = 3:5$

49. Required time $= \frac{140+120}{(132-80)\times\frac{5}{18}}$

$= \frac{260\times18}{52\times5} = 18$ sec

50. Let CP of book be ₹ x

SP = ₹ $1.2x$

New CP = ₹ $0.9x$

New SP = ₹ $1.2x + 90$

ATQ, $0.9x \times \frac{140}{100} = 1.2x + 90$

$1.26x = 1.2x + 90$

$x =$ ₹ 1500

51. I. $x = 5$

II. $y = 5$

So, $x = y$

52. I. $x^2 + 7x - 5x - 35 = 0$

$x(x+7) - 5(x+7) = 0$

$(x+7)(x-5) = 0$

$x = -7, 5$

II. $y^2 + 7y + 8y + 56 = 0$

$y(y+7) + 8(y+7) = 0$

$(y+7)(y+8) = 0$

$y = -8, -7$

So, $x \geq y$

53. I. $x = \pm 9$

II. $y = \pm 8$

So, no relation can be established

54. I. $17x^2 - 14x - 3 = 0$

$17x^2 - 17x + 3x - 3 = 0$

$17x(x-1) + 3(x-1) = 0$

$(17x+3)(x-1) = 0$

$x = -\frac{3}{17}, 1$

II. $y^2 - 2y - 35 = 0$

$y^2 - 7y + 5y - 35 = 0$

$y(y-7) + 5(y-7)=0$

$y = 7, -5$

So, no relation can be established

55. I. $x^2 + 9x - 5x - 45 = 0$

$x(x+9) - 5(x+9) = 0$

$(x-5)(x+9) = 0$

$x = 5, -9$

II. $y^2 - 5y - 8y + 40 = 0$

$y(y-5) - 8(y-5) = 0$

$(y-5)(y-8) = 0$

$y = 5, 8$

So, $x \leq y$

56. Let initial quantity of milk & water be $5x$ & $3x$ lit respectively

ATQ, $\frac{5x+8}{3x} = \frac{11}{5}$

$25x + 40 = 33x \Rightarrow x = 5$

Required difference $= 5x - 3x = 2x = 10$ lit

57. Let rate of interest be R%

ATQ, $1200 = \frac{6000\times R\times 2}{100}$

R = 10%

Since compounding is done half-yearly, rate of interest = 5%

Effective rate of interest $= 5 + 5 + \frac{5\times5}{100} = 10.25\%$

Required interest $= \frac{6000\times10.25\times1}{100} =$ ₹ 615

58. Let speed of boat in still water & speed of stream be $7x$ & $3x$ kmph respectively

ATQ, $\frac{28}{7x+3x} = \frac{42}{60}$

$x = 4$

Required difference $= \frac{40}{7x-3x} - \frac{60}{7x+3x}$

$= \frac{4}{x} = 1$ hour

59. Let amount invested by A be ₹ x

Profit ratio; A : B = $(x \times 12) : (17000 - x) \times 6 + (15500 - x) \times 6$

$= 2x : (32500 - 2x)$

ATQ, $\frac{19500}{325-2x+2x}\times(32500-2x) = 8100$

$32500 - 2x = 13500$

$x =$ ₹ 9500

Required capital of B after 6 months

$= 15500 - x =$ ₹ 6000

60. Let length & breadth of rectangle be x & y m respectively

ATQ, $1.4xy - xy = 24$

$xy = 60$ ...(*i*)

Also, $2(x + y) = 32$

$x + y = 16$ ...(*ii*)

From (*i*) & (*ii*)

$x = 10$ m, $y = 6$ m

Breadth of rectangle = 6 m

61. $? = 170 - 35$

$? = 135$

62. $(12 + 13) \times 3 = \frac{?}{5}$

$? = 375$

63. $? = (3 \times 5) \times 8$

$? = 120$

64. $\left(\frac{120}{100} \times 750\right) \div ? = 25$

$? = 900 \div 25$

$? = 36$

65. $? = (8 - 4 + 3) + \frac{6-10+7}{12}$

$? = 7\frac{1}{4}$

66. $275 + \frac{64}{100} \times 750 = 750 + ?$

$275 + 480 = 750 + ?$

$? = 5$

67. $? = 15 + 9 + 122$

$? = 146$

68. $\frac{510}{?} = 18 + 3.25$

$? = 24$

69. $\frac{12.5}{100} \times (120 + ?) = 45$

$120 + ? = 360$

$? = 240$

70. $44 \times 12 - 16 = (8)^?$

$528 - 16 = (8)^?$

$? = 3$

Previous Paper (Solved)

State Bank of India (SBI)

CLERICAL CADRE (Junior Associates)

Phase-I : Preliminary Exam 2019*

REASONING ABILITY

Directions (Qs. No. 1-5): *Study the following information carefully and answer the questions given below:*

Eight persons are sitting around a circular table facing to the center but not necessarily in the same order. Two persons sit between Q and P (either from left or right). R sits immediate to the right of Q. One person sits between R and S, who faces to T. Q and T are not immediate neighbours of each other. W sits 2nd to the left of V. Three persons sit between U and V.

1. Four of the following five are alike in a certain way and hence they form a group. Which one of the following does not belong to that group?
A. Q-W B. P-U
C. S-W D. V-T
E. Q-P

2. Who among the following sits immediate right of U?
A. W B. R
C. T D. S
E. V

3. The number of persons sit between Q and T, when counted to right of Q is same as the number of persons sit between W and .... , when counted to the left of .... ?
A. P B. S
C. T D. U
E. None of these

4. Who among the following faces R?
A. U B. V
C. P D. W
E. Q

5. Who among the following sits 3rd to the right of S?
A. P B. U
C. Q D. T
E. None of these

Directions (Qs. No. 6-10): *Study the following information carefully and answer the questions given below:*

Ten persons are sitting in two parallel rows containing five persons in each row such a way that there is an equal distance between adjacent persons. In the first row, A, B, C, D and E are seated and all of them are facing north. In the second row, P, Q, R, S and T are seated and all of them are facing south. Therefore, in the given seating arrangement, each member seated in a row faces another member of the other row.

E sits 2nd from one of the extreme end of the row. P faces the one who sits 2nd to the right of E. D sits 2nd to the left of B, who does not sit at the extreme end. Two persons sit between S and Q. R sits immediate left of S. C sits next to B.

6. Who among the following faces Q?
A. B B. D
C. A D. C
E. None of these

7. Who among the following sits at the extreme end of the row?
A. E B. T
C. C D. R
E. P

8. Four of the following five are alike in a certain way and hence they form a group. Which one of the following does not belong to that group?
A. Q B. A
C. T D. D
E. P

9. Who among the following sits 2nd to the right of P?
A. S B. R
C. Q D. T
E. None of these

10. What is the position of A with respect to E?
A. 3rd to the left
B. Immediate to the left
C. 2nd to the left
D. 3rd to the right
E. 2nd to the right

11. In the word 'PRODUCE', how many pairs of the letters have the same number of letters between them in the given word as they have in the English alphabet series?

* *Based on Memory*

A. Four
B. Two
C. One
D. Three
E. More than four

Directions (Qs. No. 12-15): *In each of the questions below are given some statements followed by some conclusions. You have to take the given statements to be true even if they seem to be at variance with commonly known facts. Read all the conclusions and then decide which of the given conclusions logically follows from the given statements disregarding commonly known facts.*

Give Answer:

A. If only conclusion II follows
B. If only conclusion I follows
C. If neither conclusion I nor II follows
D. If either conclusion I or II follows
E. If both conclusions I and II follow

12. Statements: All Chocolate are Toffee.
No Toffee is Muffin.
Only a few Muffin are Dark.

Conclusions: I. No Chocolate is Muffin.
II. Some Toffee can never be Dark.

13. Statements: No Party is Gathering.
All Summary are Gathering.
Only a few Gathering are Committee.

Conclusions: I. Some Committee can be Summary.
II. Some Party can be Committee.

14. Statements: No Market is Home.
Only a few Home are Room.
Only a few Room is Vance.

Conclusions: I. Some Home are Vance.
II. Some Market can never be Room.

15. Statements: Some Ball are Garden.
All Garden are Trade.
Only a few Trade are Pump.

Conclusions: I. Some Ball are Pump.
II. Some Garden can be Pump.

Directions (Qs. No. 16-20): *Study the following information carefully and answer the questions given below:*

Seven persons are buying different things. Only one person buy thing between C and A. B is buying thing immediately before C. Two persons buy things between C and D. C buy things after D. E buys thing immediately before D. More than three persons buy things between E and F. Only three persons buy things between D and G.

16. How many persons buy things between A and F?
A. One
B. Two
C. Three
D. Four
E. More than four

17. Who among the following buy thing immediately after F?
A. D
B. B
C. G
D. A
E. No one

18. Who among the following buy thing immediately before G?
A. D
B. B
C. C
D. A
E. No one

19. How many person buy things before A?
A. One
B. Two
C. Three
D. Four
E. More than four

20. As many as persons are buying things before D as after ....?
A. E
B. B
C. F
D. A
E. G

Directions (Qs. No. 21-23): *Study the following information carefully and answer the questions given below:*

Point S is 15 m west of point R. Point R is 30 m south of point Q. Point P is 20 m west of point Q. Point U is 15 m south of point P. Point T is 35 north of point S.

21. If point V is exactly between point Q and R, then how far and in which direction is point U with respect to V?
A. 15 m, North-East
B. 15 m, East
C. 10 m, North-West
D. 20 m, West
E. 20 m, North-East

22. Four of the following are alike in a certain way, so form a group. Which of the following does not belong to that group?
A. P, T
B. U, Q
C. R, P
D. S, Q
E. U, T

23. If point W is in 5 m east of point U, then what is the distance between point W and point S?
A. 5 m
B. 15 m
C. 25 m
D. 10 m
E. 20 m

Directions (Qs. No. 24-26): *Study the following information carefully and answer the questions given below:*

A certain number of persons are sitting in the row. All of them are facing towards north. Q sits sixth from the right of S. T sits forth to left of Q. Only two persons sit between Q and P. R sits forth to the left of S. U sits between S and T. V sits second to the right of U. W is third from any of the end. S is eight from the left end of the row. Six persons sit between W and V.

24. How many numbers of persons could sit in the row?
A. 14 B. 18
C. 23 D. 15
E. 20

25. What is the position of 'W' with respect to Q?
A. Fourth to the right
B. Fifth to the right
C. Fourth to the left
D. Eighth to the right
E. Sixth to the left

26. If X sits immediate right of V then how many persons sit between X and P?
A. Five B. Six
C. Four D. Three
E. None of these

27. If it is possible to make only one meaningful word with the 2nd, 4th, 6th and 7th letters of the word 'UNILATERAL' which would be the second letter of the word from the right end? If more than one such word can be formed give 'Y' as the answer. If no such word can be formed, give 'Z' as your answer.
A. Y B. N
C. L D. T
E. Z

Directions (Qs. No. 28-30): *In each of the question, relationships between some elements are shown in the statements. These statements are followed by conclusions numbered I and II. Read the statements and give the answer.*
A. If only conclusion I follows.
B. If only conclusion II follows.
C. If either conclusion I or II follows.
D. If neither conclusion I nor II follows.
E. If both conclusions I and II follow.

28. Statements: $A \geq B \geq C = D > E \leq F < G$

Conclusions: I. $E < B$
II. $G > E$

29. Statements: $P \leq R < T = U; Q \geq T \leq S \geq V$

Conclusions: I. $Q > P$
II. $V < R$

30. Statements: $L > M = 0 \geq P; N \leq M \geq S \geq T$

Conclusions: I. $T \leq P$
II. $N < L$

Directions (Qs. No. 31-35): *Study the following sequence and answer the given questions.*

A @ 3 4 % E N M $ 8 6 & L D S # 9 8 6 Q Y Z 1 7 % R O G @ 2 I B 2 U &

31. Which of the following element is sixth to the left of the fourteenth from the left end of the given arrangement?
A. 6 B. %
C. $ D. M
E. None of these

32. If all the symbols are dropped from the series, which element will be twelfth from the right end?
A. 9 B. Q
C. R D. Y
E. None of these

33. How many such numbers are there in the given series which are immediately preceded by a symbol and followed by a letter?
A. None B. One
C. Two D. Three
E. Four

34. How many such letters are there in the given series which are immediately preceded by number and immediately followed by a symbol?
A. One
B. Two
C. Three
D. More than three
E. None of these

35. Find the odd one out?
A. N64 B. D86
C. Y%8 D. R27
E. 8EL

NUMERICAL ABILITY

Directions (Qs. No. 36-40): *What will come in the place of question mark (?) in the following number series:*

36. 11, ?, 16, 21, 29, 41
A. 12 B. 14
C. 15 D. 13
E. 11

37. 1800, ?, 60, 15, 5, 2.5
A. 300 B. 600
C. 120 D. 240
E. 360

38. 4, 3, 4, 9, 32, ?
A. 75 B. 155
C. 125 D. 175
E. 165

39. ?, 100, 150, 375, 1312.5

A. 50 B. 100
C. 75 D. 25
E. 200

40. 0, 6, 24, 60, ?, 210

A. 130 B. 170
C. 90 D. 120
E. 150

Directions (Qs. No. 41-45): *Study the bar chart given below and answer the following questions.*

Bar chart shows the number of books read by 4 different persons (A, B, C & D) in 2005 and 2006.

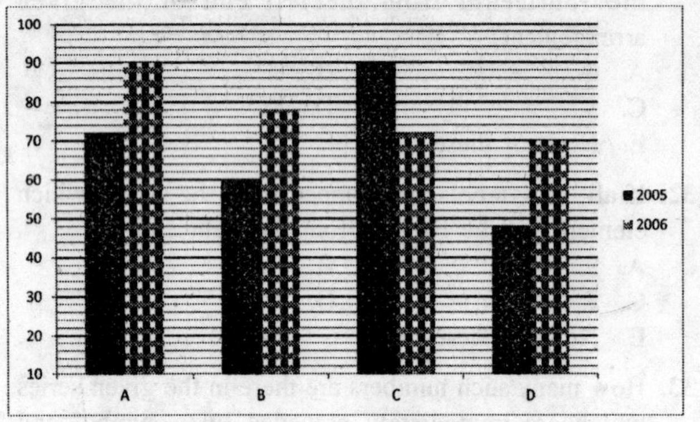

41. Find average number of books read by A, C & D in 2005.

A. 64 B. 70
C. 75 D. 60
E. 56

42. Find ratio of books read by B & C together in 2005 to books read by A & D together in 2006.

A. 15 : 16 B. 5 : 6
C. 1 : 5 D. 4 : 7
E. 2 : 3

43. Books read by A & D together in 2005 are what per cent more than books read by C in 2006?

A. $46\frac{2}{3}\%$ B. $54\frac{1}{3}\%$

C. $25\frac{2}{3}\%$ D. $33\frac{1}{3}\%$

E. $66\frac{2}{3}\%$

44. Books read by A & C together in 2005 are how much more or less than books read by B & D together in 2006?

A. 24 B. 14
C. 18 D. 22
E. 28

45. Books read by B & C together in 2006 are what per cent of books read by B in 2005?

A. 100% B. 120%
C. 250% D. 200%
E. 160%

Directions (Qs. No. 46-55): *What will come in place of (?) question mark in the following questions?*

46. $\frac{17.28 \div ?}{3.6 \times 0.2} = 200$

A. 120 B. 1.20
C. 12 D. 0.12
E. None of these

47. 486 ÷ ? × 7392 ÷ 66 = 1008

A. 54 B. 55
C. 52 D. 53
E. 51

48. $14\frac{2}{7}\%$ of $4200 \div \sqrt{576} = (?)^{\frac{1}{2}}$

A. 125 B. 225
C. 25 D. 5
E. 625

49. $\frac{2}{7} \times \frac{5}{6} \times \frac{3}{8} \times ? = 90$

A. 1208 B. 1108
C. 1008 D. 1128
E. 1348

50. (0.05 × 6.25) ÷ 2.5 = ?

A. 12.55 B. 0.125
C. 0.115 D. 1.25
E. None of these

51. 1496 ÷ 17 = ?% of 220

A. 25 B. 40
C. 50 D. 75
E. None of these

52. (36% of 180) ÷ 0.4 = ?

A. 160 B. 164
C. 166 D. 162
E. 180

53. 0.08% of 55500 – 16.4 = ?

A. 26.6 B. 28
C. 29.2 D. 30.4
E. 32

54. 35% of 150 × 16 = ? – 22

A. 865 B. 932
C. 864 D. 862
E. None of these

55. (3080 + 6160) ÷ ? = 330

A. 26 B. 22
C. 28 D. 29
E. 18

56. Difference of the compound interest received in first year and second year at 20% per annum at CI is ₹ 1200 then find the sum?

A. ₹ 25,000 B. ₹ 36,000
C. ₹ 35,000 D. ₹ 24,000
E. ₹ 30,000

57. Find the total distance covered by boat in each upstream and downstream in 7 hours if the speed of boat in still water and speed of current is 21 km/h and 3 km/h respectively?

A. 280 km B. 294 km
C. 315 km D. 301 km
E. 322 km

58. Ratio of income of A to that of B is 5 : 9. If expenditure of A is 3/8th of his income and expenditure of B is 4/9th of his income and sum of their saving is ₹ 1950 then find the difference between their income?

A. ₹ 900 B. ₹ 1000
C. ₹ 880 D. ₹ 960
E. ₹ 920

59. A alone can do a work in 12 days while A and B together can do that work in 7.5 days. Find the time taken by C alone to do that work if C takes 3 days more than that of B alone to do that work?

A. 33 days B. 30 days
C. 23 days D. 27 days
E. 28 days

60. Ratio of base and perpendicular side of a right-angled triangle is 3:4 and its base is equal to the side of a square having area 81 cm^2. Find the perimeter of the triangle?

A. 30 cm B. 36 cm
C. 33 cm D. 42 cm
E. 40 cm

Directions (Qs. No. 61-65): *In each of these questions, two equations (I) and (II) are given. You have to solve both the equations and give answer:*

A. if $x > y$ B. if $x \geq y$
C. if $x < y$ D. if $x \leq y$
E. if $x = y$ or no relation can be established between x and y.

61. I. $x^2 - 13x + 40 = 0$
II. $2y^2 - y - 15 = 0$

62. I. $5x^2 + 17x + 6 = 0$
II. $2y^2 + 11y + 12 = 0$

63. I. $7x^2 - 19x + 10 = 0$
II. $8y^2 + 2y - 3 = 0$

64. I. $x^2 - 8x + 15 = 0$
II. $y^2 - 3y + 2 = 0$

65. I. $3x^2 - 7x + 4 = 0$
II. $2y^2 - 9y + 10 = 0$

66. A person travels half of the distance at the speed of x km/h and remaining half of the distance at $4x$ km/h. Find the value of 'x' if the average speed is 36.8 km/h?

A. 21 B. 25
C. 24 D. 23
E. 20

67. A, B and C invested in a ratio of 7 : 8 : 5 in a business. They got an annual profit of ₹ 136800. If A and C withdrew their amount at the end of 3 months and 7 months respectively. Then find the difference between A and C's share of profit?

A. ₹ 12,600
B. ₹ 11,500
C. ₹ 13,500
D. ₹ 10,500
E. ₹ 13,000

68. Retailer sold one article at $33\frac{1}{3}\%$ profit and another at 100% profit. Find his overall profit percentage if the selling price of both the article is same?

A. 60% B. 55%
C. $66\frac{2}{3}\%$ D. 75%
E. $56\frac{2}{3}\%$

69. A mixture has milk and water in the ratio 4 : 1. When 50% of the mixture is taken out and replaced by 24 liters of water then the ratio of milk to water in the mixture becomes 1 : 1. Find initial quantity of mixture.

A. 80 liters
B. 45 liters
C. 70 liters
D. 60 liters
E. 75 liters

70. 4 years ago, ratio of Shivam's age to Deepak's age was 2 : 3 and ratio of Shivam's age 4 years ago to Deepak's age 5 years hence is 8 : 15. Find present age of Shivam.

A. 32 years B. 28 years
C. 40 years D. 24 years
E. 36 years

ENGLISH LANGUAGE

Directions (Qs. No. 71-78): *Read the following passage and answer the following questions based on the given passage. Some of the words are highlighted which would help you to answer some of the questions given.*

For years, world-wide organisations have become increasingly excited about the prospect of a cloud-based future. As the dream becomes an ever closer reality for many kinds of business and, Forrester predicted that enterprise spending on cloud services is **set to surge**. IDC also predicted that global spending on public cloud services and infrastructure would reach $210 bn in 2019, an increase of 24% from 2018. But one obstacle stands create friction and introduce risk: the process of migration.

As all indications point to a **massive** shift in data deployments to the cloud, it is more important than ever that the transition from on-premises to Cloud is as risk free as possible. In today's climate any loss or disruption to data can have a huge business impact. It's a complex process, is frequently underestimated and many organisations have found there's lots that can go wrong that can impact the business.

Organisations across the globe have found the cloud to be an ideal place to run modern data applications due to big data's elastic resource requirements. Furthermore, with the lack of data talent an ever-looming issue for most companies today they have been determined to **adopt** a cloud-first strategy to ensure business operations are accessible for a range of employees.

The cloud offers great promise for developers especially, as it can increase the speed at which they develop software features and increase the resilience of applications once they are deployed - along with enhanced security through the use of multiple server locations. With all this considered, it is no surprise that 42% of UK businesses leverage some kind of cloud service, according to Eurostat.

However, all the perceived benefits of leveraging the cloud are redundant if organisations come up against barriers to accessing cloud services. Cloud-based data pipelines still suffer from complexity challenges at the moment, along with the lack of visibility into cost and resource usage at the application and user level. The answer to this is automation fueled by robust Machine learning training models and artificial intelligence. These concepts and the tools that enable them can determine the prerequisites of cloud infrastructure, application dependencies, the appropriate target cloud instance profiles, and provide troubleshooting in real-time.

To summarise, the promise of the cloud has created a sense of excitement amongst enterprises, however, they have proceeded to go **full steam ahead** into adopting a cloud service, without sufficient data to **ensure** performance service level agreements (SLAs).

71. How can we tackle the risks associated with the process of migration?

A. By ensuring that organisations only migrate the apps to the cloud that will thrive in the cloud.
B. The surge in the investment in the cloud technology.
C. The use of predictive power of Artificial Intelligence.
D. The transition from on-premises to Cloud
E. None of these

72. Why the promise of the cloud has created a sense of excitement amongst enterprises?

A. As it ensures that business operations are accessible for a range of employees.
B. As the enterprise spending on cloud services is surging.
C. Reduction in the cost of operation it may entail.
D. The secure platform it provides to the data it stores.
E. None of these

73. How the process of migration stands as an obstacle to the cloud technology?

A. The expensive cost of providing safety to the data.
B. The lack of sound technology in Artificial Intelligence.
C. Complexities of the data migrated to the cloud
D. It exposes the companies to the risk of losing important information.
E. None of these

74. Which of the following statement(s) is/are correct in context of the passage?

(1) The cloud technology can help in increasing the speed at which the software features are developed.
(2) There is no risk associated with the cloud technology.
(3) Cloud technology is not a very complex process.

A. Only (2)
B. Both (1) and (2)
C. Only (3)
D. Only (1)
E. All are correct

75. What is the meaning of the phrase **"full steam ahead"**?
A. Interrupting an activity
B. Acting cautiously
C. Great increase
D. Progressing quickly
E. Prudent progression

76. Which of the following words is most similar to the word **"ADOPT"** as given in the passage?
A. Mold B. Deduce
C. Embrace D. Creative
E. Fluster

77. Which of the following words is most similar to the word **"ENSURE"** as given in the passage?
A. Confirm B. Paced
C. Redundant D. Weaken
E. Reject

78. Which of the following words is **most OPPOSITE** to the word **"MASSIVE"** as given in the passage?
A. Prominent B. Insignificant
C. Enlarged D. Filthy
E. Vouch

Directions (Qs. No. 79-85): *Read each sentence to find out if there is any error in it. The error, if any will be in one part of the sentence. The number of that part is the answer if there is no error, the answer is (E).*

79. It is widely believe (A)/ that the village which is situated on the (B)/ eastern coast of India will be wiped out (C)/ within a decade. (D)/ No error. (E)

80. Yesterday I met (A)/ an old friend (B)/ when I am going (C)/ to the market. (D)/ No error.(E)

81. The criminal was (A)/ sentenced to the (B)/ death and was (C)/ hung for his crime (D)/ No error. (E)

82. FATF strongly urges (A)/ Pakistan to swiftly complete its action plan (B)/ by October 2019 to stop (C)/ terror funding in the country (D)/ No error. (E)

83. Elon musk is determined (A)/ to be success (B)/ in whatever field (C)/ he chooses. (D)/ No error. (E)

84. New purchasing power will increasingly (A)/ come from Asia and Africa where (B)/ the demographics are still favourable (C)/ for high income growth. (D)/ No error (E).

85. Not only the (A)/ students but also (B)/ the principal were (C)/ laughing at the joke he cracked. (D)/No error (E).

Directions (Qs. No. 86-90): *In each of the following sentences, there is a blank space. Below in each sentence, there are five words out of which one can be used to fill the blank to make the sentence grammatically and coherently correct. Find the most appropriate word that fit into the blank contextually.*

86. There is nothing to indicate the building's past, ... the fireplace.
A. except B. included
C. belonged D. barred
E. foster

87. Two circus elephants that performed together .... when crossing paths 23 years later.
A. happy B. believe
C. angered D. rejoiced
E. greater

88. The law .... farmers not only to save and resow (multiply) seeds, but also to sell them to other farmers, no matter what the original source of the seed is.
A. coverts B. implements
C. emits D. permits
E. deserts

89. Small farmers must be educated and .... with proper incentive structures, to engage with agriculture.
A. fascinated B. encouraged
C. discouraged D. harvested
E. invited

90. Raipur despite being .... between two rivers, the Krishna and the Tungabhadra, it is a dust bowl in May first week.
A. surrounded B. located
C. revealed D. settle
E. None of these

Directions (Qs. No. 91-95): *Given sentences are not in their exact position. Rearrange them to make a coherent paragraph and then answer the questions given below.*

(*a*) It can even make exercise more fun and productive.

(*b*) Plus, hearing others laugh, even for no apparent reason, can often trigger genuine laughter.

(*c*) To add simulated laughter into your own life, search for laugh yoga or laugh therapy groups. Or you can start simply by laughing at other people's jokes, even if you don't find them funny.

(*d*) A Georgia State University study found that incorporating bouts of simulated laughter into an exercise program helped improve older adults' mental health as well as their aerobic endurance.

(*e*) Believe it or not, it's possible to laugh without experiencing a funny event—and simulated laughter can be just as beneficial as the real thing.

91. Which of the following should be the **FOURTH** sentence after the rearrangement?
A. (*a*) B. (*b*)
C. (*c*) D. (*d*)
E. (*e*)

92. Which of the following should be the **SECOND** sentence after the rearrangement?
A. (*a*) B. (*b*)
C. (*c*) D. (*d*)
E. (*e*)

93. Which of the following should be the **THIRD** sentence after the rearrangement?
A. (*a*) B. (*b*)
C. (*c*) D. (*d*)
E. (*e*)

94. Which of the following should be the **FIRST** sentence after the rearrangement?
A. (*a*) B. (*b*)
C. (*c*) D. (*d*)
E. (*e*)

95. Which of the following should be the **FIFTH** sentence after the rearrangement?
A. (*a*) B. (*b*)
C. (*c*) D. (*d*)
E. (*e*)

Directions (Qs. No. 96-100): *In the following questions, a sentence is divided into four parts consisting of a highlighted word in each part. Choose the option reflecting the word which is either misspelt or grammatically incorrect. If all the highlighted words are correct, choose option (E) i.e. "all are correct" as your answer choice.*

96. A British court has **ruled** that British arms **sales** to Saudi Arabia **wear** unlawful on Humanitarian **Grounds.**
A. ruled B. sales
C. wear D. Grounds
E. All are correct

97. I'm **tyred** of **hearing** politicians making **pious** pronouncements about their **devotion** to the people.
A. tyred B. hearing
C. pious D. devotion
E. All are correct

98. It is likely that weaving **prospered** and partly **relocated** towards areas **within** easy reach of the army **contractors.**
A. prospered B. relocated
C. within D. contractors
E. All are correct

99. This cat and mouse **tactic** was **purposely** designed to provoke, **inrage** and **panic** the unemployed.
A. tactic B. purposely
C. inrage D. panic
E. All are correct

100. Indian democracy's **robustness** is underscored by high voter **turnouts**, and large number of **candedates** in the **fray.**
A. robustness B. turnouts
C. candedates D. fray
E. No correction required

ANSWERS

1	**2**	**3**	**4**	**5**	**6**	**7**	**8**	**9**	**10**
A	C	B	C	B	C	B	E	A	D
11	**12**	**13**	**14**	**15**	**16**	**17**	**18**	**19**	**20**
C	B	E	B	A	C	E	C	B	E
21	**22**	**23**	**24**	**25**	**26**	**27**	**28**	**29**	**30**
D	C	B	E	A	C	B	E	A	B
31	**32**	**33**	**34**	**35**	**36**	**37**	**38**	**39**	**40**
D	D	B	A	E	D	A	B	E	D
41	**42**	**43**	**44**	**45**	**46**	**47**	**48**	**49**	**50**
B	A	E	B	C	D	A	E	C	B
51	**52**	**53**	**54**	**55**	**56**	**57**	**58**	**59**	**60**
B	D	B	D	C	E	B	D	C	B
61	**62**	**63**	**64**	**65**	**66**	**67**	**68**	**69**	**70**
A	E	A	A	C	D	A	A	A	B
71	**72**	**73**	**74**	**75**	**76**	**77**	**78**	**79**	**80**
C	A	D	D	C	C	A	B	A	C
81	**82**	**83**	**84**	**85**	**86**	**87**	**88**	**89**	**90**
D	E	B	E	C	A	D	D	B	B
91	**92**	**93**	**94**	**95**	**96**	**97**	**98**	**99**	**100**
B	A	D	E	C	C	A	E	C	C

EXPLANATORY ANSWERS

For Qs. No. 1-5.

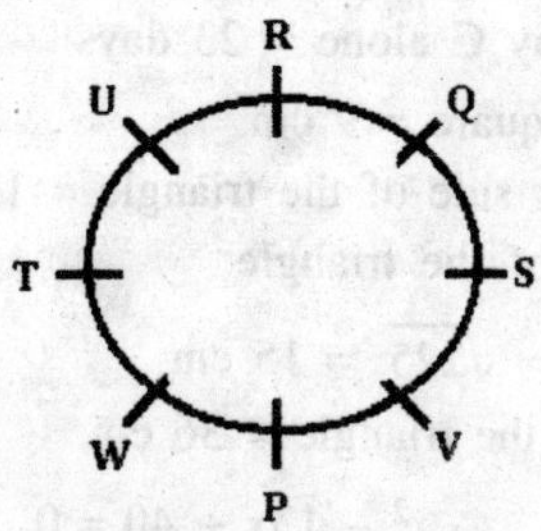

For Qs. No. 6-10.

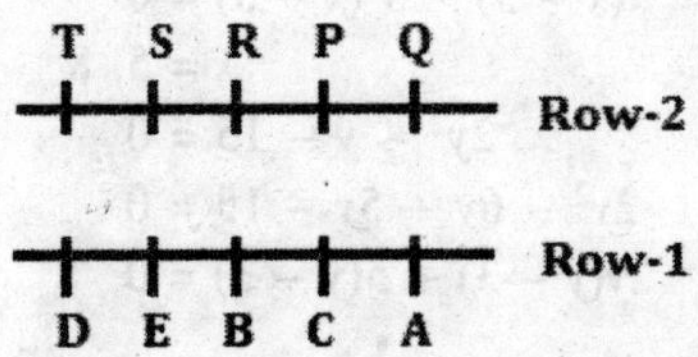

12.

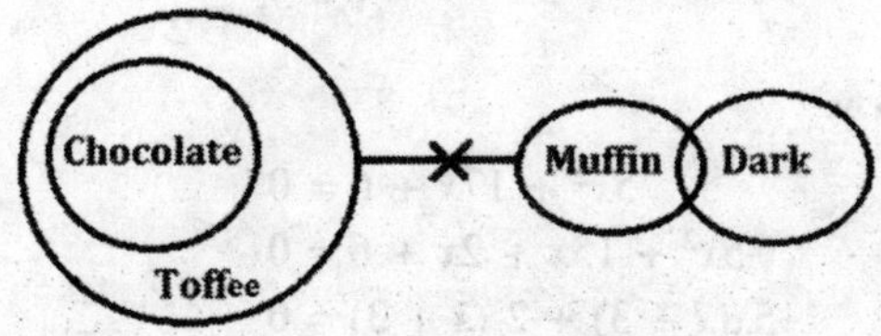

13.

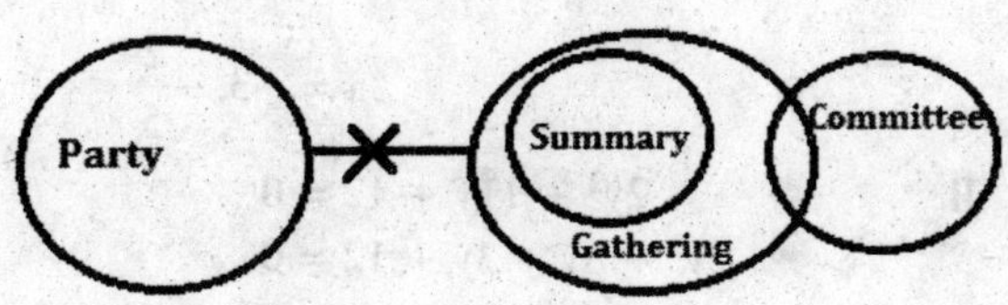

14.

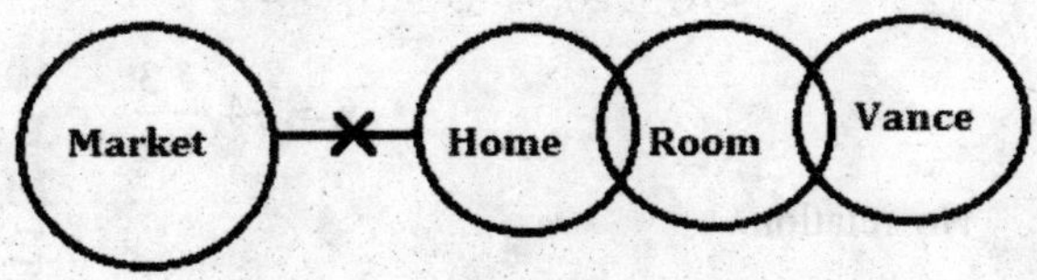

15.

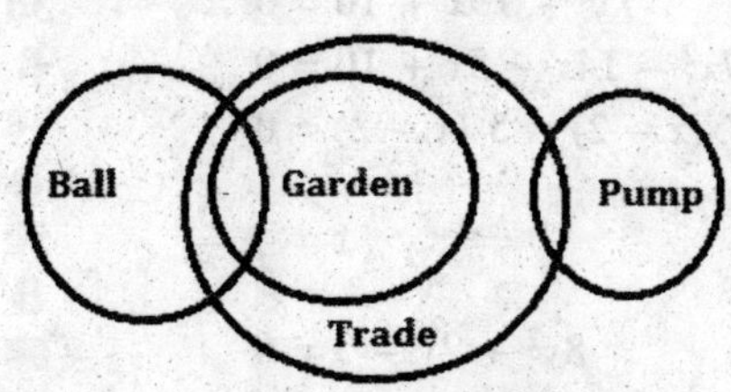

For Qs. No. 16-20.

Persons
E
D
A
B
C
G
F

For Qs. No. 24-26.

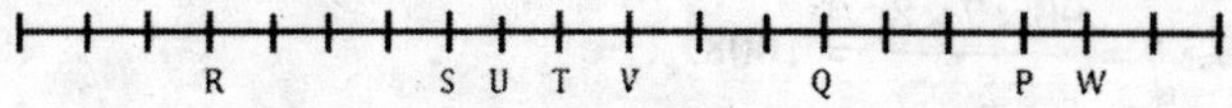

36. 11 [13] 16 21 29 41

2 3 5 8 12

1 2 3 4

37. 1800 [300] 60 15 5 2.5

÷6 ÷5 ÷4 ÷3 ÷2

38. 4 3 4 9 32 [155]

×1–1 ×2–2 ×3–3 ×4–4 ×5–5

39. [200] 100 150 375 1312.5

×0.5 ×1.5 ×2.5 ×3.5

40. 0 6 24 60 [120] 210

1^3-1 2^3-2 3^3-3 4^3-4 5^3-5 6^3-6

41. Required average $= \dfrac{72+90+48}{3} = 70$

42. Required ratio $= \dfrac{60+90}{90+70} = \dfrac{150}{160} = 15 : 16.$

43. Required %

$$= \frac{\{(72+48)-72\}}{72} \times 100 = \frac{200}{3}\% = 66\frac{2}{3}\%.$$

44. Required difference = (72 + 90) – (78 + 70) = 162 – 148 = 14.

45. Required % $= \dfrac{78+72}{60} \times 100 = \dfrac{150}{60} \times 100$

= 250%.

46. $17.28 \div ? = 200 \times 3.6 \times 0.2$

$$? = \frac{17.28}{144} = 0.12.$$

47. $\dfrac{486}{?} \times \dfrac{7392}{66} = 1008$

$$\frac{486}{?} = \frac{1008}{112}$$

$$\Rightarrow \quad ? = \frac{486}{9}$$

$$? = 54.$$

48. $\frac{100}{700} \times 4200 \times \frac{1}{24} = (?)^{\frac{1}{2}}$

$$25 = (?)^{\frac{1}{2}} \Rightarrow ? = 625$$

49. $? = \frac{90 \times 7 \times 8}{5} = 1008.$

50. $? = \frac{0.3125}{2.5} \Rightarrow ? = 0.125.$

51. $\frac{1496}{17} = \frac{?}{100} \times 220 \Rightarrow ? = 40$

52. $\frac{36}{100} \times 180 \times \frac{10}{4} = ?$

$? = 162.$

53. $0.08 \times 555 - 16.4 = ?$

$? = 44.4 - 16.4 = 28.$

54. $\frac{35}{100} \times 150 \times 16 + 22 = ?$

$? = 840 + 22 = 862.$

55. $\frac{9240}{?} = 330$

$? = 28.$

56. Let the sum be ₹ $100x$

CI in first year = ₹ $20x$

CI in two years = 44% of $100x$ = ₹ $44x$

CI in 2nd year = $44x - 20x$ = ₹ $24x$

According to the question,

$24x - 20x = 1200$

$x = 300$

Required sum = ₹ 30,000.

57. Speed in upstream = 18 km/hr

Speed in downstream = 24 km/hr

Required total distance = $(24 + 18) \times 7$

= 294 km.

58. Let income of A and B be ₹ $5x$ and ₹ $9x$ respectively

Expenditure of A = ₹$\frac{15}{8}x$

Saving of A = ₹$\frac{25}{8}x$

Expenditure of B = ₹ $4x$

Saving of B = ₹ $5x$

According to the question,

$\frac{65}{8}x = 1950$

$\Rightarrow x = 240$

Required difference = ₹ 960.

59. Let total work be 60 units (LCM of 12 and 7.5)

Efficiency of A = 5 units/day

Efficiency of A and B together = 8 units/day

Efficiency of B = 3 units/day

Time taken by B alone to do that work = 20 days

Time taken by C alone = 23 days.

60. Side of the square = 9 cm

Perpendicular side of the triangle = 12 cm

Hypotenuse of the triangle

$= \sqrt{81+144} = \sqrt{225} = 15$ cm

Perimeter of the triangle = 36 cm.

61. I.
$$x^2 - 13x + 40 = 0$$
$$x^2 - 5x - 8x + 40 = 0$$
$$x(x - 5) - 8(x - 5) = 0$$
$$x = 5, 8$$

II.
$$2y^2 - y - 15 = 0$$
$$2y^2 - 6y + 5y - 15 = 0$$
$$2y(y - 3) + 5(y - 3) = 0$$
$$y = 3, -\frac{5}{2}$$

$\therefore x > y.$

62. I.
$$5x^2 + 17x + 6 = 0$$
$$5x^2 + 15x + 2x + 6 = 0$$
$$5x(x + 3) + 2(x + 3) = 0$$
$$x = -3, -\frac{2}{5}$$

II.
$$2y^2 + 11y + 12 = 0$$
$$2y^2 + 8y + 3y + 12 = 0$$
$$2y(y + 4) + 3(y + 4) = 0$$
$$y = -4, -\frac{3}{2}$$

No relation.

63. I.
$$7x^2 - 19x + 10 = 0$$
$$7x^2 - 14x - 5x + 10 = 0$$
$$7x(x - 2) - 5(x - 2) = 0$$
$$x = 2, \frac{5}{7}$$

II.
$$8y^2 + 2y - 3 = 0$$
$$8y^2 + 6y - 4y - 3 = 0$$
$$2y(4y + 3) - 1(4y + 3) = 0$$
$$y = \frac{-3}{4}, \frac{1}{2}$$

$\therefore x > y.$

64. I.
$$x^2 - 8x + 15 = 0$$
$$\Rightarrow x^2 - 5x - 3x + 15 = 0$$
$$\Rightarrow x(x - 5) - 3(x - 5) = 0$$

$\Rightarrow$		$(x-3)(x-5) = 0$
$\therefore$		$x = 3$ or 5.
II.		$y^2 - 3y + 2 = 0$
$\Rightarrow$		$y^2 - 2y - y + 2 = 0$
$\Rightarrow$		$y(y-2) - 1(y-2) = 0$
$\Rightarrow$		$(y-1)(y-2) = 0$
$\therefore$		$y = 1$ or 2.

$\therefore x > y.$

65. I. $3x^2 - 7x + 4 = 0$

$\Rightarrow 3x^2 - 4x - 3x + 4 = 0$

$\Rightarrow (3x-4)(x-1) = 0$

$\therefore x = \frac{4}{3}$ or 1

II. $2y^2 - 9y + 10 = 0$

$\Rightarrow 2y^2 - 4y - 5y + 10 = 0$

$\Rightarrow (2y-5)(y-2) = 0$

$\Rightarrow y = \frac{5}{2}$ or 2

$\therefore y > x.$

66. Let the distance be D km

According to the question,

$$\frac{D}{\left(\frac{D}{2x} + \frac{D}{8x}\right)} = 36.8$$

$$x = 23.$$

67. Ratio of their profit sharing

A : B : C = 7 × 3 : 8 × 12 : 5 × 7 = 21 : 96 : 35

Annual profit = 136800

Difference between A and C's share of profit

$$= \frac{14}{152} \times 136800 = ₹\ 12{,}600.$$

68. Let SP of both article = $8x$

According to the question,

	Article1	Article2		
CP	$6x$	$4x$	=	$10x$
SP	$8x$	$8x$	=	$16x$

(Article1: $\times\frac{3}{4}$; Article2: $\times\frac{1}{2}$)

$$\text{Profit \%} = \frac{16x - 10x}{10x} \times 100 = 60\%.$$

69. Let initial quantity of milk and water in the mixture be '$40x$ litres' and '$10x$ litres' respectively.

According to the question,

$$\frac{\left(40x \times \frac{1}{2}\right)}{10x \times \frac{1}{2} + 24} = \frac{1}{1} \Rightarrow \frac{20x}{5x + 24} = \frac{1}{1}$$

$$20x = 5x + 24$$

$$15x = 24 \Rightarrow x = 1.6$$

So, required quantity = $40x + 10x = 50x$

= 80 litres.

70. Let age of Shivam and Deepak 4 years ago be '$2x$ years' and '$3x$ years' respectively.

According to the question,

$$\frac{2x}{3x + 4 + 5} = \frac{8}{15}$$

$$\frac{2x}{3x + 9} = \frac{8}{15}$$

$$30x = 24x + 72$$

$$6x = 72$$

$$x = 12$$

So, present age of Shivam = $2x + 4 = 28$ years.

Previous Paper (Solved)

State Bank of India

SBI-Clerical Cadre

Phase-I : Preliminary Exam 2018

ENGLISH LANGUAGE

Directions (Qs. No. 1-5): *Read the following passage carefully and answer the questions given below them. Certain words/phrases have been printed in bold to help you locate them while answering some of the questions.*

Life is messy. If we want our best and brightest in the workforce, we need to accept that they have complex lives. We need to be flexible when it comes to the realities of balancing career and family.

Being flexible at work doesn't just benefit people trying to balance their outside lives with work. An extensive body of research demonstrates the business benefits of flexible working. Yet despite this overwhelming evidence, access to flexible work and careers is not widespread. Flexible work is still regarded as an add-on, something we do for mothers for a few months when they are back from parental leave. But in the face of rapid changes to the way we work, organizations need to move beyond just having policies for flexible working or making ad-hoc adjustments for certain individuals. Companies need to fundamentally rethink the way they design work and jobs.

The World Economic Forum **predicts** that we are on the cusp of a fourth industrial revolution. Technological, socioeconomic and demographic shifts are transforming the way we work, demanding flexibility in the way individuals, teams and organizations work. We all have different things happening in our lives at different times. Not just caring for young kids, but other family members, community roles, study and volunteering. And all of these parts of our identities bring with them different skill sets. In today's workforce, fewer people identify with the stereotype of the ideal worker – a full-time, fully committed employee without personal or family commitments that impact on availability.

There are a few factors driving the demand for increased flexibility. Globalization is one. The development of a 24/7 marketplace, and the rapid expansion of the services economy are also having a transformational effect on the workplace, requiring organizations to think creatively about how they can best organize jobs and work to respond to an increasingly diverse and demanding customer base. Similarly technology is driving – and enabling – greater flexibility. It is dramatically reshaping our workplaces, blurring the boundaries between work and home and diversifying where, when and how employees work. Advances in mobile, internet and cloud technologies, the rapid development of computing power, and the digital connection between multiple objects have all driven workplace innovations such as remote working, telecommuting, co-working spaces, video/teleconferencing, and virtual teams and collaboration.

So the future of work demands new approaches to work design – but have workplaces risen to the challenge? The evidence suggests we have yet to grasp this opportunity to be more innovative.

While some employers are making flexible work more available, there is still a high prevalence of bolted-on **temporary** arrangements. These arrangements are seen as the exception to the rule, with the full-time, "face-time", long hours "ideal worker" still the model to which everyone is expected to adhere.

Many people make assumptions about flexible workers, including that they're not interested in training and development, aren't committed to the organization, or don't have any career aspirations. We need to explore and challenge these biases.

There are good international examples of successful work redesign that have involved the input of a team of employees. For example, a UK bakery sat down with their bakers and came up with a flexible system of two to three baking shifts a day to maintain a steady supply of fresh bread. The team agreed to rotate their hours each week so no team member permanently worked a shift that did not suit. After the change was made, bakery sales increased by more than 65% in the first year and employee satisfaction in the bakery has risen 10% since the change to 93%. So work redesign is not only doable, it can deliver business benefits, although it does require a completely new approach. By changing our thinking and focusing on the team and the organization as a whole, rather than the individual, we have the opportunity to create more adaptable and sustainable workplaces.

1. According to the author, how is flexible working still regarded as?
   A. the way of designing work and jobs.
   B. the way to identify the stereotype of an ideal worker.

C. an add-on, something we do for mothers for a few months when they are back from parental leave.
D. advances in mobile, internet and cloud technologies and the rapid development of computing power.
E. None of these

2. According to the passage, in today's workforce, which among the following is/are the stereotype(s) of an ideal worker?
(I) a full time worker.
(II) an employee who is fully committed to work.
(III) the employee has no personal or family commitments that impact his availability.
A. Only (II) B. Only (III)
C. Both (II) and (III) D. Both (I) and (III)
E. All of these

3. According to the passage, how is technology driving and enabling greater flexibility?
A. It is identifying the stereotype of an ideal worker.
B. It is dramatically reshaping our workplaces, blurring the boundaries between work and home and diversifying where, when and how employees work.
C. It is training the workers on how to transform the ways in which flexibility can be introduced
D. It is one of the factors that is contributing in declining the demand for flexibility at the workplace worldwide.
E. None of these

4. Which of the following were the steps taken by the UK Bakery with regards to the working time of their bakers?
(I) The UK Bakery came up with a flexible system of two to three baking shifts a day to maintain a steady supply of fresh bread.
(II) The Bakery team agreed to rotate their hours each week so no team member permanently worked a shift that did not suit.
(III) The bakery sales increased by more than 65% in the first year and employee satisfaction in the bakery has risen 10% since the change to 93%.
A. Only (III) B. Both (I) and (III)
C. Both (II) and (III) D. Both (I) and (II)
E. All of these

5. The most appropriate title of the passage is:
A. Complex lives of the workforce
B. Role of technology in increasing flexibility of workers
C. The brightest workforce requires more flexible work
D. How a UK Bakery increased their sales
E. Importance of Globalization in increasing workforce

Directions (Qs. No. 6): *Choose the word which is most nearly the SAME in meaning as the word printed in bold as used in the passage.*

6. Predict
A. ignore B. forecast
C. misunderstand D. recount
E. narrate

Directions (Qs. No. 7): *Choose the word which is most nearly the OPPOSITE in meaning as the word printed in bold as used in the passage.*

7. Temporary
A. substitute B. alternate
C. expedient D. provisional
E. permanent

Directions (Qs. No. 8-15): *Read each sentence to find out whether there is any grammatical or idiomatic error in it. The error, if any, will be in one part of the sentence. The alphabet corresponding to that part is your answer. If there is 'No error', the answer is (e). (Ignore errors of punctuation, if any.)*

8. The priest together with (*a*)/his followers were fatally injured (*b*)/in the accident which occurred last night (*c*)/near the unmanned railway crossing. (*d*)/No Error (*e*)
A. (*a*) B. (*b*)
C. (*c*) D. (*d*)
E. (*e*)

9. The young woman who is watching television in that room (*a*)/lived here for more than (*b*)/a year but she has never created (*c*)/any problem for us. (*d*)/No Error (*e*)
A. (*a*) B. (*b*)
C. (*c*) D. (*d*)
E. (*e*)

10. Each of the employees, (*a*)/whom the company has chosen to take part (*b*)/in the international seminar to be conducted (*c*)/in the City Hall, are up to the mark. (*d*)/ No Error (*e*)
A. (*a*) B. (*b*)
C. (*c*) D. (*d*)
E. (*e*)

11. Needless to say, (*a*)/no sooner were all these large and rather expensive operations finished (*b*)/when the main electricity was brought in (*c*)/and the turbine became obsolete. (*d*)/No Error (*e*)
A. (*a*) B. (*b*)
C. (*c*) D. (*d*)
E. (*e*)

12. Plastic bags less than 50 microns thick (*a*)/are banned, (*b*)/but neither the states nor the city corporations (*c*)/ cares to enforce this rule. (*d*)/No Error (*e*)

A. (*a*) B. (*b*)
C. (*c*) D. (*d*)
E. (*e*)

13. Tribal angst over economic issues (*a*)/leading to the scapegoating of nontribal longtime residents (*b*)/reflects the continued failure (*c*)/to forge a more inclusive politics in Meghalaya. (*d*)/No Error (*e*)

A. (*a*) B. (*b*)
C. (*c*) D. (*d*)
E. (*e*)

14. The Prime Minister has great power of (*a*)/ implementing some useful (*b*)/schemes but the ministers (*c*)/have even greatest ability to foil them. (*d*)/No Error (*e*)

A. (*a*) B. (*b*)
C. (*c*) D. (*d*)
E. (*e*)

15. The blunder mistake (*a*)/was the apparent failure of detectives (*b*)/to inform the Parole Board that the murderer (*c*)/had threatened to return to kill her. (*d*)/ No Error (*e*)

A. (*a*) B. (*b*)
C. (*c*) D. (*d*)
E. (*e*)

Directions (Qs. No. 16-20): *In each question below some sentences are given which are divided into five parts. The first part of the sentence (1) is correct and is given in bold followed by four parts named (a), (b), (c) and (d). Rearrange the four parts of the sentence to make a coherent paragraph. The rearranged sequence of the parts will be your answer. If the given sentence is correct as it is then choose option (E).*

16. 1. **Crashes in the early days**
(*a*) to be caused by technical faults,
(*b*) of commercial jets tended
(*c*) such as metal fatigue
(*d*) in the airframe or engines

A. (*d*)(*c*)(*a*)(*b*) B. (*a*)(*b*)(*c*)(*d*)
C. (*b*)(*a*)(*c*)(*d*) D. (*c*)(*a*)(*b*)(*d*)
E. No arrangement required

17. 1. **There have been a lot of**
(*a*) drivers not obeying
(*b*) complaints recently about
(*c*) in downtown Boston
(*d*) the speed limits

A. (*b*)(*a*)(*d*)(*c*) B. (*a*)(*b*)(*c*)(*d*)
C. (*b*)(*c*)(*a*)(*d*) D. (*c*)(*a*)(*b*)(*d*)
E. No arrangement required

18. 1. **Chinese officials say**
(*a*) dropped to a three-year
(*b*) low because of
(*c*) economic growth has
(*d*) the world economy

A. (*b*)(*a*)(*d*)(*c*) B. (*c*)(*a*)(*b*)(*d*)
C. (*b*)(*c*)(*a*)(*d*) D. (*c*)(*a*)(*b*)(*d*)
E. No arrangement required

19. 1. **I think it's a shame that**
(*a*) some foreign language teachers
(*b*) studied with a native speaker
(*c*) college without ever having
(*d*) were able to graduate from

A. (*b*)(*a*)(*d*)(*c*) B. (*c*)(*a*)(*b*)(*d*)
C. (*b*)(*c*)(*a*)(*d*) D. (*a*)(*d*)(*c*)(*b*)
E. No arrangement required

20. 1. **The Gita is a spiritual philosophy**
(*a*) addressed to all and we know that
(*b*) there are all kinds of people,
(*c*) each kind differing
(*d*) quite significantly from the other

A. (*b*)(*a*)(*d*)(*c*) B. (*c*)(*a*)(*b*)(*d*)
C. (*b*)(*c*)(*a*)(*d*) D. (*a*)(*d*)(*c*)(*b*)
E. No arrangement required

Directions (Qs. No. 21-25): *Given below are sentences consisting a blank in each. Identify the most suitable alternative among the five given that fits into the blank to make the sentence logical and meaningful.*

21. In the same amount of time it would take me to correct all the ________ in your report, I could write a better report myself.

A. mistakes B. problems
C. accuracies D. obstacles
E. disputes

22. I have recently used the services of his ________ agency to book a cruise in the Mediterranean.

A. progress B. deportation
C. travel D. transfer
E. mover

23. They would like local authorities to be given greater ________ as to how the money is spent.

A. affairs B. function
C. omission D. discretion
E. statement

24. In a 10-billion-year-old galaxy there should have been ample ________ for at least one species to escape its own mess, and to spread across the stars, filling every niche.

A. negligence B. opportunity
C. surveillance D. supply
E. advocacy

25. A true ________ of the resources involved in sport would include the unpaid labour services.

A. growth B. consideration
C. guidance D. suggestion
E. estimation

Directions (Qs. No. 26-30): *In the question given below, there is a sentence in which one part is given in bold. The part given in bold may or may not be grammatically correct. Choose the best alternative among the four given which can replace the part in bold to make the sentence grammatically correct. If the part given in bold is already correct and does not require any replacement, choose option (E), i.e. "No replacement required" as your answer.*

26. Despite of being most efficient method ever, it is still highly inefficient, and this inefficiency inspires hope.
A. Despite being the mostly efficient
B. Despite of being a most efficient
C. Despite of being the most efficient
D. Despite being the most efficient
E. No replacement required

27. A satisfactorily number of contestant must register for the contest in order for it to take place.
A. satisfactory number of contestants
B. satisfaction of number of contestants
C. satisfaction in the number of contestants
D. satisfactory number of contestant
E. no replacement required

28. The next class of wave or oscillation detector is the magnetic detector **depending in the powers of** electric oscillations to affect the magnetic state of iron.
A. depend on the power in
B. depending upon the power of
C. depends upon the power in
D. deepening upon the power of
E. no replacement required

29. James **had teaching** at the university for more than a year before he left for Asia.
A. was taught
B. had been taught
C. had been teaching
D. has been teaching
E. no replacement required

30. His tail was short and scraggly, and his harness **had been broken in** many places and fastened together again with cords and bits of wire.
A. was broke from
B. has broke from
C. have been broken in
D. have been breaking on
E. no replacement required

REASONING

Directions (Qs. No. 31-33): *Read the information carefully and answer the questions:*

A company ABC printed different number of books in different years 1947, 1956, 1987, 1998, 2002 such that number of books printed are not same in any year. 66 books were printed in an odd numbered year which is not 1947. The number of books printed in 1947 is 10 less than that printed in 1987. 59 books were printed in an year before the year in which 61 books are printed but not immediate before. The number of books printed in 2002 is 2 more than that printed in 1998.

31. How many books were printed in 1947?
A. 56
B. 66
C. 63
D. 61
E. None of these

32. What is the difference between the number of books printed in 1956 and 2002?
A. 7
B. 10
C. 8
D. 4
E. None of these

33. In how many years the number of books printed are more than that printed in 1998?
A. two
B. one
C. none
D. three
E. four

34. How many words can be formed from the 1st, 6th, 8th and 9th letter of a word 'EMANICIPATE' by using each letter once in the word?
A. two
B. one
C. none
D. three
E. more than three

35. If all the letters in the word FIGURES are arranged in alphabetical order from left to right in such a way that vowels are arranged first followed by consonants, then how many letters are there in between U and R after the arrangement?
A. two
B. one
C. none
D. three
E. four

36. If in the number 39682147, 1 is added to each of the digit which is less than five and 1 is subtracted from each of the digit which is greater than five then how many digits are repeating in the number thus formed?
A. two
B. one
C. none
D. three
E. four

Directions (Qs. No. 37 and 38): *Read the information given below and answer the questions.*

All the given members belong to the same the family. J is the brother of L. J is the only son of R. W is the father-in-law of L. D is the maternal grandfather of P, who is a male. Q is the only son of W. W is the grandfather of N and C is the daughter of N.

37. How L is related to C?
A. Mother B. Son
C. Brother D. Father
E. None of these

38. How is P related to N?
A. Mother B. Son
C. Brother D. Father
E. None of these

Direction (Qs. No. 39-41): *Read the information carefully and answer the question:*

Point U is 10 m north of point Q. Point T is 10 m east of point U. Point S is 15 m south of point T. Point P is 20 m south of point Q. Point R is 25 m east of point P. Point L is 15 m east of point S. Point M is the midpoint of point U and P.

39. What is the distance between point L and R?
A. 10 m B. 15 m
C. 5 m D. 20 m
E. 25 m

40. In which direction is point T with respect to P?
A. north-west B. south-west
C. south-east D. north-east
E. none of these

41. Which of the following points are inline?
A. P, R, S B. Q, M, L
C. U, S, T D. M, S, L
E. Q, S, L

Directions (Qs. No. 42-46): *Read the following information carefully and answer the given questions.*

Twelve persons sitting in two rows. D, E, F, K, L and M sitting in row-1 and facing north. S, T, U, X, Y and Z sitting in row-2 and facing south direction. E sits third from one of the extreme ends. S sits second to the left of the one who faces E. Only three persons sit between S and T. K sits somewhere right of M. More than three persons sit between X and T. F faces one of the immediate neighbours of T. Z sits second to the right of Y. The one who faces L sits third to the left of U. D faces S.

42. Who among the following faces K?
A. T B. S
C. X D. Y
E. None of these

43. Who among the following faces the immediate neighbour of M?
A. Z B. K
C. D D. L
E. None of these

44. Four of the following five from a group, which among the following does not belong to this group?
A. T, E B. U, D
C. Y, L D. Z, E
E. Z, K

45. Who among the following faces the one who sit to the immediate left of Y?
A. U B. D
C. X D. Z
E. None of these

46. How many persons sit between M and D?
A. one B. two
C. three D. five
E. four

Directions (Qs. No. 47): *Five people A, B, X, Y and Z live on five different floors of a building (such as ground floor numbered as 1 and top is numbered as 6). There are three floors between A and B. X lives one of the floors above Y.*

47. Who among the following lives on third floor?
A. B B. A
C. X D. Z
E. Cannot be determined

48. Which of the following elements should come in a place '?' ?
AB3 CE6 FI10 JN15 ?
A. OT20 B. TO21
C. OT21 D. TS21
E. None of these

Directions (Qs. No. 49-51): *Each of the questions below consists of a question and two statements numbered I and II given below it. You have to decide whether the data provided in the statement are sufficient to answer the question. Read both the statements and Given answer:*

A. If the data in statement I alone are sufficient to answer the question, while the data in statement II alone are not sufficient to answer the question.
B. If the data in statement II alone are sufficient to answer the question, while the data in statement I alone are not sufficient to answer the question.
C. If the data either in statement I alone or in statement II alone are sufficient to answer the question.
D. If the data even in both statements I and II together are not sufficient to answer the question.
E. If the data in both statement I and II together are necessary to answer the question.

49. Who sits immediate to the left of Ravi, who is sitting in row. All the persons who are sitting in a row facing north direction?
I. There are only two persons sit between Sahil and Geeta. More than three persons sit to the left of Geeta.
II. Not more than 8 persons can sit in a row. Ravi sits second to the left of Sahil. Diya sits 6 places away from Geeta.

50. What is the code of 'right' in a certain code language?
I. The code of 'every right to reject' is '%47 *32 $53 *95',
II. The code of 'never reject right turn' is '%62 %47 $51 *32'.

51. Find the number of boys and number of girls in the row?

I. R sits 18th from left end of the row and Y sits 11th from the right end of the row. R and Y interchange their positions, after interchanging the position R's position is 20th from left end.

II. Total 43 students are in the row and all are facing is same direction.

Directions (Qs. No. 52-56): *Study the following arrangement carefully and answer the questions given below:*

B 5 R 1 @ E K 4 F 7 © D A M 2 P 3 % 9 H I W 8 * 6 U J $ V Q #

52. Which of the following is the fifth to the left of the seventeenth from the left end of the above arrangement?

A. D B. W
C. * D. 4
E. None of these

53. Which of the following is exactly in the middle between D and U in the above arrangement?

A. % B. H
C. 9 D. 3
E. None of these

54. Four of the following five are alike in a certain way based on their position in the above arrangement and so form a group. Which is the one that does not belong to that group?

A. R1E B. F7D
C. M23 D. 9HW
E. UJ6

55. How many such symbols are there in the above arrangement each of which is immediately preceded by a number but not immediately followed by a consonant?

A. None B. One
C. Two D. Three
E. More than three

56. Which of the following is the tenth to the left end of the thirteenth from the right end?

A. F B. M
C. @ D. %
E. 3

Directions (Qs. No. 57 and 58): *Read the information carefully and answer the questions:*

Eight persons A, B, C, D, E, F, G, H are sitting around a circular table facing centre. H faces B. Two persons sit between F and B. E sits 2nd right to D. F sits 2nd right to C, who is one of the immediate neighbours of G. C is not an immediate neighbour of B.

57. Who among the following sits 3rd left to F?

A. D B. C
C. B D. A
E. None of these

58. Who among the following faces A?

A. D B. C
C. B D. G
E. None of these

Directions (Qs. No. 59 and 60): *Study the following information carefully and answer the given questions.*

In a certain code language,
'good key friends' is coded as 'xo pe cm'
'key law found' is coded as 'xo og bt'
'data key good' is coded as 'tu xo pe'

59. Which of the following is the code for 'good'?

A. xo B. pe
C. tu D. cm
E. None of these

60. Which of the following word is coded as 'og'?

A. law B. good
C. found D. Either (A) or (C)
E. key

Directions (Qs. No. 61-65): *The following questions are based on the six three digits numbers given below:*

563 218 732 491 929

61. If 2 is subtracted from the second digit of all odd numbers and 2 is added in the first digit of all even numbers, then which number is lowest number after the arrangement?

A. 218 B. 732
C. 491 D. 929
E. None of these

62. If third digit of highest number is divided by the first digit of lowest number, then what will be the resultant?

A. 4 B. 6
C. 4.5 D. 5
E. None of these

63. If all the digits in each number are arranged in increasing order, then which number will be the highest number after the rearrangement?

A. 218 B. 732
C. 491 D. 563
E. None of these

64. How many numbers will be there in the given series in which addition of first and third digit is greater than second digit?

A. One B. Two
C. Three D. Four
E. None of these

65. How many numbers will be there in the given series in which difference of first and third digit is greater than second digit?

A. One B. Two
C. Three D. Four
E. None of these

QUANTITATIVE APTITUDE

Directions (Qs. No. 66-70): *What should come in place of question mark (?) in the following questions?*

66. 18, 8, 6, 9, 32, ?
A. 248 B. 254
C. 251 D. 257
E. 260

67. 36, 18, 6, 3, 1, ?
A. 0.5 B. 0.25
C. 0.75 D. 0.3
E. 1

68. 18, 29, 42, 53, ?, 77
A. 63 B. 64
C. 65 D. 66
E. 67

69. 1, 244, 163, 190, 181, ?
A. 178 B. 184
C. 187 D. 190
E. 193

70. 250, ?, 190, 167, 148, 131
A. 215 B. 217
C. 223 D. 221
E. 219

Directions (Qs. No. 71-75): *Pie chart given below shows total number of students who opted different subjects for exam in July 2017. Study the data carefully and answer the following questions.*

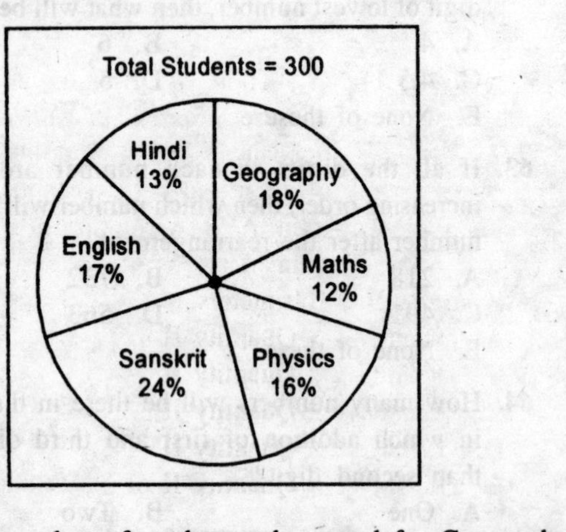

71. Total number of students who opted for Geography and Maths together is how much less than total number of students who opted for Sanskrit and Physics together?
A. 24
B. 27
C. 30
D. 33
E. 36

72. Find the total number of students who gave exams in August, 2017 if total number of students is increased by 20% in August, 2017 as compared to July, 2017.
A. 450 B. 420
C. 390 D. 330
E. 360

73. Find the central angle of total number of students who opted for Physics?
A. 57.6° B. 54°
C. 50.4° D. 43.2°
E. 64.8°

74. Find the average number of students who opted for Hindi, Geography and Sanskrit together?
A. 54 B. 55
C. 56 D. 57
E. 58

75. Find the ratio between total number of students who opted for English, Physics and Geography together to total number of students who opted for Hindi, English and Sanskrit together?
A. 8 : 9 B. 17 : 19
C. 15 : 16 D. 17 : 18
E. 5 : 6

Directions (Qs. No. 76-79): *What should come in place of question mark (?) in the following questions?*

76. $? = \sqrt{16 \times 15 + 24 \times 12 + 97}$
A. 25 B. 24
C. 28 D. 27
E. 35

77. 28% of 420 + 36% of 540 = ?
A. 312 B. 288
C. 296 D. 318
E. 324

78. 75% of 450 + 25% of 850 = ?
A. 540 B. 580
C. 550 D. 560
E. 555

79. $\sqrt{7396} + \sqrt{?} = 104$
A. 256 B. 400
C. 361 D. 289
E. 324

80. Present average age of A, B and C is 22 years. Three years ago, Average age of B and C is 18 years, then find A's age 9 years hence?
A. 24 years B. 27 years
C. 30 years D. 33 years
E. 36 years

81. Ratio between speed of boat in still water to speed of stream is 8 : 1. If 67.5 km is travelled downstream in 2.5 hours, then find the difference between speed of boat in still water to speed of stream (in kmph)?

A. 15 B. 3
C. 24 D. 21
E. 17.5

82. The perimeter of a rectangle whose length is 6 m more than its breadth is 84 m. What will be the area of the rectangle? (in m^2)

A. 446 B. 340
C. 432 D. 468
E. 348

83. Interest earned on an amount after 2 years at 20% p.a compounded yearly is ₹ 1716. Find the interest earned on same amount after 3 years at 15% p.a. at Simple interest.

A. ₹ 1620 B. ₹ 1755
C. ₹ 1665 D. ₹ 1710
E. ₹ 1750

84. In place of 18% profit an article is sold at 42% profit and seller gets ₹ 110.40 more. Find the selling price of article if it were sold at 25% profit?

A. ₹ 440 B. ₹ 460
C. ₹ 575 D. ₹ 550
E. ₹ 525

85. A and B working alone can do a work in 20 days and 15 days respectively. They started the work together but B left after sometime and A finished remaining work in 6 days. Find after how many days from start B left the work?

A. 5 days B. 4 days
C. 6 days D. 3 days
E. 7 days

Directions (Qs. No. 86-90): *In each of these questions, two equations are given. You have to solve both equations and give answer.*

A. if $x > y$ B. if $x \geq y$
C. if $x < y$ D. if $x \leq y$
E. if $x = y$ or no relation can be established between x and y.

86. (i) $x^2 = 196$
(ii) $y^2 + 2y - 48 = 0$

87. (i) $x^2 - 11x + 24 = 0$
(ii) $y^2 - 14y + 45 = 0$

88. (i) $2x^2 - 4x + 2 = 0$
(ii) $2y^2 - y - 1 = 0$

89. (i) $x^2 - 15x + 56 = 0$
(ii) $y = \sqrt{64}$

90. (i) $x^2 - x - 6 = 0$
(ii) $y^2 - 6y + 8 = 0$

Directions (Qs. No. 91-94): *What should come in place of question mark (?) in the following questions?*

91. $\sqrt{441} - \sqrt{144} = \sqrt{?}$

A. 81 B. 9
C. 100 D. 10
E. 121

92. $18\frac{2}{3} - 7\frac{1}{4} = ? + 1\frac{1}{2}$

A. 9 B. $10\frac{1}{12}$
C. $9\frac{11}{12}$ D. $9\frac{5}{6}$
E. 10

93. $\sqrt{484} \times \sqrt{169} = ? + 50\%$ of 312

A. 160 B. 150
C. 140 D. 130
E. 120

94. $15^2 + 36^2 = ? \times \sqrt[3]{2197}$

A. 127 B. 117
C. 137 D. 147
E. 153

95. The profit earned on selling two articles is ₹ 80 less than profit earned on selling three articles. If 20% profit is earned on selling one article, then find the cost price of the article?

A. ₹ 200 B. ₹ 600
C. ₹ 1200 D. ₹ 800
E. ₹ 400

96. Quantity I : 'x': Train 'A' running at a speed of 25 m/sec crosses Train 'B' coming from opposite direction running at a speed of 15 m/sec in 12 seconds. Length of train 'A' is twice of train 'B'. Length of train 'A' is 'x'.

Quantity II : 160 meters.

A. Quantity I > Quantity II
B. Quantity I < Quantity II
C. Quantity I ≥ Quantity II
D. Quantity I ≤ Quantity II
E. Quantity I = Quantity II or No relation

97. Average of three numbers b, c and d is 1 more than average of a, b and c. Average of a and d is 19.5.

Quantity I : Number 'a'.

Quantity II : 21.

A. Quantity I > Quantity II
B. Quantity I < Quantity II
C. Quantity I ≥ Quantity II
D. Quantity I ≤ Quantity II
E. Quantity I = Quantity II or No relation

98. Quantity I : 'x': A pipe alone can fill a cistern in 60 minutes. But due to leakage pipe filled only 80% of the cistern in 1 hour. 'x' is the capacity of cistern in liters if due to leakage 60 liter can be leaked out in 1 hour.

Quantity II : 250 liters.

A. Quantity I > Quantity II
B. Quantity I < Quantity II
C. Quantity I ≥ Quantity II
D. Quantity I ≤ Quantity II
E. Quantity I = Quantity II or No relation

99. Quantity I : 'x': Ratio between speed of boat in still water to speed of stream is 2 : 1. Total time taken by a man to cover 72 km in upstream and come back is 32 hours. 'x' is the downstream speed in kmph.

Quantity II : 9 kmph.

A. Quantity I > Quantity II
B. Quantity I < Quantity II
C. Quantity I ≥ Quantity II
D. Quantity I ≤ Quantity II
E. Quantity I = Quantity II or No relation

100. Quantity I : 'x': Area of a square is 324 cm^2 whose perimeter is equal to perimeter of a rectangle. Length of rectangle is 4 cm more than breadth of rectangle. 'x' is the area of rectangle.

Quantity II : 320 cm^2.

A. Quantity I > Quantity II
B. Quantity I < Quantity II
C. Quantity I ≥ Quantity II
D. Quantity I ≤ Quantity II
E. Quantity I = Quantity II or No relation

ANSWERS

1	2	3	4	5	6	7	8	9	10
C	E	B	D	C	B	E	B	B	D
11	**12**	**13**	**14**	**15**	**16**	**17**	**18**	**19**	**20**
C	D	E	D	A	C	A	B	D	E
21	**22**	**23**	**24**	**25**	**26**	**27**	**28**	**29**	**30**
A	C	D	B	E	D	A	B	C	E
31	**32**	**33**	**34**	**35**	**36**	**37**	**38**	**39**	**40**
A	D	A	A	A	B	E	C	B	D
41	**42**	**43**	**44**	**45**	**46**	**47**	**48**	**49**	**50**
D	D	A	D	B	C	E	C	E	D
51	**52**	**53**	**54**	**55**	**56**	**57**	**58**	**59**	**60**
D	A	C	E	D	A	E	D	B	D
61	**62**	**63**	**64**	**65**	**66**	**67**	**68**	**69**	**70**
A	C	D	D	B	C	A	D	B	E
71	**72**	**73**	**74**	**75**	**76**	**77**	**78**	**79**	**80**
C	E	A	B	D	A	A	C	E	D
81	**82**	**83**	**84**	**85**	**86**	**87**	**88**	**89**	**90**
D	C	B	C	C	E	E	B	E	E
91	**92**	**93**	**94**	**95**	**96**	**97**	**98**	**99**	**100**
A	C	D	B	E	A	B	A	E	E

EXPLANATORY ANSWERS

For Qs. No. 31-33.

Years	Books
1947	56
1956	59
1987	66
1998	61
2002	63

34. The 1st, 6th, 8th and 9th letter of a word 'EMANICIPATE' are E, C, P, A.
So, the words formed are PACE and CAPE.

35. The given word is: FIGURES
After the rearrangement: EIUFGRS
So, the letters between U and R will be two.

36. The given number is: 39682147
After applied operation: 48573256
So, only digit 5 is repeated in the number thus formed.

For Qs. No. 37-38.

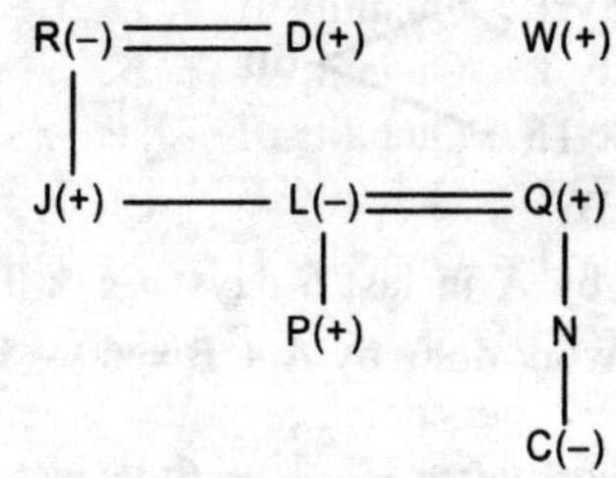

For Qs. No. 39-41.

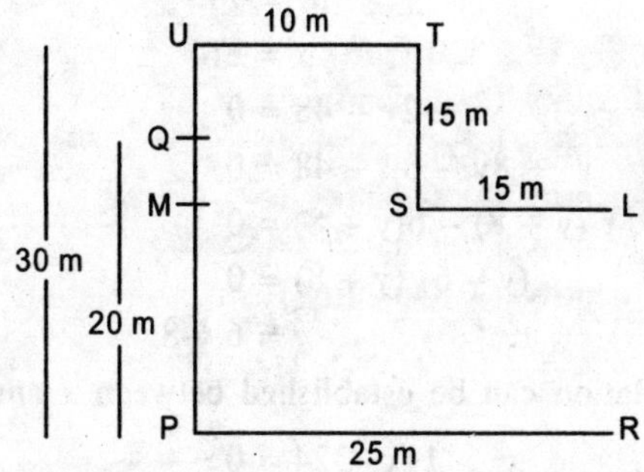

For Qs. No. 42-46.

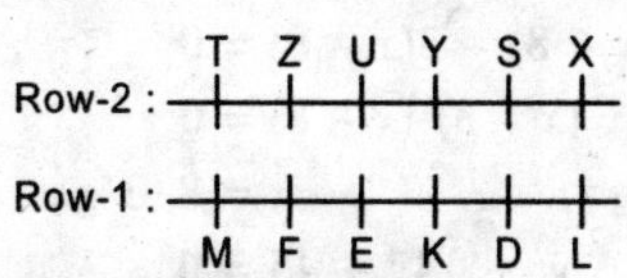

47.

Floors	Persons
5	A/B
4	X/Z
3	X/Z/Y
2	Z/Y
1	B/A

49. From both statements I and II we can find that Diya sits immediate to the left of Ravi.

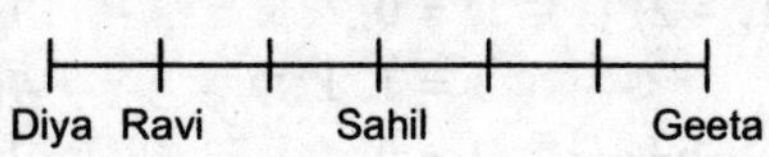

50. right can be coded either %47 or *32.

52. 5th to left of 17th from left

= 17 – 5 = 12th from left = D.

For Qs. No. 57-58.

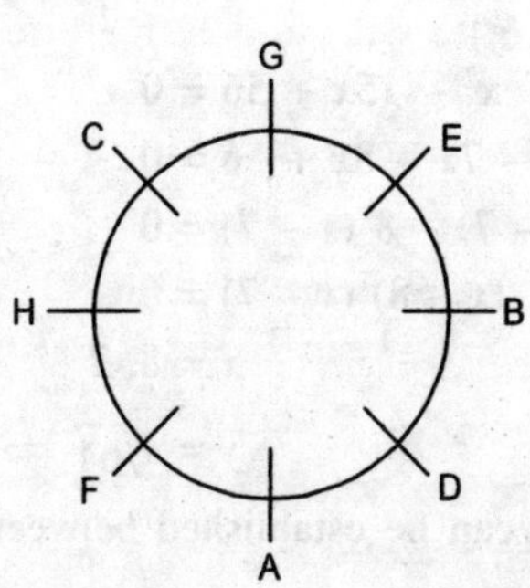

For Qs. No. 59-60.

Word	Code
friends	cm
key	xo
good	pe
law/found	og/bt
data	tu

66.

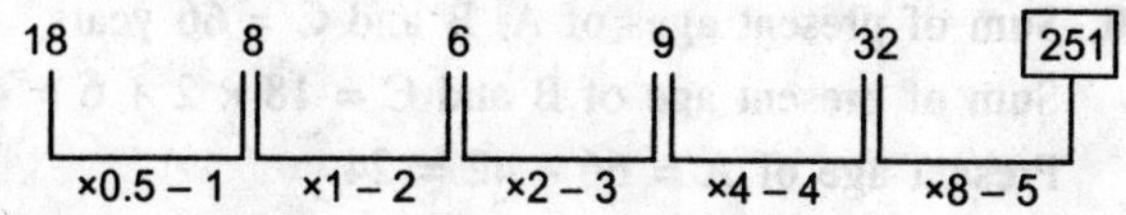

67.

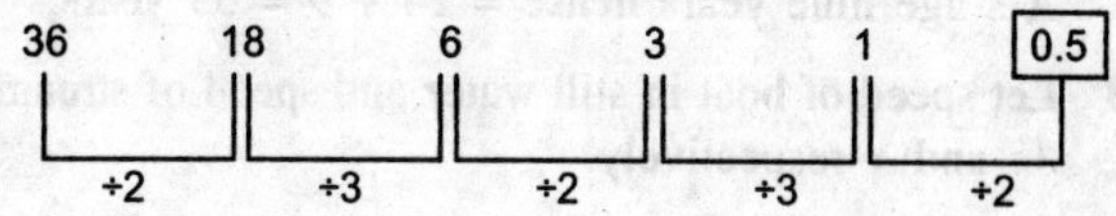

68.

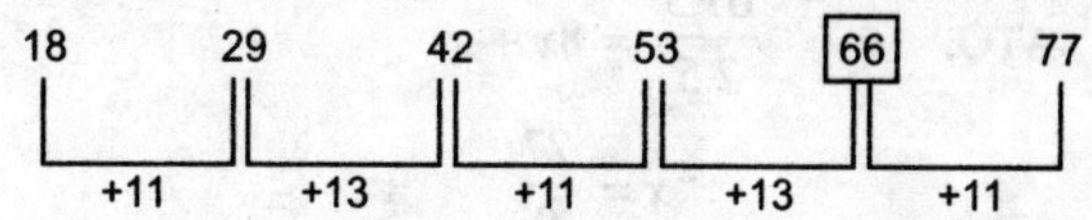

69.

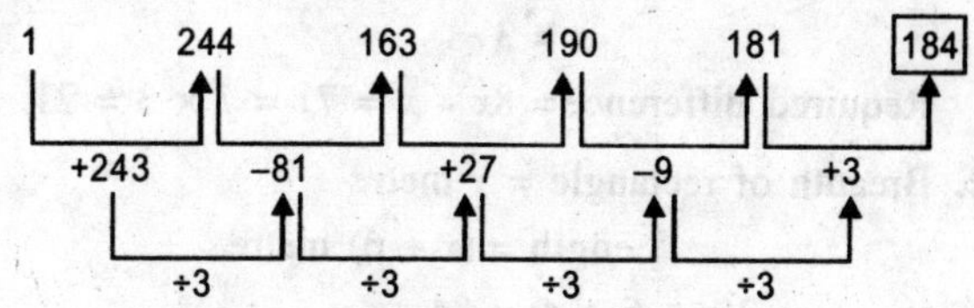

70.

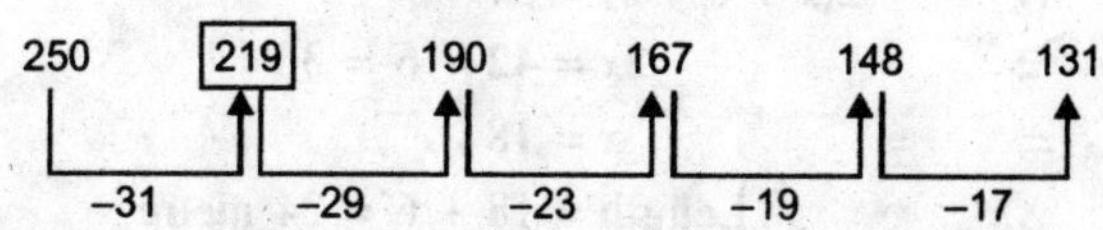

71. Required difference $= \frac{(24+16)-(18+12)}{100} \times 300$

$= (40 - 30) \times 3 = 30$

72. Total number of students who gave exam in August, 2017 $= 300 \times \frac{120}{100} = 360.$

73. Required central angle $= 16 \times 3.6 = 57.6°$.

74. Required average $= \frac{1}{3}\left(\frac{13+18+24}{100}\right) \times 300 = 55$

75. Required Ratio $= \frac{17+16+18}{13+17+24} = \frac{51}{54} = \frac{17}{18}$.

76. $? = \sqrt{16 \times 15 + 24 \times 12 + 97}$

$= \sqrt{240 + 288 + 97}$

$= \sqrt{625} = 25.$

77. $? = \frac{28}{100} \times 420 + \frac{36}{100} \times 540$

$= 117.6 + 194.4 = 312.$

78. $75\% \times 450 + 25\% \times 850 = ?$

$$? = \frac{25}{100}[3 \times 450 + 850]$$

$$= \frac{1}{4}[2200] = 550.$$

79. $\sqrt{?} = 104 - \sqrt{7396}$

$$\sqrt{?} = 104 - 86$$

$$? = (18)^2 = 324.$$

80. Sum of present ages of A, B and C = 66 years

Sum of present age of B and C = 18 × 2 + 6 = 42

Present age of A = 66 − 42 = 24

A's age nine years hence = 24 + 9 = 33 years.

81 Let speed of boat in still water and speed of stream be $8x$ and x respectively.

ATQ, $\frac{67.5}{2.5} = 8x + x$

$$x = \frac{27}{9}$$

$$x = 3$$

Required difference $= 8x - x = 7x = 7 \times 3 = 21$.

82. Breadth of rectangle = x metre

Length = $(x + 6)$ metre

$\therefore \quad 2(x + 6 + x) = 84$

$\Rightarrow \quad 2x = 42 - 6 = 36$

$\Rightarrow \quad x = 18$

$\therefore$ Length = 18 + 6 = 24 metre

$\therefore$ Area of rectangle = Length × Breadth

= 18 × 24 = 432 sq. metre

83. Overall rate for 2 years at 20% p.a. compounded yearly is equivalent to

$$20 + 20 + \frac{20 \times 20}{100} = 44\%$$

According to question,

44% of sum = 1716

100% of sum = 3900

Simple interest earned $= \frac{3900 \times 15 \times 3}{100} =$ ₹ 1755.

84. Let cost price of article = $100x$

According to question,

$$42x - 18x = 110.4$$

$$24x = 110.4 \Rightarrow x = 4.6$$

Cost price of article = 4.6 × 100 = 460

Selling price to earn 25% profit

$= 460 \times \frac{125}{100} =$ ₹ 575.

85. Efficiency — Total work

3 ← A → 20

+4 ← B → 15

7 ← A + B

(Total work = 60)

Work done by A in last 6 days = 6 × 3 = 18 work.

Remaining work done by A + B = 60 − 18 = 42 work

B left the work after $= \frac{42}{7} = 6$ days.

86. (*i*)

$$x^2 = 196$$
$$x = \pm 14$$

(*ii*)

$$y^2 + 2y - 48 = 0$$
$$y^2 + 8y - 6y - 48 = 0$$
$$y(y + 8) - 6(y + 8) = 0$$
$$(y - 6)(y + 8) = 0$$
$$y = 6, -8$$

No relation can be established between x and y.

87. (*i*)

$$x^2 - 11x + 24 = 0$$
$$x^2 - 8x - 3x + 24 = 0$$
$$x(x - 8) - 3(x - 8) = 0$$
$$(x - 3)(x - 8) = 0$$
$$x = 8, 3$$

(*ii*)

$$y^2 - 14y + 45 = 0$$
$$y^2 - 9y - 5y + 45 = 0$$
$$y(y - 9) - 5(y - 9) = 0$$
$$(y - 5)(y - 9) = 0$$
$$y = 5, 9$$

No relation can be established between x and y

88. (*i*)

$$2x^2 - 4x + 2 = 0$$
$$2x^2 - 2x - 2x + 2 = 0$$
$$2x(x - 1) - 2(x - 1) = 0$$
$$(2x - 2)(x - 1) = 0$$
$$x = 1, 1$$

(*ii*)

$$2y^2 - y - 1 = 0$$
$$2y^2 - 2y + y - 1 = 0$$
$$2y(y - 1) + 1(y - 1) = 0$$
$$(2y + 1)(y - 1) = 0$$
$$y = -\frac{1}{2}, 1 \Rightarrow x \geq y.$$

89. (*i*)

$$x^2 - 15x + 56 = 0$$
$$x^2 - 7x - 8x + 56 = 0$$
$$x(x - 7) - 8(x - 7) = 0$$
$$(x - 8)(x - 7) = 0$$
$$x = 8, 7$$

(*ii*) $y = \sqrt{64} \Rightarrow y = \pm 8$

No relation can be established between x and y.

90. (*i*)

$$x^2 - x - 6 = 0$$
$$x^2 - 3x + 2x - 6 = 0$$
$$x(x - 3) + 2(x - 3) = 0$$
$$(x - 3)(x + 2) = 0$$
$$x = 3, -2$$

(*ii*)

$$y^2 - 6y + 8 = 0$$
$$y^2 - 2y - 4y + 8 = 0$$
$$y(y - 2) - 4(y - 2) = 0$$
$$(y - 2)(y - 4) = 0$$
$$y = 2, 4$$

No relation can be established between x and y.

91.

$$\sqrt{441} - \sqrt{144} = \sqrt{?}$$
$$21 - 12 = \sqrt{?}$$
$$9 = \sqrt{?}$$
$$? = 81.$$

92.

$$18\frac{2}{3} - 7\frac{1}{4} = ? + 1\frac{1}{2}$$
$$18 - 7 + \frac{2}{3} - \frac{1}{4} = ? + 1 + \frac{1}{2}$$
$$10 + \frac{2}{3} - \frac{1}{4} - \frac{1}{2} = ?$$
$$10 + \frac{8 - 3 - 6}{12} = ?$$
$$10 - \frac{1}{12} = ?$$
$$9\frac{11}{12} = ?$$

93.

$$\sqrt{484} \times \sqrt{169} = ? + 50\% \text{ of } 312$$
$$22 \times 13 = ? + \frac{50}{100} \times 312$$
$$286 = ? + 156$$
$$? = 130.$$

94.

$$15^2 + 36^2 = ? \times \sqrt[3]{2197}$$
$$225 + 1296 = ? \times 13$$
$$\frac{1521}{13} = ?$$
$$117 = ?$$

95. **Let cost price of article = $100x$**

Selling price of one article = $120x$

According to question,

$$3 \times 20x - 2 \times 20x = 80$$
$$20x = 80$$
$$x = 4$$

Cost price of article = ₹ 400.

96. Quantity I:

Length of train 'A' = x

Length of train 'B' = $0.5x$

According to question,

$$x + 0.5x = 12 \times (25 + 15)$$
$$1.5x = 480$$
$$x = 320 \text{ meters}$$

Quantity II: 160 meters

Quantity I > Quantity II.

97. Let average of a, b and c be x

$$a + b + c = 3x$$

And, $$b + c + d = 3x + 3$$

$$\Rightarrow \quad d - a = 3$$

And, $$d + a = 39$$

$$d = 21 \text{ and } a = 18$$

Quantity I : $a = 18$

Quantity II : 21

Quantity II > Quantity I.

98. Quantity I : Due to leakage only 80% of the cistern is filled this means 20% of tank is leaked out by leakage which is equal to 60 liters

$$20\% = 60$$
$$100\% = 300 \text{ liters}$$

Capacity of tank = 300 liters

Quantity II : 250 liters

Quantity I > Quantity II.

99. Quantity I : Let speed of boat in still water and speed of stream be $2x$ and x respectively

According to question,

$$\Rightarrow \quad 32 = \frac{72}{3x} + \frac{72}{x}$$
$$\Rightarrow \quad x = \frac{96}{32} = 3$$

Downstream speed = $2x + x = 3x$ = 9 kmph

Quantity II : 9 kmph

Quantity I = Quantity II.

100. Quantity I: Side of square = $\sqrt{324}$ = 18 cm

Let length of rectangle be x and breadth of rectangle be $(x\ 4)$ cm

According to question,

$$x + x - 4 = \frac{4 \times 18}{2} = 36 \Rightarrow x = 20$$

Area of rectangle = 20×16 = 320 cm^2

Quantity II: 320 cm^2

Quantity I = Quantity II.

Previous Paper (Solved)

State Bank of India (SBI)

Junior Associates (Clerical Cadre)

Phase-I : Preliminary Exam 2016*

ENGLISH LANGUAGE

Directions (Qs. Nos. 1 to 5): *In each of the following questions, a sentence with four words in* **bold** *type is given. One of these four words given in* **bold** *may be either wrongly spelt or inappropriate in the context of the sentence. Find out the word which is wrongly spelt or inappropriate. If any, that word is your answer. If all the words given in* **bold** *are correctly spelt and also appropriate in the context of the sentence, select 'All correct' as your answer.*

1. On the basis of the forecast by the Indian Meteorological Department the government **ordered** (A)/ **district** (B)/ collectors to visit districts which are **expected** (C)/to receive heavy **rainfal.** (D)/ All correct (E).

2. **During** (A)/ the **course** (B)/ of the day many meetings were **held** (C)/ but the **agenda** (D)/ was not shared with us. All correct (E)

3. **Meazures** (A)/ to increase both financial **inclusion** (B)/ and **investment** (C)/ in infrastructure will result in **gains** (D)/ for the country. All correct (E)

4. Bringing **out** (A)/ a **family** (B)/ when you are **unemployed** (C)/ is no **picnic.** (D)/ All correct (E)

5. The **inn** (A)/ is **pucturesquly** (B)/ **situated** (C)/ on the **banks** (D)/ of the river. All correct (E)

Directions (Qs. Nos. 6 to 15): *Read the following story carefully and answer the questions given. Certain words/ phrases have been given in* **bold** *to help you locate them while answering some of the questions.*

Once there was a king who had been trying really hard to capture an elephant but that prize had proved elusive. All the hunters in the kingdom had tried but their efforts were **in vain.** So, the king announced that anyone who could capture the elephant would get half his kingdom.

The tortoise heard about this and went to the king to accept the challenge. The king was very amused. 'All my hunters have failed to capture the elephant and you think you can succeed?', asked the king. The tortoise insisted that he was up to the task and promised to deliver that elephant to the king within forty eight hours. The tortoise then dug a big hole, big enough to hold the elephant along a path leading to the village. Then he covered the hole with sticks and leaves so that it was not visible unless inspected closely. When this was done, the tortoise went in search of the elephant.

When the tortoise met the elephant, he told him, 'You know you are the largest animal in the forest and you should be a king?' The elephant had never considered this before but he thought it was not a bad idea. The tortoise told the elephant that the villagers had decided to elect the largest animal their king and were all expecting the elephant to come to the village and be crowned their king. The more the elephant heard, the more **excited** he became. The tortoise **adorned** the elephant with colourful beads and beating a gong, he sang songs **praising** the elephant while he led the way to the village. Soon they approached the trap and the tortoise being lighter and smaller walked over the trap. The elephant who was following him fell through the sticks and leaves into the deep hole and thus helped the tortoise in achieving hig goal well within the time limit.

6. As mentioned in the story, despite the king doubting his ability, the tortoise accepted the challenge as ________ .

(*a*) he was forced to do so by the villagers.
(*b*) to prove to the king that only a tortoise and his family could complete the challenge.
(*c*) he wanted the entire kingdom to himself.

A. Only (*a*)
B. Both (*a*) and (*b*)
C. Only (*b*)
D. All (*a*), (*b*) and (*c*)
E. None of these

7. Which of the following correctly explains the meaning of the phrase, 'in vain' as used in the story?

A. Were painful
B. Were unsuccessful
C. Were in order
D. Were truthful
E. Were simple

8. Which of the following could be a suitable title to the given story?

A. The Elephant Who Became the Most Popular King
B. The Wise King

* Exam held on 29 May 2016.

C. The Clever Tortoise
D. The Villagers and Their Love for the elephant
E. The Selfish Villagers

9. Which of the following is most nearly the OPPOSITE in meaning as the word 'EXCITED' as used in the story?
A. bored B. interested
C. affected D. feeling
E. merciless

10. Which of the following statements is TRUE in the context of the story?
A. The king refused to share his kingdom with the tortoise.
B. The tortoise kept his word by providing the king with what he desired.
C. It was the king's idea that helped the tortoise achieve his target.
D. The elephant was popular for his beautiful skin.
E. None of the given statements is true.

11. As mentioned in the story, the elephant followed tortoise's advice because:
(*a*) for him, the tortoise was the wisest animal in the village.
(*b*) he really believed that the villagers wanted him as the king.
(*c*) he had always wanted to become rich and powerful.
A. Only (*a*)
B. Both (*a*) and (*c*)
C. Both (*a*) and (*b*)
D. Only (*b*)
E. All three (*a*), (*b*) and (*c*)

12. Which of the following is most nearly the same in meaning as the word 'INSISTED' as used in the story?
A. requested B. revived
C. repeated D. invited
E. showed

13. Which of the following is most nearly the **opposite** in meaning as the word 'PRAISING' as used in the story?
A. insulting B. concealing
C. hiding D. refusing
E. removing

14. As mentioned in the story, which of the following can be said about the elephant?
A. He had a good sense of humour
B. He was foolish
C. He was balanced
D. He was logical
E. He was short tempered

15. Which of the following is most nearly the same in meaning as the word 'ADORNED' as used in the story?
A. touched B. adored
C. charmed D. decorated
E. stuffed

Directions (Qs. Nos. 16 to 20): *Rearrange the given six sentences/group of sentences (a), (b), (c), (d), (e) and (f) in a proper sequence so as to form a meaningful paragraph and then answer the given questions.*

(*a*) The next day Shiva appeared at Raghu's house and spotted a metal chest on the rooftop which had all the money and ornaments that Raghu owned.
(*b*) When Raghu arrived at Shiva's house. Shiva asked him to guess what fruit it was, saying that if Raghu failed he (Shiva) would carry one thing out of Raghu's house and if Raghu guessed correctly then Raghu could carry one thing out of Shiva's house.
(*c*) Seeing him Raghu thanked him saying, "Thank you for sparing my wealth and carrying out only the ladder!"
(*d*) One day Shiva hatched a plan to outwit. Raghu. He plucked a mango and wrapped it well in a piece of cloth.
(*e*) 'Oh no!' You thought that you'd hide all your wealth from me!' said Shiva going into Raghu's house and bringing out a ladder began to climb up onto the roof.
(*f*) But Raghu's guesses were incorrect.

16. Which of the following should be the FIFTH sentence after the rearrangement?
A. (*a*) B. (*b*)
C. (*d*) D. (*e*)
E. (*f*)

17. Which of the following should be the SECOND sentence after the rearrangement?
A. (*a*) B. (*b*)
C. (*c*) D. (*e*)
E. (*f*)

18. Which of the following should be the THIRD sentence after the rearrangement?
A. (*a*) B. (*b*)
C. (*c*) D. (*d*)
E. (*f*)

19. Which of the following should be the SIXTH (LAST) sentence after the rearrangement?
A. (*a*) B. (*b*)
C. (*c*) D. (*d*)
E. (*e*)

20. Which of the following should be the FIRST sentence after the rearrangement?
A. (*a*) B. (*c*)
C. (*d*) D. (*e*)
E. (*f*)

Directions (Qs. Nos. 21 to 25): *In the following sentences, read each sentence to find out whether there is any grammatical error in it. The error, if any, will be one part of the sentence. Select the part with the error as your answer. If there is no error, select 'No error' as your answer. (Ignore the errors of punctuation, if any).*

21. One should always(A)/ be happy from (B)/ whatever one has (C)/ and should not be greedy. (D)/ No error (E)

22. My friend lost (A)/ his temper on the (B)/ shopkeeper and (C)/ slapped him. (D)/ No error (E)

23. Luxurious and (A)/ expensive lights were (B)/ imported from (C)/ various countries. (D)/ No error (E)

24. They were unhappy because (A)/ the person who had a palace (B)/ had no gold and the person (C)/ who had gold had no palace. (D)/ No error (E)

25. Despite his (A)/ poor financial condition, (B)/ the auto-driver remained (C)/ honest and hard work. (D)/ No error (E)

Directions (Qs. Nos. 26 to 30): *In the following passage, there are blanks, each of which has been numbered. Against each, five words are suggested, one of which fits the blank appropriately. Find out the appropriate word in each case.*

The night fell heavy in the heights of the moun-tains and one could not see anything. All was black and the moon and the stars were covered by clouds.

As Tom was climbing only a few feet away from the top of the mountain, he ___**(26)**___ and fell in to the air, falling at great speed. He could only see black spots as he went down. He kept failing, when all of a ___**(27)**___he felt the rope tied to his waist pull at him very hard. His body was hanging in the air. Only the rope was holding him and in that moment of stillness, he had no other ___**(28)**___but to scream, 'Help me God'. All of a sudden a deep voice coming from the sky answered. 'What did you want me to do?' 'Save me God,' said Tom. 'Do you really think I can save you?' asked the voice. 'Of course you can,' ___**(29)**___Tom. 'Then cut the rope tied to your want,' said the voice. There was a moment of silence as Tom decided to hold on to the rope with all his ___**(30)**___.

The rescue team said that the next day a climber was found and frozen, his body hanging from a rope, only one foot away from the ground.

26. A. stumble B. talked C. tried D. slapped E. caused

27. A. time B. instant C. sudden D. shock E. moment

28. A. option B. person C. want D. limitation E. body

29. A. asked B. questioned C. replied D. denied E. doubted

30. A. strength B. feet C. family D. reason E. portions

QUANTITATIVE APTITUDE

31. The circumference of circle A is 75 metre more than its diameter. If the radius of circle B is 3.5 metre more than the radius of circle A, what is the circumference of circle B? (in metre)

A. 110 B. 140 C. 163 D. 96 E. 132

32. A shopkeeper sold an article at 20% discount at the marked price and earned a profit of 4%. By what per cent is the marked price of the article more than the cost price of the article?

A. 20 B. 15 C. 40 D. 25 E. 30

Directions (Qs. Nos. 33 to 37): *What will come in place of question mark (?) in the given number series?*

33. 89 86 78 63 39 ?

A. 19 B. 4 C. 9 D. 13 E. 28

34. 142 70 34 16 ? 2.5

A. 5 B. 7 C. 3 D. 12 E. 8

35. 21 37 40.2 88.2 94.6 ?

A. 211.6 B. 224.5 C. 192.3 D. 174.6 E. 182.8

36. 17 9 10 16.5 35 ?

A. 84 B. 102.5 C. 90 D. 92.5 E. 72

37. 0.75 ? 6 36 288 2880

A. 3 B. 1.5
C. 2 D. 4.5
E. 5

38. Pihu and Rani start a business together by investing ₹ 9000 and ₹ 6300 respectively. After a certain period. Pihu with drew from the business completely. If at the end of 2 years the total profit earned was ₹ 13,050 and Pihu's share was ₹ 6,750, after how many months did Pihu withdraw from business?

A. 23 months
B. 14 months
C. 20 months
D. 15 months
E. 18 months

39. Jar A contains 'x' ml of pure milk only. A 27 ml mixture of milk and water in the respective ratio of 4 : 5, is added to jar A. The new mixture thus formed in jar A contains 70% milk, what is the value of x?

A. 23 B. 30
C. 27 D. 48
E. 28

40. The speed of a boat in still water is 500% more than the speed of the current. What is the respective ratio between the speed of the boat downstream and speed of the boat upstream?

A. 9 : 2 B. 7 : 3
C. 7 : 5 D. 9 : 4
E. 4 : 3

Directions (Qs. Nos. 41 to 45): *Study the table carefully and answer the given questions.*

Number of employees in 5 organisations during 5 years

Organisations	Years 2003	2004	2005	2006	2007
A	69	55	56	59	65
B	93	100	79	101	120
C	95	89	85	75	70
D	88	109	100	99	95
E	80	132	147	164	112

41. The number of employees in organisation E increased by what per cent from 2003 to 2006?

A. 105 B. 110
C. 115 D. 102
E. 125

42. The number of employees in organisation B and C decreased by 5% and 10% respectively from 2007 to 2008. What was the total number of employees in organisation B and C together in 2008?

A. 177 B. 179
C. 175 D. 181
E. 163

43. What is the difference between total number of employees in organisation A in 2003 and 2004 together and that in organisation D in the same years together?

A. 77 B. 79
C. 73 D. 83
E. 67

44. What is the respective ratio between total number of employees in organisations B and C together in 2004 and total number of employees in organisations D and E together in 2007?

A. 21 : 22
B. 23 : 29
C. 23 : 27
D. 21 : 25
E. 21 : 23

45. What is the average number of employees in organisations A, B and E in 2005?

A. 98 B. 96
C. 92 D. 88
E. 94

46. The average runs of a cricketer in a tourna-ment, in which he played 14 matches, are 47. His average runs in the first seven matches are 57 and that in the last five matches are 44. If the runs made by him in 8th match are 15, how many runs did he make in 9th match?

A. 24 B. 32
C. 26 D. 22
E. 28

47. An equal amount of sum, ₹ P is invested in scheme A and scheme B. Both the schemes A and B offer simple interest at the rate of 12% and 9% respectively. If at the end of two years total amount received from both the schemes together was ₹ 21,780, what is the value of P?

A. ₹ 9000
B. ₹ 9600
C. ₹ 12000
D. ₹ 8400
E. ₹ 8000

Directions (Qs. Nos. 48 to 57): *What will come in place of question mark (?) in the given questions?*

48. $\frac{5}{9} \times (225.40 - 45.4) = ?^2$

A. 15 B. 5
C. 100 D. 25
E. 10

49. $80 \div 2.4 \times ? = 600$

A. 16 B. 12
C. 18 D. 14
E. 24

50. $57 - 1725 \div 69 = 4 \times ?$

A. 9 B. 11
C. 13 D. 7
E. 8

51. $\sqrt{784} \times 3 - ? = 58$

A. 26 B. 24
C. 22 D. 28
E. 25

52. $\sqrt{\dfrac{160 \times 8}{5}} \times 8 = ?$

A. 112 B. 164
C. 128 D. 116
E. 136

53. $33\frac{3}{7} + 145\frac{2}{7} + 9\frac{2}{7} = ?$

A. 188 B. 156
C. 162 D. 148
E. 192

54. $\dfrac{2.6 \times 3 + 1.8 \times 9}{6} = ?$

A. 6 B. 6.4
C. 8 D. 4.2
E. 4

55. 50% of $\left(3\frac{3}{8} + 1\frac{7}{10}\right) = ?$

A. 3.145 B. 2.3546
C. 2 D. 2.4845
E. 2.5375

56. $\sqrt{729} \div 45 \times 540 = ?^2$

A. 18 B. 324
C. 14 D. 144
E. 196

57. $8\frac{1}{3} \times 2\frac{2}{5} \times ? = 12$

A. $\frac{2}{3}$ B. $\frac{2}{5}$
C. $\frac{1}{3}$ D. $\frac{3}{5}$
E. $\frac{4}{5}$

58. The simple interest at the rate of 6% per annum received on a principal of ₹ x was ₹ 482.40 when invested for 3 years in scheme A. If scheme B offered compound interest (compounded annually) at 10% per annum what was the interest received by investing ₹ $(x - 680)$ for 2 years in scheme B?

A. ₹ 420 B. ₹ 490
C. ₹ 530 D. ₹ 540
E. ₹ 650

59. Mary paid 15% of her monthly salary towards an EMI. From the remaining salary, she paid 10% as internet bill and 20% as rent. If after the mentioned expenses she was left with ₹ 24,990, what was Mary's monthly salary?

A. ₹ 45,000
B. ₹ 48,000
C. ₹ 42,000
D. ₹ 36,000
E. ₹ 40,000

60. The sum of 4 consecutive even numbers is 47 more than the sum of three consecutive odd numbers. If the sum of smallest odd number and the smallest even number is 55, what is the smallest even number?

A. 36 B. 40
C. 32 D. 38
E. 34

61. A, B and C, each working alone, can finish a piece of work in 27, 33 and 45 days respectively. A starts by working alone for 12 days, then B takes over from A and works for 11 days. At this stage C takes over from B and completes the remaining work. In how many days the whole work was completed?

A. 33 B. 31
C. 39 D. 35
E. 37

62. A rectangular garden of length 12 m is surrounded by a 2 m wide path. If the area of the garden is 84 m^2 and the cost of gravelling is ₹ 8 per m^2, what is the total cost of gravelling the path? (in Rs.)

A. 780 B. 742
C. 724 D. 775
E. 736

63. Train A, travelling at 's' m/sec, can cross a platform double its length in 21 seconds. The same train, travelling at $(s + 5)$ m/sec. can cross the same platform in 18 seconds. What is the value of 's'?

A. 27.5 B. 32.5
C. 30 D. 35
E. 25

64. The present age of Charu is 2.5 times the present age of Harsh. Had Harsh been two years younger and Charu been 13 years older, Charu's age would have been 3.5 times Harsh's age. What is Harsh's present age?

A. 48 B. 25
C. 20 D. 28
E. 36

65. If $\frac{7}{19}$th of x is equal to y and the respective ratio between $(x + 28)$ and y is 33 : 7, what is the value of y?

A. 14 B. 32
C. 36 D. 38
E. 28

REASONING

66. Among five friends—O, P, Q, R and S—each scored different marks in an examination. P scored more than R and Q but less than O. O did not score the highest marks and R did not score the lowest marks. Who amongst the following scored the third highest?

A. Cannot be determined
B. S
C. P
D. Q
E. O

67. In a certain code language, 'CLUB' is coded as 'FKTE' and 'THEN' is coded as 'WGDQ'. In the same code language, 'ARID' will be coded as:

A. DQHG B. TQHG
C. YQKE D. DULC
E. DQLC

68. In a certain code if 'a fast train' is coded as '1 5 8' and 'train to Mumbai' is coded as '9 3 1', then what is the code for train in the given code language?

A. 8 B. 3
C. 5 D. 1
E. Either '3' or '9'

69. If three is added to each even digit and three is subtracted from each odd digit in the number 254673 and then in the new number thus formed all the digits are arranged in descending order, which of the following will be third from the right?

A. 0 B. 2
C. 9 D. 4
E. 7

70. How many such pairs of letters are there in the word 'TEACH' each of which has as many letters between them in the word (in both forward and backward directions) as they have between them in the English alphabetical series?

A. More than three B. None
C. Two D. Three
E. One

Directions (Qs. Nos. 71 to 75): *Study the following information carefully and answer the questions given below.*

Eight persons—E, F, G, H, I, J, K and L—are sitting around a circular table facing the centre but not necessarily in the same order.

- Only three persons sit between K and L. Only two persons sit between L and H.
- Only three persons sit between H and G.
- J sits second to the right of H.
- I is one of the immediate neighbours of H.
- F is neither an immediate neighbour of K nor G.

71. Which amongst the following statements is true regarding F, as per the given arrangement?

A. None of the given statements is true
B. K is one of the immediate neighbours of F
C. F sits second to the left of H
D. F sits third to the right of J
E. Only three persons sit between F and E

72. If all the persons are made to sit in alphabetical order in clockwise direction, starting from E, the positions of how many, excluding E, would remain unchanged?

A. Three B. Four
C. One D. None
E. Two

73. Four of the following five are alike in a certain way based on their positions in the given arrangement and so form a group. Which is the one that does not belong to the group?

A. GJL B. KIE
C. JHG D. HFJ
E. ILK

74. Who among the following sits to the immediate left of L?

A. H B. G
C. I D. F
E. J

75. What is the position of H with respect to E?

A. Second to the left
B. Second to the right
C. To the immediate right
D. Third to the left
E. Third to the right

Directions (Qs. Nos. 76 to 80): *Study the following information carefully and answer the questions given below.*

Seven persons, namely J, K, L, M, N, O and P watch seven different channels on seven different days of the same week starting from Monday and ending on Sunday, but not necessarily in the same order.

K watches a channel on Saturday. More than two persons watch a channel between K and N. Only one person watches a channel between N and L. J watches a channel on one of the days before L but not on Wednesday. As many persons watch a channel between L and P as between J and L. O watches a channel immediately after P.

76. On which of the following days does M watch a channel?

A. Friday B. Monday
C. Sunday D. Wednesday
E. Tuesday

77. Which of the following pairs represents the persons who watch a channel immediately before and immediately after K?

A. J, P B. M, J
C. L, O D. P, L
E. O, M

78. Which of the following statements is not true as per the given arrangement?

A. All the given statements are true
B. Only two persons watch a channel after O
C. Only two persons watch a channel between M and P
D. N watches a channel immediately before J
E. L watches a channel on Wednesday

79. Who amongst the following watches a channel on Thursday?

A. M B. P
C. L D. O
E. J

80. Four of the following five are alike in a certain way and thus form a group as per the given arrangement. Which of the following does not belong to that group?

A. OP B. NJ
C. LP D. JK
E. MK

Directions (Qs. Nos. 81 to 85): *In each of the following questions, relationship between different elements is shown in the statements. The statements are followed by two conclusions numbered I and II. Study the Conclusions based on the given statements and select the appropriate answer.*

Give answer—

A. If neither Conclusion I nor Conclusion II is true.
B. If only Conclusion I is true.
C. If both the Conclusion I and Conclusion II are true.
D. If only Conclusion II is true.
E. Is either Conclusion I or Conclusion II is true.

81. Statement : $F \leq L < U = K \geq E$
Conclusions : I. $U \geq E$ II. $F < K$

82. Statement : $B \geq O \geq N < K \leq R$; $N \geq F$
Conclusions : I. $O < R$ II. $F \leq B$

83. Statement : $C \leq D = E > F \geq G$
Conclusions : I. $C \leq F$ II. $G \geq D$

84. Statement : $L > A \geq M > P$; $R \leq A \leq N$
Conclusions : I. $M \leq N$ II. $P > R$

85. Statement : $P \leq Q \leq R = S \leq T$
Conclusions : I. $P = T$ II. $P < T$

Directions (Qs. Nos. 86 to 90): *Study the following arrangement carefully and answer the questions given below.*

Y B @ 3 E P ★ $ 5 T C Z J 4 L 7 R K 8 V ∧ F X Q U π M 6 G N % 9

86. Four of the following five are alike in a certain way based on their positions in the given arrangement and hence form a group. Which one does not belong to that group?

A. $ 5 ★ B. 6 GM
C. ZJC D. 7RL
E. BY@

87. How many alphabet are there in the English alphabetical series between the sixth element from the left end and the sixth element from the right end of the given arrangement?

A. None B. Two
C. One D. Three
E. More than three

88. Which one of the following will come next in the given sequence?

YE3 @★P E5$ ★CT ?

A. CI4 B. T4J
C. 54J D. 5JZ
E. C4Z

89. If all the symbols are deleted from the given arrangement then which of the following will be the ninth element from the right end?

A. V B. K
C. F D. 8
E. 7

90. How many such alphabet are there in the given arrangement each of which is immediately preceded by a number as well as immediately followed by a symbol?

A. One
B. Three
C. More than three
D. Two
E. None

Directions (Qs. Nos. 91 & 92): *Study the following information carefully and answer the questions given below.*

Marcus, who is standing at Point D, walks 11 m towards south and reaches Point E. He then takes a left turn and walks 7 m. He then takes a left turn, walks 5 m and reaches Point F. Point R is 18 m to the east of Point F. Point S is 6 m to the north of Point R.

91. In which direction is Point R with respect to Point D?
A. South-West
B. East
C. West
D. South-East
E. North

92. How far and in which direction is Point S with respect to Point D?
A. 11 m towards east
B. 11 m towards west
C. 17 m towards west
D. 17 m towards east
E. 25 m towards east

Directions (Qs. Nos. 93 to 95): *Study the following information carefully and answer the questions given below.*

S is the father of R. R is the only son of U. U is the daughter of J. J has only two children. K is the son of J.

93. If X is the grand daughter of J, then how is U related to X?
A. Sister
B. Mother-in-law
C. Grandfather
D. Sister-in-law
E. Cannot be determined

94. How is S related to K?
A. Brother
B. Brother-in-law
C. Cousin
D. Father
E. Uncle

95. How is R related to J?
A. Grandfather
B. Son
C. Nephew
D. Grandson
E. Son-in-law

Directions (Qs. Nos. 96 to 100): *The following questions are based on the given 3-digit numbers.*

821 547 452 935 368

96. The product of the second and the third digits in which of the following numbers is the second highest?
A. 547
B. 935
C. 368
D. 452
E. 821

97. The difference of the first and the second digits in how many of the given numbers is greater than the third digit of the same number?
A. Three
B. More than three
C. Two
D. One
E. None

98. If all the digits of the given number are arranged in ascending order within the number, what will be the sum of the second and third digits of the second highest number thus formed?
A. 12
B. 10
C. 15
D. 9
E. 14

99. If the first digit and the third digit of all the given numbers are interchanged, which of the following will become the second lowest number after performing the said operation?
A. 547
B. 452
C. 935
D. 368
E. 821

100. If '2' is added to the second digit of all even numbers and '3' is subtracted from the first digit of all odd numbers, in how many numbers thus formed will a digit appear twice?
A. None
B. Three
C. More than three
D. One
E. Two

ANSWERS

1	2	3	4	5	6	7	8	9	10
D	E	A	A	B	E	B	C	A	B

11	12	13	14	15	16	17	18	19	20
D	C	A	B	D	A	B	E	E	C
21	**22**	**23**	**24**	**25**	**26**	**27**	**28**	**29**	**30**
B	B	A	E	D	A	C	A	C	A
31	**32**	**33**	**34**	**35**	**36**	**37**	**38**	**39**	**40**
E	E	B	B	D	C	B	E	A	C
41	**42**	**43**	**44**	**45**	**46**	**47**	**48**	**49**	**50**
A	A	C	E	E	A	A	E	C	E
51	**52**	**53**	**54**	**55**	**56**	**57**	**58**	**59**	**60**
A	C	A	E	E	A	D	A	C	D
61	**62**	**63**	**64**	**65**	**66**	**67**	**68**	**69**	**70**
A	E	C	C	A	C	A	D	D	C
71	**72**	**73**	**74**	**75**	**76**	**77**	**78**	**79**	**80**
C	E	A	B	D	C	E	A	B	D
81	**82**	**83**	**84**	**85**	**86**	**87**	**88**	**89**	**90**
C	D	A	B	E	E	B	D	C	A
91	**92**	**93**	**94**	**95**	**96**	**97**	**98**	**99**	**100**
D	E	E	B	D	A	C	E	B	D

EXPLANATORY ANSWERS

31. Let the diameter of circle A be d metre.

According to the question,

$$\pi d - d = 75$$

$$\Rightarrow \quad d\left(\frac{22}{7}-1\right) = 75$$

$$\Rightarrow \quad d\left(\frac{22-7}{7}\right) = 75$$

$$\Rightarrow \quad d\times\frac{15}{7} = 75$$

$$\Rightarrow \quad d = \frac{75\times 7}{15}$$

$$= 35 \text{ metre}$$

$$\therefore \quad \text{Radius} = \frac{35}{2} = 17.5 \text{ metre.}$$

$\therefore$ Radius of circle B = 17.5 + 3.5

= 21 metre

Its circumference $= 2\times\frac{22}{7}\times 21$

= 132 metre.

32. Marked price of article = ₹ x and its cost price = ₹ 100

According to the question,

$$\frac{80x}{100} = 104$$

$$\Rightarrow \quad x = \frac{104\times 100}{80} = ₹\ 130$$

i.e., marked price is 30% above its cost price.

33. The pattern is:

89 − 3 = 86

86 − 8 (= 3 + 5) = 78

78 − 15 (= 8 + 7) = 63

63 − 24 (= 15 + 9) = 39

39 − 35 (= 24 + 11) = 4.

34. The pattern is:

$$\frac{142}{2}-1 = 71 - 1 = 70$$

$$\frac{70}{2}-1 = 35 - 1 = 34$$

$$\frac{34}{2}-1 = 17 - 1 = 16$$

$$\frac{16}{2}-1 = 8 - 1 = 7$$

$$\frac{7}{2}-1 = 3.5 - 1 = 2.5$$

35. The pattern is:

$$21 + 16 = 37$$

$$37+\frac{16\times2}{10} = 37 + 3.2 = 40.2$$

$$40.2 + 16 \times 3 = 40.2 + 48 = 88.2$$

$$88.2+\frac{16\times4}{10} = 88.2 + 6.4 = 94.6$$

$$94.6 + 16 \times 5 = 94.6 + 80 = 174.6.$$

36. The pattern is:

$$17 \times 0.5 + 0.5 = 8.5 + 0.5 = 9$$

$$9 \times 1 + 1 = 9 + 1 = 10$$

$$10 \times 1.5 + 1.5 = 15 + 1.5 = 16.5$$

$$16.5 \times 2 + 2 = 33 + 2 = 35$$

$$35 \times 2.5 + 2.5 = 87.5 + 2.5 = 90.$$

37. The pattern is:

$$0.75 \times 2 = 1.5$$

$$1.5 \times 4 = 6$$

$$6 \times 6 = 36$$

$$36 \times 8 = 288$$

$$288 \times 10 = 2880.$$

38. Let Pihu remained partner for x months

Ratio of the equivalent capitals of Pihu and Rani for 1 month

$$= 9000 \times x : 6300 \times 24$$

$$= 5x : 84$$

Sum of the terms of ratio

$$= 5x + 84$$

$\therefore$ Pihu's share $= \frac{5x}{5x+84}\times13050$

$$\therefore \frac{5x}{5x+84}\times13050 = 6750$$

$$\Rightarrow \frac{5x}{5x+84} = \frac{6750}{13050} = \frac{15}{29}$$

$$\Rightarrow 145x = 75x + 1260$$

$$\Rightarrow 145x - 75x = 1260$$

$$\Rightarrow 70x = 1260$$

$$\Rightarrow x = \frac{1260}{70}$$

$$= 18 \text{ months.}$$

39. In 27 litres of mixture,

$$\text{Milk} = \frac{4}{9}\times27 = 12 \text{ litres}$$

According to the question,

$$\frac{x+12}{x+27}\times100 = 70$$

$$\Rightarrow \frac{x+12}{x+27} = \frac{7}{10}$$

$$\Rightarrow 10x + 120 = 7x + 189$$

$$\Rightarrow 10x - 7x = 189 - 120$$

$$\Rightarrow 3x = 69$$

$$\Rightarrow x = \frac{69}{3} = 23.$$

40. Speed of current = x kmph

$\therefore$ Speed of boat in still water = $6x$ kmph.

$\therefore$ Rate downstream = $6x + x = 7x$ kmph

Rate upstream = $6x - x = 5x$ kmph

$\therefore$ Required ratio = $7x : 5x = 7 : 5$.

41. Number of employees in organisation E in 2003 = 80

Number of employees in organisation E in 2006 = 164

$$\therefore \text{Percentage increase} = \frac{164-80}{80}\times100$$

$$= \frac{840}{8} = 105\%.$$

42. Employees in 2008:

$$\text{Organisation B} \Rightarrow \frac{120\times95}{100} = 114$$

$$\text{Organisation C} \Rightarrow \frac{70\times90}{100} = 63$$

$\therefore$ Required answer = 114 + 63 = 177.

43. Required difference = (88 + 109) – (69 + 55)

= 197 – 124 = 73.

44. Required ratio = (100 + 89) : (95 + 112)

= 189 : 207 = 21 : 23.

45. Required average $= \frac{56+79+147}{3} = \frac{282}{3} = 94.$

46. Runs scored by cricketer in ninth match = x

According to the question,

$$7 \times 57 + 5 \times 44 + 15 + x = 14 \times 47$$

$$\Rightarrow 399 + 220 + 15 + x = 658$$

$$\Rightarrow 634 + x = 658$$

$$\Rightarrow x = 658 - 634 = 24.$$

47. $\text{S.I.} = \frac{\text{Principal}\times\text{Time}\times\text{Rate}}{100}$

According to the question,

$$2P+\frac{P\times12\times2}{100}+\frac{P\times9\times2}{100} = 21780$$

$\Rightarrow$ 242P = 21780 × 100

$$\therefore\ P = \frac{21780\times100}{242} = ₹\ 9000.$$

63. Length of train = x metre

Distance covered by train in crossing a platform = length of train and platform

Case I, $s = \frac{x+2x}{21} \Rightarrow 21s = 3x$

$\Rightarrow$ $x = 7s$ ...(*i*)

Case II, $s + 5 = \frac{3x}{18} \Rightarrow s + 5 = \frac{x}{6}$

$\Rightarrow$ $6s + 30 = x$ ...(*ii*)

$\therefore$ $7s = 6s + 30$

$\Rightarrow$ $s = 30.$

64. Harsh's present age = x years

$\therefore$ Charu's present age = $2.5x$ years

According to the question,

$3.5(x - 2) = 2.5x + 13$

$\Rightarrow$ $3.5x - 7 = 2.5x + 13$

$\Rightarrow$ $3.5x - 2.5x = 13 + 7 = 20$

$\Rightarrow$ $x = 20$ years.

65. According to the question,

$$\frac{7x}{19} = y$$

$\Rightarrow$ $x = \frac{19y}{7}$ ...(*i*)

Again, $\frac{x+28}{y} = \frac{33}{7}$

$$\Rightarrow \frac{\frac{19y}{7}+28}{y} = \frac{33}{7}$$

$$\Rightarrow \frac{19y+196}{7y} = \frac{33}{7}$$

$\Rightarrow$ $133y + 1372 = 231y$

$\Rightarrow$ $231y - 133y = 1372$

$\Rightarrow$ $98y = 1372$

$$\Rightarrow y = \frac{1372}{98} = 14.$$

YOUR SPACE

YOUR SPACE

Numerical Ability

1

Number Series

A series is a sequence of numbers, where the sequence of numbers is obtained by some particular pre-defined rule and applying that rule it is possible to find out the next term of the series.

(1) Arithmetic Series : An arithmetic series is one in which successive numbers are obtained by adding (or subtracting) a fixed number to the previous number. For example :
3, 5, 7 , 9 , 11 ....

(2) Geometric Series : A geometrical series is one in which each successive number is obtained by multiplying (or dividing) a fixed number to the previous number. For example, 4, 8, 16, 32, 64 ....

(3) Series of squares, cubes etc. These series can be formed by squaring or cubing every successive number. For example, 2, 4, 16, 256 ....

Some Important Rules for Number series :

1. The number in the series increases or decreases by perfect squares. For example :
$-(2)^2, -(3)^2, -(5)^2$; $2^2, 3^2, 5^2$
2. The number in the series increases or decreases by perfect cubes. For example :
$-1^3, -2^3, -3^3, -4^3$; $1^3, 2^3, 3^3, 4^3$,
3. The number in the series increase or decreases by prime number. For Example :
13, 11, 7, 5, 3 ......
4. The number in the series are multiplies of a number. For example : × 2, × 3, × 4, × 5, × 6, × 7 ......
5. The number in the series is found by dividing certain numbers. For example : ÷ 2, ÷ 4, ÷ 5, ÷ 8 ....
6. The number in the series are in AP. Here some given numbers are said to be in A.P. if the difference between two consecutive numbers is same. For example :
1, 3, 5, 7, 9, 11 ....
7. The number in the series are in G.P. Here some given numbers remains the same. For example : 32, 16, 8, 4, 2.
8. Some special rules are for special series. This can be found out by observing the series of numbers.
9. In the special series, two series may be mixed.

MULTIPLE CHOICE QUESTIONS

Directions: *What will come in place of question mark (?) in the given number series?*

1. 29 31 37 49 69 ?
(*a*) 108 (*b*) 99
(*c*) 94 (*d*) 103
(*e*) 88

2. 2 17 45 99 205 ?
(*a*) 233 (*b*) 415
(*c*) 234 (*d*) 435
(*e*) 239

3. 17 16 30 87 344 ?
(*a*) 1735 (*b*) 1760
(*c*) 1660 (*d*) 1685
(*e*) 1715

4. 8 9.4 12.2 17.8 29 ?
(*a*) 53.6 (*b*) 51.4
(*c*) 52.1 (*d*) 48.6
(*e*) 49.8

5. 26 12 11 15.5 30 ?
(*a*) 72 (*b*) 68
(*c*) 74 (*d*) 82
(*e*) 78

6.

960	839	758	709	?	675

(*a*) 698 (*b*) 694
(*c*) 684 (*d*) 648
(*e*) 680

7.

3	?	14	55	274	1643

(*a*) 5 (*b*) 6
(*c*) 7 (*d*) 8
(*e*) None of these

8.

36	38.8	42.8	?	54.4	62

(*a*) 46 (*b*) 48
(*c*) 45 (*d*) 48.2
(*e*) 49.4

9.

37	?	103	169	257	367

(*a*) 49 (*b*) 46
(*c*) 56 (*d*) 59
(*e*) 69

10.

4	6	12	?	90	315

(*a*) 25 (*b*) 27
(*c*) 30 (*d*) 45
(*e*) None of these

11. 2 4 16 96 768 ? 92160
(*a*) 7680 (*b*) 7580
(*c*) 7608 (*d*) 7090
(*e*) 7860

12. 14 36 ? 300 894 2676 8022
(*a*) 101 (*b*) 102
(*c*) 103 (*d*) 104
(*e*) None of these

13. 5 8 13 20 ? 44 61
(*a*) 29 (*b*) 30
(*c*) 31 (*d*) 32
(*e*) 37

14. 11 16 31 56 91 136 ?
(*a*) 171 (*b*) 181
(*c*) 185 (*d*) 191
(*e*) 197

15. 3 4 12 45 196 ?
(*a*) 985 (*b*) 990
(*c*) 995 (*d*) 1000
(*e*) 1005

16. 2 26 286 ? 18018 90090 270270
(*a*) 3088 (*b*) 2667
(*c*) 3862 (*d*) 2574
(*e*) 208608

17. 358 356 352 344 328 296 ?
(*a*) 232 (*b*) 247
(*c*) 225 (*d*) 255
(*e*) None of these

18. 8 ? 30 105 472.5 2598.75 16891.875
(*a*) 24 (*b*) 10
(*c*) 12 (*d*) 16
(*e*) None of these

19. 3 4 ? 21 85 110 326
(*a*) 7 (*b*) 10
(*c*) 12 (*d*) 14
(*e*) None of these

20. 50000 10000 2500 500 125 ? 6.25
(*a*) 75 (*b*) 25
(*c*) 50 (*d*) 31.5
(*e*) None of these

21. 17 98 147 172 181 (?)
(*a*) 180 (*b*) 192
(*c*) 184 (*d*) 182
(*e*) None of these

22. 11 19 31 47 67 (?)
(*a*) 80 (*b*) 81
(*c*) 86 (*d*) 96
(*e*) None of these

23. 748 460 316 244 208 (?)
(*a*) 180 (*b*) 190
(*c*) 172 (*d*) 182
(*e*) None of these

24. 1 5 13 29 ? 125 253
(*a*) 83 (*b*) 69
(*c*) 61 (*d*) 65
(*e*) None of these

25. 45 57 81 117 165 ?
(*a*) 235 (*b*) 215
(*c*) 205 (*d*) 245
(*e*) None of these

26. 353 354 351 356 349 ?
(*a*) 348 (*b*) 358
(*c*) 338 (*d*) 385
(*e*) 340

27. $\frac{1}{4}$ $\frac{1}{2}$ $\frac{3}{4}$ 1 $1\frac{1}{4}$ $1\frac{1}{2}$ $1\frac{3}{4}$?
(*a*) 2 (*b*) 4
(*c*) 6 (*d*) $1\frac{1}{5}$
(*e*) $1\frac{2}{3}$

28. 17 18 26 53 117 ? 458
(*a*) 342 (*b*) 142
(*c*) 3257 (*d*) 262
(*e*) 242

29. 36 37 46 71 ? 201 322
(*a*) 120 (*b*) 107
(*c*) 135 (*d*) 96
(*e*) None of these

30. 12 20 100 ? 8900 88900 888900
(*a*) 1000 (*b*) 900
(*c*) 800 (*d*) 500
(*e*) None of these

31. 7 7 14 42 168 ? 5040
(*a*) 672 (*b*) 850
(*c*) 740 (*d*) 800
(*e*) None of these

32. 21 30 12 39 3 ? –6
(a) 66 (b) 12
(c) 48 (d) 75
(e) None of these

33. 10 24 52 ? 220 444 892
(a) 104 (b) 98
(c) 112 (d) 108
(e) None of these

Directions (Qs. 34 to 40) : *Find the Wrong number in the following series.*

34. 905, 180, 175, 35, 30, 6, 1
(a) 6 (b) 1
(c) 175 (d) 905
(e) None of these

35. 5040, 840, 160, 42, 14, 7
(a) 7 (b) 160
(c) 14 (d) 840
(e) None of these

36. 3, 32, 363, 3993, 43923
(a) 363 (b) 3
(c) 32 (d) 43923
(e) None of these

37. 3, 18, 38, 78, 123, 178, 243
(a) 78 (b) 3
(c) 123 (d) 18
(e) None of these

38. 0, 1, 2, 2, 4, 4, 6, 8, 8, 10
(a) 6 (b) 0
(c) 1 (d) 10
(e) None of these

39. 5, 12, 16, 24, 27
(a) 12 (b) 16
(c) 24 (d) 27
(e) None of these

40. 27, 36, 45, 60, 71, 99
(a) 27 (b) 45
(c) 60 (d) 71
(e) None of these

ANSWERS

1	2	3	4	5	6	7	8	9	10
(b)	(b)	(e)	(b)	(c)	(c)	(a)	(b)	(d)	(c)
11	**12**	**13**	**14**	**15**	**16**	**17**	**18**	**19**	**20**
(a)	(b)	(c)	(d)	(e)	(d)	(a)	(c)	(c)	(b)
21	**22**	**23**	**24**	**25**	**26**	**27**	**28**	**29**	**30**
(a)	(e)	(b)	(c)	(e)	(b)	(a)	(e)	(a)	(b)
31	**32**	**33**	**34**	**35**	**36**	**37**	**38**	**39**	**40**
(e)	(c)	(d)	(d)	(b)	(c)	(b)	(d)	(c)	(d)

EXPLANATORY ANSWERS

1. 29 31 37 49 69 [99]
+1×2 +2×3 +3×4 +4×5 +5×6
Hence, 99 will come at the place of question mark.

2. 2 17 45 99 205 [415]
×2+13 ×2+11 ×2+9 ×2+7 ×2+5
Hence, 415 will come at the place of question mark.

3. 17 16 30 87 344 [1715]
×1–1 ×2–2 ×3–3 ×4–4 ×5–5
Hence, 1715 will come at the place of question mark.

4. 8 9.4 12.2 17.8 29 [51.4]
+1.4 +2×1.4 +2×2.8 +2×5.6 +2×11.2
Hence, 51.4 will come at the place of question mark.

5. 26 12 11 15.5 30 [74]
$\times\frac{1}{2}-1$ $\times 1-1$ $\times\frac{3}{2}-1$ $\times 2-1$ $\times\frac{5}{2}-1$
Hence, 74 will come at the place of question mark.

11. 2 4 16 96 768 ? 92160
2×2 4×4 16×6 96×8 768×10 7680×12
Hence, 7680 will come in place of question mark (?).

12. 14 36 ? 300 894 2678 8022
14×3–6 36×3–6 102×3–6 300×3–6 894×3–6 2676×3–6
Hence, 102 will come in place of question mark (?).

13. 5 8 13 20 ? 44 61
5+3 8+5 13+7 20+11 31+13 44+17
Added all consecutive prime numbers as 3, 5, 7, 11, 13 and 17.
Hence, 31 will come in place of question mark (?).

14. 11 16 31 56 91 136 ?
11+5 16+15 31+25 56+35 91+45 136+55
Added 5, 15, 25, 35, 45 and 55.
Hence, 191 will come in place of question mark (?).

15. 3   4   12   45   196   ?

$3\times1+1^2$ $4\times2+2^2$ $12\times3+3^2$ $45\times4+4^2$ $196\times5+5^2$

Hence, 1005 will come in place of question mark (?).

16. The pattern of the number series is:

$2 \times 13 = 26$
$26 \times 11 = 286$
$286 \times 9 = \boxed{2574}$
$2574 \times 7 = 18018$
$18018 \times 5 = 90090$

17. The pattern of the number series is:

$358 - 2 = 356$
$356 - 4 = 352$
$352 - 8 = 344$
$344 - 16 = 328$
$328 - 32 = 296$
$296 - 64 = \boxed{232}$

18. The pattern of the number series is:

$8 \times 1.5 = \boxed{12}$
$12 \times 2.5 = 30$
$30 \times 3.5 = 105$
$105 \times 4.5 = 472.5$

19. The pattern of the number series is:

$3 + 1^2 = 4$
$4 + 2^3 = \boxed{12}$
$12 + 3^2 = 21$
$21 + 4^3 = 85$
$85 + 5^2 = 110$
$110 + 6^3 = 326$

20. The pattern of the number series is:

$50000 \div 5 = 10000$
$10000 \div 4 = 2500$
$2500 \div 5 = 500$
$500 \div 4 \div 125$
$125 \div 5 = \boxed{25}$
$25 \div 4 = 6.25$

21. Difference between two consecutive terms
81, 49, 25, 9
$\Rightarrow$ 9^2, 7^2, 5^2, 3^2, 1^2
Clearly the next term = 180

22. Difference between two consecutive terms
8, 12, 16, 20, 24
$\therefore$ Next term = 91.

23. Difference between two consecutive terms are
288, 144, 72, 36, = 18
$\therefore$ Next term = 190.

24. Difference between two consecutive numbers are
4, 8, 16, $\boxed{32}$
$\therefore$ Clearly next difference = 32
$\therefore$ Required number = 61

25. Difference between two consecutive terms are
12, 24 , 36, 48, $\boxed{60}$
Next difference = 60
$\therefore$ Required number = 225.

27. Clearly difference between two terms is $\frac{1}{4}$

$\therefore$ Required number = $\frac{7}{4}+\frac{1}{4}=2$

28. Difference between two consecutive terms is
1, 8 , 27, 64, ... or $(1)^3$, $(2)^3$, $(3)^3$, $(4)^3$, $\boxed{5^3}$, ...
Clearly next difference = 5^3 = 125
$\therefore$ Required number = 242

34. The sequence followed in the series is ÷ 5, – 5 which is repeated.

900   180   175   35   30   6   1

÷ 5   – 5   ÷ 5   – 5   ÷ 5   – 5

$\therefore$ 900 should be in place of 905.

35. The numbers in the series are divided by numbers in reverse order starting from 6 to get the next number.

5040   840   168   42   14   7

÷ 6   ÷ 5   ÷ 4   ÷ 3   ÷ 2

$\therefore$ 168 should be in place of 160.

36. The numbers in this series are multiplied by 11 to get the next number.

3   33   363   3993   43923

× 11   × 11   × 11   × 11

$\therefore$ 33 should be in place of 32.

37. 3 is the only prime number in the series.

38. There are two alternate series :

+2   +2   +2   +2

0   1   2   2   4   4   6   8   8   16

× 2   × 2   × 2   × 2

Series I : 0, 2, 4, 6, 8, (addition of 2)
Series II : 1, 2, 4, 8, 16 (multiplication by 2)
$\therefore$ 16 should be in place of 10.

39. The sequence in the series is +7, +4 which is repeated, *i.e.,*

5   12   16   23   27

+7   +4   +7   +4

$\therefore$ 23 should be in place of 24.

40. All other numbers are divisible by 3.

2 Number System

Real Numbers

Rational numbers and irrational numbers taken together are known as **Real Numbers**. The set of real numbers is denoted by R. Thus, every real number is either a rational number or an irrational number.

Real numbers are classified into different system of numbers like natural numbers, whole numbers, integers, rational numbers and irrational numbers.

Rational Numbers

A rational number is a number which can be expressed in the form of $\frac{p}{q}$, where, p and q are integers without any common factor and denominator q is not zero. For example: $\frac{3}{5}, \frac{5}{2}, \frac{-2}{9}, -2, 4, 1, \frac{1}{3}$ are rational numbers.

Irrational Number

A number is irrational if and only if its decimal representation is non-terminating and non-repeating. $\sqrt{2}, \sqrt{3}, \sqrt{5},$ are irrational numbers.

Natural Numbers

Taking numbers starting from 1 are known as natural numbers *i.e.,* 1, 2, 3, ... ∞.

Whole Numbers

All natural numbers along with zero are known as Whole numbers *i.e.,* 0, 1, 2, 3, 4, 5, ... ∞.

Integers

Taking numbers both +ve and –ve along with zero are known as integers *i.e.,* – ∞, ... – 4, – 3, – 2, – 1, 0, 1, 2, ... ∞.

Surds

$\sqrt[n]{a}$ is known as a surd where 'n' is the order of surd and 'a' is radical. *e.g.,* $\sqrt{3}, \sqrt[5]{7}$ etc.

Euclid's Algorithm

For any two given positive integers a and b there exist unique whole numbers q and r.

Such that, $a = bq + r$ where, $0 \le r < b$

Here, we call a as dividend, b as divisor, q as quotient and r as remainder.

Dividend = (divisor × quotient) + remainder

Every positive even integer is in the form $2q$ and every positive odd integer is in the form $(2q + 1)$ where q is a positive integer.

Laws of Radicals:

1. If a is irrational, then $\sqrt[n]{a}$ is not a surd.
2. If $\sqrt[n]{a}$ is rational, then $\sqrt[n]{a}$ is not a surd.
3. $\left(\sqrt[n]{a}\right)^n = a$
4. $\sqrt[n]{ab} = \sqrt[n]{a} \cdot \sqrt[n]{b}$
5. $\sqrt[m]{\sqrt[n]{a}} = \sqrt[mn]{a} = \sqrt[n]{\sqrt[m]{a}}$
6. $\sqrt[n]{\frac{a}{b}} = \frac{\sqrt[n]{a}}{\sqrt[n]{b}}$
7. $\left(\sqrt[n]{a}\right)^m = \sqrt[n]{a^m}$
8. Every surd is an irrational number but every irrational number is not a surd.
9. When the product of two surds is a rational number then each of the two surds is called a rationalising factor of the other.
10. A surd which has unity only as rational factor is called a pure surd.
11. A surd which has a rational factor other than unity is called a mixed surd.

Some Important Formulae

1. $(a + b)^2 = a^2 + 2ab + b^2$
2. $(a - b)^2 = a^2 - 2ab + b^2$
3. $a^2 - b^2 = (a + b)(a - b)$
4. $a^2 + b^2 = (a + b)^2 - 2ab$
5. $(a + b + c)^2 = a^2 + b^2 + c^2 + 2ab + 2bc + 2ca$
6. $(a + b)^3 = a^3 + 3a^2b + 3ab^2 + b^3$
   $= a^3 + b^3 + 3ab(a + b)$
7. $(a - b)^3 = a^3 - 3a^2b + 3ab^2 - b^3$
   $= a^3 - b^3 - 3ab(a - b)$

8. $a^3 + b^3 = (a + b)(a^2 - ab + b^2)$ [for factorisation]

$a^3 + b^3 = (a + b)^3 - 3ab(a + b)$

[for evaluation when $a+b$ and ab are given]

9. $a^3 - b^3 = (a - b)(a^2 + ab + b^2)$

[for factorisation]

$a^3 - b^3 = (a - b)^3 + 3ab(a - b)$ [for evaluation]

10. If $a + b + c = 0$; then $a^3 + b^3 + c^3 = 3abc$

Rules of Simplification

Simplification means expressing in a simpler form. In order to simplify the arithmetic expression we use the operations in the following order which is easily remembered as "BODMAS".

1. B → Bracket [{(–)}]
2. O → Of — of
3. D → Division — ÷
4. M → Multiplication — ×
5. A → Addition — +
6. S → Subtraction — –

'BODMAS' rule is very important and should be followed strictly while solving problems on simplification. Any deviation from this rule will lead to wrong answer.

Brackets

Brackets are of four types and they are operated in the following order.

1. Vi	→	Vinuculum	—
2. Ci	→	Circular Bracket	( )
3. Cu	→	Curly Bracket	{ }
4. Sq	→	Square Bracket	[ ]

Note : This order of brackets (Vi Ci Cu Sq) is fixed and not variable.

Laws of Exponents

If a, b be any rational numbers different from zero and m and n be any integers, then

(i) $a^m \times b^m = (a \times b)^m$ *(ii)* $a^m \times a^n = a^{m+n}$

(iii) $a^m \div a^n = a^{m-n}$ *(iv)* $(a^m)^n = a^{mn}$

(v) $a^{\frac{1}{m}} \times b^{\frac{1}{m}} = (a \times b)^{\frac{1}{m}} = \sqrt[m]{a \times b} = \sqrt[m]{a} \times \sqrt[m]{b}$

(vi) $\frac{1}{a^m} = a^{-m}$

(vii) $a^{\frac{m}{n}} = (a^m)^{\frac{1}{n}}$

(viii) $a^{-\frac{m}{n}} = \frac{1}{a^{\frac{m}{n}}} = \frac{1}{(a^m)^{\frac{1}{n}}}$

> **Attention students**
>
> *(i)* Zero raisd to any power equals zero.
>
> *(ii)* Any number raised to the power zero equals 1
>
> *(iii)* A negative exponent has a special meaning. So, always look carefully in the questions of power and indeces.

Square

When a number is multiplied by itself, the product is called the squre of the number.

Square Root

The square root of a given number is that number which when multiplied by itself is equal to the given number.

We know that if we multiply 3 by 3, we get 9. Here we say that 9 is the square of 3, *i.e.*, $9 = 3^2$

In other words, we express this fact by saying that 3 is the square root of 9, *i.e.*, $3 = \sqrt{9}$

The symbol $(\sqrt{\ })$ is called *radical sign* and is used to represent the square root of a given number.

Attention students

(i) The numbers which end with 2, 3, 7 or 8, cannot be the complete square roots.

(ii) If a number ends with 1, its square root will end with either 1 or 9

(iii) If a number ends with 4, its square root will end with either 2 or 8

(iv) If a number ends with 5, its square root will end with 5

(v) If a number ends with 6, its square root will end with 4 or 6

(vi) If a number ends with 9 its square root will end with 3 or 7.

Example 1 : Find the square root of 289

Sol : $289 = 17 \times 17$

$\therefore$ Square root of 289 $= \sqrt{289} = \sqrt{17 \times 17} = 17$

Example 2 : Find the square root of 225

Sol : $225 = \underline{5 \times 5} \times \underline{3 \times 3}$

$\therefore$ Square root of 225 $= 5 \times 3 = 15$

Example 3 : Find the square root of 17956

Sol :

```
   1 | 1 79 56 ( 134
     | 1
     |------
  23 |   79
     |   69
     |------
 264 |  1056
     |  1056
     |------
     |    ×
```

$\therefore$ Square root of 17956 = 134

Example 4 : Find the square root of 0.9.

```
 9     .90 00 00 ( .948
        81
 184     900
         736
 1888    16400
         15104
          1296
```

∴ Square root of .9 correct to 2 decimal place = .948 = .95

Short-cut Method

$$\because \quad \sqrt{N-n} = \sqrt{N} - \frac{1}{2}\frac{n}{\sqrt{N}} \text{ (App)}$$

$$\therefore \quad \sqrt{.9} = \sqrt{1-.1} = \sqrt{1} - \frac{1}{2}\frac{.1}{\sqrt{1}}$$

$$= 1 - \frac{.1}{2}$$

$$= 1 - .05 = .95$$

Cube

When a number is multiplied by itself three times, the product is known as cube of the number.

Cube root

The cube root of a number is the number, the third power of which gives the number in question. The symbol used for cube root is '$\sqrt[3]{\ }$'. We can find the cube root of a number by prime factorization method only.

For example, 2 × 2 × 2 = 8

∴ Cube root of 8 is 2

Therefore cube root of 27 = $\sqrt[3]{27} = \sqrt[3]{3 \times 3 \times 3} = 3$

Cube root of 64 = $\sqrt[3]{64} = \sqrt[3]{4 \times 4 \times 4} = 4$

Cube root of 216 = $\sqrt[3]{216} = \sqrt[3]{6 \times 6 \times 6} = 6$

Attention Students

(i) The cube root of a negative number is a real number while the square root of a negative number is not a real number.

(ii) If a number ends with 0 or 1 or 4 or 5 or 6 or 9, its cube root will end with same digit.

(iii) If a number ends with 2 or 3 or 7 or 8, its cube roots will end with 8 or 7 or 3 or 2 respectively.

FRACTION

The relation to represent some part of the body to the whole body is known *Fraction*. For example $\frac{2}{5}$ is a fraction where 2 is the numerator and 5 is the denominator.

Attention Students

(i) A fraction is also called a rational number.

(ii) A fraction is unity when its numerator and denominator are equal.

(iii) When a fraction is reduced in its lowest term, its numerator and denomenator are prime to each other, *i.e.*, they have no common factor.

(iv) The value of fraction is not altered by multiplying or dividing the numerator and the denominator by the same number.

Vulgar or Common Fraction : The fraction such as $\frac{2}{9}, \frac{7}{11}, \frac{3}{10}, \frac{9}{100}$ are called vulgar fraction.

Decimal Fraction : Fractions in which denomenators are power of 10 are called decimal fractions.

For example : $\frac{1}{10}, \frac{1}{100}, \frac{7}{1000}$ etc.

Here $\frac{1}{10}$ is 1 tenths, written as .1

$$\frac{1}{100} = .01$$

$$\frac{7}{1000} = .007$$

$$\frac{13}{100} = .13 \text{ and so on.}$$

Converting a Decimal into a Vulgar Fraction

First of all write down the given number as numerator without the decimal point, and for the denominator write 1 followed by as many zeros as many are there figures after the decimal point. Now reduce the fraction to its lowest terms.

Ex : *(i)* $0.63 = \frac{63}{100}$

(ii) $0.54 = \frac{54}{100} = \frac{27}{50}$

(iii) $3.013 = 3\frac{013}{1000} = 3\frac{13}{1000}$

Attention Students

Additing zeros to the extreme right of a decimal fraction does not change its value.

For example : 0.8 = 0.80 = 0.80000

Relationship Between Two Numbers and Their L.C.M. and H.C.F.

Product of the H.C.F. and the L.C.M. of two numbers is equal to the product of the given numbers.

i.e., 1st number × 2nd number = H.C.F. × L.C.M.

If in a decimal number a digit or a set of digits is repeated again and again, the decimal is known as recurring decimal.

For example : *(i)* $2.666... = 2.\dot{6}$

(ii) $1.363636... = 1.\dot{3}\dot{6}$ or $1.\overline{36}$

(iii) $7.3424242... = 7.3\dot{4}\dot{2}$ or $7.3\overline{42}$

Recurring decimal numbers are of two types :

(i) pure and *(ii)* Mixed

(i) **Pure recurring decimals :** A decmial fraction in which all the figures after the decimal point are repeated is called a pure recurring decimal. For example,

$0.\overline{3}$, $0.\overline{37}$, $3.\overline{4579}$ etc

(ii) **Mixed recurring decimals :** A decimal fraction in which at least one figure after the decimal point is not repeated is called a mixed recurring decimal. For example,

$0.3\overline{59}$, $0.29\overline{54}$, $0.2\dot{7}$ etc.

Conversion of Recurring into Vulgar Fraction

1. Pure recurring decimals

Rule : Put as many 9's in the denominator at the number of digits under recurring and delet the recurring sign.

An example, $0.\overline{5} = \frac{5}{9}$, $0.\overline{35} = \frac{35}{99}$

$0.\overline{24} = \frac{24}{99} = \frac{8}{33}$

2. Mixed Recurring Decimals

An example,

(i) $0.1\overline{8} =$

Here, numerator = 18 − 1 = 17

and denominator = 9 × 10 = 90

$\therefore \quad 0.1\dot{8} = \frac{18-1}{90} = \frac{17}{90}$

(ii) $0.2\dot{7}\dot{9}$

Here numerator = 279 − 2 = 277

and denominator = 99 × 10 = 990

$\therefore \quad 0.2\overline{79} = \frac{279-2}{990} = \frac{277}{990}$

(iii) $0.3\overline{56} = \frac{356-3}{99 \times 10} = \frac{353}{990}$

(iv) $2.53\dot{6} = 2 + \frac{536-53}{9 \times 100} = 2 + \frac{483}{900}$

$= 2 + \frac{161}{300} = 2\frac{161}{300}$

(v) $0.43\overline{213} = \frac{43213-43}{999 \times 100} = \frac{43170}{99900} = \frac{4317}{9990}$

(vi) $5.00\overline{983} = 5 + \frac{983}{999 \times 100}$

$= 5 + \frac{983}{99900} = 5\frac{983}{99900}$

MULTIPLE CHOICE QUESTIONS

1. 20% of ? = $\sqrt{225} + 45$

(*a*) 30 (*b*) 300
(*c*) 1200 (*d*) 80
(*e*) None of these

2. $\left(8\frac{24}{27} + 1\frac{1}{9}\right) \times ? = \frac{1}{10}$

(*a*) $\frac{1}{90}$ (*b*) $\frac{1}{10}$
(*c*) $\frac{1}{50}$ (*d*) $\frac{1}{1000}$
(*e*) None of these

3. 45% of 80 + 35% of 60 = 40% of 120 + ?

(*a*) 12 (*b*) 9
(*c*) 21 (*d*) 13
(*e*) None of these

4. $\frac{(69+15) \div 12}{5 \times 5 - 4} = ?$

(*a*) $\frac{1}{3}$ (*b*) $\frac{7}{5}$
(*c*) 35 (*d*) $1\frac{12}{10}$
(*e*) None of these

5. $\frac{\sqrt{324}}{1.5} = \frac{?}{\sqrt{256}}$

(*a*) 192 (*b*) 432
(*c*) 288 (*d*) 122
(*e*) None of these

6. $\frac{(272-32)(124+176)}{17 \times 15 - 15} = ?$

(*a*) 0 (*b*) 2.25
(*c*) 300 (*d*) 400
(*e*) None of these

7. $(16)^{1.75} = ?$

(*a*) 64 (*b*) $64\sqrt{2}$
(*c*) 128 (*d*) $128\sqrt{2}$
(*e*) None of these

8. (0.333 ...) × (0.444 ...) = ?
(*a*) 0.121212 ... (*b*) 1.333 ...
(*c*) 0.777 ... (*d*) 0.148148148 ...
(*e*) None of these

9. $\frac{\sqrt{31}-\sqrt{29}}{\sqrt{31}+\sqrt{29}} = ?$
(*a*) $60-2\sqrt{899}$ (*b*) $30-\sqrt{899}$
(*c*) $30+\sqrt{899}$ (*d*) $\frac{1}{30-\sqrt{899}}$
(*e*) None of these

10. If $(125)^x = 3125$, then *x* equals
(*a*) $\frac{3}{5}$ (*b*) $\frac{5}{3}$
(*c*) $\frac{1}{4}$ (*d*) $\frac{1}{5}$
(*e*) None of these

11. The value of $(0.6\dot{3}+0.\dot{3}\dot{7})$ is
(*a*) 1.01 (*b*) .101
(*c*) $1.\dot{0}\dot{1}$ (*d*) 1.001
(*e*) None of these

12. If $\frac{1}{3.718} = .2689$, then the value of $\frac{1}{.0003718}$ is
(*a*) 2689 (*b*) 2.689
(*c*) 26890 (*d*) .2689
(*e*) None of these

13. If $\frac{5+2\sqrt{3}}{7+4\sqrt{3}} = a+b\sqrt{3}$, then
(*a*) $a = 11, b = -6$ (*b*) $a = -6, b = 11$
(*c*) $a = -11, b = 6$ (*d*) $a = -11, b = -6$
(*e*) None of these

14. If $\frac{a}{b} = \frac{4}{5}$ and $\frac{b}{c} = \frac{15}{16}$, then $\frac{c^2-a^2}{c^2+a^2} = ?$
(*a*) $\frac{1}{7}$ (*b*) $\frac{7}{25}$
(*c*) $\frac{3}{4}$ (*d*) $\frac{1}{2}$
(*e*) None of these

15. $\frac{50}{?} = \frac{?}{12\frac{1}{2}}$
(*a*) $\frac{25}{2}$ (*b*) $\frac{4}{25}$
(*c*) 4 (*d*) 25
(*e*) None of these

16. (20 ÷ 5) ÷ 2 + (16 ÷ 8) × 2 + (10 ÷ 5) × (3 ÷ 2) = ?
(*a*) 9 (*b*) 12
(*c*) 15 (*d*) 18
(*e*) None of these

17. In an examination, a student was asked to find $\left(\frac{3}{4}\right)$ of a certain number. By mistake he found $\left(\frac{3}{14}\right)$ of it. His answer was 150 more than the correct answer. The given number is
(*a*) 180 (*b*) 240
(*c*) 280 (*d*) 380
(*e*) None of these

18. If we multiply a fraction by itself and divide the product by its reciprocal, the fraction thus obtained is $18\frac{26}{27}$. The original fraction is
(*a*) $\frac{8}{27}$ (*b*) $2\frac{2}{3}$
(*c*) $1\frac{1}{3}$ (*d*) $2\frac{3}{2}$
(*e*) None of these

19. $\sqrt{0.4} = ?$
(*a*) .02 (*b*) .2
(*c*) .002 (*d*) .1
(*e*) None of these

20. If $\sqrt{24} = 4.899$, then the value of $\sqrt{\frac{8}{3}}$ is
(*a*) 0.544 (*b*) 2.666
(*c*) 1.633 (*d*) 1.333
(*e*) None of these

21. $\frac{\sqrt{32}}{\sqrt{8}}+\frac{\sqrt{48}}{\sqrt{12}} = ?$
(*a*) $\sqrt{2}$ (*b*) 2
(*c*) 4 (*d*) 8
(*e*) 5

22. If $\sqrt{2^n} = 64$, then the value of *n* is
(*a*) 2 (*b*) 4
(*c*) 6 (*d*) 12
(*e*) 10

23. If $\sqrt{3} == 1.732$ and $\sqrt{2} = 1.414$, the vlue of $\frac{1}{\sqrt{3}+\sqrt{2}}$ is
(*a*) 0.064 (*b*) 0.308
(*c*) 0.318 (*d*) 2.146
(*e*) None of these

24. Which of the following is equivalent to $\frac{15}{25}$?
(*a*) $\frac{150}{25}$ (*b*) $\frac{15}{250}$

(c) $\frac{3}{5}$ (d) $\frac{60}{75}$
(e) None of these

25. If $\frac{9*3}{3*7}$ is equivalent to $\frac{9}{7}$, the sign * is replaced by:
(a) ÷ (b) ×
(c) + (d) –
(e) None of these

26. $\frac{5}{6}$ of an hour is equal to
(a) half an hour (b) 40 minutes
(c) 50 minutes (d) 55 minutes
(e) None of these

27. An aircraft uses 2/5 of its fuel in flying 1,250 kilometres. The distance travelled on remaining fuel is
(a) 1875 km (b) 2125 km
(c) 250 km (d) 475 km
(e) None of these

28. If $\frac{4}{3} * \frac{3}{4} = \frac{16}{9}$, then * means
(a) + (b) –
(c) × (d) ÷
(e) None of these

29. Which of the following is the largest fraction?
$\frac{3}{15}, \frac{5}{20}, \frac{8}{64}, \frac{25}{1000}$
(a) $\frac{3}{15}$ (b) $\frac{5}{20}$
(c) $\frac{8}{64}$ (d) $\frac{25}{1000}$
(e) None of these

30. Six times x increased by 12 is equal to
(a) $\frac{x}{2}$ (b) $2x$
(c) $6x + 12$ (d) $12x + 6$
(e) None of these

31. Five times y diminished by 20 is equal to
(a) $5y - 20$ (b) $5y + 20$
(c) $y/4$ (d) $4y$
(e) None of these

32. The number less than 15 by 7 is
(a) $15x - 7$ (b) 15/7
(c) 15 (d) 8
(e) None of these

33. If 21 is add to four times a number, the result is 57. The number is
(a) 7 (b) 8
(c) 9 (d) 10
(e) 12

34. A number, the sum of whose fourth and fifth parts exceeds their third part by 28, is
(a) 120 (b) 240
(c) 220 (d) 160
(e) 230

35. Which fraction should be added to the sum of $5\frac{3}{4}$, $4\frac{4}{5}$ and $7\frac{3}{8}$ to make the result a whole number?
(a) $\frac{1}{40}$ (b) $\frac{2}{40}$
(c) $\frac{3}{40}$ (d) $\frac{4}{40}$
(e) None of these

36. If $\left(\frac{a}{b}\right)^{x-1} = \left(\frac{b}{a}\right)^{x-3}$, then the value of x is:
(a) $\frac{7}{2}$ (b) 2
(c) 1 (d) 1/2
(e) None of these

37. The value of $\frac{(243)^{0.13} \times (243)^{0.07}}{(7)^{0.25} \times (49)^{0.075} \times (343)^{0.2}}$ is:
(a) $2\frac{2}{7}$ (b) $1\frac{3}{7}$
(c) $\frac{7}{3}$ (d) 3/7
(e) None of these

38. $(25)^{7.5} \times (5)^{2.5} \div (125)^{1.5} = 5^?$
(a) 17.5 (b) 16
(c) 13 (d) 8.5
(e) 5.8

39. $(64)^{-1/2} - (-32)^{-4/5} = ?$
(a) $\frac{3}{16}$ (b) $\frac{1}{16}$
(c) $\frac{3}{8}$ (d) $\frac{1}{8}$
(e) None of these

40. $(17)^{3.5} \times (17)^? = 17^8$
(a) 4.5 (b) 4.25
(c) 2.75 (d) 2.5
(e) 5.2

41. $(1000)^7 \div 10^{18} = ?$
(a) 10000 (b) 1000
(c) 100 (d) 10
(e) None of these

42. $(0.04)^{-1.5} = ?$
(a) 625 (b) 250
(c) 125 (d) 25
(e) None of these

43. $(256)^{0.16} \times (256)^{0.09} = ?$
(a) 256.25 (b) 64
(c) 16 (d) 4
(e) None of these

44. If $2^{2n-1} = \frac{1}{8^{n-3}}$, then find the value of *n*.
(a) 3 (b) 2
(c) 0 (d) −2
(e) None of these

45. If $5\sqrt{5} \times 5^3 \div 5^{-3/2} = 5^{a+2}$, then find the value of *a*.
(a) 8 (b) 6
(c) 5 (d) 4
(e) 7

46. What is the value of $(4^3)^4 \div (4^2)^3$?
(a) $(4)^5$ (b) $(4)^8$
(c) $(4)^6$ (d) $(4)^{18}$
(e) None of these

47. What is the value of *m* in the following

$$\frac{\sqrt{324}}{\sqrt{49}} \times \frac{\sqrt{676}}{\sqrt{169}} \times \frac{126}{\sqrt{81}} = m$$

(a) 18 (b) 72
(c) 36 (d) 65
(e) None of these

48. What is the smallest number by which 338 is multiplied or divided to make a perfect square?
(a) 13 (b) 4
(c) 6 (d) 2
(e) None of these

49. The sum of whole numbers from 1 – 20 is
(a) 90 (b) 110
(c) 210 (d) 200
(e) None of these

50. What is the value of $(\sqrt{7}+\sqrt{5})(\sqrt{7}-\sqrt{5})$?
(a) 1 (b) 2
(c) 5 (d) 3
(e) None of these

51. The rationalising factor of $(a+\sqrt{b})$ is
(a) $a-\sqrt{b}$ (b) $\sqrt{a}-b$
(c) $\sqrt{a}-\sqrt{b}$ (d) 0
(e) None of these

52. The value of $\left(\frac{x^a}{x^b}\right)^{a+b} \times \left(\frac{x^b}{x^c}\right)^{b+c} \times \left(\frac{x^c}{x^a}\right)^{c+a}$ is
(a) 1 (b) 0
(c) x^{abc} (d) *abc*
(e) None of these

53. If $\frac{2}{3}$ part of a number is 96 then what will be $\frac{3}{4}$ of the same number?
(a) 48 (b) 192
(c) 108 (d) 72
(e) 55

54. $\sqrt{3}$ into a surd of order 6 is
(a) $\sqrt[4]{27}$ (b) $\sqrt[2]{27}$
(c) $\sqrt[5]{9}$ (d) $\sqrt[6]{27}$
(e) None of these

55. The rationalising factor of $\sqrt[4]{5}$ is
(a) $\sqrt{5}$ (b) $\sqrt[3]{5}$
(c) $\sqrt[4]{125}$ (d) $\sqrt[3]{125}$
(e) None of these

56. The rationalising factor of $\sqrt[3]{49}$ is
(a) $\sqrt{49}$ (b) $\sqrt[3]{7}$
(c) 0 (d) 1
(e) None of these

57. $\sqrt[5]{4}$ into a surd of order 10 is
(a) $\sqrt[10]{16}$ (b) $\sqrt[10]{8}$
(c) $\sqrt[10]{64}$ (d) $\sqrt[10]{4}$
(e) None of these

58. If $\sqrt{2^{x-3}} = 16$, then the value of *x* is
(a) 5 (b) 4
(c) 8 (d) 11
(e) None of these

59. What is the value of $0.\overline{57}$
(a) $\frac{57}{10}$ (b) $\frac{77}{99}$
(c) $\frac{19}{33}$ (d) $\frac{52}{9}$
(e) None of these

60. If $4^{2x} = \frac{1}{32}$, then the value of *x* is
(a) $\frac{5}{4}$ (b) $-\frac{5}{4}$
(c) $\frac{3}{4}$ (d) $-\frac{5}{2}$
(e) None of these

61. If $\left(x+\frac{1}{x}\right)=5$, then $\left(x^2+\frac{1}{x^2}\right)$ is equal to:

(*a*) 20 (*b*) 24
(*c*) 27 (*d*) 23
(*e*) None of these

62. If $\left(x+\frac{1}{x}\right)=4$, then $\left(x^4+\frac{1}{x^4}\right)$ is equal to:

(*a*) 190 (*b*) 180
(*c*) 193 (*d*) 194
(*e*) None of these

63. If $\left(x^2+\frac{1}{x^2}\right)=66$, then $\left(x-\frac{1}{x}\right)$ is equal to:

(*a*) 6 (*b*) 12
(*c*) 8 (*d*) 9
(*e*) None of these

64. If $a + b = 8$, $a - b = 4$, then $a^2 + b^2$ is equal to:

(*a*) 20 (*b*) 40
(*c*) 10 (*d*) 30
(*e*) None of these

65. If $x^2 + 5x - 2k$, is exactly divisible by $(x - 1)$, then the value of k is:

(*a*) 1 (*b*) 2
(*c*) 3 (*d*) 4
(*e*) None of these

ANSWERS

1	2	3	4	5	6	7	8	9	10
(*b*)	(*e*)	(*b*)	(*a*)	(*a*)	(*c*)	(*c*)	(*d*)	(*b*)	(*b*)
11	**12**	**13**	**14**	**15**	**16**	**17**	**18**	**19**	**20**
(*c*)	(*a*)	(*a*)	(*b*)	(*d*)	(*a*)	(*c*)	(*b*)	(*b*)	(*c*)
21	**22**	**23**	**24**	**25**	**26**	**27**	**28**	**29**	**30**
(*b*)	(*d*)	(*c*)	(*c*)	(*b*)	(*c*)	(*a*)	(*d*)	(*b*)	(*c*)
31	**32**	**33**	**34**	**35**	**36**	**37**	**38**	**39**	**40**
(*a*)	(*d*)	(*c*)	(*b*)	(*c*)	(*b*)	(*d*)	(*c*)	(*b*)	(*a*)
41	**42**	**43**	**44**	**45**	**46**	**47**	**48**	**49**	**50**
(*b*)	(*c*)	(*d*)	(*b*)	(*d*)	(*c*)	(*b*)	(*d*)	(*c*)	(*b*)
51	**52**	**53**	**54**	**55**	**56**	**57**	**58**	**59**	**60**
(*a*)	(*a*)	(*c*)	(*d*)	(*c*)	(*b*)	(*a*)	(*d*)	(*c*)	(*b*)
61	**62**	**63**	**64**	**65**					
(*d*)	(*d*)	(*c*)	(*b*)	(*c*)					

EXPLANATORY ANSWERS

2. $\left(8\frac{24}{27}+1\frac{1}{9}\right)\times ? = \frac{1}{10}$

or, $\left(9+\frac{24+3}{27}\right)\times ? = \frac{1}{10}$

or, $10 \times ? = \frac{1}{10}$ $\therefore\ ? = \frac{1}{100}$

7. $(16)^{1.75} = (2^4)^{175/100}$

$= (2^4)^{7/4} = 2^{\left(4\times\frac{7}{4}\right)} = 2^7 = 128$

9. $\frac{(\sqrt{31}-\sqrt{29})}{(\sqrt{31}+\sqrt{29})}\times\frac{(\sqrt{31}-\sqrt{29})}{(\sqrt{31}-\sqrt{29})}$

$= \frac{(\sqrt{31}-\sqrt{29})^2}{(31-29)} = \frac{31+29-2\sqrt{31}\times\sqrt{29}}{2}$

$= 30-\sqrt{899}$

10. $(125)^x = 3125 \Rightarrow 5^{3x} = 5^5$

$\Rightarrow 3x = 5 \Rightarrow x = \frac{5}{3}$

11. $0.\dot{6}\dot{3} = \frac{63}{99}$ and $0.\dot{3}\dot{7} = \frac{37}{99}$

$\therefore\ 0.\dot{6}\dot{3} + 0.\dot{3}\dot{7} = \frac{63}{99}+\frac{37}{99} = \frac{100}{99}$

$= 1\frac{1}{99} = 1.\dot{0}\dot{1}$

12. $\frac{1}{0.0003718} = \frac{10000}{3.718}$

$= 10000 \times .2689 = 2689$

13. $\frac{5+2\sqrt{3}}{7+4\sqrt{3}} = \frac{(5+2\sqrt{3})}{(7+4\sqrt{3})}\times\frac{(7-4\sqrt{3})}{(7-4\sqrt{3})}$

$= \frac{35-24+14\sqrt{3}-20\sqrt{3}}{(49-48)}$

$$= 11-6\sqrt{3}$$

Thus, $a+b\sqrt{3} = 11-6\sqrt{3}$

Hence, $a = 11$ and $b = -6$

15. Let, $\dfrac{50}{x} = \dfrac{x}{\frac{25}{2}}$

$\Rightarrow \quad x^2 = 50\times\dfrac{25}{2} = 625$

$\Rightarrow \quad x = \sqrt{625} = 25$

17. $\dfrac{3}{4}x-\dfrac{3}{14}x = 150$

$\Rightarrow \quad \dfrac{15}{28}x = 150$

$\Rightarrow \quad x = 150\times\dfrac{28}{15} = 280$

18. $x\times x\div\dfrac{1}{x} = 18\dfrac{26}{27}$

$\Rightarrow \quad x^3 = \dfrac{512}{27}$

$\Rightarrow \quad x^3 = \left(\dfrac{8}{3}\right)^3$

$\Rightarrow \quad x = \dfrac{8}{3} = 2\dfrac{2}{3}.$

21. $\dfrac{\sqrt{32}+\sqrt{48}}{\sqrt{8}+\sqrt{12}} = \dfrac{\sqrt{16\times2}+\sqrt{16\times3}}{\sqrt{4\times2}+\sqrt{4\times3}}$

$$= \frac{4\sqrt{2}+4\sqrt{3}}{2\sqrt{2}+2\sqrt{3}} = \frac{4(\sqrt{2}+\sqrt{3})}{2(\sqrt{2}+\sqrt{3})} = 2$$

22. $\sqrt{2^n} = 64 = 2^6 \Rightarrow 2^{n/2} = 2^6$

$\Rightarrow \quad \dfrac{n}{2} = 6$ or, $n = 12$

23. $\dfrac{1}{\sqrt{3}+\sqrt{2}} = \dfrac{1}{(\sqrt{3}+\sqrt{2})}\times\dfrac{(\sqrt{3}-\sqrt{2})}{(\sqrt{3}-\sqrt{2})} = \left(\dfrac{\sqrt{3}-\sqrt{2}}{3-2}\right)$

$$= \sqrt{3}-\sqrt{2} = 1.732 - 1.414 = 0.318$$

27. Remaining fuel $= 1-\dfrac{2}{5} = \dfrac{5-2}{5} = \dfrac{3}{5}$

Distance flown by $\dfrac{2}{5}$ of fuel = 1250 km.

Distance flown by full fuel $= \dfrac{1250}{2/5} = \dfrac{1250\times5}{2}$ km.

Distance flown by $\dfrac{3}{5}$ of fuel $= \dfrac{1250\times5\times3}{2\times5} = 1875$ km.

29. $\dfrac{3}{15} = \dfrac{1}{5}, \dfrac{8}{64} = \dfrac{1}{8}, \dfrac{5}{20} = \dfrac{1}{4}, \dfrac{25}{1000} = \dfrac{1}{40}$

Now, the fractions are $\dfrac{1}{5}, \dfrac{1}{4}, \dfrac{1}{8}, \dfrac{1}{40}$

$\therefore$ The largest fraction is $\dfrac{1}{4} = \dfrac{5}{20}$

33. Let the number is x

$\therefore \quad 4x + 21 = 57$ or, $4x = 57 - 21 = 36$

or, $\quad x = \dfrac{36}{4} = 9$

34. Let the number is x.

$\therefore \quad \dfrac{x}{4}+\dfrac{x}{5} = \dfrac{x}{3}+28$

$$\frac{9x}{20} = \frac{x}{3}+28$$

or, $\quad \dfrac{9x}{20}-\dfrac{x}{3} = 28$ or, $\dfrac{27x-20x}{60} = 28$

$\therefore \quad x = \dfrac{28\times60}{7} = 240$

36. Here, $\left(\dfrac{a}{b}\right)^{x-1} = \left(\dfrac{b}{a}\right)^{x-3}$

$\Rightarrow \quad x - 1 = 3 - x$

$\Rightarrow \quad 2x = 4$

$\therefore \quad x = 2$

37. $\dfrac{(243)^{0.13}\times(243)^{0.07}}{(7)^{0.25}\times(49)^{0.075}\times(343)^{0.2}} = \dfrac{(3^5)^{0.13}\times(3^5)^{0.07}}{(7)^{0.25}\times(7^2)^{0.075}\times(7^3)^{0.2}}$

$$= \frac{(3)^{0.65}\times(3)^{0.35}}{(7)^{0.25}\times(7)^{0.15}\times(7)^{0.6}} = \frac{(3)^{(0.65+0.35)}}{(7)^{(0.25+0.15+0.6)}} = \frac{3^1}{7^1} = \frac{3}{7}$$

38. $(25)^{7.5}\times(5)^{2.5}\div(125)^{1.5}$

$$= (5^2)^{7.5}\times(5)^{2.5}\div(5^3)^{1.5}$$
$$= 5^{15}\times5^{2.5}\div5^{4.5}$$
$$= 5^{(15+2.5-4.5)} = 5^{13}$$

Now, $\quad 5^? = 5^{13}$

$\therefore \quad ? = 13$

39. $(64)^{-1/2} - (-32)^{-4/5}$

$$= (2^6)^{-1/2} - (-2^5)^{-4/5}$$
$$= 2^{-3} - (-2)^{-4}$$
$$= \frac{1}{8}-\frac{1}{(-2)^4} = \frac{1}{8}-\frac{1}{16} = \frac{1}{16}$$

44. Here, $2^{2n-1} = \frac{1}{8^{n-3}}$

$\Rightarrow \quad 2^{2n-1} = (2^3)^{3-n}$

$\Rightarrow \quad 2^{2n-1} = 2^{9-3n}$

$\Rightarrow \quad 2n - 1 = 9 - 3n$

$\Rightarrow \quad 5n = 10$

$\Rightarrow \quad n = 2$

47. $\frac{\sqrt{324}}{\sqrt{49}} \times \frac{\sqrt{676}}{\sqrt{169}} \times \frac{126}{\sqrt{81}} = m$

$\frac{18}{7} \times \frac{26}{13} \times \frac{126}{9} = m$

$m = 72.$

52. $\left(\frac{x^a}{x^b}\right)^{a+b} \times \left(\frac{x^b}{x^c}\right)^{b+c} \times \left(\frac{x^c}{x^a}\right)^{c+a}$

$= (x^{a-b})^{a+b} \times (x^{b-c})^{b+c} \times (x^{c-a})^{c+a}$

$= x^{a^2-b^2} \times x^{b^2-c^2} \times x^{c^2-a^2}$

$= x^{a^2-b^2+b^2-c^2+c^2-a^2}$

$= x^0 = 1.$

53. Let, $\frac{2x}{3} = 96$

$x = \frac{96 \times 3}{2} = 144$

$\therefore \quad \frac{3}{4} \times 144 = 3 \times 36 = 108$

60. $4^{2x} = \frac{1}{32} \Rightarrow (2^2)^{2x} = \frac{1}{2^5}$

$\Rightarrow \quad 2^{4x} = 2^{-5}$

$\Rightarrow \quad 4x = -5$

$x = \frac{-5}{4}$

61. $\because \left(x + \frac{1}{x}\right) = 5$

$\therefore \quad x^2 + \frac{1}{x^2} = \left(x + \frac{1}{x}\right)^2 - 2$

$= 25 - 2 = 23$

63. $\because \quad x^2 + \frac{1}{x^2} = 66 = 64 + 2$

$x^2 + \frac{1}{x^2} - 2 = 64$

$\left(x - \frac{1}{x}\right)^2 = (8)^2$

$\therefore \quad x - \frac{1}{x} = 8$

65. $\because$ $x - 1$ is a factor of $x^2 + 5x - 2k$

$\therefore \quad x - 1 = 0$

$x = 1$

$(1)^2 + 5(1) - 2k = 0$

$6 - 2k = 0$

$2k = 0$

$\therefore \quad k = 3.$

3

L.C.M. and H.C.F.

L.C.M.

Multiple : A number is said to be multiple of other when it is exactly divisible by the other.

Common multiple : A common multiple of two or more numbers is a number which is exactly divisible by each of them. For example, for 2 and 3, common multiples are 6, 12, 18, 24 and so on.

Explanation:

Consider the two numbers 2 and 3

Multiple of 2 are 2, 4, 6, 8, 10, 12, ...

Multiple of 3 are 3, 6, 9, 12, 15, ...

$\therefore$ Common multiples are 6, 12, 18, ...

Least Common Multiple (L.C.M.) : L.C.M. of two or more given numbers is the least number which is exactly divisible by each of them. For example,

6 is a common multiple of 2 and 3

12 is also common multiple of 2 and 3

18 is also common multiple of 2 and 3

But 6 is the least common multiple (L.C.M.) of 2 and 3.

Methods to find out L.C.M.

L.C.M. of two or more given numbers is determined by following two methods:

1. By prime factorization method
2. By division method

1. By prime factorization method : Resolve the given numbers into their prime factors and then find the product of the highest power of all the factors that occur in the given numbers. This product will be the L.C.M.

Example 1 : Find the L.C.M. of 40, 50, 60 and 80.

Sol :

$$40 = 2 \times 2 \times 2 \times 5 = 2^3 \times 5$$
$$50 = 2 \times 5 \times 5 = 2 \times 5^2$$
$$60 = 2 \times 2 \times 3 \times 5 = 2^2 \times 3 \times 5$$
$$80 = 2 \times 2 \times 2 \times 2 \times 5 = 2^4 \times 5$$

Here, the prime factors that occur in the given numbers are 2, 3 and 5 and their highest powers are respectively 2^4, 5^2 and 3.

Hence the required L.C.M. = $2^4 \times 3 \times 5^2$ = 1200.

2. By division method : This is the quicker method to find the prime factors and hence L.C.M.

For determining L.C.M. of the numbers 40, 50, 60 and 80, following process of division is adopted:

2	40, 50, 60, 80
2	20, 25, 30, 40
2	10, 25, 15, 20
5	5, 25, 15, 10
	1, 5, 3, 2

Now required L.C.M. = $2 \times 2 \times 2 \times 5 \times 5 \times 3 \times 2 = 1200$

L.C.M. of decimal : First of all, we find out the L.C.M. of numbers without decimal and then, we see the number in which decimal is given in the minimum digit from right to left. We put the decimal in our result which is equal to that number of digits.

Example : Find the L.C.M. of 0.6, 9.6 and 0.36.

Sol : The given numbers are equivalent to 0.60, 9.60 and 0.36.

Now, we find out the L.C.M. of 60, 960 and 36, which is equal to 2880.

Hence, the required L.C.M. = 28.80.

L.C.M. of fraction : The L.C.M. of two or more fractions is the least fraction or integer which is exactly divisible by each of them.

If $\frac{a}{b}, \frac{c}{d}, \frac{e}{f}$ be the proper fractions, then their L.C.M. is

given by $\dfrac{\text{L.C.M. of numerators } a, c, e}{\text{H.C.F. of denominators } b, d, f}$

An example : Find the L.C.M. of $\frac{1}{2}, \frac{3}{5}, \frac{4}{7}$ and $\frac{5}{12}$

Sol :

$$\text{L.C.M.} = \frac{\text{L.C.M. of } 1, 3, 4, 5}{\text{H.C.F. of } 2, 5, 7, 12}$$
$$= \frac{60}{1} = 60$$

H.C.F.

Factor : One number is said to be a factor of other when it divides the other exactly. Hence, 5 and 7 are factors of 35.

Common factor : A common factor of two or more numbers is a number that divides each of them exactly. Hence, 5 is a common factor of 15, 25, 35 and 55.

Highest Common Factor (H.C.F.) : H.C.F. of two or more numbers is the largest number by which each given number is divisible without leaving any remainder.

An example : It is required to find the H.C.F. of 6 and 8.

Factors of 6 are 1, 2, 3, 6 and
Factors of 8 are 1, 2, 4, 8

The common factors are 1, 2, but highest of these is 2. Hence, 2 is the H.C.F.

Note : *The terms Highest Common Divisor (H.C.D.) and Greatest Common Measure (G.C.M.) are often used in the sense of Highest Common Factor (H.C.F.)*

We can find H.C.F. by two methods:

1. By prime factorization method :

An example : Find the H.C.F. of 144, 336 and 2016.

Sol : $144 = 2 \times 2 \times 2 \times 2 \times 3 \times 3 = 2^4 \times 3^2$

$336 = 2 \times 2 \times 2 \times 2 \times 3 \times 7 = 2^4 \times 3 \times 7$

$2016 = 2 \times 2 \times 2 \times 2 \times 2 \times 7 \times 3 \times 3 = 2^5 \times 7 \times 3^2$

∴ H.C.F. of given numbers $= 2^4 \times 3 = 48$.

2. By division method : Divide the greater number by the smaller number, divide the divisor by the remainder, divide the remainder by the next remainder, and so on until no remainder is left. The last divisor is the required H.C.F.

An example : Find the H.C.F. of 48, 168 and 324.

Sol :

```
48 ) 168 ( 3
     144
     ----
      24 ) 48 ( 2
           48
           --
           ××
```

Thus, the H.C.F. of 48 and 168 is 24.

Now, we find out the H.C.F. of 24 and 324

```
24 ) 324 ( 13
     24
     --
     84
     72
     --
     12 ) 24 ( 2
          24
          --
          ××
```

∴ Required H.C.F. = 12.

H.C.F. of Decimals : First of all find the H.C.F. of the given numbers ignoring decimals and then put decimal at maximum digits from right to left.

An example : Find the H.C.F. of 0.0012, 1.6 and 2.8.

Sol : First we find the H.C.F. of 12, 16 and 28, which comes to 4.

So, H.C.F. of 0.0012, 1.6 and 2.8 will be 0.0004.

H.C.F. of Fractions : If $\frac{a}{b}, \frac{c}{d}, \frac{e}{f}, \ldots$ be the proper fraction, their H.C.F. is equal to $\frac{\text{H.C.F. of numerators}}{\text{L.C.M. of denominators}}$

An example : Find the H.C.F. of $\frac{54}{9}, 3\frac{9}{17}$ and $\frac{36}{51}$

Sol : Here, $\frac{54}{9} = \frac{6}{1}$; $3\frac{9}{17} = \frac{60}{17}$ and $\frac{36}{51} = \frac{12}{17}$

Hence, the fractions are $\frac{6}{1}, \frac{60}{17}$ and $\frac{12}{17}$

∴ $\text{H.C.F.} = \frac{\text{H.C.F. of } 6, 60, 12}{\text{L.C.M. of } 1, 17, 17} = \frac{6}{17}$.

Relationship Between Two Numbers and Their L.C.M. and H.C.F.

Product of the H.C.F. and the L.C.M. of two numbers is equal to the product of the given numbers.

i.e., 1st number × 2nd number = H.C.F. × L.C.M.

MULTIPLE CHOICE QUESTIONS

1. The H.C.F. of 72 and 18 is

(*a*) 9 (*b*) 72
(*c*) 18 (*d*) 36
(*e*) 38

2. The L.C.M. of 6, 8, 10 and 12 is

(*a*) 120 (*b*) 60
(*c*) 240 (*d*) 130
(*e*) 150

3. The H.C.F. of $\frac{5}{6}, \frac{6}{7}, \frac{7}{8}, \frac{8}{9}$ and $\frac{9}{10}$ is

(*a*) $\frac{1}{2420}$ (*b*) $\frac{1}{2520}$
(*c*) $\frac{1}{2660}$ (*d*) $\frac{1}{2540}$
(*e*) None of these

4. The L.C.M. of two numbers is 85 and their product is 1020. Their H.C.F. will be

(*a*) 16 (*b*) 27
(*c*) 12 (*d*) 22
(*e*) 23

5. The largest four-digit number divisible by 48, 60 and 64 will be
(*a*) 7200 (*b*) 9600
(*c*) 8400 (*d*) 10,000
(*e*) 11,000

6. L.C.M. of 24, 28, 36 and 44 is a multiple of 24 and which of the following numbers?
(*a*) 441 (*b*) 231
(*c*) 337 (*d*) 197
(*e*) 198

7. The smallest three-digit number completely divisible by 12, 18 and 24 will be
(*a*) 72 (*b*) 144
(*c*) 180 (*d*) 224
(*e*) 225

8. The largest three-digit number, when divided by 6, 9 and 12 leaves 1 as remainder in each case, will be
(*a*) 887 (*b*) 987
(*c*) 973 (*d*) 730
(*e*) 732

9. Two numbers are in the ratio of 8 : 15. If their H.C.F. is 4, the numbers are
(*a*) 32 and 60 (*b*) 16 and 30
(*c*) 80 and 150 (*d*) 64 and 120
(*e*) 90 and 140

10. The largest number that will divide 226 and 272 leaving 1 and 2 as remainders respectively, is
(*a*) 36 (*b*) 45
(*c*) 55 (*d*) 59
(*e*) 60

11. Which of the following is the greatest common divisor of 1170 and 102?
(*a*) 8 (*b*) 4
(*c*) 6 (*d*) 3
(*e*) 1

12. A number, when 3 is added to it, becomes divisible by 36, 45 and 50. The smallest such number is
(*a*) 987 (*b*) 798
(*c*) 986 (*d*) 897
(*e*) 898

13. The product of two numbers is 2160 and their H.C.F. is 12. How many such pairs of numbers can be possibly formed?
(*a*) 3 (*b*) 1
(*c*) 2 (*d*) 12
(*e*) None of these

14. The sum of two numbers is 216 and their H.C.F. is 27. These numbers are
(*a*) 60 and 90 (*b*) 81 and 135
(*c*) 64 and 128 (*d*) 30 and 84
(*e*) 65 and 130

15. The H.C.F. and the L.C.M. of two numbers are 50 and 250 respectively. On dividing one of these numbers by 2, 50 is obtained as quotient. The numbrs are
(*a*) 100, 125 (*b*) 80, 100
(*c*) 125, 100 (*d*) 200, 250
(*e*) 130, 120

16. The H.C.F. of three numbrs is 12. If the three numbers are in the ratio of 1 : 2 : 3, then the numbers are
(*a*) 14, 28, 42 (*b*) 12, 24, 36
(*c*) 15, 30, 45 (*d*) 24, 48, 72
(*e*) None of these

17. The greatest four-digit number completely divisible by 2, 3, 4 and 5 is
(*a*) 9960 (*b*) 9690
(*c*) 8990 (*d*) 9980
(*e*) 9999

18. Three bells ring respectively at an interval of 15 seconds, 20 seconds and 24 seconds. If they ring continuously for 12 minutes then how many times, during this period, will they ring together?
(*a*) 2 times (*b*) 6 times
(*c*) 5 times (*d*) 3 times
(*e*) 4 times

19. The smallest number, on being successively divided by 5, 6, 8, 9 and 12 leaves 1 as remainder in each case and is completely divisible by 13, will be
(*a*) 4603 (*b*) 6305
(*c*) 4503 (*d*) 3601
(*e*) 5032

20. If in the process of finding H.C.F. of two numbers by continued division method, 49 is the last divisor and quotients obtained (from the beginning) are 17, 3 and 2 respectively, then the numbers are
(*a*) 432 and 4929
(*b*) 343 and 5929
(*c*) 388 and 5880
(*d*) 472 and 5930
(*e*) None of these

ANSWERS

1	2	3	4	5	6	7	8	9	10
(*c*)	(*a*)	(*b*)	(*c*)	(*b*)	(*b*)	(*b*)	(*c*)	(*a*)	(*b*)
11	**12**	**13**	**14**	**15**	**16**	**17**	**18**	**19**	**20**
(*c*)	(*d*)	(*c*)	(*b*)	(*a*)	(*b*)	(*a*)	(*b*)	(*d*)	(*b*)

EXPLANATORY ANSWERS

1. $72 = 2 \times 2 \times 2 \times 3 \times 3$

$18 = 2 \times 3 \times 3$

$\therefore$ Common factors $= 2 \times 3 \times 3 = 18$

$\therefore$ H.C.F. = 18

2. $6 = 2 \times 3;\ 8 = 2 \times 2 \times 2$

$10 = 2 \times 5;\ 12 = 2 \times 2 \times 3$

It is clear that 2 occurs as prime factor maximum three times, 3 one time and 5 one time.

$\therefore$ required L.C.M. $= 2 \times 2 \times 2 \times 3 \times 5 = 120$

3. H.C.F. of $\frac{5}{6}, \frac{6}{7}, \frac{7}{8}, \frac{8}{9}$ and $\frac{9}{10}$

$= \frac{\text{H.C.F. of } 5, 6, 7, 8 \text{ and } 9}{\text{LCM of } 6, 7, 8, 9 \text{ and } 10}$

Now H.C.F. of 5, 6, 7, 8 and 9 = 1

and L.C.M. of 6, 7, 8, 9 and 10 = 2520

$\therefore$ Required H.C.F. $= \frac{1}{2520}$

4. L.C.M. of two numbers × H.C.F. of the numbers = Product of the numbers

$\therefore$ $85 \times$ H.C.F. $= 1020$

$\therefore$ H.C.F. $= \frac{1020}{85} = 12$

5. In this question LCM of the given numbers 48, 60, 64 has to be found out.

$48 = 2 \times 2 \times 2 \times 2 \times 3;$

$60 = 2 \times 2 \times 3 \times 5$

$64 = 2 \times 2 \times 2 \times 2 \times 2 \times 2$

$\therefore$ LCM $= 2 \times 2 \times 2 \times 2 \times 2 \times 2 \times 3 \times 5 = 960$

$\because$ Largest 4-digit number = 9999

$$
\begin{array}{r}
960\ )\ 9999\ (\ 10 \\
9600 \\
\hline
399
\end{array}
$$

$\therefore$ Required number $= 9999 - 399 = 9600$

7. L.C.M. of the given numbers 12, 18 and 24

$$
\begin{array}{r|l}
2 & 12,\ 18,\ 24 \\
\hline
2 & 6,\ 9,\ 12 \\
\hline
3 & 3,\ 9,\ 6 \\
\hline
 & 1,\ 3,\ 2
\end{array}
$$

$\therefore$ L.C.M. $= 2 \times 2 \times 3 \times 3 \times 2 = 72$

$\therefore$ The required 3-digit number which is smallest as well as divisible by 12, 18, and 24 will be $72 \times 2 = 144$

9. Let the numbers be $8x$ and $15x$

$8x = 2 \times 2 \times 2 \times x$

$15x = 3 \times 5 \times x$

$\therefore$ LCM of $8x$ and $15x = 2 \times 2 \times 2 \times x \times 3 \times 5$

$= 120x$

Now, 1st number × 2nd number = HCF × LCM

$8x \times 15x = 4 \times 120x$

$120x^2 = 4 \times 120x$

$x = \frac{4 \times 120x}{120x} = 4$

$\therefore$ Numbers are $8 \times 4 = 32$ and $15 \times 4 = 60$

10. $226 - 1 = 225$ and $272 - 2 = 270$

Now, HCF of 225 and 270

$$
\begin{array}{r}
225\ )\ 270\ (\ 1 \\
225 \\
\hline
45\ )\ 225\ (\ 5 \\
225 \\
\hline
\times
\end{array}
$$

$\therefore$ The required number is 45.

12. It is clear from the given conditions of the problem that the smallest number will be 3 less than the LCM of 36, 45 and 50

$\therefore$ LCM of 36, 45 and 50

$$
\begin{array}{r|l}
3 & 36,\ 45,\ 50 \\
\hline
2 & 12,\ 15,\ 50 \\
\hline
3 & 6,\ 15,\ 25 \\
\hline
5 & 2,\ 5,\ 25 \\
\hline
 & 2,\ 1,\ 5
\end{array}
$$

$\therefore$ LCM $= 3 \times 2 \times 3 \times 5 \times 2 \times 5 = 900$

$\therefore$ Required number $= 900 - 3 = 897$

13. Product of two number = their HCF × their LCM

$2160 = 12 \times$ LCM

$\therefore$ LCM $= \frac{2160}{12}$

$= 180$

Therefore such pairs of numbers in which product of numbers is 2160 and HCF is 12 will be only 2.

i.e., 12×180 and 36×60

4

Average

AVERAGE

The average of any number of quantities of the same kind can be found by dividing their sum by their number. Thus,

$$\text{Average} = \frac{\text{Sum of quantities}}{\text{No. of quantities}}$$

$$\text{Sum of quantities} = \text{Their average} \times \text{Their number}$$

$$\text{Number of quantities} = \frac{\text{Sum of quantities}}{\text{Their average}}$$

Attention students

(*i*) Out of three numbers, first number is P times of the second number and q times of the third number. If the average of all the three numbers is r, then the first number was

$$\frac{3pqr}{pq + p + q}$$

(*ii*) A car travels from one place to another at a speed of p km/h but return at the speed of q km/h, then its average speed during the whole journey is

$$\frac{2p \times q}{p + q} \text{ km/h}$$

(*iii*) The average age of ladies and gents of a town is p years. The average age of the ladies is q years and the average age of the gents is r years. If the total number of the ladies and the gents of the town is n, then the number of gents is

$$\frac{n(p - q)}{r - q}$$

(*iv*) The average age of M persons is p years. If one new person joins them, the average age is increased by q years.

Then the age of the new comer is

$p + (1 + M)q$ years.

(*v*) The average age of M persons is p years. If N persons join them, the average age is increased by q years. Then the age of new comers is

$$p + \left(1 + \frac{M}{N}\right)q \text{ years}$$

(*vi*) The average age of M persons is p years. If N persons leave, then the average age is increased by q years. Then the average age of going persons is

$$p + \left(1 - \frac{M}{N}\right)q \text{ years}$$

(*vii*) The average age of M persons is p years. If N persons join them, the average age is decreased by q years. Then the average age of new comers is

$$p - \left(1 + \frac{M}{N}\right)q \text{ years}$$

(*viii*) The average age of M persons in p years. If N persons leave them, the average age is decreased by q years. Then the average age of going persons is

$$p - \left(1 - \frac{M}{N}\right)q \text{ years}$$

(*ix*) In a group of M persons whose average age is increased by q years when a person of p years is replaced by a new man. Then the age of new comer is

p + Mq years

(*x*) The average temperature of Monday, Tuesday, and Wednesday was F°C. The average temperature for Tuesday, Wednesday and Thursday was L°C. If the temperature for Monday was f°C, what was the temperature for Thursday?

Tricks : Let the temperature for Thursday was l°C, then

$f - l$ = no.of days (F – L)

[Here no. of days = 3, *i.e.*, from Monday to Wednesday or from Tuesday to Thursday]

MULTIPLE CHOICE QUESTIONS

1. The average of the fractions $1\frac{1}{2}, 2\frac{1}{3}, 3\frac{1}{3}$ and $4\frac{5}{6}$ is

(a) 2 (b) $2\frac{1}{2}$
(c) 3 (d) 4
(e) 5

2. The average of first nine multiples of 3 is

(a) 12.0 (b) 12.5
(c) 15.0 (d) 18.5
(e) 17.5

3. The average of 13 numbers is 68, the average of first 7 numbers is 63 and the average of last 7 numbers is 70. What is the 7th number?

(a) 43 (b) 45
(c) 47 (d) 49
(e) 50

4. One-third of a certain journey was covered at the rate of 25 km per hour, one-fourth at the rate of 30 km per hour and the rest of the 30 km per hour. What is the average speed per hour for whole journey?

(a) $33\frac{1}{3}$ kmph (b) $44\frac{1}{4}$ kmph
(c) $22\frac{1}{2}$ kmph (d) 33 kmph
(e) None of these

5. Nine men went to a hotel. Eight of them spent ₹ 3 for each over their meals and the ninth spent ₹ 2 more than the average expenditure of all the nine. What is the total money spent by them?

(a) ₹ 29.25 (b) ₹ 29.50
(c) ₹ 29 (d) ₹ 30
(e) ₹ 32

6. Average age of 8 persons increased by 2 years, when two men whose ages are 20 and 24 years are replaced by two women. What is the average age of women?

(a) 30 years (b) 31 years
(c) 28 years (d) 33 years
(e) None of these

7. A man had seven children. When their average age was 12 years, the child who was 6 years of age died. What was the average of the surviving children 5 years after the death of the child?

(a) 15 years (b) 16 years
(c) 17 years (d) 18 years
(e) None of these

8. A batman has a certain average of runs for 16 innings. In the 17th innings, he makes a score of 85 runs thereby increasing his average by 3. What is the average after the 17th inning?

(a) 33 runs (b) 34 runs
(c) 37 runs (d) 36 runs
(e) None of these

9. The average of 50 numbers is 38. If two numbers namely 45 and 55 are discarded, the average of the remaining numbers is

(a) 36.5 (b) 37
(c) 37.5 (d) 37.52
(e) 35.2

10. The average of 6 observations is 12. A new seventh observation is included and the new average is decreased by 1. The seventh observation is

(a) 1 (b) 3
(c) 5 (d) 6
(e) 7

11. A man whose bowling average is 12.4 takes 5 wickets for 26 runs and thereby decreases his average by 0.4. The number of wickets, taken by him, before his last match, is

(a) 85 (b) 78
(c) 72 (d) 64
(e) 65

12. The average of marks obtained by 120 candidates was 35. If the average of marks of passed candidates was 39 and that of failed candidates was 15, the number of candidates who passed the examination is

(a) 100 (b) 110
(c) 120 (d) 150
(e) 170

13. Out of three numbers, the first is twice the second and is half of the third. If the average of the three numbers is 56, the three numbers in order are

(a) 48, 96, 24
(b) 48, 24, 96
(c) 96, 24, 48
(d) 96, 48, 24
(e) None of these

14. Out of four numbers, the average of first three is 15 and that of the last three is 16. If the last number is 19, the first is

(a) 15 (b) 16
(c) 18 (d) 19
(e) 20

15. The average age of A, B, C and D five years ago was 45 years. By including X, the present age of all the five is 49 years. The present age of X is

(a) 64 years (b) 48 years
(c) 45 years (d) 40 years
(e) None of these

16. The average expenditure of a man for the first five months is ₹ 120 and for the next seven months it is ₹ 130. If he saves ₹ 290 in that year, his monthly average income is

(*a*) ₹ 1000 (*b*) ₹ 1800
(*c*) ₹ 2000 (*d*) ₹ 2500
(*e*) None of these

17. If *a*, *b*, *c*, *d*, *e* are five consecutive odd numbers their average is

(*a*) $5(a + 4)$ (*b*) $\frac{abcde}{5}$
(*c*) $5(a + b + c + d + e)$ (*d*) $(a + 4)$
(*e*) None of these

ANSWERS

1	2	3	4	5	6	7	8	9	10
(*c*)	(*c*)	(*c*)	(*a*)	(*a*)	(*a*)	(*d*)	(*c*)	(*c*)	(*c*)
11	**12**	**13**	**14**	**15**	**16**	**17**			
(*a*)	(*a*)	(*b*)	(*b*)	(*c*)	(*b*)	(*d*)			

EXPLANATORY ANSWERS

1. $$\text{Average} = \frac{1}{4}\left(\frac{3}{2}+\frac{7}{3}+\frac{10}{3}+\frac{29}{6}\right)$$
$$= \left(\frac{9+14+20+29}{24}\right) = \frac{72}{24} = 3$$

3. Average of 13 numbers = 68

∴ Total of 13 numbers = 13 × 68 = 884

Average of last 7 numbers = 70

∴ Total of last 7 numbers = 7 × 70 = 490

∴ Average of first 6 numbers = 884 – 490 = 394

∴ Average of first 7 numbers = 63

∴ Total of first 7 numbers = 63 × 7 = 441

∴ 7th number = 441 – 394 = 47.

5. Let the average expenditure of all the nine = ₹ *x*

Now amount spent by eight = ₹ 3 × 8 = ₹ 24

and total spent by the ninth = ₹ *x* + 2

$$\Rightarrow \frac{26 + x}{9} = x$$

∴ Average amount spent by nine = $\frac{26 + x}{9}$

Total amount spent by nine = 24 + *x* + 2 = 26 + *x*

⇒ $9x = 26 + x$ or $8x = 26$

⇒ $x = \frac{26}{8}$ = ₹ 3.25

Hence total money spent = ₹ (3.25 × 9) = **₹ 29.25**

6. Total increase in the age of 8 persons

= 2 × 8 = 16 years

Total age of two men being replaced

= 20 + 24 = 44 years

Total of the age of two women

= 44 + 16 = 60 years

⇒ The average age of women

$= \frac{60}{2} = 30$ years.

8. Average increase in the score of 17 innings = 3 runs

Total increase in the score of 17 innings

= 3 × 17 = 51 runs

∴ His average of 16 innings

= 85 – 51 = 34 runs

Hence average after the 17th innings

= 34 + 3 = **37 runs**

9. Total of 50 numbers = 50 × 38 = 1900

Total of 48 numbers = 1900 – (45 + 55) = 1800

∴ $\text{Average} = \frac{1800}{48} = 37.5$

11. Suppose the number of wickets taken before the last match = *x*

$$\Rightarrow \frac{12.4x + 26}{x + 5} = 12$$

⇒ $12.4x + 26 = 12x + 60$

⇒ $x = \mathbf{85}$

12. Let the number of candidates who passed = *x*

⇒ $39 \times x + 15 \times (120 - x) = 120 \times 35$

⇒ $24x = 4200 - 1800$

or, $x = \frac{2400}{24} = \mathbf{100}$

13. Let second number = *x*

Then, first number = 2*x*

and third number = 4*x*

∴ $\frac{x + 2x + 4x}{3} = 56 \Rightarrow \frac{7x}{3} = 56$

⇒ $7x = 56 \times 3$

⇒ $x = 24$

So, the numbers are 48, 24, 96.

5

Ratio and Proportion

RATIO

In ratio we compare two quantities of the same kind and consider what multiple, part or parts one is of the other. In comparing 8 with 4, observe that it is 2 times 4. This comparison can be represented as $8 \div 4$ or $\frac{8}{4}$.

Hence, *ratio is that relation between two numbers which is expressed by the fraction, the numerator is which is the measure of the first quantity and denominator is the measure of the second quantity.*

If the terms of a ratio be multiplied or divided by the same quantity the value of the ratio remains unaltered.

Thus 3 : 4 is the same as 9 : 12 and 9 : 12 is the same as 3 : 4

Proportion

The equality of two ratio is called proportion

Consider the two ratios:

Ist ratio	2nd ratio
5 : 15	7 : 21

Since, 5 is one-third of 15 and 7 is one-third of 21, the two ratios are equal. The equality of two ratios is called proportion and the numbers 5, 15, 7 and 21 are said to be in **proportion.**

The proportion may be written as 5 : 15 : : 7 : 21 (5 is to 15 as 7 is to 21)

or, 5 : 15 = 7 : 21

or, $\frac{5}{15} = \frac{7}{21}$

The numbers 5, 15, 7 and 21 are called the **terms.** 5 is the **first term**, 15 the **second,** 7 the **third**, and 21 the **fourth**.

The first and fourth terms, *i.e.*, 5 and 21 are called **extremes** (end terms), and the second and the third terms, *i.e.*, 15 and 7 are called the **means** (middle terms), 21 is called the **fourth** proportional.

MULTIPLE CHOICE QUESTIONS

1. If A : B = 6 : 7 and B : C = 8 : 9, then A : B : C is:
(*a*) 24 : 28 : 63 (*b*) 48 : 28 : 63
(*c*) 48 : 56 : 63 (*d*) 56 : 23 : 68
(*e*) None of these

2. The sum of two numbers is 20 and their difference is $2\frac{1}{2}$. What is the ratio of the numbers?
(*a*) 11 : 7 (*b*) 9 : 11
(*c*) 9 : 7 (*d*) 11 : 5
(*e*) None of these

3. If 10% of *x* is the same as 20% of *y*, then *x* : *y* is equal to :
(*a*) 1 : 2 (*b*) 2 : 1
(*c*) 5 : 1 (*d*) 10 : 1
(*e*) None of these

4. Two numbers are in the ratio 3 : 5. If each number is increased by 10, the ratio becomes 5 : 7. The numbers are:
(*a*) 3, 5 (*b*) 7, 9
(*c*) 13, 22 (*d*) 15, 25
(*e*) 27, 17

5. The sum of three numbers is 98. If the ratio between the first and second be 2 : 3 and that between the second and third be 5 : 8, then what is the second number?
(*a*) 20 (*b*) 30
(*c*) 10 (*d*) 40
(*e*) 50

6. One man adds 3 litres of water to 12 litres of milk and another 4 litres of water to 10 litres of milk. What is the ratio of the strenghts of the milk in the two mixtures?
(*a*) 15 : 25 (*b*) 25 : 28
(*c*) 28 : 25 (*d*) 24 : 22
(*e*) None of these

7. A vessel contains liquids P and Q in the ratio 5 :3. If 6 litres of the mixture are removed and the same quantity of liquid *q* is added, the ratio becomes 3 : 5. What quantity does the vessel hold?

(*a*) 40 litres (*b*) 50 litres
(*c*) 30 litres (*d*) 22 litres
(*e*) None of these

8. Three glasses P, Q and R with their capacities in the ratio 2 : 3 : 4 are filled with a mixture of spirit and water. The ratio of spirit to water in P, Q and R is 1 : 5, 3 : 5 and 5 : 7 respectively. If the contents of these glasses are mixed together, what is the ratio of spirit to water in the mixture?
(*a*) 14 : 27 (*b*) 23 : 47
(*c*) 25 : 47 (*d*) 46 : 22
(*e*) None of these

9. A and B are two alloys of gold and copper prepared by mixing metals in proportions 7 : 2 and 7 : 11 respectively. If equal quantities of the alloys are melted to form a third alloy C, the proportion of gold and copper in C will be
(*a*) 5 : 9 (*b*) 5 : 7
(*c*) 7 : 5 (*d*) 9 : 5
(*e*) None of these

10. The monthly salary of A, B, C is in the proportion of 2 : 3 ; 5. If C's monthly salary is ₹ 1200 more than that of A, then B's annual salary is:
(*a*) ₹ 14400 (*b*) ₹ 24000
(*c*) ₹ 1200 (*d*) ₹ 2000
(*e*) None of these

11. A certain amount was divided between Kavita and Reena in the ratio 4 : 3. If Reena's share was ₹ 2400, the amount is:
(*a*) ₹ 5600 (*b*) ₹ 3200
(*c*) ₹ 9600 (*d*) ₹ 7500
(*e*) None of these

12. In a class, the number of boys is more than the number of girls by 12% of the total strength. The ratio of the boys to girls is:
(*a*) 11 : 14 (*b*) 14 : 11
(*c*) 25 : 28 (*d*) 28 : 25
(*e*) None of these

13. A right cylinder and a right circular cone have the same radius and the same volume. The ratio of the height of the cylinder to that of the cone is:
(*a*) 3 : 5 (*b*) 2 : 5
(*c*) 3 : 1 (*d*) 1 : 3
(*e*) None of these

14. A circle and a square have same area. Therefore the ratio of the side of the square and the radius of the circle is :
(*a*) $\sqrt{\pi}:1$ (*b*) $1:\sqrt{\pi}$
(*c*) 1 : π (*d*) π : 1
(*e*) None of these

15. A, B and C can do a work in 20, 25 and 30 days respectively. They undertook to finish the work together for ₹ 2220, then the share of A exceeds that of B by:
(*a*) ₹ 120 (*b*) ₹ 180
(*c*) ₹ 300 (*d*) ₹ 600
(*e*) None of these

16. A bag contains 25 paise, 10 paise and 5 paise coins in the ratio 1 : 2 : 3. If their total value is ₹ 30, the number of 5 paise coin is:
(*a*) 50 (*b*) 100
(*c*) 150 (*d*) 200
(*e*) 250

ANSWERS

1	2	3	4	5	6	7	8	9	10
(*c*)	(*c*)	(*b*)	(*d*)	(*b*)	(*c*)	(*a*)	(*c*)	(*c*)	(*c*)
11	**12**	**13**	**14**	**15**	**16**				
(*a*)	(*b*)	(*d*)	(*a*)	(*b*)	(*c*)				

EXPLANATORY ANSWERS

1.
$$A : B = 6 : 7$$
$$B : C = 8 : 9$$
$$\therefore \quad A : B : C = 6 \times 8 : 7 \times 8 : 7 \times 9$$
$$= \mathbf{48 : 56 : 63}$$

3.
$$10\% \text{ of } x = 20\% \text{ of } y$$
$$\Rightarrow \quad \frac{10}{100}x = \frac{20}{100}y$$
$$\therefore \quad \frac{x}{10} = \frac{y}{5} \text{ or, } \frac{x}{y} = \frac{10}{5}$$
$$= \frac{2}{1} \Rightarrow x:y = \mathbf{2:1}$$

4. Let the number be 3*x* and 5*x*.

Then, $$\frac{3x+10}{5x+10} = \frac{5}{7}$$

or, $$7(3x + 10) = 5(5x + 10)$$
$$\Rightarrow \quad 21x + 70 = 25x + 50$$
$$\Rightarrow \quad 4x = 20 \Rightarrow x = 5$$

So, the numbers are **15, 25.**

6. Strength of milk in the first mixture

$$= \frac{12}{12+3} = \frac{12}{15}$$

Strength of milk in the second mixture

$$= \frac{10}{10+4} = \frac{10}{14}$$

∴ The ratio of their strengths

$$= \frac{12}{15} : \frac{10}{14} = 12 \times 14 : 15 \times 10$$

$$= \mathbf{28 : 25}$$

8. P : Q : R
2 : 3 : 4
Spirit : Water = 1 : 5, 3 : 5 and 5 : 7
When they are mixed, the ratio of spirit to water

$$= \left(2\times\frac{1}{1+5}+3\times\frac{3}{3+5}+4\times\frac{5}{5+7}\right):\left(2\times\frac{5}{1+5}+3\times\frac{5}{3+5}+4\times\frac{7}{5+7}\right)$$

$$= \left(\frac{1}{3}+\frac{9}{8}+\frac{5}{3}\right):\left(\frac{5}{3}+\frac{15}{8}+\frac{7}{3}\right) = \frac{25}{8}:\frac{47}{8} = \mathbf{25 : 47}$$

9. Gold in C $= \left(\frac{7}{9}+\frac{7}{18}\right) = \frac{21}{18} = \frac{7}{6}$

Copper in C $= \left(\frac{2}{9}+\frac{11}{18}\right) = \frac{15}{18} = \frac{5}{6}$

∴ Gold : Copper $= \frac{7}{6}:\frac{5}{6} = \mathbf{7 : 5}$

12. Let the number of boys and girls be x and y respectively.

Then $(x - y) = 12\%$ of $(x + y)$.

or, $x - y = \frac{3}{25}(x + y)$

or, $25x - 25y = 3x + 3y$

or, $22x = 28y$

or, $\frac{x}{y} = \frac{28}{22} = \frac{14}{11}$

⇒ **Ratio 14 : 11**

14. Let the side of the square be x and let the radius of the circle be y. Then,

$$x^2 = \pi y^2$$

$$\Rightarrow \frac{x^2}{y^2} = \pi \text{ or, } \frac{x}{y} = \sqrt{\pi}$$

$$\therefore \quad x : y = \sqrt{\pi} : 1$$

15. Ratio of shares of A, B, and C

$$= \frac{1}{20}:\frac{1}{25}:\frac{1}{30} = 15 : 12 : 10$$

∴ A's share $= \left(2220 \times \frac{15}{37}\right) =$ ₹ 900

B's share $= \left(2220 \times \frac{12}{37}\right) =$ ₹ 720

Thus, the share of A exceeds that of B by
= ₹ (900 − 720) = **₹ 180.**

6 Percentage

The word 'per cent' or 'percentage' means 'for every one hundred'. In other words, it gives an indication of rate per hundred. It is denoted by the symbol %.

For example, 5% means 5 out of one hundred or $\frac{5}{100}$.

Remember :

(*i*) For converting a per cent into a fraction, divide it by 100.

(*ii*) For converting a fraction into a percent, multiply it by 100.

(*iii*) For converting a per cent into a decimal, shift the decimal point two places to the left.

(*iv*) For converting one given quantity (*x*) as a percentage of another given quantity (*y*), find $\frac{x}{y}\times100$.

(*v*) There is no unit or dimension of percentage.

Some Important Tricks

1. If the price of sugar increases by *x*%, by how much per cent should a family reduce his consumption of sugar so as not to increase the expenditure on sugar?

Trick : Percentage of reduction = $\frac{x\times100}{100+x}$

2. In an election a candidate gets R% of the votes cast and loses by *x* votes to be elected. How many votes were casted at the election?

Trick : Number of votes cast = $\frac{50\times x}{50-R}$

3. A man gives *x*% of his money to his son, *y*% of the remainder to his daughter and *z*% of the remaining to his wife. If he is left now with Rs. R, what was his initial amount?

Trick: Total amount in the beginning

$$= ₹\ \frac{R\times100\times100\times100}{(100-x)(100-y)(100-z)}$$

4. If B boys and G girls appeared in an examination and *x*% of the boys and *y*% of the girls passed in it, what is the total percentage of students who passed?

Trick : Total percentage of passed students

$$=\frac{B\times x+G\times y}{B+G}$$

5. If in an examination, in which the minimum pass perentage is *x*%, a candidate secures *y* marks and fails by *z* marks, then the total numbr of marks in this examination will be $\frac{100\times(y+z)}{x}$.

6. If in an examination *x*% and *y*% candidates respectively fail in two different subjects while *z*% candidates fail in both the subjects, then the percentage of candidates who pass in both the subjects will be $[100 - (x + y - z)]\%$

MULTIPLE CHOICE QUESTIONS

1. If *x* is 90% of *y*, then what per cent of *x* is *y*?

(*a*) 90 (*b*) 190
(*c*) 101.1 (*d*) 111.1
(*e*) 110.1

2. A number exceeds 20% of itself by 40. The number is:

(*a*) 50 (*b*) 60
(*c*) 80 (*d*) 320
(*e*) 70

3. The price of an article is cut by 10%. To restore it to the former value, the new price must be increased by:

(*a*) 10% (*b*) $9\frac{1}{11}\%$
(*c*) $11\frac{1}{9}\%$ (*d*) 11%
(*e*) None of these

4. 5% income of A is equal to 15% income of B and 10% income of B is equal to 20% income of C. If income of C is 2000, then total income of A, B and C is:

(*a*) ₹ 6000 (*b*) ₹ 18000

(c) ₹ 20000 (d) ₹ 14000
(e) None of these

5. A student who secures 20% marks in an examination fails by 30 marks. Another student who secures 32% gets 42 marks more than those required to pass. The percentage of marks required to pass is:
(a) 20 (b) 25
(c) 28 (d) 30
(e) 40

6. In a college election, a candidate secured 62% of the votes and is elected by a majority of 144 votes. The total number of votes polled is:
(a) 600 (b) 800
(c) 925 (d) 1200
(e) 1000

7. P is six times as large as *q*. The per cent that *q* is less than *p*, is:
(a) $83\frac{1}{3}$ (b) $16\frac{2}{3}$
(c) 90 (d) 60
(e) 50

8. The price of an article has been reduced by 25%. In order to restore the original price, the new price must be increased by:
(a) $33\frac{1}{3}\%$ (b) $11\frac{1}{9}\%$
(c) $9\frac{1}{11}\%$ (d) $66\frac{2}{3}\%$
(e) None of these

9. In 40% of the perople read newspaper X, 50% read newspaper Y, and 10% read both the papers. What percentage of the people read neither newspaper?
(a) 10% (b) 15%
(c) 20% (d) 25%
(e) None of these

10. The population of a village is 4500. $\frac{5}{9}$th of them are males and rest females. If 40% of the males are married, then the percentage of married female is:
(a) 35 (b) 40
(c) 50 (d) 60
(e) 40

11. A's income is 10% more than B's. How much per cent is B's income is less than A's?
(a) 10% (b) 7%
(c) $9\frac{1}{11}\%$ (d) $6\frac{1}{2}\%$
(e) None of these

12. If the price of a television set is increased by 25%, then by what percentage should the new price be reduced to bring the price back to original level?
(a) 15% (b) 20%
(c) 25% (d) 30%
(e) None of these

13. The number of grams of water needed to reduce 9 grams of shaving lotion containing 50% alcohol to a lotion containing 30% alcohol, is:
(a) 4 (b) 5
(c) 6 (d) 7
(e) 8

14. The length of a given rectangle is increased by 20% and the breadth of the rectangle is decreased by 20%. Then, the new area is:
(a) remains the same (b) is increased by 4%
(c) is increased by 5% (d) is decreased by 4%
(e) None of these

15. If the sides of a square is increased by 30%, its area is increased by:
(a) 9% (b) 30%
(c) 60% (d) 69%
(e) None of these

16. If the income tax is decreased by 26%, a man's net income increases by $\frac{2}{3}\%$. The rate of income tax is :
(a) $3\frac{1}{2}\%$ (b) $2\frac{1}{2}\%$
(c) $1\frac{1}{2}\%$ (d) 3%
(e) None of these

17. The gross income of a person is ₹ 20000. 10% of his income is exempted from income tax and his net income is ₹ 19100. The rate of income tax is:
(a) 3% (b) 2%
(c) 4% (d) 5%
(e) None of these

18. The gross income of a person is ₹ 15000, 20% of his income is exempted from income tax and the rate of income tax is ₹ 4%.
The net income is:
(a) 14520 (b) 14620
(c) 15520 (d) 15620
(e) None of these

ANSWERS

1	2	3	4	5	6	7	8	9	10
(d)	(a)	(c)	(b)	(b)	(a)	(a)	(a)	(c)	(c)
11	**12**	**13**	**14**	**15**	**16**	**17**	**18**		
(c)	(b)	(c)	(d)	(d)	(b)	(d)	(a)		

EXPLANATORY ANSWERS

1. $x = 90\%$ of $y \Rightarrow x = \frac{90}{100}y$

Let $z\%$ of $x = y$

Then, $\frac{z}{100} \times x = y$

$\Rightarrow \frac{z}{100} \times \frac{90}{100} y = y$

$\Rightarrow z = \frac{100 \times 100}{90} = 111.1$

3. Let original price be ₹ 100

Then, new price = ₹ 90

Increase on Rs. 90 = ₹ 10

$\therefore$ Increase % $= \left(\frac{10}{90} \times 100\right)\% = 11\frac{1}{9}\%$

4. 5% A = 15% B, and 10% B = 20% C

$\therefore \frac{A}{20} = \frac{3B}{20}$ and $\frac{B}{10} = \frac{C}{5}$

$\Rightarrow B = 2C$

$\therefore \frac{A}{20} = \frac{3}{20} \times 2C = \frac{3}{10}C = \frac{3}{10} \times 2000 = 600$

$\therefore A = (600 \times 20) = 12000$

$B = (2 \times 2000) = 4000$

$\therefore A + B + C = 12000 + 4000 + 2000 = 18000$

6. (62% of x – 38% of x) = 144

$\Rightarrow$ 24% of $x = 144$

$\Rightarrow x = \frac{144 \times 100}{24} = 600$

8. Let Original price be ₹ 100

$\therefore$ Reduced price = ₹ 75

Increase on ₹ 75 = ₹ 25

$\therefore$ Increase on ₹ 100 $= \left(\frac{25}{75} \times 100\right)\% = 33\frac{1}{3}\%$

9. $n(A) = 40, n(B) = 50$

$n(A \cap B) = 10$

$\therefore n(A \cup B) = n(A) + n(B) - n(A \cap B)$

$= 40 + 50 - 10 = 80$

$n(\text{not A and not B}) = n(A^C \cap B^C) = n(A \cup B)^C$

$= 100 - n(A \cup B)$

$= 100 - 80 = 20$

10. Males $= \left(\frac{5}{9} \times 4500\right) = 2500$

Females = 2000

$\therefore$ Married males $= \frac{40}{100} \times 2500 = 1000$

and married females = 1000

$\therefore$ Precentage of married females

$= \left(\frac{1000}{2000} \times 100\right)\% = 50\%$

12. Let original price = ₹ x

$\therefore$ New price $= \frac{125}{100} \times x = \frac{5x}{4}$

Reduction on $\frac{5x}{4} = \left(\frac{5x}{4} - x\right) = \frac{x}{4}$

$\therefore$ Reduction on $100 = \left(\frac{x}{4} \times \frac{4}{5x} \times 100\right)\% = 20\%$

16. 26% of income tax $= \frac{2}{3}\%$ of the net income

$\therefore$ Income tax $= \left[\frac{2}{3} \times \frac{100}{26}\right]\%$ of the net income

$= \frac{100}{39}\%$ of the net income

Let net income = ₹ 3900

$\therefore$ Income tax $= 3900 \times \frac{100}{39 \times 100} =$ ₹ 100

Gross income = ₹ 3900 + ₹ 100 = ₹ 4000

$\therefore$ Rate % of income tax $= \left(\frac{100}{4000} \times 100\right)\% = 2\frac{1}{2}\%$

18. Gross income = ₹ 15000

Income exempted from income tax

= 20% of gross income

Income on which income tax is changeable

= (100 – 20)% = 80% of gross income

$= 15000 \times \frac{80}{100} =$ ₹ 12000

$\therefore$ Income tax paid @ 4%

$= 12000 \times \frac{4}{100} =$ ₹ 480

$\therefore$ Net income = 15000 – 480 = 14520.

7

Profit and Loss

A consumer who goes to the market and buys certain goods. The buyer is called a customer and the shopkeeper who sells the goods to him is called a retailer. The retailer purchases goods in turn in bulk from a wholesaler who keeps a large stock of good and in this case, the retailer becomes the customer.

1. Cost price : Cost price (C.P.) is that price at which a particular article is bought. Profit and loss both are marked at cost price.

2. Selling Price (S.P.) : Selling price is that price at which a particular article is sold.

3. Overheads : The expenses incurred on transportation, maintenance, packaging, advertisements and the like are included as *Overhead.* These overheads and the profit when added to the cost price determine the selling price.

4. Profit or Gain : Whenever a person sells an article at price greater than the cost price he is said to have made a profit or gain. Profit or Gain = S.P. – C.P.

5. If S.P. is less than the C.P. there is loss.

Loss = C.P – S.P

Remember :

(*i*) Loss or gain are always reckoned on cost price
(*ii*) Gain on ₹ 100 is Gain percent
(*iii*) Loss on ₹ 100 is Loss percent.

Some Basic Formulae :

(*i*) Gain = S.P. – C.P.

(*ii*) Loss = C.P. – S.P.

(*iii*) $\text{Gain \%} = \dfrac{\text{S.P.}-\text{C.P.}}{\text{C.P}} \times 100\% = \dfrac{\text{Gain} \times 100}{\text{C.P.}}$

(*iv*) $\text{Loss \%} = \dfrac{\text{C.P.}-\text{S.P.}}{\text{C.P.}} \times 100\% = \dfrac{\text{Loss} \times 100}{\text{C.P.}}$

From these we can write direct expressions for S.P. and C.P.

(*v*) $\text{S.P.} = \left(\dfrac{100+\text{Gain\%}}{100}\right) \times \text{C.P.}$

in case of gain or profit

(*vi*) $\text{S.P.} = \left(\dfrac{100-\text{Loss\%}}{100}\right) \times \text{C.P.}$ in case of loss

These can be rewritten as

$\text{C.P.} = \dfrac{100}{100+\text{Gain\%}} \times \text{S.P.}$ in case of profit

$\text{C.P.} = \dfrac{100}{100-\text{Loss\%}} \times \text{S.P.}$ in case of loss

MULTIPLE CHOICE QUESTIONS

1. The C.P. of an article is 40% of the S.P. The per cent that the S.P is of C.P. is
(*a*) 40 (*b*) 80
(*c*) 220 (*d*) 250
(*e*) 200

2. Ashok bought 25 kg of rice at the rate of ₹ 6 per kg and 35 kg of rice at the rate of ₹ 7 per kg. He mixed the two and sold the mixture at the rate of ₹ 6.75 per kg. What was his gain or loss in the transaction?
(*a*) ₹ 16 gain (*b*) ₹ 16 loss
(*c*) ₹ 10 gain (*d*) ₹ 15 loss
(*e*) None of these

3. When the price of fans was ruduced by 20%, the number of fans sold increased by 40%. What was the effect on the sales in rupees?
(*a*) 12% increase (*b*) 12% decrease
(*c*) 40% decrease (*d*) 40% inrease
(*e*) None of these

4. A horse and a cow were sold for Rs. 12000 each. The horse was sold at a loss of 20% and the cow at a gain of 20%. The entire transaction resulted in
(*a*) no loss or gain (*b*) loss of ₹ 1000
(*c*) gain of ₹ 1000 (*d*) loss of ₹ 2000
(*e*) None of these

5. Profit after selling a commodity for ₹ 425 is same as loss after selling it for ₹ 335. The cost of the commodity is:
(*a*) ₹ 285 (*b*) ₹ 390
(*c*) ₹ 295 (*d*) ₹ 400
(*e*) None of these

6. Bhajan Singh purchased 120 reams of paper at ₹ 80 per ream. He spent ₹ 280 on transportation, paid octroi at the rate of 40 paise per ream and paid ₹ 72 to the coolie. If he wants to have a gain of 8%, what must be the selling price per ream?
(a) ₹ 86 (b) ₹ 86.48
(c) ₹ 79 (d) ₹ 90
(e) None of these

7. Ram bought 4 dozen apples at ₹ 12 per dozen and 2 dozen at ₹ 16 per dozen. He sold all of them to earn 20%. At what price per dozen did he sell the apples?
(a) ₹ 14.40 (b) ₹ 16.00
(c) ₹ 16.80 (d) ₹ 16.20
(e) None of these

8. Jimmy bought paper sheets for ₹ 7200 and spent ₹ 200 in transport. Paying ₹ 600 he had 330 boxes made, which he sold at ₹ 28 each. What is his profit percentage?
(a) 15.5 (b) 40
(c) 50 (d) 60
(e) None of these

9. A owns a house worth ₹ 10000. He sells it to B at a profit of 10% based on the worth of the house. B sells the house back to A at a loss of 10%. In this transaction A gets:
(a) no profit no loss (b) profit of ₹ 1000
(c) profit of ₹ 1100 (d) profit of ₹ 1200
(e) None of these

10. At what price must Kantilal sell a mixture of 80 kg sugar at ₹ 6.75 per kg with 120 kg at ₹ 8 per kg to gain 20%?
(a) ₹ 7.50 per kg (b) ₹ 8.20 per kg
(c) ₹ 8.35 per kg (d) ₹ 9 per kg
(e) None of these

11. A dealer marks his goods 20% above cost price. He then allows some discount on it and makes a profit of 8%. The rate of discount is:
(a) 12% (b) 10%
(c) 6% (d) 4%
(e) None of these

12. The difference between a discount of 40% on ₹ 500 and two successive discounts of 36% and 4% on the same amount is:
(a) 10 (b) 2
(c) 1.93 (d) 7.20
(e) None of these

13. A trader lists his articles 20% above C.P. and allows a discount of 10% on cash payment. His gain percent is:
(a) 10% (b) 8%
(c) 6% (d) 4%
(e) None of these

14. Tarun bought a T.V. with 20% discount on the labelled price. Had he bought it with 25% discount, he would have saved ₹ 500. At what price did he buy the T.V.?
(a) ₹ 5000 (b) ₹ 10000
(c) ₹ 11000 (d) ₹ 12000
(e) None of these

15. The purchase tax on an article is levied at the rate of $66\frac{2}{3}\%$ of its wholesale price, while the retailer's profit amounts to 20% of the retail price of the article. What is the wholesale price of an article which is retailed at ₹ 12.50?
(a) ₹ 4 (b) ₹ 6
(c) ₹ 8 (d) ₹ 2
(e) None of these

16. A tradesman sells one kind of sugar at ₹ 3 per kg and loses 20 per cent and another kind of sugar at ₹ 5 per kg and gain 25 per cent. He mixes them together in equal proportion and sells the mixture at ₹ 6 per kg. What is his gain %?
(a) $53\frac{26}{31}\%$ (b) $51\frac{31}{26}\%$
(c) $54\frac{26}{31}\%$ (d) $55\frac{26}{31}\%$
(e) None of these

17. At a cricket match the contractor provided dinner for 24 persons, and fixed the price so as to gain $12\frac{1}{2}\%$ upon his total outlay. Three of the circketers being absent, the remaining 21 paid the fixed price for their dinner, and as such the contractor lost 1 rupee. What was the charge of the dinner?
(a) ₹ 2 (b) ₹ 3
(c) ₹ 4 (d) ₹ 5
(e) None of these

18. A merchant buys 200 kilograms of rice at ₹ 1.25 per kilogram, 400 kilograms of rice at 75 paise per kilogram. He mixes them and sells one third of the mixture at one rupee per kilogram. At what rate should he sell the remaining mixture so that he may earn a profit of 25% on the whole outlay?
(a) ₹ 1.20 (b) ₹ 1.22
(c) ₹ 1.30 (d) ₹ 1.32
(e) None of these

19. The price of an article was increased by $p\%$. Later the new price was decreased by $p\%$. If the latest price was ₹ 1, the original price was :
(a) ₹ 1 (b) ₹ $\left(\frac{1-p^2}{100}\right)$

(c) ₹ $\left(\dfrac{10000}{10000-p^2}\right)$ (d) ₹ $\left(\dfrac{\sqrt{1-p^2}}{100}\right)$

(e) None of these

20. A businessman sells an old machine for ₹ 1150 after taking some profit. Had he sold it for ₹ 910 his loss would have been $\frac{7}{5}$ of the profit. What was the cost price of that machine?

(a) ₹ 1000 (b) ₹ 1050

(c) ₹ 1100 (d) ₹ 1150

(e) None of these

ANSWERS

1	2	3	4	5	6	7	8	9	10
(d)	(c)	(a)	(b)	(b)	(d)	(b)	(a)	(c)	(d)
11	**12**	**13**	**14**	**15**	**16**	**17**	**18**	**19**	**20**
(b)	(d)	(b)	(b)	(b)	(c)	(b)	(b)	(c)	(b)

EXPLANATORY ANSWERS

2. C.P. of 60 kg mix = ₹ (25 × 6 + 35 × 7) = ₹ 395

S.P. of 60 kg mix = ₹ (60 × 6.75) = ₹ 405

∴ Gain = ₹ (405 – 395) = ₹ 10

4. Loss % = $\left(\dfrac{20}{10}\right)^2 = (2)^2 = 4\%$

Total S.P. = ₹ 24000

and Total C.P. = $\left(\dfrac{100}{96}\times 24000\right)$ = ₹ 25000

∴ Loss = ₹ (25000 – 24000) = ₹ 1000

5. Let C.P. = ₹ x

Then, $425 - x = x - 355$

or, $2x = 780 \Rightarrow x = 390$

7. C.P. of 6 dozen apples = ₹ (12 × 4 + 16 × 2) = ₹ 80

Gain = 20%

∴ S.P. = $\left(\dfrac{120}{100}\times 80\right)$ = ₹ 96

∴ S.P. per dozen = $\left(\dfrac{96}{6}\right)$ = ₹ 16

9. C.P. of B = 110% of ₹ 10000 = ₹ 11000

Loss of B = 10%

∴ S.P. of B = 90% of ₹ 11000 = ₹ 9900

Thus, C.P. of A = ₹ 9900

So, A gets [(10% of ₹ 10000) + (10000 – 9900)] = ₹ 1100

13. Let C.P. be ₹ 100

Then, marked price = ₹ 120

S.P. = 90% of ₹ 120 = $\left(\dfrac{90}{100}\times 120\right)$ = ₹ 108

∴ Gain % = $\left(\dfrac{8}{100}\times 100\right)\%$ = 8%

14. Let the labelled price = ₹ 100

∴ S.P. in 1st case = ₹ 80

and S.P. in 2nd case = ₹ 75

If saving is ₹ 5, labelled price = ₹ 100

If saving is ₹ 500, labelled price

= $\left(\dfrac{100}{5}\times 500\right)$ = ₹ 10000

17. Let the charge for the dinner be ₹ 1.

∴ Total charge from 24 persons = ₹ 24

Since he gains $12\frac{1}{2}\%$ upon his total outlay

∴ His total C.P. = $\dfrac{24\times 100}{\left(100+\dfrac{25}{2}\right)} = \dfrac{24\times 200}{225} = \dfrac{64}{3}$

But, charge from 21 person at the rate of ₹ 1 paid = ₹ 21

∴ Actual loss = $\dfrac{64}{3} - 21 = \dfrac{1}{3}$

But actual total loss = ₹ 1

If loss is $\frac{1}{3}$, then charge per head = ₹ 1

If loss is 1, then charge per head = ₹ 3

20. Difference in the selling price

= ₹ (1150 – 910) = ₹ 240

⇒ ₹ 240 = Profit in 1st case + Loss in 2nd case

Profit + $\frac{7}{5}$ of the profit = $\left(1+\frac{7}{5}\right)$ of the profit

= $\frac{12}{5}$ of the profit

∴ Profit = $240\times\frac{5}{12}$ = ₹ 100

Hence, the C.P. = ₹ (1150 – 100) = ₹ 1050.

8 Simple Interest

INTEREST

Interest is the money paid for the use of money borrowed, i.e., extra money paid for using other's money is called *interest.*

The sum borrowed is called the principal. The sum of interest and principal is called the *Amount.* If the interest on a certain sum borrowed for a certain period is reckoned uniformly, then it is called simple interest, denoted by S.I.

Thus, if A = Amount

P = Principal

I = Interest

T = Time (in year)

R = Rate percent per annum, then

we can recognise the following useful relations:

(*a*) $I = \frac{P \times R \times T}{100}$ (*b*) $P = \frac{100 \times I}{R \times T}$

(*c*) $T = \frac{100 \times I}{P \times R}$ (*d*) $R = \frac{100 \times I}{P \times T}$

(*e*) $P = \frac{100\,A}{100 + RT}$ (*f*) A = P + I.

MULTIPLE CHOICE QUESTIONS

1. If the simple interest on a certain sum of money at 6% per annum for 3 years is ₹ 90, the sum will be:

(*a*) ₹ 500 (*b*) ₹ 450
(*c*) ₹ 525 (*d*) ₹ 560
(*e*) None of these

2. If the simple interest on ₹ 1 for 1 month is 1 paise, the rate per cent p.a. will be:

(*a*) 10% (*b*) 8%
(*c*) 12% (*d*) 6%
(*e*) None of these

3. A sum of money doubles itself in 20 years. In how many years will it triple itself at the same rate of simple interest?

(*a*) 30 years (*b*) 50 years
(*c*) 40 years (*d*) 45 years
(*e*) None of these

4. After what time will the sum of ₹ 2000 become ₹ 2240 at 4% per annum simple interest?

(*a*) 3 years (*b*) 2 years
(*c*) 5 years (*d*) 4 years
(*e*) None of these

5. A sum of money amounts to ₹ 1150 in 3 years and to ₹ 1250 in 5 years at a certain rate per cent p.a. simple interest. The rate per cent p.a. will be:

(*a*) 5% (*b*) 8%
(*c*) 7% (*d*) 6%
(*e*) None of these

6. The simple interest on a sum of ₹ 892 lent out at 6% p.a. for 8 months will be :

(*a*) ₹ 36.68 (*b*) ₹ 35.68
(*c*) ₹ 48.58 (*d*) ₹ 33.38
(*e*) None of these

7. A lent a sum of ₹ 1250 to B at a certain rate of interest for 3 years and a sum of ₹ 1500 to C at the same rate of interest for 2 years. If he was paid total ₹ 258.75 as interest in both cases, find the rate of interest at which money was lent by him.

(*a*) $4\frac{1}{6}\%$ (*b*) $6\frac{1}{4}\%$
(*c*) $2\frac{1}{7}\%$ (*d*) $3\frac{5}{6}\%$
(*e*) None of these

8. A man lends ₹ 500 for 4 years and ₹ 600 for 3 years at a certain rate of simple interest. If he gets total ₹ 190 as interest in both cases, the rate per cent per annum is:

(*a*) 8% (*b*) 5%
(*c*) 10% (*d*) 4%
(*e*) None of these

9. What annual instalment should be paid to clear the debt of ₹ 645 in 4 years at the rate of 5% p.a. simple interest?

(*a*) ₹ 160 (*b*) ₹ 185
(*c*) ₹ 150 (*d*) ₹ 190
(*e*) None of these

10. If a certain sum of money at simple interest amounts to ₹ 1900 in 3 years and to ₹ 2050 in 5 years, the rate per cent per annum is :

(a) 4½% (b) 3½%
(c) 2½% (d) 5¼%
(e) None of these

11. Which of the following sum of money will amount to ₹ 1050 in 5 years at 8% per annum simple interest?

(a) ₹ 750 (b) ₹ 825
(c) ₹ 775 (d) ₹ 730
(e) None of these

12. A certain sum of money lent out on simple interest amounts to ₹ 1760 in 2 years and to ₹ 2000 in 5 years. Find the sum

(a) ₹ 1650 (b) ₹ 1500
(c) ₹ 1580 (d) ₹ 1600
(e) None of these

13. A sum of ₹ 2444 is divided among three parts in such a manner that simple interest on the three divided parts at 6% p.a. after 3, 4 and 5 years respectively remains equal. Such three parts will be :

(a) ₹ 780, ₹ 1040, ₹ 624
(b) ₹ 1040, ₹ 780, ₹ 624
(c) ₹ 624, ₹ 780, ₹ 1040
(d) ₹ 940, ₹ 880, ₹ 624
(e) None of these

14. Amount received by a money lender on lending out a certain sum of money at 3% per annum simple interest for 4 years is same as the amount received by him on lending out the sum of ₹ 6384 at 4% p.a. for 6 years. The sum will be:

(a) ₹ 7168 (b) ₹ 7278
(c) ₹ 7078 (d) ₹ 7068
(e) None of these

15. If the sum of 8097 is divided among A, B and C in such a manner that amount received from these parts at 4% p.a. simple interest after 4, 5 and 6 years respectively remains equal, then A's part will exceed the B's part by:

(a) ₹ 85 (b) ₹ 93
(c) ₹ 75 (d) ₹ 63
(e) None of these

ANSWERS

1	2	3	4	5	6	7	8	9	10
(a)	(c)	(c)	(a)	(a)	(b)	(d)	(b)	(c)	(a)
11	12	13	14	15					
(a)	(d)	(b)	(d)	(b)					

EXPLANATORY ANSWERS

2. Principal = ₹ 1 = 100 paise

Time = 1 month = $\frac{1}{12}$ years

Simple Interest = 1 paise

$$\therefore \quad \text{Rate} = \frac{\text{S.I.}\times 100}{\text{P}\times\text{T}} = \frac{1\times 100}{100\times\frac{1}{12}} = 12\%.$$

4. $\because$ Amount = Principal $\left(1+\frac{\text{Rate}\times\text{Time}}{100}\right)$

$$\text{or,} \quad \text{Time} = \frac{(\text{Amount}-\text{Principal})\times 100}{\text{Principal}\times\text{Rate}}$$

$$= \frac{(2240-2000)\times 100}{2000\times 4} = \frac{240\times 100}{2000\times 4}$$

= 3 years.

6. P = ₹ 892, R = 6%

and Time = 8 months or $\frac{8}{12} = \frac{2}{3}$ year

$$\therefore \quad \text{S.I.} = \frac{892\times 6\times\frac{2}{3}}{100} = ₹\ 35.68$$

8. Suppose the rate per cent p.a. = x%

∴ In the first case,

$$\text{S.I.} = \frac{500\times 4\times x}{100} = ₹\ 20x$$

In the second case,

$$\text{S.I.} = \frac{600\times 3\times x}{100} = ₹\ 18x$$

According to question,

Total simple interest in both cases = ₹ 190

∴ $20x + 18x = 190$ or, $38x = 190$

or, $x = \frac{190}{38} = 5$

Hence, the rate percent p.a. in both cases is 5%.

10. Amount after 3 years = ₹ 1900

Amount after 5 years = ₹ 2050

∴ Simple interest for 2 years

$= ₹\ 2050 - ₹\ 1900 = ₹\ 150$

∴ Simple interest for 1 year

$= \frac{150}{2} = ₹\ 75$

∴ Simple interest for 3 year

$= ₹\ 75 \times 3 = ₹\ 225$

∴ Principal = Amount after 3 years – S.I. for 3 years

$= ₹\ 1900 - ₹\ 225 = ₹\ 1675$

∴ Rate $= \frac{225 \times 100}{1675 \times 3} = 4\frac{1}{2}\%$ (Approx.)

12. Amount after 5 years = ₹ 2000

Amount after 2 years = ₹ 1760

∴ Interest for 3 years

$= ₹\ 2000 - ₹\ 1760 = ₹\ 240$

∴ Interest for 1 year

$= \frac{240}{3} = ₹\ 80$

And interest for 2 years

$= ₹\ 80 \times 2 = ₹\ 160$

∴ Principal sum = Amount after 2 years – Interest for 2 years

$= ₹\ 1760 - ₹\ 160 = ₹\ 1600$

13. Ratio among such three parts of ₹ 2444

$$= \frac{1}{6 \times 3} : \frac{1}{6 \times 4} : \frac{1}{6 \times 5} = \frac{1}{3} : \frac{1}{4} : \frac{1}{5} = 20 : 15 : 12$$

Sum of proportionals

$= 20 + 15 + 12 = 47$

∴ Ist part $= \frac{20}{47} \times 2444 = ₹\ 1040$

2nd part $= \frac{15}{47} \times 2444 = ₹\ 780$

and, 3rd part $= \frac{12}{47} \times 2444 = ₹\ 624$

9 Compound Interest

COMPOUND INTEREST

In business transaction if interest as it becomes due is not paid to the lender but is added on to the principal, the money is said to be lent at *compound interest* and the total sum owed after a given time is called the amount at compound interest for that time. After a certain period, the difference between the amount and the original principal is called the compound Interest (C.I.).

Some Important Formulae

Let, Principal = P,
Time = n years,
Rate = $r\%$ p.a.
then,

(*a*) the amount, when interest is compounded annually: Amount $= P\left(1+\frac{r}{100}\right)^n$

(*b*) the amount, when interest is compounded half yearly: Amount $= P\left(1+\frac{r/2}{100}\right)^{2n}$

(*c*) when interest is compounded quarterly :

$$\text{Amount} = P\left(1+\frac{r/4}{100}\right)^{4n}$$

(*d*) when time is fraction of a year, say $4\frac{1}{3}$ years,

then, Amount $= P\left(1+\frac{r}{100}\right)^4 \times \left(1+\frac{\frac{1}{3}r}{100}\right)$

Important Facts

1. The difference between compound interest and simple interest on Rs. P for 2 years and $r\%$ p.a.

$$\text{Difference} = P\left(\frac{r}{100}\right)^2$$

2. The difference between compound interest and simple interest on Rs. P for 3 years at $r\%$ p.a.

$$\text{Difference} = P\left(\frac{r}{100}\right)^2\left(\frac{r}{100}+3\right)$$

3. The amount of Rs. P for 3 years when the rate of interest for first year is $r_1\%$, for second year is $r_2\%$ and third year is $r_3\%$.

$$\text{Amount} = P\left(1+\frac{r_1}{100}\right)\left(1+\frac{r_2}{100}\right)\left(1+\frac{r_3}{100}\right)$$

4. If a certain sum of money becomes m times in t years put at compound interest, in how many years will it be n times?

$$\text{Required time} = \frac{t \log n}{\log m} \text{ years.}$$

5. If a sum of money put out at compound interest amount in t_1 years to Rs. x and in t_2 years to Rs. y, then the rate of interest per cent per annum.

$$\text{Rate } \% = \left[\left(\frac{y}{x}\right)^{1/n} - 1\right] \times 100 \quad \text{where, } n = t_2 - t_1$$

$$\text{or, Rate} = \frac{100(y-x)}{x \times n}\% \quad (\text{where } n = t_2 - t_1)$$

6. If a loan of Rs. P at $r\%$ compound interest p.a. is to be repaid in two equal yearly instalments, then the value of each instalments

$$= \frac{P}{\left(\frac{100}{100+r}\right)+\left(\frac{100}{100+r}\right)^2}$$

7. If a loan of Rs. P at $r\%$ compound interest p.a. is to be repaid in three equal yearly instalments, then the value of each instalment is

$$= \frac{P}{\left(\frac{100}{100+r}\right)+\left(\frac{100}{100+r}\right)^2\left(\frac{100}{100+r}\right)^3}$$

8. When the compound interest of a certain sum for n years at $r\%$ p.a. be C.I., then the simple interest of the same sum for the same time at the same rate of interest is

(*a*) when $n = 2$ and C.I = x; S.I. $= \frac{2x}{2+\frac{r}{100}}$

(*b*) when $n = 3$ and C.I = x; S.I. $= \frac{3x}{3+\frac{3r}{100}+\left(\frac{r}{100}\right)^2}$

MULTIPLE CHOICE QUESTIONS

1. What will be the compound interest on ₹ 8000 for 3 years at 5% p.a.?
(*a*) ₹ 1361 (*b*) ₹ 1261
(*c*) ₹ 1260 (*d*) ₹ 1250
(*e*) None of these

2. Find the amount of ₹ 4000 borrowed for 2 years at 2½% per annum compound interest.
(*a*) ₹ 4202.50 (*b*) ₹ 4102.50
(*c*) ₹ 5202.50 (*d*) ₹ 4000.50
(*e*) None of these

3. What will be the amount if a sum of ₹ 2500 is invested for 1 year at 4% per annum compound interest, interest being compounded half-yearly?
(*a*) ₹ 2625 (*b*) ₹ 2601
(*c*) ₹ 2830 (*d*) ₹ 2901
(*e*) None of these

4. After how many years will ₹ 3375 become ₹ 4096 at $6\frac{2}{3}\%$ per annum compound interest?
(*a*) 4 years (*b*) 2 years
(*c*) 2½ years (*d*) 3 years
(*e*) None of these

5. The present population of a city is 80,000. If the rate of growth is 5% per year, find its population after 3 years.
(*a*) 88,100 (*b*) 95,600
(*c*) 92,610 (*d*) 84,600
(*e*) None of these

6. First year's interest on a sum of money placed at compound interest at the rate of 8% per annum is ₹ 72. What will be interest for the second year?
(*a*) ₹ 77.76 (*b*) ₹ 78.66
(*c*) ₹ 85.66 (*d*) ₹ 78.76
(*e*) None of these

7. In how many years will a sum of ₹ 19200 placed at 10% per annum compound interest yield an interest of ₹ 4032?
(*a*) 1½ years (*b*) 2½ years
(*c*) 2 years (*d*) 3 years
(*e*) None of these

8. The simple interest on a sum of ₹ 4800 for 2 years is ₹ 768. What will be the compound interest on the same sum at the same rate and for the same period?
(*a*) ₹ 798.72
(*b*) ₹ 870.75
(*c*) ₹ 920.69
(*d*) ₹ 884.20
(*e*) None of these

9. If the first year's interest on a certain sum of money placed at 5% p.a. compound interest is ₹ 1200, what will be the interest for the third year?
(*a*) ₹ 1220 (*b*) ₹ 1323
(*c*) ₹ 1423 (*d*) ₹ 1330
(*e*) None of these

10. A man deposits ₹ 1200 in a bank on the 1st day of each year. If the bank pays 5% per annum compound interest on deposited sum of money, what will be the amount to his credit on the 10th day of the second year?
(*a*) ₹ 2560 (*b*) ₹ 2460
(*c*) ₹ 2370 (*d*) ₹ 2860
(*e*) None of these

11. The difference between simple and compound interest on a sum of ₹ P for 2 years at *r*% per annum will be:
(*a*) $P\left(\frac{100}{r}\right)^2$ (*b*) $\frac{\left(\frac{100}{r}\right)^2}{P}$
(*c*) $\frac{P}{\left(\frac{100}{r}\right)^2}$ (*d*) $\frac{\left(\frac{r}{100}\right)^2}{P}$
(*e*) None of these

12. A man purchased a sewing machine for ₹ 5000. If due to sustained use value of this sewing machine depreciates by 6% annually, find its value after 3 years.
(*a*) ₹ 3775.67 (*b*) ₹ 4152.92
(*c*) ₹ 4250.25 (*d*) ₹ 4356.25
(*e*) None of these

13. What will be the difference between compound and simple interest on ₹ 11,000 for 2 years at 6% per annum?
(*a*) ₹ 39.60 (*b*) ₹ 41.40
(*c*) ₹ 38.70 (*d*) ₹ 35.50
(*e*) None of these

14. Find the sum on which the difference between compound and simple interest for 3 years at 10% per annum will be ₹ 868.
(*a*) ₹ 29500 (*b*) ₹ 27625
(*c*) ₹ 28500 (*d*) ₹ 28000
(*e*) None of these

15. Two friends A and B jointly lent out ₹ 81,600 at 4% per annum compound interest, payable annually. 2 years after A gets the same amount as B gets after 3 years. The investment made by B was :
(*a*) ₹ 30,000 (*b*) ₹ 40,000
(*c*) ₹ 45,000 (*d*) ₹ 38,000
(*e*) None of these

ANSWERS

1	2	3	4	5	6	7	8	9	10
(*b*)	(*a*)	(*b*)	(*d*)	(*c*)	(*a*)	(*c*)	(*a*)	(*b*)	(*b*)
11	**12**	**13**	**14**	**15**					
(*c*)	(*b*)	(*a*)	(*d*)	(*b*)					

EXPLANATORY ANSWERS

3. Here, P = ₹ 2500, R = 4% p.a. = 4/2% = 2% half yearly, Time = 1 year

i.e., 1 × 2 = 2 half years

∴ $n = 2$

$$\therefore \quad A = 2500\left(1+\frac{2}{100}\right)^2 = 2500\left(\frac{51}{50}\right)^2$$

$$= \frac{2500\times51\times51}{50\times50} = ₹\ 2601$$

4. ∵ P = ₹ 3375, R = $6\frac{2}{3}\% = \frac{20}{3}\%$

Amount = ₹ 4096

Using the formula, $A = P\left(1+\frac{R}{100}\right)^n$,

we get $4096 = 3375\left(1+\frac{20}{3\times100}\right)^n$

or, $\frac{4096}{3375} = \left(1+\frac{1}{15}\right)^n$ or $\left(\frac{16}{15}\right)^3 = \left(\frac{16}{15}\right)^n$

or, $n = 3$

∴ Required time = 3 years.

6. Second year's interest = 1st year's interest + Interest on 1st year's interest

∴ Second year's interest = 72 + 8% of 72

$$= 72+\frac{72\times8}{100}$$

= 72 + 5.76 = ₹ 77.76

9. Since for the first year simple interest is equal to the compound interest.

$$\therefore \quad P = \frac{S.I.\times100}{R\times T} = \frac{1200\times100}{5\times1} = ₹\ 24000$$

Principal for the second year

= ₹ 24000 + ₹ 1200 = ₹ 25200

∴ Interest for the second year

$$= \frac{25200\times5\times1}{100} = ₹\ 1260$$

Principal for the third year

= ₹ 25200 + ₹ 1260 = ₹ 26460

∴ Interest for the third year

$$= \frac{26460\times5\times1}{100} = ₹\ 1323$$

10. 1st year's interest on ₹ 1200 = $\frac{1200\times5\times1}{100}$ = ₹ 60

∴ Amount to his credit at the beginning of the first year

= ₹ 1200 + ₹ 60 = ₹ 1260

He deposits another ₹ 1200 on the 1st day of the second year.

∴ The amount to his credit on the 10th day of the second year

= ₹ 1260 + ₹ 1200 = ₹ 2460.

11. According to rule 3 it is clear that difference between C.I. and S.I. for 2 year = $P\Big/\left(\frac{100}{r}\right)^2$

13. According to formula

P = ₹ 11000, R = 6%, Difference between C.I. & S.I. = x = ?

$$x = \frac{P}{\left(\frac{100}{R}\right)^2} = \frac{11000}{\left(\frac{100}{6}\right)^2}$$

$$= \frac{11000\times6\times6}{100\times100} = ₹\ 39.60.$$

14. According to formula,

∵ R = 10%

Difference between C.I. and S.I. (x) = ₹ 868

Since Time = 3 years

$$\therefore \quad \text{Sum of money} = \frac{x\times100^3}{R^2(300+R)} = \frac{868\times100^3}{10^2(300+10)}$$

$$= \frac{868\times100^3}{100\times310} = ₹\ 28000$$

Hence, the required sum is ₹ 28000.

10

Discount

Discount is the reduction or an allowance made from the amount of a bill in lieu of its immediate cash payment. The reduction made in consideration of making immediate payment is called discount or *true discount* (T.D.). The immediate cash payment is called *present worth* (P.W.) or present value.

Important Formulae

(*i*) Sum Due (S.D.) = P.W. + T.D.

(*ii*) P.W. = S.D. – T.D.

$$= \frac{100 \times \text{S.D.}}{100+(\text{T}\times\text{R})} \text{ at Simple Interest}$$

$$= \frac{\text{S.D.}}{\left(1+\frac{\text{R}}{100}\right)^n} \text{ at Compound Interest}$$

(*iii*) T.D. = S.D. – P.D.

(*iv*) T.D. on Sum Due = Interest on P.W.

(*v*) $\text{T.D.} = \frac{\text{S.D.}\times\text{R}\times\text{T}}{100+(\text{R}\times\text{T})}$

(*vi*) $\text{T} = \frac{100\times\text{T.D.}}{\text{P.W.}\times\text{R}}$

(*vii*) $\text{R} = \frac{100\times\text{T.D}}{\text{P.W.}\times\text{T}}$

Banker's Discount (B.D.)

In business when a trader buys goods from wholesaler, the payment is generally made by a bill. If wholesaler wants money at earlier date, bill is sold to the banker for ready money and it is said to be discounted and the amount which the banker deducts is called Banker's discount.

Banker's Discount (B.D.) is the same as the simple interest on the amount of bill for the number of days the bill has yet to run.

Banker's Gain (B.G.)

It is the difference between the simple interest on the sum due and that on the Present Worth of the sum due.

Important Formulae

(*i*) $\text{B.D.} = \frac{\text{S.D.}\times\text{T}\times\text{R}}{100} = \frac{\text{T.D.}\times\text{S}}{\text{P.W}}$

(*ii*) B.G. = B.D. – T.D.

(*ii*) $\text{S.D.} = \frac{\text{B.D}\times\text{T.D.}}{\text{B.D.}-\text{T.D}} = \frac{\text{S.I.}\times\text{T.D.}}{\text{S.I.}-\text{T.D.}}$

(*iv*) $\text{S.D.} = \frac{\text{B.D.}\times 100}{\text{R}\times\text{T}}$

(*v*) $\text{Time} = \frac{\text{B.D.}\times 100}{\text{S.D.}\times\text{R}}$

(*vi*) $\text{Rate} = \frac{\text{B.D.}\times 100}{\text{T}\times\text{S.D.}}$

(*vii*) Money paid by the banker = S.D. – B.D.

(*viii*) Banker's Discount = T.D. + Interest on True Discount

(*ix*) $\text{T.D.} = \sqrt{\text{P.W.}\times\text{B.G}}$

Note : *Three days of grace are always added while calculating time in questions on Banker's Discount.*

MULTIPLE CHOICE QUESTIONS

1. Find the true discount on a bill for ₹ 1270 due 7 months hence at 10% per annum.

(*a*) ₹ 10 (*b*) ₹ 35
(*c*) ₹ 70 (*d*) ₹ 170
(*e*) None of these

2. The sum due 219 days hence whose present worth at $5\frac{1}{2}$% of ₹ 400 is :

(*a*) ₹ 300 (*b*) ₹ 312
(*c*) ₹ 390 (*d*) ₹ 413.20
(*e*) None of these

3. What is the rate of interest when the P.W. of ₹ 8175 due in 5 months ₹ 8000?

(*a*) 4% (*b*) 5%
(*c*) $5\frac{1}{4}$% (*d*) $5\frac{1}{2}$%
(*e*) None of these

4. If the interest on ₹ 50 at $4\frac{1}{2}\%$ be equal to the discount of ₹ 59 for the same time and at the same rate when is the latter sum due?

(a) 3 years (b) 4 years
(c) 5 years (d) 2 years
(e) None of these

5. The interest on a certain sum of money is ₹ 67.20 and the discount on the same sum of money for the same time and at the same rate is ₹ 60. What is the sum?

(a) ₹ 560 (b) ₹ 500
(c) ₹ 460 (d) ₹ 400
(e) None of these

6. The relation between T.D., P.W. and B.G. is :

(a) $(PW)^2 = BG \times TD$ (b) $(TD)^2 = PW \times BG$
(c) $BG = BD \times TD$ (d) $PW \times BG = TD$
(e) None of these

7. A banker discounts 4 months bill of ₹ 5000 at 3% discount. What rate of interest per annum is he charging?

(a) 3% (b) $3\frac{1}{33}\%$
(c) $33\frac{1}{3}\%$ (d) $3\frac{1}{3}\%$
(e) None of these

8. The difference between the banker's discount and the true discount at 3% for 1 year is ₹ 27. Find the sum.

(a) ₹ 3090 (b) ₹ 30900
(c) ₹ 309 (d) ₹ 30.90
(e) None of these

9. The difference between S.I. and T.D. on a sum of money due 2 years hence at 5% p.a. is Rs. 11. What is the sum?

(a) ₹ 1200 (b) ₹ 1210
(c) ₹ 1225 (d) ₹ 1235
(e) None of these

10. If B.D. and T.D. on a certain sum for the same time and at the same rate be ₹ 172 and ₹ 160 respectively, find the sum.

(a) ₹ $229\frac{1}{3}$ (b) ₹ $2290\frac{1}{3}$
(c) ₹ $2293\frac{1}{3}$ (d) ₹ 2293
(e) None of these

ANSWERS

1	2	3	4	5	6	7	8	9	10
(c)	(d)	(c)	(b)	(a)	(b)	(b)	(b)	(b)	(c)

EXPLANATORY ANSWERS

1. $$\text{T.D.} = \frac{A \times R \times T}{100 + RT} = \frac{1270 \times 10 \times 7}{\left(100 + 10 \times \frac{7}{12}\right)12}$$

$$= \frac{1270 \times 10 \times 7}{1270} = ₹\ 70.\ \textbf{Ans.}$$

3. Present Worth = ₹ 8000

Interest on ₹ 8000 for $\frac{5}{12}$ year

= ₹ 8175 – ₹ 8000 = ₹ 175

∴ Interest on ₹ 100 for 1 year

$$= \frac{175}{8000} \times \frac{100}{5} \times 12 = ₹\ \frac{21}{4}$$

∴ Rate = $5\frac{1}{4}\%$

5. ∵ Interest on Sum – T.D. = Interest on T.D.

∴ ₹ 67.20 – ₹ 60 = Interest on ₹ 60

∴ $7\frac{1}{5}$ = Interest on ₹ 60

∴ ₹ 1 = Interest on $\dfrac{60}{7\frac{1}{5}}$

∴ $67\frac{1}{5}$ = Interest on $\dfrac{60}{7\frac{1}{5}} \times 67\frac{1}{5}$

∴ The required sum = $\dfrac{60}{7\frac{1}{5}} \times 67\frac{1}{5}$

= ₹ 560. **Ans.**

10. $$\text{S.D.} = \frac{\text{B.D.} \times \text{T.D.}}{\text{B.D.} - \text{T.D.}} = \frac{172 \times 160}{172 - 160}$$

$$= \frac{172 \times 160}{12} = \frac{6880}{3}$$

$$= ₹\ 2293\frac{1}{3}.\ \textbf{Ans.}$$

11 Partnership

When two or more than two persons agree to invest money to run a business jointly, this association or deal is called *partnership* and those who invest money are called *pertners.* The total investment is called the *capital.*

Kind of partners : There are two kinds of partners.

1. Working or active partner : When a partner devotes his time for the business in addition to invest his money, he is called a working partner. With mutual agreement, the active partners get some fixed percentage of profit as *working allowance.*

2. Sleeping or non-active partner : A partner who simply invests money, but does not attend to the business is called a sleeping partner.

King of partnership :

(*i*) **Simple partnership :** If the capitals of several partners are invested for the same period. It is called a simple partnership.

(*ii*) **Compound or complex partnership :** If the capitals of the partners are invested for diffrent intervals of time, the partnership is called compound or complex.

Attention Students

In every examination the questions are generally set on compound partnership. But such questions are first to be converted into simple partnership and then solved.

Some Important Formulae

1. If the capitals of two partners are invested for the same duration of period A_1 and A_2 be their investments and total profit is Rs. P, then share of the partners in the profits are Rs. $\frac{A_1 \times P}{A_1 + A_2}$ and Rs. $\frac{A_2 \times P}{A_1 + A_2}$.
2. If the capitals of two partners be Rs. A_1 and A_2 for the periods t_1 and t_2 respectively and the profit be Rs. P, then shares of the partners in the profit are Rs. $\frac{A_1 \times t_1 \times P}{A_1 t_1 + A_2 t_2}$ and Rs. $\frac{A_2 t_2 \times P}{A_1 t_1 + A_2 t_2}$

MULTIPLE CHOICE QUESTIONS

1. A and B started a business with the investment of ₹ 80000 and ₹ 60000 respectively. At the end of the year total profit in the business will be divided between them in the ratio of :

(*a*) 2 : 3 (*b*) 3 : 4
(*c*) 2 : 1 (*d*) 4 : 3
(*e*) None of these

2. A and B started a business in partnership with the investment of ₹ 4000 and ₹ 6000 respectively. If at the end of the year total profit is ₹ 2250, what will each of them get?

(*a*) ₹ 900, ₹ 1350 (*b*) ₹ 800, ₹ 1450
(*c*) ₹ 1000, ₹ 1250 (*d*) ₹ 1200, ₹ 1050
(*e*) None of these

3. Sonu, Monu and Mohit together start a business with the investment of ₹ 1800, ₹ 1500 and ₹ 1600 respectively. If at the end of the year, Monu gains a profit of ₹ 900 the total profit in the business is:

(*a*) ₹ 2880 (*b*) ₹ 2940
(*c*) ₹ 3200 (*d*) ₹ 3240
(*e*) None of these

4. Omdutt started a business with a capital of ₹ 8000. After six months, Sanjay joined him with investment of some capital. If at the end of the year each of them gets equal amount as profit, how much did Sanjay invest in the business?

(*a*) ₹ 18000 (*b*) ₹ 17500
(*c*) ₹ 16000 (*d*) ₹ 16500
(*e*) None of these

5. A, B and C buy a farm for ₹ 100000. A contributes ₹ 40000 in it. They sell it, and from the profit B gets ₹ 2750 and C gets ₹ 1750. What would be the profit of A?

(*a*) ₹ 2780 (*b*) ₹ 3000
(*c*) ₹ 3280 (*d*) ₹ 2785
(*e*) None of these

6. A and B jointly invest ₹ 2100 and ₹ 3100 respectively in a firm. A is an active partner and hence he gets 25%

of the profit separately. If their business yields them total ₹ 1040 as profit, what will be the gain of each of them?

(a) ₹ 415, ₹ 625 (b) ₹ 575, ₹ 465
(c) ₹ 515, ₹ 525 (d) ₹ 560, ₹ 480
(e) None of these

7. Two partners invested ₹ 12500 and ₹ 8500 respectively in a business and decided that 60% of the profit incurred from the business will be equally divided between them while remaining profit will be assumed as interest on their capitals. If one of the partners gets ₹ 300 more profit than the other, what is the total profit in the business?

(a) ₹ 3937.50 (b) ₹ 4940.50
(c) ₹ 3936.50 (d) ₹ 4156
(e) None of these

8. Neeraj and Birju are partners in a business. They divide between them the profit incurred in the business in such a proportion that $\frac{2}{5}$th portion of the profit gained by Neeraj is equal to $\frac{1}{3}$rd portion of the profit gained by Birju. If total profit in the business is ₹ 1210, find the profit earned by Birju.

(a) ₹ 780 (b) ₹ 550
(c) ₹ 680 (d) ₹ 590
(e) None of these

9. A, B and C together took under lease a pasture ground for ₹ 888. If in this pasture ground A put his 20 sheeps out to graze for 2½ months, B put his 30 sheeps out to graze for 4 months and C put his 36 sheeps out to graze for 3½ months, find the lease amount paid by each of them.

(a) ₹ 205, ₹ 315, ₹ 378 (b) ₹ 150, ₹ 360, ₹ 378
(c) ₹ 170, ₹ 360, ₹ 358 (d) ₹ 228, ₹ 360, ₹ 300
(e) None of these

10. A, B and C started a business with the investment of ₹ 5000, ₹ 6000 and ₹ 4000 respectively. A is an active partner and therefore he gets 30% of the profit separately. Rest of the profit in divided in the ratio of their capitals. If at the end of year, A's profit is ₹ 200 more than the sum of the profits made by B and C, find the profit made by each of them.

(a) ₹ 1620, ₹ 1242, ₹ 1178
(b) ₹ 1720, ₹ 1252, ₹ 1228
(c) ₹ 1510, ₹ 1187, ₹ 1133
(d) ₹ 1600, ₹ 840, ₹ 560
(e) None of these

ANSWERS

1	2	3	4	5	6	7	8	9	10
(d)	(a)	(b)	(c)	(b)	(b)	(a)	(b)	(b)	(d)

EXPLANATORY ANSWERS

1. The two partners invest their capitals for the same period

∴ Profit will be divided between them in the ratio of their capitals

∴ Ratio between their profits = 80000 : 60000 = 4 : 3

3. Sonu, Monu and Mohit invest their capitals for the same period

∴ Ratio of their profits = 1800 : 1500 : 1600 = 18 : 15 : 16

Sum of proportionals = 18 +15 + 16 = 49

Monu's profit = ₹ 900

∴ Total profit in the business

$= \frac{900}{15} \times 49 =$ ₹ 2940

4. Investment by Omdutt = ₹ 8000 for 12 months

∴ Capital of Omdutt = ₹ 8000 × 12 = ₹ 96000 for 1 month

Suppose Sanjay invested ₹ x for 6 months

∴ Capital of Sanjay = ₹ $x \times 6$ = ₹ $6x$ for 1 month

Since they get equal amounts as profit

∴ Their investment will also be same

Therefore, $6x = 96000$

or, $x = \frac{96000}{6} = 16000$

∴ Sanjay invested ₹ 16000 in the business.

5. Capital of (A + B + C) = ₹ 100000

Capital of A = ₹ 40000

∴ Capital of (B + C) = ₹ (100000 − 40000) = ₹ 60000

Profit of (B + C) = ₹ (2750 + 1750) = ₹ 4500

∴ A's profit $= 4500 \times \frac{40000}{60000} =$ ₹ 3000

8. According to question :

2/5 portion of profit made by Neeraj = 1/3rd portion of profit made by Birju

∴ Ratio between profits of Neeraj and Birju

$= \frac{2}{5} : \frac{1}{3} = 6 : 5$

Where total profit = ₹ 1210

In the above proportion, sum of proportionals = 6 + 5 = 11

∴ Share of Birju in the profit $= \frac{5}{11} \times 1210 =$ ₹ 550

12 Area and Perimeter

In mensuration we often have to deal with the problem of finding the areas and perimeters of plane figures.

Triangle

1. Perimeter = 3 × side
2. Area = $\frac{1}{2} \times \text{base} \times \text{height}$, or

   Area = $\sqrt{s(s-a)(s-b)(s-c)}$

   where *a*, *b*, *c*, are the lengths of the sides of triangle

   and $s = \frac{a+b+c}{2}$

Right Angled Triangle

It is one where one of the angles is right angle, i.e., 90°.

1. $(\text{Hypotenuse})^2 = (\text{Perpendicular})^2 + (\text{Base})^2$
2. Area = $\frac{1}{2} \times \text{Base} \times \text{Perpendicular}$

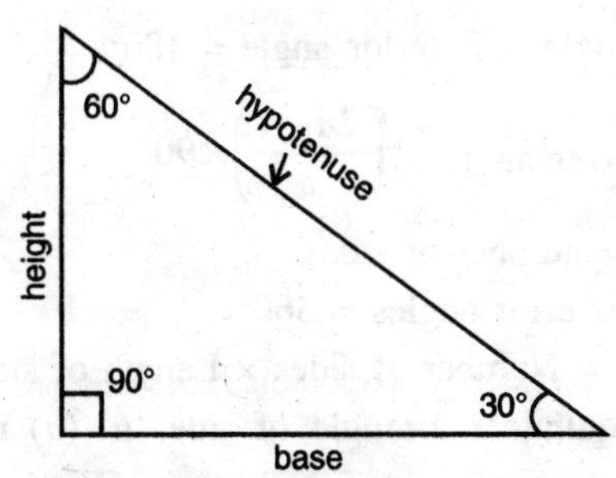

N.B. : 30-60-90 triangle is a special case of right angled triangle, where the three angles are equal to 30°, 60° and 90°.

Here,

3. Side opposite to the angle 30° = $\frac{1}{2} \times \text{Hypotenuse}$
4. Side opposite to the angle 60° = $\frac{\sqrt{3}}{2} \times \text{Hypotenuse}$

Equilateral Triangle

All three sides are equal in length and all three angles are equal to 60°

1. Area = $\frac{\sqrt{3}}{4} \times (\text{Side})^2$
2. Area = $\frac{(\text{Height})^2}{\sqrt{3}}$
3. Height = $\frac{\sqrt{3}}{2} \times \text{side}$
4. Perimeter = 3 × side

Isosceles Triangle

Two sides are equal in lengths.

1. Area = $\frac{b}{4}\sqrt{4a^2 - b^2}$

   where *a* = lengths of opposite sides

   b = length of unequal side
2. In an isosceles right triangle,

   (*a*) Hypotenuse = $\sqrt{2} \times \text{congruent side (a)}$

   (*b*) Area = $\frac{1}{2} \times a^2$

   (*c*) Perimeter = $\sqrt{2} \times a(\sqrt{2}+1)$

Rectangle

1. Area = length(*l*) × breadth(*b*)
2. Perimeter = 2(*l* + *b*)
3. Diagonal = $\sqrt{l^2 + b^2}$
4. Area of the path (inside of the rectangle) = $2x\,(l + b - 2x)$ where, *x* is the width of path.
5. Area of the path (Outside of the rectangle) = $2x\,(l + b + 2x)$

Square :

1. Area = $(\text{Side})^2$
2. Perimeter = 4 × side
3. Diagonal = $\text{side} \times \sqrt{2}$
4. Area of path (outside of square) = $4x \times (a + x)$ [where *a* = side, *x* = width of path]
5. Area of path (inside of square) = $4x \times (a - x)$

Parallelogram

In parallelogram opposite sides are parallel and equal. The two diagonals are not always equal but they bisect each other at the point of intersection.

Area = Base × Height.

Trapezium

It is a quadrilateral whose one pair of opposite sides is parallel. Other two opposite sides are oblique.

1. Area $= \frac{1}{2} \times$ Height $\times$ (Sum of parallel sides). Here, height is the distance between the two parallel sides.

2. Median $= \left(\frac{1}{2} \times \text{Sum of parallel side}\right)$. Here, median is the segment joining the midpoints of oblique sides.

3. Height $= \frac{2}{K}\sqrt{s(s-k)(s-c)(s-d)}$
(where $k = a - b$, *i.e.*, the difference between the parallel sides and c and d are the two non-parallel sides.)
Also $s = \frac{k+c+d}{2}$

Rhombus

It is parallelogram whose all sides are equal and diagonals are bisect each other at right angle.

1. Area $= \frac{1}{2} \times$ Product of diagonals
2. Side $= \sqrt{\left(\frac{d_1}{2}\right)^2 + \left(\frac{d_2}{2}\right)^2}$, where d_1 and d_2 are diagonals
3. Perimeter = 4 × side
4. Area of a rhombus (with one side and one diagonal given)
$= \text{diagonal} \times \sqrt{(\text{side})^2 - \left(\frac{\text{diagonal}}{2}\right)^2}$
5. Other diagonal $= 2 \times \sqrt{(\text{side})^2 - \left(\frac{\text{diagonal}}{2}\right)^2}$

Quadrilateral

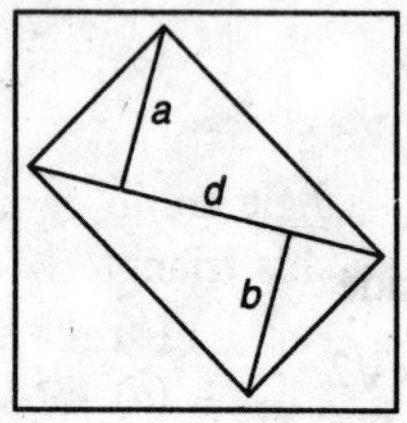

Area $= \frac{1}{2} \times$ One diagonal $\times$ (Sum of perpendicular to it from the opposite vertices) $= \frac{1}{2} \times d \times (a+b)$

Circle :

1. Diameter = 2 × Radius
2. Area $= \pi r^2 = \frac{\pi}{4} d^2$ [where d = diameter $= \sqrt{\frac{4A}{\pi}}$
3. Circumference $= 2\pi r = \pi d$
4. Radius $= \frac{\text{Circumference}}{2\pi} = \frac{\sqrt{\text{Area}}}{\pi}$
5. Length of an Arc $= \frac{\theta}{360^\circ} \times 2\pi r$
6. Area of sector $= \frac{\theta}{360^\circ} \times \pi r^2 = \frac{1}{2} \times \text{Arc} \times r$
7. Area of the ring or circular path $= \pi (R + r)(R - r)$

Remember some tricks for plane figures.

(*i*) If area related each side is increased by $a\%$, then

(*a*) Percentage increase in the area $= 2a + \frac{a^2}{100}$

(*b*) $\frac{\text{New Area}}{\text{Old Area}} = \left(1 + \frac{a}{100}\right)^2$

(*ii*) If area related to each side is decreased by $a\%$, then

(*a*) Percentage decrease in area $= 2a - \frac{a^2}{100}$

(*b*) $\frac{\text{New Area}}{\text{Old Area}} = \left(1 - \frac{a}{100}\right)^2$

(*iii*) If the perimeter of a rectangle, circle, quadrilateral and triangle are same, then area of the circle will be the largest.

Polygone :

1. Interior angle + Exterior angle = 180°
2. Each interior angle $= \left(\frac{2n-4}{n}\right) \times 90^\circ$
where n = number of sides
3. Sum of Exterior angles = 360°
4. Perimeter = Number of sides × Length of side.
5. For an equilateral triangle of side '*a*' (*a*) radius of inscribed circle $= \frac{a}{2\sqrt{3}}$ and side of the triangle $= 2\sqrt{3}r$, (*b*) radius of circumcircle $= \frac{a}{\sqrt{3}}$
6. Area of regular polygon $= \frac{1}{2}$(No. of sides) (Radius of the incribed circle)
7. Area of regular hexagon $= \frac{3\sqrt{3}}{2}(\text{side})^2 = 2.598\ (\text{side})^2$
8. Area of a regular octagon $= 2\left(\sqrt{2}+1\right)(\text{side})^2 = 4.828\ (\text{side})^2$
9. Area of cyclic quadrilateral A
$= \sqrt{s(s-a)(s-b)(s-c)(s-d)}$ where, $s = \frac{a+b+c+d}{2}$
and, $\angle A + \angle C = \angle B + \angle D = 180^\circ$

MULTIPLE CHOICE QUESTIONS

1. A rectangle measures 50 cm × 25 cm. Its area is
(*a*) 1150 sq. cm. (*b*) 1250 sq. cm.
(*c*) 1275 sq. cm. (*d*) 1280 sq. cm.
(*e*) None of these

2. A field is in the form of a square whose perimeter is 580 m. Area of this field is
(*a*) 20025 sq. m. (*b*) 20225 sq. m.
(*c*) 30025 sq. m. (*d*) 19975 sq. cm.
(*e*) None of these

3. Find the area of the square whose each side measures 20 cm.
(*a*) 300 sq. cm. (*b*) 380 sq. cm.
(*c*) 360 sq. cm. (*d*) 400 sq. cm.
(*e*) None of these

4. Area of a circle is 154 sq. cm. Its circumference will be
(*a*) 44 cm (*b*) 48 cm
(*c*) 54 cm (*d*) 68 cm
(*e*) None of these

5. The base and the height of a triangle is 8 cm and 10 cm respectively. Its area will be
(*a*) 40 sq. cm. (*b*) 20 sq. cm.
(*c*) 49 sq. cm. (*d*) 64 sq. cm.
(*e*) None of these

6. If it is given that the parallel sides of a trapezium are 15 m and 25 m while the distance between them is 10 m. its area will be
(*a*) 150 sq. m. (*b*) 225 sq. m.
(*c*) 200 sq. m. (*d*) 270 sq. m.
(*e*) None of these

7. Perimeter of a rectangular field is 760 m and its length and breadth are in the ratio 11 : 8. Area of this rectangular field is
(*a*) 35200 sq. m. (*b*) 34700 sq. m.
(*c*) 35600 sq. m. (*d*) 45200 sq. m.
(*e*) None of these

8. If side of a square is reduced by 50%, its area will be reduced by
(*a*) 50% (*b*) 75%
(*c*) 80% (*d*) 60%
(*e*) None of these

9. If area of a square is equal to the area of a rectangle 6.4 m long and 2.5 m wide, then each side of this square measures
(*a*) 8 m (*b*) 5.4 m
(*c*) 3.8 m (*d*) 4 m
(*e*) None of these

10. If perimeter of a right angled triangle is six times its smallest side, then the three sides of this triangle are in the ratio of
(*a*) 13 : 5 : 12 (*b*) 13 : 12 : 5
(*c*) 12 : 5 : 13 (*d*) 13 : 5 : 10
(*e*) None of these

11. The perimeter of a square is 24 m and that of another is 32 m. Find the perimeter of a third square area of which is equal to sum of the areas of these two squares
(*a*) 40 m (*b*) 51 m
(*c*) 37 m (*d*) 42 m
(*e*) None of these

12. If each side of a square is doubled, its area will become
(*a*) double (*b*) four times
(*c*) three times (*d*) eight times
(*e*) None of these

13. The difference between the areas of two squares is 225 sq. metres and each side of the bigger square is 25 metres. The side of the smaller square is
(*a*) 18 m (*b*) 21 m
(*c*) 20 m (*d*) 22 m
(*e*) None of these

14. If the perimeter of an equilateral triangle is 72 cm, its area will be
(*a*) $144\sqrt{3}$ sq. cm (*b*) $142\sqrt{3}$ sq. cm
(*c*) $154\sqrt{2}$ sq. cm. (*d*) $144\sqrt{2}$ sq. cm.
(*e*) None of these

15. The radii of two circles are 5 cm and 12 cm respectively. Find the radius of a circle which is equal in area to these two circles.
(*a*) 15 cm (*b*) 13 cm
(*c*) 10 cm (*d*) 8 cm
(*e*) None of these

16. If the circumference of a circle is equal to the perimeter of a square, then their areas are in the ratio of
(*a*) 14 : 11 (*b*) 7 : 8
(*c*) 14 : 13 (*d*) 13 : 11
(*e*) None of these

17. Three sides of a triangle are in the ratio of 17 : 15 : 8. If the perimeter of this triangle is 40 m, find its area
(*a*) 50 sq. m. (*b*) 49 sq. m.
(*c*) 60 sq. m. (*d*) 69 sq. m.
(*e*) None of these

18. If the length of a rectangle is increased by 20% and width is decreased by 15%, then its area
(*a*) decreased by 4% (*b*) increases by 2%
(*c*) decreases by 2% (*d*) increases by 3%
(*e*) None of these

19. Find the perimeter of a rhombus whose diagonals measure 16 cm and 12 cm.
(*a*) 38 cm (*b*) 40 cm
(*c*) 41 cm (*d*) 46 cm.
(*e*) None of these

20. If the difference between the circumference and the radius of a circle is 37 cm, find its diameter.
(*a*) 11 cm (*b*) 12 cm
(*c*) 16 cm (*d*) 14 cm
(*e*) None of these

21. If the diagonal of a square is doubled to make another square, the area of the new square will
(*a*) become fourfold (*b*) become twofold
(*c*) become sixfold (*d*) become eightfold
(*e*) None of these

22. The areas of two concentric circles, forming a ring, are 154 sq. cm and 616 sq. cm. respectively. The width of the ring is
(*a*) 6 cm (*b*) 7 cm
(*c*) 9 cm (*d*) 11 cm
(*e*) None of these

23. If the length of a rectangle is increased by 20%, then by how much percent its breadth must be decreased so as to keep its area unaltered?
(*a*) 25% (*b*) $8\frac{1}{3}\%$
(*c*) $16\frac{2}{3}\%$ (*d*) 20%
(*e*) None of these

24. Each side of a given square is 5 cm and assuming the two opposite sides of this square as diameters, two semicircles are drawn in the inside of the square. If these semicircles are cut out from the square, then the area of the remaining portion of the given square will be
(*a*) $(9 - 6.25\pi)$ sq. cm. (*b*) $(25 - 6.25\pi)$ sq. cm.
(*c*) $(25 - 4.25\pi)$ sq. cm. (*d*) $(36 - 6.25\pi)$ sq. cm.
(*e*) None of these

25. If area of a traingle whose base is 6 cm is equal to the area of a circle of radius 6 cm, find the height of this triangle.
(*a*) 10 cm (*b*) 22 cm
(*c*) 12 cm (*d*) 18 cm
(*e*) None of these

26. If areas of two squares are in the ratio of 25 : 16, their perimeters will be in the ratio of
(*a*) 5 : 4 (*b*) 4 : 5
(*c*) 5 : 2 (*d*) 2 : 3
(*e*) None of these

27. The length and breadth of a room are in the ratio 2 : 1. If the cost of cementing the floor at 75 paise per sq. metre comes to be ₹ 864 and the cost of polishing the walls at ₹ 3.25 per sq. metre comes to be ₹ 884, then the height of the room is
(*a*) $2\frac{8}{9}$m (*b*) $1\frac{8}{9}$m
(*c*) $1\frac{2}{9}$m (*d*) $1\frac{7}{9}$m
(*e*) None of these

28. A garden is 24 m long and 14 m wide. There is a path 1 m wide outside the garden along its sides. If the path is to be constructed with square marble tiles 20 cm × 20 cm, find the number of tiles required to cover the path.
(*a*) 1800 (*b*) 2200
(*c*) 2000 (*d*) 2150
(*e*) None of these

29. Two adjacent sides of a parallelogram are 40 m and 30 m respectively. If one diagonal of the parallelogram measures 50 m, find its area.
(*a*) 1100 sq. m. (*b*) 1200 sq. m.
(*c*) 1400 sq. m. (*d*) 1500 sq. m.
(*e*) None of these

30. Four sides of a trapezium are 50 cm, 17 cm, 25 cm and 12 cm respectively. If the first of the four sides is parallel to the third, find the area of this trapezium.
(*a*) 280 sq. cm. (*b*) 810 sq. cm.
(*c*) 270 sq. cm. (*d*) 225 sq. cm.
(*e*) None of these

ANSWERS

1	2	3	4	5	6	7	8	9	10
(*b*)	(*a*)	(*d*)	(*a*)	(*a*)	(*c*)	(*a*)	(*b*)	(*d*)	(*b*)
11	**12**	**13**	**14**	**15**	**16**	**17**	**18**	**19**	**20**
(*a*)	(*b*)	(*c*)	(*a*)	(*b*)	(*a*)	(*c*)	(*b*)	(*b*)	(*d*)
21	**22**	**23**	**24**	**25**	**26**	**27**	**28**	**29**	**30**
(*a*)	(*b*)	(*c*)	(*b*)	(*c*)	(*a*)	(*b*)	(*c*)	(*b*)	(*c*)

EXPLANATORY ANSWERS

2. Perimeter of the square = 4 × side

According to question :

$$4 \times \text{side} = 580 \Rightarrow \text{side} = \frac{580}{4} = 145 \text{ m}$$

$$\therefore \quad \text{Area} = (\text{side})^2 = (145)^2 = 20025 \text{ sq. m.}$$

4. Area of the circle $= \pi r^2$

$$\therefore \quad \pi r^2 = 154$$

$$\Rightarrow \quad r^2 = \frac{154 \times 7}{22}$$

$$\Rightarrow \quad r^2 = 7 \times 7 \Rightarrow r = 7 \text{ cm}$$

∴ Circumference of the circle

$$= 2\pi r = 2\times\frac{22}{7}\times 7 = 44 \text{ cm.}$$

7. Suppose length and breadth of the rectangular field are $11x$ m and $8x$ m.

∴ Perimeter of the field $= 2(11x + 8x)$

$= 2 \times 19x = 38x$ m.

According to question :

Perimeter of the field = 760 m

∴ $38x = 760 \Rightarrow x = \frac{760}{38} = 20$

∴ Length of the field $= 11 \times 20 = 220$ m

Breadth of the field $= 8 \times 20 = 160$ m

∴ Aea of the field $= 220 \times 160 = 35200$ sq. m.

8. Suppose side of the square = x m

In the first case :

Area of the square = x^2 sq. m.

In the second case :

On effecting 50% reduction in the side of the square,

Side of the new square $= x - 50\%$ of $x = \frac{x}{2}$ m

∴ Area of the new square $= \left(\frac{x}{2}\right)^2 = \frac{x^2}{4}$ sq. m.

∴ Reduction in area of the square

$$= x^2 - \frac{x^2}{4} = \frac{3x^2}{4} \text{ sq. m.}$$

∴ Percentage reduction $= \frac{3x^2/4}{x^2}\times 100 = 75\%$

Hence, area of the square will be reduced by 75%.

9. Area of the rectangle $= 6.4 \times 2.5 = 16.00$ sq. m.

According to question :

Area of the square = Area of the rectangle

∴ Area of the square = 16 sq. m.

∴ Side of the square $= \sqrt{16} = \sqrt{4\times 4} = 4$ m.

11. Perimeter of the 1st square = 24 m

∴ Side of the 1st square $= \frac{24}{4} = 6$ m

Perimeter of the 2nd square = 32 m

∴ Side of the 2nd square $= \frac{32}{4} = 8$ m

According to question :

Area of the third square = Area of the first two squares

∴ Area of the third square = Areas of the 1st square + Area of the 2nd square

$= 6^2 + 8^2 = 36 + 64 = 100$ sq. m.

∴ Side of the third square $= \sqrt{100} = 10$ m

∴ Perimeter of the third square

$= 4 \times$ side $= 4 \times 10 = 40$ m.

12. In the first case :

Side of the square = x m

∴ Area of the square = x^2 sq. m

In the second case :

Side of the square = $2x$ m.

∴ Area of the square $= (2x)^2 = 4x^2$ sq. m

Hence, it is clear that if side of a square is doubled, its area becomes four times.

15. ∵ Radius of the first circle = 5 cm

∴ Area of the first circle $= \pi \times 5^2 = 25\pi$ sq. cm and

Radius of the second circle = 12 cm

∴ Area of the second circle $= \pi \times 12^2 = 144\pi$ sq. cm

According to question :

Area of the new circle = Sum of the areas of the two circles

∴ Area of the new circle $= 25\pi + 144\pi = 169\pi$ sq. cm.

$= \pi(13)^2$ sq. cm

Hence, it is clear that the radius of the new circle will be 13 cm.

17. Suppose sides of the triangle are $17x$ m, $15x$ m and $8x$ metres

∴ Perimeter $= 17x + 15x + 8x = 40x$

According to question :

Perimeter of triangle = 40 m

∴ $40x = 40$

⇒ $x = 1$ m

Therefore, the sides are $17 \times 1 = 17$ m, $15 \times 1 = 15$ m and $8 \times 1 = 8$ m

∵ $(17)^2 = (15)^2 + (8)^2$,

i.e., it is a right angled triangle

∴ Area of the right angled triangle $= \frac{1}{2}\times$ base $\times$ height

$$= \frac{1}{2}\times 8\times 15 = 60 \text{ sq.m.}$$

19. Side of rhombus

$$= \sqrt{\left(\frac{\text{One diagonal}}{2}\right)^2 + \left(\frac{\text{Other diagonal}}{2}\right)^2}$$

$$= \sqrt{\left(\frac{16}{2}\right)^2 + \left(\frac{12}{2}\right)^2} = \sqrt{8^2 + 6^2}$$

$$= \sqrt{64+36} = \sqrt{100} = 10 \text{ cm.}$$

∴ Perimeter of the rhombus

$= 4 \times$ side $= 4 \times 10 = 40$ cm.

20. Suppose radius of the circle = R cm

∴ Circumference of the circle = $2\pi R$ cm.

According to question :

$$2\pi R - R = 37$$

$$\Rightarrow \quad R\left(2\times\frac{22}{7}-1\right) = 37$$

$$\Rightarrow \quad R(44 - 7) = 37 \times 7 \Rightarrow R \times 37 = 37 \times 7$$

$$\Rightarrow \quad R = \frac{37\times7}{37} = 7$$

$\therefore$ Radius of the circle = 7 cm

Hence, diameter of the circle = 2R = 2 × 7 = 14 cm.

25. Radius of the circle = 6 cm

$\therefore$ Area of the circle = 36 sq. cm

According to question :

Area of the triangle of base 6 cm = Area of the circle of radius 6 cm

$$\therefore \quad \frac{1}{2}\times\text{base}\times\text{height} = 36 \Rightarrow \frac{1}{2}\times6\times\text{height} = 36$$

$$\Rightarrow \text{Height of the triangle} = \frac{36\times2}{6} = 12 \text{ cm.}$$

26. Suppose sides of the first and the second squares are x and y respectively

$\therefore$ Area of the first square = x^2 sq. unit

And area of the second square = y^2 sq. unit

According to question :

Areas of the two circles are in the ratio 25 : 16

$$\therefore \quad x^2 : y^2 = 25 : 16$$

$$\Rightarrow \quad x : y = 5 : 4$$

Ratio of perimeters of the two squares

$= 4x : 4y$

$= x : y = 5 : 4.$

28. Area of the garden = 24 × 14 = 336 sq. m

Area of the (garden + path) = 26 × 16 = 416 sq. m

$\therefore$ Area of the path = 416 – 336 = 80 sq. m

Area of 1 tile = 20 × 20 = 400 sq. cm

= .04 sq. m

$\therefore$ Number of tiles required to cover the path

$$= \frac{80}{.04} = 2000.$$

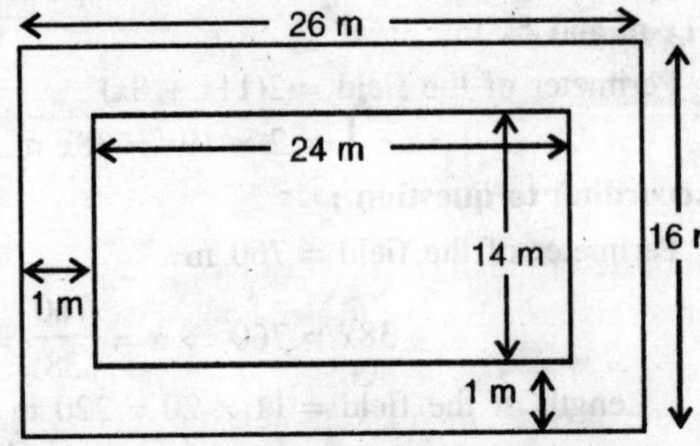

29. Suppose in the parallelogram ABCD,

AB = 40 m, BC = 30 m, AB = CD, BC = AD

Area of the parallelogram ABCD

= Area of (ΔABC + ΔADC)

= 2 × Area of the ΔABC

Since $50^2 = 40^2 + 30^2$

$\therefore$ Two two triangles, *i.e.*, ΔABC and ΔADC are right angled triangle.

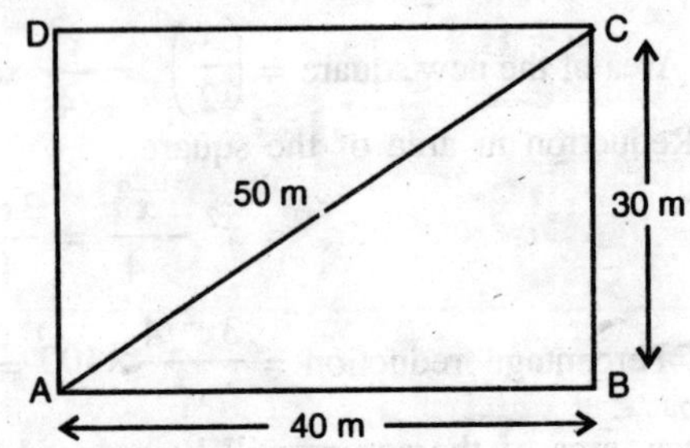

$\therefore$ Area of parallelogram ABCD

$$= \frac{1\times30\times40}{2} + \frac{1\times30\times40}{2}$$

$= 600 + 600 = 1200$ sq. metres.

13 Distance and Time

Introduction : If a man walks a distance 3 km in each hour, we say that his speed is 3 km per hour, i.e., 3 km/L.

Thus the *speed* of a body is the rate at which it is moving, i.e., distance travelled in unit time and is measured by the distance which the body should move through in a given time.

Main Formulae

1. Speed = Distance ÷ Time
2. Distance = Time × Speed
3. Time = Distance ÷ Speed
4. x km/hr = $\left(x \times \frac{5}{18}\right)$ m/sec
5. x metres/sec = $\left(x \times \frac{18}{5}\right)$ km/hr.
6. If the speed of a body is changed in the ratio $m : n$, then the ratio of the time taken changes in the ratio $n : m$.

Average Speed : When a certain distance is covered by a body in parts at different speeds, then the average speed

$$= \frac{\text{Total distance covered by a body}}{\text{Total time taken}}$$

Caution : In such cases, average speed should not be calculated as average of different speeds, i.e.,

$$\text{Ave. speed} \neq \frac{\text{Sum of speed}}{\text{No. of different speed}}$$

There are two different cases when average speed is required.

Case I : When time remains constant and speed varies :

Rule : If a man travels at the rate of x km/h for t hours and again at the rate of y km/h for another t hours, then for the whole journey, his average speed is given by

$$\text{Average speed} = \frac{\text{Total distance}}{\text{Total time taken}}$$

$$= \frac{xt + yt}{t + t} = \frac{x + y}{2} \text{ kmph.}$$

Case II : When the distance covered remains same and the speeds vary :

Rule : When a man covers a certain distance with a speed of x km/h and another equal distance at the rate of y km/h, then for the whole journey, the average speed is given by

$$\text{Average speed} = \frac{2xy}{x + y} \text{ km/h.}$$

Velocity : The speed of a moving body is called as its velocity if the direction of motion is also taken into consideration.

$$\text{Velocity} = \frac{\text{Net displacement of the body}}{\text{Time taken}}$$

Relative Speed : (*a*) Bodies moving in same direction:

(*i*) When two bodies move in the same direction, then the difference of their speeds is called the relative speed of one with respect to the other.

(*ii*) When two bodies move in the same direction, the distance between them increases (or decreases) at the rate of difference of their speeds.

MULTIPLE CHOICE QUESTIONS

1. A car moving at 48 km/hr completes a journey in 10 hours. By how much the speed of this car should be increased so as to do this journey in 8 hours?
(*a*) 8 km/hr. (*b*) 12 km/hr
(*c*) 10 km/hr (*d*) 15 km/hr
(*e*) None of these

2. Starting from a point at a speed of 4 km/hr a man reaches at a cerain place and returns back to the point from where he had started journey on bicycle at the speed of 16 km/hr. His average speed during the entire journey will be:
(*a*) 6.4 km/h (*b*) 8.4 km/h
(*c*) 5.4 km/h (*d*) 10 km/h
(*e*) None of these

3. A motorist covers a certain distance at a average speed of 48 km/h in 45 minutes. What speed in km/h he must maintain to cover the same distance in 30 minutes?
(*a*) 66 km/h (*b*) 79 km/h
(*c*) 80 km/h (*d*) 72 km/h
(*e*) None of these

4. Two points A and B are 150 km apart. A man completes his onward journey from A to B in 3 hours 20 minutes and return journey from B to A in 4 hours 10 minutes. His averate speed during the entire journey will be less than his average speed during the journey from A to B by:
(*a*) 5 km/h (*b*) 7.5 km/h
(*c*) 9 km/h (*d*) 3 km/h
(*e*) None of these

5. The speed of a boat in still water is 8 km/hr. If it can travel 12 km upstream at the same time as it can travel 20 km down stream, the rate of flow of stream in km/h is:
(*a*) 4 km/h (*b*) 2 km/h
(*c*) 4.5 km/h (*d*) 5.5 km/h
(*e*) None of these

6. A man can row his boat at the rate of 5 km/h in still water and at the rate of 3.5 km/h against a stream. At what rate can he row down the same stream?
(*a*) 6.5 km/h (*b*) 7.5 km/h
(*c*) 2.5 km/h (*d*) 4.5 km/h
(*e*) None of these

7. A policeman saw a thief at a distance of 200 m. The policeman and the thief started running at the same time. If the policeman runs at a speed of $4\frac{1}{6}$ m per second and the thief at a speed of $3\frac{1}{3}$m per second, after what time the policeman will catch the thief?
(*a*) 12 min (*b*) 10 min
(*c*) 9 min (*d*) 4 min
(*e*) None of these

8. Kanchan walks from her home at 4 kms per hour and reaches her school 5 minutes late. If she walks at 5 kms per hour, she reaches the school 2½ minutes earlier. How far is the school from her home?
(*a*) 3.5 kms (*b*) 2.5 kms
(*c*) 2.75 kms (*d*) 3.2 kms
(*e*) None of these

9. A monkey wants to climb up a glazed pole. He climbs 12 metres in 1 minute and then he slips back 3 metres in the next minute. If the pole is 63 metre high, how long does he take to climb at the top of the pole?
(*a*) $11\frac{1}{4}$ min (*b*) $12\frac{1}{2}$ min
(*c*) $12\frac{3}{4}$ min (*d*) $14\frac{3}{4}$ min
(*e*) None of these

10. A and B start walking at the same time on a circular path with circumference 35 metre. If they walk in the same direction at 4 km/hr and 5 km/hr respectively, after what time will they meet together?
(*a*) 35 hours (*b*) 27 hours
(*c*) 24 hours (*d*) 40 hours
(*e*) None of these

11. While walking at $\frac{3}{5}$ of his usual speed Kamalkant reaches at his destination late by 30 minutes. His usual time consumed in reaching to his destination is:
(*a*) 32 min (*b*) 40 min
(*c*) 45 min (*d*) 42 min
(*e*) None of these

12. The distance between two stations A and B is 300 km. A train leaves the station A with a speed of 40 km/hr. At the same time another train departs from the station B with a speed of 50 km/hr. How much time will these two trains take to cross each other?
(*a*) 3 hrs 40 min (*b*) 3 hrs 20 min
(*c*) 2 hrs 20 min (*d*) 3 hrs 45 min
(*e*) None of these

13. Gulshan starts from a place P at 2 p.m. and walks to Q at 5 km per hour. Tarun starts from P at 3 p.m. and follows Gulshan on bicycle at 10 km per hour. By when Tarun will catch Gulshan?
(*a*) At 5.30 p.m. (*b*) At 4.00 p.m.
(*c*) At 4.30 p.m. (*d*) At 6.00 p.m.
(*e*) None of these

ANSWERS

1	2	3	4	5	6	7	8	9	10
(*b*)	(*a*)	(*d*)	(*a*)	(*b*)	(*a*)	(*d*)	(*b*)	(*c*)	(*a*)
11	**12**	**13**							
(*c*)	(*c*)	(*b*)							

EXPLANATORY ANSWERS

1. Distance covered by the car in 10 hrs at 48 km/hr = 48 × 10 = 480 km

In the second case :

Distance = 480 km, Time = 8 hours

$\therefore$ Speed of the car = $\frac{480}{8}$ = 60 km/hr.

$\therefore$ Increase that should be effected in the speed of the car = 60 – 48 = 12 km/hr.

2. According to the given rule:

∵ Distances covered by the man in the two cases are equal

Here, $x = 4$ km/hr, $y = 16$ km/hr.

∴ Average speed during the entire journey

$$= \frac{2xy}{x+y} = \frac{2\times4\times16}{4+16}$$

$$= \frac{8\times16}{20} = 6.4 \text{ km/hr.}$$

3. Distance covered by the motorist in 45 minutes at 48 km/hr = 48 × 45/60 = 36 km

[∵ 45 minutes = 45/60 hours]

In the second case :

Distance = 36 km, Time

$= 30 \text{ minutes} = \frac{1}{2}$ hours

∴ Speed of the motorist $= \frac{36}{1/2}$

= 36 × 2 = 72 km/hr

6. Speed of the boat in still water = 5 km/hr.

Against the stream :

Speed of the boat = 3.5 km/hr

i.e., Speed of the boat in still water – Rate of flow of stream = 3.5 km/hr.

∴ 5 – Rate of flow of stream = 3.5

or, Rate of flow of the stream = 5 – 3.5 = 1.5 km/hr.

Down the stream:

Speed of the boat = Speed of the boat in still water + Rate of flow of the stream = 5 + 1.5 = 6.5 km/hr.

7. Suppose the policeman will catch the thief after t seconds

∴ Distance covered by the policeman in t seconds at $4\frac{1}{6}$ m/s. $= 4\frac{1}{6}\times t = \frac{25t}{6}$ metres

Distance covered by the thief in t second at $3\frac{1}{3}$ m/s

$= 3\frac{1}{3}\times t = \frac{10}{3}t$ metres

∵ Distance covered by the policeman = 200 m + distance covered by the thief

$$\therefore \quad \frac{25t}{6} = 200+\frac{10t}{3}$$

$$\text{or,} \quad \frac{5t}{6} = 200 \text{ or } t = \frac{200\times6}{5}$$

= 240 seconds = 4 minutes

∴ The policeman will catch the thief after 4 minutes.

10. The two persons walk in the same direction

∴ Their relative speed = 5 – 4 = 1 km/hr

Distance covered in 1 round on the circular path = 35 km

∴ They will meet after $\frac{35}{1}$ = 35 hours.

12. The two trains are moving in the opposite directions

∴ Relative speed = 40 + 50 = 90 km/hr.

Distance between the two stations = 300 km

∴ Time taken to cross each other $= \frac{300}{90} = 3\frac{1}{3}$ hours

or, 3 hours 20 minutes.

13. Gulshan starts 1 hour before Taurn

∴ Distance covered by Gulshan in 1 hour at 5 km/hr = 5 × 1 = 5 km

Hence Gulshan will be 5 km ahead of Tarun at sharp 3 p.m.

Both of them move in the same direction

∴ Relative speed = 10 – 5 = 5 km/hr.

∴ Time of meeting after 3 p.m. $= \frac{5}{5}$ = 1 hour

∴ Tarun will catch Gulshan at 4 p.m.

14 Questions on Trains

Important Facts

1. The time taken by a train in passing a signal post or a telegraph pole or a man standing near a railway line = $\frac{\text{Length of the train}}{\text{Speed of the train}}$

2. The time taken by a train passing a railway bridge or a platform or a tunnel or a train at rest $= \frac{x+y}{\text{Speed}}$

   where, x = length of the train

   y = length of the bridge or platform or standing train or tunnel

3. (*a*) Time taken by faster train to pass the slower train in the same direction

   $$= \frac{x+y}{u-v}$$

   where x = length of the first train

   y = length of the second train

   u = speed of the first train

   v = speed of the second train and $u > v$

   (*b*) Time taken by the trains in passing each other while moving in opposite direction

   $$= \frac{x+y}{u+v}$$

4. (*a*) Time taken by the train to cross a man $= \frac{x}{u-v}$

   where, both are moving in the same direction and x = length of the train

   u = speed of the train and

   v = speed of the man.

   (*b*) Time taken by the train to across a man running in the opposite direction $= \frac{x}{u+v}$

5. If two trains start at the same time from two points A and B towards each other and after crossing, they take a and b hours in reaching B and A respectively.

   Then, A's speed : B's speed $= \left(\sqrt{b}:\sqrt{a}\right)$

6. A train starts from a place at u km/h and another fast train starts from the same place after t hours at v km/h in the same direction. Find at what distance from the starting place both the trains will meet and also find the time of their meeting.

   Distance $= \frac{u \times v \times t}{v-u}$ km, time $= \frac{u \times t}{v-u}$ hours

7. The distance between two places A and B is x km. A train starts from A to B at u km/h. One another train after t hours starts from B to A at v km/h. At what distance from A will both the train meet and also find the time of their meeting.

   Time $= \frac{x - u \times t}{u+v} + t$ hours

   Distance from A $= u\left(\frac{x - u \times t}{u+v} + t\right)$ km.

8. Two trains starts simultaneously from the stations A and B towards each other at the rates of u and v km/h rspectviely. When they meet it is found that the second train had travelled x km more than the first. Then the distance between the two stations (i.e., between A and B) $= \frac{x(u+v)}{v-u}$ km.

MULTIPLE CHOICE QUESTIONS

1. A train runs at 45 km per hour. How far does it go in 6 seconds?

   (*a*) 72 m (*b*) 60 m
   (*c*) 75 m (*d*) 70 m
   (*e*) None of these

2. A man whose speed is 9 km/hr. in still water can swim 9 km upstream in 3 hours. Which of the following is actual speed of the stream?

   (*a*) 3 km/hr. (*b*) 6 km/hr.
   (*c*) 9 km/hr. (*d*) 12 km/hr.
   (*e*) None of these

3. A man takes a trip at an average speed of 30 km/hr. He returns by the same route at an averave speed of 20 km/hr. His average speed for the entire journey is:

   (*a*) 10 km/hr. (*b*) 24 km/hr.
   (*c*) 24.5 km/hr. (*d*) 25 km/hr.
   (*e*) None of these

4. A motorist covers a distance of 39 km in 45 minutes, by moving at a speed of x km/hr for the first 15 minutes, then moving at double the speed for the next 20 minutes and then again moving at his original speed for the rest of journey. Then x is equal to :
(*a*) 31.2 (*b*) 36
(*c*) 40 (*d*) 52
(*e*) None of these

5. A train travels 82.6 km/hr. How many metres will it travel in 15 minutes?
(*a*) 206.50 m (*b*) 2065 m
(*c*) 20650 m (*d*) 20.65 m
(*e*) None of these

6. On a tour a man travels at the rate of 64 km per hour for the first 160 km, then travels the next 160 km at the rate of 80 km per hour. What is the average speed for the first 320 km of the tour?
(*a*) 35.55 km/hr (*b*) 36 km/hr
(*c*) 71.11 km/hr (*d*) 72 km/hr
(*e*) None of these

7. If a train running at 72 km/hr crosses a coconut tree standing by the side of the track in 7 seconds, the length of the train is :
(*a*) 104 m (*b*) 140 m
(*c*) 504 m (*d*) 540 m
(*e*) None of these

8. Two trains are moving in the same direction at 45 km/hr and 25 km/hr. The faster train crosses a passenger travelling in the slower one in 18 seconds. The length of the faster train is:
(*a*) 100 m (*b*) 120 m
(*c*) 150 m (*d*) 180 m
(*e*) None of these

9. Two trains are moving at 50 km/hr and 70 km/hr in an opposite direction. Their lengths are 150 m and 100 m respectively. The time they will take to pass each other completely is :
(*a*) 3 seconds (*b*) $4\frac{1}{2}$ second
(*c*) 5 seconds (*d*) $7\frac{1}{2}$ second
(*e*) None of these

10. A train leaves Delhi at 9 A.M. at a speed of 30 km/hr. Another train leaves at 2 P.M. at a speed of 40 km/hr on the same day and in the same direction. How far from Delhi, will the two trains meet?
(*a*) 300 km (*b*) 400 km
(*c*) 600 km (*d*) 650 km
(*e*) None of these

ANSWERS

1	2	3	4	5	6	7	8	9	10
(*c*)	(*b*)	(*b*)	(*b*)	(*c*)	(*c*)	(*b*)	(*a*)	(*d*)	(*c*)

EXPLANATORY ANSWERS

1. Distance covered in 3600 sec. = 45000 m

$$\text{Distance covered in 1 sec.} = \frac{45000}{3600} \text{ m}$$

$$\text{Distance covered in 6 sec.} = \frac{45000}{3600} \times 6 = 75 \text{ m. } \textbf{Ans.}$$

2. Speed of man in still water = 9 km/hr.
In 3 hours he swims upstream = 9 km

$$\therefore \text{ In 1 hour he swims upstream} = \frac{9}{3} = 3 \text{ km}$$

$\therefore$ Speed upstream = 3 km/hr.
$\therefore$ Speed of the stream = 9 – 3 = 6 km/hr. **Ans.**

3. Let distance = x km

$$\text{Time taken in first journey} = \frac{x}{30} \text{ hours}$$

$$\text{Time taken in return journey} = \frac{x}{20} \text{ hrs}$$

Total time taken in entire journey

$$= \frac{x}{30} + \frac{x}{20} = \frac{x}{12} \text{ hours}$$

Total distance covered = $x + x = 2x$ km

$$\text{Average speed} = \frac{\text{Distance}}{\text{Time}} = \frac{2x}{x/12}$$

$$= 2x \times \frac{12}{x} = 24 \text{ km/hr.}$$

4. Distance = Speed × Time

$$39 = x \times \frac{15}{60} + 2x \times \frac{20}{60} + x \times \frac{10}{60}$$

or, $$39 = x\left[\frac{1}{4} + \frac{2}{3} + \frac{1}{6}\right] \text{ or, } 39 = \frac{13}{12}x$$

$$\therefore \quad x = \frac{39 \times 12}{13} = 36.$$

7. Distance covered in 3600 seconds = 72000 m

$$\text{Distance covered in 1 second} = \frac{72000}{3600} \text{ m}$$

$$\text{Distance covered in 7 seconds} = \frac{72000}{3600} \times 7 = 140 \text{ m.}$$

15 Time and Work

The problems on Time and Work are based on the calculation of time required by a given number of work-force (which may include men, women and children) to complete the given job.

Sometimes we are required to find the work done in a given period. Thus it can be said that the problems on Time and Work fall in two categories.

1. To find the time required to complete a given job, and
2. To find the work done in a given period.

Now we will find the relationship between the three variables, i.e., the amount of work (W), the number of persons doing it (P) and the time period of doing work (T). If 'P_1' persons can do 'W_1' works in 'T_1' days and 'P_2' persons can do 'W_2' works in 'T_2' days, then we have a very general formula $P_1T_1W_1 = P_2T_2W_2$. From our common sense, we can also derive the following relations :

1. *More work requires more time and vice-versa.* If the number of persons engaged to do the work remains same, i.e., for constant P, W and T have directly proportional relationship.
$W \propto T$
2. *More persons requires less time and vice-versa.* If the amount of work (W) to be done is kept unchanged, i.e., to say, P and T have inversely proportional relationship when W is kept constant.
$$P \propto \frac{1}{T}$$
3. *More work requires more persons and vice-versa.* If time to finish the work remains unchanged, i.e., for constant T, P and W have directly proportional relationship. $P \propto W$

We can combine the above three relations between P, T and W

$$\frac{PT}{W} = \text{Constant}$$

or $$\frac{P_1T_1}{W_1} = \frac{P_2T_2}{W_2}$$

MULTIPLE CHOICE QUESTIONS

1. 12 boys can do a piece of work in 16 days. In how many days can 6 boys do the same work?
(*a*) 16 days (*b*) 32 days
(*c*) 23 days (*d*) 24 days
(*e*) None of these

2. A can do a piece of work in 8 days while B can do the same work in 16 days. If they start working together, how long would they take to complete half portion of this work?
(*a*) $2\frac{2}{3}$ days (*b*) $3\frac{5}{7}$ days
(*c*) $4\frac{1}{2}$ days (*d*) $3\frac{1}{2}$ days
(*e*) None of these

3. A can do a piece of work in 4 days. B is 50% more efficient than A. How long would B alone take to finish this work?
(*a*) $3\frac{1}{3}$ days (*b*) $5\frac{1}{4}$ days
(*c*) $2\frac{2}{3}$ days (*d*) $1\frac{2}{3}$ days
(*e*) None of these

4. A and B working together complete a work in 35 days. If A takes 60 days to complete it, how long would B alone take to complete it?
(*a*) 64 days (*b*) 72 days
(*c*) 81 days (*d*) 84 days
(*e*) None of these

5. 10 men or 18 boys can do a piece of work in 15 days. In how many days would 25 men and 15 boys complete the same work working together?
(*a*) $5\frac{1}{2}$ days (*b*) $4\frac{1}{2}$ days
(*c*) $6\frac{2}{3}$ days (*d*) $2\frac{1}{3}$ days
(*e*) None of these

6. A can do a piece of work in 40 days. He starts working, but having some other engagements he drops out after 5 days. Thereafter B completes this work in 21 days. How many days would A and B take to complete this work working together?

(*a*) 15 days (*b*) 16 days
(*c*) 17 days (*d*) 11 days
(*e*) None of these

7. Two taps can fill a tank in 24 minutes and 30 minutes respectively. Both of them are opened together, but the first tap is turned off after 8 minutes. Now find how long would the second tap take to fill the tank?

(*a*) $24\frac{1}{2}$ minutes (*b*) $13\frac{2}{3}$ minutes
(*c*) 12 minutes (*d*) 15 minutes
(*e*) None of these

8. Two persons A and B can complete a piece of work in 8 hours and 16 hours respectively. If they work at it alternately for an hour, A starting first, in how many hours will the work be finished?

(*a*) $9\frac{1}{3}$ hours (*b*) $10\frac{1}{2}$ hours
(*c*) $11\frac{1}{2}$ hours (*d*) $8\frac{1}{2}$ hours
(*e*) None of these

9. Two taps A and B can fill a cistern in 12 minutes and 15 minutes respectively. Both are opened together but after 3 minutes A is turned off. After how much further time will the cistern be filled?

(*a*) $7\frac{2}{3}$ min (*b*) $8\frac{1}{2}$ min
(*c*) $10\frac{1}{2}$ min (*d*) $8\frac{1}{4}$ min
(*e*) None of these

10. A and B working together can complete a piece of work in 12 days and B and C working together can complete the same work in 16 days. A worked at it for 5 days and B worked at it for 7 days. C finished the remaining work in 13 days. How many days would C alone take to complete it?

(*a*) 10 days (*b*) 24 days
(*c*) 32 days (*d*) 40 days
(*e*) None of these

11. A cistern is filled by a tap in $3\frac{1}{2}$ hours. Due to a leak in the bottom of the cistern, it takes half an hour longer to fill the cistern. If the cistern is full, how long will it take the leak to empty it?

(*a*) 28 hours (*b*) 29 hours
(*c*) $31\frac{1}{3}$ hours (*d*) 38 hours
(*e*) None of these

12. Two pipes can fill a tank in 8 hours and 12 hours respectively whereas an escape pipe can empty it in 6 hours. If the three pipes are opened at 1 p.m., 2 p.m. and 3 p.m. respectively, at what time will the tank be filled?

(*a*) 7.00 a.m. (*b*) 8.00 a.m.
(*c*) 5.00 a.m. (*d*) 7.30 a.m.
(*e*) None of these

13. Two men undertake to do a piece of work for ₹ 1400. First man alone can do this work in 7 days while the second man alone can do this work in 8 days. If they working together complete this work in 3 days with the help of a boy, how should money be divided?

(*a*) ₹ 600, ₹ 500, ₹ 300
(*b*) ₹ 600, ₹ 525, ₹ 275
(*c*) ₹ 600, ₹ 550, ₹ 250
(*d*) ₹ 500, ₹ 525, ₹ 375
(*e*) None of these

14. If 3 men and 5 women can do a piece of work in 8 days and 2 men and 7 boys can do the same work in 12 days, find the number of boys, the work done by whom can equate the work done by 10 women.

(*a*) 19 boys (*b*) 21 boys
(*c*) 23 boys (*d*) 15 boys
(*e*) None of these

15. A, B and C can complete a piece of work in 20, 12 and 18 days respectively. They start the work together but A drops out after 4 days and B drops out 2 days before the completion of work. The work is finished in :

(*a*) $2\frac{22}{25}$ days (*b*) $6\frac{24}{29}$ days
(*c*) $5\frac{24}{25}$ days (*d*) $6\frac{24}{25}$ days
(*e*) None of these

ANSWERS

1	2	3	4	5	6	7	8	9	10
(*b*)	(*a*)	(*c*)	(*d*)	(*b*)	(*a*)	(*c*)	(*b*)	(*d*)	(*b*)
11	**12**	**13**	**14**	**15**					
(*a*)	(*a*)	(*b*)	(*b*)	(*d*)					

EXPLANATORY ANSWERS

1. 12 boys can do a piece of work in = 16 days

$\therefore$ 1 boy will do 1 work in = 16 × 12 days

$\therefore$ 6 boys will do 1work in = $\frac{16 \times 12}{6}$ = 32 days

3. A does the work in = 4 days

$\therefore$ B will do this work in = $4 \times \frac{100}{150} = \frac{8}{3} = 2\frac{2}{3}$ days

6. Work done by A in 5 days = 5/40 = 1/8

$\therefore$ Remaining work = 1 – 1/8 = 7/8

$\because$ B completes 7/8 work in 21 days

$\therefore$ B would complete 1 work in $\frac{21 \times 8}{7}$ = 24 days

According to direct formula

$\because$ Here, $x = 40$, $y = 24$

$\therefore$ Working together, A and B would complete this work in

$$= \frac{xy}{x+y} = \frac{40 \times 24}{40+24} = \frac{40 \times 24}{64} = 15 \text{ days}$$

11. Tap fills the cistern in 1 hour = $\frac{1}{3\frac{1}{2}} = \frac{2}{7}$ part

Due to leakage and filling, part of the cistern filled in 1 hour = $\frac{1}{4}$

Leak empties the water out of the cistern in 1 hour

$= \frac{1}{4} - \frac{2}{7} = -\frac{1}{28}$ part of the cistern (– sign indicates leakage)

The leak empties the water from $\frac{1}{28}$ part of the cistern in = 1 hour

$\therefore$ The leak will empty the water from 1 part (whole) of the cistern in = 28 hours.

12. Suppose the tank gets filled x hours after opening the first tap

$\therefore$ 1st tap works for x hours, 2nd tap works for $(x - 1)$ hours and 3rd tap works for $(x - 2)$ hours

$\therefore$ Portion of the tank filled in x hours + portion of the tank filled in $(x - 1)$ hours – portion of the tank emptied in $(x - 2)$ hours = Total tank filled

$$\therefore \quad \frac{x}{8} + \frac{x-1}{12} - \frac{x-2}{6} = 1$$

or, $\frac{3x+2x-2-4x+8}{24} = 1$ or $x + 6 = 24$

or, $x = 18$

Therefore, it will take 18 hours to fill the tank

$\therefore$ 1 p.m. + 18 hours = 19.00 hours

i.e., 7.00 a.m.

13. According to direct formula

Wages of the first man for 3 days = work done by him in 3 days × ₹ 1400

$= \frac{3}{7} \times 1400$ = ₹ 600

Wages of the second man for 3 days = work done by him in 3 days × ₹ 1400

$= \frac{3}{8} \times 1400$ = ₹ 525

$\therefore$ Wages of the boy for 3 days

= ₹ 1400 – ₹ (600 + 525)

= ₹ (1400 – 1125) = ₹ 275

$\therefore$ Their shares will be ₹ 600, ₹ 525 and ₹ 275 respectively.

15. Suppose work is finished in x days

$\therefore$ A works for 4 days, B works for $(x - 2)$ days and C works for x days

$\because$ work done by A in 4 days + work done by B in $(x - 2)$ days + work done by C in x days = 1 work

$$\therefore \quad \frac{4}{20} + \frac{x-2}{12} + \frac{x}{18} = 1$$

or, $\frac{36+15x-30+10x}{180} = 1$ or $25x + 6 = 180$

or, $25x = 174$

or $x = \frac{174}{25} = 6\frac{24}{25}$ days

Therefore, work is finished in $6\frac{24}{25}$ days.

16 Problems Based on Age

Generally, problems based on ages are essentially being asked in all competitive examinations. These questions are solved with the help of Algebra. Therefore, students are required the knowledge of linear equations. This method needs some basic concepts as well as some more time than it deserves. We have tried to evaluate some easier tricks to solve this type of questions.

Important Facts

1. The present age of the father is x times the age of his son. T years hence, the father's age become y times the age of his son. Then the present age of the father and his son are:

$$\text{peresent age of the son} = \frac{(y-1)\,T}{x-y}$$

$$\text{and fathers age} = \frac{(y-1)T\times x}{x-y} \text{ years.}$$

Memory trick

Father : Son
Present age = x : 1
After T years = y : 1

$$\text{Then, son's age} = \frac{1\times T(y-1)}{\text{difference of cross product}}$$

$$\text{Father's age} = \frac{x\times T(y-1)}{\text{diff. of cross product}}$$

2. T years ago, the father's age was x times that of his son and at present the father's age is y times the age of his son. Then their present ages are :

$$\text{Son's age} = \frac{T(x-1)}{x-y} \text{ years}$$

$$\text{Father's age} = \frac{T(x-1)}{x-y}\times y \text{ years.}$$

Memory Tricks

Father : Son
Present age = y : 1
before T years = x : 1

$$\text{Then Son's age} = \frac{1\times T(x-1)}{\text{diff. of cross product}}$$

$$\text{Father's age} = \frac{y\times T(x-1)}{\text{diff. of cross product}}$$

3. The ratio between the present ages of the father and his son is $m : n$ and the sum of their present ages is x years. Then the age of each, i.e.,

$$\text{Age of the father} = \frac{m\times x}{m+n} \text{ years}$$

$$\text{Son's age} = \frac{n\times x}{m+n} \text{ years.}$$

MULTIPLE CHOICE QUESTIONS

1. Harsha is 40 years old and Rith is 60 years old. How many years ago was the ratio of their ages 3 : 5?
(*a*) 10 years (*b*) 20 years
(*c*) 37 years (*d*) 5 years
(*e*) None of these

2. The ratio of present ages of two brothers is 1 : 2 and 5 years back the ratio was 1 : 3. What will be the ratio of their ages after 5 years?
(*a*) 1 : 4 (*b*) 2 : 3
(*c*) 3 : 5 (*d*) 5 : 6
(*e*) None of these

3. The ratio of the ages of Mohan and Meera is 3 : 4. Four years earlier the ratio was 5 : 7. Find the present ages of Mohan and Meera.
(*a*) 24 years, 32 years (*b*) 30 years, 20 years.
(*c*) 32 years, 24 years (*d*) 25 years, 18 years
(*e*) None of these

4. The ratio of the ages of A and B is 3 : 11. After 3 years the ratio becomes 1 : 3. What are the ages of A and B?
(*a*) 9 years, 33 years (*b*) 10 years, 40 years
(*c*) 9 years, 18 years (*d*) 8 years, 35 years
(*e*) None of these

5. In 10 years, A will be twice as old as B was 10 years ago. If A is now 9 years older than B, find the present age of B?

(*a*) 39 years (*b*) 40 years
(*c*) 41 years (*d*) 38 years
(*e*) None of these

6. Aruna got married 6 years ago. Today her age is $1\frac{1}{4}$ times her age at the time of marriage. Her Son's age is (1/10) times her age. Her Son's age is :
(*a*) 1 years (*b*) 2 years
(*c*) 3 years (*d*) 4 years
(*e*) None of these

7. The ratio between Ram's and Mohan's ages two years ago was 3 : 2 and at present it is 7 : 5. Find their present ages.
(*a*) 14 years, 10 years (*b*) 15 years, 20 years
(*c*) 13 years, 9 years (*d*) 10 years, 25 years
(*e*) None of these

8. Jayant is as much younger to Arun as he is older to Prashant. If the sum of the ages of Arun and Prashant is 48 years, what is the age of Jayant?
(*a*) 21 years (*b*) 22 years
(*c*) 23 years (*d*) 24 years
(*e*) None of these

ANSWERS

1	2	3	4	5	6	7	8
(*a*)	(*c*)	(*a*)	(*a*)	(*a*)	(*c*)	(*a*)	(*d*)

EXPLANATORY ANSWERS

1. Let x years ago the ratio of their ages was 3 : 5.

∴ By question

$$\frac{40-x}{60-x} = \frac{3}{5}$$

$$\Rightarrow \quad 200 - 5x = 180 - 3x \Rightarrow 2x = 20$$

$$\therefore \quad x = 10 \text{ years.}$$

4. Let $x : y = 3 : 11$

and $T = 3$ years

$P : q = 1 : 3$

Now applying direct formula,

$$\text{A's age} = x \times \left|\frac{(p-q)T}{xq-yp}\right|$$

$$= 3 \times \left|\frac{(1-3)\times 3}{9-11}\right| = 3 \times 3 = 9 \text{ years}$$

$$\text{Hence, B's age} = y \times \left|\frac{(p-q)T}{xq-yp}\right|$$

$$= 11 \times 3 = 33 \text{ years.}$$

5. Let the present age of B = x years.

then, A's age is $(x + 9)$ years.

∴ By question.

$$(x + 9 + 10) = 2(x - 10)$$

or, $$x + 19 = 2x - 20$$

or, $$x = 39 \text{ years}$$

Hence, B's age is 39 years at present

6. 6 years ago, let Aruna's age = x years.

Then Aruna's present age = $(x + 6)$ years

∴ By question,

$$x + 6 = \frac{5}{4} \times x$$

$$\Rightarrow \quad (x + 6) \times 4 = 5x$$

$$\Rightarrow \quad x = 24$$

∴ Aruna's present age = 24 + 6 = 30 years.

∴ Son's present age $= \frac{1}{10} \times 30 = 3$ years.

8. Let Arun's age = x years

then Prashant's age = $(48 - x)$ years.

Now, let the age of Jayant is y years.

Then, by question,

$$(x - P) = P - (48 - x) \Rightarrow P = 24 \text{ Ans.}$$

17

Pipe and Cistern

The fundamental concepts for solving problems on pipes and cistern are similar to those for Time and Work. Here the work may be positive or negative, i.e, filling or emptying of the tank respectively. Work is done by pipes instead of persons.

An inlet pipe (i.e, a pipe connected with a tank and fills it) fills the tank and hence its work is taken as positive. An exit or outlet pipe (i.e., a pipe connected with a tank and empties it) empties the tank and hence its work is taken as negative. A leakage is equivalent to an exit pipe.

Since the work here can be positive as well as negative, care must be taken in using proper sign convention.

Attention Students

1. If a pipe can fill a tank in x hours, then the part filled in 1 hour $= \frac{1}{x}$.

2. If a pipe can empty a tank in y hour, then the part of the full tank emptied in 1 hour $= \frac{1}{y}$.

3. If two pipes can fill a tank in x and y hours respectively and both the pipes are opened simultaneously then,

time taken to fill the tank $= \frac{xy}{x+y}$ hours.

4. (*a*) A tap fills a cistern in x hours and the other can empty the cistern in y hours. If both the taps are opened simultaneously, then,

time taken to fill the tank $= \frac{xy}{y-x}$ hours

(*b*) A tap can fill a tank in x hours. Due to a leak in the bottom it is filled in y hours. If the tank is full, the time taken by the leak to empty the tank $= \frac{xy}{y-x}$ hours.

5. If two taps A and B together can fill a tank in x hours and the tap A only can fill the tank in y hours, how many hours will take B alone to fill the tank?

Required time $= \frac{xy}{y-x}$ hours.

6. Two pipes can fill a cistern in x and y hours respectively. How much after opening the both pipes, second pipe should be turned off so that the cistern be filled in z hours?

Required time $= \frac{y(x-z)}{x}$ hours.

7. Three taps A, B and C can fill a tank in x, y and z hours respectively.

If all the three taps are opened simultaneously, then

time taken to fill the tank $= \frac{zyz}{xy+yz+zx}$ hours.

8. Two pipes A and B can fill a cistern in x hours and y hours respectively. A third pipe C can empty the cistern in z hours.

If all the three pipes are opened at the same time, then

time taken to completely fill the cistern

$= \frac{xyz}{yz+zx-xy}$ hours.

9. Two taps can fill a cistern in n min. and $(n + 1)$ min. respectively.

If these taps are opened alternately for a minute, in what time will be cistern be filled?

time taken to fill the cistern

$= 2\left(\text{whole number of } \frac{n(n+1)}{n+(n+1)}\right) + \frac{\text{remainder}}{(n+1)}$

MULTIPLE CHOICE QUESTIONS

1. A cistern which could be filled in 9 hours takes one hour more to be filled owing to a leak in its bottom. If the cistern is full, in what time will the leak empty it?
(*a*) 70 hours (*b*) 80 hours
(*c*) 90 hours (*d*) 100 hours
(*e*) None of these

2. Two pipes P and Q can fill a cistern in 12 and 15 minutes respectively. Both are opened together, but at the end of 3 minutes the first is turned off. How much longer will the cistern take to fill?
(*a*) $8\frac{1}{4}$ (*b*) $11\frac{1}{4}$
(*c*) $7\frac{1}{4}$ (*d*) $15\frac{1}{4}$
(*e*) None of these

3. Two pipes A and B would fill a cistern in 20 and 34 minutes respectively. Both pipes being opened, find when the first pipe must be turned off so that the cistern may be just filled in 17 minutes?
(*a*) 10 min. (*b*) 30 min.
(*c*) 17 min. (*d*) 34 min.
(*e*) None of these

4. Pipe A and B can fill a tank in 10 hours and 15 hours respectively. Both together can fill it in:
(*a*) 6 hours (*b*) 7 hours
(*c*) 8 hours (*d*) 9 hours
(*e*) None of these

5. A cistern is normally filled in 8 hours but takes two hours longer to fill because of a leak in its bottom. If the cistern is full, the leak will empty it in:
(*a*) 20 hours (*b*) 30 hours
(*c*) 40 hours (*d*) 50 hours
(*e*) None of these

6. A tap can fill a tank in 12 hours, whereas another can empty it in 18 hours. If both the taps are opened simultaneously, how much time will the tank take to fill?
(*a*) 36 hours. (*b*) 72 hours
(*c*) 18 hours (*d*) 12 hours
(*e*) None of these

7. Two taps can fill a tank in 2 hours and 3 hours respectively. If both of them are opened at the same time, the tank will be filled up in:
(*a*) 2 hours 12 min. (*b*) 1 hours 12 min
(*c*) 5 hours (*d*) None of these
(*e*) None of these

8. A tank can be filled separately by two taps A and B in 45 minutes and 36 minutes respectively. A tap C at the bottom can empty the full cistern in 30 minutes. If the tap C is opened 7 minutes after the two taps A and B are opened, find when the cistern will be full?
(*a*) 46 minutes (*b*) 25 minutes
(*c*) 14 minutes (*d*) None of these
(*e*) None of these

9. There is a leak in the bottom of a cistern. When the cistern had no leak, it was filled in 2½ hours. If now takes half an hour longer. If the cistern is full of water, how long would it take in leaking itself empty, in case the water leaks out at double the rate after half the cistern becomes empty?
(*a*) 10 hours 10 min. (*b*) 11 hours 15 min.
(*c*) 9 hours (*d*) 15 hours 10 min.
(*e*) None of these

10. When the waste pipe is closed, two taps can separately fill a cistern in 10 and 12 minutes respectively. When the waste pipe is open they together fill it in 15 minutes. How long does it take waste pipe to empty the cistern, when the taps are closed?
(*a*) 8 min. 34 sec. (*b*) 7 min. 10 sec.
(*c*) 12 min. (*d*) 10 min.
(*e*) None of these

11. Two pipes A and B can fill up a tank in 6 minutes and 7 minutes respectively. If they are opened for one minute alternately, A beginning, in how much time will they fill up the tank?
(*a*) $6\frac{3}{7}$ minutes (*b*) 7 minutes
(*c*) 6 minutes (*d*) 3 minutes
(*e*) None of these

ANSWERS

1	2	3	4	5	6	7	8	9	10	11
(*c*)	(*a*)	(*a*)	(*a*)	(*c*)	(*a*)	(*b*)	(*a*)	(*b*)	(*a*)	(*a*)

EXPLANATORY ANSWERS

1. Time taken to empty by the leak = $\frac{9\times10}{10-9}$ = 90 hours.

2. Let the cistern will take x min to fill.
then by applying formula

$$\frac{12(15-x)}{15} = \frac{3}{1} \Rightarrow 180 - 12x = 45$$

$$\Rightarrow \quad x = \frac{45}{4} \text{ min} = 11\frac{1}{4} \text{ min}$$

$\therefore$ Cistern take to fill when p is turned off

$$= 11\frac{1}{4} - 3 = 8\frac{1}{4}\text{ min}$$

3. Ist Method

$\therefore$ The part of the cistern filled by B in 17 min

$$= \frac{1}{34} \times 17 = \frac{1}{2}$$

$\therefore$ Rest of the cistern is to be filled by A.

Now, A shall fill $\frac{1}{2}$ of the cistern in 10 minutes so that pipe A must be turned off after 10 min.

IInd Method :

Let, x = 20 min, y = 34 min, z = 17 min

then, after applying formula

$$\text{Required time} = \frac{x(y-z)}{y}\text{ min}$$

$$= \frac{20(34-17)}{34} = \frac{20 \times 17}{34}$$

= 10 min.

4. Required time $= \frac{10 \times 15}{10 + 15} = \frac{150}{25} = 6$ hours.

5. Time taken by the leak to empty the cistern

$$= \frac{8 \times 10}{10 - 8} = \frac{80}{2} = 40 \text{ hours}$$

6. Time taken to fill the tank

$$= \frac{12 \times 18}{18 - 12} = \frac{12 \times 18}{6} = 36 \text{ hours.}$$

7. Time taken to fill the tank $= \frac{2 \times 3}{2 + 3} = \frac{6}{5}$ hour

8. In 7 minutes (A + B) together will fill

$$= 7 \times \left(\frac{1}{45} + \frac{1}{36}\right) = 7 \times \frac{1}{20} = \frac{7}{20} \text{ tank}$$

Unfilled portion of tank after 7 minutes

$$= 1 - \frac{7}{20} = \frac{13}{20} \text{ tank}$$

Now, tank filled in 1 minute when A, B and C are opened

$$= \frac{1}{45} + \frac{1}{36} - \frac{1}{30} = \frac{4+5-6}{180} = \frac{1}{60}$$

$\therefore$ Time required to fill $\frac{13}{20}$ tank

$$= 60 \times \frac{13}{20} = 39 \text{ minutes}$$

Hence, total time required to fill the tank

= 7 + 39 = 46 minutes

9. When there was no leak, the cistern was filled in $\frac{5}{2}$ hours

$\therefore$ The cistern filled in 1 hour $= \frac{2}{5}$ of the cistern

Now, when there was leak, the cistern was filled in 3 hours.

$\therefore$ The cistern filled in 1 hour $= \frac{1}{3}$ of the cistern

$\therefore$ The cistern emptied in 1 hour $= \frac{2}{5} - \frac{1}{3} = \frac{1}{15}$ of the cistern i.e., 1 cistern is emptied in 15 hours

$\therefore \frac{1}{2}$ cistern is emptied in $\frac{15}{2}$ hours.

Now, by question,

remaining half cistern is emptied in

$$\frac{15}{2} \times \frac{1}{2} = \frac{15}{4} \text{ hours}$$

$\therefore$ Total time taken to empty the cistern

$$= \frac{15}{2} + \frac{15}{4} = \frac{45}{4} \text{ hours.} = 11 \text{ hours } 15 \text{ min.}$$

10. When the waste pipe is closed, then portion of cistern filled up by 1st tap in

$$1 \text{ minute} = \frac{1}{10}$$

and portion of cistern filled up by 2nd tap in

$$1 \text{ minute} = \frac{1}{12}$$

$\therefore$ Cistern filled up by 1st and 2nd tap in 1 minute

$$= \frac{1}{10} + \frac{1}{12} = \frac{6+5}{60} = \frac{11}{60}$$

Now, when the waste pipe is open,

$\therefore$ work of tap 1st and 2nd in 1 min $= \frac{1}{15}$

$\therefore$ The waste pipe can empty in 1 min

$$= \frac{11}{60} - \frac{1}{15} = \frac{7}{60} \text{ of the cistern}$$

Hence, the waste pipe can empty the cistern in $\frac{60}{7}$ minutes, i.e., 8 minutes 34 sec. (approx)

11. Applying, direct formula

time taken to fill the cistern

$$= 2\left(\text{whole no. of } \frac{6 \times 7}{6 + 7}\right) + \frac{\text{Remainder}}{7}$$

$$= 2 \times 3 + \frac{3}{7} = \frac{45}{7} = 6\frac{3}{7} \text{ minutes.}$$

18

Boat and Stream

When we simply say speed of a boat and swimmer, it usually means speed in still water. If the boat or the swimmer moves against the stream, then it is called *Upstream* and if it moves with the stream, it is called *Downstream.*

Hence, if x km per hour be the man's rate in still water, and y km per hour the rate of the current then

(*i*) $x + y$ = man's rate with the current (called the down rate)

(*ii*) $x - y$ = man's rate against current (called the up rate)

(*iii*) $x = \frac{1}{2}(\text{down rate} + \text{up rate})$

(*iv*) $y = \frac{1}{2}(\text{down rate} - \text{up rate})$

Important Facts

1. A man can row x km/hr in still water. In a stream flowing at y km/hr if it takes him t hours to row to a point and come back, the distance between the two points is given by $t\left(\frac{x^2 - y^2}{2x}\right)$
2. A man rows a certain distance downstream in t_1 hours and returns the same distance in t_2 hours. If the speed of stream be x km/hours then the speed of the man in still water is given by $x\left(\frac{t_2 + t_1}{t_2 - t_1}\right)$ km/hr.
3. If a man swims down stream d_1 km in t_1 hours and upstream d_2 km in t_2 hours, then
   (*a*) the speed of man in still water is $\frac{1}{2}\left[\frac{d_1t_2 + d_2t_1}{t_1t_2}\right]$ km/hr.
   (*b*) Speed of the stream is $\frac{1}{2}\left[\frac{d_1t_2 - d_2t_1}{t_1t_2}\right]$ km/hr.
4. A man can row a boat S_1 km upstream and d_1 km downstream in t_1 hours. Also, he can row S_2 km upstream and d_2 km downstream in t_2 hours, then
   (*a*) his upstream speed = $\frac{S_1d_2 - S_2d_1}{t_1d_2 - t_2d_1}$
   (*b*) downstream speed = $\frac{S_1d_2 - S_2d_1}{t_2S_1 - t_1S_2}$

Memory Trick

Here numerator is same for both (upstream and downstream) speed, but for denominator, it has downstream distances for upstream speed and upstream distances for downstream speed.)

MULTIPLE CHOICE QUESTIONS

1. If the speed of a boat in still water is 5 km/hr and its speed against the current is 2.5 km/hr, then what is its speed in the direction of the current?
   (*a*) 11.5 km/hr (*b*) 12 km/hr
   (*c*) 10 km/hr (*d*) 14 km/hr
   (*e*) None of these
2. The speed of a motorboat in still water is 9 km/hr and the speed of the stream is 2.5 km/hr. Find the time taken by the motorboat to go 9.1 km against the stream?
   (*a*) 1 hour 24 minutes (*b*) 2 hours 24 minutes
   (*c*) 3 hours 24 minutes (*d*) 4 hours 24 minutes
   (*e*) None of these
3. The boat goes 40 km upstream in 8 hours and 36 km downstream in 6 hours. Find the speed of the boat in still water?
   (*a*) 5.5 km/hr (*b*) 6 km/hr
   (*c*) 6.5 km/hr (*d*) 7 km/hr
   (*e*) None of these
4. A boat goes 6 km upstream and back to the starting point in 2 hours. If the current of the stream runs at the rate of 4 km/hr find the speed of the boat in still water?
   (*a*) 6 km/hr (*b*) 8 km/hr
   (*c*) 10 km/hr (*d*) 12 km/hr
   (*e*) None of these

5. A man can swim 3 km/hr in still water. If the velocity of the stream be 2 km/hr, find the time taken by him to swim to a point 10 km upstream and back?

(*a*) 12 hours (*b*) 10 hours
(*c*) 8 hours (*d*) 6 hours
(*e*) None of these

6. A boat covers 24 km upstream and 36 km downstream in 6 hours, while it covers 36 km upstream and 24 km downstream in $6\frac{1}{2}$ hours. Find the speed of the current?

(*a*) 2 km/hr (*b*) 4 km/hr
(*c*) 6 km/hr (*d*) 8 km/hr
(*e*) None of these

7. A swimmer can swim a certain distance in the direction of current in 5 hours and return the same distance in 7 hours. If the stream flows at the rate of 1 km/hr, find the speed of the swimmer in still water?

(*a*) 3 km/hr (*b*) 4 km/hr
(*c*) 5 km/hr (*d*) 6 km/hr
(*e*) None of these

8. A man can row 5 km/hr in still water and the speed of the stream is 1.5 km/hr. He takes an hour when he travels upstream to a place and back again to the starting point. How far is the place from the starting point?

(*a*) 2.275 km (*b*) 3.5 km
(*c*) 1.5 km (*d*) 4.5 km
(*e*) None of these

9. A man can row three quarters of a kilometre against the stream in $11\frac{1}{4}$ minutes and return in $7\frac{1}{2}$ minutes. Find the speed of the man in still water?

(*a*) 3 km/hr. (*b*) 4 km/hr.
(*c*) 5 km/hr (*d*) 6 km/hr.
(*e*) None of these

10. A boat covers 12 km upstream and 18 km downstream in 3 hours while it covers 36 km upstream and 24 km downstream in $6\frac{1}{2}$ hours. Find the speed of the current?

(*a*) 1 km/hr. (*b*) 2 km/hr.
(*c*) 3 km/hr (*d*) 4 km/hr
(*e*) None of these

ANSWERS

1	2	3	4	5	6	7	8	9	10
(*a*)	(*a*)	(*a*)	(*b*)	(*a*)	(*a*)	(*d*)	(*a*)	(*c*)	(*b*)

EXPLANATORY ANSWERS

1. Let the speed of boat downstream = x km/h. then by applying direct formula, the speed of boat in still water

$$= \frac{1}{2}(\text{down rate} + \text{up rate})$$

$$\Rightarrow \quad 7 = \frac{1}{2}(x + 2.5)$$

$$\Rightarrow \quad x = 14 - 2.5 = 11.5 \text{ km/hr.}$$

2. The speed of a boat upstream

$$= (9 - 2.5) \text{ km/h} = 6.5 \text{ km/h}$$

$$\therefore \quad \text{Required time} = \frac{9.1}{6.5} = \frac{7}{5} = 1 \text{ hour 24 min.}$$

5. By applying direct formula,

$$\text{Distance between two points} = t\left(\frac{x^2 - y^2}{2x}\right)$$

$$\Rightarrow \quad 10 = t\left(\frac{3^2 - 2^2}{2 \times 3}\right)$$

$$\Rightarrow \quad \frac{10 \times 6}{5} = t$$

$$\therefore \quad t = 12 \text{ hours.}$$

7. Speed of the swimmer in still water = $x\left(\frac{t_2 + t_1}{t_2 - t_1}\right)$

[Here x = 1 km/hr., t_1 = 5 hours, t_2 = 7 hours]

$$= 1\left(\frac{7+5}{7-5}\right) = \frac{12}{2} = 6 \text{ km/hr.}$$

8. Distance between two points

$$= t\left(\frac{x^2 - y^2}{2x}\right)$$

$$= 1\left(\frac{5^2 - 1.5^2}{2 \times 5}\right) = \frac{25 - 2.25}{10}$$

$$= \frac{22.75}{10} = 2.275 \text{ km.}$$

19 Permutation & Combination

Combination

Each of the groups or selections which can be made by taking some or all a number of things without reference to the order of things in each group is called combination.

Permutation

Each of arrangements which can be made by taking some or all of a number of things is called a permutation. If the arrangement is in a line, then it is a linear permutation, if it is in a circle, then it is a circular permutation.

FUNDAMENTAL THEOREM

I. If a certain thing can be done in m ways and when it has been done in any one these ways, a second thing can be done in n ways in which two things can be done in mn ways.

II. The number of permutations of n different thing taking r at a time

$$^{n}P_r = \frac{n!}{(n-r)!} = n(n-1)(n-2)...(n-r+1)$$

where $(0 \le r \le n)$, $^{n}P_0 = 1, {}^{n}P_1 = n$

Note : *In the above, repetition was not allowed, so that if we could fill the first place in n ways, then second can be filled in (n –1), third in (n –2) ....and rth in (n –r + 1) ways. Hence, total place could be filled in n(n – 1)(n – 2) ...(n – r + 1) ways.*

Now, if repetition is allowed, then each of the r places can be filled in n ways.

Hence, by fundamental theorem all the r places can be filled in $n.n.n...r$ times *i.e.,* n^r ways.

III. Number of permutations of n different things taken all at a time :

$$^{n}P_n = n(n-1)(n-2)...[n-(n-1)]$$

$= n(n-1)(n-2)...3.2.1$

$= n!$

IV. Number of combinations of n different things taken r at a time :

$$^{n}C_r = \frac{n!}{(n-r)!r!} = \frac{^{n}P_r}{r!}$$

V. Number of combinations of n different things taken all at a time is

$$^{n}C_n = \frac{n!}{n!(n-n)!} = \frac{1}{0!} = 1$$

VI. Number of permutations of n things taken all at a time when p of them are similar of one type, q of them are similar of another type, r of them are simliar of a third type and the remaining $n-(p+q+r)$ are all different is

$$\frac{n!}{p!q!r!}$$

VII. If some or all of n things be taken at a time, then the number of combinations is given by $^{n}C_1 + {}^{n}C_2 + ... + {}^{n}C_n = 2^n - 1$

VIII. $^{n}C_r = {}^{n}C_{n-r}$; $^{n}C_0 = {}^{n}C_n = 1$, $^{n}C_1 = n$

IX. $^{n}C_x = {}^{n}C_y \Leftrightarrow x = y$ or $x + y = n$

X. $^{n}C_r + {}^{n}C_{r-1} = {}^{n+1}C_r$

XI. The number of combinations of n distinct things taken r at a time when k particular things always occur is:

$$^{n-k}C_{r-k}$$

If k particular objects never occur, then no. of combinations of n distinct objects taken r at a time is

$$^{n-k}C_r$$

XII. The number of permutations of n distinct things taken r at a time when k particular things always occur is

$$^{n-k}C_{r-k} \cdot r!$$

If k particular things never occur, then the no. of permutations of n distinct things taken r at a time is

$$^{n-k}C_r . r!$$

Circular Permutation

A circular table has no head and arrangements like those are considered indentical.

Here, having fixed one thing, the remaining $(n-1)$ things can be arranged round the table in $(n-1)!$ ways.

n beads on a circular wire can be arranged in $\frac{1}{2}(n-1)!$ different ways.

MULTIPLE CHOICE QUESTIONS

1. A five-digit number divisible by 3 is to be formed using the numerals 0, 1, 2, 3, 4 and 5 without repetition. The total number of ways in which this can be done is:

(*a*) 216 (*b*) 240
(*c*) 600 (*d*) 3125
(*e*) 2500

2. The sum $\sum_{i=0}^{m}\binom{10}{i}\binom{20}{m-i}$ where $\binom{p}{q}=0$ if $(p<q)$ is maximum when m is:

(*a*) 5 (*b*) 10
(*c*) 15 (*d*) 20
(*e*) 25

3. The number of arrangements of word BANANA in which two N's do not appear adjacently is:

(*a*) 40 (*b*) 60
(*c*) 80 (*d*) 100
(*e*) 120

4. Let T_n denote the number of triangles which can be formed using the vertices of a regular polygon of side n. If $T_{n+1} - T_n = 21$, then n equals:

(*a*) 5 (*b*) 7
(*c*) 6 (*d*) 4
(*e*) 3

5. If ${}^nC_r$ denotes the number of combinations of n things taken r at a time, then the expression ${}^nC_{r+1} + {}^nC_{r-1} + 2\ {}^nC_r$ equal:

(*a*) ${}^{n+2}C_r$ (*b*) ${}^{n+2}C_{r+1}$
(*c*) ${}^{n+1}C_r$ (*d*) ${}^{n+1}C_{r+1}$
(*e*) None of these

6. A student is to answer 10 out of 13 questions in an examination such that he must choose at least 4 from the first five questions. The number of choices available to him is:

(*a*) 140 (*b*) 196
(*c*) 280 (*d*) 346
(*e*) 370

7. The number of ways in which 6 men and 5 women can dine at a round table if no two women are to sit together is given by:

(*a*) $6! \times 5!$ (*b*) 30
(*c*) $5! \times 4!$ (*d*) $7! \times 5!$
(*e*) None of these

8. The number of ways in which 5 male and 2 female members of a committee can be seated around a round table so that the two females are not seated together is:

(*a*) 840 (*b*) 720
(*c*) 600 (*d*) 480
(*e*) 510

9. The total number of 9-digit numbers which have all different digits are:

(*a*) 8 (7!) (*b*) 9 (9!)
(*c*) 10 (9!) (*d*) None of these
(*e*) –

10. There are 10 lamps in a hall. Each one of them can be switched on independently. The number of ways in which the hall can be illuminated is:

(*a*) 10! (*b*) 10^2
(*c*) 1023 (*d*) 2^{10}
(*e*) None of these

11. The number of numbers that can be formed by the digits 1, 2, 3, 4, 3, 2, 1 with odd digits at odd places is given by:

(*a*) 430 (*b*) 36
(*c*) 18 (*d*) None of these
(*e*)

12. The number of ways of dividing 52 cards amongst four players so that three players have 17 cards each and the fourth player just one card is:

(*a*) $\dfrac{52!}{(17!)^3}$ (*b*) 52!

(*c*) $\dfrac{52!}{17!}$ (*d*) $\dfrac{52!}{(17!)^2}$

(*e*) None of these

13. How many different words can be formed out of the letters of the word ALLAHABAD?

(*a*) 91 (*b*) 504
(*c*) 7560 (*d*) 1036
(*e*) None of these

14. How many words can be formed by taking 4 letters at a time out of the letters of the word CONDITION?

(*a*) 610 (*b*) 858
(*c*) 738 (*d*) 126
(*e*) None of these

15. How many 5-letter words can be formed that contain at least one of the 5 vowels?

(*a*) $\binom{16}{5}-1$ (*b*) $26^5 - 21^5$

(*c*) $\sum_{r=1}^{5}\binom{21}{5-r}\binom{5}{r}$ (*d*) $26^2 - 21^2$

(*e*) None of these

ANSWERS

1	2	3	4	5	6	7	8	9	10
(*a*)	(*c*)	(*a*)	(*b*)	(*b*)	(*b*)	(*a*)	(*d*)	(*b*)	(*c*)
11	**12**	**13**	**14**	**15**					
(*c*)	(*a*)	(*c*)	(*d*)	(*b*)					

EXPLANATORY ANSWERS

1. Sum of 0, 1, 2, 3, 4, 5 is 15.

If a five digit number is to be divisible by 3, then out of the six digits we shall have to leave either 0 or 3. If we leave 0, then remaining digits can be arranged in $^5P_5 = 5!$ ways.

Again if we leave 3, then the remaining digits can be arranged in $^5P_5 - {^4P_4} = 5! - 4!$ ways.

Hence the total number of such 5 digit numbers is

$= 5! + 5! - 4!$

$= 120 + 120 - 24 = 216.$

3. Two N's do not appear together

= Total – together

$= \frac{6!}{3!\,2!} - \frac{5!}{3!}$

$= 60 - 20 = 40$

4. According to the question,

$T_n = {^nC_3}$

$\therefore \quad T_{n+1} - T_n = 21$

$\Rightarrow \quad {^{n+1}C_3} - {^nC_3} = 21$

$\Rightarrow \quad {^nC_2} = 21$; as ${^nC_r} + {^nC_{r+1}} = {^{n+1}C_{r+1}}$

$\Rightarrow \quad {^nC_2} = {^7C_2} \quad \Rightarrow n = 7$

5. ${^nC_{r+1}} + {^nC_{r-1}} + 2\ {^nC_r}$

$= {^nC_{r+1}} + {^nC_r} + {^nC_{r-1}} + {^nC_r}$

$= {^{n+1}C_{r+1}} + {^{n+1}C_r}$

$= {^{n+2}C_{r+1}}$

7. The number of ways to sit men = 5! and the number of ways to sit women = $^6C_5 \times 5!$

Total number of ways $= 5! \times {^6C_5} \times 5!$

$= 5! \times 6 \times 5! = 6!\ 5!$

8. Let the males be seated firstly. This can be done in $(5 - 1)!$ *i.e.,* 4! ways.

Now 2 females can be arranged in 6 places in $^5P_2$ ways, so that no two females sit together.

Required number of ways

$= 4! \times {^5P_2}$

$= 24 \times (5 \times 4) = 480.$

10. Each bulb has two choices, either switched on or off.

$\therefore$ required number of ways $= 2^{10} - 1 = 1023$

(since in one way when all are switched off, the hall will not be illuminated).

13. In the words ALLAHABAD, there are 9 letters, in which there are four A's, two l's and 3 different letters.

Required number of ways $= \frac{9!}{4!\,2!}$

$= \frac{5 \times 6 \times 7 \times 8 \times 9}{2} = 7560$

15. Total number of 5-letters words

$= 26 \times 26 \times 26 \times 26 \times 26 = (26)^5$

The words which have no vowels

$= 21 \times 21 \times 21 \times 21 \times 21 = (21)^5$

The words which have at least one vowel

$= (26)^5 - (21)^5$

20 Probability

The concept of probability is extremely important. It is extensively used in the development of all Physical Science and daily life events. The chance of happening of an event when expressed quantitatively is known as probability.

If an experiment results in $(m + n)$ mutually exclusive, exhaustive and equally likely outcomes and an event E can occur in m ways then probability of E is given as

$$P[E] = \frac{m}{m+n}$$

i.e., probability of an event is the ratio of favourable ways of that event upon total ways of the experiment

$$P[E] = \frac{\text{Favourable ways of event E}}{\text{Total ways}}$$

Thus, an event can occur in m ways and fails in n ways, this statement at times is given as odds in favour of the event E are n to m.

1. Random Experiment

If an experiment is conducted and its result is unpredictable, *i.e.*, its outcome can be one of the many outcomes, then such an experiment is called random experiment.

2. Sample Space

The collection of all outcomes of a random experiment in a form of set is called a sample space *e.g.*, if a die is thrown then the set S = {1, 2, 3, 4, 5, 6} is called a sample space.

3. Simple Event

Each outcome of an experiment is called a simple event.

4. Event

Any combination of simple events is called an event, it is denoted by E.

Example : *If a card is drawn from a pack of cards, there are 52 possible outcomes, each of them is simple event and the card is a king is an event as it consists of four events. i.e., king of each unit.*

5. Mutually Exclusive Event

A set of events is called mutually exclusive, if the happening of one event excludes the happening of the other *e.g.*, tossing of a coin will result in either head or tail, happening of head excludes the happening of tail and vice-versa, if A and B are two mutually exclusive events then

$$A \cap B = \phi$$

6. Exhaustive Events

All the outcomes of the experiment put together are called exhaustive events as no other result outside this can happen as a result of this experiment.

7. Equally Likely Event

If any outcome of the experiment is not favoured or disfavoured compared to other outcomes they are called equally likely *e.g.*, drawing a card from a pack of cards result in 52 equally likely events.

8. Union of Events

If there are two events A and B in a sample space, if we write $A \cup B$ it means either of the event can happen and it is called A union (b)

9. Intersection of Events

If both events happen simultaneously, it is written as $A \cap B$ and it is read as A intersection (b)

10. Complement of the Event

The complement of event A contains all the outcomes of sample space except those of A it is denoted by $\overline{A}$ or A^C.

(*a*) **Addition Theorem:** For happening of either of two events A and B

$$P(A \cup B) = P(A) + P(B) - P(A \cap B)$$

If A and B are mutually exclusive, then

$$A \cap B = \phi \Rightarrow (A \cap B) = 0$$

Then $P(A \cup B) = P(A) + P(B)$

(*b*) **Multiplication Theorem:** If A and B are two independent events, then the probability of simultaneous occurrence is given as

$$P(A \cap B) = P(A).P(B)$$

(*c*) **Conditional Probability:** It is probability of the happening of one event with an assumption that another event has already happened if

$$P(A / B) = \frac{P(A \cap B)}{P(B)}$$ here B has happened.

or, $P\left(\frac{B}{A}\right) = \frac{P(A \cap B)}{P(A)}$ here A has happened.

MULTIPLE CHOICE QUESTIONS

1. The probability of getting heads in both trials when a balanced coin is tossed twice, will be :

(a) $\frac{1}{4}$ (b) $\frac{1}{2}$

(c) 1 (d) $\frac{3}{4}$

(e) None of these

2. Two cards are drawn at random from a pack of 52 cards. The probability of these two being aces is :

(a) $\frac{1}{26}$ (b) $\frac{1}{12}$

(c) $\frac{1}{2}$ (d) $\frac{1}{13}$

(e) None of these

3. A card is drawn from a well shuffled pack of 52 cards, the probability of getting a queen of club or king of heart is :

(a) $\frac{1}{52}$ (b) $\frac{1}{26}$

(c) $\frac{1}{13}$ (d) $\frac{2}{13}$

(e) None of these

4. A single letter is selected at random from the word "PROBABILITY" the probability that it is vowel is :

(a) $\frac{3}{11}$ (b) $\frac{4}{11}$

(c) $\frac{2}{11}$ (d) 0

(e) None of these

5. The probability that leap year selected at random contains 53 Sunday is :

(a) $\frac{7}{366}$ (b) $\frac{26}{183}$

(c) $\frac{1}{7}$ (d) $\frac{2}{7}$

(e) None of these

6. Three mangoes and three apples are in a box. If two fruits are chosen at random, the probability that one is a mango and the other is an apple is :

(a) $\frac{2}{3}$ (b) $\frac{3}{5}$

(c) $\frac{1}{3}$ (d) $\frac{1}{7}$

(e) None of these

7. The probability of getting more than 7 when a pair of dice are thrown is :

(a) $\frac{7}{36}$ (b) $\frac{7}{12}$

(c) $\frac{5}{12}$ (d) $\frac{5}{13}$

(e) None of these

8. Three letters are written to different persons and addresses on three envelopes are also written without looking at the address, the probability that the letters go into right envelopes is :

(a) $\frac{1}{27}$ (b) $\frac{1}{6}$

(c) $\frac{1}{9}$ (d) $\frac{1}{3}$

(e) None of these

9. Three identical dice are rolled, the probability that the same number will appear on each of them is :

(a) $\frac{1}{6}$ (b) $\frac{1}{8}$

(c) $\frac{1}{36}$ (d) $\frac{2}{13}$

(e) None of these

10. One die and one coin are tossed simultaneously the probability of getting 6 on die and head on coin is :

(a) $\frac{1}{2}$ (b) $\frac{1}{6}$

(c) $\frac{1}{12}$ (d) $\frac{2}{13}$

(e) None of these

11. A card is drawn at random from a pack of 100 cards numbered 1 to 100, the probability of drawing a number which is a square is :

(a) $\frac{1}{5}$ (b) $\frac{2}{5}$

(c) $\frac{1}{10}$ (d) $\frac{1}{13}$

(e) None of these

12. The probabilities of so solving a problem by three students A, B, C are $\frac{1}{2}, \frac{1}{3}, \frac{1}{4}$ respectively. The probability that the problem will be solved is :

(a) $\frac{1}{4}$ (b) $\frac{1}{2}$

(c) $\frac{3}{4}$ (d) $\frac{1}{3}$

(e) None of these

13. The probability that a marksman will hit a target is given as $\frac{1}{5}$, then his probability of at least one hit in 10 shots is :

(*a*) $1-\left(\frac{4}{5}\right)^{10}$ (*b*) $\frac{1}{5^{10}}$

(*c*) $1-\frac{1}{5^{10}}$ (*d*) $\frac{1}{3^{10}}$

(*e*) None of these

14. From a pack of cards two are drawn, the first being replaced before the second is drawn, the probability that the first is a diamond and the second is a king will be :

(*a*) $\frac{13}{4}$ (*b*) $\frac{4}{13}$

(*c*) $\frac{1}{52}$ (*d*) 52

(*e*) None of these

15. Two cards are drawn successively with replacement from a well shuffled pack of 52 cards, the probability of drawing two aces is :

(*a*) $\frac{1}{13}\times\frac{1}{13}$ (*b*) $\frac{1}{13}\times\frac{1}{17}$

(*c*) $\frac{1}{52}\times\frac{1}{51}$ (*d*) $\frac{1}{13}\times\frac{4}{51}$

(*e*) None of these

16. You are given a box with 20 cards in it, 10 of these cards have the letter *I* printed on them, the other ten have the letter *T* printed on them, if you pick up 3 cards at random and keep them in the same order, the probability of making the word *IIT* is :

(*a*) $\frac{9}{80}$ (*b*) $\frac{1}{8}$

(*c*) $\frac{4}{27}$ (*d*) $\frac{5}{38}$

(*e*) None of these

17. In a box containing 100 bulbs, 10 are defective. What is the probability that out of a sample of 5 bulbs, none is defective?

(*a*) 10^{-5} (*b*) $\left(\frac{1}{2}\right)^5$

(*c*) $\left(\frac{9}{10}\right)^5$ (*d*) $\frac{9}{10}$

(*e*) None of these

18. The chance of throwing an ace first only of two successive throws with an ordinary die is :

(*a*) $\frac{1}{36}$ (*b*) $\frac{5}{36}$

(*c*) $\frac{25}{36}$ (*d*) $\frac{1}{6}$

(*e*) None of these

19. The mean number of heads in three tosses of a coin is:

(*a*) $\frac{3}{2}$ (*b*) $\frac{5}{2}$

(*c*) $\frac{1}{2}$ (*d*) $\frac{1}{8}$

(*e*) None of these

20. The value of *P*(2) in a Binomial distribution when $P=\frac{1}{6}$ and $n = 5$ is :

(*a*) $\frac{3125}{7776}$ (*b*) $\frac{250}{7776}$

(*c*) $\frac{1250}{7776}$ (*d*) $\frac{25}{7776}$

(*e*) None of these

21. A die is thrown once. What is the probability of getting a number other than 3?

(*a*) $\frac{5}{6}$ (*b*) $\frac{1}{6}$

(*c*) $\frac{2}{6}$ (*d*) $\frac{3}{13}$

(*e*) None of these

22. A die is thrown once. What is the probability of getting the number 5?

(*a*) $\frac{2}{6}$ (*b*) $\frac{5}{6}$

(*c*) $\frac{1}{6}$ (*d*) $\frac{2}{13}$

(*e*) None of these

23. One card is drawn from a well shuffled deck of 52 cards. What is the probability of drawing an ace?

(*a*) $\frac{1}{52}$ (*b*) $\frac{1}{13}$

(*c*) $\frac{4}{13}$ (*d*) $\frac{3}{13}$

(*e*) None of these

24. A box contains 3 blue marbles, 2 white marbles and 4 red marbles. If a marble is taken out at random from the box, what is the probability that it will be a white one?

(*a*) $\frac{2}{9}$ (*b*) $\frac{1}{9}$

(*c*) $\frac{7}{9}$ (*d*) $\frac{4}{13}$

(*e*) None of these

25. 15 cards numbered 1, 2, 3, ... 15 are put in a box and mixed. One person draws a card from the box. Find the probability that the number in the card is a prime number.

(*a*) $\frac{7}{15}$ (*b*) $\frac{8}{15}$

(*c*) $\frac{2}{5}$ (*d*) $\frac{4}{5}$

(*e*) None of these

26. 1000 tickets of a lottery were sold and there are 5 prizes on these tickets. If Saket has purchased one lottery ticket. What is the probability of winning a prize?

(*a*) 0.002 (*b*) 0.005

(*c*) 0.05 (*d*) 0.5

(*e*) None of these

27. A bag contains 5 red balls and some blue balls. If the probability of drawing a blue ball is double that of a red ball, find the number of blue balls in the bag?

(*a*) 5 (*b*) 8

(*c*) 10 (*d*) 6

(*e*) 12

28. A box contains 20 balls bearing numbers 1, 2, 3, 4, 5, ... 20. A ball is drawn at random from the box. What is the probability that number on the ball is composite number?

(*a*) $\frac{11}{20}$ (*b*) $\frac{8}{20}$

(*c*) $\frac{9}{20}$ (*d*) $\frac{7}{20}$

(*e*) None of these

29. In tossing a fair die, the probability of getting an odd number less than 4 is

(*a*) $\frac{2}{3}$ (*b*) $\frac{3}{4}$

(*c*) 2 (*d*) $\frac{1}{2}$

(*e*) None of these

30. The probability of getting 9 with two dice is

(*a*) $\frac{1}{36}$ (*b*) $\frac{1}{27}$

(*c*) $\frac{2}{9}$ (*d*) $\frac{1}{9}$

(*e*) None of these

ANSWERS

1	2	3	4	5	6	7	8	9	10
(*a*)	(*b*)	(*b*)	(*b*)	(*d*)	(*b*)	(*c*)	(*b*)	(*c*)	(*c*)
11	**12**	**13**	**14**	**15**	**16**	**17**	**18**	**19**	**20**
(*c*)	(*c*)	(*a*)	(*c*)	(*a*)	(*d*)	(*c*)	(*b*)	(*a*)	(*c*)
21	**22**	**23**	**24**	**25**	**26**	**27**	**28**	**29**	**30**
(*a*)	(*c*)	(*b*)	(*a*)	(*c*)	(*b*)	(*c*)	(*a*)	(*a*)	(*d*)

EXPLANATORY ANSWERS

1. Probability of getting head in one trial $= \frac{1}{2}$

$\therefore$ Probability of getting heads in both the trials $= \frac{1}{2} \times \frac{1}{2} = \frac{1}{4}$.

2. Required probability $= \frac{{}^4C_2}{{}^{52}C_2} = \frac{4 \times 3}{52 \times 51} = \frac{1}{221}$.

3. Total ways = 52

There is one queen of club and one king of heart favourable ways = 1 + 1 = 2

$\therefore$ Required probability $= \frac{2}{52} = \frac{1}{26}$.

4. Total ways are 11, there are three vowels and one is repeated. So favourable case = 4

So, required probability $= \frac{4}{11}$.

5. In a leap year, there are 366 days, it means 52 full weeks and two days. These two days can be Mon., Tues.; Tues.; Wed.; Wed.; Thurs. Thurs.; Friday; Fri. Sat.; Sat.; Sun.; Sun.; Mon.

So, required probability $= \frac{2}{7}$.

6. Total ways $= {}^6C_2 = 15$

Favourable ways $= {}^3C_1 \times {}^3C_1 = 9$.

Reqd. Probability $= \frac{9}{15} = \frac{3}{5}$.

7. $P(8) + P(9) + P(10)$.

8. Total no. of ways = 3! = 6 and favourable no. of ways = 1.

9. Total ways = 6 × 6 × 6 favourable ways are 6, *i.e.*, (1,1,1) (2,2,2) (3,3,3)

(4,4,4) (5,5,5) (6,6,6)

So, required probability $=\frac{6}{6\times6\times6}=\frac{1}{36}$.

10. A die has 6 outcomes, coin has two. So, total ways = 6 × 2 = 12, favourable ways = 1.

So, required prob. $=\frac{1}{12}$.

11. Total ways = 100, Squares of following no's lie between 1 and 100, $1^2, 2^2, 3^2, 4^2, 5^2, 6^2, 7^2, 8^2, 9^2, 10^2$ which are 10 in number.

So, required probability $=\frac{10}{100}=\frac{1}{10}$.

13. He will hit the target, $P(A)=\frac{1}{5}$. He will not hit the target, $P(\bar{A})=\frac{4}{5}$. Probability that he will not hit the target in 10 shoots is $\left(\frac{4}{5}\right)^{10}$ · So, at least once, target will be heat.

Required probability $=1-\left(\frac{4}{5}\right)^{10}$

14. The required probability

$$=\frac{^{13}C_1}{^{52}C_1}\cdot\frac{^4C_1}{^{51}C_1}=\frac{13}{52}\cdot\frac{4}{52}=\frac{1}{52}.$$

15. Required probability

$$\left(\frac{4}{52}\times\frac{4}{52}\right)=\left(\frac{4}{52}\right)^2=\frac{1}{13}\times\frac{1}{13}.$$

16. As we have to consider order for IIT, the required probability

$$=\frac{10}{20}\times\frac{9}{19}\times\frac{10}{18}=\frac{5}{38}.$$

17. Probability of non-defective piece $=\frac{90}{100}=\frac{9}{10}$ in a sample of five none defective, the required probability

$$=\frac{9}{10}\times\frac{9}{10}\times\frac{9}{10}\times\frac{9}{10}\times\frac{9}{10}=\left(\frac{9}{10}\right)^5$$

18. ∴ Probability of throwing an ace $=\frac{1}{6}$ and of not throwing ace $=\frac{5}{6}$. Hence, required probability

$$=\frac{1}{6}\times\frac{5}{6}=\frac{5}{36}.$$

19. We know that mean of binomial distribution is *np* here

$n=3, p=\frac{1}{2}$. So, mean $=3\times\frac{1}{2}=\frac{3}{2}$.

20. For Binomial distribution, $p(r)={}^nC_rp^rq^{n-r}$ Here,

$p=\frac{1}{6},\ q=\frac{5}{6},\ n=5,\ r=2.$

So, $p(2)={}^5C_2\left(\frac{1}{6}\right)^2\left(\frac{5}{6}\right)^3=\frac{1250}{7776}$.

21. Possible outcomes are 1, 2, 3, 4, 5, 6

∴ Required probability $=\frac{5}{6}$.

22. Possible outcomes are 1, 2, 3, 4, 5, 6
Favourable outcomes in this case is 5

∴ Required probability $=\frac{1}{6}$.

23. Possible outcomes = 52
Favourable outcomes = 4

∴ Required probability $=\frac{4}{52}=\frac{1}{13}$.

24. Total number of marbles = 9
Number of white marble = 2

∴ Required probability $=\frac{2}{9}$.

25. Total number of possible outcomes = 15
Favourable outcomes are 2, 3, 5, 7, 11, 13 = 6

∴ Required probability $=\frac{6}{15}=\frac{2}{5}$.

26. Total number of outcomes = 1000
Favourable outcomes = 5

∴ Required probability $=\frac{5}{1000}=0.005$.

28. Possible outcomes = 20
Favourable outcomes are 4, 6, 8, 9, 10, 12, 14, 15, 16, 18, 20 = 11

∴ Required probability $=\frac{11}{20}$.

29. Total number of outcomes = 6
Favourable outcomes are = 1, 2, 3, 5 = 4

∴ Required probability $=\frac{4}{6}=\frac{2}{3}$.

30. Total number of possible outcomes = 6 × 6 = 36
Number of outcomes = 4

∴ Required probability $=\frac{4}{36}=\frac{1}{9}$.

21

Data Analysis

Data analysis is the technique of interpreting the information given in the form of (*i*) Tables (*ii*) Graphs, or (*iii*) Charts. Questions are framed from the information given in the tables, graphs and charts. For solving such types of questions, candidates are required to go through the given table or graph very carefully and then interpret the information to the best of his abilities.

TABLES

Tables are often used in reports, magazines and newspaper to present a set of numerical data. It is one of the easiest and most accurate ways of presenting data. One of the main purposes of tables is to make complicated information easier to understand. Hence, the advantage of presenting data in a table is that one can see the information at a glance. We present below an example of tabular presentation of annual expenditure of 5 families for last 4 years.

Annual Expenditure of 5 families (in Rs. Thousands)

Years → *Families* ↓	*2011*	*2012*	*2013*	*2014*
A	35	50	55	60
B	40	60	65	75
C	45	50	70	80
D	30	40	45	50
E	50	55	60	70

Essentials of a Table :

(*i*) **Title :** Heading of the table

(*ii*) **Stub :** The section of the table containing row headings in called Stub.

(*iii*) **Column Captions :** The heading of each column is designated as column caption.

(*iv*) Body (*v*) Footnotes (*vi*) Source

Attention Students :

(*i*) Do not waste time in memorising a table. You can refer to it as many times as you want.

(*ii*) Your answer should be based on precise data given in the table.

(*iii*) Don't include your own information in answering questions, however accurate you may be.

(*iv*) Be careful about minor details.

CIRCLE GRAPH

These are used to show the share of various sectors in the total. Circle graphs are called Pie-Charts. They usually show the percentage share of each sector in the whole (taken as 100%). In such representation the total quantity in question is distributed over a total angle of 360°. The area of each sector is proportional to the relative proquency of the class represented by the sector.

$$\text{Sector angle} = \frac{\text{Class frequency}}{\text{Total frequency}} \times 360^\circ$$

For example: *Distribution of Expenditure of a family*

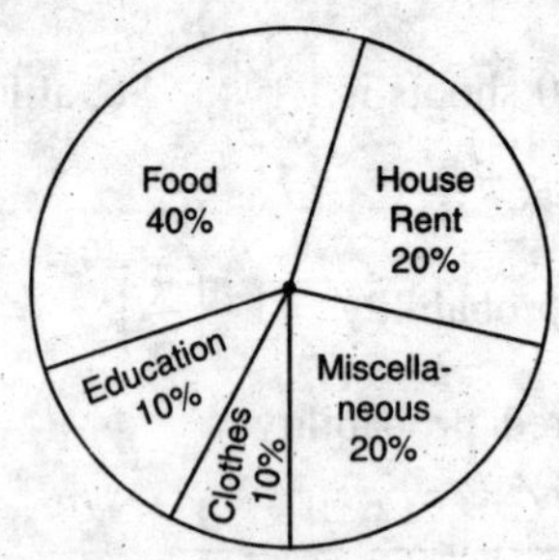

LINE GRAPHS

Line graphs are used to show how a quantity changes continuously. If the line goes up, the quantity is increasing; if the line goes down, the quantity is decreasing; if the line is horizontal, the quantity is not changing.

For example:

Demand and Production of rubber (in thousand tones) in various years

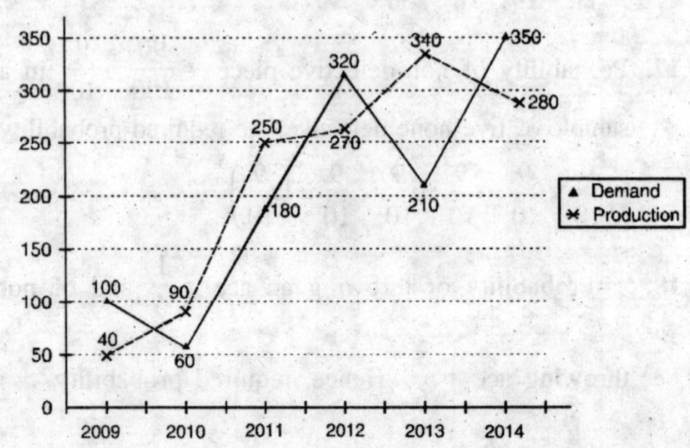

BAR GRAPHS

Given quantity of a bar graph can be compared by the height or length. A bar graph can have either vertical or horizontal bars. You can compare different quantities or the same quantity at the different times. The bars may be placed adjacent to each other or may be separated from each other by spaces depending upon the problem.

For example:

Registration of New Vehicles in Delhi (in thousands)

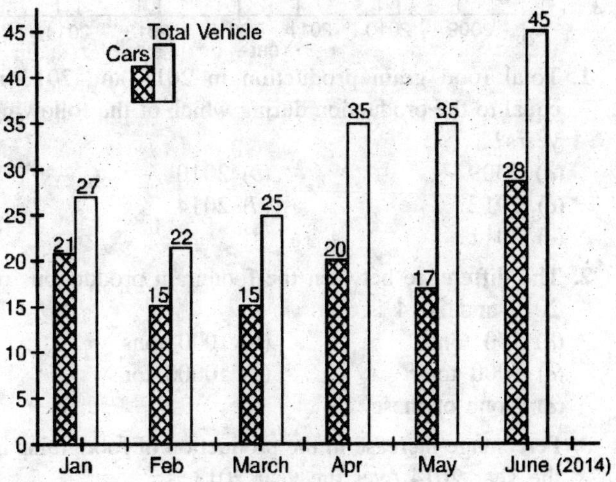

CUMULATIVE GRAPH

These are usually bar or line graphs where the height of the bar or line is divided up proportionally among various quantities presented in the graph. The representation of quantities may be done in terms of either percentage of the total or in absolute figures. These are also called sub-divided graphs. Thus, cumulative graph may be conveniently used for making comparisions.

For example:

The Results of B.Sc. Students of a college for three years

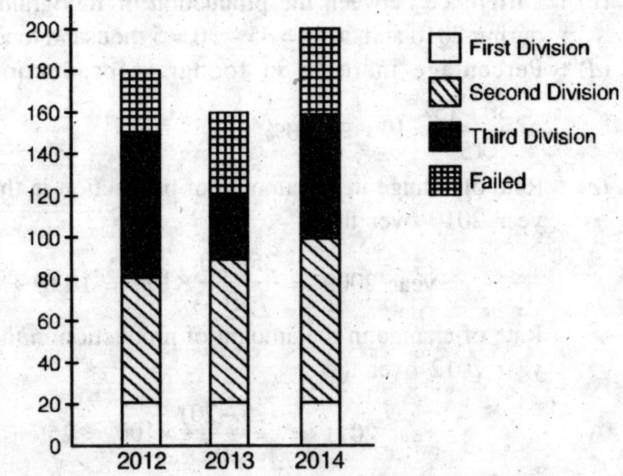

EXERCISE-1

Directions : *Study the following table and answer the questions given below :*

Categories of students according to their enrolment in various courses in a vocational college.

Courses	*Categories (Faculty)*			
	Arts		*Science*	
	Boys	*Girls*	*Boys*	*Girls*
1. Business Management	25	45	25	65
2. Typewriting	23	186	20	32
3. Stenography	25	120	12	58
4. Typewriting and Stenography	12	100	3	5

1. If 60% boys and 70% girls pass in their respective courses, then total pass precentage is :

(*a*) 58% (*b*) 66%
(*c*) 54% (*d*) 62%
(*e*) 60%

2. The total number of students who have opted the course of Business Management and the course of Stenography exceeds the number of students studying in typewriting course by :

(*a*) 44% (*b*) 66%
(*c*) 33% (*d*) 55%
(*e*) 58%

3. In which of the following courses, percentage of girls is the highest?

(*a*) Stenography
(*b*) Business Management
(*c*) Typewriting
(*d*) Typewriting and Stenography
(*e*) None of these

4. In the art faculty number of students who have opted the course of stenography is how much percent of the total student in the faculty?

(*a*) 27% (*b*) 10%
(*c*) 18% (*d*) 15%
(*e*) 20%

5. Total number of boys studying in the college exceeds the total number of girls in the college by :

(*a*) 321% (*b*) 280%
(*c*) 308% (*d*) 250%
(*e*) 300%

Solution

1. (*d*) : ∵ Total boys

$= 45 + 186 + 120 + 100 + 65 + 32 + 58 + 5 = 611$

∴ Number of boys who pass in their respective courses = 60% of 611

$$= 611 \times \frac{60}{100} = 366.60$$

Total number of girls
= 25 + 23 + 25 + 12 + 25 + 20 + 12 + 3 = 145

Number of girls who pass in their respective courses

$$= 70\% \text{ of } 145 = \frac{145 \times 70}{100} = 101.50$$

∴ Combined pass percent

$$= \frac{(366.6 + 101.5) \times 100}{611 + 145}$$

$$= \frac{46810}{756} = 61.92 \text{ or } 62\%.$$

2. (*a*) : ∵ Number of students in Business Management course = 160

Number of students in typewriting course = 261

Number of students in stenography course = 215

$$\therefore \text{Required per cent} = \left(\frac{160 + 215 - 261}{261}\right) \times 100$$

= 44% (approx.).

3. (*b*) : Percentage of girls in Business Management course

$$= \frac{(25 + 25) \times 100}{160}$$

= 31.25

Percentage of girls in typewriting course

$$= \frac{(23 + 20) \times 100}{261}$$

= 16.47

Percentage of girls in stenography course

$$= \frac{(25 + 12) \times 100}{215} = 12.56$$

And percentage of girls in typewriting and stenography course

$$= \frac{(12 + 3) \times 100}{120} = 12.50$$

Hence, it is clear from the above that percentage of girls in Business Management course is the highest.

4. (*a*) : Required percentage

$$= \frac{(25 + 120) \times 100}{536} \times 100 = 27.$$

5. (*a*) : Total number of boys =
45 + 65 + 186 + 32 + 120 + 58 + 100 + 5
= 611

Total number of girls
= 25 + 23 + 25 + 12 + 25 + 20 + 12 + 3 = 145

∴ Required percentage

$$= \left(\frac{611 - 145}{145}\right) \times 100$$

= 321%

EXERCISE-2

Directions : *The following bar graph shows the production of food grains in India during certain year. Study the graph carefully and answer the questions given below :*

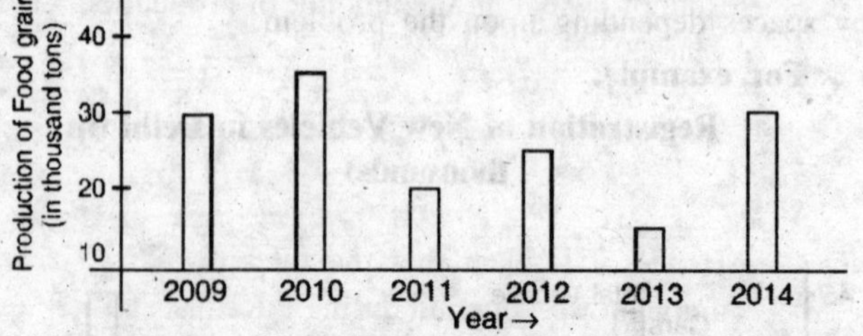

1. Total food grain production in 2011 and 2013 is equal to the production during which of the following years?

(*a*) 2009 (*b*) 2010
(*c*) 2012 (*d*) 2014
(*e*) 2011

2. The difference between the foodgrain productions of 2010 and 2014 is :

(*a*) 500 tons (*b*) 1000 tons
(*c*) 5000 tons (*d*) 10000 tons
(*e*) None of these

3. Percentage increase in the production of foodgrains in the year 2014 over the year 2013 is :

(*a*) 15% (*b*) 30%
(*c*) 50% (*d*) 100%
(*e*) 80%

4. Rate of change in quantity of production in which of the following two consecutive years is at the minimum level?

(*a*) 2009 and 2010 (*b*) 2011 and 2012
(*c*) 2013 and 2014 (*d*) 2012 and 2013
(*e*) None of these

Solution

1. (*b*) : Total production in 2011 and 2013 = 20 + 15 = 35 thousand tons. This total production is equal to the production in the year 2010.

2. (*c*) : Difference between the production of foodgrains during 2010 and 2014 = 35 – 30 = 5 thousand tons.

3. (*d*) : Percentage increase in foodgrain production

$$= \frac{30 - 15}{15} \times 100 = 100\%.$$

4. (*c*) : Rate of change in the amount of production in the year 2010 over the

$$\text{year } 2009 = \frac{35 - 30}{30} \times 100 = 16.67\%$$

Rate of change in the amount of production in the year 2012 over the

$$\text{year } 2011 = \frac{(25 - 20)}{20} \times 100 = 25\%$$

Rate of change in the amount of production in the year 2014 over the

$$\text{year 2013} = \frac{(30-15)}{15}\times 100$$
$$= 100\%$$

Rate of change in the amount of production in the year 2013 over the

$$\text{year 2012} = \frac{(25-15)}{15}\times 100$$
$$= 66.67\%$$

Hence, it is clear that the rate of change in the amount of production during the consecutive years 2013 and 2014 is at the highest level.

EXERCISE-3

Directions : *The bar graph as shown below gives information about the sale and profit details of a departmental store during the years from 2008–2015. Study the graph carefully and answer the questions asked here under.*

Sale and Profit details (2008–15)

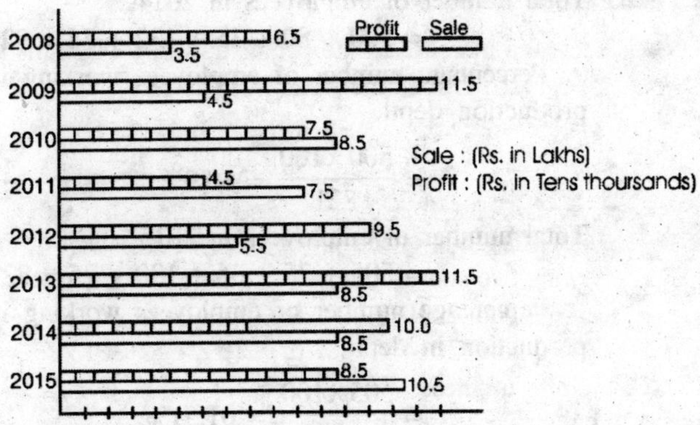

1. Mean of annual increase in sale from 2010 to 2015 (rupees in lakhs) is :

(*a*) 0.1 (*b*) 0.2
(*c*) 0.3 (*d*) 0.4
(*e*) 0.5

2. Annual mean profit of the store (rupees in ten thousands) is approximately :

(*a*) 8.5 (*b*) 8.6
(*c*) 8.7 (*d*) 9.0
(*e*) 8.0

3. During which of the following years percentage of profit earned by the store on the total sale was at the highest level?

(*a*) 2008 (*b*) 2009
(*c*) 2010 (*d*) 2012
(*e*) 2014

4. Assuming the profit earned during the year 2008 as base (100), the profit made by the store during the year 2015 was :

(*a*) 76 (*b*) 105
(*c*) 121 (*d*) 131
(*e*) 120

5. During which year between 2008 to 2013 profit made by the store as compared to the previous year was more than 100%?

(*a*) 2015 (*b*) 2014
(*c*) 2012 (*d*) 2010
(*e*) 2013

Solution

1. (*d*) : Mean of annual increase in sale from 2010 to 2015

$$= \frac{10.5-8.5}{5} = .4$$

2. (*c*) : Annual mean profit of the store (rupees in thousands)

$$= \frac{(6.5+11.5+7.5+4.5+9.5+11.5+10.0+8.5)}{8}$$

$$= \frac{69.5}{8} = 8.7 \text{ (approx.)}$$

3. (*b*) : Percentage of profit on the total sale in 2008

$$= \frac{6.5\times 10000\times 100}{3.5\times 100000} = 1.86$$

Percentage of profit on the total sale in 2009

$$= \frac{11.5\times 10000\times 100}{4.5\times 100000} = 25.56$$

Percentage of profit on the total sale in 2010

$$= \frac{7.5\times 10000\times 100}{8.5\times 100000} = 8.82$$

And percentage of profit on the total sale in 2012

$$= \frac{9.5\times 10000\times 100}{5.5\times 100000} = 17.27.$$

$\therefore$ Percentage of profit on the total sale in 2009 was at the highest level.

4. (*d*) : Required profit

$$= \frac{100\times 8.5}{6.5} = 131.$$

5. (*c*) : Profit percent during the year 2012 as compared to the previous year

$$= \frac{(9.5-4.5)\times 100}{4.5} = 111.11\%$$

Hence, profit in the year 2012 was more than 100% as compared to the preivous year.

EXERCISE-4

Directions : *Study the following table carefully and answer the questions given below :*

Number of Employees Working in Various departments of a Factory

Year	*Production Deptt.*	*Sale Deptt.*	*Procure-ment Deptt.*	*Admini-stration & Accounts Deptt.*	*Reserarch & Development Deptt.*
2010	150	25	50	45	75
2011	225	40	45	62	70
2012	450	65	30	90	73
2013	470	73	32	105	70
2014	500	80	35	132	74
2015	505	75	36	130	75

1. During which of the following years number of employees working in production deptt. of the factory was less than 50% of the total employees of the factory?
(*a*) 2010 (*b*) 2012
(*c*) 2013 (*d*) 2014
(*e*) 2015

2. During which year the number of employees working in each department was more than those in the previous year?
(*a*) 2014 (*b*) 2013
(*c*) 2012 (*d*) 2011
(*e*) 2015

3. In which department of the factory number of employees remained nearly same during the years from 2010 to 2015
(*a*) Production
(*b*) Sale
(*c*) Research and Development
(*d*) Administration and Accounts
(*e*) Procurement

4. In which department of the factory number of employees remained less than 10% of the total employees of the factory continuously from 2010 to 2015.
(*a*) Procurement
(*b*) Sale
(*c*) Research and Development
(*d*) Administration and Accounts
(*e*) Sale and Procurement

5. During which year number of employees in the factory became nearly double the total number of employees working in the factory during 2010
(*a*) 2015 (*b*) 2014
(*c*) 2013 (*d*) 2012
(*e*) 2011

Solution

1. (*a*) : Number of total employees in 2010
$= 150 + 25 + 50 + 45 + 75 = 345$

$\therefore$ Percentage number of employees working in production deptt.

$$= \frac{150\times100}{345} = 43.48\%$$

Number of total employees in 2011
$= 225 + 40 + 45 + 62 + 70 = 442$

$\therefore$ Percentage number of employees working in production deptt.

$$= \frac{225\times100}{442} = 50.9\%$$

Number of total employees in 2012
$= 450 + 65 + 30 + 90 + 73 = 708$

$\therefore$ Percentage number of employees working in production deptt.

$$= \frac{450\times100}{708} = 63.56\%$$

Total number of employees in 2013
$= 470 + 73 + 32 + 105 + 70 = 750$

$\therefore$ Percentage number of employees working in production deptt.

$$= \frac{470\times100}{750} = 62.67\%$$

Total number of employees in 2014
$= 500 + 80 + 35 + 132 + 74 = 821$

$\therefore$ Percentage number of employees working in production deptt.

$$= \frac{500\times100}{821} = 60.9\%$$

Total number of employees in 2015
$= 505 + 75 + 36 + 130 + 75 = 821$

$\therefore$ Percentage number of employees working in production in deptt.

$$= \frac{505\times100}{821} = 61.51\%.$$

Hence, it is clear that percentage number of employees working in production deptt. was less than 50% in 2010.

2. (*a*) : It is clear from the table that it was the year 2014 when the number of employees working in each department was more than that in the previous year.

3. (*c*) : According to the table in the research and development department number of employees remained nearly same during the year from 2010 to 2015.

4. (*a*) : Candidates may solve this question of their own.

5. (*d*) : Total number of employees in 2010 = 345
Total number of employees in 2012 = 708
Hence, it was the year 2012 when total number of employees in the factory became nearly double the total number of employees working in the factory during 2010.

EXERCISE-5

Directions : *The pie-chart given below shows the household expenditure of a family on different items. Study the chart carefully and answer the questions that follow :*

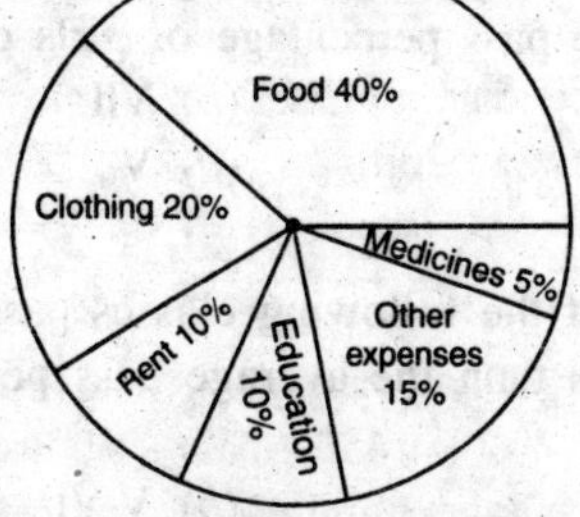

1. If the family's expenditure on education is Rs. 375 then the same amount is being expent by this family on which of the following items?
   (*a*) Medicines (*b*) Other expenses
   (*c*) Rent (*d*) Clothing
   (*e*) None of these
2. If the family expends Rs. 750 per month on food, what is the annual expenditure of this family on education?
   (*a*) Rs. 2150 (*b*) 1022.50
   (*c*) Rs. 2250 (*d*) 1400
   (*e*) Rs. 1500
3. If total expenditure of this family is Rs. 4500, find the expenditure of this family on clothing?
   (*a*) Rs. 800 (*b*) Rs. 900
   (*c*) Rs. 840 (*d*) Rs. 950
   (*e*) Rs. 850
4. What is the angle subtended on the centre by the segment representing other expenses?
   (*a*) 64° (*b*) 54°
   (*c*) 36° (*d*) 15°
   (*e*) 30°
5. What is the ratio of total expenses on rent and clothing to the total expenses on medicines and other expenses of this family?
   (*a*) 2 : 3 (*b*) 3 : 4
   (*c*) 3 : 5 (*d*) 3 : 2
   (*e*) None of these

Solution

1. (*c*) : Both segments representing education and rent rspectively are each subtending a central angle of 36°. Hence, family's expenditure on these two items will be equal, *i.e.*, Rs. 375 will be expent on rent.

2. (*c*) : Expenditure of food= Rs. 750

$\therefore$ Total expenditure $= \frac{100 \times 750}{40}$ = Rs. 1875

$\because$ Expenditure on education = 10%

$\therefore$ Amount spent on education

$= \frac{1875 \times 10}{100}$ = Rs. 187.50

$\therefore$ Annual expenditure of the family on education = 187.50 × 12 = Rs. 2250.00

3. (*b*) : Expenditure on clothing = 20%

$\therefore$ Total expenditure on clothing

$= \frac{20}{100} \times 4500$ = Rs. 900

4. (*b*) : Central angle for 15% $= \frac{15}{100} \times 360° = 54°$.

5. (*d*) : Expenditure on rent and clothing = 10% + 20% = 30%

Expenditure on medicine and other expenses = 5% + 15% = 20%

$\therefore$ Ratio of the two = 30% : 20% = 3 : 2.

EXERCISE-6

Directions : *The pie chart, drawn here, shows the spending of a country on various sports during a particular year. Study the graph carefully and answer the questions that follow :*

Percent of Money Spent on Various Sports for One Year

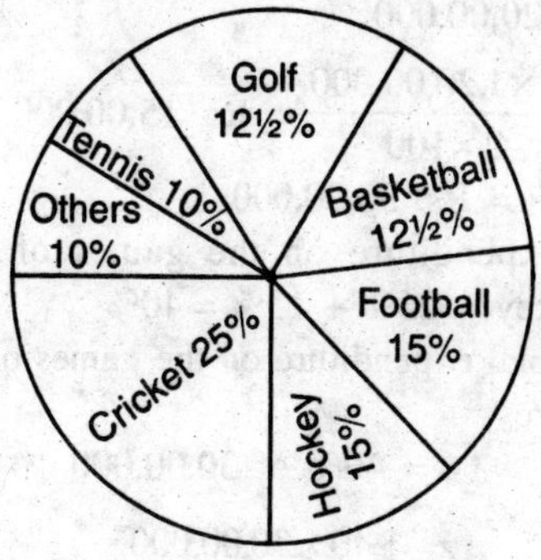

1. Graph shows that the most popular game of the country is :
   (*a*) Football (*b*) Hockey
   (*c*) Cricket (*d*) Tennis
   (*e*) Golf
2. Out of the following the country spent the same amount on :
   (*a*) Hockey and Cricket (*b*) Hockey and Football
   (*c*) Hockey and Golf (*d*) Tennis and Golf
   (*e*) None of these
3. The ratio of the total amount spent on football to that spent on hockey is :
   (*a*) 2 : 1 (*b*) 1 : 1
   (*c*) 1 : 2 (*d*) 3 : 2
   (*e*) 1 : 3
4. If the total amount spent on sports during the year was Rs. 1,20,00,000, how much was spent on basketball?

(*a*) Rs. 16,00,000 (*b*) Rs. 18,00,000
(*c*) Rs. 3,00,000 (*d*) Rs. 15,00,000
(*e*) None of these

5. If the total amount spent on sports during the year was Rs. 30,00,000, the amount spent on cricket and hockey together was :
(*a*) Rs. 18,00,000 (*b*) Rs. 12,00,000
(*c*) Rs. 15,00,000 (*d*) Rs. 20,00,000
(*e*) None of these

Solution

1. (*c*) : According to the graph, expenditure on cricket is the maximum. Therefore cricket is the most popular game.

2. (*b*) : According to the graph, equal amount has been spent on Hockey and Football.

3. (*b*) : Expenditure on the game of Football = 15% of total amount spent
Expenditure on the game of Hockey = 15% of total amount spent
Therefore the ratio of the expenditure on the two games = 1 : 1.

4. (*d*) : 100% = Rs. 1,20,00,000
∴ Expenditure on the game of Basketball = 12½% of 1,20,00,000

$$= \frac{25 \times 1,20,00,000}{2 \times 100} = \text{Rs. } 15,00,000.$$

5. (*b*) : 100% = Rs. 30,00,000
∴ Expenditure on the games of Cricket and Hockey = 25% + 15% = 40%
∴ Total expenditure on the games of Cricket and Hockey
= 40% of 30,00,000

$$= \frac{40 \times 30,00,000}{100} = \text{Rs. } 12,00,000.$$

EXERCISE-7

Directions : *The graph given below shows annual result of different classes of a school. Study the graph carefully and attempt the questions that follow :*

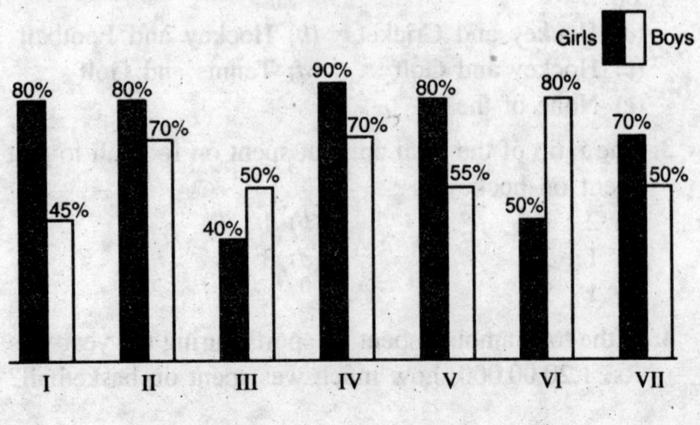

1. Result of which class shows maximum difference between pass percentage of the girls and the boys?
(*a*) I (*b*) IV
(*c*) III (*d*) VI
(*e*) V

2. In which class pass percentage of boys is more than the average pass percentage of girls of the school?
(*a*) VI (*b*) VII
(*c*) III (*d*) V
(*e*) IV

3. In which of the following classes pass percentage of girls is less than the average pass percentage of the school?
(*a*) III-VI (*b*) V-VI
(*c*) VI-VII (*d*) III-IV
(*e*) IV-V

4. In which class number of failed girls is minimum?
(*a*) I (*b*) III
(*c*) IV (*d*) VII
(*e*) II

5. Average pass percentage of boys in classes II and III is equal to average pass percentage of girls in which of the following classes?
(*a*) II-VI (*b*) I-V
(*c*) VI-VII (*d*) V-VI
(*e*) None of these

Solution

1. (*a*) : Difference between pass percentage of girls and boys in class I = 80 – 45 = 35%
Difference between pass percentage of girls and boys in class II = 80 – 70 = 10%.
Differene between pass percentage of girls and boys in class III = 50 – 40 = 10%
Difference between pass percentage of girls and boys in class IV = 90 – 70 = 20%
Difference between pass percentage of girls and boys in class V = 80 – 55 = 25%
Difference between pass percentage of girls and boys in class VI = 80 – 50 = 30%
Difference between pass percentage of girls and boys in class VII = 70 – 50 = 20%
Hence, it is clear that result of class I shows maximum difference between pass percentage of the girls and the boys.

2. (*a*) : Average pass percentage of girls

$$= \frac{80+80+40+90+80+50+70}{7} = \frac{490}{7} = 70\%$$

Therefore, in class VI pass percentage of boys is more than the average pass percentage of girls.

3. (*a*) : Average pass percentage of the school

$$= \frac{80+45+80+70+40+50+90+70+80+55+50+80+70+50}{14}$$

$$= \frac{910}{14} = 65\%$$

Therefore, it is clear that pass percentage of the girls in III and VI classes is less than the average pass percentage of the school.

4. (*c*) : In class IV pass percentage of girls is the highest. Therefore in this class only number of failed girls is the minimum.

5. (*c*) : Average pass percentage of the boys in classes II and III $= \frac{70+50}{2} = \frac{120}{2} = 60\%$

Average pass percentage of the girls in class VI and VII $= \frac{50+70}{2} = 60\%$

Therefore, average pass percentage of boys in classes II and III is equal to the average pass percentage of girls in classes VI and VII.

EXERCISE-8

Directions : *Study carefully the graph given below and answer the questions that follow :*

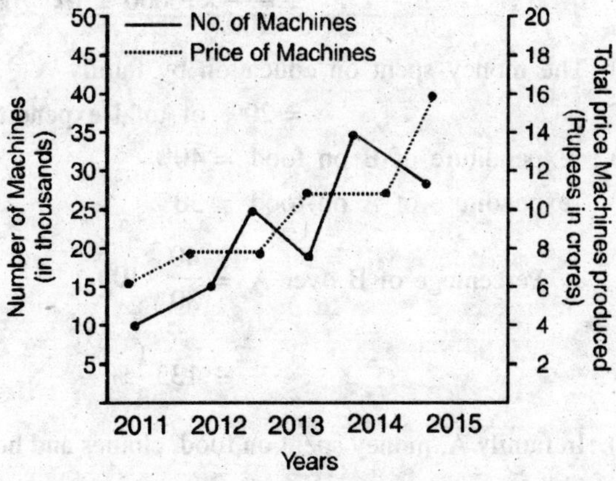

1. Price of a machine during 2012 was :

(*a*) Rs. $5\frac{1}{3}$ thousand

(*b*) Rs. 50 thousand

(*c*) Rs. 5103

(*d*) Rs. 3 thousand

(*e*) None of these

2. The percentage decrease in the production in 2014 over the previous year 2013 was :

(*a*) 5% (*b*) 20%

(*c*) 25% (*d*) 30%

(*e*) 35%

3. The difference in revenue collection from the sale of machines during 2014 and 2015 was :

(*a*) Rs. 10 lakhs (*b*) Rs. 1 crore

(*c*) Rs. 4 crores (*d*) Rs. 6 crores

(*e*) None of these

4. Had the company sold its machines in 2015 at 25% inhanced price, what would have been the total selling price of machines produced during the year?

(*a*) Rs. 35 crores

(*b*) Rs. 20 crores

(*c*) Rs. 12.5 crores

(*d*) Rs. 15.5 crores

(*e*) None of these

5. Difference between the price of a machine in the year 2013 and that in the year 2014 was :

(*a*) Rs. 1500 (*b*) Rs. 2500

(*c*) Rs. 1800 (*d*) Rs. 3200

(*e*) Rs. 2000

Solution

1. (*a*) : No. of machines produced during the year 2012

= 15000

And price of the machines

= Rs. 8,0000000

∴ Price of 1 machine in 2012

$$= \text{Rs.}\frac{80000000}{15000}$$

$$= \text{Rs. } 5\frac{1}{3} \text{ thousand}$$

2. (*b*) : Percentage decrease in production of machines during 2014 over the previous year 2013

$$= \frac{(25-20)\times 100}{25} = 20\%$$

3. (*d*) : Difference in revenue collected from sale of machines during 2014 and 2015

= 16 – 10

= Rs. 6 crores.

4. (*c*) : On enhancing price by 25% in 2015, total price of the machines produced during the year 2015

$$= \frac{10\times 125}{100} = \text{Rs. 12.5 crores.}$$

5. (*c*) : Price of 1 machine in 2013

$$= \frac{80000000}{25000} = \text{Rs. 3200}$$

Price of 1 machine in 2014

$$= \frac{100000000}{20000} = \text{Rs. 5000}$$

∴ Required difference

= Rs. (5000 – 3200)

= Rs. 1800.

EXERCISE-9

Direction : *Following bar diagram shows the monthly expenditure of two families on food, clothing, education, fuel, house rent and miscellaneous (in percentage).*

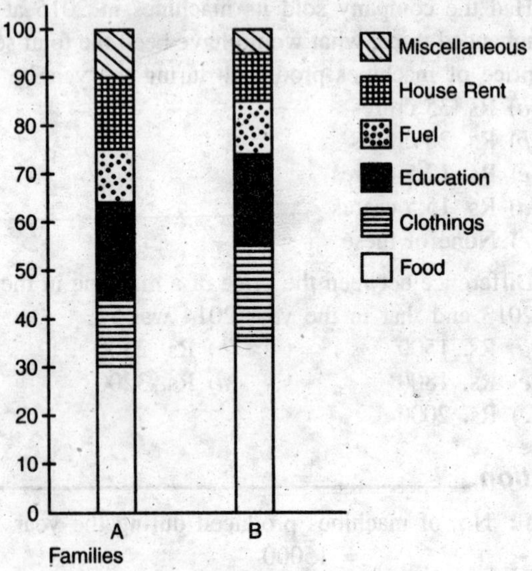

Study the above diagram and mark a tick against the correct answer in each question.

1. If both families have the same expenditure, which one spends more on education and miscellaneous together?
(*a*) Family A
(*b*) Family B
(*c*) both (*a*) and (*b*)
(*d*) Cannot be determined
(*e*) None of these

2. If total annual expenditure of family B is Rs. 10,000 then money spent on clothes during the year is :
(*a*) Rs. 200
(*b*) Rs. 2000
(*c*) Rs. 600
(*d*) Rs. 6000
(*e*) None of these

3. What fraction of the total expenditure is spent on education in family A?
(*a*) 20% of total expenditure
(*b*) 30% of total expenditure
(*c*) 15% of total expenditure
(*d*) 25% of total expenditure
(*e*) None of these

4. What percentage is B's expenditure on food over A's expenditure on food? (Taking equal total expenditure)
(*a*) $120\frac{1}{2}\%$ (*b*) $130\frac{1}{3}\%$
(*c*) $133\frac{1}{3}\%$ (*d*) $110\frac{1}{3}\%$
(*e*) None of these

5. If the total annual expenditure of family A is Rs. 30,000 then money spent on food, clothes and house rent is :
(*a*) Rs. 18,500
(*b*) Rs. 18,000
(*c*) Rs. 21,000
(*d*) Rs. 15,000
(*e*) None of these

Solution

1. (*a*) : Total spent on education & miscellaneous by family A = (20 + 10) = 30%

Total spent on education & miscellaneous by family B = (15 + 5) = 20%

Hence, family A spends more on these hands.

2. (*b*) : The money spent on clothes by family B

$= 20\%$ of total expenditure

$= \frac{20}{100} \times 10000 = \text{Rs. } 2000,$

3. (*a*) : The money spent on education by family A

$= 20\%$ of total expenditure

4. (*c*) : Expenditure of B on food = 40%

expenditure of A on food = 30%

$\therefore$ Percentage of B over A $= \frac{40}{30} \times 100$

$= 133\frac{1}{3}\%$

5. (*b*) : In family A, money spent on food, clothes and house rent

$= (30 + 15 + 15)\%$

$= 60\%$ of total expenditure

$= \text{Rs.}\left(\frac{60}{100} \times 30{,}000\right)$

$= \text{Rs. } 18{,}000.$

Reasoning Ability

1

Syllogism

INTRODUCTION

Syllogism was introduced by Aristotle (a reasoning consisting two premises and a conclusion). Aristotle gives the following definition of syllogism in his fundamental treatise Organon.

"A syllogism is discourse, in which, certain things being stated, something other than what is stated follows of necessity from their being so." Things that have stated are known as premises and the one that follows from the premises is known as the conclusion of the syllogism.

A categorical syllogism is a type of argument with two premises and one conclusion. Each of these three propositions is one of four forms of categorical proposition.

Type	Form	Example
A	All S are P	All monkeys are mammals
E	No S is P	No monkeys are birds
I	Some S are P	Some philosophers are logicians
O	Some S are not P	Some logicians are not philosophers

These four type of proposition are called A, E, I and O type propositions, the variables S and P are place-holders for terms which represent out a class or category of thing, hence the name "categorical" proposition.

A categorical syllogism contains precisely three terms: the major term, which is the predicate of the conclusion; the minor term, the subject of the conclusion; and the middle term, which appears in both premises but not in the conclusion.

Aristotle noted following five basic rules governing the validity of categorical syllogisms.

1. The middle term must be distributed at least once (distributed term refers to all members of the denoted class, as in all S are P and no S is P).
2. A term distributed in the conclusion must be distributed in the premise in which it occurs.
3. Two negative premises imply no valid conclusion.
4. If one premise is negative, then the conclusion must be negative.
5. Two affirmatives imply an affirmative.

John Venn, an English logician, in 1880 introduced a method for analyzing categorical syllogisms, known as the Venn diagram. In a paper entitled "on the Diagrammatic and Mechanical Representation of proposition's and Reasoning" in the "philosophical magazine and journal of science," Venn shows the different ways to represent propositions by diagrams. For categorical syllogism three overlapping circles are drawn to represent the classes denoted by the three terms. Universal propositions (all S are P, no S is P) are indicated by shading the sections of the circles representing the excluded classes. Particular propositions (some S are P, some S are not P) are indicated by placing some mark, usually an "x", in the part of the circle representing the class whose members are specified. The conclusion may then be inferred from the diagram.

Venn diagrams has similarity with Euler diagrams, invented by Leonhard Euler in the 18th century, but Venn diagrams are visually more complex than the Euler diagrams.

Solving Syllogism problems are usually moderate time consuming by traditional methods and considered difficult by most of the students. **New RAVAL NOTATION** solves Syllogism problems very quickly and accurately. This method solves any categorical syllogism problem with same ease and is as simple as ABC...

Method: In **RAVAL NOTATION,** each premise and conclusion is written in abbreviated form, and then conclusion is reached simply by connecting abbreviated premises.

NOTATION: Statements (both premises and conclusions) are represented as follows:

Statements	Notation:
(*a*) All S are P	SS-P
(*b*) Some S are P	S-P
(*c*) Some S are not P	(S/P)
(*d*) No S is P	SS/PP

(-implies are and/implies are not)

All is represented by double letters; Some is represented by single letter. Some S are not P is represented as (S/P) in statement notation. *This statement is written uniquely in brackets because one cannot include this statement in deriving any conclusion. (Some S are not P does not imply some P are not S).* No S is P implies No P is S so its notation contains double letters on both sides.

RULES

1. Conclusions are reached by connecting Notations. Two notations can be linked only through common linking terms. When the common linking term multiplies (becomes double from single), divides (becomes single from double) or remains double then conclusion is arrived between terminal terms. (Aristotle's rule: the middle term must be distributed at least once).
2. If both statements linked are having – signs, resulting conclusion carries – sign (Aristotle's rule: two affirmatives imply an affirmative).
3. Whenever statements having – and/signs are linked, resulting conclusion carries/sign. (Aristotle's rule: if one premise is negative, then the conclusion must be negative).
4. Statement having/sign cannot be linked with another statement having/sign to derive any conclusion. (Aristotle's rule: two negative premises imply no valid conclusion).
5. Whenever statement carrying / sign is involved in deducting conclusion then terminating point in statement carrying – sign should be in double letters to have any valid conclusion. (When the terminating term is in double letters, it limits the terminating term to the maximum up to common term. Hence valid conclusion follows only in this case when / sign is involved)

Following illustrations will make the above rules very clear.

Illustration for Rule 5:

1. Statements: **Notation**

(*a*) No S is P. (*a*) SS / PP

(*b*) All Q is P (*b*) QQ – P

Valid Conclusion:

1. No S is Q 1. SS / QQ

Explanation: From

(*a*) SS / PP (*b*) QQ – P

1. SS / QQ follow because common linking term (P) divides and terminating term Q is in double letters.

Representation by Euler's method

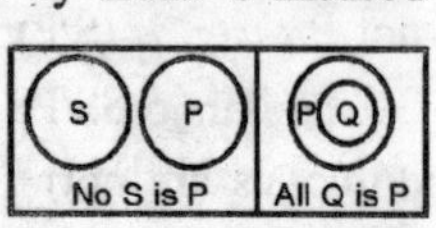

All Q is P can be combined with No S is P as shown below.

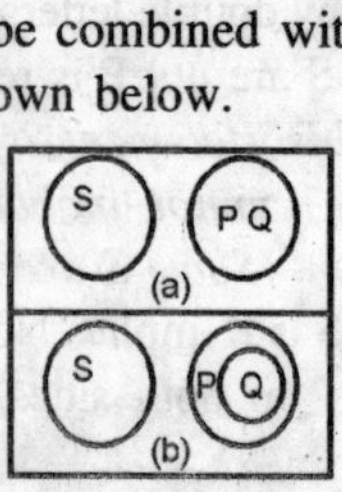

Hence No S is Q follow in both (a) and (b)

2. Statements: **Notation:**

(*a*) No S is P (*a*) SS / PP

(*b*) All P is Q (*b*) PP – Q

Wrong Conclusion:

1. Some S are not Q 1. S / Q

Explanation: From

(*a*) SS / PP (*b*) PP – Q

1. S / Q does not follow, though common linking term (P) is in double letters but terminating term Q is in single letter.

Representation by Euler's method

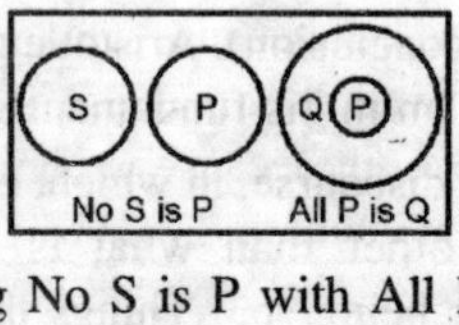

On combining No S is P with All P is Q. One of the possible cases is shown below. It is clear from the diagram that Some S are not Q does not follow in this case

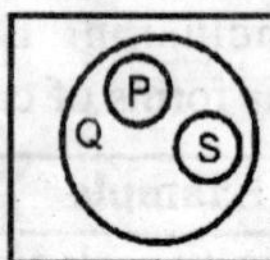

No S is Q does not follow

3. Statements: **Notation:**

(*a*) All S are P (*a*) SS – P

(*b*) All P are Q (*b*) PP – Q

Valid Conclusions:

1. All S are Q	1. SS – Q
2. Some S are Q	2. S – Q
3. Some Q are S	3. Q – S
4. Some P are S	4. P – S
5. Some Q are P	5. Q – P
6. Some S are P	6. S – P
7. Some P are Q	7. P – Q

Wrong Conclusions:

1. All Q are S	1. QQ – S
2. All P are S	2. PP – S
3. All Q are P	3. QQ – P
4. Some S are not Q	4. S / Q
5. Some Q are not S	5. Q / S
6. Some P are not S	6. P / S

Valid Conclusions explanation: From

(*a*) SS – P (*b*) PP – Q

1. SS – Q follows, because here common linking term (P) multiplies.
2. S – Q follows, because "Some" is part of All (S is included in SS but not vice versa) and common linking term (P) multiplies.
3. Q – S follows, because here common linking term (P) divides.
4. P – S follows from the main statement SS – P (by reverse reading).

5. Q – P follows from the main statement PP – Q (by reverse reading, one can isolate P from PP).
6. S – P follows from the main statement SS – P.
7. P – Q follows from the main statement PP – Q.

Wrong Conclusions explanation:

1. QQ – S does not follow because we don't have any QQ in statement notation.
2. PP – S does not follow because there is no common linking term between PP and S.
3. QQ – P does not follow because we don't have any QQ in statement notation.
4. S / Q is ruled out because we don't have any / sign in statement notation.
5. Q / S is ruled out because we don't have any / sign in statement notation.
6. P / S is ruled out because we don't have any / sign in statement notation.

4. Statements: **Notation:**

(*a*) All S are P (*a*) SS – P
(*b*) Some P are Q (*b*) P – Q

Valid Conclusions:

1. Some S are P 1. S – P
2. Some P are S 2. P – S
3. Some Q are P 3. Q – P

Wrong Conclusions:

1. All S are Q 1. SS – Q
2. All P are S 2. PP – S
3. Some Q are S 3. Q – S
4. Some Q are not S 4. Q / S

Valid Conclusions explanation: From
(*a*) SS – P (*b*) P – Q

1. S – P follows from statement SS – P
2. P – S follows from statement SS – P (reverse reading)
3. Q – P follows from statement P – Q (reverse reading)

Wrong Conclusions explanation:

1. SS – Q does not follow because common linking term (P) remains singular.
2. PP – S does not follow because PP is not present in any statement notation.
3. Q – S does not follow because common linking term (P) remains singular.
4. Q / S is ruled out because we don't have any / sign in statement notation.

5. Statements: **Notation:**

(*a*) Some S are P (*a*) S – P
(*b*) Some P are Q (*b*) P – Q

Valid Conclusions:

1. Some P are S 1. P – S
2. Some Q are P 2. Q – P

Wrong Conclusions:

1. Some S are Q 1. S – Q
2. Some Q are S 2. Q – S
3. All P are S 3. PP – S
4. All Q are S 4. QQ – S

Valid Conclusions explanation: From
(*a*) S – P (*b*) P – Q

1. P – S follows from statement S – P (reverse reading).
2. Q – P follows from statement P – Q (reverse reading).

Wrong Conclusions explanation:

1. S – Q does not follow because common linking term (P) remains singular.
2. Q – S does not follow because common linking term (P) remains singular.
3. PP – S does not follow because PP is not present in any statement notation.
4. QQ – S does not follow because QQ is not present in any statement notation.

6. Statements: **Notation:**

(*a*) All S are P (*a*) SS – P
(*b*) No P is Q (*b*) PP / QQ

Valid Conclusions:

1. No S is Q 1. SS / QQ
2. No Q is S 2. QQ / SS
3. No Q is P 3. QQ/ PP
4. Some S are not Q 4. S / Q
5. Some Q are not S 5. Q / S
6. Some P are not Q 6. P / Q
7. Some Q are not P 7. Q / P

Wrong Conclusions:

1. Some Q are P 1. Q – P
2. All P are S 2. PP – S

Valid Conclusions explanation: From
(*a*) SS – P (*b*) PP/QQ

1. SS / QQ follows because common linking term (P) multiplies (Whenever – and / are linked result carries / sign).
2. QQ / SS follow because common linking term (P) divides.
3. QQ / PP follow from statement *(b)* on reverse reading.
4. S / Q follows because common linking term (P) multiplies (one can read S from SS and Q from QQ).
5. Q / S follow (by reverse reading) because common linking term (P) divides and terminating term S is in double letters.
6. P/Q follow from PP/QQ.
7. Q/P follows from PP/QQ (reverse reading).

Wrong Conclusions explanation:

1. Q – P does not follow because Q is linked with P via / sign.
2. PP – S does not follow from SS – P.

7. Statements: **Notation:**

(*a*) No S is P (*a*) SS / PP
(*b*) No P is Q (*b*) PP / QQ

Wrong Conclusions:

1. No S is Q 1. SS / QQ
2. No Q is S 2. QQ / SS
3. Some P is S 3. P – S
4. Some Q is S 4. Q – S

Wrong Conclusions explanation: From
(a) SS / PP (b) PP / QQ

1. SS / QQ do not follow because both statements have / sign so statements (a) and (b) cannot be combined to deduce any conclusion.
2. QQ / SS do not follow because both statements have / sign.
3. P – S does not follow because we don't have – sign between P and S anywhere in statement notation.
4. Q – S does not follow because both statements have / sign.

8. Statements:

Statements	Notation
(a) Some S are P	(a) S – P
(b) No P is Q	(b) PP / QQ
(c) All T are Q	(c) TT – Q
Valid Conclusions:	
1. Some S are not Q	1. S / Q
2. Some P are not T	2. P / T
3. Some T are not P	3. T / P
4. Some S are not T	4. S / T
Wrong Conclusions:	
1. Some Q are not S	1. Q / S
2. Some T are not S	2. T / S

Valid Conclusions explanation: From
(a) S – P (b) PP / QQ
(c) TT – Q

1. S / Q follows because common linking term (P) multiply.
2. P / T follow because common linking term (Q) divides and terminating term T is in double letters.
3. T / P follow because common linking term (Q) multiplies.
4. S / T follows because first common linking term (P) multiplies then second linking term (Q) divides and terminating term T is in double letters.

Wrong Conclusions explanation:

1. Q / S do not follow because terminating term S is in single letter.
2. T / S do not follow because terminating term S is in single letter.

9. Statements:

Statements	Notation
(a) Some S are P	(a) S – P
(b) All P are Q	(b) PP – Q
(c) All Q are T	(c) QQ – T
Valid Conclusions:	
1. Some S are T	1. S – T
2. Some T are S	2. T – S

Valid Conclusions explanation: From
(a) S – P (b) PP – Q
(c) QQ – T

1. S – T follows, when we move from S towards T, P multiplies so we reach Q since Q also multiplies we get S – T.
2. T – S follows, when we move from T towards S, Q divides so we reach PP, since PP also divides we get T – S.

Complementary pair (in conclusions): In a complementary pair, at least one of the two statements is always true. For example: Conclusions 1. Some S are P, 2. Some S are not P. Obviously one of these conclusions must be true, therefore if answer options contain either 1 or 2 is true and none of them is individually true then this answer option is correct one. As in traditional methods, in RAVAL'S NOTATION too complementary pair options are to be found by mere inspection.

Exclusive statements: Statements beginning with "only", "alone", "none but", "none else but" are called exclusive statements. Such statements can be reduced in desired forms

Let the given exclusive statement be	*Then it can be reduced as*	*Notation*
Only S is P or S alone is P or None but S is P or No one else but S is P	All P are S or No non-S is P	PP – S or non-S non-S/PP

MULTIPLE CHOICE QUESTIONS

Directions (Qs. Nos. 1 to 10): *In each question below are given two statements followed by two conclusions numbered I and II. You have to take the given two statements to be true even if they seem to be at variance from commonly known facts. Read the conclusion and then decide which of the given conclusions logically follows from the two given statements, disregarding commonly known facts.*

Give answer:

A. If only conclusion I follows
B. If only conclusion II follows
C. If either I or II follows
D. If neither I nor II follows and
E. If both I and II follow.

1. Statements: I. All tables are chalks.
II. All chalks are chairs.
Conclusions: I. All chairs are tables.
II. All tables are chairs.

2. Statements: I. Some radios are stones.
II. All stones are rods.
Conclusions: I. Some stones are radios.
II. All Radios being roads is a possibility.

3. Statements: I. Some birds are flowers.
II. Some flowers are books.
Conclusions: I. Some birds are books.
II. No book is a flower.

4. Statements: I. Some cows are jackals.
II. No fox is a cow.
Conclusions: I. Some jackals are foxes.
II. Some jackals are not foxes.

5. Statements: I. Only cats are animals.
II. No dog is an animal.
Conclusions: I. Some cats are not dogs.
II. Some dogs are cats.

6. Statements : I. All shoes are carpets.
II. No carpet is a pullover.
Conclusions: I. No shoes are pullovers.
II. All carpets are shoes.

7. Statements: I. No window is a wall.
II. No wall is a door.
Conclusions: I. No window is a door.
II. No door is a window.

8. Statements: I. All players are tall.
II. Johan is tall.
Conclusions: I. Johan is a player.
II. Johan is not a player.

9. Statements: I. All dogs are wolves.
II. Some wolves are tigers.
Conclusions: I. Some dogs are tigers.
II. Tigers which are wolves are not dogs.

10. Statements: I. All cars fly.
II. Some cycles fly.
Conclusions: I. All cars are cycles.
II. Some cycles do not fly.

Directions (Qs. Nos. 11 to 20): *In each question below are given three statements followed by two conclusions numbered I and II. You have to take the given two statements to be true even if they seem to be at variance from commonly known facts. Read the conclusion and then decide which of the given conclusions logically follows from the two given statements, disregarding commonly known facts.*

Give answer:
A. If only conclusion I follows
B. If only conclusion II follows
C. If either I or II follows
D. If neither I nor II follows and
E. If both I and II follow.

11. Statements: I. Some spoons are pots.
II. All pots are cups.
III. Some cups are cards.
Conclusions: I. Some cards are spoons.
II. Some cups are spoons.

12. Statements: I. Some keys are locks.
II. Some locks are doors.
III. Some doors are windows.
Conclusions: I. Some windows are locks.
II. Some doors are keys.

13. Statements: I. Some boys are flowers.
II. All flowers are jungles.
III. All jungles are houses.
Conclusions: I. Some houses are flowers.
II. Some houses are boys.

14. Statements: I. All bottles are tanks.
II. All tanks are drums.
III. All drums are pipes.
Conclusions: I. Some pipes are tanks.
II. Some drums are bottles.

15. Statements: I. All sticks are brushes.
II. No brush is a fruit.
III. Some fruits are trees.
Conclusions: I. Some trees are sticks.
II. No tree is stick.

16. Statements: I. Some shirts are pants.
II. All pants are clothes.
III. Some clothes are napkins.
Conclusions: I. Some napkins are shirts.
II. Some clothes are shirts.

17. Statements: I. All packets are tents.
II. All tents are houses.
III. Some boxes are houses.
Conclusions: I. Some houses are packets.
II. Some boxes are tents.

18. Statements: I. Some nuts are bolts.
II. Some bolts are hammers.
III. Some hammers are nails.
Conclusions: I. Some nails are bolts.
II. No nail is a bolt.

19. Statements: I. All windows are doors.
II. No door is mountain.
III. Some mountains are roads.
Conclusions: I. Some roads are windows.
II. Some roads are doors.

20. Statements: I. Some phones are bangles.
II. Some bangles are rings.
III. All rings are sticks.
Conclusions: I. Some rings are phones.
II. Some sticks are bangles.

Directions (Qs. Nos. 21 to 25): *In each question below are given four statements followed by four conclusions numbered I, II, III and IV. You have to take the given two statements to be true even if they seem to be at variance from commonly known facts. Read the conclusion and then decide which of the given conclusions logically follows from the two given statements, disregarding commonly known facts.*

21. Statements: I. All silver are metals.
II. All metals are steel.
III. Some steel are stones.
IV. All stones are stands.
Conclusions: I. Some stands are metals.
II. Some stones are silver.
III. Some stands are steel.
IV. Some stones are steel.
A. Only conclusions III and IV follow
B. Only conclusion I follows

C. Only conclusion II follows
D. Only conclusion III follows
E. None of these

22. Statements: I. All chairs are tables.
II. All tables are songs.
III. Some songs are rhythms.
IV. Some rhythms are pillows.
Conclusions: I. Some tables are chairs.
II. All tables are rhythms.
III. All chairs are songs.
IV. Some pillows are songs.
A. Only conclusions I and III follow
B. Only conclusions I and IV follow
C. Only conclusion I follows
D. Only conclusion III follows
E. None of these

23. Statements: I. Some mobiles are pens.
II. Some pens are covers.
III. Some covers are plates.
IV. All plates are papers.
Conclusions: I. All mobiles are covers.
II. Some pens are papers.
III. All plates are pens.
IV. Some papers are mobiles.
A. Only conclusion I follows
B. Only conclusion II follows
C. Only conclusions I and IV follow
D. Only conclusions II and IV follow
E. None follows

24. Statements: I. All shoes are tables.
II. Some tables are lanes.
III. All caps are lanes.
IV. Some lanes are row.
Conclusions: I. Some tables are rows.
II. Some tables are shoes.
III. Some rows are caps.
IV. Some lanes are shoes.
A. Only conclusions I and II follow
B. Only conclusion II follows
C. Only conclusion III follows
D. Only conclusion I either or conclusion IV follows
E. None of these

25. Statements: I. Some symbols are numbers.
II. Some numbers are letters.
III. All alphabets are symbols.
IV. All pianos are letters.
Conclusions: I. Some symbols are letters.
II. Some numbers are pianos.
III. No letter is symbol.
IV. Some symbols are alphabets.
A. Only conclusion I follows
B. Only conclusion II follows
C. Only conclusions III and IV follow
D. Only conclusion IV follows
E. Only either I or III and IV follow

Directions : *In each question below are given two statements followed by two conclusions numbered I and II. You have to take the two given statements to be true even if they seem to be at variance from commonly known facts and then decide which of the given conclusions logically follows from the two given statements, disregarding commonly known facts. Read both the statements and—*

Give answer
A. if only conclusion I follows;
B. if only conclusion II follows;
C. if either I or II follows;
D. if neither I nor II follows;
D. if both I and II follows.

26. Statements: I. All tomatoes are red.
II. All grapes are tomatoes.
Conclusions: I. All grapes are red.
II. Some tomatoes are grapes.

27. Statements: I. All painters are smilling.
II. Some authors are painters.
Conclusions: I. All smiling authors are painters.
II. Some authors are smiling.

28. Statements: I. All peons in this office are efficient.
II. Ramu is not efficient.
Conclusions: I. Ramu is not peon in this office.
II. Ramu should be more efficient.

29. Statements: I. All weavers are hard working.
II. No hard working men are foolish.
Conclusions: I. No weavers are foolish.
II. Some foolish are weavers.

30. Statements: I. All fishes are cars.
II. All cars are vegetables.
Conclusions: I. Some vegetables are cars.
II. Some vegetables are fishes.

31. Statements: I. Some dogs are pups.
II. All horses are pups.
Conclusions: I. Some dogs are horses.
II. Some horses are dogs.

32. Statements: I. All beautiful women are mothers.
II. All mothers are understanding.
Conclusions: I. All beautiful women are understanding.
II. All mothers are beautiful women.

33. Statements: I. Some toys are tables.
II. No table is black.
Conclusions: I. Some toys are black.
II. Some toys are not black.

34. Statements: I. All rivers are mountains.
II. Some rivers are deserts.
Conclusions: I. Some mountains are deserts.
II. Some deserts are not mountains.

35. Statements: I. All men are horses.
II. All horses are elephants.

Conclusions: I. All men are elephants.
II. All elephants are men.

36. Statements: I. Some artworks are paintings.
II. All paintings are masterpieces.
Conclusions: I. All masterpieces are paintings.
II. Some masterpieces are artworks.

37. Statements: I. Some men are genius.
II. No brother is genius.
Conclusions: I. Some brothers are men.
II. Some brothers are not men.

38. Statements: I. All pants are skirts.
II. No shirt is a skirt.
Conclusions: I. Some skirts are pants.
II. All shirts are pants.

39. Statements: I. All planes are tyres.
II. All tyres are engines.
Conclusions: I. No engine is a plane.
II. No tyre is a plane.

40. Statements: I. Some cartoons are funny.
II. Some cartoons are silly.
Conclusions: I. All funny are cartoons.
II. Some silly are cartoons.

Directions : *In the following questions, select the set of conclusion which logically follows from the given statements.*

41. Statements: I. All foxes are plates.
II. All plates are trees.
Conclusions: I. All foxes are trees.
II. All trees are foxes.
III. Some trees are foxes.
IV. Some trees are plates.

A. All conclusions are correct.
B. Only conclusions I, III, and IV follow.
C. Only conclusions II, III, and IV follow.
D. Only conclusions I and IV follow.
E. None of the above.

42. Statements: I. Some cubes are squares.
II. All squares are circles.
Conclusions: I. All cubes are circles.
II. Some circles are cubes.
III. Some circles are squares.
IV. All squares are cubes.

A. Only conclusion I follows.
B. Only conclusion I, II and III follow.
C. All conclusions are correct.
D. Only conclusions II and III follow.
E. None of the above.

43. Statements: I. All cups are goats.
II. All goats are tins.
Conclusions: I. All goats are cups.
II. All tins are goats.
III. No cups are tins.
IV. No tins are cups.

A. Only conclusions III and IV follow.
B. Only conclusios I and II follow.
C. Only conclusions I, II and III follow.
D. All conclusions are correct.
E. None of the above.

44. Statements: I. All bombs are bags.
II. Some bags are jets.
Conclusions: I. All bombs are jets.
II. All jets are bombs.
III. Some jets are bombs.
IV. Some bombs are jets.

A. Only conclusion III follows.
B. Only conclusions I and II follow.
C. All conclusions are correct.
D. Only conclusions III and IV follow.
E. None of the above.

45. Statements: I. Some thorns are jackets.
II. Some jackets are boats.
Conclusions: I. No thorns are boats.
II. All jackets are boats.
III. Some boats are thorns.
IV. No jackets are thorns.

A. Either conclusion I or IV follows.
B. Either conclusion I or II follows.
C. Either conclusion I or III follows.
D. No conclusion is correct.
E. All conclusions are correct.

ANSWERS

1	2	3	4	5	6	7	8	9	10
B	E	D	B	A	A	D	C	D	D
11	**12**	**13**	**14**	**15**	**16**	**17**	**18**	**19**	**20**
B	D	E	E	C	B	A	C	D	B
21	**22**	**23**	**24**	**25**	**26**	**27**	**28**	**29**	**30**
A	A	E	B	E	E	B	A	A	E
31	**32**	**33**	**34**	**35**	**36**	**37**	**38**	**39**	**40**
D	A	C	E	A	B	C	A	D	B
41	**42**	**43**	**44**	**45**					
B	D	E	E	D					

EXPLANATORY ANSWERS

1. [A + A = A, All tables are chairs]

2. [I + A = I, Some radios are roads. Also, some radios are stones *conversion* Some stones are radios.]

3. [I + I = no conclusion]

4. [Change order of the statements to align. Now, No fox is a cow + Some cows are jackals = E + I = O*, Some jackals are not foxes.]

5. [Change order first. Now, No dog is an animal + Only cats are animals *implies* No dog is an animal + All animals are cats = E + A = O*, Some cats are not dogs.]

6. [A + E = E]

7. [E + E = no conclusion]

8. [Align: Johan is tall + Some tall are players = A + I = no conclusion. But, Johan should either be a player or a non-player. Hence either of the two choices follows.

9. [A + I = no conclusion]

10. [After alignment, All cars fly + Some fly are cycles = no conclusion]

11. [Some spoons are *pots,+ All pots* are cups. I + A = I type of conclusion "Some spoons are cups". Conclusion II is converse of it.]

12. [All the three premises are I type. No conclusion follows from two I premises.]

13. Some boys are *flowers.* + *All flowers* are jungles. I + A = I type conclusion, "Some boys are jungles". Some boys are flowers + *All jungles* are houses. I + A = I type conclusion, "Some boys are houses". Conclusion II is converse of it.

14. All bottles are tanks. + All tanks are drums. A + A = A – type of conclusion *i.e.* "all bottles are drums". Conclusion II is converse of it. All tanks are drums + All drums are pipes A + A implies A-type of conclusion "All tanks are pipes". Conclusion I is converse of it.

15. All sticks are brushes + No brush is fruit. *i.e.* A + E = E type of conclusion. "No stick is fruit". No brush is fruit + Some fruits are trees. *i.e.* E + I = O*, "Some trees are not brushes". Conclusions I and II forms a complementary pair. Therefore, either I or II follows.

16. Some shirts are pants + All pants are clothes = Some shirts are clothes. Conclusion II is converse of it.

17. All packets are tents + All tents are houses = All packets are houses. Conclusion I is the converse of it.

18. All the three premises are particular affirmative. No conclusion can be reached from two particular premises (I type).

19. All windows are doors + No door is mountain = No window is mountain. No door is mountain + Some mountains are roads = Some roads are not doors.

20. Some bangles are rings + All rings are sticks = Some bangles are sticks. Conclusion II is converse of the third premise.

21. All silver are metals + All metals are steel = All silver are steel. Some steel are stones + All stones are stands = Some steel are stands conversion Conclusion III. Conclusion IV is converse of the third premise.

22. All chairs are tables + All tables are songs = All chairs are songs (Conclusion III) Conclusion I is converse of first premise.

23. Some covers are plates + All plates are papers = Some covers are papers.

24. All shoes are tables + Some tables are lanes = no conclusion. Conclusion II is the converse of the first premise.

25. All alphabets are symbols + Some symbols are numbers = no conclusion. Conclusion IV follows from the conversion of the third premise. Conclusion I and III form complementary pair.

26. When all tomatoes are red and all grapes are tomatoes, then all grapes are also red. When all grapes are tomatoes, then some tomatoes must be grapes. Therefore, both conclusions I and II are correct.

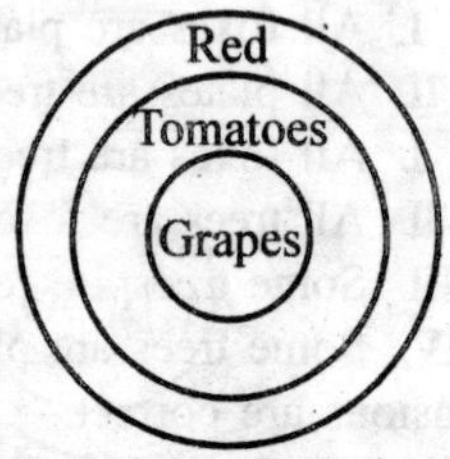

27. When all painters are smiling and some authors are painters, then some authors are smiling. Therefore, only conclusion II is correct.

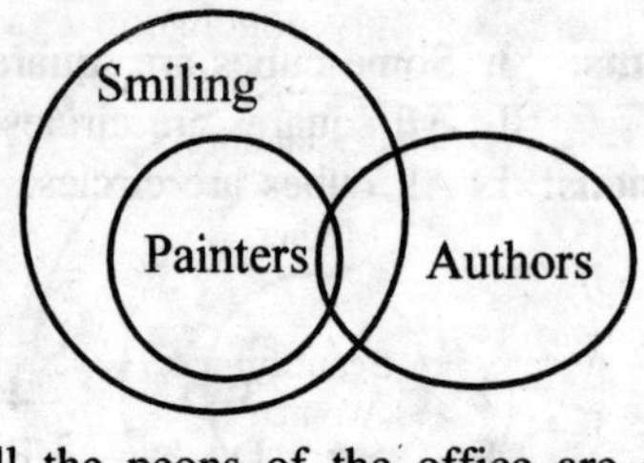

28. When all the peons of the office are efficient, then Ramu cannot be a peon in this office. Therefore, only conclusion I is correct.

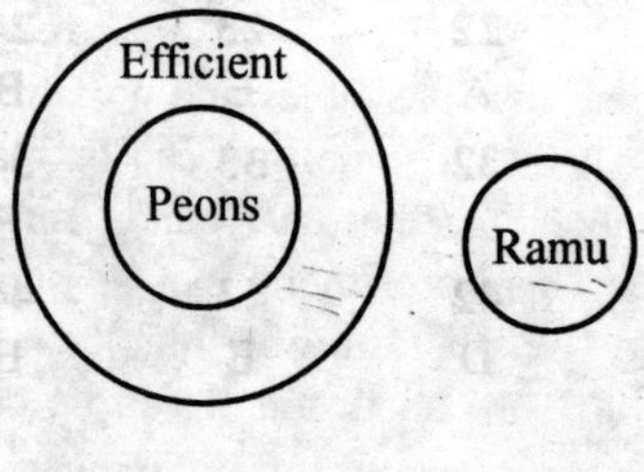

29. When all weavers are hardworking and no hardworking men are foolish, then no weavers are foolish. Therefore, only conclusion I is correct.

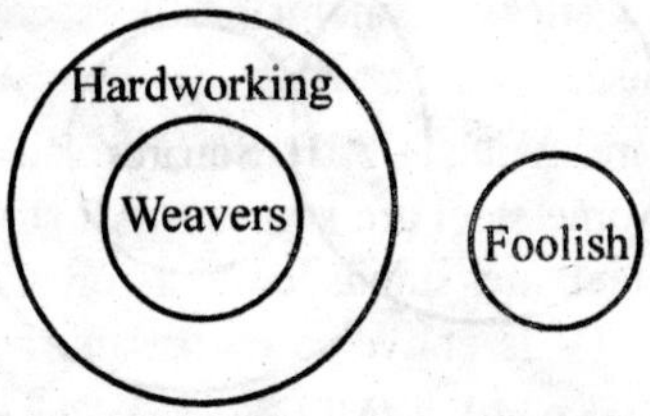

30. When all fishes are cars and all cars are vegetables, then all fishes will naturally be vegetables. This means that some vegetables are fishes. And when all cars are vegetables, then some vegetables will be cars naturally. Therefore, both the conclusions I and II are correct.

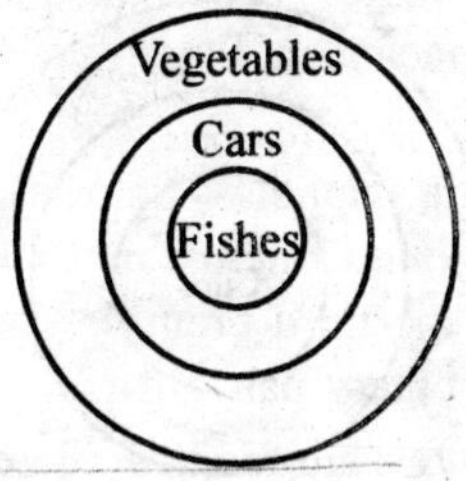

31. No relationship can be established between the two statements. Therefore, neither conclusion I nor conclusion II is correct.

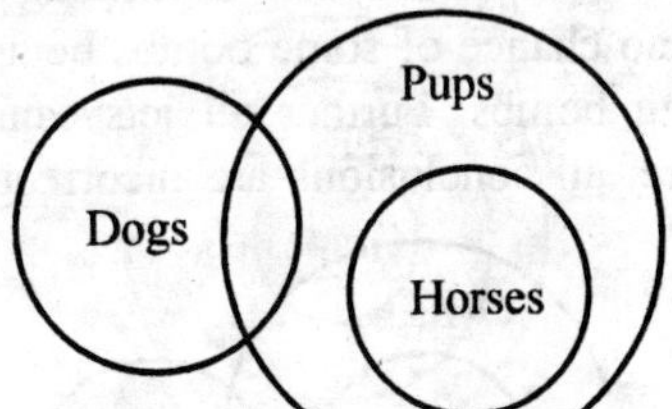

32. When all beautiful women are mothers and all mothers are understanding, then naturally all beautiful women are understanding. All mothers need not be beautiful women. Therefore, only conclusion I is correct.

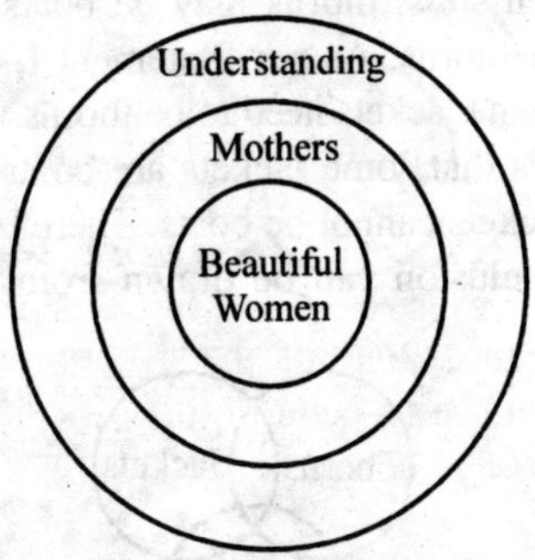

33. When some toys are tables and no table is black, then it is indicated that some toys can be black, as all toys are not tables. On the other hand, some toys may not be black. Therefore, there is a possibility that some toys may or may not be black. As such, either conclusion I or conclusion II can be correct.

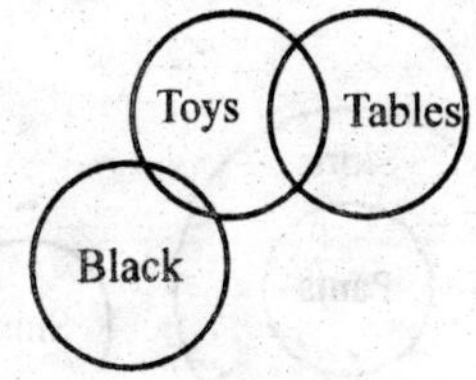

34. When all rivers are mountains and some rivers are deserts, then some deserts cannot be mountains and also, some mountains need not be deserts. Therefore, both conclusion I and conclusion II are correct.

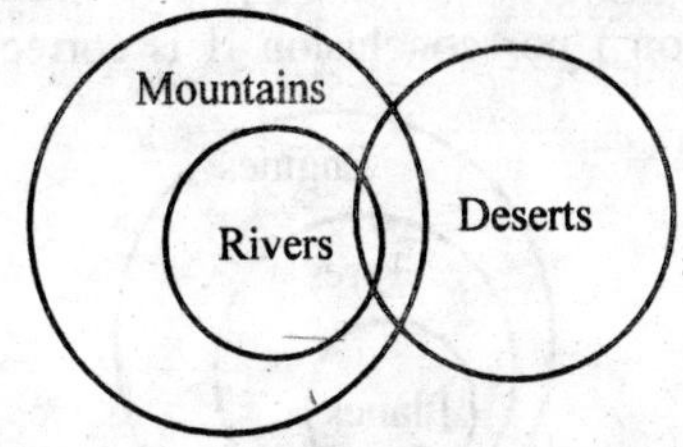

35. When all men are horses and all horses are elephants then, naturally all men are elephants, but all elephants need not be men. Therefore, only conclusion I is correct.

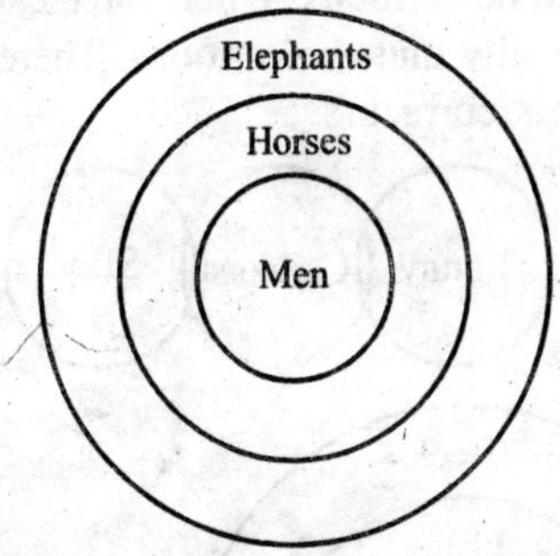

36. When some artworks are paintings which are all masterpieces, then some masterpieces must be artwork. When all paintings are masterpieces then some (not all) masterpieces must be paintings. Therefore, only conclusion II is correct.

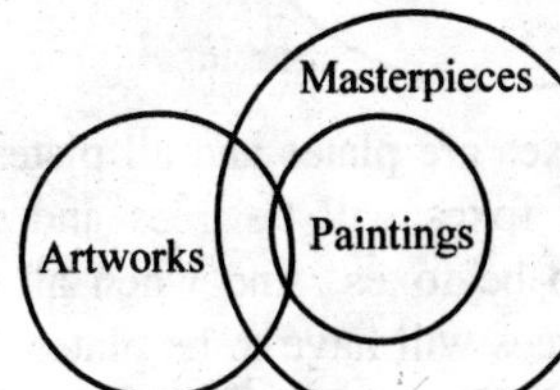

37. Some men are genius and no brother is a genius. Some men who are not genius may or may not be brothers, *i.e.* some brothers may or may not be men. Therefore, either conclusion I or conclusion II is correct.

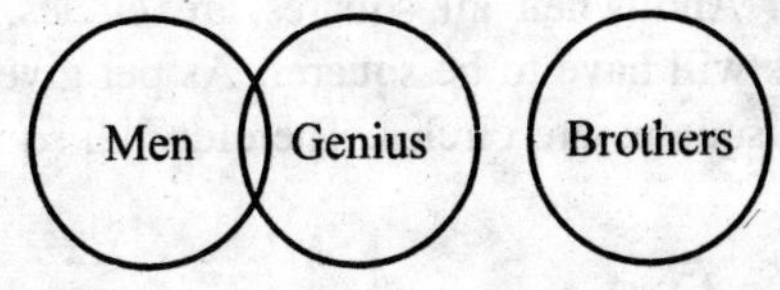

38. When all pants are skirts then some skirts must be pants. When no shirt is a skirt and all pants are skirts, then shirts cannot be pants. Therefore, only conclusion I is correct.

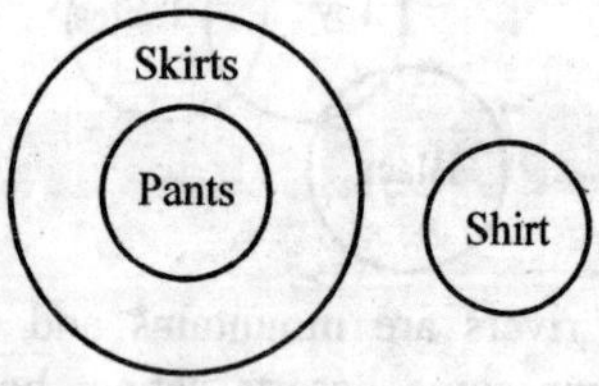

39. When all planes are tyres then some tyres must be planes. When all planes are tyres which are all engines then some engines must be planes. Therefore, neither conclusion I nor conclusion II is correct.

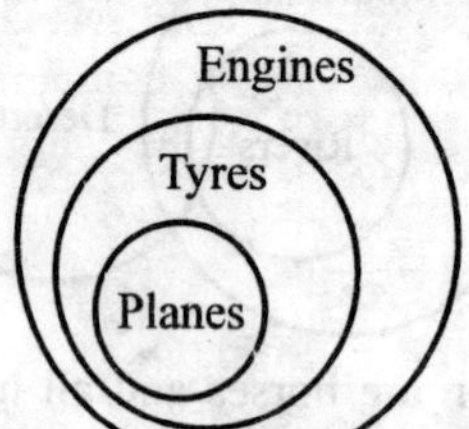

40. When some cartoons are funny then some (not all) funny must be cartoons. When some cartoons are silly, then some silly must be cartoons. Therefore, only conclusion II is correct.

41.

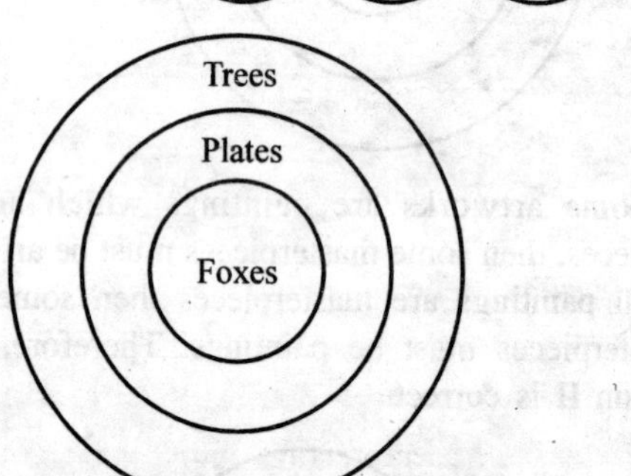

When all foxes are plates and all plates are trees, then naturally all foxes will be trees and some trees will then have to be foxes. And when all plates are trees then some trees will have to be plates. Therefore, only conclusions I, III and IV are correct.

42. When it is given that some cubes are squares and all squares are circles, then some cubes will naturally be circles, though all cubes cannot be circles. When some cubes are circles, then some circles will have to be cubes. And when all squares are circles, then some circles will have to be squares. As per given statement II, all squares are circles. Therefore all squares cannot be cubes. As such only conclusions II and III are correct.

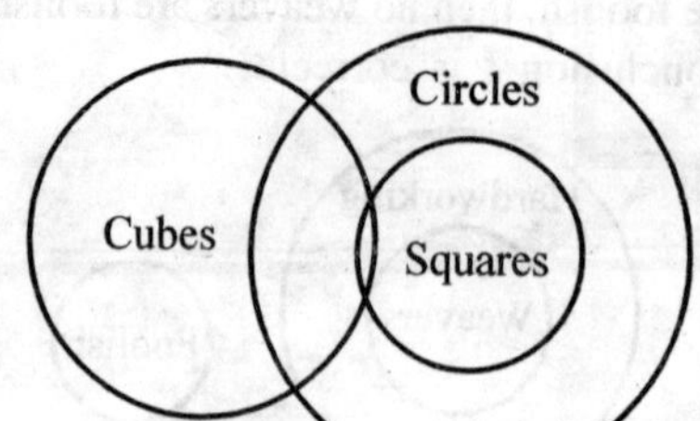

43. When all cups are goats, then only some goats can be cups. When all goats are tins, then only some tins can be goats. When all cups are goats and all goats are tins, then naturally all cups are tins and some tins must be cups. Therefore, all the conclusions are incorrect.

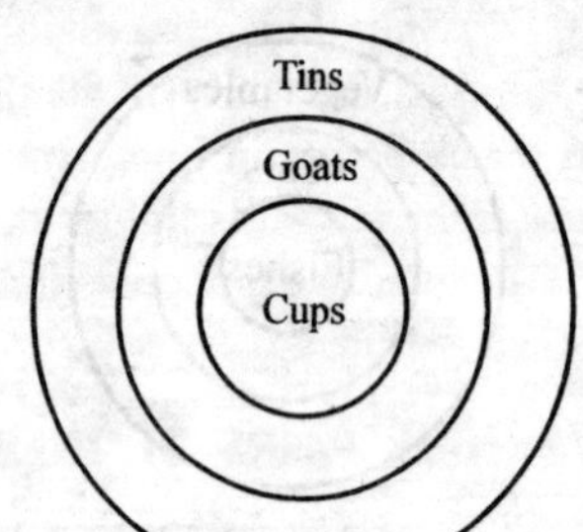

44. When all bombs are bags and some bags are jets then all bombs cannot be jets. 'Some bags' indicate that there is no chance of some bombs being jets, or some jets being bombs. Further all jets cannot be bombs. Therefore, all conclusions are incorrect.

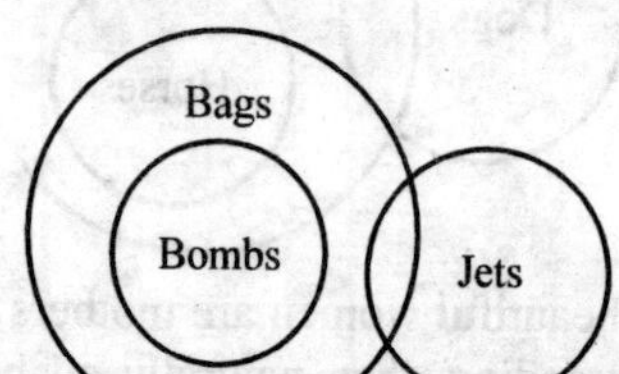

45. When some thorns are jackets and some jackets are boats, then some thorns may be boats but some boats cannot be thorns. As per Statement I, some thorns are jackets, some jackets need to be thorns. When Statement II conveys that some jackets are boats, then it is clear that all jackets cannot be boats. Therefore, no particular given conclusion can be drawn from the given statements.

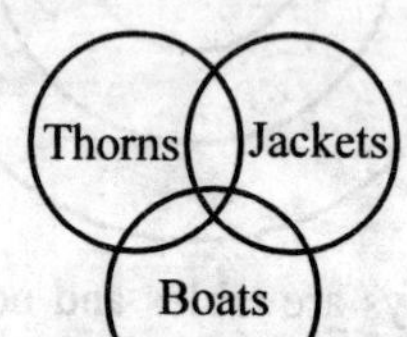

●●●

2 Coded Inequalities

To solve coded inequalities problem one's primarily task is to combine (visualise) two or more inequalities in to one combined notation.

Rule-Carry one directional lightest inequality to deduce conclusion from combined inequality. Whenever inequalities are combined together in one combined notation writing common terms only once then conclusion will follow between any two terms if and only if all the inequalities between these two terms points in one same direction and conclusion will carry lightest ('<' is lighter than '≤' and '>' is lighter than '≥') inequality sign present between these two terms.

Basics of above rule

1. Two inequalities can be combined if and only if they have a common term.
2. Two inequalities can be combined (to give valid conclusion) if and only if the common term is greater than (or 'greater than or equal to') one and less than (or 'less than or equal to') the other.
3. The conclusion – inequality will have an '≥' sign (or a '≤' sign) if and only if both the signs in the combined inequality were '≥'(or '≤', as the case may be).

VARIOUS PAIRS OF INEQUALITIES AND THEIR CONCLUSIONS (IF POSSIBLE)

First inequality	Second inequality	Combined notation	Conclusion inequality	Explanation for conclusion inequality
$S > P$	$P < Q$	$S > P < Q$	None	inequality signs points in opposite direction
$S < P$	$P > Q$	$S < P > Q$	None	inequality signs points in opposite direction
$S \geq P$	$P < Q$	$S \geq P < Q$	None	inequality signs points in opposite direction
$S > P$	$P \leq Q$	$S > P \leq Q$	None	inequality signs points in opposite direction
$S > P$	$P > Q$	$S > P > Q$	$S > Q$	inequality signs points in same direction (>)
$S < P$	$P < Q$	$S < P < Q$	$S < Q$	inequality signs points in same direction (<)
$S \geq P$	$P > Q$	$S \geq P > Q$	$S > Q$	inequality signs points in same direction (lightest is '>')
$S > P$	$P \geq Q$	$S > P \geq Q$	$S > Q$	inequality signs points in same direction (lightest is '>')
$S \leq P$	$P < Q$	$S \leq P < Q$	$S < Q$	inequality signs points in same direction (lightest is '<')
$S < P$	$P \leq Q$	$S < P \leq Q$	$S < Q$	inequality signs points in same direction (lightest is '<')
$S \geq P$	$P \geq Q$	$S \geq P \geq Q$	$S \geq Q$	inequality signs points in same direction (both inequalities carry '≥' sign)
$S \leq P$	$P \leq Q$	$S \leq P \leq Q$	$S \leq Q$	inequality signs points in same direction (both inequalities carry '≤' sign)

MULTIPLE CHOICE QUESTIONS

Directions (Qs. 1-5): *In the following questions, the symbols @, #, %, $ and * are used with the following meaning as illustrated below.*

'A @ B' means 'A is not smaller than B'.

'A # B' means 'A is neither smaller than nor equal to B'.

'A % B' means 'A is neither smaller than nor greater than B'.

'A $ B' means 'A is not greater than B'.

'A * B' means 'A is neither greater than nor equal to B'.

Now in each of the following the questions assuming the given statements to be true, find which of the two conclusions (*a*) and (*b*) given below is/are definitely true?

Give answer

A. If only conclusion (*a*) is true.

B. If only conclusion (*b*) is true.

C. If either conclusion (*a*) or (*b*) is true.
D. If neither conclusion (*a*) nor (*b*) is true.
E. If both conclusions (*a*) and (*b*) are true.

1. Statements : T @ V, V # M, M % F
Conclusions : (*a*) T # M (*b*) T @ F

2. Statements : L $ N, N * F, R % L
Conclusions : (*a*) F # R (*b*) R $ N

3. Statements : H # I, I @ J, J $ P
Conclusions : (*a*) H # J (*b*) H # P

4. Statements : L * D, D # K, K $ J
Conclusions : (*a*) L * K (*b*) D $ J

5. Statements : Q $ W, W % E, E @ K
Conclusions : (*a*) Q $ K (*b*) W @ K

Directions (Qs. Nos. 6 to 10): *In the following questions, the symbols $, •, %, Ω and @ are used with the following meaning as illustrated below :*

'P • Q' means 'P is neither greater than nor equal to Q'.
'P @ Q' means 'P is neither smaller than nor equal to Q'.
'P Ω Q' means 'P is not greater than Q'.
'P % Q' means 'P is not smaller than Q'.
'P $ Q' means 'P is neither greater than nor smaller than Q'.

6. Statements : R % W, W @ F, F $ Z
Conclusions : (*a*) F • R (*b*) Z • W

7. Statements : B @ K, K % J, J • M
Conclusions : (*a*) J • B (*b*) M @ B

8. Statements : D $ T, T Ω H, H @ N
Conclusions : (*a*) H $ D (*b*) H @ D

9. Statements : H Ω N, N • K, K Ω D
Conclusions : (*a*) D @ N (*b*) H • K

10. Statements : W % E, E @ K, K $ J
Conclusions : (*a*) J Ω E (*b*) W % K

Directions (Qs. 11-15): *In the following questions, the symbols @, ©, %, $ and # are used with the following meaning as illustrated below.*

'P % Q' means 'P is either smaller than or equal to Q'
'P © Q' means 'P is greater than Q'
'P # Q' means 'P is neither greater than nor smaller than Q'
'P $ Q' means 'P is smaller than Q'
'P @ Q' means 'P is either greater than or equal to Q'

11. Statements : B # F, F $ H, H © K
Conclusions : (*a*) H @ B (*b*) K $ B

12. Statements : H @ T, T © N, N $ W
Conclusions : (*a*) N $ H (*b*) W $ H

13. Statements : H $ F, F % M, M © J
Conclusions : (*a*) J $ F (*b*) M © H

14. Statements : M $ T, T % R, M © N
Conclusions : (*a*) M $ R (*b*) N $ T

15. Statements : D $ T, T % B, B @ F
Conclusions : (*a*) D # T (*b*) D @ F

Directions (Qs. Nos. 16 to 20): *In the following questions, the symbols @, ©, $, % and • are used with the following meanings as illustrated below:*

P © Q means P is not smaller than Q.
P • Q means P is not greater than Q.
P @ Q means P is neither greater than nor smaller than Q.
P $ Q means P is neither smaller than nor equal to Q.
P % Q means P is neither greater than nor equal to Q.

Now in each of the following questions assuming the given statements to be true, find which of the conclusions I, II, III and IV given below them is/are definitely true and give your answers accordingly.

16. Statements : K © L, L % O, O @ M, M • N
Conclusions : I. N © O II. M $ L III. K • N IV. L @ N

A. Only II is true
B. Only I and II are true
C. Only I is true
D. Either I or II is true
E. None is true

17. Statements : A • B, B $ C, C % D, D © E
Conclusions : I. D $ A II. B $ D III. E % C IV. A @ E

A. Only I is true
B. Only either I or II is true
C. Only I and IV are true
D. None is true
E. Only IV is true

18. Statements : F $ P, P @ R, R © S, S % T
Conclusions : I. R % F II. S • P III. P © T IV. S % F

A. Only I, II and III are true
B. Only I and II are true
C. Only III and IV are true
D. Only I, II and IV are true
E. All are true

19. Statements : G % H, H • I, I $ J, J @ K
Conclusions : I. G % I II. G % J III. K $ I IV. H • J

A. Only I is true
B. Only II is true
C. Only I, II and III are true
D. Only either I or II and III are true
E. All are true

20. Statements : V @ W, W % X, X • Y, Y $ Z
Conclusions : I. Z $ X II. Y © V III. W % Y IV. Y @ W

A. Only I and III are true
B. Only II is true
C. Only III is true
D. None is true
E. Only III and IV are true

Directions (21-25) : *In the following questions, the symbols @, #, $, © and % are used with the following meaning as illustrated below.*

'P @ Q' means 'P is not smaller than Q'

'P # Q' means 'P is not greater than Q'

'P $ Q' means 'P is neither greater than nor equal to Q'

'P © Q' means 'P is neither smaller than nor equal to Q'

'P % Q' means 'P is neither greater than nor smaller than Q'

21. Statements : V $ W, W @ T, T # H
Conclusions : (*a*) V © T (*b*) H % W

22. Statements : H © M, M @ E, E $ C
Conclusions : (*a*) C © M (*b*) H © E

23. Statements : N @ J, J % R, R © H
Conclusions : (*a*) R # N (*b*) N © H

24. Statements : L @ K, K © A, A $ W
Conclusions : (*a*) W $ L (*b*) L # W

25. Statements : J # R, R © D, D @ F
Conclusions : (*a*) F $ R (*b*) F % R

Directions (Qs. Nos. 26 to 30): *In the following questions, the symbols &, @, #, $ and % are used with the following meaning:*

A & B means A is greater than B.

A @ B means A is either greater than or equal to B.

A # B means A is equal to B.

A $ B means A is smaller than B.

A % B means A is either smaller than or equal to B.

Now in each of the following questions assuming the given statements to be true, find which of the two conclusions I and II given below them is/are Definitely true?

Give answer:

A. if only conclusion I is true
B. if only conclusion II is true
C. if either conclusion I or II is true
D. if neither conclusion I nor II is true
E. if both conclusions I and II are true

26. Statements : M $ L, O & P, M # N, O % N
Conclusions : I. M & O II. M # O

27. Statements : W $ N, S # Q, R @ N, S $ R
Conclusions : I. W $ R II. N # Q

28. Statements : A $ B, D % E, C # D, C @ B
Conclusions : I. E & B II. B # E

29. Statements : W & U, Y # X, Z $ Y, X @ W
Conclusions : I. Z # W II. X & Z

30. Statements : R @ A, U & L, A # H, H @ U
Conclusions : I. H # L II. L $ H

Directions (Qs. Nos. 31 to 35): *In the following questions, the symbols @, ©, %, $ and β are used with the following meaning as illustrated below:*

'P © Q' means 'P is smaller than Q'.

'P @ Q' means 'P is either smaller than or equal to Q'.

'P % Q' means 'P is greater than Q'.

'P $ Q' means 'P is either greater than or equal to Q'.

'P β Q' means 'P is equal to Q'.

Now in each of the following questions assuming the given statements to be true, find which of the two conclusions I and II given below them is/are Definitely true?

Give answer:

A. if only conclusion I is true
B. if only conclusion II is true
C. if either conclusion I or II is true
D. if neither conclusion I nor II is true
E. if both conclusions I and II are true

31. Statements : B © T, T β M, M % F
Conclusions : I. B © M II. B © F

32. Statements : M β R, R % T, T $ K
Conclusions : I. K @ M II. K © M

33. Statements : W © D, D @ H, H β N
Conclusions : I. N $ D II. W © N

34. Statements : W @ D, D $ R, R © K
Conclusions : I. R β W II. R % W

35. Statements : F $ J, J % V, V © N
Conclusions : I. N $ F II. N % J

Directions (Qs. Nos. 36 to 40): *In the following questions, certain symbols have been used to indicate relationships between elements as follows:*

A % B means A is neither smaller nor greater than B.

A $ B means A is greater than B.

A & B means A is either greater than or equal to B.

A @ B means A is smaller than B.

A # B means A is either smaller than or equal to B.

In each question, three statements showing relationships have been given, which are followed by two conclusions I and II. Assuming that the given statements are true, find out which conclusion(s) is/are definitely true.

Mark answer :

A. if only conclusion I is true
B. if only conclusion II is true
C. if either conclusion I or II is true
D. if neither conclusion I nor II is true
E. if both conclusions I and II are true

36. Statements : P & Q, Q $ R, Q % S
Conclusions : I. P @ S II. R @ P

37. Statements : F & G, G % H, H $ K
Conclusions : I. H @ F II. F % H

38. Statements : T # V, V $ X, X & Y
Conclusions : I. V $ Y II. X # T

39. Statements : C % E, E # W, W @ Z
Conclusions : I. W & C II. C @ Z

40. Statements : L # M, M @ N, N $ P
Conclusions : I. L # N II. M & P

ANSWERS

1	2	3	4	5	6	7	8	9	10
A	E	A	D	B	E	A	C	E	D
11	**12**	**13**	**14**	**15**	**16**	**17**	**18**	**19**	**20**
D	A	B	E	D	B	D	D	A	C
21	**22**	**23**	**24**	**25**	**26**	**27**	**28**	**29**	**30**
D	B	E	D	A	C	A	C	B	B
31	**32**	**33**	**34**	**35**	**36**	**37**	**38**	**39**	**40**
A	B	E	D	D	B	C	A	E	D

EXPLANATORY ANSWERS

(Ans. 1 to 5) :

'A @ B' means 'A is not smaller than B' → A ≥ B

'A # B' means 'A is neither smaller than nor equal to B' → A > B

'A % B' means 'A is neither smaller than nor greater than B' → A = B

'A $ B' means 'A is not greater than B' → A ≤ B

'A * B' means 'A is neither greater than nor equal to B' → A < B

1. T @ V, V # M, M % F → T ≥ V, V > M, M = F → T ≥ V > M = F

Conclusion *(a)* → T # M → T > M

The relation between T and M in the statement T ≥ V > M = F : T > M. So, it is true.

Conclusion *(b)* → T @ F → T ≥ F

The relation between T and F in the statement T ≥ V > M = F : T > F. So, it is not true.

(T > M = F → T > F)

2. L $ N, N * F, R % L → L ≤ N, N < F, R = L → R = L ≤ N < F

Conclusion *(a)* → F # R → F > R

The relation between F and R in the statement R = L ≤ N < F : R < F. So, it is true.

(R ≤ N < F → R < F)

Conclusion *(b)* → R $ N → R ≤ N

The relation between R and N in the statement R = L ≤ N < F : R ≤ N. So, it is true.

3. H # I, I @ J, J $ P → H > I, I ≥ J, J ≤ P → H > I ≥ J ≤ P

Conclusion *(a)* → H # J → H > J

The relation between H and J in the statement H > I ≥ J ≤ P : H > J. So, it is true.

Conclusion *(b)* → H # P → H > P

The relation between H and P in the statement H > I ≥ J ≤ P : H > P or H < P or H = P. So, it is not true.

4. L * D, D # K, K $ J → L < D, D > K, K ≤ J → L < D > K ≤ J

Conclusion *(a)* → L * K → L < K

The relation between L and K in the statement L < D > K ≤ J : L = K or L > K or L < K. So, it is not true.

Conclusion *(b)* → D $ J → D ≤ J

The relation between D and J in the statement L < D > K ≤ J : D = J or D > J or D < J. So, it is not true.

5. Q $ W, W % E, E @ K → Q ≤ W, W = E, E ≥ K → Q ≤ W = E ≥ K

Conclusion *(a)* → Q $ K → Q ≤ K

The relation between Q and K in the statement Q ≤ W = E ≥ K : Q = K or Q > K or Q < K. So, it is not true.

Conclusion *(b)* → W @ K → W ≥ K

The relation between W and K in the statement Q ≤ W = E ≥ K : W ≥ K. So, it is true.

(6–10): • → <, @ → >, Ω → ≤, % → ≥, $ → =

6. Statements: R % W → R ≥ W,
W @ F → W > F,
F $ Z → F = Z

Therefore, R ≥ W > F = Z

Conclusions:

(a) F • R → F < R : True

(b) Z • W → Z < W: True

7. Statements: B @ K → B > K,
K % J → K ≥ J,
J • M → J < M

Therefore, B > K ≥ J < M

Conclusions:

(a) J • B → J < B : True

(b) M @ B → M > B : False

8. Statements: D $ T → D = T,
T Ω H → T ≤ H,
H @ N → H > N

Therefore, D = T ≤ H > N

Conclusions:

(a) H $ D → H = D : False

(*b*) H @ D → H > D: False
H is greater than or equal to D.
So either I or II is true

9. Statements: H Ω N → H ≤ N,
N • K → N < K,
K Ω D → K ≤ D
Therefore, H ≤ N < K ≤ D
Conclusions:
(*a*) D @ N → D > N : True
(*b*) H • K → H < K : True

10. Statements: W % E → W ≥ E,
E @ K → E > K,
K $ J → K = J
Therefore, W ≥ E > K = J
Conclusions:
(*a*) J Ω E → J ≤ E : False
(*b*) W % K → W ≥ K : False

(For Ans. 11-15)
'P % Q' means 'P is either smaller than or equal to Q' → P ≤ Q
'P © Q' means 'P is greater than Q' → P > Q
'P # Q' means 'P is neither greater than nor smaller than Q' → P = Q
'P $ Q' means 'P is smaller than Q' → P < Q
'P @ Q' means 'P is either greater than or equal to Q' → P ≥ Q

11. B # F, F $ H, H © K → B = F, F < H, H > K → B = F < H > K
Conclusion (*a*) → H @ B → H ≥ B
The relation between H and B in the statement B = F < H > K : B < H. So, it is not true.
Conclusion (*b*) → K $ B → K < B
The relation between K and B in the statement B = F < H > K : K = B or K > B or K < B. So, it is not true.

12. H @ T, T © N, N $ W → H ≥ T, T > N, N < W → H ≥ T > N < W
Conclusion (*a*) → N $ H → N < H
The relation between N and H in the statement H ≥ T > N < W : H > N. So, it is true.
Conclusion (*b*) → W $ H → W < H
The relation between W and H in the statement H ≥ T > N < W : W = H or W > H or W < H. So, it is not true.

13. H $ F, F % M, M © J → H < F, F ≤ M, M > J → H < F ≤ M > J
Conclusion (*a*) → J $ F → J < F
The relation between J and F in the statement H < F ≤ M > J : J = F or J < F or J > F. So, it is not true.
Conclusion (*b*) → M © H → M > H
The relation between M and H in the statement H < F ≤ M > J : M > H. So, it is true.

14. M $ T, T % R, M © N → M < T, T ≤ R, M > N → N < M < T ≤ R
Conclusion (*a*) → M $ R → M < R
The relation between M and R in the statement N < M < T ≤ R : M < R. So, it is true.
Conclusion (*b*) → N $ T → N < T
The relation between N and T in the statement N < M < T ≤ R : N < T. So, it is true.

15. D $ T, T % B, B @ F → D < T, T ≤ B, B ≥ F → D < T ≤ B ≥ F
Conclusion (*a*) → D # T → D = T
The relation between D and T in the statement D < T ≤ B ≥ F : D < T. So, it is not true.
Conclusion (*b*) → D @ F → D ≥ F
The relation between D and F in the statement D < T ≤ B ≥ F : D < F. So, it is not true.

(16 – 20): © → ≥ • → ≤ @ → =
$ → > % → <

16. K © L → K ≥ L, L % O → L < O,
O @M → O = M, M • N → M ≤ N
Therefore, K ≥ L < O = M ≤ N
Conclusions:
I. N © O → N ≥ O : True
II. M $ L → M > L : True
III. K • N → K ≤ N : False
IV. L @ N → L = N : False

17. A • B → A ≤ B, B $ C → B > C,
C % D → C < D, D © E → D ≥ E
Therefore, A ≤ B > C < D ≥ E
Conclusions:
I. D $ A → D > A : False
II. B $ D → B > D : False
III. E % C → E < C : False
IV. A @ E → A = E : False

18. F $ P → F > P, P @ R → P = R,
R © S → R ≥ S, S % T → S < T
Therefore, F > P = R → S < T
Conclusions:
I. R % F → R < F : True
II. S • P → S ≤ P : True
III. P © T → P ≥ T : False
IV. S % F → S < F : True

19. G % H → G < H, H • I → H ≤ I,
I $ J → I > J, J @ K → J = K
Therefore, G < H ≤ I > J = K
Conclusions:
I. G % I → G < I : True
II. G % J → G < J: False
III. K $ I → K > I : False
IV. H • J → H ≤ J : False

20. V @ W → V = W, W % X → W < X,
X • Y → X ≤ Y, Y $ Z → Y > Z
Therefore, V = W < X ≤ Y > Z
Conclusions:
I. Z $ X → Z > X : False

II. Y © V → Y ≥ V : False
III. W % Y → W < Y : True
IV. Y @ W → Y = W : False

(Ans. 21-25)
'P @ Q' means 'P is not smaller than Q' → P ≥ Q
'P # Q' means 'P is not greater than Q' → P ≤ Q
'P $ Q' means 'P is neither greater than nor equal to Q' → P < Q
'P © Q' means 'P is neither smaller than nor equal to Q' → P > Q
'P % Q' means 'P is neither greater than nor smaller than Q' → P = Q

21. V $ W, W @ T, T # H → V < W, W ≥ T, T ≤ H → V < W ≥ T ≤ H
Conclusion *(a)* → V © T → V > T
The relation between V and T in the statement V < W ≥ T ≤ H : V = T or V > T or V < T. So, it is not true.
Conclusion *(b)* → H % W → H = W
The relation between H and W in the statement V < W ≥ T ≤ H → H = W or H > W or H < W. So, it is not true.

22. H © M, M @ E, E $ C → H > M, M ≥ E, E < C → H > M ≥ E < C
Conclusion *(a)* → C © M → C > M
The relation between C and M in the statement H > M ≥ E < C → M > C. So, it is not true.
Conclusion *(b)* → H © E → H > E
The relation between H and E in the statement H > M ≥ E < C → H > E. So, it is true.

23. N @ J, J % R, R © H → N ≥ J, J = R, R > H → N ≥ J = R > H
Conclusion *(a)* → R # N → R ≤ N
The relation between R and N in the statement N ≥ J = R > H : N ≥ R. So, it is true.
Conclusion *(b)* → N © H → N > H
The relation between N and H in the statement N ≥ J = R > H : N > H. So, it is true.

24. L @ K, K © A, A $ W → L ≥ K, K > A, A < W → L ≥ K > A < W
Conclusion *(a)* → W $ L → W < L
The relation between W and L in the statement L ≥ K > A < W : W = L or W > L or W < L. So, it is not true.
Conclusion *(b)* → L # W → L ≤ W
The relation between L and W in the statement L ≥ K > A < W : L = W or L < W or L > W. So, it is not true.

25. J # R, R © D, D @ F → J ≤ R, R > D, D ≥ F → J ≤ R > D ≥ F
Conclusion *(a)* → F $ R → F < R
The relation between F and R in the statement J ≤ R > D ≥ F : R > F. So, it is true.
Conclusion *(b)* → F % R → F = R
The relation between F and R in the statement J ≤ R > D ≤ F : R > F. So, it is not true.

26. Statements : M < L, O > P, M = N, O ≤ N
Combined notation: P < O ≤ N = M < L
Conclusions:
I. M > O II. M = O
We have M ≥ O, So either I or II follows

27. Statements : W < N, S = Q, R ≥ N, S < R
Combined notation: W < N ≤ R > S = Q
Conclusions:
I. W < R : True II. N = Q : False

28. Statements : A < B, D ≤ E, C = D, C ≥ B
Combined notation: A < B ≤ C = D ≤ E
Conclusions:
I. E > B II. B = E
We have B ≤ E, So either I or II follows

29. Statements : W > U, Y = X, Z < Y, X ≥ W
Combined notation: Z < Y = X ≥ W > U
Conclusions:
I. Z = W : False II. X > Z : True

30. Statements: R ≥ A, U > L, A = H, H ≥ U
Combined notation: R ≥ A = H ≥ U > L
Conclusions:
I. H = L : False II. L < H : True

(31-35): © → < @ → ≤ % → > $ → ≥ β → =

31. B © T → B < T,
T β M → T = M,
M % F → M > F
Therefore, B < T = M > F
Conclusions:
I. B © M → B < M : True
II. B © F → B < F : False

32. M β R → M = R,
R % T → R > T,
T $ K → T ≥ K
Therefore, M = R > T ≥ K
Conclusions:
I. K @ M → K ≤ M : False
II. K © M → K < M : True

33. W © D → W < D,
D @ H → D ≤ H,
H β N → H = N
Therefore, W < D ≤ H = N
Conclusions:
I. N $ D → N ≥ D : True
II. W © N → W < N : True

34. W @ D → W ≤ D,
D $ R → D ≥ R,
R © K → R < K
Therefore, W ≤ D ≥ R < K
Conclusions:
I. R β W → R = W : False
II. R % W → R > W : False

35. F $ J → F ≥ J,
J % V → J > V,
V © N → V < N
Therefore, F ≥ J > V < N
Conclusions:
I. N $ F → N ≥ F : False
II. N % J → N > J : False

(36-40): A % B → A = B, A $ B → A > B, A & B → A ≥ B, A @ B → A < B, A # B → A ≤ B

36. P & Q → P ≥ Q,
Q $ R → Q > R,
Q % S → Q = S
Therefore, P ≥ Q = S > R
Conclusions:
I. P @ S → P < S : False
II. R @ P → R < P : True

37. F & G → F ≥ G,
G % H → G = H,
H $ K → H > K
Therefore, F ≥ G = H > K
Conclusions:
I. H @ F → H < F : False
II. F % H → F = H : False
H is either smaller than or equal to F.

38. T # V → T ≤ V,
V $ X → V > X,
X & Y → X ≥ Y
Therefore, T ≤ V > X ≥ Y
Conclusions:
I. V $ Y → V > Y : True
II. X # T → X ≤ T : False

39. C % E → C = E,
E # W → E ≤ W,
W @ Z → W < Z
Therefore, C = E ≤ W < Z
Conclusions:
I. W & C → W ≥ C : True
II. C @ Z → C < Z : True

40. L # M → L ≤ M,
M @ N → M < N,
N $ P → N > P
Therefore, L ≤ M < N > P
Conclusions:
I. L # N → L ≤ N : False
II. M & P → M ≥ P : False

●●●

3

Coded Relations

Coded relations problem involves interpreting a given relation—string which is coded in a particular way and then matching it with the relation mentioned in the questions. The process of decoding each and every relation and then interpreting from the given relation—string the final relation is a cumbersome process and doing it for all the choices makes it very time consuming. However systematic representation and some clever common sense observations may give a speedy solution.

BLOOD RELATIONSHIPS

While attempting questions on blood relations, one should be clear of all the relation patterns that can exist between any two individuals. Very well-known relations are:

Mother	Grandmother
Father	Grandfather
Son	Grandson
Daughter	Granddaughter
Brother	Brother-in-law
Sister	Sister-in-law
Niece	Father-in-law
Nephew	Mother-in-law
Uncle	Son-in-law
Aunt	Daughter-in-law
Husband	Cousin
Wife	

The patterns of some relationships which help in solving questions in these tests are :

Father's or Mother's Father	– Grandfather (Paternal or Maternal)
Father's or Mother's Mother	– Grandmother (Paternal or Maternal)
Father's or Mother's Son	– Brother
Father's or Mother's Daughter	– Sister
Father's Brother	– Paternal Uncle
Father's Sister	– Paternal Aunt
Mother's Brother	– Maternal Uncle
Mother's Sister	– Maternal Aunt
Uncle or Aunt's Son or Daughter	– Cousin
Son's Wife	– Daughter-in-law
Daughter's Husband	– Son-in-law
Husband's or Wife's Brother	– Brother-in-law
Husband's or Wife's Sister	– Sister-in-law
Brother's Wife	– Sister-in-law
Sister's Husband	– Brother-in-law
Brother's Son	– Nephew
Brother's Daughter	– Niece

MULTIPLE CHOICE QUESTIONS

Directions (Qs. 1-5): *These questions are based on the following information.*

'P = Q' means 'Q is the father of P'
'P # Q' means 'P is the sister of Q'
'P ? Q' means 'Q is the mother of P'
'P $ Q' means 'P is the brother of Q'
'P £ Q' means 'Q is the son of P'
'P × Q' means 'P is the daughter of Q'

1. Which of the following is not correct?
A. L £ M # O means O is the sister of L
B. M # O £ P = Q means Q and O are husband & wife
C. P = Q ? R means R is the grandmother of P
D. R × S ? T means R is the granddaughter of T
E. All are correct

2. Which of the following is correct?
A. L £ M $ R means R is the paternal uncle of L
B. M $ R # D ? V means M is the son of V
C. D ? V × T means D is the granddaughter of T
D. V × T # P means P is the maternal uncle of V
E. None is correct

3. Which of the following indicates 'A is the grandfather of B'?
A. M × A = N = B   B. B $ L × Q × A
C. L # B = S $ Q = A   D. B × L × A
E. None of these

4. Which of the following means 'F is the paternal uncle of G'?
A. L = F $ Q £ G   B. G × M # F $ L

C. N $ F $ L × G D. G × L $ F $ N
E. None of these

5. 'S × M # B = F $ D' reveals which of the following relations?
A. M is the maternal uncle of F
B. S is the granddaughter of F
C. B is the paternal uncle of S
D. F and B are brother and sister
E. None of the above relations gets revealed

Directions (Qs. 6-8): *These questions are based on the following information.*

'P × Q' means 'P is father of Q'
'P – Q' means 'P is sister of Q'
'P + Q' means 'P is mother of Q'
'P ÷ Q' means 'P is brother of Q'

6. In the expression B + D × M ÷ N, how is M related to B?
A. granddaughter
B. son
C. grandson
D. granddaughter or grandson
E. None of these

7. Which of the following represents 'J is son of F'
A. J ÷ R – T × F B. J + R – T × F
C. J ÷ M – N × F D. Can't be determined
E. None of these

8. Which of the following represents 'R is niece of M'?
A. M ÷ K × T – R B. M – J + R – N
C. R – M × T ÷ W D. Can't be determined
E. None of these

Directions (Qs. 9-13): *These questions are based on the following information.*

'P © Q' means 'Q is the brother of P'
'P # Q' means 'P is the daughter of Q'
'P = Q' means 'Q is the sister of P'
'P £ Q' means 'P is the son of Q'
'P * Q' means 'P is the father of Q'
'P @ Q' means 'P is the mother of Q'

9. Which of the following can be a correct conclusion drawn from the expression 'Q £ N @ S © M = P'?
A. S is the brother of P
B. N has two sons and two daughters
C. S is the sister of Q
D. P is the sister of Q
E. None of these

10. What does the expression 'P @ R = S © T £ V' mean?
A. V is the husband of P
B. R is the son of V
C. R is the daughter of V
D. V is the wife of P
E. None of these

11. Which of the following indicates that 'C is the paternal uncle of D'?
A. C £ V # N @ L © D
B. C £ V £ L @ N © D
C. D £ L £ N @ V © C
D. D £ N # V @ L © C
E. None of these

12. Which of the following indicates that 'Q is the daughter of N'?
A. Q * P # C @ N @ V
B. N * P # C @ Q @ V
C. M @ N # R * Q
D. M © Q = V # N
E. None of these

13. Which of the following can be the correct conclusion drawn from the expression 'L = M # N © P * Q'?
A. Q is the grandson of M
B. L is the uncle of N
C. N is the uncle of Q
D. Q is the niece of N
E. None of these

14. If P + Q means P is the brother of Q; P × Q means P is the father of Q and P – Q means P is the sister of Q, which of the following relations shows that I is the niece of K?
A. K + Y + Z – I
B. K + Y × I – Z
C. Z – I × Y + K
D. K × Y + I – Z
E. None of these

15. If X + Y means X is the daughter of Y; X – Y means X is the brother of Y; X % Y means X is the father of Y and X × Y means X is the sister of Y. Which of the following means I is the niece of J?
A. J – N % C × I
B. I × C – N % J
C. J + M × C % I
D. I × C + N – J
E. None of these

16. If P + Q means P is the brother of Q; P × Q means P is the wife of Q and P % Q means P is the daughter of Q then which of the following means D is the uncle of A?
A. A % B × C + D
B. A × B + C % D
C. A + C % B × D
D. None of these
E. Cannot be determined

Directions (Qs. Nos. 17 and 18): *Read the following information to answer the questions:*

A + B means A is the father of B
A – B means A is the sister of B

A × B means A is the husband of B
A % B means A is the wife of B

17. Which of the following means 'T is the nephew of Q'?
A. Q × R – S + T
B. Q + R % S + T
C. Q – R % S + T
D. None of these
E. Cannot be determined

18. Which of the following means S is granddaughter of R?
A. R + P % Q + S
B. K % R + P × Q – L + S
C. K % R + P % Q + S – L
D. K % R + P % Q + S + L
E. None of these

19. If 'A + B' means 'A is brother of B', 'A – B' means 'A is sister of B', 'A × B' means 'A is wife of B' and 'A % B' means 'A is father of B', then which of the following indicates 'S is the son of P'?
A. P × Q % R + S – T
B. P × Q % S – R + T
C. P × Q % R – T + S
D. P × Q % R – S + T
E. None of these

Directions (Qs. Nos. 20 and 21): *Read the following information to answer the questions.*

P # Q means Q is father of P.
P * Q means Q is mother of P.
P @ Q means Q is brother of P.
P $ Q means Q is sister of P.

20. Which of the following means X is grandmother of Y?
A. Z $ X * K # L @ Y
B. Y @ L # K * X $ Z
C. X * K # L @ Y
D. Can't be determined
E. None of these

21. Which of the following means C is aunt of F?
A. E @ F # D # C * B
B. F @ E # D $ C * B
C. B * C $ D # E @ F
D. Can't be determined
E. None of these

22. If A + B means B is the brother of A; A × B means B is the husband of A; A – B means A is the mother of B and A % B means A is the father of B, which of the following relations shows that Q is the grandmother of T?
A. Q – P + R % T
B. P × Q % R – T
C. P × Q % R + T
D. P + Q % R – T
E. None of these

23. 1. A3P means A is the mother of P
2. A4P means A is the brother of P
3. A9P means A is the husband of P
4. A5P means A is the daughter of P
Which of the following means that K is the mother-in-law of M?
A. M9N3K4J
B. M9N5K3J
C. K5J9M3N
D. K3J9N4M
E. None of these

24. If P $ Q means P is the father of Q; P # Q means P is the mother of Q and P * Q means P is the sister of Q, then N # L $ P * Q shows which of the relation of Q to N?
A. Grandson
B. Granddaughter
C. Nephew
D. Data is inadequate
E. None of these

25. B5D means B is the father of D.
B9D means B is the sister of D.
B4D means B is the brother of D.
B3D means B is the wife of D.
Which of the following means F is the mother of K?
A. F3M5K
B. F5M3K
C. F9M4N3K
D. F3M5N3K
E. None of these

ANSWERS

1	2	3	4	5	6	7	8	9	10
A	B	C	D	B	C	E	B	D	A
11	**12**	**13**	**14**	**15**	**16**	**17**	**18**	**19**	**20**
C	B	E	B	D	D	D	C	D	B
21	**22**	**23**	**24**	**25**					
B	A	B	D	A					

EXPLANATORY ANSWERS

1. L £ M # O → M is son of L, M is sister of O → M is a male here, he can not become sister to O. So, this is not correct.

2. L £ M $ R → M is son of L, M is brother of R → R is not paternal uncle of L, R is either son or daughter to L.

M $ R # D ? V → M is brother of R, R is sister of D, V is mother of D. V is mother of M, R and D. So, M is son of V.

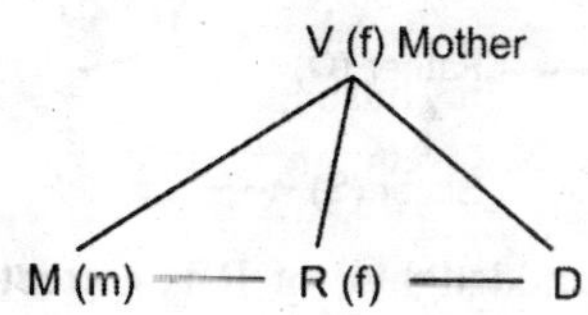

3. A is grandfather of B means A must be a male. In 1, 2 and 4 options there is no confirmation of A's gender. In all these options A is either male or female. So, all these options can be eliminated. But in third option A is a male. So we have to check that option.

L # B = S $ Q = A → L and B are children to S and S and Q are children to A.

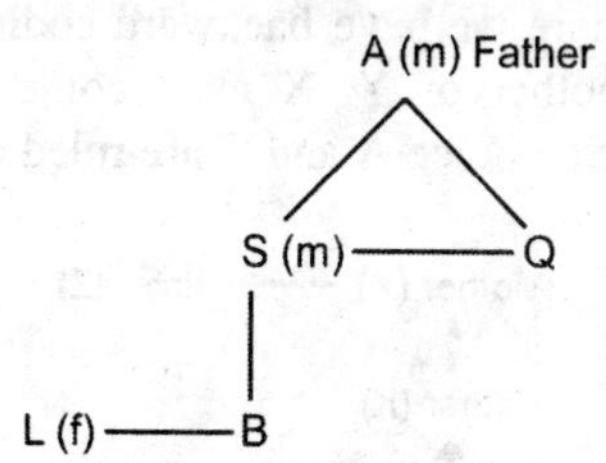

4. F is paternal uncle of G means F must be a male. In all options F is male.

G × L $ F $ N → L, F and N are siblings and G is L's daughter. And F is paternal uncle of G.

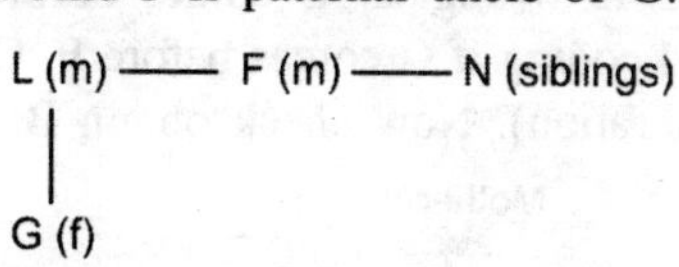

5. S × M # B = F $ D → S is daughter of M and M is mother of S and sister of B. B and M are children of F and F is brother of D. So, S is granddaughter of F and F is maternal grandfather of S. D is maternal grandmother or grandfather to S.

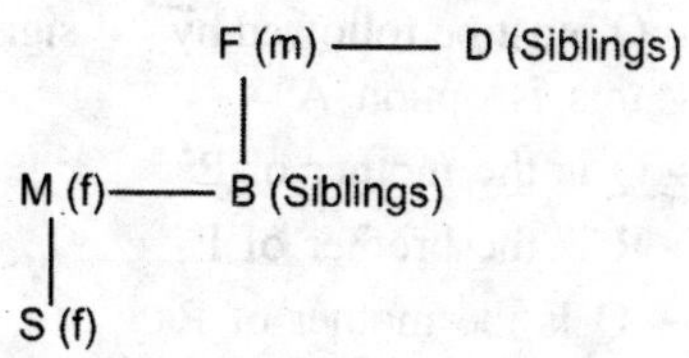

6. B + D × M ÷ N → B is mother of D, D is father of M and M is brother of N.

B is M's father's mother. So, M is grandson of B.

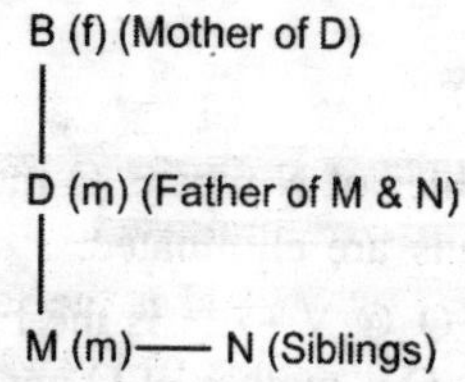

7. J is son F means J must be a male. If 'J' is followed by '÷' or '×', then F must be a male. So, we can eliminate 2nd option.

J ÷ R – T × F → J is brother of R, R is sister of T and T is father of F. Here, J is paternal uncle of F.

J ÷ M – N × F → J is brother of M, M is sister of N and N is father of F. Here, J is paternal uncle of F.

8. R is niece of M means R must be a female. If R is followed by '–' or '+', then R must be a female. So, we can eliminate 1st option. M – J + R – N → M is sister of J, J is mother of R, R is sister of N. Here, M is maternal aunt to R and R is niece of M (M's sister's daughter).

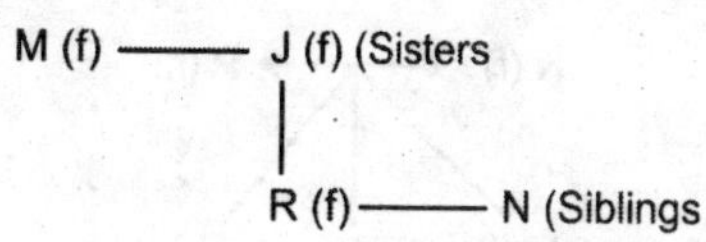

9. Q £ N @ S © M = P → Q is son of N, N is mother of S, M is brother of S and P is sister of M. N is the mother and she has 4 children among whom Q and M are sons, P is daughter and S is son or daughter.

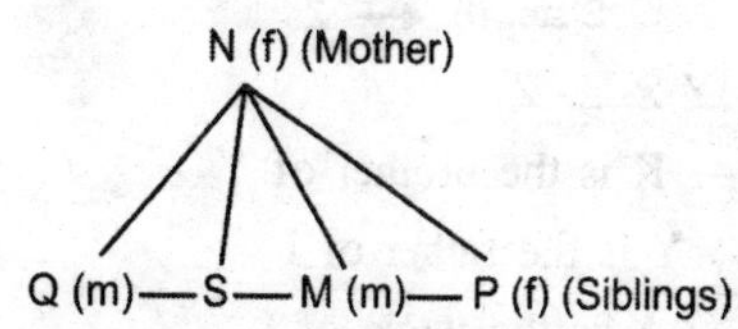

10. P @ R = S © T £ V → P is mother of R, S is sister of R, T is brother of S and T is the son of V. P and V are wife and husband and their children are R, S and T among whom S is their daughter, T is their son and R is their son or daughter.

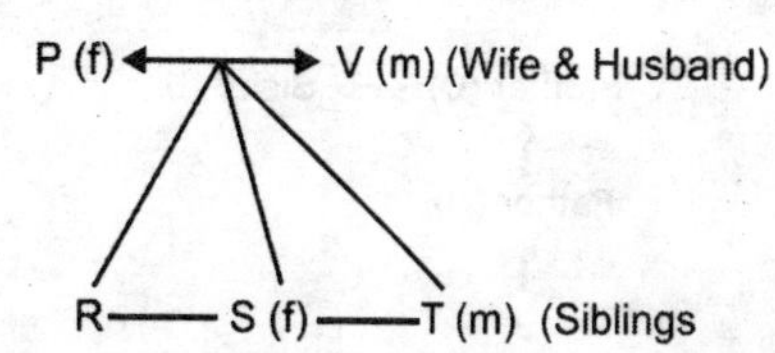

11. C is the paternal uncle of D means C must be a male. D £ L £ N @ V © C → D is son of L, L is son of N, N is mother of V and C is brother of V.

N is the mother and N has 3 children among whom L and C are her sons and V is her son or daughter. D is son of L and V is D's paternal uncle or aunt and C is

D's paternal uncle and D is nephew to V and C.

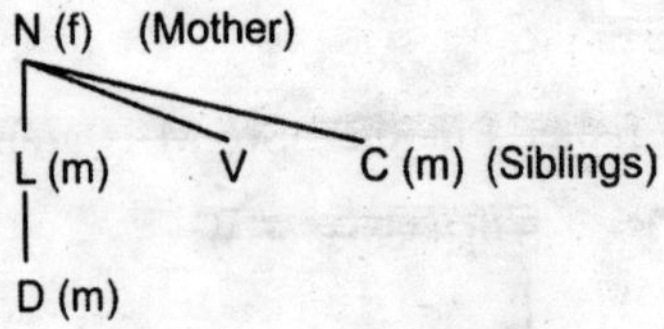

12. Q is the daughter of N means Q must be a female. 1, 3 and 4 options are eliminated.

N * P # C @ Q @ V → N is the father of P, P is the daughter of C, C is mother of Q and Q is mother of V. N and C are husband and wife. Their daughters are P and Q. Q is mother of V.

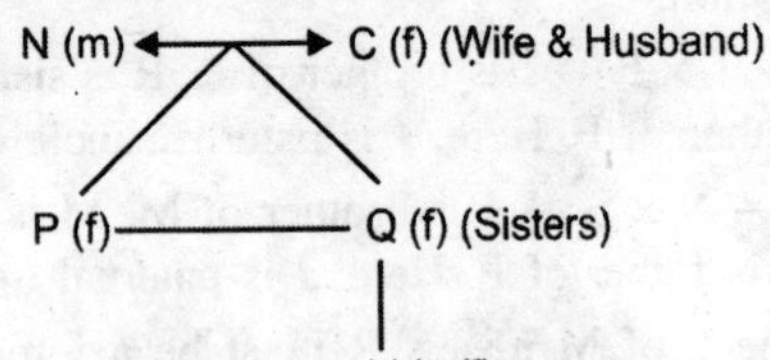

13. L = M # N © P * Q → M is sister of L, M is daughter of N, P is brother of N and P is father of Q. Here, N is wife and her husband is P. Their children are M, L and Q.

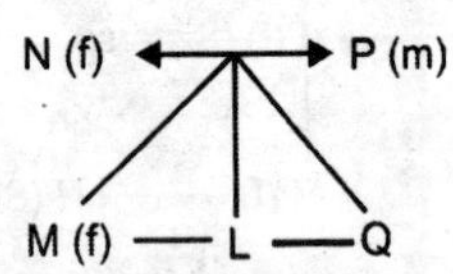

14. As option 'A' has 'I' at last position, it is ruled out.

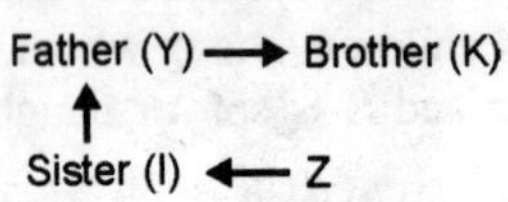

B. K + Y × I – Z

K + Y → K is the brother of Y

Y × I → Y is the father of I

Hence, → K is the uncle of I

and I – Z → I is the sister of Z

Hence, → I is the niece of K.

15. As options (A) and (C) has 'I' at last positions they are ruled out.

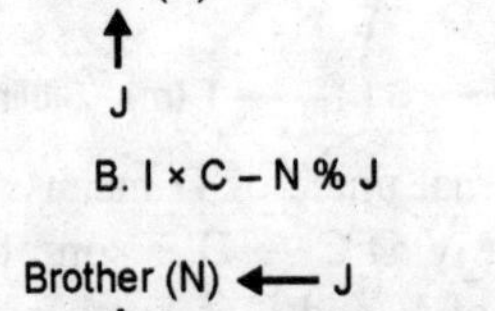

B. I × C – N % J

D. I × C + N – J

I × C → I is the sister of C

C + N → C is the daughter of N

and N – J → N is the brother of I.

Hence, I is niece of J.

16. All options have 'D' at last place, so none follows.

17. Since 'T is the nephew of Q' so 'T' must be a male but sex of 'T' cannot be established in any of the option.

18. Choice A, B is not correct as sex of S is not known. D is ruled out because S is a male here. Representation for choice C is as follows:

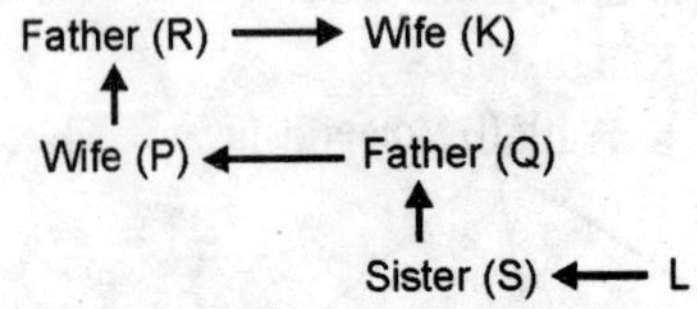

So, S is granddaughter of R is correct here.

19. As 'S' is female in option A and B, both are rejected directly. The sex of 'S' in option C is not known, hence it is also eliminated. Now, check option D.

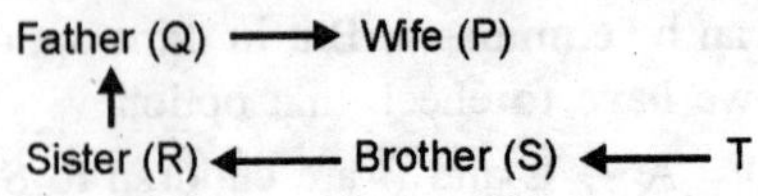

Clearly, S is son of P.

20. Note that here we have backward coding so if X is to be grandmother of Y, X must come after Y in the sequence. So choice A and C are ruled out. Now check option B.

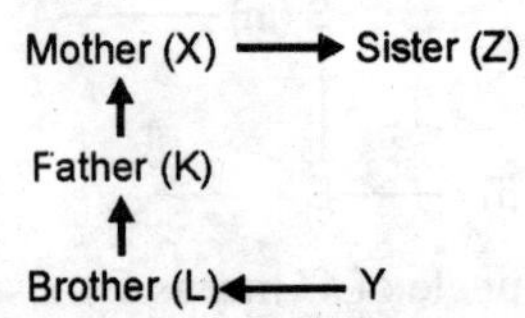

Clearly, X is grandmother of Y.

21. Option C is wrong as C is male here (C is father of D). Option C is wrong as C comes before F here. (In backward coding if C comes before F, C must be of a later generation). Now check option B.

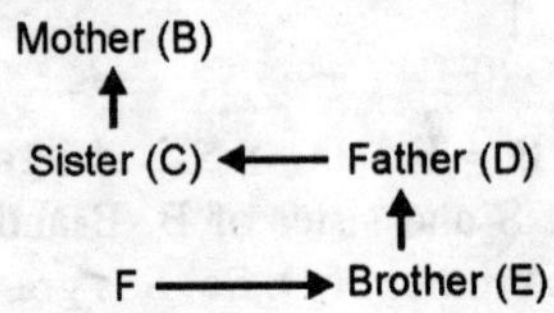

Clearly, C is aunt of F.

22. We can note that as Q is definitely a female in correct option, so Q must be followed by '-' sign. Only option satisfying this is option A

Q – P → Q is the mother of P

P + R → R is the brother of P

Hence, → Q is the mother of R

R % T → R is the father of T.

Hence, Q is the grandmother of T.

23. We can note that in the correct option K must be followed by '5' or '3' as K must be a female. So option A is ruled out.

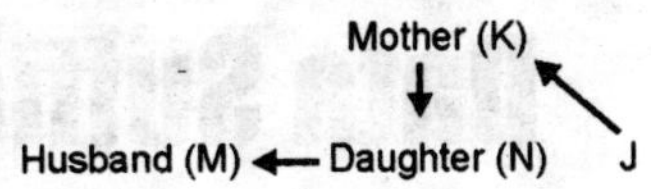

B. M9N5K3J

M9N → M is the husband of N

N5K → N is the daughter of K

Hence, → M is the son-in-law of K

K3J → K is the mother of J

Hence, → K is a lady

Hence, → K is the mother-in-law of M.

24. As 'Q' occupies last position in question statement, we can note that its sex is not known.

As the sex of Q is not known, hence, data is inadequate.

25.

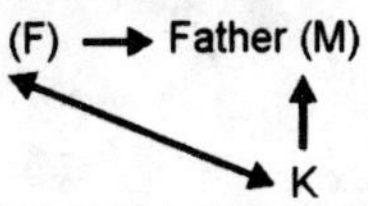

A. F3M5K

F3M → F is the wife of M

M5K → M is the father of K

Therefore, F is the mother of K.

As F is a female, so 'F' should be followed by either '3' or '9' so option 'B' is ruled out.

●●●

4 Data Sufficiency

Data sufficiency is most common in the examinations. Every question in this topic can be solved based on some data provided in the question itself. Questions are given with data as statements.

There can be two or more statements. We have to check these statements sufficiency to solve the problem. Please note that questions can be solved using one or more statements and even cannot be solved at all using all statements. We have to choose particular option as answer.

Points to remember

- There is no need to solve the question to get exact answer.
- There is only need to check data sufficiency to get the answer.
- Questions asked in the banking exams are almost from general topics like profit and loss, interest, time and distance, ratio and proportion, pipe and cistern etc.

MULTIPLE CHOICE QUESTIONS

Directions (Qs. No. 1-5) : *Each of the questions given consists of a question and two statements I & II given below it. You have to decide statement's sufficiency to solve the question. Give answer—*

A. If the statement I alone is sufficient but II alone is not.

B. If the statement II alone is sufficient but I alone is not.

C. If either statement I alone or II alone is sufficient.

D. If the data given in both statement I and II are not sufficient.

E. If both statement I and II is required to solve the question.

1. What is the speed of running train?

I. If train covers a bridge in 40 seconds.

II. If train crosses another train in 10 seconds.

2. What is the value of X – (Y/45)?

I. X is the largest possible four digit no. and Y is the smallest three digit no.

II. If (X – Y) is known.

3. C is the brother of D. How is D related to C?

I. D is the sister of E.

II. F is the huband of D.

4. Among Neera, Meera, Pummi and Ajay, who came last in the race?

I. Neera came after Meera but not after Ajay.

II. Pummi came after Ajay but not after Nutan.

5. Who is at the fourteenth position of this row from left?

I. The last person is Shyam and first person is Sita.

II. The person 4th to the left of Shyam is Mohan. Who is at 17th position from the right of Sita.

6. What is the code of 'pi' in the code language?

I. In the code language 'la pi ni' means 'you are beautiful'.

II. In the same code language 'pa pi pu' means 'boys are beautiful'.

7. A, B, C, D and E are sitting around a circle facing at the centre. Who is second to left of B?

I. B is sitting between C and D. D is sitting to the immediate left of E.

II. A is sitting third right of B.

8. In which direction is Ajay going now?

I. If Ajay turns to the right and again to right, he will be facing west.

II. If Ajay turns to the left and walks 01 km and then takes left turn and walks 01 km, he will be facing South.

9. How much money I have in my bank account?

I. I save ₹ 5,000 every month and fix in my account. I opened this account 03 years back.

II. I have ₹ 1 lakh more than you. You save ₹ 3,000 every month and keep in your account. You opened your account 01 years back.

10. How many persons saw the Mela today?

I. Each pass holder can bring two person with him/her.

II. In all 200 passes are sold till today.

11. What is Nitin's rank from the top in a class of forty students?

Statements:

I. There are ten students between Nitin and Deepa.

II. Deepa is twentieth from the top.

12. Among A, B, C, D, E and F, who is the heaviest?
Statements:
I. A and D are heavier than B, E and F but none of them is the heaviest.
II. A is heavier than D but lighter than C.

13. Among A, B, C, D and E, who is in the middle while standing in a row?
Statements:
I. C, who is third to the left of D, is to the immediate right of A and second to the left of E.
II. C is second to the left of E, who is not at any of the ends and who is third to the right of A. D is at one of the ends.

14. On which day in April is Gauri's birthday?
Statements:
I. Gauri was born exactly 28 years after her mother was born.
II. Her mother will be 55 years 4 months and 5 days on August 18 this year.

15. How many visitors saw the exhibition yesterday?
Statements:
I. Each entry pass holder can take up to three persons with him/her.
II. In all, 243 passes were sold yesterday.

16. What is the numerical code for 'sky' in a certain code?
Statements:
I. The code for 'give me sky' is '719'.
II. The code for 'you can bring sky for me' is written as '574186'.

17. Who among P, Q, T, V and M is exactly in the middle when they are arranged in ascending order of their heights?
Statements:
I. V is taller than Q but shorter than M.
II. T is taller than Q and M but shorter than P.

18. Gopi ranks eighteenth from the top in a class. What is his rank from the last?
Statements:
I. There are 47 students in the class.
II. Jatin who ranks 10th in the same class, ranks 38th from the last.

19. Among five friends, who is the tallest?
Statements:
I. D is taller than A and C.
II. B is shorter than E but taller than D.

20. How many speeches were delivered in the two days' programme?
Statements:
I. 18 speakers were invited to give at least one speech (maximum of two speeches), out of which one-sixth of the speakers could not come.
II. One-third of the speakers gave two speeches each.

21. In a row of five buildings—P, Q, R, S and T, which building is in the middle?
Statements:
I. Buildings S and Q are at the two extreme ends of the row.
II. Building T is to the right of building R.

22. What is the rank of S from the bottom in a class of 30 students?
Statements:
I. M is third from the top and there are five students between M and S.
II. The rank of K is fourth from the bottom and there are 17 students between K and S.

23. What time did the train leave today?
Statements:
I. The train normally leaves on time.
II. The scheduled departure is at 14 : 30.

24. What does '$' mean in a code language?
Statements:
I. '5$#3' means 'flowers are really good'.
II. '7#35' means 'good flowers are available'.

25. What is the colour of the new grass?
Statements:
I. Blue is called green, red is called orange, orange is called yellow.
II. Yellow is called white, white is called black, green is called brown and brown is called purple.

26. Which train did Amit catch to go to office?
Statements:
I. Amit missed his usual train of 10.25 a.m. A train comes in every 5 minutes.
II. Amit did not catch the 10.40 a.m. train or any train after that time.

27. What is the monthly salary of Prasha?
Statements:
I. Prasha gets 15% more than Sumit while Sumit gets 10% less than Lokesh.
II. Lokesh's monthly salary is ₹ 2500.

28. The Chairman of a big company visits one department on Monday of every week except for the Monday of third week of every month. When did he visit the Purchase department?
Statements:
I. He visited Accounts department in the second week of September after having visited Purchase department on the earlier occasion.
II. He had visited Purchase department immediately after visiting Stores department but before visiting Accounts department.

29. On which day of the week did Hetal visit the zoo?
Statements:
I. Hetal did not visit zoo either on Tuesday or on Thursday.

II. Hetal visited zoo two days before her mother reached his house which was day after Monday.

30. How many gift boxes were sold on Monday?

Statements:

I. It was 10% more than the boxes sold on the earlier day *i.e.* Sunday.

II. Every third visitor to the shop purchased the box and 1500 visitors were there on Sunday.

31. What is Sheela's position from the right end in a row of children?

Statements:

I. There are 10 children between Sheela and Rajan.

II. Rajan is twentieth from the left end of the row of children.

32. It is 8.00 p.m., when can Hemant get next bus for Ramnagar from Khanpur?

Statements:

I. Buses for Ramnagar from Khanpur leave after every 30 minutes, till 10 p.m.

II. Fifteen minutes ago, one bus has left for Ramnagar from Khanpur.

33. What is Sandhya's rank from the top in a class of 25 students?

Statements:

I. Sandhya ranks three ranks above Amit who ranks 18th from the bottom.

II. Sandhya's rank from the top is two ranks below Deepti who ranks 23rd from the bottom.

34. Among M, N, D, P and K, who earns more than only the least earner among them?

Statements:

I. N earns more than M and P but less than only D.

II. M earns more than P who earns less than K.

35. How many employees of Bank M opted for VRS?

Statements:

I. 18% of the 950 officer cadre employees and 6% of the 1100 other cadre employees of Bank M opted for VRS.

II. 28% of the employees in the age-group of 51 to 56 and 17% of the employees in all other age-groups of Bank M opted for VRS.

36. In a row of five children A, B, C, D and E, who is standing in the middle?

Statements:

I. D is to the immediate right of E and B is to the immediate left of E.

II. B is at the extreme left of the row.

37. How many girls are taller than Shravan in his class?

Statements:

I. When students of Shravan's class are ranked in descending order of their heights, Shravan's rank is 17th from the top among all the students and 12th among boys.

II. Shravan's rank from the bottom on the basis of height among boys is 18th and among all students, 29th.

Directions (Qs. Nos. 38-50): *In each of the following problems, there is one question and three statements I, II and III given below the question. You have to decide whether the data given in the statements is sufficient to answer the question. Read all the statements carefully and find which of the statements is/are sufficient to answer the given question. Choose the correct alternative in each question.*

38. Who among Siddhartha, Nitin, Vipul and Mukul is the youngest?

Statements:

I. Vipul is younger than Mukul but older than Siddhartha and Nitin.

II. Mukul is the oldest.

III. Siddhartha is older than Nitin.

A. Only I B. Only I and II
C. Only II and III D. Only I and III
E. None of these

39. What is Suman's rank from the top in a class of forty students?

Statements:

I. Suman is 3 ranks below Deepa from the top.

II. Deepa's rank from the bottom is 23.

III. Suman is 3 ranks above Deepa from the bottom.

A. Any two of the three B. Only I and II
C. Only II and III D. All I, II and III
E. Only II and either I or III

40. In which year was Sanju born?

Statements:

I. Sanju is six years older than Gopal.

II. Gopal's brother was born in 1982.

III. Sanju's brother is two years younger than Gopal's brother who was eight years younger than Gopal.

A. Only I and II B. Only II and III
C. Only I and III D. All I, II and III
E. None of these

41. How is 'DATE' written in the code language?

Statements:

I. DEAR is written as $#@? in that code.

II. TREAT is written as %?#@% in that code.

III. TEAR is written as %#@? in that code.

A. Only I and II
B. Only II and III
C. All I, II and III
D. Only I and either II or III
E. None of these

42. Five persons—A, B, C, D and E are sitting in a row. Who is sitting in the middle?

Statements:

I. B is between E and C.

II. B is to the right of E.

III. D is between A and E.

A. Only I and II
B. Only II and III
C. Only I and III
D. All I, II and III
E. None of these

43. Who is the tallest among six boys P, T, N, D, Q and R?

Statements:

I. P is taller than D and N but not as tall as T.
II. R is taller than Q but not as tall as T.
III. Q is not taller than T and R.

A. Only I and II
B. Only II and III
C. Only I and III
D. All I, II and III
E. Only I and either II or III

44. In a certain code, 'XYZ' means 'We are friends'. Which letter stands for 'We'?

Statements:

I. 'PYN' means 'They are classmates'.
II. 'ZMS' means 'We love them'.
III. 'PX' means 'Hello friends'.

A. Only II
B. Only I and III
C. All I, II and III
D. Either I only or II only
E. None of these

45. Among P, Q, R, S and T, Q is the second tallest and S is immediate taller than the shortest. Who among them is in the middle when they stand in the order of their heights?

Statements:

I. T is not the shortest.
II. R is taller than S but shorter than Q.
III. P ranks third in height above S when all are arranged in the order of height.

A. Only I and II
B. Either II only or I and III only
C. Only II
D. Only II and III
E. None of these

46. What is the total monthly salary of Akki?

Statements:

I. Akki's basic salary is ₹ 100 more than Rajan's salary who also serves in Akki's company.
II. Other allowances drawn by Rajan besides his basic salary are ₹ 2000 per month which is ₹ 50 less than Akki's salary.
III. Rajan's basic salary is ₹ 1550 per month.

A. Only II
B. Only II and III
C. Only I and II
D. Only I and III
E. All I, II and III

47. Four subjects—Physics, Chemistry, Mathematics and Biology—were taught in our consecutive periods of one hour each starting from 8.00 a.m. At what time was the Chemistry period scheduled?

Statements:

I. Mathematics period ended at 10.00 a.m., which was preceded by Biology.
II. Physics was scheduled in the last period.
III. Mathematics period was immediately followed by Chemistry.

A. Only I
B. Either I only or II only
C. Only II
D. Only II and III
E. Only I and either II or III

48. How many sons does X have?

Statements:

I. Q and U are brothers of T.
II. R is sister of P and U.
III. R and T are daughters of X.

A. Only I and II
B. Only II and III
C. All I, II and III
D. I, II and III together are not sufficient
E. None of these

49. What does 'come' represent in a code language?

Statements:

I. 'pit na tac' means 'come and go' in that code language.
II. 'ja ta da' means 'you are good' in that code language.
III. 'na da rac' means 'you can come' in that code language.

A. Only I and II
B. Only II and III
C. Only I and III
D. All I, II and III
E. None of these

50. How is the girl in the photograph related to Kamal?

Statements:

I. Pointing to the photograph, Kamal said, "She is the mother of my father's only granddaughter".
II. Kamal has no siblings.
III. Pointing to the photograph, Kamal said, "She is the only daughter-in-law of my mother."

A. Any two of the three
B. Only I and II
C. Only II and III
D. Either only III or only I and II
E. None of these

51. How many daughters does W have?

Statements:

I. B and D are sisters of M.
II. M's father T is husband of W.
III. Out of the three children which T has, only one is a boy.

A. Only I and III
B. All I, II, and III are required to answer the question
C. Only II and III
D. Question cannot be answered even with all I, II and III
E. Only I and II

52. Who among A, B, C, D, E and F each having a different height, is the tallest?

Statements:

I. B is taller than A but shorter than E.

II. Only two of them are shorter than C.

III. D is taller than only F.

A. Only I and II
B. Only I and III
C. Only II and III
D. All I, II and III are required to answer the question
E. All I, II and III are not sufficient to answer the question

53. How is 'go' written in a code language?

Statements:

I. 'Now or never again' is written as 'tom ka na sa' in that code language.

II. 'You come again now' is written as 'ja ka ta sa' in that code language.

III. 'Again go now or never' is written as 'na ho ka sa tom' in that code language.

A. Only I and III
B. Only II and III
C. Only I and II
D. All I, II, and III are required to answer the question
E. None of the above

54. Towards which direction is village J from village W?

Statements:

I. Village R is to the west of village W and to the north of Village T.

II. Village Z is to the east of Village J and to the south of village T.

III. Village M is to the north east of Village J and north of Village Z.

A. Only I and II
B. Only II and III
C. All I, II and III are required to answer the question
D. All I, II and III are not sufficient to answer the question
E. None of the above

55. On which day of the week starting from Monday did Suresh visit Chennai?

Statements:

I. Suresh took leave on Wednesday.

II. Suresh visited Chennai the day after his mother's visit to his house.

III. Suresh's mother visited Suresh's house neither on Monday nor on Thursday.

A. Only II and III
B. Only I and II
C. Only I and III
D. All I, II and III are required to answer the question
E. Question cannot be answered even with all I, II and III

ANSWERS

1	2	3	4	5	6	7	8	9	10
D	-	C	E	D	E	E	C	D	D
11	**12**	**13**	**14**	**15**	**16**	**17**	**18**	**19**	**20**
D	A	C	E	D	D	E	C	E	E
21	**22**	**23**	**24**	**25**	**26**	**27**	**28**	**29**	**30**
D	C	D	E	B	D	E	A	B	E
31	**32**	**33**	**34**	**35**	**36**	**37**	**38**	**39**	**40**
D	E	C	D	A	E	A	D	E	D
41	**42**	**43**	**44**	**45**	**46**	**47**	**48**	**49**	**50**
D	D	A	E	B	E	E	D	C	D
51	**52**	**53**	**54**	**55**	**56**	**57**	**58**	**59**	**60**
B	D	A	A	E					

EXPLANATORY ANSWERS

1. As we know that to calculate the speed, we need distance covered in particular time. So, we need these two data in the statements. But in the above example, it is obvious that both data are insufficient.

3. Data provided by both statement I and II show that D is female. So, both statement alone are sufficient.

9. However, the data provided by each statement can be used to solve the problem in question. But the final answer cannot be concluded due to two different answers by different statement.

10. Because, even by using both statements exact number of Mela viewers cannot be calculated.

11. Since there are ten students between Nitin and Deepa, so Nitin may be eleven ranks above or below Deepa. Thus, Nitin may be 9th or 31st from the top.

12. From I, we conclude that since none of A and D is the heaviest and each one of B, E and F is lighter than both A and D, so C is the heaviest.

13. From each one of I and II, we get the order : A, C, B, E, D. Clearly, B is in the middle.

14. Clearly, the birthday of Gauri's mother can be found out from II and then Gauri's birthday can be determined using the fact given in I.

15. From I and II, we find that maximum (243 × 3) *i.e.* 729 visitors saw the exhibition.

But the exact number cannot be determined.

16. In I and II, the common words are 'me' and 'sky' and the common code numbers are '7' and '1'. So, the code for 'sky' is either '7' or '1'.

17. From I, we have: M > V > Q.

From II, we have: T > Q, T > M, P > T.

Combining the above two, we have: P > T > M > V > Q *i.e.* Q < V < M < T < P.

Clearly, M is in the middle.

18. From I, we conclude that in a class of 47 students, Gopi ranks 18th from the top and hence 30th from the last.

From II, we conclude that there are 9 students above and 37 students below Jatin in rank. Thus, there are (9 + 1 + 37) = 47 students in the class.

So, Gopi who ranks 18th from the top, is 30th from the last.

19. From I, we have: D > A, D > C.

From II, we have: E > B > D.

Combining the above two, we get: E > B > D > A > C or E > B > D >C > A.

Thus, E is the tallest.

20. From I, we find that number of speakers who attended programme = 18 – (1/6) of 18 = 15.

From II, we find that one-third of 15 *i.e.* 5 speakers gave 2 speeches each, while each of the remaining 10 speakers delivered only one speech.

So, total number of speeches delivered
= (5 × 2 + 10 × 1) = 20.

21. From I, we have the order : S, –, –, –, Q. From II, we have the order : R, T.

Combining the above two, we get two possible orders: S, R, T, P, Q or S, P, R, T, Q. Thus, either T or R is in the middle.

22. From I, we conclude that S is 9th from the top. Thus, in a class of 30 students, S ranks 22nd from the bottom.

From II, we conclude that P is 22nd from the bottom.

23. Clearly, even both I and II together do not reveal the exact time of departure of the train today.

24. In I and II, the common codes are '5', '#' and '3' and the common words are 'flowers', 'are' and 'good'. Thus, in I, the remaining code '$' stands for 'really'.

25. The colour of new grass is 'green' and as given in II, 'green' is called 'brown'. So, the colour of new grass is 'brown'.

26. From I and II, we conclude that Amit went to office by either 10.30 a.m. or 10.35 a.m. train.

27. From both I and II, we find that: Prasha's salary = 115% of (90% of ₹ 2500) = ₹ 2587.50.

28. From I, we can conclude that the Chairman visited Purchase department on Monday of the first week of September. The time of visit of no department is mentioned in II, which is, therefore, insufficient.

29. According to I, Hetal visited the zoo on any of the week days except Tuesday and Thursday.

According to II, Hetal's mother reached her house day after Monday *i.e.* on Tuesday. Thus, Hetal visited zoo two days before Tuesday *i.e.* on Sunday.

30. From II, we can conclude that (1500 * 3) = 500 boxes were sold on Sunday. Thus, from I, we find that number of boxes sold on Monday = 500 + 10% of 500 = 550.

31. Clearly, neither the number of children in the row is given nor the position of Sheela relative to Rajan is mentioned in any one of I or II.

32. II reveals that the previous bus had left at 7.45 p.m. As given in I, the next bus would leave after 30 minutes *i.e.* at 8.15 p.m.

33. From I, we know that in a class of 25 students, Amit ranks 18th from the bottom and 8th from the top. Sandhya is three ranks above Amit and so, Sandhya ranks 5th from the top.

From II, Deepti ranks 23rd from the bottom and hence, 3rd from the top. Sandhya, being 2 ranks below Deepti, is, thus, 5th from the top.

34. From I, we have: N > M, N > P, D > N. Thus, we have: D > N > M > P or D > N > P > M.

But, from II, M earns more than P *i.e.* D > N > M > P. Also, since P earns less than K and N earns less than only D, so we have: D > N > K > M > P or D > N > M > K > P.

Hence, either K or M earns more than only the least earner *i.e.* P.

35. From I, we have: number of employees who opted for VRS = 18% of 950 + 6% of 1100 = 171 + 66 = 237.

From II, we cannot get the required answer until and unless the number of employees in age-group 51 to 56 and other age-groups is known.

36. From I, we have the order: B, E, D. From II, B is at the extreme left of the row. Thus, considering both I and II, we conclude that among the five children, D is the third and hence the middle child in the row.

37. From I, we conclude that there are 16 students and 11 boys taller than Shravan. This implies that there are 5 girls taller than Shravan.

In II, Shravan's rank from the bottom is mentioned and to ascertain the number of girls taller than him, we need to know his rank from the top for which the number of students in the class is required, which is not given.

38. From I, we have: M > V, V > S, V > N ...(i)
From II, we have: Mukul is the oldest ...(ii)
From III, we have: S > N ...(iii)
Combining (i) and (iii), we get : M > V, V > S > N or M > V > S > N. Clearly, Nitin is the youngest.

39. From II, we conclude that in a class of 40, Deepa ranks 23rd from the bottom *i.e.* 18th from the top.
From I and II, we find that Suman is 3 ranks below 18th rank from the top *i.e.* she ranks 21st from the top.
From II and III, we find that Suman is 3 ranks above 23rd rank from the bottom *i.e.* she ranks 20th from the bottom or 21st from the top.

40. From II, we know that Gopal's brother was born in 1982.
From III, we find that Gopal's brother was 8 years younger to him *i.e.* Gopal was born in 1974.
From I, we find that Sanju is 6 years older than Gopal. Thus, Sanju was born in 1968.

41. Observing I, II and III, we find that similar letters have similar code symbols at the corresponding places in the code. So, this is direct-coding.
Thus, to find the code for DATE, we need the code for D which can be obtained from I only (*i.e.* $.) and the codes for A, T and E which can be obtained either from II or III (@, # and % respectively).

42. From I, the order is : E, B, C or C, B, E. From II, the order is : E, B. From III, the order is: A, D, E. Combining the above three, we get the order as : A, D, E, B, C. Clearly, E is sitting in the middle.

43. From I, we have: P > D, P > N, T > P *i.e.* T > P > D > N or T > P > N > D ...(i)
From II, we have: R > Q, T > R *i.e.* T > R > Q ...(ii)
From III, we have: T > Q, R > Q ...(iii)
Clearly, from (i) and (ii), we conclude that T is taller than each one of P, N, D, R and Q. So, T is the tallest.

44. To find the code for 'we', we need to have any of the following:
(i) 'We are friends' should have only 'We' common with another statement, as in II;
(ii) 'We are friends' should have only 'are' and 'friends' common with another single or two statements, as in I and III. Thus, we need Either II only or I and III only.

45. From the given statement, the descending order of heights is :__, Q,__, S,__. From II, we have the order: __, Q, R, S,__. Thus, R is in the middle.
From III, we have the order : P, Q,__, S,__. But, according to I, T is not the shortest. So, R is the shortest. Thus, we have the order : P, Q, T, S, R. So, T is in the middle.

46. From III, we have: Rajan's basic salary = ₹ 1550.
From I, we have: Akki's basic salary = ₹ (1550 + 100) = ₹ 1650.
From II, we have: Rajan's other allowances = ₹ 2000 and Akki's other allowances = ₹ 2050.
Therefore Akki's monthly salary = ₹ (1650 + 2050) = ₹ 3700.

47. From I and II, we conclude that Mathematics period began at 9.00 a.m., Biology period began at 8.00 a.m. and Physics period began at 11 a.m. So, the Chemistry period began at 10.00 a.m.
From I and III, we conclude that Mathematics period ended and Chemistry period began at 10.00 a.m.

48. From I, II and III, we conclude that all P, Q, R, T and U are children of X. Of these, Q and U are male while R and T are female. But the sex of P cannot be determined.

49. To find the code for 'come', we need to have two statements which have one common code word and 'come' as the common word, which is there in I and III.

50. From I, we conclude that the girl is either Kamal's or his brother's wife. But, according to II, Kamal has no siblings.
So, from both I and II, we conclude that the girl is Kamal's wife.
From III, we find that the girl is the only daughter-in-law of Kamal's mother *i.e.* she is Kamal's wife.

51. Combining statements I and II we have:

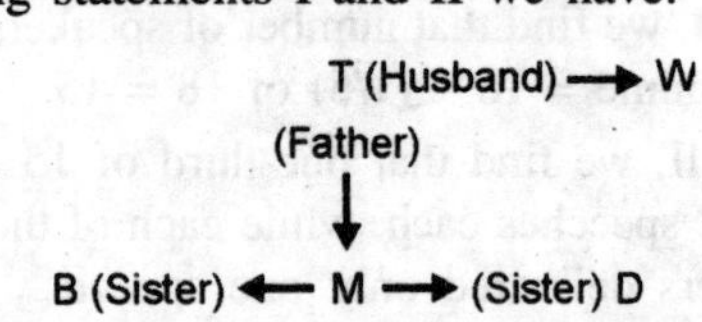

still it is not clear how many children does W have and what is the sex of M. By adding statement II one can conclude that M is a male and W has two daughters.

52. From I we have: A < B < E
From II we have: - - C - - -
From III we have: F < D < - < - < - < -
Combining I, II, III we get: F < D < C < A < B < E.

53. I and III have only 'go' as non common element.

54. 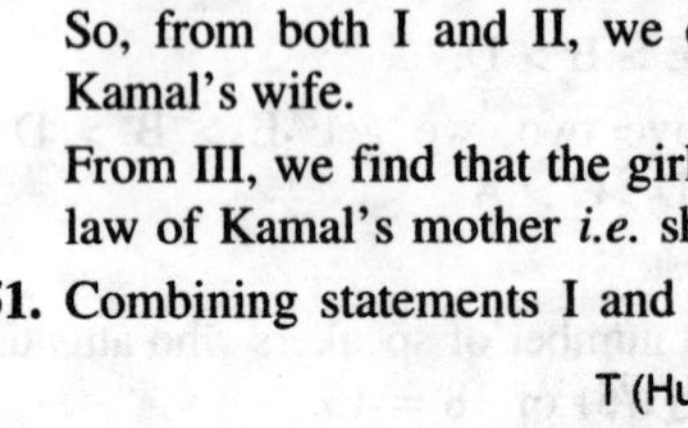

Combining I and II we get : 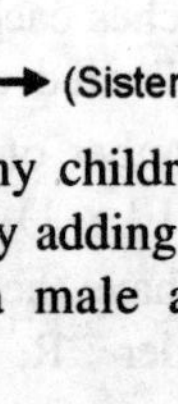

●●●

5 Direction Sense

DIRECTION SENSE TEST TRICKS

There are four main directions—East, West, North and South. There are four cardinal directions—North-East (N-E), North-West (N-W), South-East (S-E) and South-West (S-W) as shown below:

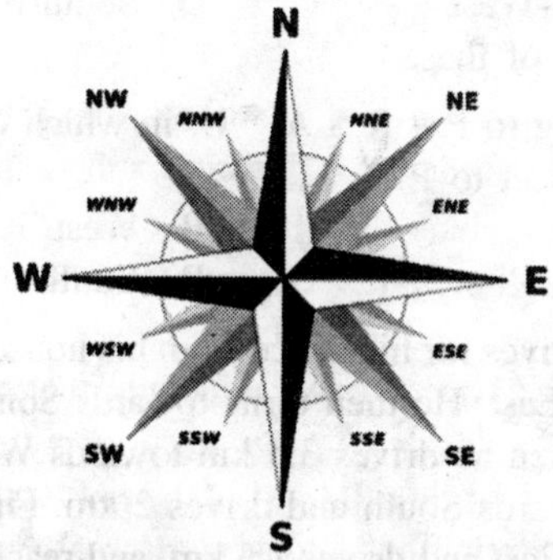

At the time of sunrise if a man stands facing the east, his shadow will be towards west.

At the time of sunset the shadow of an object is always in the east.

If a man stands facing the North, at the time of sunrise his shadow will be towards his left and at the time of sunset it will be towards his right.

At 12:00 noon, the rays of the sun are vertically downward hence there will be no shadow.

There are 4 main type of questions on directions which are frequently asked in examinations:

Type 1

Panas started from his house goes 5 km in the East, and then he turns to his left and goes to 4 km. Finally he turns left and cover 5 km. How far and in which direction he is from his house.

Explanation:

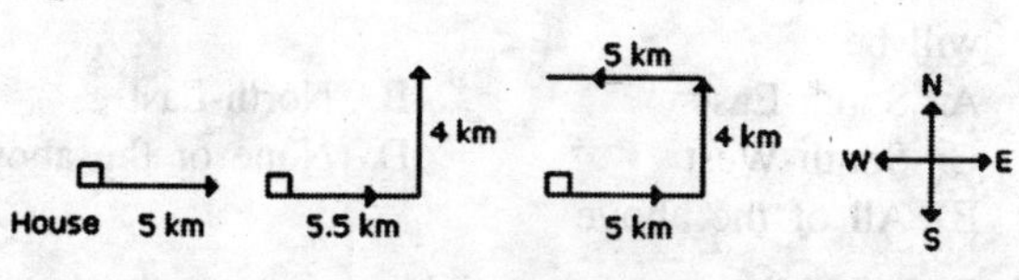

From third position it is clear he is 4 km from his house and is in North direction.

Type 2

Mukesh starting from his house goes 4 km in the East, and then he turns to his right and goes 3 km. What minimum distance will be covered by him to come back to his house?

Explanation:

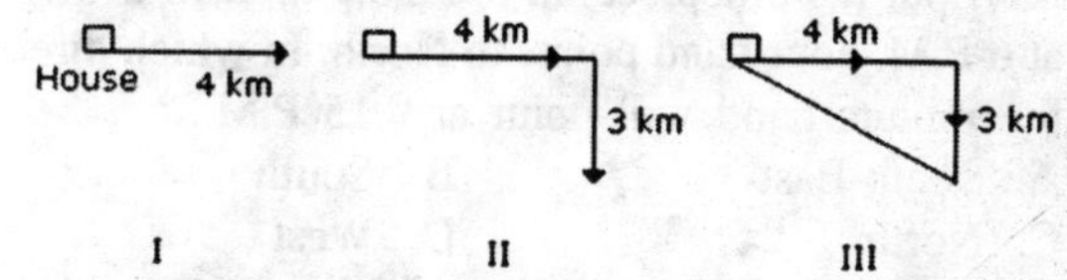

Minimum distance

$= \sqrt{(4)^2 + (3)^2} = \sqrt{16+9} = \sqrt{25} = 5$ km.

Type 3

One morning after sunrise Juhi while going to school met Lalli at boring road crossing. Lalli's shadow was exactly to the right of Juhi. If they were face to face, which direction was Juhi facing?

Explanation: In the morning sunrise in the east

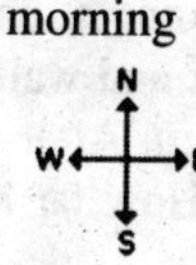

So, in morning the shadow falls towards the west.

Now, Lalli's shadow falls to the right of Juhi. Hence, Juhi is facing South.

Type 4

Tina starting from her house walked 5 km to reach the crossing of Palace. In which direction she was going, a road opposite to this direction goes to Hospital. The road to the right goes to station. If the road which goes to station is just opposite to the road which IT-Park, then in which direction to Tina is the road which goes to IT-Park?

Explanation:

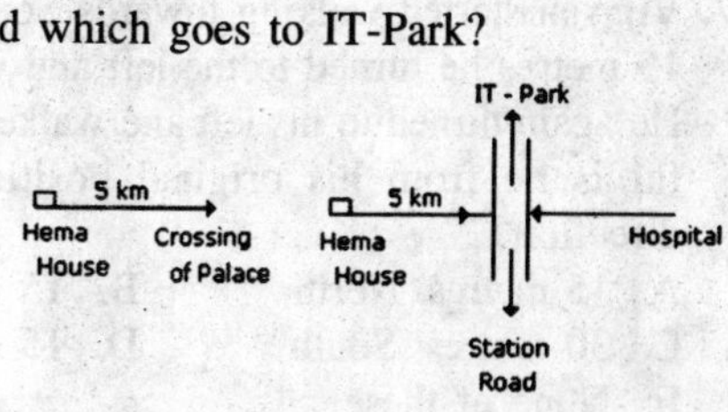

From II it is clear that the road which is going to IT Park is left to Hema.

MULTIPLE CHOICE QUESTIONS

1. One morning Urmilla and Vishal were talking to each other face to face at a crossing. If Vishal's shadow was exactly to the left of Urmilla, which direction was Urmilla facing?
A. East B. West
C. North D. South
E. None of these

2. If South-East becomes North, North-East becomes West and so on. What will West become?
A. North-East B. North-West
C. South-East D. South-West
E. None of these

3. Ravi put his timepiece on the table in such a way that at 6 P.M. hour hand points to North. In which direction the minute hand will point at 9.15 P.M. ?
A. South-East B. South
C. North D. West
E. None of these

4. Rakesh walked 20 m towards north. Then he turned right and walks 30 m. Then he turns right and walks 35 m. Then he turns left and walks 15 m. Finally he turns left and walks 15 m. In which direction and how many metres is he from the starting position?
A. 15 m, West B. 30 m, East
C. 30 m, West D. 45 m, East
E. 45 m, West

5. Starting from the point X, John walked 15 m towards west. He turned left and walked 20 m. He then turned left and walked 15 m. After this he turned to his right and walked 12 m. How far and in which directions is now John from X?
A. 32 m, South B. 47 m, East
C. 42 m, North D. 27 m, South
E. None of these

6. Suman is 40 metres South-West of Ashok, Prakash is 40 metres South-East of Ashok. Prakash is in which direction of Suman?
A. South B. West
C. East D. North-East
E. None of these

7. Vijayan started walking towards South. After walking 15 metres he turned to the left and walked 15 metres. He again turned to his left and walked 15 metres. How far is he from his original position and in which direction?
A. 15 metres, North B. 15 metres, East
C. 30 metres, South D. 15 metres, West
E. None of these

Directions (8 to 10): *Each of the following questions is based on the following information:*

1. P # Q means B is at 1 metre to the right of P.
2. P $ Q means B is at 1 metre to the North of P.
3. P * Q means B is at 1 metre to the left of P.
4. P @ Q means B is at 1 metre to the south of P.
5. In each question first person from the left is facing North.

8. According to X @ B * P, P is in which direction with respect to X?
A. North (b) South
C. North-East D. South-West
E. None of these

9. According to M # N $ T, T is in which direction with respect to M?
A. North-West B. North-East
C. South-West D. South-East
E. None of these

10. According to P # R $ A * U, in which direction is U with respect to P?
A. East B. West
C. North D. South

11. A man drives for his office from his house, drives 2 km towards East. He then turns towards South and drives 1 km. Then he drives 3.5 km towards West and again turns towards South and drives 2 km. Finally he turns towards East and drives 1.5 km. and reaches his office. How far and towards which direction is his office with reference to his house?
A. 2 km towards East B. 3 km towards East
C. 4 km towards South D. 2.5 km towards North
E. None of these

12. I was walking in South-East direction. After a while I turned 90° to the right and walked ahead. Later I turned 45° to the right. In which direction am I walking now?
A. North B. North-East
C. South-West D. East
E. None of these

13. If a person is walking towards North, what direction should he follow so that he is walking towards West?
A. right, right, left (b) left, left, right
C. left, right, left D. left, left, left
E. None of these

14. If all the directions are changed in the manner that North becomes South and vice versa, then North-West will be :
A. South-East B. North-East
C. South-West D. None of the above
E. All of the above

15. Ravi travelled four km straight towards south. He turned left and travelled six km straight, then turned right and travelled four km straight. How far is he from the starting point?

A. 8 km
B. 10 km
C. 12 km
D. 18 km
E. 20 km

Directions (Qs. 16 to 20): *P, Q, R and S are standing on four corners of a square piece of plot as shown in the given figure. They start moving, and the movements are explained in each of the questions. Read the question and select the right alternative.*

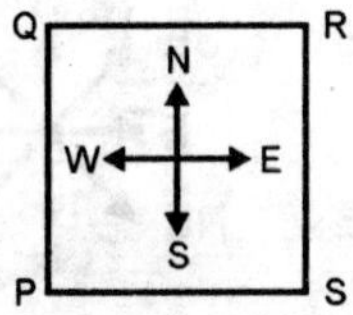

16. P, Q , R and S walk diagonally to opposite corners and from there Q and R walk one and a half sides anti-clockwise while P and S walk one side clockwise along the sides. Where is S now?
A. At the North-West corner
B. At the North-East
C. At the South-West corner
D. At the East-West
E. None of these

17. Q travelled straight to R, a distance of 10 m. He turned right and walked 7 m towards S, again he turned right and walked 8 m, and then finally turned right and walked 7m. How far is he from his original position?
A. 7 m
B. 8 m
C. 2 m
D. 3 m
E. 5 m

18. From the original position, S starts crossing the field diagonally. After walking half the distance he turns right; walks some distance and turns left. Which direction is S facing now?
A. South-East
B. North-West
C. South-West
D. North
E. None of these

19. P and S walk one and a half length of the side clockwise and anti-clockwise respectively. Which one of the following statements is true?
A. P is at midpoint between Q and R and S at the corner originally occupied by P
B. P and S are both at the midpoint between R and S
C. P and S are both at the midpoint between Q and R.
D. S is at midpoint between Q and R and P is at the midpoint between original side of R and S
E. None of these

20. P, Q, R and S walk one and a half sides clockwise. Who is on the left of Q if he is facing West?
A. P
B. R
C. S
D. Both A and B
E. None of these

ANSWERS

1	2	3	4	5	6	7	8	9	10
C	C	D	D	A	C	B	D	B	C
11	**12**	**13**	**14**	**15**	**16**	**17**	**18**	**19**	**20**
D	A	B	A	B	B	C	B	C	B

EXPLANATORY ANSWERS

1.

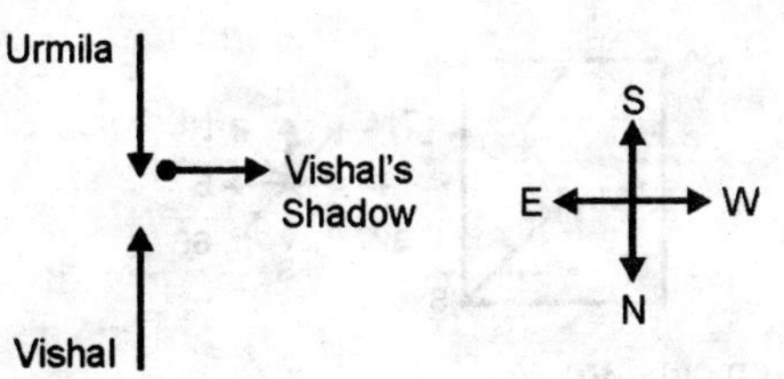

2.

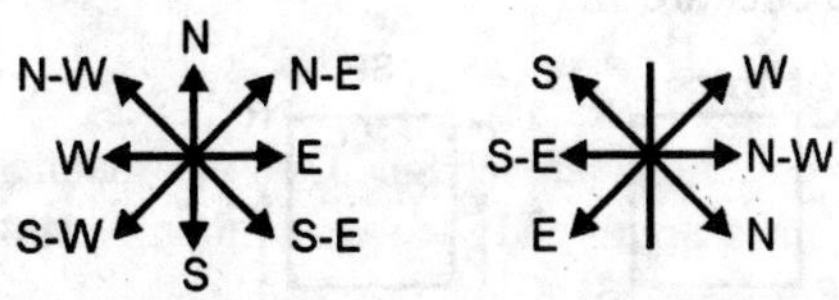

It is clear from the diagrams that new name of West will become South-East.

3.

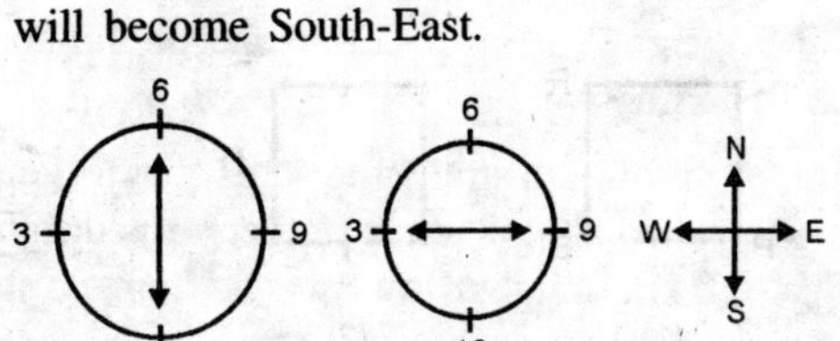

At 9.15 P.M., the minute hand will point towards west.

4.

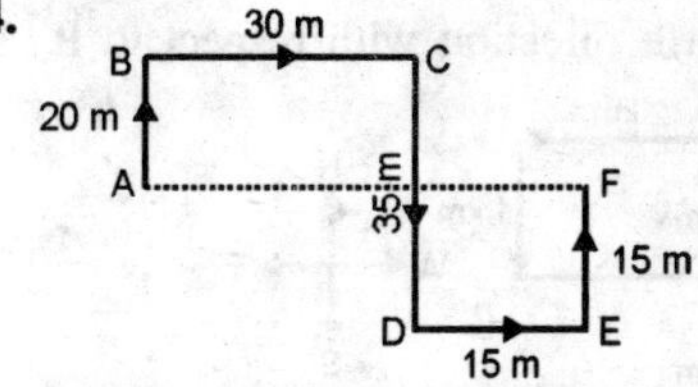

Required distance = AF = 30 + 15 = 45 m. From the above figure, F is in East direction from A. So the answer is '45 m East'.

5.

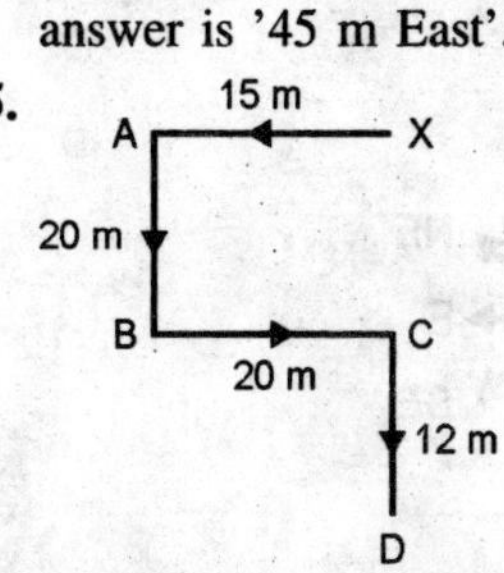

Required distance = 20 + 12 = 32 m South.

6.

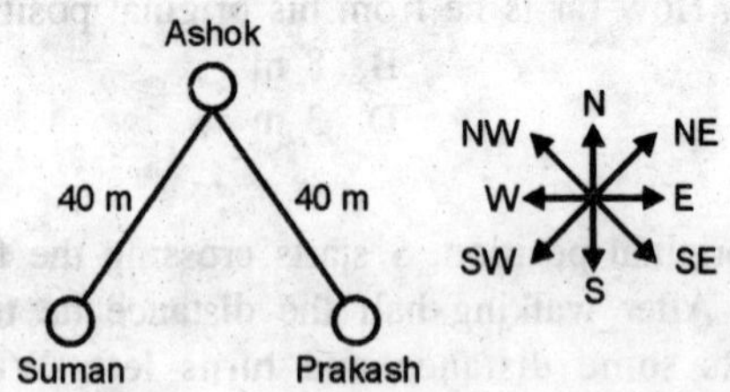

7.

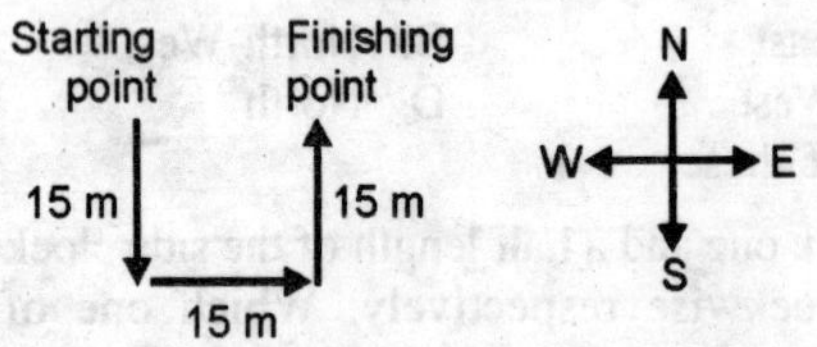

8. According to X @ B * Y

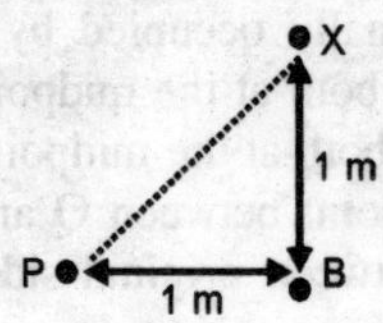

Hence P is in South-West of X.

9. According to M # N $ T

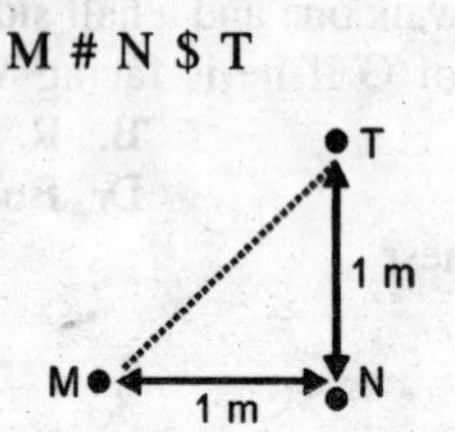

Hence T is in the North-East of M.

10. According to P # R $ A * U

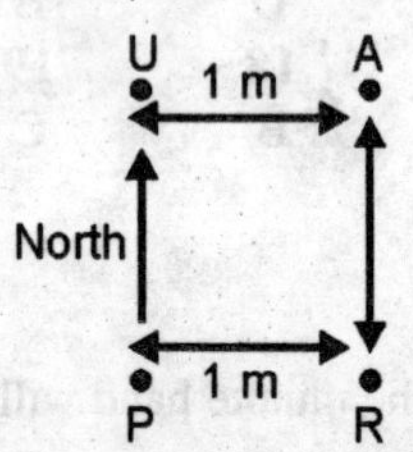

Hence U is in North direction with respect to P.

11.

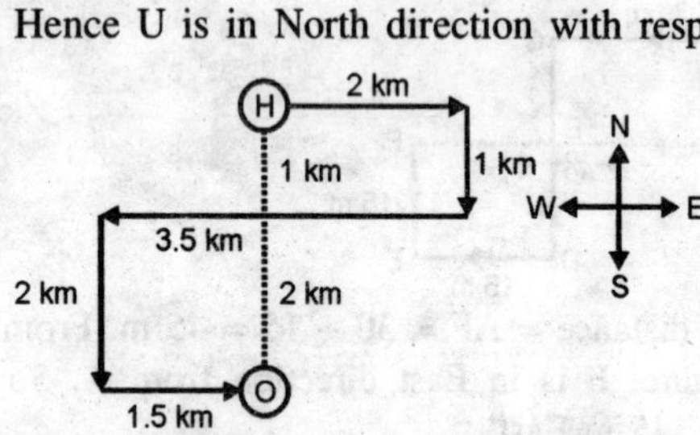

12.

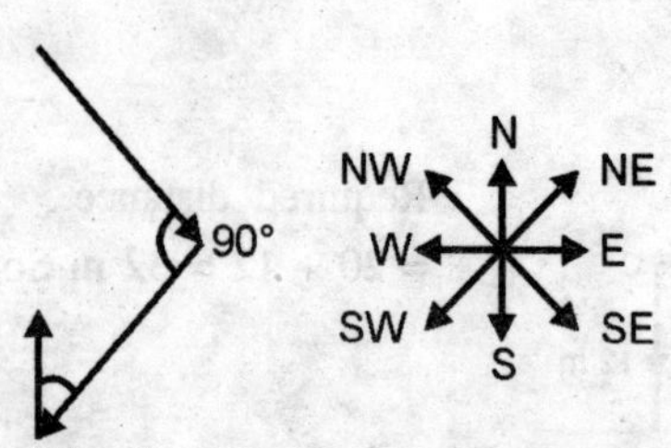

13.

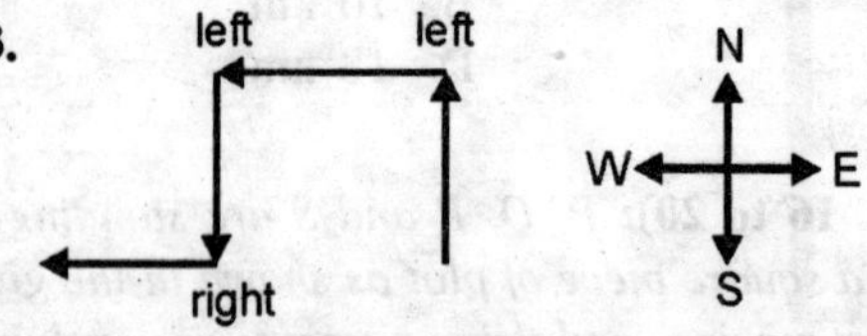

14. Original Directions Changed Directions

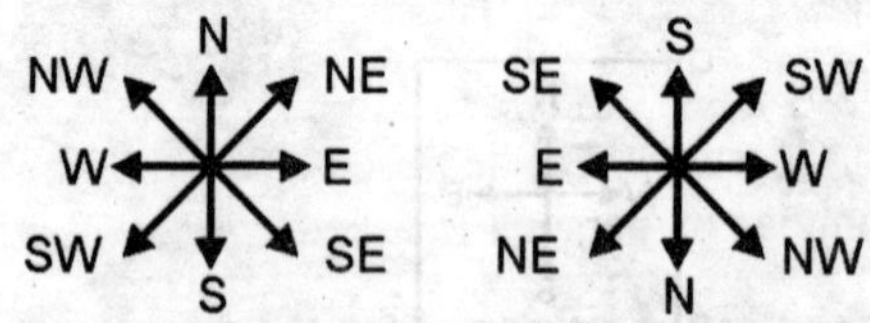

15.

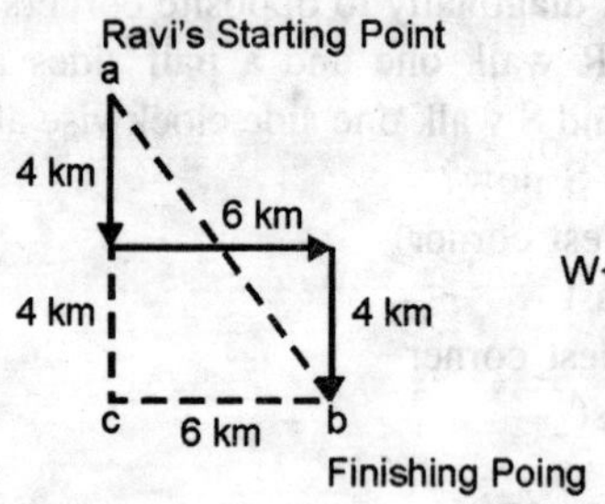

ab = Ö(bc^2 + ca^2) = Ö(6^2 + 8^2) = Ö(36 + 64) = 10 km

16.

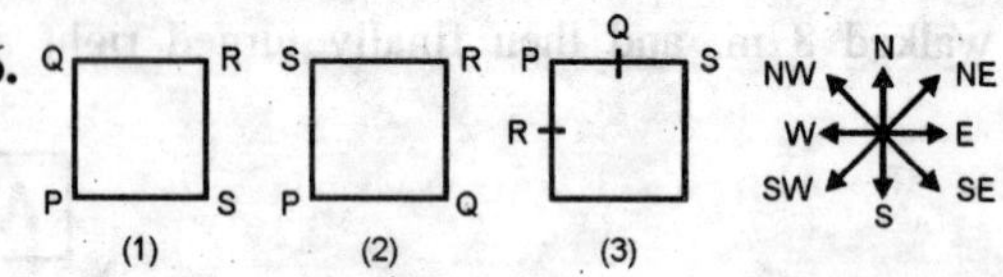

17. (10 m – 8 m = 2 m)

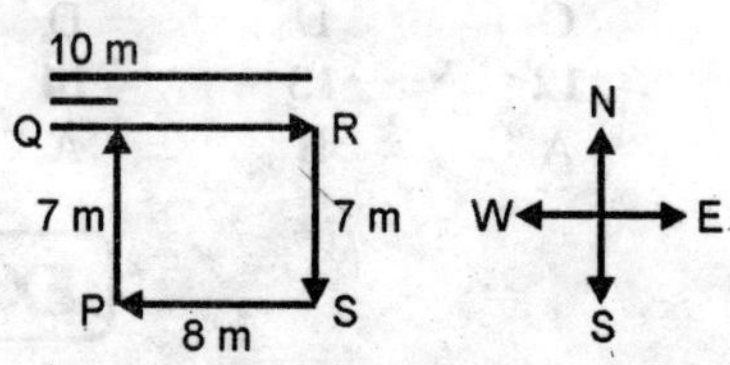

18.

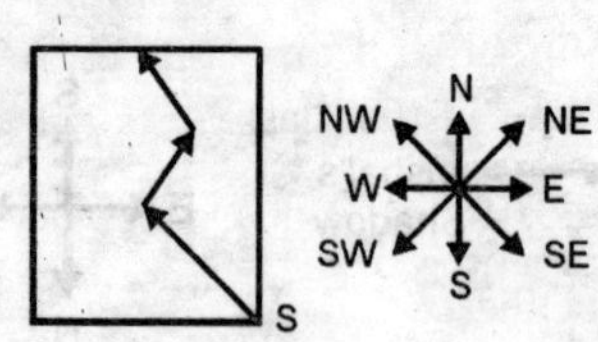

19. The movements are :

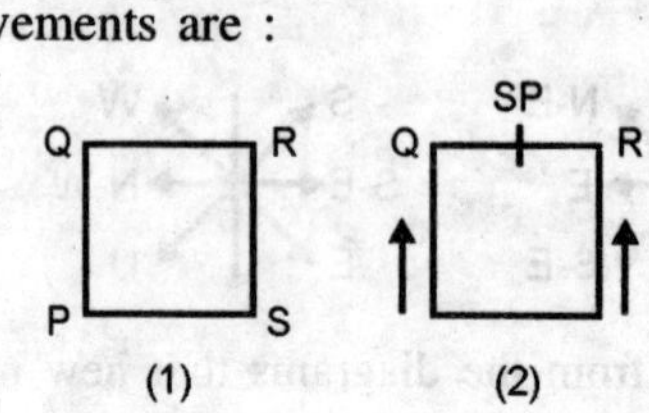

20.

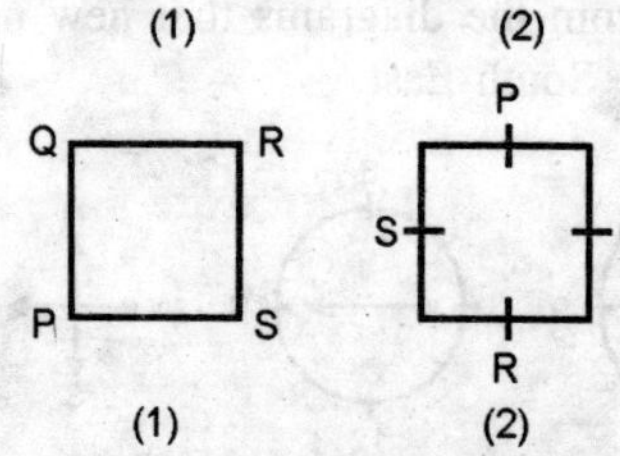

6 Ranking Test

In Ranking Test Questions will be posed about the ranks of a person both from the top and from the bottom are mentioned and the total number of persons is asked.

Important Tricks for Ranking Test

- Rank of a person from lower or right end = (Total number of persons in row) – (Rank of that person from upper or left end) + 1
- Rank of a person from upper or left end = (Total number of persons in row) – (Rank of that person from lower or right end) + 1
- Total number of persons in a row or class = (Rank of a person from upper end or left end) = (Rank of that person from lower or right end) – 1

MULTIPLE CHOICE QUESTIONS

1. Anu and Vinay are ranked seventh and eleventh respectively from the top in a class of 31 students. What will be their respective ranks from the bottom in the class?

A. 20th and 24th B. 24th and 20th
C. 25th and 21st D. None of these
E. Data inadequent

2. In a class of 42 students, Mahesh's rank is 16th from the bottom. What is his rank from the top?

A. 25th B. 26th
C. 24th D. 27th
E. None of these

3. A class of boys stands in a single line. One boy is nineteenth in order from both the ends. How many boys are there in the class?

A. 27 B. 37
C. 38 D. 39
E. None of these

4. In a queue, Amrita is 10th from the front while Mukul is 25th from behind and Mamata is just in the middle of the two. If there be 50 persons in the queue, what position does Mamata occupy from the front?

A. 20th B. 19th
C. 18th D. 17th
E. None of these

5. In a row of trees, one tree is 8th from one end and 3rd from the other. How many trees are there in the row?

A. 11 B. 9
C. 10 D. 12
E. None of these

6. If Janki is 12 ahead in rank of Pallavi who ranks 15th from last, then how many students are there in the class if Janki ranks 4th in order of merit?

A. 23 B. 27
C. 31 D. 30
E. None of these

7. In a row of trees, one tree is fifth from either end of the row. How many trees are in the row?

A. 11 B. 8
C. 10 D. 9
E. None of these

8. Jaya ranks 5th in a class of 53. What is her rank from the bottom in the class?

A. 49th B. 48th
C. 47th (d) 50th
E. None of these

9. Mohan ranks twenty- first in a class of sixty-five students. What will be his (Mohan's) rank if the lowest candidate is assigned rank 1?

A. 44th B. 45th
C. 46th D. Data inadequate
E. None of these

10. In a row of boys, Rajan is tenth from the right and Suraj is tenth from the left. When Rajan and Suraj interchange their positions, Suraj will be twenty-seventh from the left. Which of the following will be Rajan's position from the right?

A. Tenth B. Twenty- sixth
C. Twenty-ninth D. Twenty-fifth
E. None of these

11. Uma ranked 8th from the top and 37th from bottom in a class. How many students are there in the class?
A. 47 B. 46
C. 45 D. 48
E. None of these

12. In a queue, Sadiq is 14th from the front and Joseph is 17th from the end, while Jane is in between Sadiq and Joseph. If Sadiq be ahead of Joseph and there be 48 persons in the queue, how many persons are there between Sadiq and Jane?
A. 5 B. 6
C. 7 D. 8
E. None of these

13. Rohan ranked eleventh from the top and twenty-seventh from the bottom among the students who passed the annual examination in a class. If the number of students who failed in the examination was 12, how many students appeared for the examination?
A. 48
B. 49
C. 50
D. Cannot be determined
E. None of these

14. There are five different houses, A to E, in a row. A is to the right of B and E is to the left of C and right of A, and B is to the right of D. Which of the houses is in the middle?
A. B B. A
C. D D. E
E. None of these

ANSWERS

1	2	3	4	5	6	7	8	9	10
C	D	B	C	C	C	D	A	B	E
11	**12**	**13**	**14**						
E	D	B	B						

EXPLANATORY ANSWERS

1. Number of students behind Anu in rank
= (31 − 7) = 24

So, Anu is 25th from the bottom.
So, Number of students behind Vinay in rank
= (31 − 11) = 20

So, Vinay is 21st from the bottom.
Trick : This question can be solved easily by using formula,
Anu's rank from the bottom = 31 − 7 + 1 = 25th
Vinay's rank from the bottom = 31 − 11 + 1 = 21st.

2. Number of students ahead Mahesh in rank = 42 − 16 = 26
So, Mahesh's rank is 27th from the top.
Trick : This question can be solved by formula also.
Mahesh's rank from the top = 42 − 16 + 1 = 27th.
Formula Rank of a person from upper or left end = (Total number of persons in row) − (Rank of that person from lower or right end) + 1.

3. Clearly, number of boys in the row
= (18 + 18 + 1) = 37
Trick : The question can be solved by formula also, total number of boys in the row = 19 + 19 − 1 = 37
Formula total number of persons in a row or class = (Rank of a person from upper end or left end) + (Rank of that person from lower or right end) − 1.

4. Number of persons between Amrita and Mukul
= 50 − (10 + 25) = 15.

Since Mamta lies in middle of these 15 persons, So Mamta's position is 8th from Amrita *i.e.*, 18th from the front.

5. The number of trees in the row are :

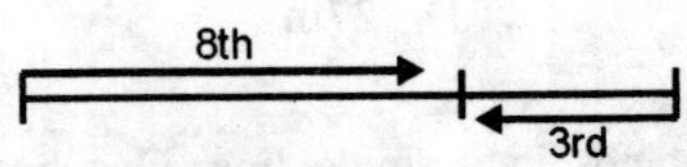

(8 + 3) − 1 = 10

6.
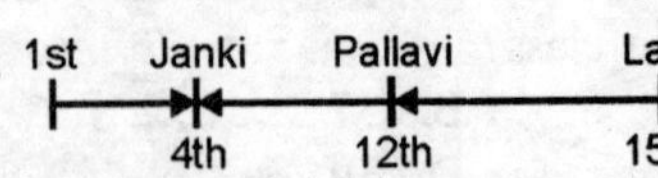

The total number of students are :
4 + 12 + 15 = 31

7.
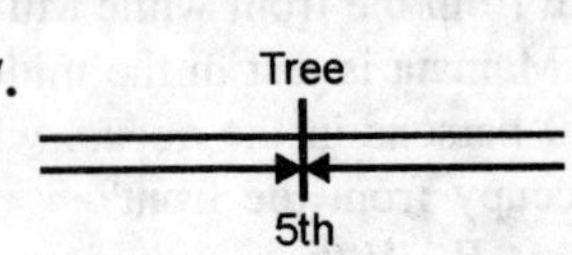

Total number of trees in the row are :
(5 + 5) − 1 = 9

8.
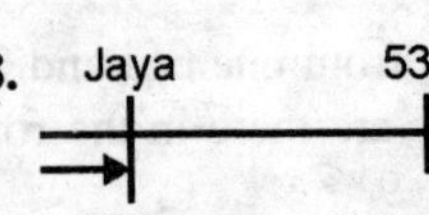

Jaya's rank from the bottom is :
(53 − 5) + 1 = 49th.

9. 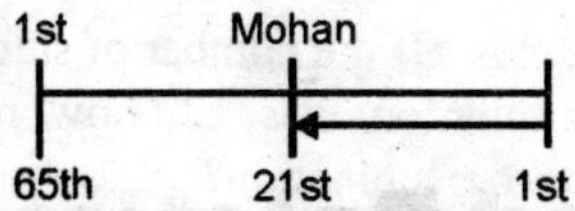

Question asked means Mohan's rank from the last. Mohan's rank is (65 – 21) + 1 = 45th

10. 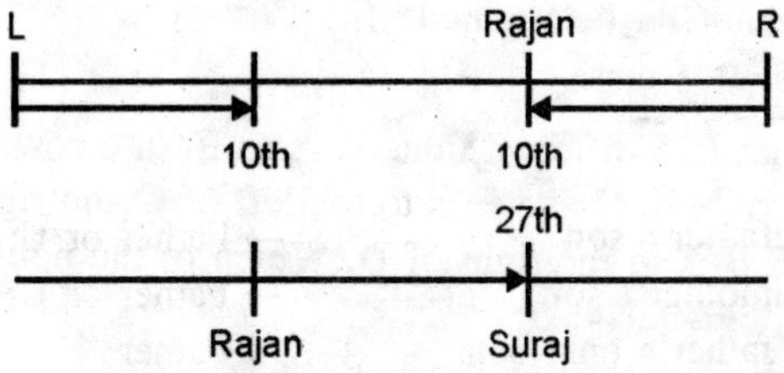

As the position of boys is equal from both ends, Rajan will also be 27th from the right after changing positions.

11. 

Total number of students in the class are :
(8 + 37) – 1= 44

12. 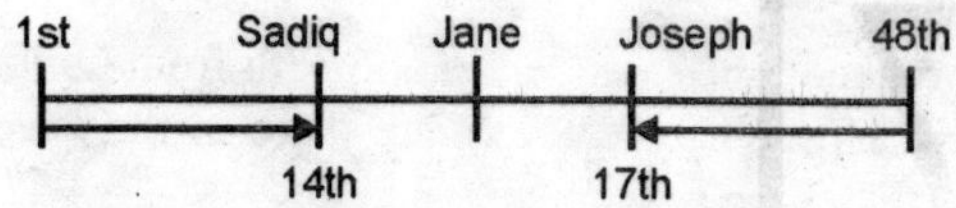

Sadiq's position from last is :

(48 – 14) + 1 = 35th

Number of persons between Sadiq and Joseph are = (35 – 17) – 1 = 17

Jane is in between Sadiq and Joseph i.e., at 9th position between Sadiq and Joseph.

So, there are 8 persons between Sadiq and Jane.
Note : (8 + 8) + 1 = 17

13. 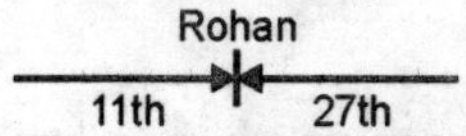

Number of students who passed the examination (11 + 27) – 1 = 37

Those who failed = 12

Total number of students who appeared in the examination = 37 + 12 = 49.

14. The houses in the row are: D B A E C.

●●●

7 Blood Relations

Definition

A person who is related to another by birth rather than by marriage.

Module objective

Blood relations of a group of persons are given in jumbled form. In these tests, the success of a candidate depends upon knowledge of the Blood Relations, some of which are summarized below. The questions which are asked in this section depend upon Relation.

Prerequisites

To remember easily the relations may be divided into two sides as given below:

1. Relations of Paternal side

1. Father's father → Grandfather
2. Father's mother → Grandmother
3. Father's brother → Uncle
4. Father's sister → Aunt
5. Children of uncle → Cousin
6. Wife of uncle → Aunt
7. Children of aunt → Cousin
8. Husband of aunt → Uncle

2. Relations of Maternal side

1. Mother's father → Maternal grandfather
2. Mother's mother → Maternal grandmother
3. Mother's brother → Maternal uncle
4. Mother's sister → Aunt
5. Children of maternal uncle → Cousin
6. Wife of maternal uncle → Maternal aunt

3. Relations from one generation to next

Generation I: Grandfather, grandmother, maternal grandfather, maternal grandmother

↓

Generation II: Mother, father, uncle, aunt, maternal uncle, maternal aunt

↓

Generation III: Self, sister, sister-in-law, brother, brother-in-law

↓

Generation IV: Son, daughter, nephew, niece

Relations

1. Grandfather's son → Father or Uncle
2. Grandmother's son → Father or Uncle
3. Grandfather's only son → Father
4. Grandmother's only son → Father
5. Mother's or father's mother → Grandmother
6. Son's wife → Daughter-in-Law
7. Daughter's husband → Son-in-Law
8. Husband's or wife's sister → Sister-in-Law
9. Brother's son → Nephew
10. Brother's daughter → Niece
11. Uncle or aunt's son or daughter → Cousin
12. Sister's husband → Brother-in-Law
13. Brother's wife → Sister-in-Law
14. Grandson's or grand daughter's daughter → Great grand daughter

Solved Examples

Type-1

1. If A + B means A is the mother of B; A × B means A is the father of B; A $ B means A is the brother of B and A @ B means A is the sister of B then which of the following means P is the son of Q?

A. Q + R @ P @ N B. Q + R * P @ N
C. Q × R $ P @ N D. Q × R $ P $ N
E. None of these

Solution: (D)

Q × R = Q is the mother of R [–Q, ±R]
R $ P = R is the brother of P [+R, ±P]
P $ N = P is the brother of N [+P, ±N]
Therefore P is the son of Q.

Type-2

2. A has 3 children, B is the brother of C and C is the sister of D, E who is the wife of A is the mother of D. There is only one daughter of the husband of E. What is the relation between D and B?

Solution: With the chart

+A –E
↓
+ B + D – C

Therefore, D is a boy because there is only one daughter of E. Hence, B is the brother of D.

Type-3

3. Pointing to a photograph, Rekha says to Lalli, "The girl in the photo is the second daughter of the wife of only son of the grandmother of my younger sister." How this girl of photograph is related to Rekha?

Solution: First Method

1. Grandmother of younger sister of Rekha → Grandmother of Rekha
2. Wife of only son of grandmother → Mother of Rekha
3. Younger daughter of the mother → Younger sister.

4. Pointing to a photograph Arun said, 'she is the mother of my brother's son's wife's daughter'. How is Arun related to the lady?

A. Uncle B. Daughter-in-law
C. Cousin D. Both A and C
E. None of these

Explanation: The woman in the photograph is Arun Brother's daughter-in-law. Because son's wife's daughter is daughter-in-law to his brother.

5. If D is the brother of B, how B is related to C? To answer this question which of the statements is/are necessary?

1. The son of D is the grandson of C.
2. B is the sister of D.

A. Only 1
B. Only 2
C. Either 1 or 2
D. 1 and 2 both are required
E. None of these

Ans. (D) Given: D is the brother of B.
From statement 1, we can detect that D is son of C (son of D is the grandson of C). From statement 2, we can detect that B is 'Female' (sister of D). Therefore, B is daughter of C.

Directions (Qs. 6-10) : *Read the following information carefully and answer the questions given below:*

A B D F G H and K are seven members of a family. They belong to three generations. There are two married couples belonging to two different generations. D is son of H and is married to K. F is granddaughter of B. G's father is grandfather of A. B's husband is father-in-law of K. H has only one son.

6. How is F related to G?

A. Son B. Nephew
C. Niece D. data inadequate
E. None of these

Ans. A

7. How is H related to B?

A. Father B. Father-in-law
C. Uncle D. data inadequate
E. None of these

Ans. E

8. How is K related to G?

A. Sister-in-law B. Sister
C. Niece D. data inadequate
E. None of these

Ans. C

9. Which of the following is the pair of married ladies?

A. HK B. HD
C. KF D. BF
E. None of these

Ans. D

10. How many female members are there among them?

A. Two B. Three
C. Four D. data inadequate
E. None of these

Ans. E

MULTIPLE CHOICE QUESTIONS

1. P is the mother of K; K is the sister of D; D is the father of J. How is P related to J?

A. Mother
B. Grandmother
C. Aunt
D. Data inadequate
E. None of these

2. If P $ Q means P is the father of Q; P # Q means P is the mother of Q and P * Q means P is the sister of Q, then N # L $ P * Q shows which of the relation of Q to N?

A. Grandson
B. Granddaughter
C. Nephew
D. Data is inadequate
E. None of these

3. If A $ B means A is the brother of B; A @ B means A is the wife of B; A # B means A is the daughter of B and A * B means A is the father of B, which of the following indicates that U is the father-in-law of P?

A. P @ Q $ T # U * W
B. P @ W $ Q * T # U
C. P @ Q $ W * T # U
D. P @ Q $ T # W * U
E. None of these

4. Introducing a man, a woman said, "He is the only son of the mother of my mother". How is the woman related to the man?

A. Mother B. Sister
C. Niece D. Maternal aunt
E. None of these

5. Pointing to Gopi, Nalni says, "I am the daughter of the only son of his grandfather". How Nalni is related to Gopi?

A. Niece B. Daughter
C. Sister D. Cannot be determined
E. None of these

6. A's son B is married with C whose sister D is married to E the brother of B. How D is related to A?

A. Sister B. Daughter's-in-law
C. Sister-in-law D. Cousin
E. None of these

7. Pointing to a lady a person said, "The son of her only brother is the brother of my wife." How is the lady related to the person?

A. Maternal aunt B. Grandmother
C. Sister of father-in-law D. Cannot be determined
E. None of these

8. 1. B5D means B is the father of D.
2. B9D means B is the sister of D.
3. B4D means B is the brother of D.
4. B3D means B is the wife of D.

Which of the following means F is the mother of K?

A. F3M5K B. F5M3K
C. F9M4N3K D. F3M5N3K
E. None of these

9. A $ B means A is the father of B; A # B means A is the sister of B; A * B means A is the daughter of B and A @ B means A is the brother of B. Which of the following indicates that M is the wife of Q?

A. Q $ R # T @ M B. Q $ R @ T # M
C. Q $ R * T # M D. Q $ R @ T * M
E. None of these

10. If A $ B means A is the brother of B; B * C means B is the son of C; C @ D means C is the wife of D and A # D means A is the son of D, how C is related to A?

A. Maternal grandmother B. Maternal aunt
C. Aunt D. Mother
E. None of these

11. If A $ B means B is the father of A; A # B means B is the mother of A; A * B means B is the sister of A and A @ B means B is the husband of A, which of the following indicates that N is the grandmother of P?

A. P * Q # M $ N B. P @ Q $ M # N
C. P # Q $ N * M D. Both A and B
E. None of these

12. Anupam said to a lady sitting in a car, "The only daughter of the brother of my wife is the sister-in-law of the brother of your sister". How the husband of the lady is related to Anupam?

A. Maternal uncle B. Uncle
C. Father D. Son-in-law
E. None of these

13. If P + Q means P is the brother of Q; P × Q means P is the wife of Q and P % Q means P is the daughter of Q then which of the following means D is the uncle of A?

A. A % B × C + D B. A × B + C % D
C. A + C % B × D D. Both A and B
E. None of these

14. A is the son of C; C and Q are sisters; Z is the mother of Q and P is the son of Z. Which of the following statements is true?

A. P and A are cousins
B. P is the maternal uncle of A
C. Q is the maternal grandfather of A
D. C and P are sisters
E. None of these

15. M is the father of N who is the son of V. In order to know the relation of M to P, which of the statement/statements is/are necessary?

1. P is the brother of V.
2. The daughter of N is the granddaughter of V.

A. Only (1) B. Only (2)
C. Either (1) or (2) D. (1) and (2) both
E. None of these

16. If X + Y means X is the daughter of Y; X – Y means X is the brother of Y; X % Y means X is the father of Y and X × Y means X is the sister of Y. Which of the following means I is the niece of J?

A. J – N % C × I B. I × C – N % J
C. J + M × C % I D. I × C + N – J
E. None of these

Directions (Qs. 17 and 18): *Each of these questions is based on the following information:*

1. A + B means A is the mother of B.
2. A – B means A is the sister of B.
3. A * B means A is the father of B.
4. A β B means A is the brother of B.

17. Which of the following means Q is the grandfather of P?

A. P + N * M * Q B. Q * N * M + P
C. Q β M β N * P D. Both A and B
E. None of these

18. Which of the following means that N is the maternal uncle of M?

A. N β P – L + E – M
B. N – Y + A β M
C. M – Y * P – N
D. N β C + F * M
E. None of these

Directions (Qs. no. 19 and 20): *Each of these questions is based on the following information:*

1. M % N means M is the son of N.
2. M @ N means M is the sister of N.
3. M $ N means M is the father of N.

19. Which of the following shows the relation that C is the granddaughter of E?
A. C % B $ F $ E   B. B $ F $ E % C
C. C @ B % F % E   D. E % B $ F $ C
E. None of these

20. Which of the following shows the relation that S is the father of Q?
A. S @ P $ Q   B. Q @ P % S
C. Q $ S @ P   D. All of these
E. None of these

21. I am only son for my parents. The man in picture is my Father's son. Who is he?
A. He himself   B. Father
C. Brother   D. Cannot be determined
E. None of these

22. If A + B means A is the sister of B; A × B means A is the wife of B, A % B means A is the father of B and A – B means A is the brother of B. Which of the following means T is the daughter of P?
A. P × Q % R + S – T   B. P × Q % R – T + S
C. P × Q % R + T – S   D. P × Q % R + S + T
E. None of these

23. Pointing to a woman, Abhijit said, "Her granddaughter is the only daughter of my brother." How is the woman related to Abhijit?
A. Sister   B. Grandmother
C. Mother-in-law   D. Mother
E. None of these

24. Amit said, "This girl is the wife of the grandson of my mother". How is Amit related to the girl?
A. Father   B. Grandfather
C. Husband   D. Father-in-law
E. None of these

25. A and B are children of D. Who is the father of A? To answer this question which of the statements (1) and (2) is necessary?
1. C is the brother of A and the son of E.
2. F is the mother B.
A. Only (1)   B. Only (2)
C. Either (1) or (2)   D. (1) and (2) both
E. None of these

26. Pointing to a man on the stage, Rita said, "He is the brother of the daughter of the wife of my husband." How is the man on the stage related to Rita?
A. Husband   B. Cousin
C. Nephew   D. Son
E. None of these

27. A party consists of grandmother, father, mother, four sons and their wives and one son and two daughters to each of the sons. How many females are there is all?
A. 14   B. 16
C. 18   D. 24
E. None of these

28. Lakshmi and Meena are Rohan's wives. Shalini is Meena's Step-daughter. How is Lakshmi related to Shalini?
A. Sister   B. Mother-in-Law
C. Mother   D. Step-mother
E. None of these

29. Daya has a brother Anil. Daya is the son of Chandra. Bimal is Chandra's father. In terms of relationship, what is Anil of Bimal?
A. Son   B. Grandson
C. Brother   D. Grandfather
E. None of these

30. Dikshitha's mother is the only daughter of Monika's father. How is Monika's husband related to Dikshitha?
A. Uncle   B. Father
C. Grandfather   D. Brother
E. Data inadequate

31. If (*i*) M is brother of N; (*ii*) B is brother of N; and (*iii*) M is brother of D, then which of the following statements is definitely true?
A. N is brother of B   B. N is brother of D
C. M is brother of B   D. D is brother of M
E. None of these

32. Deepak is brother of Ravi. Rekha is sister of Atul. Ravi is son of Rekha. How is Deepak related to Rekha?
A. Son   B. Brother
C. Nephew   D. Father
E. None of these

33. A is B's sister. C is B's mother. D is C's father. E is D's mother. Then, how is A related to D?
A. Grandmother   B. Grandfather
C. Daughter   D. Granddaughter
E. None of these

34. Given that:
1. A is brother of B.
2. C is father of A
3. D is brother of E.
4. E is daughter of B.
The uncle of D is
A. A   B. B
C. C   D. E
E. None of these

35. Pointing to a girl Sandeep said, "She is the daughter of the only sister of my father." How is Sandeep related to the girl?
A. Uncle   B. Cousin
C. Father   D. Grandfather
E. None of these

36. Pointing to a boy in the photograph Reena said, "He is the only son of the only child of my grandfather." How Reena is related to that boy?
A. Mother   B. Sister
C. Aunt   D. Cannot be determined
E. None of these

37. A * B means A is the sister of B
1. A $ B means B is the mother of A
2. A + B means A is the brother of B
3. A = B means B is the father of A.
Which of the following means M is the maternal uncle of N?
A. M = P + Q * N B. N + P = Q * M
C. N * P $ Q * M D. Data is inadequate
E. None of these

38. If M × N means M is the daughter of N; M + N means M is the father of N; M % N means M is the mother of N and M – N means M is the brother of N then P % Q + R – T × K indicates which relation of P to K?
A. Daughter-in-law B. Sister-in-law
C. Aunt D. Both A and B
E. None of these

39. If P + Q means P is the brother of Q; P × Q means P is the father of Q and P – Q means P is the sister of Q, which of the following relations shows that I is the niece of K?
A. K + Y + Z – I B. K + Y × I – Z
C. Z – I × Y + K D. K × Y + I – Z
E. None of these

40. Pointing towards a girl, Abhisek says, "This girl is the daughter of only a child of my father." What is the relation of Abhisek's wife to that girl?
A. Daughter B. Mother
C. Aunt D. Sister
E. None of these

41. Pointing towards a man, a woman said, "His mother is the only daughter of my mother." How is the woman related to the man?
A. Mother B. Grandmother
C. Sister D. Daughter
E. None of these

42. If P $ Q means P is the brother of Q; P # Q means P is the mother of Q; P * Q means P is the daughter of Q in A # B $ C * D, who is the father?
A. D B. B
C. C D. Data is inadequate
E. None of these

43. Introducing Suchendra, Naman says, "She is the wife of only nephew of only brother of my mother." How Suchendra is related to Naman?
A. Wife B. Sister
C. Sister-in-law D. Data is inadequate
E. None of these

44. If A + B means A is the brother of B; A % B means A is the father of B and A × B means A is the sister of B. Which of the following means M is the uncle of P?
A. M % N × P B. N × P % M
C. M + S % R % P D. M + K % T × P
E. None of these

45. Pointing to Varman, Madhav said, "I am the only son of one of the sons of his father." How is Varman related to Madhav?
A. Nephew B. Uncle
C. Father or Uncle D. Father
E. None of these

46. Introducing a woman, Shashank said, "She is the mother of the only daughter of my son." How that woman is related to Shashank?
A. Daughter B. Sister-in-law
C. Wife D. Daughter-in-law
E. None of these

47. If A + B means B is the brother of A; A × B means B is the husband of A; A – B means A is the mother of B and A % B means A is the father of B, which of the following relations shows that Q is the grandmother of T?
A. Q – P + R % T B. P × Q % R – T
C. P × Q % R + T D. P + Q % R – T
E. None of these

48. 1. A3P means A is the mother of P
2. A4P means A is the brother of P
3. A9P means A is the husband of P
4. A5P means A is the daughter of P
Which of the following means that K is the mother-in-law of M?
A. M9N3K4J B. M9N5K3J
C. K5J9M3N D. K3J9N4M
E. None of these

49. Pointing to a photograph Anjali said, "He is the son of the only son of my grandfather." How is the man in the photograph related to Anjali?
A. Brother B. Uncle
C. Son D. Data is inadequate
E. None of these

50. Pointing to a person, Deepak said, "His only brother is the father of my daughter's father". How is the person related to Deepak?
A. Father B. Grandfather
C. Uncle D. Brother-in-law
E. None of these

ANSWERS

1	2	3	4	5	6	7	8	9	10
B	D	A	C	C	B	C	A	D	D

11	12	13	14	15	16	17	18	19	20
D	D	D	B	A	D	D	A	C	B
21	**22**	**23**	**24**	**25**	**26**	**27**	**28**	**29**	**30**
A	B	D	D	B	D	A	C	B	B
31	**32**	**33**	**34**	**35**	**36**	**37**	**38**	**39**	**40**
C	A	D	A	B	B	D	D	B	B
41	**42**	**43**	**44**	**45**	**46**	**47**	**48**	**49**	**50**
A	A	A	D	C	D	A	B	A	C

EXPLANATORY ANSWERS

1. P is the mother of K
K is the sister of D
D is the father of J.
Therefore, J is the nephew or niece of K and P is the grandmother of J.

2. As the sex of Q is not known, hence, data is inadequate.

3. P @ Q → P is the wife of Q ....(1)
Q $ T → Q is the brother of T ...(2)
T # U → T is the daughter of U
Hence, → Q is the son of U ...(3)
U * W → U is the father of W.
From (1) and (3), U is the father-in-law of P.

4. The man is the only son of the mother of the woman. Hence, the man is the maternal uncle of the woman. So, the woman is the niece of the man.

5. Nalni is the daughter of the only son of Gopi's grandfather. Hence, it's clear that Nalni is the sister of Gopi.

6. Since E is the brother of B. Therefore, A is the father of E, but D is the wife of E.
Hence, D is the daughter-in-law of A.

7. Brother of person's wife → brother-in-law of the person. Hence, the son of lady's brother is brother-in-law of the person. Therefore, the brother of the lady is the father-in-law of the person. Hence, the lady is the sister of the person's father-in-law.

8. F3M → F is the wife of M
M5K → M is the father of K
Therefore, F is the mother of K.

9. Q $ R → Q is the father of R
R @ T → R is the brother of T
Hence, → Q is the father of T
T * M → T is the daughter of M
Hence, → M is the mother of T
Hence, M is the wife of Q.

10. A $ B → A is the brother of B
B * C → B is the son of C
Hence, → A is the son of C
C @ D → C is the wife of D
Hence, → C is the mother of A.

12. Anupam's son-in-law is the brother of the lady who was sitting in the car. Hence, the husband is also the son-in-law of Anupam.

14. C and Q are sisters and A is the son of C. Hence, C is the mother of A or Z is the mother Q.
Hence, Z is the maternal grandmother of A. P is the son of Z. Hence, P is the maternal uncle of A.

15. M is the father of N and N is the son of V.
Hence, V is the mother of N.
From (1), P is the brother of V
Therefore, M is the brother-in-law of P because V is the wife of M.
From (2), the daughter of N, is the granddaughter of V.
From this we do not get any relation of M to P.

16. I × C → I is the sister of C
C + N → C is the daughter of N and N – J → N is the brother of I.
Hence, I is niece of J.

18. N β P → N is the brother of P
P – L → P is the sister of L
L + E → L is the mother of E
E – M → E is the sister of M.
Hence, L is the mother of M, P is the maternal aunt of M and N is the maternal uncle of M.

19-20. Each of these questions is based on the following information:
1. M % N means M is the son of N.
2. M @ N means M is the sister of N.
3. M $ N means M is the father of N.

19. C @ B → C is the sister of B
B % F → B is the son of F
Hence, → C is the daughter of F
F % E → F is the son of E
Hence, → C is the granddaughter of E.

20. Q is sister of P and P is son of S *i.e.* S is father of P. As Q is sister of P hence S is father of Q also.
So, answer is option B.

22. P × Q → P is the wife of Q
Q % R → Q is the father of R
R – T → R is the brother of T
T + S → T is the sister of S.
Therefore, T is the daughter of P.

23. Daughter of Abhijit's brother → niece of Abhijit. Thus the granddaughter of the woman is Abhijit's niece. Hence, the woman is the mother of Abhijit.

24. The girl is the wife of grandson of Amit's mother *i.e.*, the girl is the wife of son of Amit. Hence, Amit is the father-in-law of the girl.

25. A and B are children of D.
From (1), C is the brother B and son of E.
Since, the sex of D and E are not known. Hence (1) is not sufficient to answer the question.
From (2). F is the mother of B. Hence, F is also the mother of A. Hence D is the father of A.
Thus, (2) is sufficient to answer the question.

26. Wife of Husband - Herself; Brother of daughter - Son. So, the man is Rita's Son.

35. The girl is the daughter of the sister of Sandeep's father. Hence, the girl is the cousin or Sandeep is the cousin of the girl.

36. The boy in the photograph is the only son of Reena's grandfather's only son; *i.e.,* the boy is the only son of Reena's father. Hence, the boy is the brother of Reena or Reena is the sister of the boy.

38. P % Q → P is the mother of Q
Q + R → Q is the father of R
R – T → R is the brother of T
Hence, → Q is the father of T
T × K → T is the daughter of K
Hence, → Q is the husband of K
Therefore, P is the mother-in-law of K

39. K + Y → K is the brother of Y
Y × I → Y is the father of I
Hence, → K is the uncle of I
and I – Z → I is the sister of Z
Hence, → I is the niece of K.

40. Only the child of my father means 'Abhisek' himself. This means the girl is the daughter of Abhisek. Hence, Abhisek's wife is the mother of the girl.

41. Only daughter of my mother → myself.
Hence, the woman is the mother of the man.

42. A is the mother of B, B is the brother of C and C is the daughter of D. Hence, D is the father.

A (Parents) D
| |
B - is - Brother - of – C

43. Brother of mother means maternal uncle.
Hence only nephew of Naman's maternal uncle means Naman himself. Therefore Suchendra is the wife of Naman.

44. M + K → M is the brother of K
K % T → K is the father of T
T × P → T is the sister of P
Therefore, K is the father of P and M is the uncle of P.

45. Madhav is the only son of one of the sons of Varman's father → Either Varman is the father or uncle of Madhav.

46. The woman is the mother of Shashank's grand-daughter. Hence, the woman is the daughter-in-law of Shashank.

47. Q – P → Q is the mother of P
P + R → R is the brother of P
Hence, → Q is the mother of R
R % T → R is the father of T.
Hence, Q is the grandmother of T.

48. M9N → M is the husband of N
N5K → N is the daughter of K
Hence, → M is the son-in-law of K
K3J → K is the mother of J
Hence, → K is a lady
Hence, → K is the mother-in-law of M.

49. The man in the photograph is son of Anjali's grandfather's son *i.e.,* the son of Anjali's father. Hence, the boy is the brother of Anjali.

50. Father of Deepak's daughter's father → Deepak's father. Hence, the person in the brother of Deepak's father. Therefore, the person is the uncle of Deepak.

●●●

8 Statement Analysis

In these questions, a series of interlinked information or data is given. Quantitatively analysis of given information or data provides certain conclusions.

In Statement Analysis (Problem Solving) questions, all given information has to be interpreted and arranged step-by-step. One should be careful that no given data is left incorporated. A brief glimpse to all questions asked on given data is helpful in preparing the solution format.

Solved Examples

Directions: *Read the following information carefully and answer the questions given below:*

In a family of six persons—A, B, C, D, E and F—there are three males and three females. There are two married couples and two persons are unmarried. Each one of them reads different newspapers, viz. Times of India, Indian Express, Hindustan Times, Financial Times, Navbharat Times and Business Standard. E, who reads Indian Express, is mother-in-law of A, who is wife of C. D is the father of F and he does not read Times of India or Business Standard. B reads Navbharat Times and is the sister of F, who reads Hindustan Times. C does not read Business Standard.

1. Who among the following reads the Times of India?

A. C
B. D
C. A
D. Data inadequate
E. None of these

2. How is F related to E?

A. Daughter
B. Brother
C. Son
D. Data inadequate
E. None of these

3. Which of the following is one of the married couples?

A. D-B
B. D-E
C. B-F
D. E-F
E. None of these

4. Which of the following newspapers is read by 'A'?

A. Times of India
B. Navbharat Times
C. Financial Times
D. Data inadequate
E. None of these

5. How many sons does E have?

A. Four
B. Three
C. Two
D. One
E. None of these

MULTIPLE CHOICE QUESTIONS

Directions (Qs. No. 1-5) : *Study the following information carefully and answer the questions given below:*

A, B, C, D, E, F and G are 7 friends left for 7 different cities – Delhi, Chennai, Hyderabad, Bangalore, Kolkata, Chandigarh and Jaipur, each one on a different day of the week. C left for Jaipur on Monday. On the last day of the week, the person left for Bangalore. E left the next day of A who left for Chandigarh and on the previous day of G. D left for Kolkata on Friday. B didn't leave for either Hyderabad or Bangalore and G left for Delhi.

1. On which day of the week did B leave?

A. Sunday B. Saturday
C. Monday D. Tueday
E. None of these

2. Who left for Bangalore?

A. E B. B
C. G D. F
E. None of these

3. Who left on Tuesday?

A. A B. C

C. G	D. F
E. None of these

4. On which day of the week did E leave?
A. Friday	B. Sunday
C. Wednesday	D. Thursday
E. None of these

5. Which of the following Combination is not right?
A. C – Jaipur	B. F – Bangalore
C. A – Chandigarh	D. E – Kolkata
E. None of these

Directions (Qs. No. 6-10) : *Study the following information carefully and answer the questions given below:*

Eight friends – Romil, Ramesh, Rakesh, Rohit, Rahul, Abhijit, Abhishek and Anil – are sitting around a circular table, not necessarily in the same order. Four of them are facing inside others are facing outside. They are belong to eight different cities – Bhopal, Patna, Kolkata, Delhi, Gwalior, Bengaluru, Chennai and Rajkot, but not necessarily in the same order. Abhijit faces the Centre and sits third to the right of Rakesh. Rohit belongs to Kolkata and faces the person who belongs to Bengaluru. Abhishesk sits third to the right of Ramesh, who stays in Bhopal. The persons who belong to Delhi and Gwalior are facing to the same direction (inside or outside). Rahul is sitting between the person who belongs to Kolkata and the one from Rajkot respectively. Romil belongs to Gwalior and Rakesh belongs to Patna. The person who belongs to Chennai is facing outward and immediate neighbour of Rajkot. Anil is immediate neighbour of the persons who belong to Gwalior and Chennai. Rahul is immediate left of Rohit.

6. Who belongs to Bengaluru?
A. Romil	B. Rohit
C. Anil	D. Abhishek
E. Rahul

7. Immediate neighbours of Romil?
A. Romesh and Rakesh	B. Rahul and Rohit
C. Anil and Ramesh	D. Abhishek and Rahul
E. Rohit and Abhijit

8. Which of the following pair is true?
A. Romil – Bhopal	B. Anil – Bengaluru
C. Rohit – Delhi	D. Abhijit – Delhi
E. Abhishek – Patna

9. Position of Ramesh with respect to Rahul?
A. Third to the right	B. Fourth to the left
C. Fifth to the right	D. Second to the right
E. Third to the left

10. If Rohit and Anil interchange their positions and similarly Abhijit and Rakesh interchange their positions then what is the position of Romil with respect to Rakesh?
A. Third to the left	B. Third to the right
C. Second to the left	D. Immediate left
E. None of these

Directions (Qs. No. 11-15) : *Study the following information carefully and answer the questions given below:*

There are six persons A, B, C, D, E and F in school. Each of the teachers teaches two subjects, one compulsory subject and the other optional subject. D's optional subject was History while three others have it as compulsory subject. E and F have Physics as one of their subjects. F's compulsory subject is Mathematics which is an optional subject of both C and E. History and English are A's subjects but in terms of compulsory and optional subjects, they are just reverse of those of D's. Chemistry is an optional subject of only one of them. The only female teacher in the school has English as her compulsory subject.

11. What is C's compulsory subject?
A. History	B. Physics
C. Chemistry	D. English
E. Mathematics

12. Who is a female member in the group?
A. A	B. B
C. C	D. D
E. E

13. Which of the following has same compulsory and optional subjects as those of F's?
A. D	B. B
C. A	D. C
E. None of these

14. Disregarding which is the compulsory and which is the optional subject, who has the same two subject combination as F?
A. A	B. B
C. E	D. D
E. None of these

15. Which of the following groups has History as the compulsory subject?
A. A, C, D	B. B, C, D
C. C, D	D. A, B, C
E. A, D

Directions (Qs. No. 16-20) : *Study the following information carefully and answer the questions given below:*

Seven boys A, D, Y, U, P, Q and J live in three different buildings – Ashiana, Top-view and Ridge. Each of them is flying kites of different colours i.e. red, green, blue white, black, yellow and pink, not necessarily in that order. Not more than three or less than two stay in any of the buildings. Q is flying a pink and does not live in Ridge building. U does not live in the same building as A or P and is flying a yellow coloured kite. D lives in Ridge building with only one more person and is flying a green kite. None in the Top-view building flies a white kite. P does not fly a blue kite.

16. Who live in Ridge building?
A. D, U	B. D, A, P
C. Y, A, P	D. A, P
E. None of these

17. Who is flying the blue kite?
A. A B. J
C. P D. Data inadequate
E. None of these

18. Who flies the red kite?
A. A B. J
C. P D. Data inadequate
E. None of these

19. Who stay in Top-view building?
A. Y, J, P B. A, P
C. A, P, D D. Y, U, J
E. None of these

20. What coloured kite is J flying?
A. Blue B. White
C. Black D. Data inadequate
E. None of these

Directions (Qs. No. 21-25) : *Study the following information carefully and answer the questions given below:*

Six exams Maths, Science, History, Economics, English and Hindi are to be scheduled starting from 2nd March and ending on 8th march wit Sunday being an off day, not necessarily in the same order. Each of the exam has different time duration: 40 mins, 50 mins, 60 mins, 75 mins, 90 mins and 100 mins, again not necessarily in the same order. 8th march is not sunday and an exam of 40 mins is scheduled on that day. Maths exam is for less than 60 mins and is scheduled immediately before English exam. There are two exams scheduled between Hindi exam which is for 100 mins and History exam which is for 60 mins. English exam is before Sunday and there are two days between sunday and maths exam. Economics exam which is for 75 mins is not scheduled on 2nd March. The exam schedules on saturday is of 100 mins.

21. How many exams are scheduled before sunday?
A. Two B. One
C. Five D. Three
E. None of these

22. Which of the following combinations of exam - Day - Time Duration is correct?
A. English -Wednesday - 75 mins
B. Maths - Thursday - 50 mins
C. History - Thursday - 60 mins
D. Hindi - Tuesday - 100 mins
E. None is correct

23. What is the time duration of science exam?
A. 90 mins B. 75 mins
C. 50 mins D. 40 mins
E. None of these

24. On which day is Economics exam scheduled?
A. Monday B. Saturday
C. Tuesday D. Friday
E. Cannot be determined

25. Which day is sunday?
A. 3rd March B. 2nd March
C. 5th March D. 6th March
D. Cannot be determined

Directions (Qs. No. 26-30) : *Study the following information carefully and answer the questions given below:*

Seven persons namely Paramjit, Tarun, Morya, Jeeva, Vaani, Ram and Waqar are good friends and are studying in M.Com, M.A. and M.Sc courses. Three are doing M.Com, two are in M.A. and another two are in M.Sc. Each of them has a very distinct and favourite colour choice ranging from blue, red, yellow, white, black, pink and brown but not necessarily in the same order. None doing M.Com like either red or black. Morya is doing M.A. and he likes blue. Ram is doing M.Sc and likes brown. Jeeva is doing M.Com and likes yellow. Paramjit who does not like red is in the same discipline of Ram. Tarun is in the same discipline of Morya. Vaani does not like pink.

26. Which among the following groups is doing M.Com?
A. Jeeva, Vaani and Waqar
B. Vaani, Waqar and Tarun
C. Jeeva, Vaani and Tarun
D. Jeeva, Paramjit and Ram
E. None of these

27. What is the colour combination choice of those who are in M.Sc discipline?
A. Brown and Pink B. Black and White
C. Black and Brown D. Yellow and Black
E. None of the above

28. Which colour does Vaani like?
A. Yellow B. Pink
C. White D. Brown
E. None of the above

29. What is the colour combination choice of those who are in M.A. discipline?
A. Red and Black
B. Blue and Red
C. Blue and Black
D. Data inadequate
E. None of these

30. Morya is related with which discipline?
A. M.Sc B. M.A.
C. M.Com D. M.Phil
E. None of these

Directions (Qs. No. 31-35) : *Study the following information carefully and answer the questions given below:*

M, K, J, T, R, D and W are seven members of a family. There are two married couples among them belonging to two different generations. Each of them has a different choice of cuisine - Chinese, Continental, Thai, Punjabi, South India, Gujarati and Malwani. The grandfather in the family likes Gujarati food. None of the ladies likes Continental or Thai food. T is the son of M, who likes Chinese food. W is J's daughter-in-law and she likes South Indian food. K is grandfather of D, who likes Punjabi food. J is mother of R, who likes Continental food.

31. How is R related to D?
A. Father B. Brother
C. Uncle D. Data inadequate
E. None of these

32. How many male members are there in the family?
A. 3 B. 4
C. 5 D. Data inadequate
E. None of these

33. Which of the following group contains one each from the same generations?
A. JRT B. JRW
C. MRD D. MWT
E. None of these

34. Which food does T like?
A. Gujarati B. Thai
C. Malwani D. Data inadequate
E. None of these

35. Which of the following combinations represents favourite food of the two married ladies?
A. Malwani, South Indian B. South Indian, Punjabi
C. Punjabi, Malwani D. Data inadequate
E. None of these

Directions (Qs. No. 36-40) : *Study the following information carefully and answer the questions given below:*

Four people were being interviewed for the same job, on the same day but in different rooms (R1, R2, R3 and R4), at different time and by different interviewers. (First sentence – what do you do? Make a table!)

Determine which candidate was interviewed by whom, at which time and in which room. (What can be arranged first in the table? What can logically be the first coloumn? – Room numbers, because other information cannot be logically arranged!)

(*i*) Teena's appointment was just after Mr. Sharma's, which was just after that of the person in room R2.

(*ii*) Mr. Narurkar's appointment was atleast two hours later than Bimal's.

(*iii*) Mr. Joshi's appointment was just after the person who had an interview in room R4, who had an appointment just after Chirag.

(*iv*) Three of the four people were: (1) Deepak, (2) the one with interview in room R1, and (3) the one who was interviewed at 1 p.m. (This is a crazy one!)

(*v*) Interview times were – 11 a.m., 12 noon, 1 p.m., and 2 p.m. (This could be a row heading.)

(*vi*) Sharma, Narurkar, Joshi and Zaidi were interviewers and Teena, Bimal, Chirag and Deepak were the interviewees.

36. Sharma's appointment is with
A. Teena B. Bimal
C. Chirag D. Deepak
E. None of these

37. Deepak's appointment was in room
A. R1 B. R3
C. R2 D. R4
E. None of these

38. Mr. Zaidi interviewed
A. Deepak B. Teena
C. Bimal D. Chirag
E. None of these

39. Who interviewed at 2 p.m.?
A. Mr. Joshi B. Mr. Zaidi
C. Mr. Narurkar D. Mr. Sharma
E. None of these

40. Which candidate was interviewed last?
A. Deepak B. Teena
C. Bimal D. Chirag
E. None of these

Directions (Qs. No. 41-45) : *Study the following information carefully and answer the questions given below:*

P, Q, R, S, T, U and V are 7 friends who travel to college everyday by a particular train which stops at 5 stations – 1, 2, 3, 4 and 5 respectively after it leaves base stations. 3 among them get in the train at the base station. S gets down at the next station at which U gets down. Q gets in with 2 persons and does not get down with either P or T. V alone gets in at station 3 and gets down with R after 1 station. P travels between only 2 stations and gets down at station 5. None of them gets in at station 2. R gets in with U but does not get in with either Q or S. T gets in with 2 others and gets down alone after S. Q and S going to same college and they get down together at station 3. None of them gets down at station 1.

41. At which station does T get down?
A. Station 2 B. Station 4
C. Station 3 D. Station 5
E. None of these

42. At which station does R, U get in?
A. Base station B. Station 2
C. Station 1 D. Station 3
E. None of these

43. After how many station does Q get down?
A. 4 B. 3
C. 1 D. 2
E. None of these

44. At which of the following station does Q and T get in?
A. Base Station B. Station 1
C. Station 2 D. Station 3
E. None of these

45. Which of the following is correct?
A. T gets in at the base station
B. R gets in at the Station 3
C. V gets down at Station 5
D. U gets down at Station 2
E. None of these

Directions (Qs. No. 46-50) : *Study the following information carefully and answer the questions given below:*

A building has eight floors from 1 to 8 in such a way that ground floor is numbered 1, the above floor is numbered 2 and so on. The top most floor is numbered 8. Eight persons G, P, M, R, Q, A, D and C are staying each on one of these floors. A is staying on floor 6. There is a gap of three persons between G and R. C is staying on the topmost floor. Neither P nor M is staying on the floor 5. Q is staying middle of P and M. R is staying on the floor 1. M is not an immediate neighbour of G.

46. Who is staying on the floor no. 7?
A. A　B. P
C. D　D. R
E. M

47. How many persons are staying between D and P?
A. Three　B. Four
C. Two　D. One
E. None of these

48. Who is staying on the second floor?
A. Q　B. M
C. P　D. A
E. Q or M

49. If all persons are arranged in alphabetical order such as A occupies floor 1 then who will occupy floor 5?
A. G　B. Q
C. R　D. M
E. P

50. Immediate neighbours of the person who is staying in floor 3?
A. R and P　B. A and P
C. G and M　D. P and M
E. D and G

Directions (Qs. No. 51-55) : *Study the following information carefully and answer the questions given below:*

Madan and Rohit are in the same team of hockey. Parth defeated Rohit in badminton but lost to Sachin in tennis. Nitin teams with Sagar in football and with Sachin in hockey. Rohit defeated Sachin in chess. Those who play cricket do not play badminton, volleyball or tennis. Madan and Parth are in opposite teams of basketball. Nitin represents his state in cricket while Sagar does so at the district level. Boys who play chess do not play football, basketball or volleyball. Madan and Parth are together in the volleyball team. Boys who play football also play hockey.

51. Name the boys who do not play football.
A. Sachin, Nitin　B. Rohit, Sagar
C. Rohit, Sachin　D. Rohit, Nitin
E. None of these

52. Who plays both hockey and tennis?
A. Sachin　B. Rohit
C. Nitin　D. Parth
E. None of these

53. Which is the most popular game with this group?
A. Cricket　B. Hockey
C. Football　D. Badminton
E. None of these

54. Who plays the largest number of games?
A. Sagar　B. Rohit
C. Parth　D. Nitin
E. None of these

55. Which boy plays both badminton and hockey?
A. Sachin　B. Rohit
C. Nitin　D. Parth
E. None of these

Directions (Qs. No. 56-60) : *Study the following information carefully and answer the questions given below:*

Six friends Abhi, Deep, Myank, Prince, Rambo and Sumit married within a year in the months of February, April, July, September, November and December and in the cities of Ahmedabad, Bengaluru, Chennai, Delhi, Mumbai and Kolkata but not necessarily following the above order. The brides names were Geetu, Jasmeet, Harman, Bindia, Inpreet and Vanshika, once again not following any order. The following are some facts about their weddings.

(*i*) Myank's wedding took place in Chennai, however he was not married to Geetu or Vanshika.
(*ii*) Abhi's wedding took place in Ahmedabad and Rambo's in Delhi; however neither of them was married to Jasmeet or Bindia.
(*iii*) The wedding in Kolkata took place in February.
(*iv*) Harman's wedding took place in April, but not in Ahmedabad.
(*v*) Geetu and Inpreet got married in February and November and in Chennai and Kolkata but not following the above order.
(*vi*) Prince visited Bengaluru and Kolkata only after his marriage in December.
(*vii*) Sumit was married to Jasmine to September.

56. Harman's husband is
A. Abhi　B. Deep
C. Rambo　D. Prince
E. Myank

57. Deep's wedding took place in
A. Bengaluru　B. Mumbai
C. Kolkata　D. Delhi
E. Chennai

58. In Mumbai, the wedding of one of the friends took place in the month of
A. April　B. September
C. November　D. December
E. July

59. Sumit's wedding was held in
A. Bengaluru B. Chennai
C. Kolkata D. Delhi
E. Mumbai

60. Geetu was married to
A. Mayank B. Deep
C. Prince D. Both A and B
E. None of these

ANSWERS

1	2	3	4	5	6	7	8	9	10
B	D	A	C	D	C	C	B	E	A
11	**12**	**13**	**14**	**15**	**16**	**17**	**18**	**19**	**20**
A	D	E	C	D	A	A	C	E	B
21	**22**	**23**	**24**	**25**	**26**	**27**	**28**	**29**	**30**
E	B	D	A	D	A	C	C	B	B
31	**32**	**33**	**34**	**35**	**36**	**37**	**38**	**39**	**40**
C	D	A	B	A	C	B	C	A	A
41	**42**	**43**	**44**	**45**	**46**	**47**	**48**	**49**	**50**
B	C	D	A	A	C	C	B	D	D
51	**52**	**53**	**54**	**55**	**56**	**57**	**58**	**59**	**60**
C	A	B	C	B	C	C	D	A	B

EXPLANATORY ANSWERS

Qs. 1-5

Day	Person	City
Monday	C	Jaipur
Tuesday	A	Chandigarh
Wednesday	E	Hyderabad
Thursday	G	Delhi
Friday	D	Kolkata
Saturday	B	Chennai
Sunday	F	Bangalore

Qs. 6-10

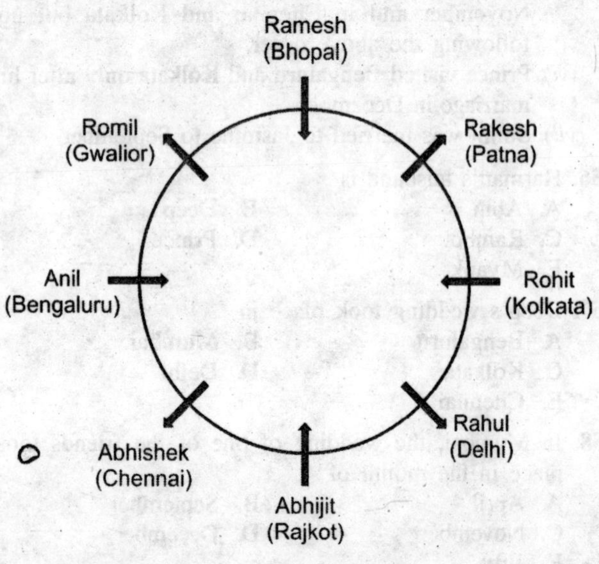

Qs. 15-20

Boy	Building	Kite
A	Top-View	Blue
D	Ridge	Green
Y	Top-View	Black
U	Ridge	Yellow
P	Top-View	Red
Q	Ashiana	Pink
J	Ashiana	White

Qs. No. 21-25

Date	Day	Exam	Time Duration
2nd March	Wednesday	History	60 mins
3rd March	Thursday	Maths	50 mins
4th March	Friday	English	90 mins
5th March	Saturday	Hindi	100 mins
6th March	Sunday	Off	Off
7th March	Monday	Economics	75 mins
8th March	Tuesday	Science	40 mins

Qs. 26-30 :

Persons	Courses	Colours
Jeeva	M.Com	Yellow
Vaani	M.Com	White
Waqar	M.Com	Pink
Morya	M.A.	Blue
Tarun	M.A.	Red
Ram	M.Sc.	Brown
Paramjit	M.Sc.	Black

Qs. 31-35 :

Person	Cuisine	Generation	Relationships
K (Male)	Gujarati	1st	Father of M and R, Grandfather of D and T
J (Female)	Malwani	1st	Wife of K
M (Male)	Chinese	2nd	Son of K and J
W (Female)	South Indian	2nd	Wife of M
R (Male)	Continental	2nd	Brother of M
D (male/ Female)	Punjabi	3rd	Son/Daughter of M &W
T (Male)	Thai	3rd	Son of M

31. R is the brother of M, who is father of D. So, R is uncle of D.

32. We can not determine because there is nothing mentioned about D in the question.

33. J belongs to 1st generation, R belongs to 2nd generation and T belongs to 3rd generation.

34. Thai food

35. J likes Malwani and W likes South Indian.

Qs. 36-40

Interviewee	Interviewer		11 a.m.	12 p.m.	1 p.m.	2 p.m.
Chirag	Sharma	R1	X	Definite	X	X
Bimal	Zaidi	R2	Definite	X	X	X
Deepak	Joshi	R3	X	X	X	Definite
Teena	Narurkar	R4	X	X	Definite	X

Qs. 41-45

Station	Person Get in	Person Get down
Base	Q, S, T	
1	R, U	None
2	None	U
3	V	Q, S
4	P	T
5		P, R, V

Qs. 46-50

Floor No.	Persons
8	C
7	D
6	A
5	G
4	P
3	Q
2	M
1	R

Qs. 51-55

	Madan	Rohit	Parth	Sachin	Nitin	Sagar
Hockey	Y	Y		Y	Y	Y
Badminton		Y	Y		N	N
Tennis			Y	Y	N	N
Chess		Y		Y		
Football		N		N	Y	Y
Basketball	Y	N	Y	N		
Volleyball	Y	N	Y	N	N	N
Cricket					Y	Y

Qs. 56-60

Husband	Wife	Place	Month
Abhi	Vanshika	Ahmedabad	July
Deep	Geetu	Kolkata	February
Myank	Inpreet	Chennai	November
Prince	Bindia	Mumbai	December
Rambo	Harman	Delhi	April
Sumit	Jasmeet	Bengaluru	September

●●●

9 Letter-Number Symbols

These problems involves simple coding. Letters, numbers are coded as numbers/symbols and some special conditions are applicable.

MULTIPLE CHOICE QUESTIONS

Directions (Qs. Nos. 1 to 6): *In each question below is given a group of letters followed by four combinations of digits/symbols numbered A, B, C and D. You have to find out which of the combinations correctly represents the group of letters based on the following coding system and the conditions and mark the numbers of that combination as your answer. If none of the four combinations correctly represents the group of letters, give E i.e. 'None of these' as your answer.*

Letters	A	M	P	J	E	I	R	T	W	B	U	K	Y	Z	H
Digit/Symbol	1	9	2	@	3	©	4	8	7	$	6	%	5	•	Ω

Conditions:

(*i*) If the first letter is a consonant and the last letter is a vowel, their codes are to be interchanged.

(*ii*) If the first letter is a vowel and the last letter is a consonant, both are to be coded as the code for the vowel.

1. UPAMYE
A. 612953 B. 321956
C. 621956 D. 621953
E. None of these

2. JPERTB
A. @3248$ B. @2348@
C. $2348@ D. @23485
E. None of these

3. IMPBEZ
A. ©92$3© B. •92$3•
C. •92$3© D. ©9$23©
E. None of these

4. JETWBH
A. Ω387$@ B. @387$@
C. @387$Ω D. @387$Ω
E. None of these

5. KHAPYI
A. %Ω125% B. ©Ω125%
C. ©Ω215© D. ©Ω125©
E. None of these

6. BPTRKA
A. $284%1 B. 1284%$
C. 1284%1 D. $284%$
E. None of these

Directions (Qs. Nos. 7 to 11): *In each question below is given a set of digits followed by four combinations of letters numbered A, B, C and D. You have to find out which of the combinations correctly represents the set of digits based on the following coding system and the conditions and mark the numbers of that combination as your answer. If none of the four combinations correctly represents the set of digits, give E i.e. 'None of these' as your answer.*

Digit	1	2	3	4	5	6	7	8	9
Letter Code	R	J	I	M	T	K	F	D	B

Conditions:

(*i*) If the first digit is odd and the last digit is even, their codes are to be interchanged.

(*ii*) If the first digit is even and the last digit is odd, both are to be coded as the code for the even digit.

(*iii*) If both the first and the last digits are odd, both are to be coded as 'Z'.

7. 5469381
A. ZMKBIDR B. TMKBIDR
C. ZMKBIDZ D. RMKBIDT
E. None of these

8. 7859624
A. MDTBKJF B. FDTBKJM
C. FDTBKJF D. MDTBKJM
E. None of these

9. 3492618
A. IMBJKRD B. DMBJKRI
C. IBJMKRD D. IMBJKRD
E. None of these

10. 4578369
A. MTFDIKM B. BTFDIKM
C. BTFDIKB D. MTFDIKB
E. None of these

11. 6843192
A. KDMIRBK B. JDMIRBK
C. DIMKRBJ D. KDMIRBJ
E. None of these

Directions (Qs. Nos. 12 to 16): *Read the following information to answer the questions:*

Number:	1	2	3	4	5	6	7	8	9
Symbol :	×	*	?	÷	$	•	+	!	Ω

(*i*) If any number begins by odd number then the odd number is symbolized by @.
(*ii*) If any number ends by even number then the even number is symbolized as ©.

12. Which of the following will be the symbol of 673258?
A. • + ? $! B. @ + ? * !
C. @ ? + $ * ! D. • + ? * $ ©
E. None of these

13. Which of the following will be the symbol of 236475?
A. ? * • ÷ × B. © ? • ÷ + @
C. × ? • ÷ + @ D. © ? ! ÷ + $
E. None of these

14. Which of the following will be the symbol of 846721?
A. © ÷ • + * × B. ! ÷ • + * @
C. ! ÷ • + * × D. © ÷ • + * ×
E. None of these

15. Which of the following will be the symbol of 178524?
A. @ + ! $ * © B. × + ! $ ©
C. @ + ! $ * ÷ D. * + ! $ ÷ Ω
E. None of these

16. Which of the following will be the symbol of 25486?
A. * $ ÷ ! Ω B. * $ ÷ ! ©
C. © $ ÷ ! • D. * $! ÷ •
E. None of these

Directions (Qs. Nos. 17 to 21): *Study the following arrangement carefully and answer the questions given below:*

4 $ 3 Z Y A 5 6 Ω © @ 7 P L E T Q S B 2 8 C 1 M U I X %

17. Which of the following is the fourth to the left of the tenth from the right end of the above arrangement?
A. B B. 7
C. L D. E
E. None of these

18. How many such numbers are there in the above arrangement, each of which is immediately preceded by a number and not immediately followed by a letter?
A. None B. One
C. Two D. Three
E. More than three

19. If all the symbols and letters from the above arrangement are dropped which of the following will be fifth from the left end of the above arrangement?
A. 4 B. 3
C. 5 D. 7
E. 8

20. How many such consonants are there in the above arrangement, each of which is immediately preceded by a letter and immediately followed by a vowel?
A. None B. One
C. Two D. Three
E. More than three

21. Four of the following five are alike in a certain way based on their positions in the above arrangement and so form a group. Which is the one that does not belong to that group?
A. 4ZA B. $Y5
C. CU% D. PTS
E. @LT

Directions (Qs. Nos. 22 to 24): *Study the following series I and II comprising letters/digits/symbols and answer the questions given below.*

Series I: N P Q * 5 4 B Z $ # 3 7 D 9 A ↑ F 8 G H 1 + D K 6

Series II: 7 4 £ J M 1 © Y P 8 Q R 5 T N 6 2 ↓ U A 3 9 @ I S

22. What is the total number of **symbols** in series I each of which is immediately followed by a digit and immediately preceded by a letter **together with** the number of **letters** in series II which are immediately preceded by a symbol and immediately followed by a letter?
A. 5 B. 4
C. 1 D. 3
E. None of these

23. If the first ten elements of series I are picked up and written in reverse order followed by last ten elements of series II without changing the order, which of the following pairs of elements will indicate sixteenth element from left and the eighth element to its left respectively?
A. A, Q B. 3, Q
C. 3, Z D. A, Z
E. None of these

24. If the letters, the digits and the symbols from each series are counted separately, which of the following is lowest in count?
A. Symbols in series I B. Letters in series I
C. Digits in series II D. Symbols in series II
E. None of these

Directions (Qs. Nos. 25 to 28): *Answer these questions referring to the symbol-letter-number sequence given below:*

Reena : 3 # R U 2 + > A P Y B 4
Kareena : Q £ 5 N → F G 8 * D 7 Y
Jessica : O * H T 6 @ C 9 Z K Ω 1

25. If all the symbols from Reena's series, all the letters from Kareena's series and all the numbers from Jessica's series are respectively arranged in the same given order one after the other from the left end, which of the following will be the fifth to the right of the third element from your left?

A. F   B. G
C. Q   D. Y
E. None of These

26. If each symbol which immediately precedes a number in Reena's series, each number which immediately follows a letter in Kareena's series, and each letter which immediately precedes a symbol in Jessica's series are selected, what will be the total number of these elements?

A. Six   B. Three
C. Five   D. Seven
E. None of these

27. Four of the following five are similar in some respect. Find the Odd man out.

A. AF@   B. Y*9
C. 47K   D. P8C
E. BDZ

28. What is the difference between the total letters and total symbols, which are used in the series of Reena, Kareena and Jessica?

A. Eight   B. Five
C. Six   D. Seven
E. None of these

Directions (Qs. Nos. 29 to 34): *In each question below is given a group of letters followed by four combinations of digits/symbols numbered A, B, C and D. You have to find out which of the combinations correctly represents the group of letters based on the following coding system and the conditions and mark the numbers of that combination as your answer. If none of the four combinations correctly represents the group of letters, give E. i.e. 'None of these' as your answer.*

Letters	P	Z	K	A	F	I	D	R	M	G	Q	E	W	S
Digit/Symbol	6	9	3	8	$	2	4	7	#	1	©	5	%	@

Conditions:

(*i*) If the second letter is a consonant and the last letter is a vowel, their codes are to be interchanged.

(*ii*) If the second as well as last letter is a consonant, each one is to be coded as the code for the letter 'F'.

(*iii*) If the third as well as fourth letter is a vowel, then each one is to be coded as 'β'

29. SDGPIA

A. @81624   B. @82614
C. @41628   D. @26184
E. None of these

30. ZIEAKM

A. 923#ββ   B. 92853#
C. 92ββ3#   D. 92583#
E. None of these

31. WARMFQ

A. %©7#$8   B. %87#$©
C. %β7#$β   D. %78©$#
E. None of these

32. EDSKIM

A. 5@4#32   B. 54@32#
C. 5$@3$2   D. 5@32
E. None of these

33. DEQGFA

A. 45©1$8   B. $584©1
C. 8$145©   D. 81$54©
E. None of these

34. MKEZAI

A. #35982   B. #25983
C. #53982   D. #25398
E. None of these

ANSWERS

1	2	3	4	5	6	7	8	9	10
D	E	A	C	B	B	C	A	B	A
11	**12**	**13**	**14**	**15**	**16**	**17**	**18**	**19**	**20**
D	D	E	C	A	B	D	B	D	C
21	**22**	**23**	**24**	**25**	**26**	**27**	**28**	**29**	**30**
C	A	B	D	E	E	A	E	A	C
31	**32**	**33**	**34**						
B	E	A	B						

EXPLANATORY ANSWERS

1. U P A M Y E
↓ ↓ ↓ ↓ ↓ ↓
6 2 1 9 5 3

2. J P E R T B
↓ ↓ ↓ ↓ ↓ ↓
@ 2 3 4 8 $

3. I M P B E Z
↓ ↓ ↓ ↓ ↓ ↓
© 9 2 $ 3 ©

Condition (*ii*) is applicable

4. J E T W B H
↓ ↓ ↓ ↓ ↓ ↓
@ 3 8 7 $ Ω

5. K H A P Y I
↓ ↓ ↓ ↓ ↓ ↓
© Ω 1 2 5 %
Condition (*i*) is applicable

6. B P T R K A
↓ ↓ ↓ ↓ ↓ ↓
1 2 8 4 % $
Condition (*i*) is applicable

7. 5 4 6 9 3 8 1
↓ ↓ ↓ ↓ ↓ ↓ ↓
Z M K B I D Z
Condition (*iii*) is applicable

8. 7 8 5 9 6 2 4
↓ ↓ ↓ ↓ ↓ ↓ ↓
M D T B K J F
Condition (*i*) is applicable

9. 3 4 9 2 6 1 8
↓ ↓ ↓ ↓ ↓ ↓ ↓
D M B J K R I
Condition (*i*) is applicable

10. 4 5 7 8 3 6 9
↓ ↓ ↓ ↓ ↓ ↓ ↓
M T F D I K M
Condition (*ii*) is applicable

11. 6 8 4 3 1 9 2
↓ ↓ ↓ ↓ ↓ ↓ ↓
K D M I R B J

12. 6 7 3 2 5 8
↓ ↓ ↓ ↓ ↓ ↓
• + ? * $ ©
Condition (*ii*) is applicable

13. 2 3 6 4 7 5
↓ ↓ ↓ ↓ ↓ ↓
* ? • ÷ + $

14. 8 4 6 7 2 1
↓ ↓ ↓ ↓ ↓ ↓
! ÷ • + * ×

15. 1 7 8 5 2 4
↓ ↓ ↓ ↓ ↓ ↓
@ + ! $ * ©
Both condidtions are applicable.

16. 2 5 4 8 6
↓ ↓ ↓ ↓ ↓
* $ ÷ ! ©
Condition (ii) is applicable.

17. 4th to the left of the 10th from the right end means 14th from the right end, *i.e.*, E.

18. Number Number Symbol or Number Number Number, 5 6 Ω is only one such combination.

19. The new sequence would be 4 3 5 6 7 2 8 1

5th from the left

20. Letter Consonant Vowel, such combinations are ZYA, PLE.

21.

4	+3	Z	+2	A
$	+3	Y	+2	5
C	+3	U	+2	%
P	+3	T	+2	S
@	+3	L	+2	T

22. Series I: N P Q * 5 4 B Z $ # 3 7 D 9 A ↑ F 8 G H 1 + D K 6
Series II: 7 4 £ J M 1 © Y P 8 Q R 5 T N 6 2 ↓ U A 3 9 @ I S.
Now, total = 1 + 4 = 5.

23. The new sequence is :
$ Z B 4 5 * Q P N 6 2 ↓ U A 3 9 @ I S.

24.

Series	Letters	Digits	Symbols
I	12	8	2
II	12	9	4

25. The new series will be: # + > Q N F G D Y 6 9 1 (3 + 5 =) 8th from the left in the new series is D

26. Reena: 3 # R U 2 + > A P Y B 4
No symbol precedes a number in Reena's series.
Kareena: Q £ 5 N → F G 8 * D 7 Y
Jessica: O * H T 6 @ C 9 Z K Ω 1
There are total 4 such elements.

27. The first, second and third element of each group is taken from Reena, Kareena and Jessica series respectively. Suppose the position value of first element is 'N' from the left end, then the position value of the second element is (N – 1) and that of third element is (N – 2) from the left end in their respective groups. Option A violates the pattern.

28. Total letters = 18, total symbols = 9.
Hence, difference = (18 – 9 =) 9.

29. S D G P I A
↓ ↓ ↓ ↓ ↓ ↓
@ 8 1 6 2 4 Condition (*i*) is applicable

30. Z I E A K M
↓ ↓ ↓ ↓ ↓ ↓
9 2 β β 3 # Condition (*iii*) is applicable

31. W A R M F Q
↓ ↓ ↓ ↓ ↓ ↓
% 8 7 # $ ©

32. E D S K I M
↓ ↓ ↓ ↓ ↓ ↓
5 $ @ 3 2 $ Condition (*ii*) is applicable

33. D E Q G F A
↓ ↓ ↓ ↓ ↓ ↓
4 5 © 1 $ 8

34. M K E Z A I
↓ ↓ ↓ ↓ ↓ ↓
2 5 9 8 3 Condition (*i*) is applicable

10 Seating Arrangement

The process of making a group of people to sit as per a prefixed manner is called **Seating Arrangement.** In these questions, some conditions are given, on the basis of which students are required to arrange objects, either in a row or in a circular order. While making arrangements, it should be noted that all the conditions given are compiled with.

These type of the questions are most common that are asked in various examinations like CAT, XAT, IIFT, FMS and Bank PO. These type of questions generally involve five to eight individuals arranged in a certain fashion. They may have to be arranged in a row or in a circle.

Sometimes these questions are made more difficult by allowing an individual to a particular position with some conditions.

General Guide Lines to Solve 'Seating Arrangement' Questions

Guide Line 1: First of all take a quick glance on the given information. After performing this step, you would get an idea of the situation of people or objects.

Guide Line 2: Next, determine the usefullness of each informations and classify them accordingly into 'definite information', 'comparative informaton' and 'negative information'.

Guide Line 3: When the place of any person or object is definitely mentioned then we say that it is a *definite information.* e.g., A is sitting on the right end of the bench.

Guide Line 4: When the place of any person or object is not mentioned definitely but mentioned only in the comparison of another person or object, then we say that it is a *comparative information.* e.g., A is sitting second to the right of E. This type of information can be helpful when we can get the definite information about E.

Guide Line 5: A part of definite information may consist of *negative information.* A negative information does not tell us anything definitely but it gives an idea to eliminate a possibility. e.g., C is not sitting on the immediate left of A.

Types of Questions Asked in Different Examinations

There are multiple types of questions which are asked from the chapter 'Seating Arrangement,' so it is quite difficult to predict exact type of questions that are asked, but on the basis of *Observation, Analysis* and *Experience,* here we are giving different types of questions that are usually asked in the examination. Almost all the questions at this chapter can be categorized into these types. Also, this description of type will make your study easy and streamline.

LINEAR ARRANGEMENT

In this type of arrangement, we arrange people or objects in a line or row. The arrangement is done only on one 'axis' and hence, the position of people or objects assumes importance in terms of order like first position, second position... last position. In this type of arrangement, we take directions according to our left and right.

There are few words which must be paid adequate attention, *i.e.,* 'between' means sandwiched, 'immediate left' is different from 'to the left'. To understand it let us see some pictorial representation.

One Row Sequence

(A) When direction of face is not clear, then we take ourself as base and then the diagram will be as follows:

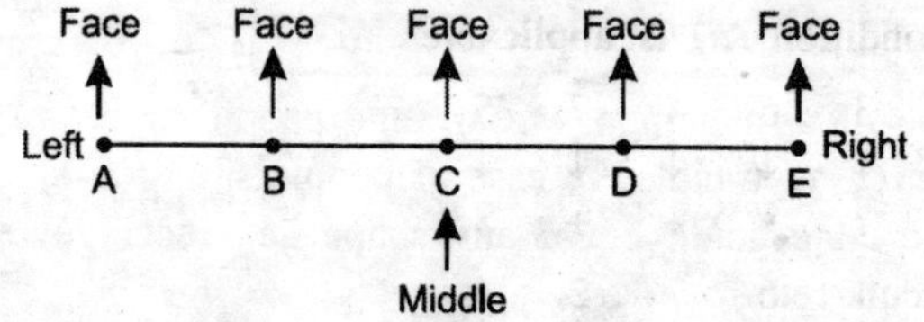

From the above diagram, it is clear that

(*i*) B, C, D, E are right of A but only B is the immediate right of A.

(*ii*) D, C, B, A are left of E but only D is the immediate left of E.

(*iii*) C, D, E are right of B only C is the immediate right of B.

(*iv*) C, B, A are left of D but only C is the immediate left of D.

(*v*) D and E are right of C but only D is the immediate right of C.

(*vi*) B and A are left of C but only B is the immediate left of C.

(*vii*) A is the immediate left of B while E is the immediate right of D.

(B) When direction of face is towards you, then the diagram will be as follows:

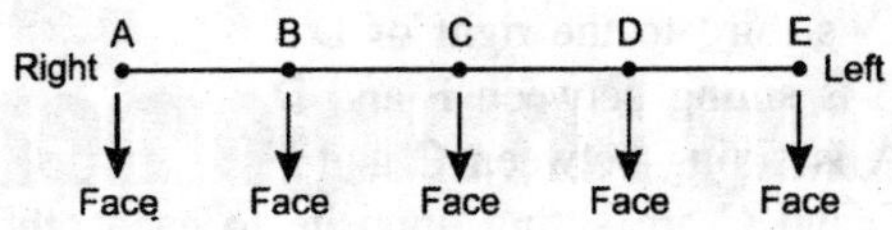

From the above diagram, it is clear that

(*i*) Left of A = B, C, D and E

(*ii*) Right of E = D, C, B and A

(*iii*) B is immediate left of A; C is immediate left of B; D is immediate left of C and E is immediate left of D.

(*iv*) D is immediate right of E; C is immediate right of D; B is immediate right of C; and A is immediate right of B.

Two Rows Sequence

Let us see 6 persons seating in two rows

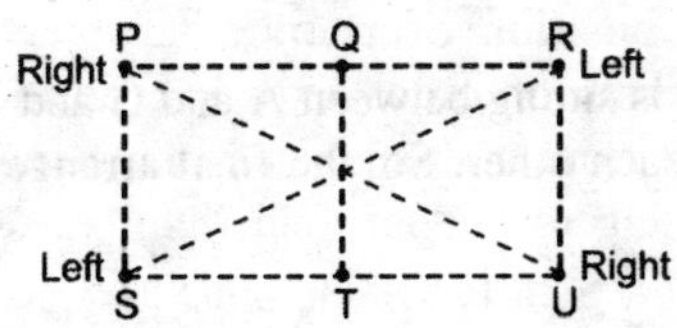

From the above diagram, it is clear that

(*i*) P is sitting opposite S

(*ii*) Q is sitting opposite T

(*iii*) R is sitting opposite U

(*iv*) P and U are sitting at diagonally opposite positions.

(*v*) S and R are sitting at diagonally opposite positions.

CIRCULAR ARRANGEMENT

In this type of arrangement we arrange people or objects around a circle or a table. In case of people sitting around a table, the table could be of any shape i.e., rectangular, square, circular etc.

Circular Sequence

In this arrangement, sime persons are sitting around a circle and they are facing the centre.

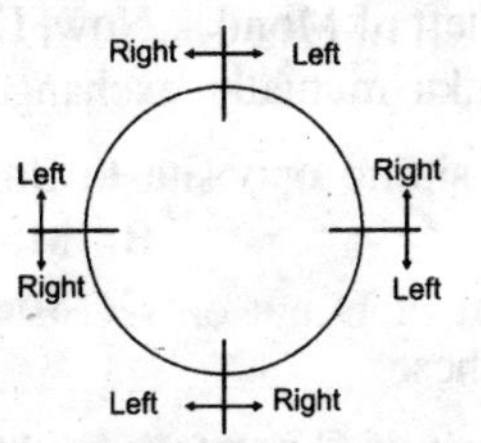

1. Left movement is called clockwise rotation.
2. Right movement is called anti-clockwise rotation.

(*i*) The above presentation is for 4 persons but for any number of persons, the direction is taken in the same manner.

(*ii*) For rectangular and sequence arrangement, directions are taken as discussed in two rows sequence.

The information given in questions specify the position of some or all the persons in the arrangement. The positions are specified through conditions like a particular person is sitting right or left of another person.

After reading the given information, you should draw the shape specified in the question. Following two shapes are of six and eight persons sitting around a circle.

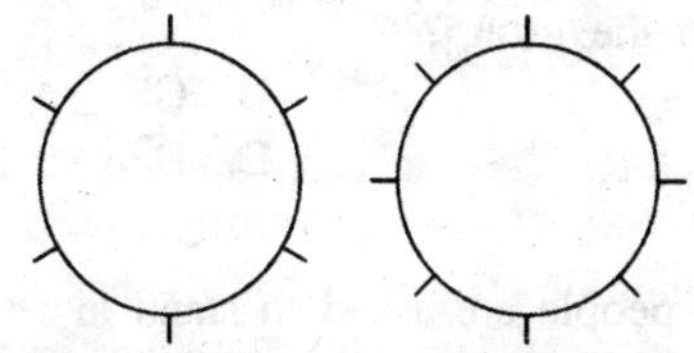

Six persons   Eight persons

Solved Examples

Example 1. A, B, C, D, E, F, G and H are sitting in a row facing North.

(*i*) A is fourth to the right of E

(*ii*) H is fourth to the left of D

(*iii*) C and F, which are not at the ends, are neighbours of B and E respectively.

(*iv*) H is next to the left of A and A is the neighbour of B. Who are sitting at the extreme ends?

Solution : From information (*i*), we get that there are three persons between A and E.

E X X X A

In the information (*iv*), it is given that H is next to the left of A and B is the neighbour of A. Using the information with (*i*), we get E X X H A B

By the information (*ii*), E X X H A B X D By the information (*iii*),

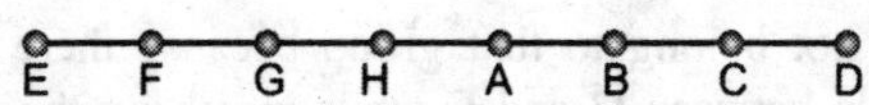

So, E and D are sitting at the extreme ends.

Directions (Example Nos. 2 to 6) : *Read the following information carefully and answer the questions given below:*

Six people : C, D, E, F, G and H are standing in a straight line facing North not necessarily in the same order. D is standing second to the right of F. C is standing fourth to the left of H and H is not standing on the extreme end of the line. E is standing second to the right of D.

2. What is the position of G with respect to E?

A. Immediate left   B. Second to the left
C. Third to the left   D. Third to the right
E. None of these

3. Which of the following pairs represents the people standing at the extreme ends of the line?

A. FH   B. CE
C. DE   D. CH
E. None of these

4. Who is standing second to the right of C?

A. F B. D
C. G D. E
E. None of these

5. Four of the following five are alike in a certain way based on their positions in the above arrangement and so form a group. Which of the following does not belong to the group?

A. CG B. GE
C. GH D. DE
E. FD

6. If all the people are asked to stand in an alphabetical order from left to right, the positions of how many will remain unchanged?

A. One B. Two
C. Three D. Four
E. None of these

Solutions (2 to 6) : D is standing second to the right of F. *i.e.,* F * D. E is standing second to the right of D *i.e.,* F * D * E. H is not standing on the extreme end of line and C is standing fourth to the left of H.

So, H must be standing between D and E.
Final position will be as following:

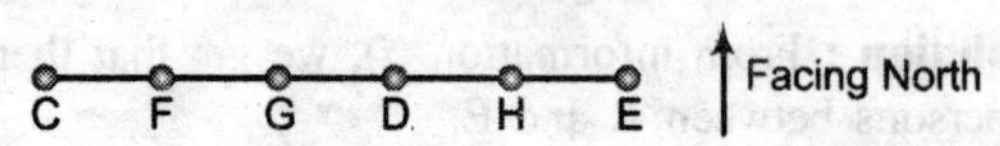

2. G is standing third to the left of E. Hence, correct answer is C.

3. C and E are standing on the extreme ends of the line. Hence, correct answer is B.

4. G is standing second to the right of C. Hence, correct answer is C.

5. GE does not belong to that group because there are two people between G and E while in others, there is only one person. Hence, correct answer is B.

6. Present order C F G D H E
Alphabetical order C D E F G H

So, position of C will remain unchanged. Hence, correct answer is A.

Directions (Example Nos. 7 & 8) : *Read the following information and answer the questions based on it.*

Eight friends A, B, C, D, E, F, G and H are sitting in a circle facing the centre. B is sitting between G and D. H is third to the left of B and second to the right of A. C is sitting between A and G and B and E are not sitting opposite to each other.

7. Who is third to the left of D?

A. F
B. E
C. A
D. Cannot be determined
E. None of these

8. Which of the following statements is not correct?

A. D and A are sitting opposite to each other
B. C is third to the right of D
C. E is sitting between F and D
D. A is sitting between C and F
E. E and C are sitting opposite to each other

Solution (7 to 8) : First of all draw a circular figure having eight persons. Now, B is sitting between G and D. H is third to the left of B and second to the right of A.

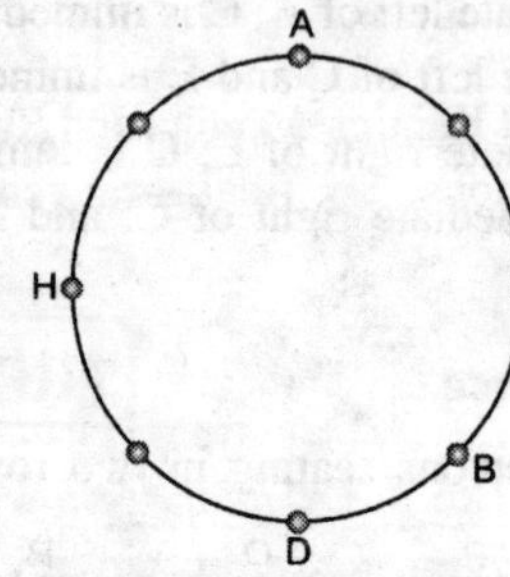

Now, C is sitting between A and G and B and E are not opposite to each other. So, the final arrangement will be as following:

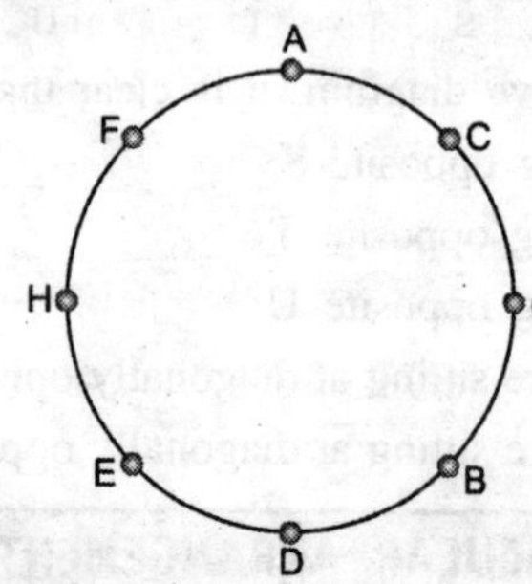

7. F is third to the left of D. So, correct answer is A.
8. E is not sitting between F and D. So, correct answer is C.

Directions (Example Nos. 9 to 11) : *Read the following information and answer the questions given below:*

Six girls are sitting in a circle. Sonia is sitting opposite to Radhika. Poonam is sitting right of Radhika but left of Deepti. Monika is sitting left of Radhika. Kamini is sitting right of Sonia and left of Monika. Now, Deepti and Kamini, Monika and Radhika mutually exchange their positions.

9. Who will be sitting opposite to Sonia?

A. Radhika B. Monika
C. Kamini D. Sonia
E. None of these

10. Who will be sitting left of Kamini?

A. Poonam B. Deepti
C. Radhika D. Sonia
E. None of these

11. Who will be sitting left of Deepti?

A. Sonia B. Monika
C. Radhika D. Poonam
E. Cannot be determined

Solutions (9 to 11) : *From the given information, initial arrangement will be as following:*

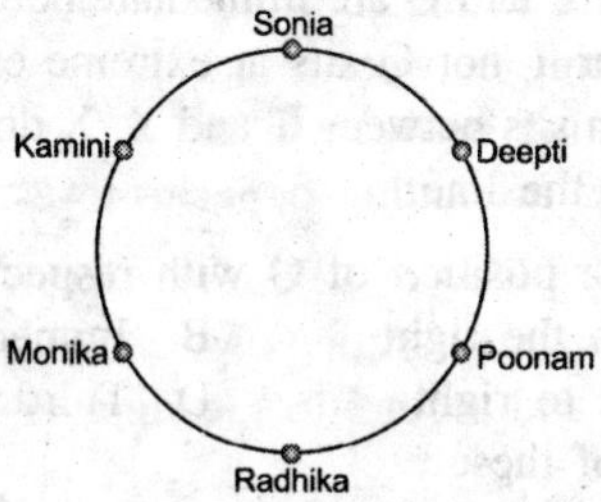

Now, Deepti and Kamini, Monika and Radhika mutually exchange their positions. So, final arrangement will be as following.

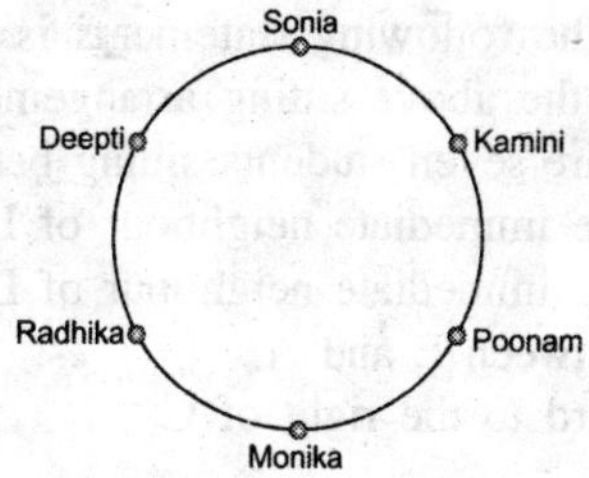

9. Monika is sitting opposite to Sonia. So, the correct answer is B.

10. Poonam is sitting left of Kamini. So, the correct answer is A.

11. Sonia is sitting left of Deepti. So, the correct answer is A.

MULTIPLE CHOICE QUESTIONS

Directions (Q. Nos. 1 to 3) : *Read the following information carefully and answer the questions given below.*

(*i*) A, B, C, D, E, F, G and H are standing in a row facing North.
(*ii*) B is not neighbour of G.
(*iii*) F is to the immediate right of G and neighbour of E.
(*iv*) G is not at the extreme end.
(*v*) A is sixth to the left of E.
(*vi*) H is sixth to the right of C.

1. Who among the following are neighbours?
A. AB B. CG
C. FH D. CA
E. None of these

2. Which one among the following defines the position of D?
A. Fourth to the right of H
B. Third to the right of A
C. Neighbour of B and F
D. To the immediate left of B
E. None of these

3. Which of the following is true?
A. C is to the immediate left of A
B. D is neighbour of B and F
C. G is to the immediate right of D
D. A and E are at the extreme ends
E. None of the above

Directions (Q. Nos. 4 to 8) : *Study the following information to answer the given questions.*

A, B, C, X, Y and Z are seated in a straight line facing North. C is third to the right of Z and B sits second to the right of C. X sits to the immediate right of A.

4. Which of the following represents the pair of persons sitting exactly in the middle of the line?
A. XB B. ZB
C. BX D. XC
E. XY

5. What is X's position with respect to Z?
A. Immediate right of Z B. Second to the left
C. Third to the right D. Second to the right
E. None of these

6. Four of the following five are alike in a certain way based on their sitting positions in the above arrangement and so form a group. Which is the one that does not belong to the group?
A. ZA B. XC
C. CY D. YB
E. XA

7. How many persons are seated between A and C?
A. One B. Two
C. Three D. Four
E. None of these

8. If A : X and Z : A, then Y : ?
A. Y B. B
C. A D. X
E. None of these

Directions (Q. Nos. 9 to 13) : *Study the following information carefully and answer the given questions following it.*

(*i*) Eleven students A, B, C, D, E, F, G, H, I, J and K are sitting in the first row of a class facing the teacher.
(*ii*) D, who is on the immediate left of F, is second to the right of C.
(*iii*) A is second to the right of E, who is at one of the ends.
(*iv*) J is the immediate neighbour of A and B and third to the left of G.
(*v*) H is on the immediate left of D and third to the right of I.

9. Who is sitting midway between E and H?
A. J B. B
C. I D. G
E. None of these

10. Which of the following statements is not true in the context of the above sitting arrangements?

A. There are seven students sitting between K and D
B. G is the immediate neighbour of I and C
C. H is the immediate neighbour of D and F
D. K is between E and A
E. F is third to the right of C

11. To obtain the respective seats of all the persons which statement given above is not required?

A. I B. II
C. III D. IV
E. None of these

12. Besides 'E', who among the following is at the extreme end?

A. K B. F
C. B D. Can't say
E. None of these

13. Which of the following groups is at the left of I?

A. AJB B. GCH
C. HDF D. GCH
E. None of these

Directions (Q. Nos. 14 to 16) : *Read the following information carefully and answer the questions given below.*

(*i*) There are five friends.
(*ii*) They are standing in a row facing South.
(*iii*) Jayesh is to the immediate right of Alok.
(*iv*) Pramod is between Bhagat and Subodh.
(*v*) Subodh is between Jayesh and Pramod.

14. Who is at the extreme left end?

A. Alok B. Bhagat
C. Subodh D. Data inadequate
E. None of these

15. Who is in the middle?

A. Bhagat B. Jayesh
C. Pramod D. Subodh
E. None of these

16. To find answers of the above two questions, which of the given statements can be dispensed with?

A. Only (*i*) B. Only (*v*)
C. Only (*iii*) D. Only (*ii*)
E. None of these

17. Six students are sitting in a row in an examination hall. K is sitting between V and R. V is sitting next to M. M is sitting next to B. B is sitting on the extreme left and Q is sitting next to R. Who are sitting adjacent to V?

A. M and R B. M and K
C. K and R D. M and Q
E. None of these

Directions (Qs. Nos. 18 to 22) : *Study the following information to answer the given questions.*

P, Q, R, S, T, V, X and Y are seated in a straight line facing North. P sits fourth to the left of V. V sits either sixth from the left end of the line or fourth from the right end of the line. S sits second to right of R. R is not an immediate neighbour of V. T and Q are immediate neighbours of each other but neither T nor Q sits at extreme ends of the line. Only one person sits between T and X. X does not sit at the extreme end of the line.

18. What is the position of Q with respect to P?

A. Fifth to the right B. Immediate neighbour
C. Second to right D. Third to left
E. None of these

19. Which of the following represents persons seated at the two extreme ends of the line?

A. P, V B. Y, S
C. R, V D. Y, P
E. R, Y

20. How many persons are seated between R and T?

A. One B. Two
C. Three D. Four
E. None of these

21. If P is related to Q and S is related to T in a certain way, to which of the following would V be related to following the same pattern?

A. Y B. P
C. R D. S
E. X

22. Who amongst the following sits exactly in the middle of the persons who sit second from the left and the person who sits fifth from the right?

A. V B. Q
C. T D. S
E. P

Directions (Qs. Nos. 23 to 25) : *Read the following information carefully and answer the questions given below.*

Six girls A, B, K, D, E and P are standing in a row. B is between D and P. A does not stand next to either P or D. K does not stand next to D. E stands between A and K.

23. P stands between

A. B and K B. E and A
C. D and B D. A and K
E. Can't be determined

24. Who occupy the extreme ends of the row?

A. D and E B. D and A
C. A and P D. B and E
E. None of these

25. K stands between

A. P and B B. P and D
C. P and E D. E and A
E. None of these

Directions (Q. Nos. 26 to 30) : *Study the following information carefully to answer these questions.*

Eight members P, Q, R, S, T, V, H and L are sitting in two rows with equal number of members in each row.

Members of one row are facing North and those in the other row are facing South. Each member in one row is sitting exactly opposite a member in the other row.

P sits in the row facing North, to the immediate right of H who is exactly opposite of R. L is to the immediate right of R and S is exactly opposite of T who is to the immediate right of P. V does not sit at any of the ends of any row.

26. Which of the following members sit at the ends of the same row?

A. TH B. SR
C. LQ D. LT
E. None of these

27. Who sits opposite of P?

A. L B. Q
C. V D. Can't be determined
E. None of the above

28. Which of the following members sit exactly opposite each other?

A. VQ B. LV
C. VH D. VP
E. None of these

29. Who is to the left of V?

A. T B. S
C. R D. L
E. None of these

30. Who sits to the right of Q?

A. H B. L
C. V D. R
E. None of these

Directions (Q. Nos. 31 to 35): *Study the following information to answer the given questions.*

Seven friends T, U, V, W, X, Y and Z are sitting in a straight line facing North. W sits fifth to the right of T. W does not sit at any of extreme ends. Two people sit between Z and X. Y sits third to the left of U. Y sits exactly in the middle. Z is not an immediate neighbour of Y.

31. What is Z's position with respect to W?

A. Second to the left B. Third to the right
C. Fourth to the left D. Third to the left
E. Fourth to the right

32. Who is second to the right of T?

A. Y B. X
C. U D. V
E. None of these

33. Four of the following five are alike in a certain way based on their sitting positions inthe above line and so form a group. Which is the one that does not belong to the group?

A. UW B. XV
C. ZT D. YV
E. WX

34. If all the seven friends are made to sit alphabetically from right to left, positions of how many will remain unchanged?

A. None B. One
C. Two D. Three
E. Four

35. Who sit at the extreme ends of the line?

A. XZ B. VX
C. YZ D. XT
E. TU

Directions (Q. Nos. 36 to 40) : *Study the following information carefully and answer the questions that follow.*

(*i*) Seven members of a family J, K, L, M, N, O and P are to be seated in a row from left to right. (The one standing at the left end will be called the 1st; the one standing at the right end, the 7th.)

(*ii*) Their professions are lawyer, accountant, social worker, IAS, housewife, commissioner and student, though not necessarily in that order.

(*iii*) The third person is the housewife.

(*iv*) M, who is not the commissioner, will stand after the person who immediately follows N.

(*v*) J is the social worker.

(*vi*) The lawyer stands sixth.

(*vii*) The accountant stands to the immediate left of the commissioner.

(*viii*) P stands to the immediate right of O and to the immediate left of K.

(*ix*) N, the student, stands fifth.

36. The person standing first from left is

A. O B. the social worker
C. P D. the commissioner
E. L

37. The person standing to the immediate left of M is

A. the housewife B. J
C. the lawyer D. K
E. the commissioner

38. Which of the following correctly matches a person with his/her profession?

A. O-IAS B. K-housewife
C. L-commissioner D. P-lawyer
E. M-accountant

39. Suppose, P has to go on account of an emergency and the family brings in the family servant Q, who stands to the immediate right of L. The sixth person from the left is now

A. K B. J
C. N D. Q
E. M

40. If in addition to the changes described in Q. 39 the housewife and her husband, the IAS, agree to interchange places, which of the following will be true?

A. M will stand after O but before J
B. K will be the only person to the right of L
C. There will be an equal number of persons to the left and to the right of J
D. There will be only one person to the right of N and to the left of K
E. The first and last person will be the same as before

41. In a college party, 5 girls are sitting in a row. P is sitting to the left of M and to the right of O. R is sitting to the right of N but to the left of O. Who is sitting in the Middle?

A. O B. R
C. P D. M
E. P

42. Six persons M, N, O, P, Q, R are sitting in two rows. Each row has three persons Q is not at the ends of any row. P is second to the left of R. O is the neighbour of Q and diagonally opposite to P. N is the neighbour of R. Who is opposite of N?

A. R B. Q
C. P D. M
E. None of these

43. From A to E, five buildings are in a row. A is to the right of B; E is to the left of C and to the right of A; B is to the right of D. Which building is exactly in the middle?

A. E B. A
C. B D. D
E. None of these

Directions (Q. Nos. 44 to 48) : *Study the following information carefully and answer the questions given below.*

A, B, C, D, E, F, G, H and K are sitting around a circle facing the centre. B is fourth to the left of G who is second to the right of C. F is fourth to the right of C and second to the left of K. A is fourth to the right of K. D is not immediate neighbour of either K or B, H is third to the right of E.

44. Who is fourth to the right of D?

A. K B. H
C. E D. B
E. None of these

45. In which of the following combinations is the third person sitting in between the first and second persons?

A. EKB B. CHB
C. AGC D. FGD
E. None of these

46. Who is third to the right of H?

A. A B. D
C. G D. F
E. None of these

47. Who is the fourth to the left of E?

A. A B. C
C. G D. Data inadequate
E. None of the above

48. Who is second to the right of?

A. C B. H
C. F D. E
E. Data inadequate

Directions (Q. Nos. 49 to 53) : *Study the following information carefully to answer these questions.*

Eight friends A, B, C, D, E, F, G and H are sitting around a circle facing the centre. B is third to the right of A, who is third to the right of C. F is second to the right of E who is not an immediate neighbour of B. D sits second to the left of H, who sits second to the left of G.

49. Who sits second of the left of A?

A. G B. D
C. H D. E
E. None of these

50. Who sits to the immediate left of B?

A. G B. F
C. D D. H
E. None of these

51. What is the position of H with respect to F?

A. To the immediate right B. Third to the left
C. Second to the left D. Second to the right
E. Third to the right

52. Four of the following five are alike in a certain way based on their positions in the given arrangement and so form a group. Which is the one that does not belong to the group?

A. AD B. HG
C. EF D. BF
E. CE

53. Which of the following pairs has the first person sitting to the immediate right of the second person?

A. BH B. DF
C. CF D. EA
E. None of these

Directions (Q. Nos. 54 to 58) : *Study the following information and answer these questions.*

I. A, B, C, D, E, F, G and H are eight friends sitting in a circle facing the centre.
II. F is on the immediate right of D while B is on the immediate left of E.
III. A is sitting opposite neither C nor H. And A is not the neighbour of H.
IV. E and H are sitting adjacent to C.

54. Which of the following is wrong?

I. F is to the immediate left of G.
II. A is to the immediate right of D.
III. H and D are sitting opposite each other.

A. Only I B. Only II
C. Only III D. II and III
E. All I, II and III

55. Which of the following are two pairs of adjacent members?
A. AF and BC B. FH and BG
C. AG and CE D. BG and AG
E. None of the above

56. What is the position of G?
A. Fourth to the left of F
B. Third to the left of B
C. Third to the right of B
D. Second to the left of D
E. None of these

57. Which of the following is/are correct?
I. D is third to the left of E.
II. D is fifth to the right of E.
III. A and F are adjacent to each other.
A. Only I B. Only II
C. I and II D. II and III
E. All I, II and III

58. If A and E interchange places and so do F and H, then
A. G and C are adjacent to F
B. D and B are adjacent to A
C. E is not sitting opposite A
D. H is not sitting opposite F
E. H is fourth to the left of C

Directions (Q. Nos. 59 to 63) : *Study the following information carefully and answer the given questions.*

A, B, C, D, E, F, G and H are sitting around a square table facing the centre in such a way that four of them sit at four corners of the square while four sit inthe middle of each of the four sides.

(*i*) A sits second to right of F. F sits in the middle of one of the sides of the table.

(*ii*) G who does not sit at any of the corners of the table sits second to the right of D.

(*iii*) Only two people sit between D and B (taken from one side).

(*iv*) C is not an immediate neighbour of G.

(*v*) H is sit second to left of B.

(*vi*) E is not an immediate neighbour of G or F.

59. Who sits exactly between F and A?
A. B B. C
C. E D. H
E. None of these

60. How many persons sit between A and H when counted in anti-clockwise direction from A?
A. None B. One
C. Two D. Three
E. Four

61. Four of the following five are alike in a certain way based on their sitting positions in the above arrangement and so form a group. Which is the one that does not belong to that group?
A. D B. F
C. A D. E
E. G

62. What is the position of F with respect to C?
A. Third to the left
B. Immediate to the right
C. Second to the left
D. Third to the right
E. Immediate to the left

63. What will come in place of the question mark (?) based upon the given sitting arrangement?
AE EH HF ?
A. FE B. HC
C. FD D. DB
E. FH

Directions (Q. Nos. 64 to 68) : *Study the following information carefully and answer the questions given below.*

P, Q, R, S, T, V, W and Z are sitting around a circle facing the centre. T is second to the right of R who is third to the right of P. S is second to the left of P and fourth to the right of Q. Z is third to the right of V who is not an immediate neighbour of P.

64. In which of the following combinations is the first person sitting in between the second and the third persons?
A. VTS B. TZS
C. QRV D. PWQ
E. VRT

65. Who is second to the right of T?
A. S B. Z
C. P D. R
E. None of these

66. What is P's position with respect to S?
A. Fourth to the left B. Fourth to the right
C. Fifth to the left D. Sixth to the left
E. Third to the right

67. Who is the immediate left to Z?
A. T B. P
C. S D. V
E. None of these

68. Who is second to the right of W?
A. R B. Q
C. Z D. S
E. None of these

Directions (Q. Nos. 69 to 73) : *Study the following information carefully and answer the questions given below.*

A, B, C, D, E, F, G and H are sitting around a circle facing the centre. B is second to the right of D who is third to the right of F. C is second to the left of A who is second to the left of F. G is third to the right of E.

69. In which of the following combinations is the first person sitting between the second and the third persons?

A. GCD B. FGH
C. EFH D. ABE
E. None of these

70. Who is third to the right of H?

A. G B. D
C. C D. Data inadequate
E. None of these

71. Who is to the immediate right of A?

A. B B. E
C. F D. Data inadequate
E. None of these

72. What is H's position with respect to B?

A. Fifth to the right B. Third to the left
C. Fifth to the left D. Third to the right
E. Fourth to the left

73. Who is to the immediate left of G?

A. H B. F
C. D D. Data inadequate
E. None of these

Directions (Q. Nos. 74 to 78) : *Study the following information carefully and answer the questions given below.*

A, B, C, D, E, F, G, H and K are sitting around a circle facing the centre. F is fourth to the right of A who is third to the right of B. K is fourth to the left of B and third to the right of D. C is third to the right of H. E is second to the left of G.

74. Who is to the immediate right of F?

A. B B. G
C. E D. Data inadequate
E. None of these

75. Who is third to the right of K?

A. F B. E
C. G D. Data inadequate
E. None of these

76. What is E's position with respect to B?

A. Second to the left B. Third to the right
C. Fourth to the right D. Third to the left
E. Fifth to the right

77. Who is fourth to the left of G?

A. C B. A
C. D D. K
E. Data inadequate

78. In which of the following combinations is the third person sitting between the first and the second persons?

A. GFB B. BGH
C. ADC D. KEC
E. EGF

Directions (Q. Nos. 79 to 83) : *Study the following information to answer the given questions.*

(*i*) Eight persons E, F, G, H, I, J, K and L are seated around a square table-two on each side.

(*ii*) There are three lady members and they are not seated next to each other.

(*iii*) J is between L and F.

(*iv*) G is between I and F.

(*v*) H, a lady member is second to the left of J.

(*vi*) F, a male member is seated opposite to E, a lady member.

(*vii*) There is a lady member between F and I.

79. Who among the following are the three lady members?

A. E, H and J
B. E, G and J
C. G, H and J
D. Cannot be determined
E. None of these

80. Which of the following is true about J?

A. J is a male member
B. J is a female member
C. Sex of J cannot be determined
D. Position of J cannot be determined
E. None of the above

81. Who among the following is seated between E and H?

A. I B. J
C. F D. Cannot be determined
E. None of these

82. Who among the following is to the immediate left of F?

A. G B. J
C. I D. Cannot be determined
E. None of these

83. How many persons are seated between K and F?

A. One B. Two
C. Three D. Cannot be determined
E. None of these

84. Six friends are playing cards sitting around a circle and facing the centre. Kanny is sitting to the left of Danny; Michel is sitting between Boby and Johny Rozer is between Kanny and Boby. Who is sitting to the left of Michel?

A. Danny B. Johny
C. Canny D. Boby
E. None of these

85. Radha, Sheela, Mahima and Seeta are sitting around a rectangular table. Radha is sitting to the right of Sheela. Mahima is sitting to the left of Seeta. Which of the following pair is sitting opposite each other?

A. Sheela-Seeta B. Radha-Seeta
C. Radha-Sheela D. Mahima-Radha
E. None of these

ANSWERS

1	2	3	4	5	6	7	8	9	10
D	B	C	D	D	E	A	B	B	C
11	12	13	14	15	16	17	18	19	20
E	B	A	A	D	A	B	C	E	C
21	22	23	24	25	26	27	28	29	30
A	D	A	B	C	E	C	D	B	A
31	32	33	34	35	36	37	38	39	40
C	D	B	A	E	A	C	B	D	A
41	42	43	44	45	46	47	48	49	50
A	B	B	D	D	C	A	B	A	C
51	52	53	54	55	56	57	58	59	60
E	D	B	E	C	D	C	A	B	C
61	62	63	64	65	66	67	68	69	70
D	E	C	E	B	D	C	A	D	C
71	72	73	74	75	76	77	78	79	80
B	E	A	B	C	D	A	E	E	A
81	82	83	84	85					
E	B	C	D	B					

EXPLANATORY ANSWERS

Solutions (Q. Nos. 1 to 3) : *According to the given information, the final arrangement is as following*

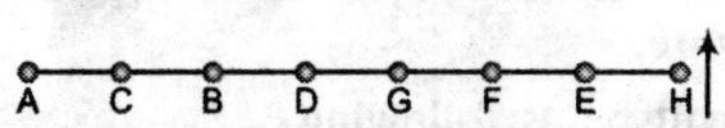

1. C and A are neighbours.

2. D is third to the right of A.

3. G is to the immediate right of D.

Solutions (Q. Nos. 4 to 8) : *According to the given information, the final arrangement is as following*

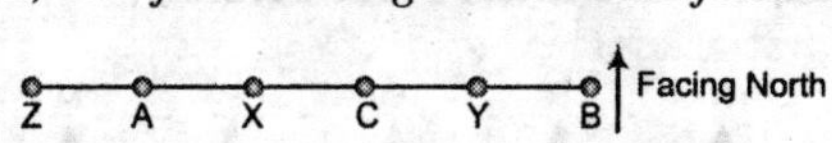

4. X and C are sitting exactly middle of the line.

5. X is second to the right of Z.

6. XA does not belong to that group because in this pair, second person is sitting to the immediate left of first person, while in others first person is sitting to the immediate right of first person.

7. Only X is sitting between A and C.

8. In the given two pairs, second person is sitting to the immediate right first person. B is sitting immediate right of Y.

Solutions (Q. Nos. 9 to 13):

From (*iii*), A is second to the right of E, who is at one of the ends. So, E is at the left end.

From (*iv*), J is the immediate neighbour of A and B, it implies that J is sitting on the immediate right of A and B is sitting immediate right of J.

E * A J B * G ...(*a*)

From (*ii*) and (*v*), we get the following arrangement

I C H D F ...(*b*)

From the arrangements (*a*) and (*b*), we can get the final arrangement

E K A J B I G C H D F

9. There are seven persons which are sitting between E and H. B is in the midway of them.

10. H is not the immediate neighbour of D and F

11. To get the final arrangement, we require all the statements.

12. F is at the extreme end.

13. A, J and B are at the left of L.

Solutions (Q. Nos. 14 to 16) : *According to the given information, the final arrangement is as following*

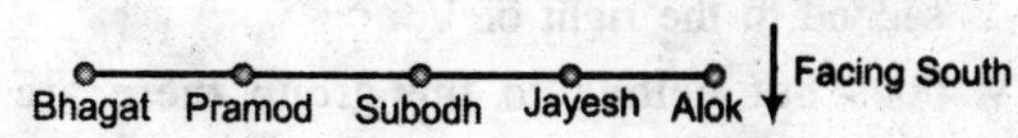

14. Alok is at the extreme left end.

15. Subodh is in the middle.

16. Statemment I is superfluous.

17. According to the given information, the final arrangemnet is as following

So, M and K are sitting adjacent to V.

Solutions (Q. Nos. 18 to 22) : *According to the given information, the final arrangement is as following*

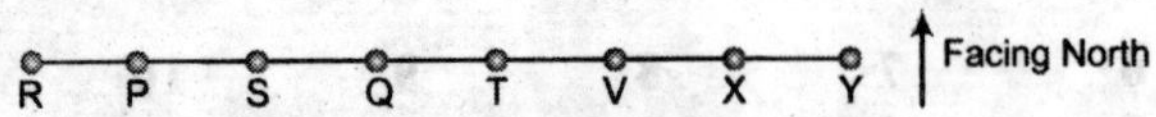

18. A is second to the right of P.

19. R and Y are sitting on the extreme ends of line.

20. Three persons P, S and Q are seated between R and T.

21. In the given pairs, second person is seated second to the right of first person. So, V be related to Y as Y is sitting second to the right of V.

22. Second from the left is P and fifth from the right is Q. S is sitting between P and Q.

Solutions (Q. Nos. 23 to 25) : *B is between D and P. So, DBP or PBD.*

E stands between A and K. So, AEK or KEA.

A does not stand next to either P or D and K does not stand to next D. So, the final arrangement will be as following

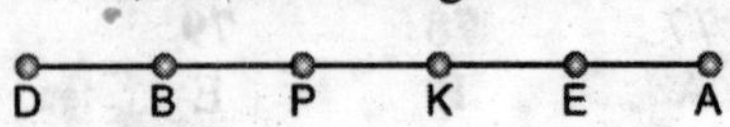

23. P stands between B and K.

24. D and A occupy the extreme ends of the row.

25. K stands between P and E.

Solutions (Q. Nos. 26 to 30) : *According to given information, the final arrangement is as following*

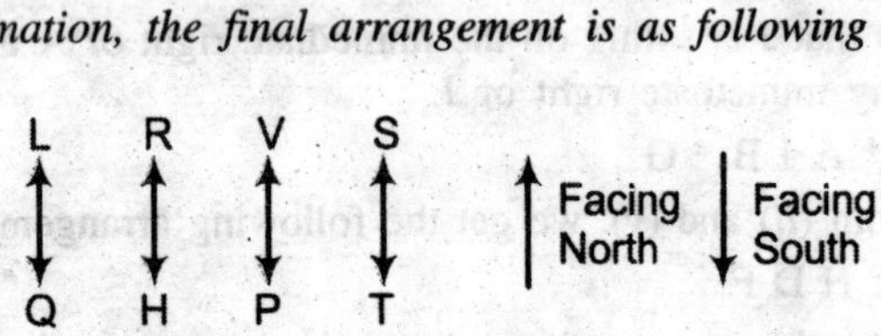

26. LS and QT sit at the ends of same row.

27. V sits opposite of P.

28. V and P sit exactly opposite to each other.

29. S is to the left ofV.

30. H sits to the right of Q.

Solutions (Q. Nos. 31 to 35) : *According to given information, the final arrangement is as following.*

31. Z is fourth to the left of W.

32. V is second to the right of V.

33. XV does not belong to the group there are not immediate neighbours while other pairs are immediate neighbours.

34. Actual position TZVYXWU

Alphabetical position ZYXWVUT

So, the position of none of the friends will remain unchanged.

35. T and U sit at the extreme ends of line.

Solutions (Q. Nos. 36 to 40) : *From statements (iii), (vi) and (ix), we can get the following arrangement*

Position	1	2	3	4	5	6	7
Name					N		
Profession			House wife		Student	Lawyer	

Now, from (*iv*) and (*vii*) statements,

Position	1	2	3	4	5	6	7
Name					N		M
Profession	Acc.	Comm.	House wife		Student	Lawyer	

J must be at position 4 and from statement (*viii*), O, P and K are together. So, they are at positions 1, 2 and 3 respectively. The final arrangement will be as following

Position	1	2	3	4	5	6	7
Name	O	P	K	J	N	L	M
Profession	Acc.	Comm.	House wife	Social worker	Student	Lawyer	IAS

36. The person standing first from left is O.

37. The person standing to the immediate left of M is the lawyer.

38. K is the house wife.

39. The new order will be as following

OKJNLQM

So, sixth person from the left is Q.

40. The new order will be as following

OMJNLQK

So, M will stand after O but before J.

41.

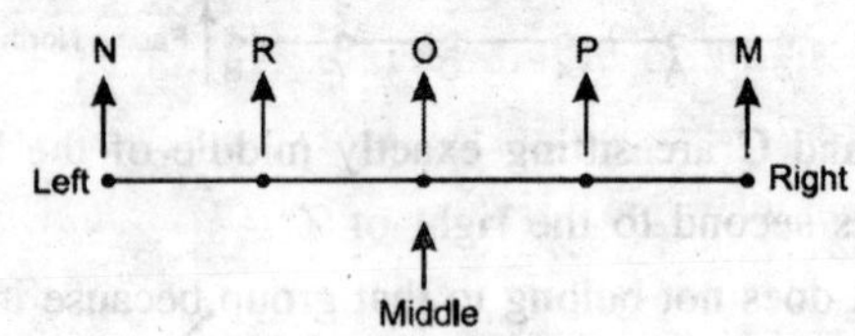

42.

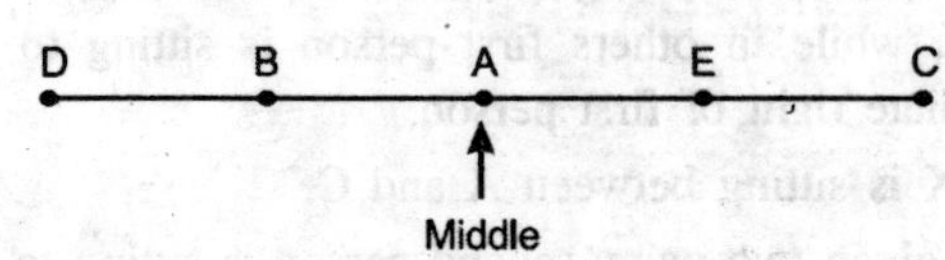

43.

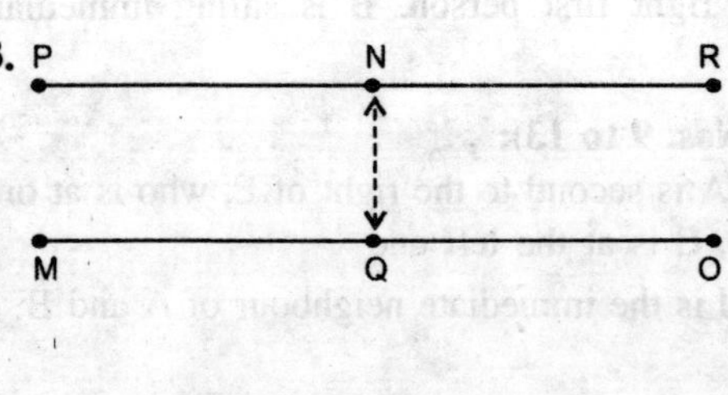

Solutions (Q. Nos. 44 to 48) : *According to given information, the final arrangement is as following*

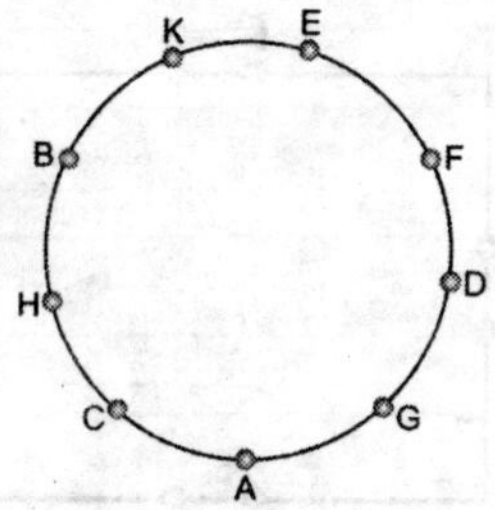

44. B is fourth to the right of D.

45. D is sitting between F and G.

46. G is third to the right of H.

47. A is fourth to the left of E.

48. H is second to the right of K.

Solutions (Q. Nos. 49 to 53) : *According to the given information, the final arrangement is as following*

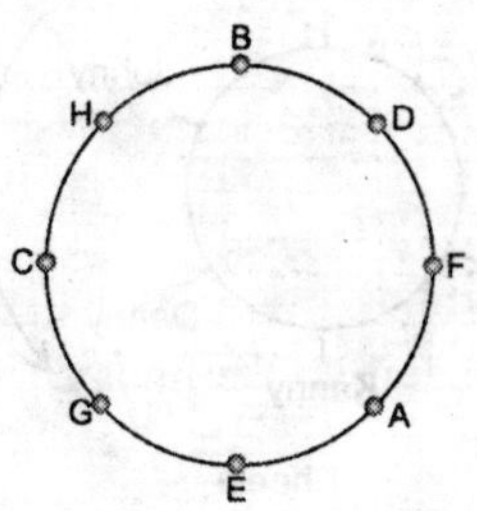

49. G sits second to the left of A.

50. D sits to the immediate left of B.

51. H is third to the right of F.

52. BF does not belong to that group because in this pair, second person is sitting second to the left of first person while in other pairs, second person is sitting second to the right of first person.

53. D is sitting to the immediate right of F.

Solutions (Q. Nos. 54 to 58) : *According to given information, the final arrangement is as following*

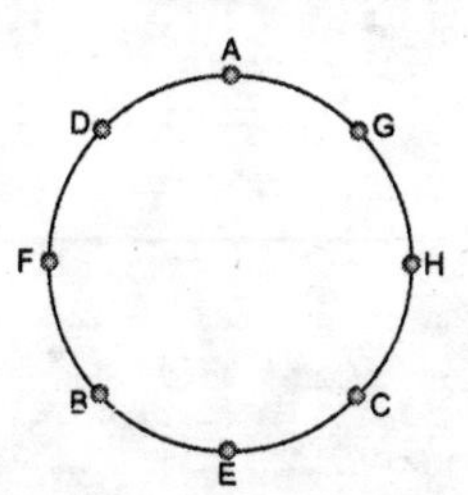

54. All the three statements I, II and III are wrong.

55. AG and CE are two pairs of adjacent members.

56. G is second to the left of D.

57. D is third to the left of E and he is also fifth to the right of E. So, Statements I and II are correct.

58. The new arrangement will be as following

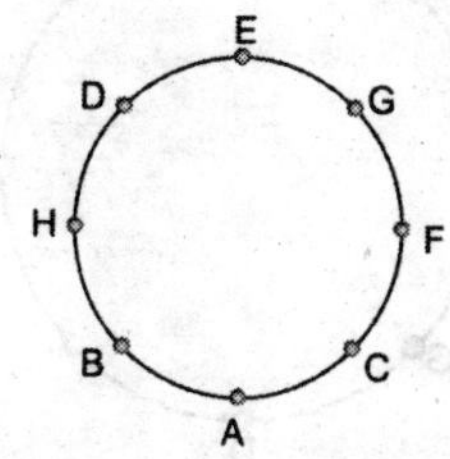

Solutions (Q. Nos. 59 to 63) : *According to given information, the final arrangement is as following*

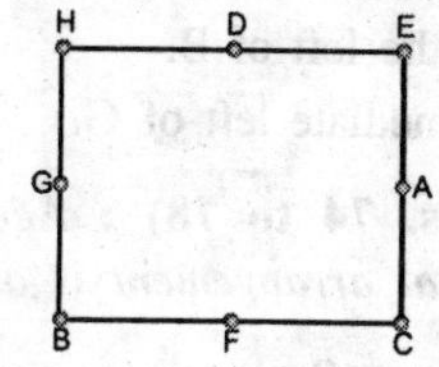

59. C is between F and A.

60. There are two persons E and D that are sitting between A and H, when counted in anti-clockwise direction from A.

61. E does not belong to this group because E is sitting on a corner while all others are sitting in the middle of each side.

62. F is to the immediate left of C.

63. One more person sits in each successive pair of persons. Hence, three persons (C, A and E) are sitting between F and D.

Solutions (Q. Nos. 64 to 68) : *According to given information, the final arrangement is as following*

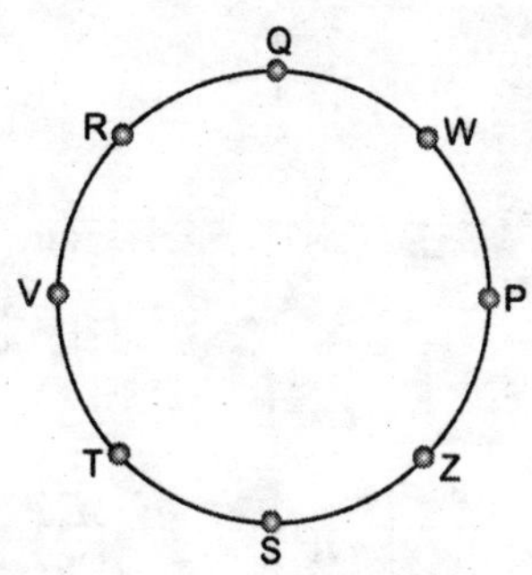

64. V is sitting between R and T.

65. Z is second to the right of T.

66. P is sixth to the left of S.

67. S is to the immediate left of Z.

68. R is second to the right of W.

Solutions (Q. Nos. 69 to 73) : *According to given information, the final arrangement is as following*

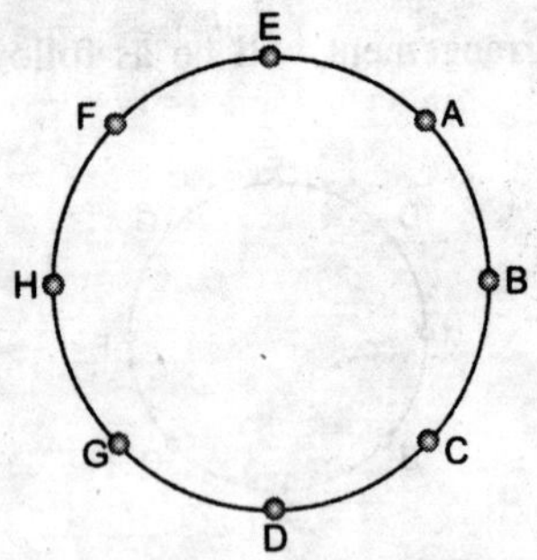

69. A is sitting between B and E.

70. C is third to the right of H.

71. E is to the immediate right of A.

72. H is fourth to the left of B.

73. H is to the immediate left of G.

Solutions (Q. Nos. 74 to 78) : *According to given information, the final arrangement is as following*

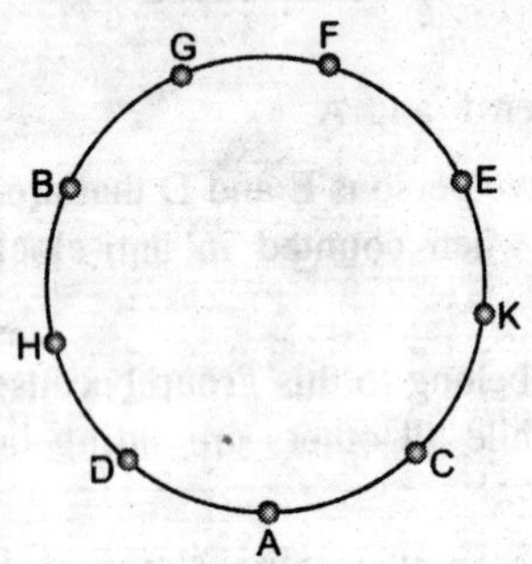

74. G is to the immediate right of F.

75. G is third to the right of K

76. E is third to the left of B.

77. C is fourth to the left of G.

78. F is sitting between E and G.

Solutions (Q. Nos. 79 to 83) : *According to given information, the final arrangement is as following*

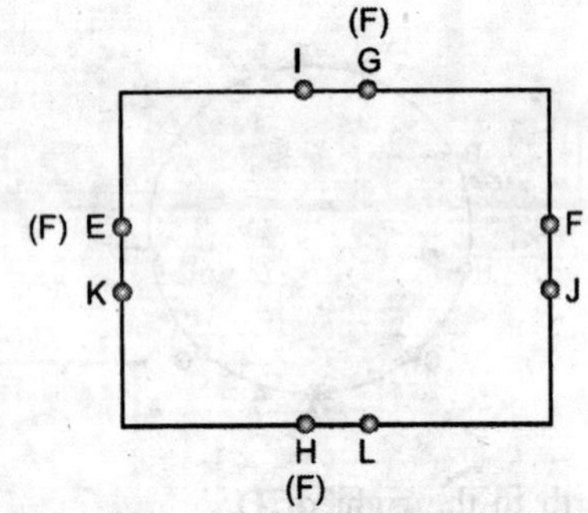

79. E, H and G are lady members.

80. J is a male member.

81. K is sitting between E and H.

82. J is to the immediate left of H.

83. Three persons (H, L and J) are seated between K and F.

84.

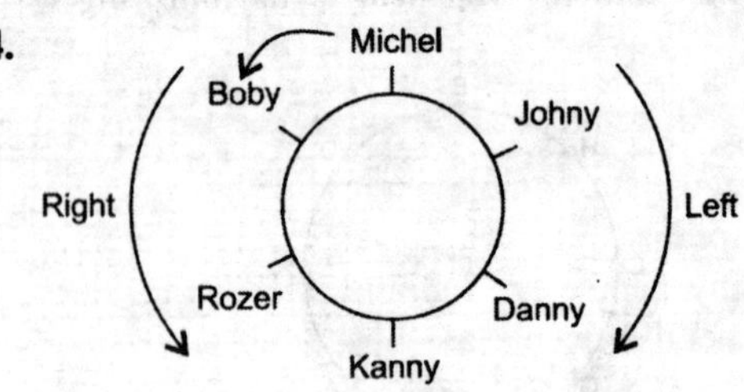

85.

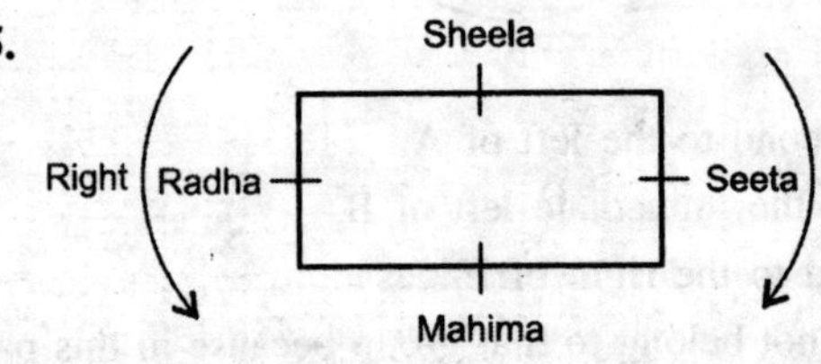

●●●

11 Statement and Assumptions

MULTIPLE CHOICE QUESTIONS

Directions (Q. 1–35): *In each question below a statement is given followed by two assumptions numbered I and II. You have to consider the statement and the following assumptions and decide which of the assumptions is implicit in the statement.*

Give answer

A. If only assumption I is implicit
B. If only assumption II is implicit
C. If either I or II is implicit
D. If neither I nor II is implicit
E. If both I and II are implicit.

1. Statement: Be humble even after being victorious.
Assumptions:
I. Many people are humble after being victorious.
II. Generally people are not humble.

2. Statement: The government has decided to pay compensation to the tune of ₹ 1 lakh to the family members of those who are killed in railway accidents.
Assumptions:
I. The government has enough funds to meet the expenses due to compensation.
II. There may be reduction in incidents of railway accidents in near future.

3. Statement: Films have become indispensable for the entertainment of people.
Assumptions:
I. Films are the only media of entertainment.
II. People enjoy films.

4. Statement: Of all the newspapers published in Mumbai, readership of the 'Times' is the largest in the Metropolis.
Assumptions:
I. 'Times' is not popular in mofussil areas.
II. 'Times' has the popular feature of cartoons on burning social and political issues.

5. Statement: Apart from the entertainment value of television, its educational value cannot be ignored.
Assumptions:
I. People take television to be a means of entertainment only.
II. The educational value of television is not realised properly.

6. Statement: The State government has decided to appoint four thousand primary school teachers during the next financial year.
Assumptions:
I. There are enough schools in the state to accommodate four thousand additional primary school teachers.
II. The eligible candidates may not be interested to apply, as the government may not finally appoint such a large number of primary school teachers.

7. Statement: A warning in a train compartment—"To stop train, pull chain. Penalty for improper use ` 500."
Assumptions:
I. Some people misuse the alarm chain.
II. On certain occasions, people may want to stop a running train.

8. Statement: If it is easy to become an engineer, I don't want to be an engineer.
Assumptions:
I. An individual aspires to be a professional.
II. One desires to achieve a thing which is hard earned.

9. Statement: The concession in rail fares for a journey to hill stations has been cancelled because it is not needed for people who can spend their holidays there.
Assumptions:
I. Railways should give concession only to needy persons.
II. Railways should not encourage people to spend their holidays at hill stations.

10. Statement: "The bridge was built at the cost of ₹ 128 crores and even civil bus service is not utilizing it, what a pity to see it grossly underutilized." A citizen's view on a new flyover linking east and west sides of a suburb.
Assumptions:
I. The building of such bridges does not serve any public objective.
II. There has to be some accountability and utility of money spent on public projects.

11. **Statement:** Beware of dogs, our dogs do not bark, but they are trained to distinguish between genuine guests and intruders.
Assumptions:
I. Barking dogs bite rarely.
II. Our dogs could be dangerous for intruders.

12. **Statement:** Because of the large number of potholes in road X, reaching airport in time has become difficult.
Assumptions:
I. Reaching airport in time may not always be necessary.
II. There is no other convenient road to the airport.

13. **Statement:** Safety and health practices in many Indian companies are well below the international standards.
Assumptions:
I. International standards of health and safety are ideal and unrealistic.
II. Indian organizations do not consider safety and health management as their prime social responsibility.

14. **Statement:** Greater public participation results in good civic governance. Statement of Municipal Commissioner of City A.
Assumptions:
I. The municipal office is not competent to effect good civic administration.
II. Good civic governance is a matter of collective will and effort of the people and administration.

15. **Statement:** The regulatory authority has set up a review committee to find out the reasons for unstable stock prices.
Assumptions:
I. The investors may regain confidence in stock market by this decision.
II. The review committee has the expertise to find out the causes for volatility in the stock market.

16. **Statement:** 'Please note that the company will provide accommodation to only outside candidates if selected.' A condition in an advertisement.
Assumptions:
I. The local candidates would be having some other arrangement for their stay.
II. The company plans to select only local candidates.

17. **Statement:** Cases of food poisoning due to consumption of liquor are increasing in rural areas.
Assumptions:
I. Percentage of people consuming liquor is more in rural areas.
II. There are many unauthorized spurious liquor shops in the rural areas.

18. **Statement:** Shalini made an application to the bank for a loan of ₹ 1,80,000 by mortgaging her house to the bank and promised to repay it within five years.
Assumptions:
I. The bank has a practice of granting loans for ₹ 1,00,000 and above.
II. The bank accepts house as collateral security against such loans.

19. **Statement:** "Computer education should start at schools itself."
Assumptions:
I. Learning computers is easy.
II. Computer education fetches jobs easily.

20. **Statement:** "As there is a great demand, every person seeking tickets of the programme, will be given only five tickets."
Assumptions:
I. The organizers are not keen on selling the tickets.
II. No one is interested in getting more than five tickets.

21. **Statement:** Please consult us before making any decision on investment.
Assumptions:
I. You may take a wrong decision if you don't consult us.
II. It is important to take a right decision.

22. **Statement:** The Parent Teacher Association (PTA) of a school has informed the Principal that they will not send their children to the school unless the school-authority reduces the fees with immediate effect.
Assumptions:
I. Majority of the parents may agree with the PTA and may not send their wards with the school.
II. The school authority may accede to the demand of the PTA and reduce the fees.

23. **Statement:** The company has the right to reject any application form without furnishing any reason while sorting the list of candidates for interview—A condition mentioned in the employment notice.
Assumptions:
I. It is desirable to call only eligible candidates for interview.
II. The company believes in following impartial practice in all its functions.

24. **Statement:** Kartik left for Delhi on Tuesday by train to attend a function to be held on Friday at his uncle's house in Delhi.
Assumptions:
I. Kartik may reach Delhi on Wednesday.
II. Kartik may reach Delhi before Friday.

25. **Statement:** "Avon Cycles—Fast, easy to ride, impressive, reliable, crafted and up-to-date automation." An advertisement.
Assumptions:
I. There is no other cycle with any of these features.
II. People do not bother about the cost.

26. Statement: The entire north India, including Delhi and the neighbouring states remained 'powerless' the whole day of 19th December as the northern grid supplying electricity to the seven states collapsed yet again.

Assumptions:

1. The northern grid had collapsed earlier.
2. The grid system of providing electricity to a group of states is an ineffective type of power supply system.

27. Statement: It is through participative management policy alone that indiscipline in our industries can be contained and a quality of life can be ensured to the worker.

Assumptions:

I. Quality of life in our industries is better.

II. Indiscipline results in poor quality of life.

28. Statement: Municipal Corporation has decided to ban the entry of vehicles from sub-urban areas to the main city through main routes during peak hours to avoid traffic congestion.

Assumptions:

I. The people of sub-urban areas should not bring their vehicles during peak hours.

II. There is no traffic congestion by the vehicles of people residing in the main city.

29. Statement: World Health Organisation has decided to double its assistance to various health programmes in India as per-capita expenditure on health in India is very low compared to many other countries.

Assumptions:

I. The enhanced assistance may substantially increase the per-capita expenditure on health in India and bring it on a par with other countries.

II. The Government funding is less than adequate to provide medical facilities in India.

30. Statement: The General Administration Department has issued a circular to all the employees informing them that henceforth the employees can avail their lunch break at any of the half-hour slots between 1.00 p.m. and 2.30 p.m.

Assumptions:

I. The employees may welcome the decision and avail lunch break at different time slots.

II. There may not be any break in the work of the organization as the employees will have their lunch break at different time slots.

31. Statement: Government aided schools should have uniformity in charging various fees.

Assumptions:

I. The Government's subsidy comes from the money collected through taxes from people.

II. The Government while giving subsidy may have stipulated certain uniform conditions regarding fees.

32. Statement: In spite of less than normal rainfall in the catchment areas during the first two months of monsoon of the lakes supplying water to the city, the authority has not yet affected any cut in the water supply to the city.

Assumptions:

I. The rainfall during the remaining period of the monsoon may be adequate for normal water supply.

II. The present water level of the lakes supplying water to the city may be adequate for normal supply.

33. Statement: The head of the organization congratulated the entire staff in his speech for their sincere effort to bring down the deficit and urged them to give their best for attaining a more profitable position in future.

Assumptions:

I. The employees may get motivated and will maintain and if possible, enhance their present level of work.

II. The employees may now relax and slow down in their day to day work as there is no immediate threat of huge deficit.

34. Statement: The host in one of the popular T.V. programmes announced that the channel will contact the viewers between 9.00 a.m. to 6.00 p.m. on weekdays and the lucky ones will be given fabulous prizes.

Assumptions:

I. The people may remain indoors to receive the phone call.

II. More people may start watching the programme.

35. Statement: There is big boom in drug business and a number of jhuggi-jhopari dwellers in Delhi can be seen pedalling with small pouches of smack and brown sugar.

Assumptions:

I. Drug addiction is increasing in the country, specially in the capital.

II. Most of the jhuggi-jhopari dwellers would do anything for the money.

ANSWERS

1	2	3	4	5	6	7	8	9	10
B	A	B	D	E	A	E	B	A	B
11	**12**	**13**	**14**	**15**	**16**	**17**	**18**	**19**	**20**
B	B	B	B	E	A	B	E	A	D
21	**22**	**23**	**24**	**25**	**26**	**27**	**28**	**29**	**30**
E	E	A	B	D	A	B	D	E	B
31	**32**	**33**	**34**	**35**					
B	E	A	E	D					

EXPLANATORY ANSWERS

1. Clearly, nothing is mentioned about the nature of the people. So, assumption I is not implicit. Also, the statement gives an advice of being humble even after being victorious. This means that generally people are not humble. So, assumption II is implicit.

2. Clearly, the amount of compensation must have been decided keeping in mind the monetary position of the Government. So, assumption I is implicit. However, nothing can be said about the frequency of railway accidents in future. So, assumption II is not implicit.

3. 'Films are indispensable' does not mean that they are the only means of entertainment. So, assumption I is not implicit. Clearly, assumption II follows from the statement. So, it is implicit.

4. Neither the volume of readership of the 'Times' in areas other than the Metropolis nor the reason for its huge acclamation is evident from the statement. So, neither assumption I nor II is implicit.

5. The statement makes the first assumption clear though educational value is not to be ignored. So, assumption I is implicit. Educational value must not be ignored also shows that the educational value is not realised properly. So, assumption II is also implicit.

6. Such decisions as given in the statement are taken only after taking the existing vacancies into consideration. So, assumption I implicit while II isn't.

7. Clearly, the penalty is imposed to prevent people from misusing the alarm chain. This means that some people misuse it. So, assumption I is implicit. The alarm chain is provided to stop the running train in times of urgency. So, assumption II is also implicit.

8. Clearly, nothing is mentioned about the professional nature of the job. So, assumption I is not implicit. The statement hints that one rejects a thing that is easy to achieve. So, assumption II is implicit.

9. The statement mentions that concessions should not be given to people who can afford to spend holidays in hill stations. This means it should be given only to needy persons. So, assumption I is implicit. But, II does not follow the statement and is not implicit.

10. Clearly, the statement expresses grave concern over a newly-built flyover not being utilized by public. This implies that such projects need to be taken up only after working out their utility and that the huge expenditure incurred on building such structures is worthwhile only if they prove useful for the public. Thus, only assumption II is implicit.

11. The statement clearly warns the visitors to beware of dogs as they are trained to welcome the guests and intruders differently. So, assumption II is implicit. assumption I is vague and hence, it is not implicit.

12. The statement presents the issue of 'not reaching airport in time' as a problem. This means that reaching airport in time is necessary. So, assumption I is not implicit. Besides, it is mentioned that reaching airport in time has become difficult due to large number of potholes in road X. This implies that road X is the only possible way. So, assumption II is implicit.

13. The statement talks about the safety and health practices in Indian companies being far below international standards. It is clearly a criticism of Indian organizations not paying considerable attention to these aspects. So, assumption II is implicit. The international standards demand perfection and are, in no way, non-achievable. So, assumption I is not implicit.

14. The statement stresses on the fact that though civic governance is the task of the municipal body, but all the tasks done come out to be more fruitful if the general public lends a helping hand in the same. So, only assumption II is implicit.

15. Clearly, assumption I mentions the aim for which the step talked about in the statement, has been undertaken while assumption II mentions the essential requirement for it. So, both assumption I and II are implicit.

16. The statement mentions that the company intends to provide accommodation only to outside candidates. This means that local candidates would have to arrange accommodation on their own and that the company may select local as well as outside candidates. Thus, only assumption I is implicit.

17. The statement talks of number of cases of food poisoning due to consumption of liquor and not of the number of cases consuming liquor. So, assumption I is not implicit. Besides, the statement indicates that people in rural areas are getting spurious or low-grade liquor and no check is being kept on shops selling liquor there. So, assumption II is implicit.

18. The fact that Shalini has applied for a loan of ₹ 1,80,000 implies that the bank can grant a loan above ₹ 1,00,000. So, assumption I is implicit. assumption II also follows directly from the statement and so is implicit.

19. Clearly, computer education can be started at the school level only if it is easy. So, assumption I is implicit. In the statement, nothing is mentioned about the link between jobs and computer education. So, assumption II is not implicit.

20. Clearly, the organisers are adopting this policy not to reduce the sale but to cope up with great demand so that everyone can get the ticket. So, assumption I is not implicit. Also, due to great demand, the maximum number of tickets one person can get has been reduced to five. So, assumption II is also not implicit.

21. Clearly, the statement was spoken for fear that the other person may take a wrong decision. So, assumption I is implicit. Again, the statement confirms that it is important to take the right decision. So, assumption II is also implicit.

22. The PTA is an association which would surely reflect the parents' interests and act to get them fulfilled. So, both assumption I and II are implicit.

23. Since the statement talks of the company short-listing the candidates to be called for interview, so assumption I is implicit. However, nothing can be deduced about whether the company would make a partial or fair selection of candidates. So, assumption II is not implicit.

24. Clearly, it cannot be deduced as to which day Kartik would reach Delhi. But Kartik has left for Delhi to attend a function to be held on Friday. So, he must have planned his journey to reach Delhi before Friday. Thus, only assumption II is implicit.

25. The advertisement is for Avon cycles and nothing about the cost or the features of other brands of cycles, are mentioned. So, neither assumption I nor II is implicit.

26. The statement mentions that the northern grid collapsed 'yet again'. This means that it had collapsed earlier also. So, assumption I is implicit. Also, the statement talks of a particular fault in the system but does not condemn the grid system. So, assumption II is not implicit.

27. The statement mentions that participative management policy 'will' provide quality life to the workers. So, assumption I is not implicit. Clearly, the statement mentions that participative management will contain the indiscipline and ensure quality life to workers. So, assumption II is implicit.

28. It is mentioned that entry only through main routes has been banned. So, assumption I is not implicit. Besides, the entry has been banned to reduce the volume of traffic on roads and ease congestion. It could only be done at the entrances to the city and not within the city itself. So, congestion by the city vehicles is unavoidable. Hence, assumption II is also not implicit.

29. The fact that WHO has extended its assistance to India implies that government funding here is not adequate. So, assumption II is implicit. Besides, WHO has decided to provide assistance to health programmes in India keeping in mind the considerably low per-capita expenditure on health. So, assumption I is also implicit.

30. The employees' reaction to the new decision cannot be deduced from the statement. So, assumption I is not implicit. However, assumption II denotes the most probable consequence of the new decision. So, assumption II is implicit.

31. Nothing about the source of Government's subsidy can be deduced from the statement. So, assumption I is not implicit. However, assumption II follows from the statement and so it is implicit.

32. The statement clearly indicates that at present the water level of the lakes is adequate. There is nothing of a shortage to induce a cut in water supply and still there is time to wait and watch the performance of rains during the remaining monsoon period. So, both assumption I and II are implicit.

33. The appreciation received from the head of the organization would surely motivate the employees to keep up their spirits and strive hard for the progress of the organization. So, only assumption I is implicit.

34. Clearly, the organisers of the programme have adopted the viewer interaction scheme and announced prizes for some lucky viewers so that more people are enticed into staying at home and viewing the programme. So, both assumption I and II are implicit.

35. The statement talks of boom in drug business and cites examples from the capital city. This makes I implicit. Further, it is given that most jhuggi-jhopari dwellers are seen to indulge in transactions of drug pouches. This implies that they give in to their lust for money quite easily and do not hesitate to get involved in illegal activities or the same. So, assumption II is implicit.

●●●

12 Courses of Action

MULTIPLE CHOICE QUESTIONS

Directions (Q. 1–25): *In each question below a statement is given followed by two courses of action numbered I and II. You have to assume everything in the statement to be true and on the basis of the information given in the statement, decide which of the suggested courses of action logically follow(s) for pursuing.*

Give answer

A. If only I follows
B. If only II follows
C. If either I or II follows
D. If neither I nor II follows
D. If both I and II follow.

1. Statement: Since its launching in 1881, Vayudoot has so far accumulated losses amounting to ₹ 153 crore.

Courses of Action:

I. Vayudoot should be directed to reduce wasteful expenditure and to increase passenger fare.

II. An amount of about ₹ 300 crore should be provided to Vayudoot to make the airline economically viable.

2. Statement: Exporters in the capital are alleging that commercial banks are violating a Reserve Bank of India directive to operate a post shipment export credit denominated in foreign currency at international rates from January this year.

Courses of Action:

I. The officers concerned to the commercial banks are to be suspended.

II. The RBI should be asked to stop giving such directives to commercial banks.

3. Statement: A large number of people die every year due to drinking polluted water during the summer.

Courses of Action:

I. The government should make adequate arrangements to provide safe drinking water to all its citizens.

II. The people should be educated about the dangers of drinking polluted water.

4. Statement: If the retired professors of the same institute are also invited to deliberate on restructuring the organisation, their contribution may be beneficial to the institute.

Courses of Action:

I. Management may seek opinion of the employees before calling retired professors.

II. Management should involve experienced people for the systematic restructuring of the organisation.

5. Statement: There is an unprecedented increase in migration of villagers to urban areas as repeated crop failures have put them into precarious financial situation.

Courses of Action:

I. The villagers should be provided with alternate source of income in their villages which will make them stay put.

II. The migrated villagers should be provided with jobs in the urban areas to help them survive.

6. Statement: Most of those who study in premier engineering colleges in India migrate to developed nations for better prospects in their professional pursuits.

Courses of Action:

I. All the students joining these colleges should be asked to sign a bond at the time of admission to the effect that they will remain in India at least for ten years after they complete education.

II. All those students who desire to settle in the developed nations should be asked to pay entire cost of their education which the government subsidises.

7. Statement: Doordarshan is concerned about the quality of its programmes particularly in view of stiff competition it is facing from STAR and other satellite TV channels and is contemplating various measures to attract talents for its programmes.

Courses of Action:

I. In an effort to attract talents the Doordarshan has decided to revise its fee structure for the artists.

II. The fee structure should not be revised until other electronic media also revise it.

8. Statement: The Chairman stressed the need for making education system more flexible and regretted that the curriculum has not been revised in keeping with the pace of the changes taking place.

Courses of Action:

I. Curriculum should be reviewed and revised periodically.

II. System of education should be made more flexible.

9. Statement: The availability of imported fruits has increased in the indigenous market and so the demand for indigenous fruits has been decreased.

Courses of Action:

I. To help the indigenous producers of fruits, the Government should impose high import duty on these fruits, even if these are not of good quality.

II. The fruit vendors should stop selling imported fruits. So that the demand for indigenous fruits would be increased.

10. Statement: On an average, about twenty people are run over by trains and die every day while crossing the railway tracks through the level crossing.

Courses of Action:

I. The railway authorities should be instructed to close all the level crossings.

II. Those who are found crossing the tracks, when the gates are closed, should be fined heavily.

11. Statement: It is necessary to adopt suitable measures to prevent repetition of bad debts by learning from the past experiences of mounting non-performing assets of banks.

Courses of Action:

I. Before granting loan to customers, their eligibility for loan should be evaluated strictly.

II. To ensure the payment of instalments of loan, the work, for which loan was granted, should be supervised minutely on regular basis.

12. Statement: There has been an unprecedented increase in the number of requests for berths in most of the long distance trains during the current holiday season.

Courses of Action:

I. The railway authority should immediately increase the capacity in each of these trains by attaching additional coaches.

II. The people seeking accommodation should be advised to make their travel plan after the holiday.

13. Statement: It is reported that though Vitamin E present in fresh fruits and vegetables is beneficial for human body, capsule Vitamin E does not have the same effect on human body.

Courses of Action:

I. The sale of capsule Vitamin E should be banned.

II. People should be encouraged to take fresh fruits and vegetables to meet the body's requirement of Vitamin E.

14. Statement: There has been less than forty per cent voter turnout in the recent assembly elections.

Courses of Action:

I. The election commission should cancel the entire election process as the votes cast are not adequate to represent people.

II. The election commission should take away the voting rights of those who did not exercise their rights.

15. Statement: The Committee has criticized the institute for its failure to implement a dozen of regular programmes despite an increase in the staff strength and not drawing up a firm action plan for studies and research.

Courses of Action:

I. The broad objectives of the institute should be redefined to implement a practical action plan.

II. The institute should give a report on reasons for not having implemented the planned programmes.

16. Statement: India has been continuously experiencing military threats from its neighbouring countries.

Courses of Action:

I. India should engage into an all out war to stop the nagging threats.

II. India should get the neighbours into a serious dialogue to reduce the tension at its borders.

17. Statement: Financial stringency prevented the State Government from paying salaries to its employees since April this year.

Courses of Action:

I. The State Government should immediately curtail the staff strength at least by 30%.

II. The State Government should reduce wasteful expenditure and arrange to pay the salaries of its employees.

18. Statement: Courts take too long in deciding important disputes of various departments.

Courses of Action:

I. Courts should be ordered to speed up matters.

II. Special powers should be granted to officers to settle disputes concerning their department.

19. Statement: Footpaths of a busy road are crowded with vendors selling cheap items.

Courses of Action:

I. The help of police should be sought to drive them away.

II. Some space should be provided to them where they can earn their bread without blocking footpaths.

20. Statement: Many medical and engineering graduates are taking up jobs in administrative services and in banks.

Courses of Action:

I. All the professionals should be advised to refrain from taking up such jobs.

II. The government should appoint a committee to find out the reasons for these professionals taking up such jobs and to suggest remedial measures.

21. Statement: Due to substantial reduction in fares by different airline services, large number of passengers so far travelling by upper classes in trains have switched over to airline services.

Courses of Action:

I. The railways should immediately reduce the fare structure of the upper classes substantially to retain its passengers.

II. The railways should reduce the capacity of upper classes in all the trains to avoid loss.

22. Statement: There has been large number of cases of internet hacking in the recent months creating panic among the internet users.

Courses of Action:

I. The government machinery should make an all out effort to nab those who are responsible and put them behind bars.

II. The internet users should be advised to stay away from using internet till the culprits are caught.

23. Statement : Although the Indian economy is still heavily dependent on agriculture, its share in global agricultural trade is less than the share of agricultural exports to total exports.

Courses of Action :

I. Efforts should be made to increase our agricultural production.

II. The exports of non-agricultural commodities should be reduced.

24. Statement : About 30 to 40 per cent of children who are enrolled, do not attend school on any given day.

Courses of Action :

I. More schools should be started.

II. Reasons for this absenteeism should be found out.

25. Statement : Certain mining industries in Gujarat may come to a standstill because of the notification issued by the Ministry of Environment and Forest banning mining operations and industries alike within 25 kms of National Park, the bird sanctuary and reserve forest areas.

Courses of Action :

I. The Ministry should be asked to immediately withdraw the notification.

II. The Government should make efforts to shift the parks, sanctuaries and reserve forests to other non-mining areas.

ANSWERS

1	2	3	4	5	6	7	8	9	10
A	D	E	B	A	B	A	E	D	B
11	**12**	**13**	**14**	**15**	**16**	**17**	**18**	**19**	**20**
E	A	B	D	E	B	B	E	E	B
21	**22**	**23**	**24**	**25**					
A	A	D	D	D					

EXPLANATORY ANSWERS

1. Clearly, for better economic gain, losses should be reduced and income increased. So, only course I follows.

2. The statement mentions that the commercial banks violate a directive issued by the RBI. The remedy is only to make the banks implement the Act. So, none of the courses follows.

3. The situation demands creating awareness among people about the dangers of drinking polluted water so that they themselves refrain from the same, and at the same time taking steps to provide safe drinking water. So, both the courses follow.

4. Clearly, the statement stresses that the contribution of retired professors shall be beneficial. This means that these people's experience of working in the organisation is helpful. So, only course II follows.

5. Clearly, increased migration would add extra burden on city's infrastructure. So, attempts should be made to make the villagers feel comfortable in the villages itself. So, only course I follows.

6. Clearly, no student can be bound to live and work in the country against their wish. So, course I does not follow. However, it is quite right to recover the extra benefits awarded to students if they do not serve their own country. So, only course II follows.

7. Clearly, the decision to revise its fee structure for artists is taken by Doordarshan as a remedy to the challenging problem that had arisen before it. It cannot wait till other media take action. So, only course I follows.

8. Clearly, the situation demands making the education system more flexible and changing it periodically according to the needs of the time. So, both the courses follow.

9. The ideas suggested in both course I and II represent unfair means to cut competition. The correct way would be to devise methods and techniques such that the indigenous producers could produce better quality fruits and make them available in the market at prices comparable with those of the imported ones. Hence, neither course I nor II follows.

10. The accidents can clearly be prevented by barring people from crossing the tracks when the gates are closed, So, only course II follows.

11. To ensure that debts taken are repaid promptly, the customer's requirements and future prospects ought to be studied and their work constantly checked. Thus, both the courses follow.

12. People cannot be deprived of going to a certain destination merely for lack of berths. Instead it, it is the duty of the railway authority to accommodate all the bookings by all means. So, only course I follows.

13. The statement implies that capsule Vitamin E does not function so effectively as natural Vitamin E. Since no negative effect of capsule Vitamin E is mentioned, so course I does not follow. Hence, only course II follows.

14. Re-election would demand repeated expenses and following course II would reduce the voter base permanently. Instead, awareness should be created among the people to use their right to vote effectively. So, neither course I nor II follows.

15. The problem is that despite an increase in staff strength, the institute has failed in its objective of implementing its plan. So, either there should be reasons for the failure or the plans are a failure and must be revised for practical implementation. Thus, both the courses follow.

16. Clearly, war is the last resort. First, peaceful talks and negotiations should be indulged in, to settle the issues of dispute. So, only course II follows.

17. Clearly, curtailing of the staff strength will only increase the panic and discontent, and the satisfaction of the employees is a must. So, the Government should arrange for payment of wages. Thus, only course II follows.

18. Clearly, either the work in the court needs to be sped up or the system be reorganised so that more number of problems can be resolved at the lower levels itself, to provide speedy justice to the people. So, both the courses follow.

19. Crowding on footpaths is a great inconvenience for walkers. So, stern action needs to be taken to remove the vendors. But at the same time these people ought to be provided alternative means of livelihood. So, both the courses follow.

20. Following course I would be an infringement of the right to freedom of individuals. However, if the lacking of their respective fields are found out and removed, the professionals would surely give up the idea of opting for other jobs. Hence, only course II follows.

21. Airlines, being convenient and faster means of transport, people would surely prefer it to the railways if there is a marginal difference between the fares. Hence, a considerable gap between the two fares is a must for the railways. So, course I follows. Following course II would reduce the volume of passengers. Hence, course II does not follow.

22. Clearly, internet users should not suffer on account of certain individuals who indulge in internet hacking. However, such wrong-doers ought to be penalised so that there are no hassles in the use of internet. So, only course I follows.

23. India's share in global agricultural trade is less than the share of agricultural exports to total exports. Therefore, there is no necessity of increasing the agricultural production. Reducing the exports of non-agricultural commodity will not affect the share of agricultural exports. So, neither course of action follows.

24. About 30 to 40 per cent of enrolled children do not attend schools. Therefore, the decision to start more schools is pointless. The statement does not mention that a particular group of children do not attend schools. This means the percentage of absent children comprises of various children who are absent at different times. There cannot be specific reasons for this absenteeism. So, neither course of action follows.

25. The department cannot withdraw the notification because environment pollution must be checked around the sanctuary and reserve forest areas. Further, it is coherent to shift the mining industries. So, neither course of action follows.

●●●

13 Cause and Effect

MULTIPLE CHOICE QUESTIONS

Directions (Q. 1–20): *In each of the questions below two statements I and II are given. These statements may be either independent causes or may be effects of independent causes or a common cause. One of these statements may be the effect of the other statements. Read both the statements and decide which of the following answer choice correctly depicts the relationship between these two statements.*

Mark Answer

A. If statement I is the cause and statement II is its effect.
B. If statement II is the cause and statement I is its effect.
C. If both the statements I and II are independent causes.
D. If both the statements I and II are effects of independent causes.
E. If both the statements I and II are effects of some common cause.

1. Statements:

I. Rural and semi-urban areas in the country have been suffering due to load-shedding for quite some time.

II. If the Government is not able to overcome the power crisis, load-shedding will be extended even to the urban areas.

2. Statements:

I. The Government has increased rates of petrol and diesel by 10% with immediate effect.

II. Oil producing countries have decided to increase 10% of production on crude oil from the last quarter.

3. Statements:

I. The vegetable prices in the local market have increased manifold during the past few days.

II. Incessant rain have created flood like situation in most rural parts of the State.

4. Statements:

I. The performance of Indian sports persons in the recently held Olympics could not reach the level of expectations the country had on them.

II. The performance of Indian sports person in the last Asian games was far better than any previous games.

5. Statements:

I. Large numbers of people have fallen sick after consuming sweets from a particular shop in the locality.

II. Major part of the locality is flooded and has become inaccessible to outsides.

6. Statements:

I. The life today is too fast, demanding full of variety in all aspects which at times leads to stressful situation.

II. Number of suicide cases among teenagers is on increase.

7. Statements:

I. The university authority has instructed all the colleges under its jurisdiction to ban use of cell phones inside the college premises.

II. Majority of the teachers of the colleges signed a joint petition to the university, complaining about the disturbances caused by cell phone ring tones inside the classrooms.

8. Statements:

I. The Government has reduced the prices of petroleum products by five per cent a week after increasing the prices by ten per cent.

II. The rate of inflation dropped marginally during the last week.

9. Statements:

I. The committee appointed by the Government on the fee structure of the professional courses has drastically reduced the fees of various courses in comparison to those charged in the last year.

II. The parents of aspiring students seeking admission to professional courses had launched a severe agitation protesting against the high fees charged by the professional institutes and the admission process was delayed considerably.

10. Statements:

I. The Government has decided to hold a single entrance test for admission to all the medical colleges in India.

II. The State Government has debarred students from other States to apply for the seats in the medical colleges in the State.

11. Statements:

I. Large number of Primary Schools in the rural areas are run by only one teacher.

II. There has been a huge dropout from the primary schools in rural areas.

12. Statements:

I. The car manufacturing companies have recently increased the prices of mid-sized cars.

II. The Government recently increased the duty on mid-sized cars.

13. Statements:

I. The State Government has announced special tax package for the new industries to be set-up in the State.

II. Last year the State Government had hiked the taxes for all industrial activities in the State.

14. Statements:

I. Standard of living among the middle class society is constantly going up since part of few years.

II. Indian Economy is observing remarkable growth.

15. Statements:

I. The Meteorological Department has issued a statement mentioning deficient rainfall during monsoon in many parts of the country.

II. The Government has lowered the revised estimated GDP growth from the level of earlier estimates.

16. Statements:

I. The staff of Airport Authorities called off the strike they were observing in protest against privatization.

II. The staff of Airport Authorities went on strike anticipating threat to their jobs.

17. Statements:

I. A huge truck overturned in the middle of the road last night.

II. The police had cordoned off entire area in the locality this morning for half of the day.

18. Statements:

I. Importance of yoga and exercise is being realized by all sections of the society.

II. There is an increasing awareness about health in the society particularly among middle-age group of people.

19. Statements:

I. The prices of food grains and other essential commodities in the open market have risen sharply during the past three months.

II. The political party in opposition has given a call for general strike to protest against the government's economic policy.

20. Statements:

I. The employees of the biggest bank in the country have given an indefinite strike call starting from the third of the next month.

II. The employees of the Central Government have withdrawn their week long demonstrations.

ANSWERS

1	2	3	4	5	6	7	8	9	10
E	D	B	E	D	E	B	D	B	E
11	**12**	**13**	**14**	**15**	**16**	**17**	**18**	**19**	**20**
A	B	B	A	D	D	A	B	A	A

EXPLANATORY ANSWERS

1. If certain preventive measures are practiced at the rural and semi-urban areas, the problem will be solved. But if the same is not practiced even at the cities, the problem may roll into the city also, so the two effects are of some common cause.

2. Both statements I and II are the effects of independent causes.

3. The transportation gets effect due to the flood created by incessant rains in the most rural parts of State. Therefore, on account of this, it is possible to increase the vegetable prices in the local market.

4. Both the statements are effects of some common cause.

5. Both statements I and II are the effects of independent causes.

6. Both the statements are effects of some common cause.

7. Since the teachers of the colleges complained to the university about the disturbances caused by cell phone ring-tones inside the class-rooms, the university authority has instructed all the colleges under its jurisdiction to ban use of cell phones inside the college premises.

8. Both the statements I and II are effects of independent causes.

9. Since the parents of aspiring students seeking admission to professional courses had launched a severe agitation protesting against the high fees charged by the professional institutes.

So, the committee was appointed by the Government on the fee structure of professional courses has drastically reduced the fees of various courses.

10. Both the statements are effects of some common cause.

11. Since large number of primary schools in the rural areas are run by only one teacher so, there has been a huge dropout from the primary schools in rural areas.

12. Since the government has recently increased the duty on mid-sized cars, therefore, the car manufacturing companies have recently increased the prices of mid-sized cars.

13. Because of the hike in taxes last year, the State Government has announced special tax package for the new industries to be set up in the State.

14. Since the standard of living among the middle class society is constantly going up so, Indian Economy is observing remarkable growth.

15. Both the statements I and II are effects of independent causes.

16. Both the statements I and II are effects of independent causes.

17. Since a huge truck overturned in the middle of the road last night, the police had cordoned off the entire area in the locality last morning for half of the day.

18. As the awareness about health in the society is increasing particularly, among middle-aged group of peole, the importance of Yoga and exercise is being realized by all sections of the society.

19. Since the prices of food grains and other essential commodities in the open market have been raised sharply during the past three months, the political party in opposition has given a call for general strike to protest against the government's economic policy.

20. Both the statements are effects of different causes.

●●●

14 Number and Alphabet Problem

Number and Alphabet problems are fun to attempt. They are based on given number sequences, mathematical calculations or on alphabetical series in natural as well as in reverse order.

Natural Order:

A B C D E F G H I J K L M N O P Q R S T U V W X Y Z

Reverse Order:

Z Y X W V U T S R Q P O N M L K J I H G F E D C B A

Note: The series starts from A on reaching Z and from Z on reaching A. Of these A E I O U are vowels and the rest are consonants.

Solved Examples

1. How many 6's are there in the following series of numbers which are preceded by 7 but not immediately followed by 9?
6 7 9 5 6 9 7 6 8 7 6 7 8 6 9 4 6 7 7 6 9 5 7 6 3

A. One B. Two
C. Three D. Four
E. More than 4

Ans.: C. 6 7 9 5 6 9 7 6 8 7 6 7 8 6 9 4 6 7 7 6 9 5 7 6 3

2. If the first ten letters of the following alphabet are written in the reverse order, which of the following letters will be the seventh to the left of the twelfth letter from the right end?

A. H B. C
C. I D. B
E. None of these

Ans.: B. The new series after reversing the first ten letters will be

JIHGFEDCBAKUMNOPORSTUVWXYZ

7th 12th

12th letter from right end, counting from 'Z' will be 'O' and 7th letter to the left of 'O' is 'C'.

MULTIPLE CHOICE QUESTIONS

1. How many even numbers are there in the following series of numbers, each of which is immediately preceded by an odd number, but not immediately followed by an even number?
5 3 4 8 9 7 1 6 5 3 2 9 8 4 3 5

A. Nil B. 1
C. 2 D. 3
E. None of these

2. In the following number sequence how many such even numbers are there which are exactly divisible by its immediate preceding number but not exactly divisible by its immediate following number?
3 8 4 1 5 7 2 8 3 4 8 9 3 9 4 2 1 5 8 2

A. Two B. Three
C. Four D. More than four
E. One

3. Which pair of numbers has least and maximum frequency in the given sequence?
8 7 5 6 4 5 8 3 8 6 7 2 3 5 8 3 5 7 6 4 7 6 5

A. 4 and 5 B. 2 and 6
C. 3 and 8 D. 2 and 5
E. None of these

Directions (Qs. Nos. 4 to 10): *The following questions are based on alphabet series in natural or reverse order and the combinations that can be made by changing the position of alphabet in given words.*

4. In the following list of letters, how many D's are followed by F, but not preceded by E?
X M N D F P R S T D D F O C E D F B T E D K

A. 4 B. 3
C. 2 D. 1
E. None of these

5. If the positions of the first and sixth letters of the word BENEFICIAL are interchanged, similarly the positions of the second and seventh are interchanged and so on, which letter will be third from the right end after rearrangement?

A. E B. N
C. C D. F
E. None of these

6. If it is possible to make a meaningful word with the second, the fifth, the tenth and the twelfth letters of the word METROPOLITAN, which of the following will be the third letter of that word? If no such word can be made, give 'X' as the answer and if more than one such word can be made, give 'M' as the answer.

A. N
B. T
C. Q
D. X
E. M

7. From the word "LAPAROSCOPY", how many independent meaningful English words can be made without changing the order of the letters and using each letter only once?

A. 1
B. 2
C. 3
D. 4
E. More than 4

8. The letter given in the centre can be used more than once, while each other letter is to be used only once to form a meaningful word. The third letter of that meaningful word is the answer. If no such meaningful word can be made, give 'X' as the answer and if more than one such meaningful word can be made, give 'M' as the answer.

A. P
B. R
C. O
D. X
E. M

9. If a meaningful word can be formed by using the first, third, fifth and seventh letters of the word INFORMAL, what will be the last letter?

A. N
B. F
C. M
D. R
E. No new word can be made

10. From the word CATCHMENTAREA how many independent meaningful words can be made without changing the order of the letters and using each letter only once?

A. 1
B. 2
C. 3
D. 4
E. More than 4

Directions (11-13): *Following questions are based on the five three digit numbers given below:*

518 849 365 783 291

11. If the positions of first and third digits in each number are interchanged, which of the following will be the second digit of third highest number ?

A. 1
B. 4
C. 8
D. 9
E. 6

12. If the first digit in all the numbers starting with an even digit is replaced by a number preceding it, then which of the following will be the sum of the first digit of the resulting highest and the lowest numbers?

A. 4
B. 8
C. 7
D. 6
E. 3

13. If the positions of the first and the second digits in each number are interchanged, which of the following will be the second highest number ?

A. 849
B. 365
C. 783
D. 291
E. 518

Directions (14-17): *Following questions are based on the five three digit numbers given below:*

518 723 496 375 254

14. What is the sum of digits of the third highest number?

A. 14
B. 12
C. 19
D. 15
E. 11

15. If '1' is added to the first digit of each number and '1' is subtracted from the third digit of each number, which of the following will be the new second lowest number ?

A. 518
B. 723
C. 496
D. 375
E. 254

16. If the positions of the first and the second digits of each of the above numbers are interchanged, which of the following will be the third digit of the lowest number?

A. 8
B. 3
C. 6
D. 5
E. 4

17. If the positions of the first and the third digits of each of the above numbers are interchanged, which of the following will be the second digit of the highest number?

A. 1
B. 2
C. 9
D. 7
E. 5

Directions (18-22): *These questions are based on the following set of numbers.*

937 483 765 572 684

18. If in each number the first two digits are replaced by their sum, which number will be the largest?

A. 937
B. 483
C. 765
D. 572
E. 684

19. If in each number the positions of first and the second digits are interchanged, which number will be the smallest?

A. 937
B. 483
C. 765
D. 572
E. 684

20. If in each number the order of digits is reversed and then the numbers are arranged in descending order, which number will be second?
A. 937 B. 483
C. 765 D. 572
E. 684

21. If '1' is added to the second digit and then the first and second digits are interchanged which number will be third?
A. 684 B. 765
C. 572 D. 937
E. 483

22. If in each number '1' is added to the last digit and then the position of second and the third digits are interchanged which number will be the largest?
A. 483 B. 937
C. 572 D. 765
E. 684

ANSWERS

1	2	3	4	5	6	7	8	9	10
C	A	D	C	B	E	B	E	D	C
11	**12**	**13**	**14**	**15**	**16**	**17**	**18**	**19**	**20**
E	B	C	C	D	A	A	E	A	C
21	**22**								
C	B								

EXPLANATORY ANSWERS

1. 5 3 4 8 9 7 1 6 5 3 2 9 8 4 3 5

2. 3 8 4 1 5 7 2 8 3 4 8 9 3 9 4 2 1 5 8 2

3. 2 appears only once and 5 appears five times 8 7 5 6 4 5 8 3 8 6 7 2 3 5 8 3 5 7 6 4 7 6 5

4. D's followed by 'F' but not preceded by 'E' are :
X M N D F P R S T D D F O C E D F B T E D K

5. The position of letters after interchanging the places of letters in word BENEFICIAL will be : ICIALBENEF 3rd letter from right end will be 'N'.

6. The 2nd, 5th, 10th and 12th letters of the word METROPOLITAN are E, O, T and N. The words that can be made by using these four letters are : NOTE and TONE.

7. The words are : LAP and COPY

8. The words formed are REPORT and PORTER

9. INFORMAL The 1st, 3rd, 5th and 7th letters are IFRA. The formed is FAIR; its last letter is 'R'.

10. The words formed are : CATCH, MEN, AREA.

11. 518 → 815; 849 → 948; 365 → 563;
783 → 387; 291 → 192
So third highest number is 563

12. 518 → 518; 849 → 749; 365 → 365;
783 → 783; 291 → 191;
So Highest Number is 783 and lowest number is 191.
Required Sum = 7 + 1 = 8

13. 518 → 158; 849 → 489; 365 → 635; 783 → 873; 291 → 921;
Second Highest Number → 873 → 783

14. Third highest number → 496, 4 + 9 + 6 = 19

15. 518 → 617; 723 → 822; 496 → 595; 375 → 474; 254 → 353 Second lowest number → 474 → 375

16. 518 → 158; 723 → 273; 496 → 946; 375 → 735; 254 → 524
Lowest number → 158 ?518

17. 518 → 815; 723 → 327; 496 → 694; 375 → 573; 254 → 452;
Highest number → 815 → 518

18. 937 → 127; 483 → 123; 765 → 135; 572 → 122; 684 → 144; Highest number is 144 → 684

19. 937 → 397; 483 → 843; 765 → 675 ; 572 → 752; 684 → 864
Smallest number is 397 → 937

20. 937 → 739; 483 → 384; 765 → 567; 572 → 275; 684 → 486; 739 > 567 > 486..... 567 → 765

21. 684 → 694 → 964; 765 → 775 → 775; 572 → 582 → 852; 937 → 947 → 497; 483 → 493 → 943;
Third highest number is 852 → 572.

22. 483 → 484 → 448; 937 → 938 → 983; 572 → 573 → 537; 765 → 766 → 766; 684 → 685 → 658.
Largest number → 983 → 937.

●●●

15

Series

LETTER SERIES

In letter series, the letters follow a definite order. The given series of letters can be in natural order or in reverse order or combination of both. The letters may be skipped or repeated or consecutive. The given series may be single or may comprise two different series merged at alternate positions. While attempting questions on letter series one should note the pattern of alphabet series.

Alphabets in natural series

A B C D E F G H I J K L M N O P Q R S T U V W X Y Z
1st 5th 10th 15th 20th 25th

are:

Alphabets in reverse series

Z Y X W V U T S R Q P O N M L K J I H G F E D C B A
1st 5th 10th 15th 20th 25th

Note: On reaching Z, the series restarts from A and on reaching A, it restarts from Z.

Solved Example

1. A Z B Y C ?

A. D B. X C. U
D. E E. None of these

Ans.: (B) There are two alternate series.

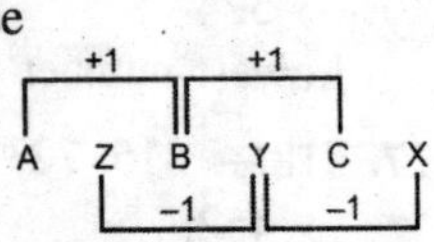

Series I : A B C (Consecutive letters in natural series)

Series II : Z Y X (Consecutive letters in reverse series)

REPEAT SERIES

In this type of series small letters of the alphabet are used to make a set of letters which are repeated. The candidate has to find the set of letters which will fit the blanks left in the given series in such a manner that one section of the series is further repeated in the same manner.

Solved Example

2. Which of the following groups of letters will complete the given series? ba-b-aab-a-b

A. baab B. abba C. abaa
D. babb E. None of these

Ans.: (B) The series is baab, baab, baab. Here the section 'baab' is repeated in the series. Solving steps : The candidate has to look for clues to solve such series pattern. 'aab' in the series indicates that 'b' in this series is preceded by two 'a' so, the first blank and the last blank will be filled by 'a'. Now the first set is formed, *i.e.*, 'baab' in the beginning. This set is repeated, so the second and third blanks will have 'b' filling them.

NUMBER SERIES

In this type of series, the set of given numbers in a series are related to one another in a particular pattern or manner. The relationship between the numbers may be (i) consecutive odd/even numbers; (ii) consecutive prime numbers; (iii) squares/cubes of some numbers with/without variation of addition or subtraction of some number; (iv) sum/product/difference of preceding numbers; (v) addition/subtraction/multiplication/division by some number; and (vi) many more combinations of the relationships given above.

Solved Example

3. Complete the given series. 2, 14, 98, 686, ?

A. 1976 B. 2548 C. 980
D. 4802 E. None of these

Ans.: (D) The numbers are multiplied by 7 to obtain the next numbers.

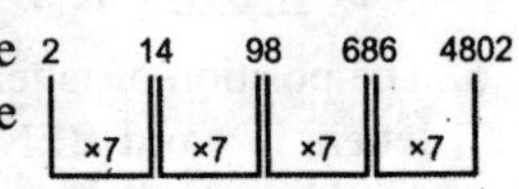

The given series may also comprise of two alternate series merged as one.

MIXED SERIES

Mixed series comprises of the combinations of letters and numbers. In this type of series, the letters and numbers may have a common sequence pattern or may have separate sequence patterns.

Solved Example

4. What should come in the place of question mark in the following letter-number combination?

F6, H8, J10, L12, ?

A. N15 B. O14 C. N14
D. O13 E. None of these

Ans.: (C) The letters are moved two steps forward and the number indicates the position of the letter in the alphabet series.

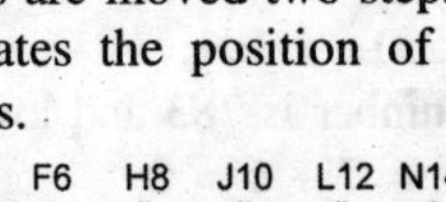

MULTIPLE CHOICE QUESTIONS

Directions (Qs. 1 to 8): *In each of the following series determine the order of the letters. Then from the given options select the one which will complete the given series.*

1. GH, JL, NQ, SW, YD, ?
A. EJ B. FJ
C. EL D. FL
E. None of these

2. AI, BJ, CK, ?
A. DL B. DM
C. GH D. LM
E. None of these

3. b e d f ? h j ? l
A. i m B. m i
C. i n D. j m
E. None of these

4. ADVENTURE, DVENTURE, DVENTUR, ?, VENTU
A. DVENT B. VENTURE
C. VENTUR D. DVENTU
E. None of these

5. PERPENDICULAR, ERPENDICULA, RPENDICUL, ?
A. PENDICUL B. PENDIC
C. ENDIC D. ENDICU
E. None of these

6. ATTRIBUTION, TTRIBUTIO, RIBUTIO, IBUTI,?
A. IBU B. UT
C. UTI D. BUT
E. None of these

7. M, N, O, L, R, I, V, ?
A. A B. E
C. F D. H
E. Z

8. A, CD, GHI, ?, UVWXY
A. LMNO B. MNO
C. MNOP D. NOPQ
E. None of these

Directions (Qs. 9 to 15): *Which letter(s) in each of the following series is wrong or is misfit in the series?*

9. Z A W B X C
A. D B. C
C. X D. W
E. None of these

10. M L O N Q P T R
A. T B. O
C. Q D. L
E. None of these

11. D K R Y F L
A. L B. D
C. R D. Y
E. None of these

12. L N Q T W Z C F
A. C B. Q
C. L D. F
E. None of these

13. XW, DC, CB, NM, PQ, QP
A. NM B. CB
C. PQ D. XW
E. None of these

14. B E I N S A I
A. A B. E
C. S D. I
E. None of these

15. Z T P K H F
A. Z B. P
C. T D. F
E. None of these

Directions (Qs. Nos. 16 to 20): *In each of the following letter series, some of the letters are missing which are given in that order as one of the alternatives below it. Choose the correct alternative.*

16. ba _ cb _ b _ bab _
A. acbb B. bacc
C. bcaa D. cabb
E. None of these

17. c _ bba _ cab _ ac _ ab _ ac
A. abebe B. acbcb
C. babec D. bcacb
E. None of these

18. ab _ _ baa _ _ ab _
A. aaaaa B. aabaa
C. aabab D. baabb
E. None of these

19. _ bc _ ca _ aba _ c _ ca
A. abcbb B. bbbec
C. bacba D. abbec
E. None of these

20. ab _ aa _ bbb _ aaa _ bbba
A. abba B. baab
C. aaab D. abab
E. None of these

Directions (Qs. 21 to 25): *Choose the correct alternative that will continue the same pattern and replace the question mark in the given series.*

21. 3, 9, 27, 81, 243, ?
A. 486 B. 729
C. 972 D. 359
E. None of these

22. 1, 6, 12, 19, 27 ?
A. 38 B. 35
C. 36 D. 54
E. None of these

23. 125, 80, 45, 20, ?
A. 5 B. 8
C. 10 D. 12
E. None of these

24. 120, 99, 80, 63, 48, ?
A. 35 B. 38
C. 39 D. 40
E. None of these

25. 589654237, 89654237, 8965423, 965423, ?
A. 58965 B. 65423
C. 89654 D. 96542
E. None of these

Directions (Qs. 26–33): *In each series given below, what would come in place of the question-mark?*

26. 2B, 4C, 8E, 14H, ?
A. 20L B. 22L
C. 21I D. 16K
E. None of these

27. C(1)L, F(4)O, I(9)R, L(16)U, ?
A. P(27)W B. N(24)Y
C. M(23)X D. O(25)X
E. None of these

28. 3F, 6G, 11I, 18L, ?
A. 27P B. 21O
C. 27Q D. 25N
E. None of these

29. W(1)A, X(4)Z, Y9Y, ?, A(25)W
A. X(11)Z B. Z(21)A
C. Z(16)X D. Z(14)X
E. None of these

30. 81Y, 27S, 9N, 3J, ?
A. 0H B. IG
C. 0F D. IE
E. None of these

31. E5, K11, Q17, ?
A. X20 B. Y24
C. V22 D. W25
E. None of these

32. D2, I3, N6, S18, ?
A. V72 B. W36
C. Y90 D. X108
E. None of these

33. 3J, 6M, 12L, ?, 48N
A. 24O B. 8M
C. 26M D. 22O
E. None of these

Directions (Qs. Nos. 34 and 35) : *Which of the following does not fit in the letter number series given below?*

34. G4T, J10R, M20P, P43N, S90L
A. J10R B. S90L
C. M20P D. G4T
E. None of these

35. B0R, G3U, E3P, J7S, H9N
A. E3P B. J7S
C. H9N D. G3U
E. None of these

ANSWERS

1	2	3	4	5	6	7	8	9	10
D	A	A	C	E	C	B	C	D	A
11	**12**	**13**	**14**	**15**	**16**	**17**	**18**	**19**	**20**
A	C	C	C	B	B	B	B	A	B
21	**22**	**23**	**24**	**25**	**26**	**27**	**28**	**29**	**30**
B	C	A	A	D	B	D	A	C	B
31	**32**	**33**	**34**	**35**					
C	D	A	A	B					

EXPLANATORY ANSWERS

1. 1st letter:

G —(+3)→ J —(+4)→ N —(+5)→ S —(+6)→ Y —(+7)→ (F)

2nd letter:

H —(+4)→ L —(+5)→ Q —(+6)→ W —(+7)→ D —(+8)→ (L)

2. 1st letter: A —(+1)→ B —(+1)→ C —(+1)→ (D)

2nd letter: I —(+1)→ J —(+1)→ K —(+1)→ (L)

3. The series may be divided into groups as shown: b e d / f ? h / j ? l. Clearly in the first group, the second and third letters are respectively three and two steps ahead of the first letter. A similar pattern would follow in the second and third groups.

4. One letter from the beginning and one from the end of a term are removed, one by one, in alternate steps.

5. Each term of the series is obtained by removing two letters from the preceding term one from the beginning and one from the end. So, the missing term is PENDICU.

6. In the first step, one letter from the beginning and one from the end of a term are removed to give the next term. In the second step, two letters from the beginning of a term are removed. These two steps are repeated alternately.

7. The given sequence is a combination of two series: I. M, O, R, V and II. N, L, I, ?

The pattern in I is: M $\xrightarrow{+2}$ O $\xrightarrow{+3}$ R $\xrightarrow{+4}$ V

The pattern in II is: N $\xrightarrow{-2}$ L $\xrightarrow{-3}$ I $\xrightarrow{-4}$ (E)

8. Each term consists of consecutive letters in order. The number of letters in the terms goes on increasing by one at each step. Also, there is a gap of one letter between the last letter of the first term and the first letter of the second term; a gap of two letters between the last letter of the second term and the first letter of the third term; and so on. So, there should be a gap of three letters between the last letter of the third term and the first letter of the desired term.

9. There are two alternate series I. Z, Y, X and II. A, B, C

The pattern in I is : Z $\xrightarrow{-1}$ (Y) $\xrightarrow{-1}$ X

The pattern in II is : A $\xrightarrow{+1}$ B $\xrightarrow{+1}$ C

10. Two consecutive letters are written backwards.

ML ON OP SR (← ← ← ←) S should be in place of T.

11. The pattern in this series is moving the letters seven steps forward.

D K R Y F (M) (+7 +7 +7 +7 +7) M should be in place of L.

12. The pattern in the series is +3

(K) N Q T W Z C F (+3 +3 +3 +3 +3 +3 +3) K should be in place of L.

13. The series is made with any two consecutive letters written backwards.

XW DC CB NM QP (← ← ← ← ←) Q should come before P in the series.

14. The difference between the letters is increased by one at each step.

B E I N (T) A I (+3 +4 +5 +6 +7 +8) T should be in place of S.

15. The difference between the letters is decreased by one at each step.

Z T O K H F (-6 -5 -4 -3 -2) O should be in place of P.

16. The series is babc/babc/babc. Thus, the pattern 'babc' is repeated.

17. The series is cabbac/cabbac/cabbac. Thus, the pattern 'cabbac' is repeated.

18. The series is aba/aba/aba/aba. Thus, the pattern 'aba' is repeated.

19. The series is abc/bca/cab/abc/bca. Thus, the letters change places in a cyclic order.

20. The series is abb/aaabbb/aaaabbbb/a. Thus, the letters are repeated twice, then thrice, then four times and so on.

21. The numbers in the series are multiplied by 3 to get the next numbers.

22. The difference between the numbers in the series increases by 1, after beginning from 5, *i.e.*,

1 6 12 19 27 36 (+5 +6 +7 +8 +9)

23. The pattern is –45, –35, –25, ...
So, missing term = 20 – 15 = 5.

24. The pattern is –21, –19, –17, –15,.....
So, missing term = 48 – 13 = 35.

25. The digits are removed one-by-one from the beginning and the end in order alternately, so as to obtain the subsequent terms of the series.

26. The sequence of numbers is +2, +4, +6, +8 and sequence of letters is +1, +2, +3, +4.

27. The corresponding letters are moved 3 steps forward and the sequence of numbers is +3, +5, +7, +9.

28. The sequence of numbers is +3, +5, +7, +9 and the letters are moved 1, 2, 3, 4 steps forward.

29. The letters on the left are in reverse series, the letters on the right are in natural series, and the numbers are squares of numbers in natural order starting from 1.

30. The numbers are divided by 3 at each step and the letters are moved 6, 5, 4, 3 steps backward.

31. The series comprises of random letters and numbers indicate the position of the letter in alphabet series.

32. The letters are moved five steps forward and every third number is the product of two preceding numbers.

33. Every number is double the previous number and the sequence of letters is +3, –1 (3 steps forward, 1 step backward) which is repeated.

34. The letters on the left are moved 3 steps forward, the letters on the right are moved 2 steps backward and the sequence of numbers is (4 × 2) +1, (9 × 2) +2, (20 × 2) +3, (43 × 2) +4. So, J9R should be in place of J10R.

35. The sequence of letters on the left is +5, –2 (5 steps forward, 2 steps backward) which is repeated, the sequence of letters on the right is +3, –5 (3 steps forward, 5 steps backward) which is repeated, and the numbers are the sum of two preceeding numbers. So, J6S should be in place of J7S.

●●●

16

Analogy

WORD ANALOGY

In Analogy Tests, the relationship between two given words is established and then applied to the other words. The type of relationship may vary, so while attempting such questions the first step is to identify the type of relationship, which can be any one of the following.

NUMBER ANALOGY

In number analogy also, the relationship between the given numbers is detected and then applied to the second part to find the missing numbers.

This relationship between the numbers can be based on any of the following patterns :

(*i*) numbers can be odd/even/prime numbers;

(*ii*) numbers can be multiples of one number;

(*iii*) numbers can be squares/cubes of different numbers;

(*iv*) some numbers can be added to/subtracted from/multiplied to/divided into the first number to get the second number;

(*v*) the second number can be the sum/product/difference of the digits of first number; and

(*vi*) combinations of any mathematical calculations given above can apply to the relationship between the two given numbers.

MULTIPLE CHOICE QUESTIONS

Directions : *In the questions given below one term is missing. Based on the relationship of the two given words find the missing term from the given options.*

1. HUNGER : FOOD : : THIRST : ?
A. Water B. Drink
C. Tea D. Coffee
E. None of these

2. HUNTER : GUN : : WRITER : ?
A. Book B. Pen
C. Poem D. Page
E. None of these

3. WOOL : SHEEP : : SILK : ?
A. Saree B. String
C. Silkworm D. Moth
E. None of these

4. FOOD : STOMACH : : FUEL : ?
A. Engine B. Automobile
C. Rail D. Aeroplane
E. None of these

5. WATER : SAND : : OCEAN : ?
A. Island B. River
C. Desert D. Waves
E. None of these

6. ADULT : BABY : : FLOWER : ?
A. Seed B. Bud
C. Fruit D. Butterfly
E. None of these

7. WRITER : READER : : PRODUCER : ?
A. Creator B. Contractor
C. Creature D. Consumer
E. None of these

8. ENTRANCE : EXIT : : LOYALTY : ?
A. Treachery B. Patriotism
C. Fidelity D. Reward
E. None of these

9. MOTHER : MATERNAL : : FATHER : ?
A. Eternal B. Detrimental
C. Paternal D. Formidable
E. None of these

10. PEARL : NECKLACE : : FLOWER : ?
A. Plant
B. Garden
C. Petal
D. Bouquet
E. None of these

11. ALPHABET : WORD : : WORD : ?
A. Sound
B. Music
C. Sentence
D. Dictionary
E. None of these

12. LIFE : DEATH : : HOPE : ?
A. Cry
B. Pain
C. Despair
D. Sad
E. None of these

13. GOOD : BAD : : VIRTUE : ?
A. Blame
B. Sin
C. Despair
D. Vice
E. None of these

14. BIRD : FLY : : SNAKE : ?
A. Timid
B. Clatter
C. Crawl
D. Hole
E. None of these

15. CAT : MOUSE : : BIRD : ?
A. Cage
B. Trap
C. Eagle
D. Worm
E. None of these

16. STATE : EXILE
A. Police : Arrest
B. Judge : Convict
C. Constitution : Amendment
D. Church : Excommunicate
E. None of these

17. CAPRICIOUSNESS : RELIABILITY
A. Extemporaneous : Predictability
B. Unreliable : Inhuman
C. Tenacious : Practicality
D. Arbitrary : Whimsical
E. None of these

18. LOATH : COERCION
A. Detest : Caressing
B. Irritate : Caressing
C. Irate : Antagonism
D. Reluctant : Persuasion
E. None of these

19. SCALES : FISH
A. Lady : Dress
B. Tree : Leaves
C. Bird : Feather
D. Skin : Man
E. None of these

20. TREE : SAPLING
A. Hut : Mansion
B. Giant : Dwarf
C. Horse : Foal
D. Ant : Elephant
E. None of these

21. CHALK : BLACKBOARD
A. Door : Handle
B. Table : Chair
C. Ink : Paper
D. Type : Paint
E. None of these

22. PRIMEVAL : MEDIEVAL
A. Dinosaur : Dragon
B. Gorilla : Soldier
C. Evolution : Revelation
D. Thorn : Rose
E. None of these

23. TRILOGY : NOVEL
A. Rice : Husk
B. Milk : Cream
C. Fabric : Weaving
D. Serial : Episode
E. None of these

24. PEDANT : ERUDITION
A. Prude : Modesty
B. Blunt : Politician
C. Diplomats : Tactless
D. Enemy : Friendly
E. None of these

25. FURY : IRE
A. Convulsion : Spasm
B. Amusement : Happiness
C. Joke : Laugh
D. Dispassion : Emotion
E. None of these

Directions : *In the following questions, select the number from the given options which follows the same relationship as shared between the first two numbers.*

26. 1 : 11 : : 2 : ?
A. 20
B. 22
C. 24
D. 44
E. None of these

27. $\frac{1}{7} : \frac{1}{14} : : \frac{1}{9} : ?$
A. $\frac{1}{88}$
B. $\frac{1}{80}$
C. $\frac{1}{81}$
D. $\frac{1}{18}$
E. None of these

28. 0.16 : 0.0016 : : 1.02 : ?
A. 10.20
B. 0.102
C. 0.0102
D. 1.020
E. None of these

29. 663 : 884 : : 221 : ?
A. 332
B. 554
C. 773
D. 442
E. None of these

30. 16 : 0.16 : : ?
A. 2 : 0.02
B. 7 : 0.007
C. 1.3 : 0.13
D. 0.01 : 0.001
E. None of these

31. $3 : \frac{1}{3} : : ?$
A. 6 : 12
B. 5 : 2/15
C. 8 : 1/8
D. 9 : 27
E. None of these

32. 65 : 13 : : 180 : ?
A. 93
B. 36
C. 133
D. 102
E. None of these

33. 125 : 27 : : 343 : ?
A. 729 B. 64
C. 216 D. 512
E. None of these

34. 357 : 73 : : ?
A. 429 : 94 B. 201 : 21
C. 138 : 38 D. 93 : 39
E. None of these

35. 731 : 902 : : 655 : ?
A. 646 B. 800
C. 793 D. 556
E. None of these

36. 162 : 9 : : 310 : ?
A. 33 B. 27
C. 16 D. 4
E. None of these

37. 13 : 17 : : 15 : ?
A. 19 B. 11
C. 21 D. 16
E. None of these

38. 225 : 15 : : 256 : ?
A. 26 B. 16
C. 20 D. 28
E. None of these

39. 46 : 48 : : 54 : ?
A. 59 B. 40
C. 67 D. 62
E. None of these

40. 33 : 36 : : 21 : ?
A. 9 B. 18
C. 25 D. 32
E. None of these

ANSWERS

1	2	3	4	5	6	7	8	9	10
A	B	C	A	C	B	D	A	C	D
11	**12**	**13**	**14**	**15**	**16**	**17**	**18**	**19**	**20**
C	C	D	C	D	D	C	D	D	C
21	**22**	**23**	**24**	**25**	**26**	**27**	**28**	**29**	**30**
C	A	D	A	B	B	D	C	D	A
31	**32**	**33**	**34**	**35**	**36**	**37**	**38**	**39**	**40**
C	B	A	A	A	D	A	B	B	A

EXPLANATORY ANSWERS

1. Hunger is satiated by food, thirst by water.

2. Weapon of a hunter is a gun, weapon of a writer is a pen.

3. Wool is obtained from sheep, silk is obtained from silkworm.

4. Food is consumed in stomach, fuel is consumed in engine.

5. The related words are near opposites.

6. The youngone of an adult is a baby and that of a flower is a bud.

7. A writer aims to please the readers by his writings, a producer aims to please the consumers by his products.

8. The related words are opposites.

9. Relations on the mother's side are maternal and on the father's side paternal.

10. Many pearls make a necklace, many flowers make a bouquet.

11. More than one alphabet make a word, more than one word make a sentence.

12. The related words are opposites.

13. The related words are opposites.

14. Birds fly, snakes crawl.

15. Cat chases the mouse, bird chases the worm.

16. Punishment of leaving the State is exile, punishment of leaving the Church is excommunication.

17. The related words are antonyms.

18. Loathing is the result of constant coersion, reluctance is the result of constant persuasion.

19. Covering of the fish is scales, covering of man is skin.

20. Young tree is a sapling, young horse is a foal.

21. Chalk is used to write on blackboard, ink is used to write on paper.

22. The related words represent almost the same time period and answer option represents almost the same sized creatures.

23. Trilogy is section of a novel, episode is a section of a serial.

24. The related words are synonyms.

25. Fury causes ire, amusement causes happiness.

26. The first number is repeated to obtain the second number.

27. The first fraction is multiplied by half to obtain the second fraction.

$$\frac{1}{7} : \frac{1}{14} :: \frac{1}{9} : \frac{1}{18}$$

$$\times\frac{1}{2} \qquad \times\frac{1}{2}$$

28. The decimals are divided by 100.

0.16 : 0.0016 :: 1.02 : 0.0102

÷ 100 ÷ 100

29. The digits at tens and hundreds place is same but the digit at the units place is half the other identical digits.

66 3 : 88 4 :: 22 1 : 44 2

30. Of the two related numbers, the second number is the result of first number divided by 100.

16 : 0.16 :: 2 : 0.02

÷ 100 ÷ 100

31. Of the two related numbers, the second number is the part fraction of the first number, *i.e.* 3 is related to one-third $\left(\frac{1}{3}\right)$. Similarly, 8 will be related to one-eighth $\left(\frac{1}{8}\right)$.

32. The first number is divided by 5 to get the second number.

65 : 13 :: 180 : 36

÷ 5 ÷ 5

33. The numbers are cubes of different odd numbers.

125 : 27 :: 343 : 729

↓ ↓ ↓ ↓

5^3 3^3 7^3 9^3

34. The central digit of the first number is left out and the corner digits written in reverse order to get the second number.

357 : 73 :: 429 : 94

35. The sum of the digits of both the numbers is same.

731 : 902 → 7 + 3 + 1 = 9 + 0 + 2 *i.e.* 11 = 11

655 : 646 → 6 + 5 + 5 = 6 + 4 + 6 *i.e.* 16 = 16

36. The sum of the digits of the first number is the second number.

162 : 9 :: 310 : 4

1 + 6 + 2 3 + 1 + 0

37. First number plus 4 gives the second number.

13 : 17 :: 15 : 19

+4 +4

38. The root of first number is the second number.

225 : 15 :: 256 : 16

$\sqrt{225}$ $\sqrt{256}$

39. The product of the digits of first number is multiplied by 2 to get the second number.

46 : 48 :: 54 : 40

(4 × 6) 2 (5 × 4) 2

40. The square of the sum of the digits of the first number is the second number.

33 : 36 :: 21 : 9

$(3 + 3)^2$ $(2 + 1)^2$

●●●

17 Classification

In this type of classification, four words/numbers/groups of letters are given out of which three are almost same in matter or meaning and only one word/number/group of letters is different from the common three. One has to find out the one which is different from the rest.

MULTIPLE CHOICE QUESTIONS

Directions : *In each of the following questions, three words are alike in some manner. Spot the odd one out.*

1. A. Green B. Red C. Colour D. Orange E. None of these

2. A. Stable B. Hole C. Canoe D. Sty E. None of these

3. A. Nose B. Eyes C. Skin D. Teeth E. None of these

4. A. Venus B. Moon C. Pluto D. Mars E. None of these

5. A. Happy B. Gloomy C. Lively D. Cheerful E. None of these

Directions : *Three of the following four in each question are alike in a certain way and so form a group. Select the group of letters that does not belong to that group.*

6. A. ACE B. LOR C. GIK D. VXZ E. None of these

7. A. TSR B. LKJ C. PQO D. HGF E. None of these

8. A. EF LM B. KJ SR C. XW HG D. ED YX E. None of these

9. A. JOPK B. BOPC C. QOPR D. TOPS E. None of these

10. A. DfH B. MoQ C. UwY D. InO E. None of these

Directions : *In each of the following questions, there are four options. Three numbers, in these options, are alike in certain manner. Only one number does not fit in. Choose the one which is different from the rest.*

11. A. 1948 B. 2401 C. 966 D. 1449 E. None of these

12. A. 182 B. 169 C. 130 D. 158 E. None of these

13. A. 129 B. 130 C. 131 D. 132 E. None of these

14. A. 3215 B. 9309 C. 4721 D. 2850 E. None of these

15. A. 1776 B. 2364 C. 1976 D. 3776 E. None of these

Directions : *In the following questions select the pair which is different from the other three.*

16. A. Chair - Furniture B. Shirt - Garment C. Necklace - Jewellery D. Bogie - Engine E. None of these

17. A. Crayon - Paper B. Pencil - Lead C. Pen - Ink D. Brush - Paint E. None of these

18. A. War - Peace B. Real - Natural C. Premiere - First D. Wrath - Anger E. None of these

19. A. Finger - Thimble B. Head - Cap C. Waist - Tiara D. Foot - Shoe E. None of these

20. A. Day - Night B. Clever - Foolish C. Clear - Blurred D. Arrive - Come E. None of these

Directions : *In the following questions, which of the following pair of letters is different from the other three?*

21. A. FGH - HIJ B. PQR - RST C. MNO - OPQ D. CDE - DEF E. None of these

22. A. JuM - jUm B. iLo - Ilo C. PSa - psA D. ZeX - zEx E. None of these

23. A. NQT - JMP B. CFI - RUX C. ADG - FGH D. SVY - ORU E. None of these

24. A. DXD - XDX B. KUK - UKU C. FHF - EHE D. RSR - SRS E. None of these

25. A. AYT - BZU B. FNG - EMF C. RWO - QVN D. HJD - GIC E. None of these

ANSWERS

1	2	3	4	5	6	7	8	9	10
C	C	D	B	B	B	C	A	D	D
11	**12**	**13**	**14**	**15**	**16**	**17**	**18**	**19**	**20**
A	D	C	B	B	D	A	A	C	D
21	**22**	**23**	**24**	**25**					
D	B	C	C	A					

EXPLANATORY ANSWERS

1. All others are types of colour.

2. Canoe is a boat. Others are resting places of birds/animals.

3. All others are sense organs.

4. All others are planets.

5. All others are expressions of joy.

6. The sequence in each group is +2. Only option (*b*) has sequence in +3, *i.e.*,

A B C D E (+2 +2) L M N O P Q R (+3 +3)

G H I J K (+2 +2) V W X Y Z (+2 +2)

7. The sequence of alphabet in each group is in reverse order. Only option (C) has sequence in disturbed order.

8. Two consecutive alphabet in each group are in reverse sequence (–1), *i.e.*,

K J (–1) S R (–1) ; X W (–1) H G (–1) ; E D (–1) Y X (–1)

Only in option (A) the sequence is in natural order (+1), *i.e.*, E F (+1) L M (+1)

9. In each group, letters 'OP' are common. The two corner alphabet are in natural order (+1); *i.e.*,

JOPK (+1) ; BOPC (+1) ; QOPR (+1)

Only in option (D) they are in reverse order (–1); *i.e.*,

TOPS (–1)

10. In other groups, only the alphabet in the centre is of lower case. In this option letter 'L' on the left is also in lower case.

11. Other numbers are divisible by 7.

12. Other numbers are multiples of 13.

13. 131 is a prime number.

14. In other numbers, no digit is repeated.

15. In other numbers, the last two digits are same.

16. Bogie is a part of train which is a type of conveyance. Chair, Shirt and Necklace are types of furniture, garment and jewellery respectively.

17. The medium used for writing with pencil is lead, with pen it is ink and with brush, it is paint. With crayon it should be wax.

18. The pair of words are opposite. Other pairs are synonyms.

19. Tiara is worn on the head.

20. Other words are opposite to each other.

21. In all other groups, the letters are in natural series and the last letter of first part is the first letter of the second part.

22. In all other groups, only the vowel is in lower case in the first part and in second part the case is reversed.

23. In all other groups, the letters jump two letters in between them.

24. In all other groups, the single letter in first part is repeated in the second and vice versa.

25. In all other groups, the letters in the first part are one step forward than the corresponding letters in the second part.

18

Coding and Decoding

Coding is a secretive language which is used to change the representation of the actual term/word/value. This coded language can be framed by

(*i*) moving the letters one or more steps forward or backward;

(*ii*) substituting numbers for letters and vice-versa;

(*iii*) writing the letters of the given word in reverse order in part or in whole; and

(*iv*) replacing the letters in their natural series by the same positioned letters in their reverse series.

Alphabet in natural series are :

A B C D E F G H I J K L M N O P Q R S T U V W X Y Z

1st 5th 10th 15th 20th 25th

Alphabet in reverse series are :

Z Y X W V U T S R Q P O N M L K J I H G F E D C B A

1st 5th 10th 15th 20th 25th

Note : On reaching Z, the series restarts from A and on reaching A, it restarts from Z.

Solved Examples

1. If FACE is coded as GBDF, then BADE will be coded as :

A. CBEF B. CEBF

C. CFBE D. CBFE

E. None of these

Ans.: (A) The word is coded by moving the letters one step forward

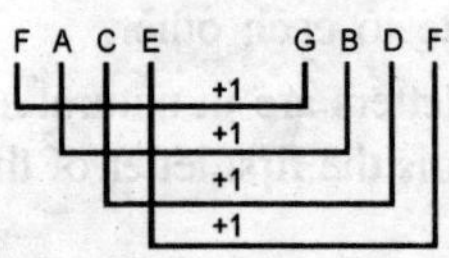

Similarly,

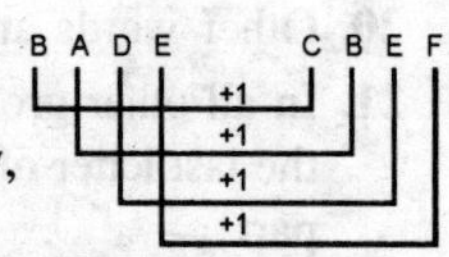

2. If RESULT is coded as 798206, LET will be coded as :

A. 680 B. 092

C. 096 D. 086

E. None of these

Ans.: (C) The letters are coded by numbers, and to code the given word, select the respective coded numbers.

R E S U L T → letters

7 9 8 2 0 6 → code

So, code for LET will be

L E T → letters

0 9 6 → code

3. In a certain code 'ra mei ket' means 'he is rich'; 'rui pha jeu' means 'run for money'; and 'pha rui ket' means 'money for rich'. Which of the following is the code for 'rich'?

A. ra B. pha

C. ket D. jeu

E. None of these

Ans.: (C) The given information is :

	Code	**Sentence**
1.	ra mei ket	he is rich
2.	rui pha jeu	run for money
3.	pha rui ket	money for rich

After comparing codes and sentences 1 and 3, it is clear that word 'rich' is common and so is the code 'ket'.

4. If 'banana' is called 'jelly', 'jelly' is called 'green', 'green' is called 'apple'. 'apple' is called 'mango', what is the colour of leaf?

A. green B. mango

C. apple D. banana

E. None of these

Ans.: (C) Leaf is green in colour and according to the codes in the question 'green' is called 'apple'.

In another form of coding, the Digits and its coded Letters or vice versa are already given. One has to find out the answers to the given questions just by tallying the given codes.

5.

Digits :	3	7	2	0	1	9	8	5	4
Letters :	A	X	M	W	Z	B	L	N	D

Which of the following options has the correct coded form of the given number 90342?

A. BMADX B. BWADX

C. BWADM D. BMADW

E. None of these

Ans.: (C) In another format, the capital letters A to Z are coded by using the small letters a to z. With the help of the coding pattern, one has to find the right code from the columns which has equivalent to the group of capital letters.

MULTIPLE CHOICE QUESTIONS

Directions (Qs. Nos. 1 to 10): *In the following questions select the right option which indicates the correct code for the word or letter given in the question.*

1. In a certain code PROFESSION is written as EFORPNOISS. In the same code DICTIONARY will be written as :

A. YRANOITCID B. ITCIDYRANO
C. ITCIDYRNAO D. ITCDIYARNO
E. None of these

2. If THOUSAND is coded as SGNTRZMC, then FUMING will be coded as :

A. GVNJOH B. ETHLMF
C. EVLJMH D. ETLHMF
E. None of these

3. If COUNTRY is coded in a certain way as EMWLVPA, ELECTORATE will be coded in the same manner as :

A. CJCEVQPYWC B. GJGERQTYVG
C. CNCERQPCRG D. GJGAVMTYVC
E. None of these

4. If m is coded as g, g as o, a as *i* and *i* as y, then 'imagination' will be written as :

A. ygagynatyin B. ygioynityog
C. ygioynityon D. ygioyintyon
E. None of these

5. If OUT is coded as 152120, IN will be coded as :

A. 1015 B. 819
C. 1813 D. 914
E. None of these

6. If MOTHERLAND is coded as 9501623748, how will DREAM be coded ?

A. 82697 B. 86297
C. 82769 D. 82679
E. None of these

7. If HARD is coded as 1357 and SOFT as 2468, what will 21448 stand for?

A. SHAFT B. SHORT
C. SHOOT D. SHART
E. None of these

8. If FACE is coded as 6135, BIG as 297, HAD as 814 and BADGE as 21475, then what is the code for 'A'?

A. 3 B. 1
C. 2 D. 4
E. None of these

9. In a certain code ELECTION is written as GLGCVIQN, then VOTER will be coded as :

A. XOVET
B. VOXET
C. WPUFU
D. VQTGR
E. None of these

10. If EXAMINATION is coded as 83690567045, the codes for 'N' and 'A' are :

A. 7, 5 B. 5, 6
C. 6, 5 D. 5, 7
E. None of these

Directions (Qs. Nos. 11 to 15): *In the following questions study the coded patterns and then select the right option from the given alternatives.*

11. In a certain code, (i) 'juka lal mit sut' stands for 'Hello, how are you?; (ii) 'mudi sut em nif' for 'Where are they going ?'; (iii) 'hu zul met sut' for 'What are their names?'; and (iv) 'lal sut zul pe' for 'Are you going too?. Which of the following words in the above code language stand for 'are you'?

A. sut mit B. mudi sut
C. juka nif D. sut lal
E. None of these

12. If 'luma papa jano' stands for 'he speaks softly', 'papa lo hedi lami' for 'wind blows softly downhill'; and 'lo puki luma jano lami sod' for 'he sings like wind blows whisper; then what word will be written for 'downhill'?

A. papa B. lami
C. hedi D. lo
E. None of these

13. In a certain code language,

1. 'Gor Paku' Means 'Best Gift'
2. 'Mull Gor Sot' Means 'Gift of Love'
3. 'SotHed Paku' Means 'Best of Luck' and
4. 'Hed Sot Paku' Means 'Love is Best'

Which of the following codes stand for the word 'Love'?

A. Paku B. Hed
C. Sot D. Mull
E. None of these

14. In a certain code '7 8 6' means 'bring me apple', '9 5 8' means 'peel green apple' and '6 4 5' means 'bring green fruit'. Which of the following is the code for 'me'?

A. 8 B. 6
C. 7 D. Cannot be determined
E. None of these

15. In a certain code language '1 2 3' means 'hot filter coffee','3 5 6' means 'very hot day' and '5 8 9' means 'day and night'. Which digit in that language means 'very'?

A. 8 B. 6
C. 9 D. 5
E. None of these

Directions : (Qs. 16-17): *In a code language, A. 'pit dar na' means 'you are good'; B. 'dar tok pa' means 'good and bad'; C. 'tim na tak' means 'they are bad'.*

16. In that language, which word stands for 'they'?

A. na B. tof

C. tim
D. None of these
E. None of these

17. To find the answer to the above question, which of the following statements can be dispensed with?
A. Only A
B. Only B
C. A or B
D. None of these
E. None of these

Directions (Qs. Nos. 18 to 20): *In a certain code language : A. '1 3 4' means 'you are well' B. '7 5 8' means 'they go home' C. '8 3 9' means 'we are home'.*

18. Which of the following represents 'they' in that code language?
A. 5
B. 7
C. 3
D. Data inadequate
E. None of these

19. Which of the statements can be dispensed with while answering the above question?
A. A only
B. B only
C. A or C only
D. B and C only
E. None of these

20. Which of the following represents 'are' in that code language?
A. 1
B. 3
C. 4
D. 7
E. None of these

Directions (Qs. Nos. 21 to 25): *Read the given coded information and choose the correct answer from the given options.*

21. If 'water' is called 'blue', 'blue' is called 'red', 'red' is called 'white', 'white' is called 'sky', 'sky' is called 'rain', 'rain' is called 'green', 'green' is called 'air' and 'air' is called 'table', which of the following is the colour of milk?
A. white
B. rain
C. sky
D. green
E. air

22. If 'light' is called 'dark', 'dark' is called 'green', 'green' is called 'blue', 'blue' is called 'red', 'red' is called 'white' and 'white' is called 'yellow', what is the colour of blood?
A. red
B. dark
C. white
D. yellow
E. None of these

23. If 'sky' is called 'sea', 'sea' is called 'water', 'water' is called 'air', 'air' is called 'cloud' and 'cloud' is called 'river', then what do we drink when thirsty?
A. sky
B. air
C. water
D. sea
E. cloud

24. If 'yellow' means 'red', 'white' means 'green', 'red' means 'orange', 'blue' means 'white' and 'green' means 'blue', then the colour of sky is:
A. white
B. green
C. blue
D. yellow
E. red

25. If 'land' is called 'sky', 'sky' is called 'air', 'air' is called 'water', 'water' is called 'sand' and 'sand' is called 'solid', where do fishes swim?
A. air
B. sky
C. water
D. solid
E. sand

Directions (Qs 26 to 30) : *The following questions are based on the code pattern given below:*

Digits :	2	6	4	1	0	8	3	7	5	9
Letters :	M	E	N	H	V	F	I	W	L	X

Which of the given options has the correct coded form of the given numbers?

26. 435216
A. HILMNE
B. NILMHE
C. VFLMNE
D. NILHME
E. None of these

27. 897615
A. FXWEHL
B. VXLENH
C. FXLWHE
D. VXELHI
E. None of these

28. 146738
A. HNEIWF
B. HNWEIF
C. HENWIF
D. HNEWIF
E. None of these

29. 092863
A. VXMFEI
B. VXMIFE
C. VXMIEF
D. VXFMEI
E. None of these

30. 702439
A. LVMIEX
B. INEMHV
C. WVMNIX
D. VWNMEX
E. None of these

ANSWERS

1	2	3	4	5	6	7	8	9	10
B	D	D	C	D	D	B	B	A	B
11	**12**	**13**	**14**	**15**	**16**	**17**	**18**	**19**	**20**
D	C	C	C	B	C	D	B	A	B
21	**22**	**23**	**24**	**25**	**26**	**27**	**28**	**29**	**30**
C	C	B	A	E	B	A	D	A	C

EXPLANATORY ANSWERS

1. The word is divided into two equal parts and the letters of each part are written backwards.

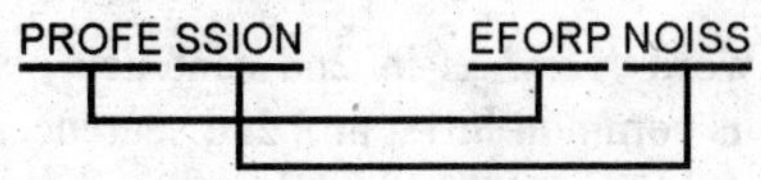

Similarly,

2. The word is coded by moving the alphabet one step backwards, i.e.,

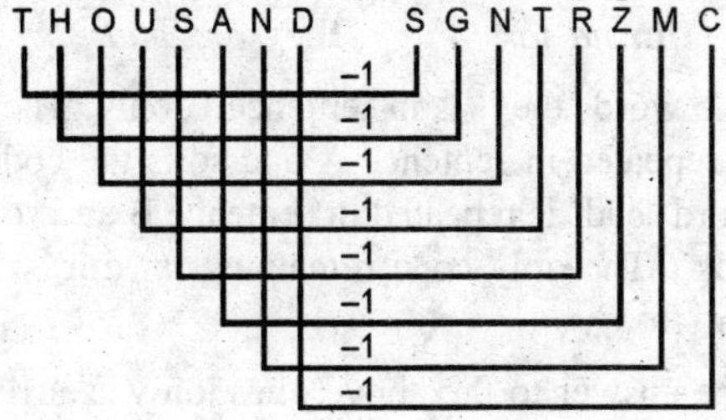

Similarly,

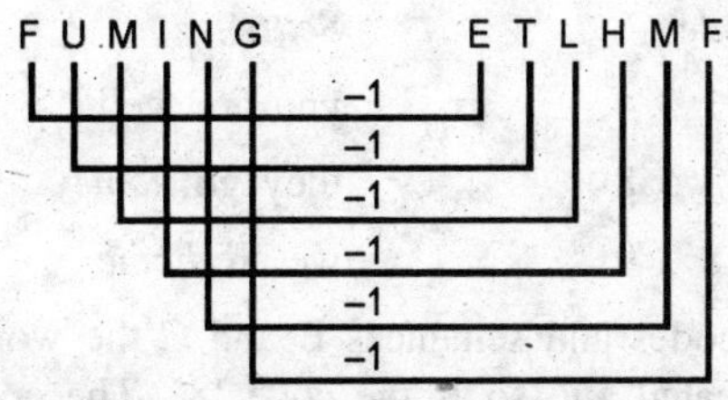

3. The word is coded by moving the alphabet two steps forward and two steps backward alternately, i.e.,

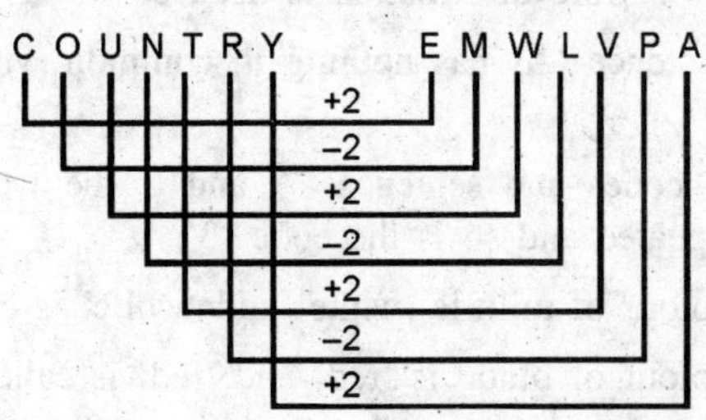

Similarly,

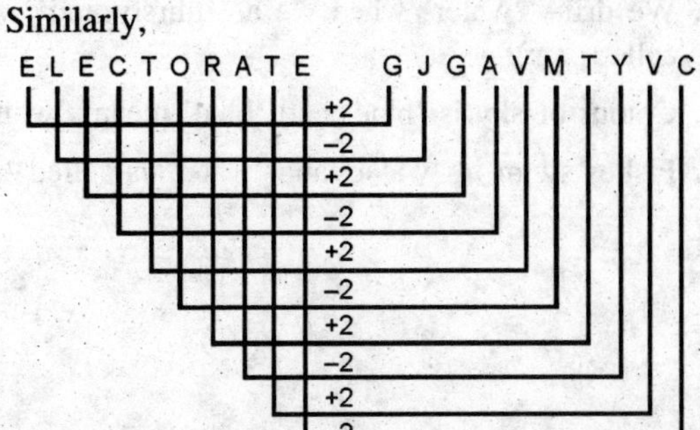

4. Alphabet whose codes are given

m → g   g → o

a → i   i → y

All other alphabet will remain unchanged so, 'imagination' will be coded as :

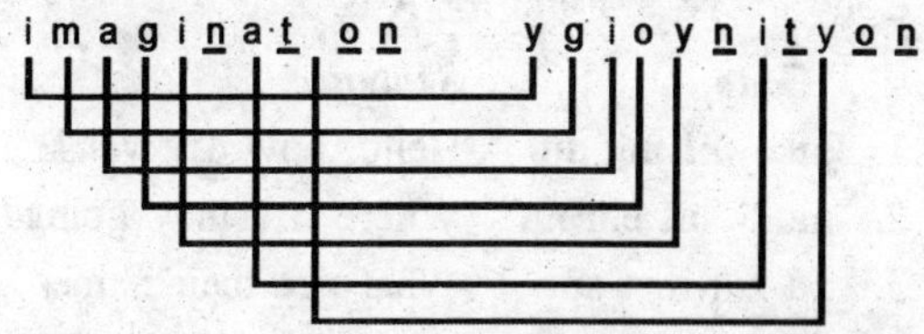

5. The coded number signifies the position of the alphabet in its natural alphabetical series (ABCD...)

O U T → OUT

15th 21st 20th → 152120

Similarly,

I N → IN

9th 14th → 914

6. The letters of the word are coded by numbers. So to find the code for DREAM select the respective numbers.

M O T H E R L A N D → letters

9 5 0 1 6 2 3 7 4 8 → codes So,

D R E A M → letters

8 2 6 7 9 → answer codes

7. The numbers represent letters and to find the answer, select the respective letters.

1 3 5 7   2 4 6 8 → codes

H A R D   S O F T → letters

So,

2 1 4 4 8 → codes

S H O O T → answer letters

8. The letter 'A' is present in three words and so is the number '1' in all the three words.

FACE   HAD   BADGE

6135   814   21475

9. Only the letters at the odd positions are moved two steps forward.

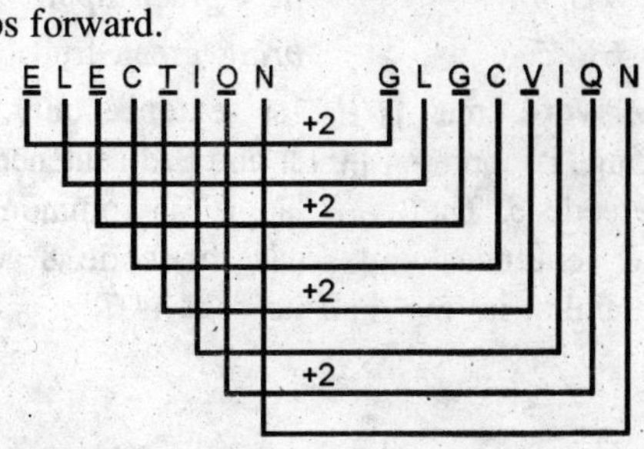

Similarly,

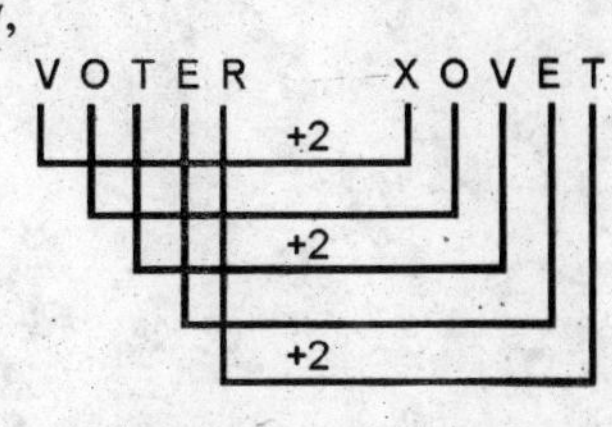

10. The word is coded as :

E X A M I N A T I O N

8 3 6 9 0 5 6 7 0 4 5

Code for N is 5 and for A is 6.

11.

	Code	Sentence
1.	juka *lal* mit **sut**	Hello, how **are** *you*?
2.	mudi **sut** em nif	Where **are** they going?
3.	hu zul met **sut**	What **are** their names?
4.	*lal* **sut** zul pe	**Are** *you* going too?

The word 'are' is present in all the four sentences and so is the code 'sut'. The word 'you' is common in 1st and 4th sentences and so is the code 'lal'.

12.

	Code	Sentence
1.	luma *papa* jano	he speaks *softly*
2.	*papa lo* **hedi** *lami*	*wind blows softly* **downhill**
3.	*lo* puki luma jano *lami* sod	he sings like *wind blows* whisper

Code 'papa' is repe-ated in 1st and 2nd sentence but the word 'downhill' is not.

Of the other coded words in 2nd sentence 'lo' and 'lami' are repeated in 3rd sentence, but again the word 'downhill' is not. The only code remaining is 'hedi' which should mean 'downhill'.

13.

	Code	Sentence
1.	Gor Paku	Best Gift
2.	Mull Gor *Sot*	Gift of *Love*
3.	SotHed Paku	Best of Luck
4.	Hed *Sot* Paku	*Love* is Best

Only in sentences 2nd and 4th, the word 'Love' is repeated and the only code repeated is 'Sot'.

14.

	Code	Sentence
1.	7 8 6	*bring* **me** *apple*
2.	9 5 8	peel green *apple*
3.	6 4 5	*bring* green fruit

The word 'me' is in 1st sentence only. The word 'bring' is common in 1st and 3rd sentences and so is the code 6. The word 'apple' is common in 1st and 2nd sentences and so is the code 8. Only word remaining is 'me' and its code is 7.

15.

	Code	Sentence
1.	1 2 3	*hot* filter coffee
2.	3 5 **6**	**very** hot day
3.	5 8 9	*day* and night

The word 'very' is in 2nd sentence only. The word 'hot' is common in 1st and 2nd sentences and so is the code '3'. The word 'day' is common in 2nd and 3rd sentences and so is the code '5'. The only code remaining is '6' which stands for 'very'.

16.

	Code	Sentence
A.	pit dar na	you are good
B.	dar *tok* pa	good and *bad*
C.	**tim** *na tak*	**they** *are bad*

The word 'they' is in sentence B only. The word 'are' is repeated in sentence A and so is the code 'na'. The word 'bad' is repeated in sentence B and so is the code 'tok'. The only code remaining is 'tim' which stands for 'they'.

17. The answer to the above question was arrived at only after comparing all the three codes and sentences.

18.

	Code	Sentence
A.	1 3 4	you are well
B.	7 5 8	they go *home*
C.	8 3 9	we are *home*

In codes and sentences B and C the word 'home' is repeated and so is the code '8'. The code for word 'they' can be either '7' or '5'. The same applies for 'go'. More information is needed.

19. Sentence 'A' has nothing in common with sentence 'B'.

20. In codes and sentences A and C the word 'are' is repeated and so is the code '3'.

21. Colour of milk is 'white' and 'white' is called 'sky'.

22. Colour of blood is 'red' and 'red' is called 'white'.

23. We drink 'water' when we are thirsty and 'water' is called 'air'.

24. Colour of sky is 'blue' and 'blue' means 'white'.

25. Fishes swim in 'water' and 'water' is called 'sand'.

19 Machine–Input and Output

In input-output problems one is asked to imagine that there is some computer or a word-processing machine and it performs some operation on a given input. These operations are performed repeatedly as per a pre-fixed pattern and subsequently one has different output in different steps. One's primarily job is to deduce the rule followed by computer/machine in arranging numbers and words. One should analyze final arranged step while deducing rule applied.

MULTIPLE CHOICE QUESTIONS

Directions (Qs. Nos. 1 to 5): *A word-number arrangement machine, when given an input as a set of words and numbers, rearranges them following a particular rule and generates stepwise outputs till the rearrangement is complete following that rule.*

Followings is an illustration of input and steps of rearrangement till the last step.

Input	: pour	ask	57	dear	39	fight	17	28
Step I	: ask	pour	57	dear	39	fight	17	28
Step II	: ask	57	pour	dear	39	fight	17	28
Step III	: ask	57	dear	pour	39	fight	17	28
Step IV	: ask	57	dear	39	pour	fight	17	28
Step V	: ask	57	dear	39	fight	pour	17	28
Step VI	: ask	57	dear	39	fight	28	pour	17

and Step VI is the last output.

As per the rule followed in the above steps find out the answer to each of the following questions:

1. If step II of an input is "cut 97 38 end for 29 46 down", which of the following will be the last step?

A. Fifth B. Fourth
C. Sixth 4 D. Seventh
E. None of these

2. If the 4th step of an input is "ago 85 elite 79 exile fat 26 41", which of the following will definitely be the 2nd step of the input?

A. ago 85 79 elite fat 41 26 exile
B. ago 85 exile elite 41 26 fat 79
C. ago 85 26 exile 41 elite 79 fat
D. Cannot be determined
E. None of these

3. If the 1st step of an input is "car 17 vas tiger 92 87 like 52", which of the following will be the 4th step?

A. car 92 like 87 tiger 52 17 vas
B. car 92 like 87 17 vas tiger 52
C. car 92 like 87 tiger 17 vas 52
D. car 92 like 17 vas tiger 87 52
E. None of these

4. Input: zeal for 49 31 high 22 track 12
Which of the following will be the 3rd step?

A. for 49 high 31 track 22 zeal 12
B. for 49 high 31 zeal 22 track 12
C. for 49 high zeal 31 22 track 12
D. for 49 high 31 track zeal 22 12
E. None of these

5. Input : 19 feat 34 28 dog bag take 43
Which of the following steps would be "bag 43 dog 19 feat 34 28 take"?

A. Second B. Fourth
C. First D. Cannot be determined
E. None of these

Directions (Qs. Nos. 6 to 10): *A word-number arrangement machine, when given an input as a set of words and numbers, rearranges them following a particular rule and generates stepwise outputs till the rearrangement is complete following that rule.*

Followings is an illustration of input and steps of rearrangement till the last step.

Input : sine 88 71 cos theta 14 56 gamma delta 26
Step I : cos sine 71 theta 14 56 gamma delta 26 88
Step II : delta cos sine theta 14 56 gamma 26 88 71
Step III : gamma delta cos sine theta 14 26 88 71 56
Step IV : sine gamma delta cos theta 14 88 71 56 26
Step V : theta sine gamma delta cos 88 71 56 26 14

And Step V is the last Step of the arrangement of the above input as the intended arrangement is obtained.

As per the rules followed in the above steps, find out in each of the following questions the appropriate steps for the given input, Input for the questions

Input : for 52 all 96 25 jam road 15 hut 73 bus stop 38 46 (all numbers are in two digits)

6. Which word/number would be at the 6th position from the left in Step V?

A. 25 B. stop

C. jam
D. all
E. road

7. Which of the following would be the Step III?
A. hut for bus all 25 jam road 15 stop 38 96 73 52 46
B. for us all 25 jam road 15 hut 38 stop 96 46 73 52
C. hut for bus all jam road 15 stop 38 96 73 52 46 25
D. for bus all 25 jam road 15 hut stop 38 46 96 73 52
E. None of the above

8. Which word/number would be at the 8th position from the right in Step IV?
A. 15
B. road
C. hut
D. jam
E. stop

9. Which of the following would be Step VII?
A. stop road jam hut for bus all 15 96 73 52 46 38 25
B. road jam hut for bus all stop 15 25 38 46 52 73 96
C. stop road jam hut for bus all 96 73 52 46 38 25 15
D. jam hut for bus all 25 road stop 15 96 73 52 46 38
E. There will be no such step as the arrangement gets established at Step VI

10. Which step number would be the following output? bus all for 52 25 jam road 15 hut stop 38 46 96 73
A. There will be no such step
B. III
C. II
D. V
E. VI

Directions (Qs 11 to 14): *A word-number arrangement machine, when given an input as a set of words and numbers, rearranges them following a particular rule and generates stepwise outputs till the rearrangement is complete following that rule.*

Input : tall 48 13 rise alt 99 76 32 wise jar high 28 56 barn

Followings is an illustration of input and steps of rearrangement till the last step.

Input : tall 48 13 rise alt 99 76 32 wise jar high 28 56 barn
Step I : 13 tall 48 rise 99 76 32 wise jar high 28 56 barn alt
Step II : 28 13 tall 48 rise 99 76 32 wise jar high 56 alt barn
Step III : 32 28 13 tall 48 rise 99 76 wise jar 56 alt barn high
Step IV : 48 32 28 13 tall rise 99 76 wise 56 alt barn high jar
Step V : 56 48 32 28 13 tall 99 76 wise alt barn high jar rise
Step VI : 76 56 48 32 28 13 99 wise alt barn high jar rise tall
Step VII : 99 76 56 48 32 28 13 alt barn high jar rise tall wise

Step VII is the last step of the above input, as desired arrangement is obtained.

As per the rules followed in the above steps, find out in each of the following questions the appropriate steps for the given input.

Input : 84 why sit 14 32 not best ink feet 51 27 vain 68 92
(All the numbers are two digit numbers)

11. Which step number is the following output? 32 27 14 84 why sit not 51 vain 92 68 feet best ink
A. Step V
B. Step VI
C. Step IV
D. Step III
E. There is no such step

12. Which word/number would be at 5th position from the right in Step V?
A. 14
B. 92
C. feet
D. best
E. why

13. How many elements (words or numbers) are there between 'feet' and '32' as they appear in the last step of the output?
A. One
B. Three
C. Four
D. Five
E. Seven

14. Which of the following represents the position of 'why' in the fourth step?
A. Eighth from the left
B. Fifth from the right
C. Sixth from the left
D. Fifth from the left
E. Seventh from the left

Directions (Qs. Nos. 15 to 19): *Given an input a machine generates pass codes step-by-step following certain rules as illustrated below:*

Input : talk seven 37 48 given 83 likely 62
Step I : 37 talk seven 48 given 83 likely 62
Step II : 37 talk 48 seven given 83 likely 62
Step III : 37 talk 48 seven 62 likely given 83
Step IV : 37 talk 48 seven 62 likely 83 given

Step IV is the last step for this input.

In the following questions same logic as illustrated above is to be used.

15. Step II for an input is "23 working 48 32 park blossom 26 garden". What will be the fifth step?
A. 23 working 26 park 48 32 blossom garden
B. 23 working 26 park 32 48 blossom garden
C. 23 working 26 32 park 48 blossom garden
D. 23 working 26 48 park 32 blossom garden
E. None of these

16. Second step of an input "12 where 82 33 great wall 49 just". Which step will be the last step?
A. VI
B. VII
C. VIII
D. IV
E. None of these

17. What will be step III for the following input?
Input: phone computer 32 link 18 75 46 dairy
A. 18 phone 46 link computer 75 32 dairy
B. 18 phone 32 link 46 computer 75 dairy
C. 18 phone 32 computer link 75 46 dairy
D. 18 phone 32 link computer 75 46 dairy
E. None of these

18. Step IV of an input "22 united 37 trading killer 45 72 jogger". What will be the input definitely?
A. united 22 37 jogger 45 trading 72 killer
B. united trading 22 37 jogger 45 72 killer
C. united 22 trading jogger 37 killer 45 72
D. Cannot be determined
E. None of these

19. What will be the third step of an input whose first step is " 17 45 follow rule examination 36 85 hut"?
A. 17 rule 36 45 follow examination 85 hut
B. 17 rule 36 45 follow 85 examination hut
C. 17 rule 36 45 examination follow 85 hut
D. Cannot be determined
E. None of these

Directions (Qs. Nos. 20 to 25): *A word-number arrangement machine, when given an input as a set of words and numbers, rearranges them following a particular rule and generates stepwise outputs till the rearrangement is complete following that rule.*

Followings is an illustration of input and steps of rearrangement till the last step.

Input : rose girl 13 petal 16 go 35 ate 71 wild 22 87
Step I : go rose girl 13 petal 16 35 ate 71 wild 22 87
Step II : go 13 rose girl petal 16 35 ate 71 wild 22 87
Step III : go 13 ate rose girl petal 16 35 71 wild 22 87
Step IV : go 13 ate 16 rose girl petal 35 71 wild 22 87
Step V : go 13 ate 16 girl rose petal 35 71 wild 22 87
Step VI : go 13 ate 16 girl 22 rose petal 35 71 wild 87
Step VII : go 13 ate 16 girl 22 rose 35 petal 71 wild 87
Step VIII : go 13 ate 16 girl 22 rose 35 wild petal 71 87
Step IX : go 13 ate 16 girl 22 rose 35 wild 71 petal 87
and Step IX is the last step of the rearrangement.

20. Input: man 79 over 63 like 43 joy 15 never climbed 21 56
How many steps will be required to complete the arrangement?
A. Eight B. Nine
C. Ten D. Eleven
E. None of these

21. Step II of an input: to 13 world news 73 29 win 52. How many more steps will be required to complete the arrangement?
A. Six B. Four
C. Five D. Two
E. None of these

22. Input : no 11 19 94 join for 81 style 37 matched. Which of the following steps will be the last?
A. VI B. VII
C. VIII D. IX
E. None of these

23. Step III of an input is : we 12 you 19 meet 17 discuss 15 result 16.
Which of the following will be step II?
A. we 12 you 17 meet 19 discuss 15 result 16
B. we 12 17 you meet 19 discuss 15 result 16
C. we 12 you 15 17 meet 19 discuss result 16
D. Cannot be determined
E. None of these

24. Which of the following cannot be definitely Step V of an input?
A. be 13 did 27 eye 43 soon 34 39 wonder
B. be 13 did 27 eye 43 soon 39 34 wonder
C. be 13 did 27 soon 43 eye 39 wonder 34
D. Cannot be determined
E. None of these

25. If two given inputs gives identically same output, which of the following is definitely true?
A. Both require same number of steps for final arrangement.
B. Two inputs are identically same
C. Both contains same elements which may or may not be in same sequence
D. 2nd last step for both arrangements will be same
E. None of these

Directions (Qs. 26 to 29): *Study the following information carefully and answer the questions given below :*

The admission ticket for an exhibition bears a password which is changed after every clock hour based on set of words chosen for each day. The following is an illustration of the code and steps of rearrangement for subsequent clock hours. The time is 9 a.m. to 2 p.m. *Day's first password:*
First Batch: 9 a.m. to 10 a.m.
is not ready cloth simple harmony burning.
Second Batch: 10 a.m. to 11 a.m.
ready not is cloth burning harmony simple.
Third Batch: 11 a.m. to 12 noon
cloth is not ready simple harmony burning.
Fourth Batch: 12 noon to 1 p.m.
not is cloth ready burning harmony simple.
Fifth Batch: 1 p.m to 2 p.m.
ready cloth is not simple harmony burning.

26. If the password for 11 a.m. to 12 noon was— "soap shy miss pen yet the she", what was the password for the first batch?
A. shy miss pen soap yet the she
B. pen miss shy soap she the yet
C. miss soap pen shy she the yet
D. soap pen miss shy she the yet
E. None of these

27. If the password for the first batch was—"rate go long top we let have", which batch will have the password—"go rate top long have let we?"
A. Second
B. Third
C. Fourth
D. Fifth
E. None of these

28. Day's first password—" camel road no toy say me not", what will be the password for fourth batch, *i.e.*, 12 noon to 1 p.m.?
A. toy camel road no say me not
B. toy no road camel not me say
C. no road camel toy not me say
D. road camel toy no not me say
E. None of these

29. If the batch 2 of the day has following password—"came along net or else eky lot", what would be the password for batch 4, (*i.e.*, 12 noon to 1 p.m.)?
A. along net or came else key lot
B. or net along came lot key else
C. came or net along lot key else
D. net or came along else key lot
E. None of these

Directions (Qs. 30 to 34) : *Study the following information carefully and answer the questions given below:*

An export processing unit has a computerized machine which generates six codes to distinguish product of each of seven batches produced in a day. The machine is fed code for first batch of each day. Based on that, the machine generates 6 codes by rearrangement of words for subsequent batches. Following is an illustration of generation of codes for some batches of a day.

Day's first batch — who nut cream page for table.
Day's second batch — who for cream page nut table.
Day's third batch — who for page cream nut table.
Day's fourth batch — table for page cream nut who.
Day's fifth batch — page table for nut who cream.
Day's sixth batch — page who for nut table cream.

and so on till seventh batch. Next day based on the same rule, new set of words will be introduced as given above :

30. If the first batch code of a day is 'five gave it close to mine', which of the following will be the code for fourth batch?
A. five to it close gave mine
B. mine to close it gave five
C. five to close it gave mine
D. close five to gave mine it
E. None of these

31. If the code of fifth batch of a day is 'same is tea at now then', which of the following would definitely be the first code of that day?
A. tea same is now then at
B. same now tea at is then
C. now at then same tea is
D. now tea is same then at
E. None of these

32. If the code of fourth batch is 'so when clean get lemon dust', which of the following would be the code for seventh batch?
A. get dust lemon when so clean
B. clean so when lemon dust get
C. when get dust so clean lemon
D. clean dust lemon when so get
E. None of these

33. If the code of sixth batch of the day is 'very say could man on fire', which of the following batch codes would read as 'say could very fire man on'?
A. Second
B. Third
C. Fourth
D. Fifth
E. None of these

34. If the seventh batch of the day is 'from door no leaf glass but', which of the following would be the first three words of the code of batch third of that day?
A. door leaf from.....
B. door leaf but.....
C. glass leaf from.....
D. but door no.....
E. None of these

ANSWERS

1	2	3	4	5	6	7	8	9	10
A	D	B	C	E	A	D	B	C	A
11	**12**	**13**	**14**	**15**	**16**	**17**	**18**	**19**	**20**
E	D	B	C	B	A	D	D	A	C
21	**22**	**23**	**24**	**25**	**26**	**27**	**28**	**29**	**30**
B	A	D	C	C	A	C	D	A	B
31	**32**	**33**	**34**						
C	D	B	A						

EXPLANATORY ANSWERS

1.

Step II : cut 97 38 end for 29 46 down
⑥ 5 ⑥ ⑥ 4 3

Step II : cut 97 38 end for 29 46 down

Step III : cut 97 down 38 end for 29 46

Step IV : cut 97 down 46 38 end for 29

Step V : cut 97 down 46 end 38 for 29

2.

Step I : car 17 vas tiger 92 87 like 52
2 4 3

Step I : car 17 vas tiger 92 87 like 52

Step II : car 92 17 vas tiger 87 like 52

Step III : car 92 like 17 vas tiger 87 52

Step IV : car 92 like 87 17 vas tiger 52

4.

Input : zeal for 49 31 high 22 track 12
1 2 3

Step I : for zeal 49 31 high 22 track 12

Step II : for 49 zeal 31 high 22 track 12

Step III : for 49 high zeal 31 22 track 12

5.

Input : 19 feat 34 28 dog bag take 43
3 1 2

Input : 19 feat 34 28 dog bag take 43

Step I : bag 19 feat 34 28 dog take 43

Step II : bag 43 19 feat 34 28 dog take

Step III : bag 43 dog 19 feat 34 28 take

Solution (6 to 10) : Here in Step I word which come first in dictionary takes first position from left and rest elements shifts one position rightwards and in the same step largest number takes first position from right and other elements shifts one step leftwards. In next step, same methodology is applied to only unarranged ones. Process continues until all words are arranged fzrom left to right in reverse dictionary order and numbers are arranged in increasing sequence from right to left.

Input : sine 88 71 cos theta 14 56 gamma delta 26
4 1B 2B 1 5 5B 3B 3 2 4B

Here, to get final arrangement sequence will be : 5 4 3 2 1 1B 2B 3B 4B 5B

(Note here first unnumbered from left or right will not be circled as no element could arrive at arranged position)

Input : for 52 all 96 25 jam road 15 hut 73 bus stop 38 46
3 3B 1 1B 6B 5 6 7B 4 2B 2 7 5B 4B

Input : for 52 all 96 25 jam road 15 hut 73 bus stop 38 46

Step I : all for 52 25 jam road 15 hut 73 bus stop 38 46 96

Step II : bus all for 52 25 jam road 15 hut stop 38 46 96 73

Step III : for bus all 25 jam road 15 hut stop 38 46 96 73 52

Step IV : hut for bus all 25 jam road 15 stop 38 96 73 52 46

Step V : jam hut for bus all 25 road 15 stop 96 73 52 46 38

Step VI : road jam hut for bus all 15 stop 96 73 52 46 38 25

Step VII : stop road jam hut for bus all 96 73 52 46 38 25 15

Solution (11 to 14) : Here in Step I smallest number takes first position from left and rest elements shifts one position rightwards and in the same step word which comes first in dictionary takes first position from right and rest elements shifts one position leftwards. In next step, same methodology is applied to only unarranged ones. Process continues until all numbers are arranged in decreasing sequence from left to right and all words are arranged in reverse dictionary order from right to left.

Input : 84 why sit 14 32 not best ink feet 51 27 vain 68 92
6 7B 5B 1 3 4B 1B 3B 2B 4 2 6B 5 7

Here, to get final arrangement sequence will be:
7 6 5 4 3 2 1 1B 2B 3B 4B 5B 6B 7B

(Note here first unnumbered from left or right will not be circled as no element could arrive at arranged position)

Input : 84 why sit 14 32 not best ink feet 51 27 vain 68 92

Step I : 14 84 why sit 32 not best ink feet 51 27 vain 68 92 best

Step II : 27 14 84 why sit 32 not ink 51 vain 68 92 best feet

Step III : 32 27 14 84 why sit not 51 vain 68 92 best feet ink

Step IV : 51 32 27 14 84 why sit vain 68 92 best feet ink not

Step V : 68 51 32 27 14 84 why vain 92 best feet ink not sit

Step VI : 84 68 51 32 27 14 why 92 best feet ink not sit vain

Step VII : 92 84 68 51 32 27 14 best feet ink not sit vain why

Solution (15 to 19) : Here numbers and words are arranged alternately. Numbers are arranged in increasing order while words are arranged in decreasing order of their dictionary placements. If a number or word is already arranged, then next member is arranged in the same step.

15.

Step II : 23 working 48 32 park blossom 26 garden
5 4 3

Step II : 23 working 48 32 park blossom 26 garden

Step III : 23 working 26 48 32 park blossom garden

Step IV : 23 working 26 park 48 32 blossom garden

Step V : 23 working 26 park 32 48 blossom garden

16.

Step II : 12 where 82 33 great wall 49 just
⑦ 3 ⑦ 4 5 6

Step II : 12 where 82 33 great wall 49 just

Step III : 12 where 33 82 great wall 49 just

Step IV : 12 where 33 wall 82 great 49 just

Step V : 12 where 33 wall 49 82 great just

Step VI : 12 where 33 wall 49 just 82 great

Hence Step VI will be the last step.

17.

Input : phone computer 32 link 18 75 46 dairy
2 2 3 1

Input : phone computer 32 link 18 75 46 dairy

Step I : 18 phone computer 32 link 75 46 dairy

Step II : 18 phone 32 computer link 75 46 dairy

Step III : 18 phone 32 link computer 75 46 dairy

18. Input cannot be determined by any given step

19.

Step I : 17 45 follow rule examination 36 85 hut.
2 3

Step I : 17 45 follow rule examination 36 85 hut.

Step II : 17 rule 45 follow examination 36 85 hut.

Step III : 17 rule 36 45 follow examination 85 hut.

Here words and number are arranged alternately. Words are arranged according to number of letters it contains, word having minimum number of letters is arranged first, if two words contains same number of letters then the word which comes first in dictionary is arranged first while numbers are arranged in increasing order

20.

Input: man 79 over 63 like 43 joy 15 never climbed 21 56
③ 6 9 4 5 1 2 8 10 3 7

Input : man 79 over 63 like 43 joy 15 never climbed 21 56

Step I : joy man 79 over 63 like 43 15 never climbed 21 56

Step II : joy 15 man 79 over 63 like 43 never climbed 21 56

Step III : joy 15 man 21 79 over 63 like 43 never climbed 56

Step IV : joy 15 man 21 like 79 over 63 43 never climbed 56

Step V : joy 15 man 21 like 43 79 over 63 never climbed 56

Step VI : joy 15 man 21 like 43 over 79 63 never climbed 56

Step VII : joy 15 man 21 like 43 over 56 79 63 never climbed

Step VIII : joy 15 man 21 like 43 over 56 never 79 63 climbed

Step IX : joy 15 man 21 like 43 over 56 never 63 79 climbed

Step X : joy 15 man 21 like 43 over 56 never 63 climbed 79

21.

Step II : to 13 world news 73 29 win 52
⑦ 5 ⑦ 4 3 6

Step II : to 13 world news 73 29 win 52

Step III : to 13 win world news 73 29 52

Step IV : to 13 win 29 world news 73 52

Step V : to 13 win 29 news world 73 52

Step VI : to 13 win 29 news 52 world 73

This is the final arrangement.

22.

Input : no 11 19 94 join for 81 style 37 matched
① ① ② ⑦ 2 1 5 4 3 6

Input : no 11 19 94 join for 81 style 37 matched

Step I : no 11 for 19 94 join 81 style 37 matched

Step II : no 11 for 19 join 94 81 style 37 matched

Step III : no 11 for 19 join 37 94 81 style matched

Step IV : no 11 for 19 join 37 style 94 81 matched

Step V : no 11 for 19 join 37 style 81 94 matched

Step VI : no 11 for 19 join 37 style 81 matched 94

This is the final arrangement.

23. Previous steps cannot be determined.

24. Step V of any input should have at least five elements arranged.

Solution (26 to 29): Following rule is followed here: Out of seven words, the sixth word does not change at all. The fifth and the seventh word exchange their places alternately. In the first four words, in the 2nd and 4th step the third word becomes the first word and the word preceding it follows it in the new sequence. But in the 3rd and 5th step 1st and 4th words and 2nd and 3rd words interchange their position.

1st Batch : is not ready cloth simple harmony burning. According to rule followed, in the 2nd step the third word 'ready' should become the first word. The fifth and seventh word should interchange their position. Thus the second sequence should be "ready not is cloth burning harmony simple".

Whereas in the third sequence the words (1st and 4th and 2nd and 3rd should interchange their position as well as 5th and 7th word should interchange).

The third sequence should thus be :
cloth is not ready simple harmony burning.
Both of these correlate with the sequences given.
Based on these the questions can be easily solved.

Solution (30 to 34) : The operations are as follows :

Ist batch → IInd batch :
2nd and 5th words are interchanged.
IInd Batch → IIIrd Batch :
3rd and 4th words are interchanged.
IIIrd Batch → IVth Batch :
1st and 6th words are interchanged.
IVth Batch → Vth Batch :
1st, 2nd, 3rd, 4th, 5th, 6th words become 2nd, 3rd, 1st, 6th, 4th, 5th respectively.
Vth Batch → VIth Batch :
2nd and 5th words are interchanged [Same as (1)]
VIth Batch → VIIth Batch :
3rd and 4th words are interchanged [Same as (2)]

30. I Batch → five gave it close to mine
II Batch → five to it close gave mine
III Batch → five to close it gave mine
IV Batch → mine to close it gave five

31. V Batch → same is tea at now then
IV Batch → is tea same then at now
III Batch → now tea same then at is
II Batch → now tea then same at is
I Batch → now at then same tea is

32. IV Batch → so when clean get lemon dust
V Batch → clean so when lemon dust get
VI Batch → clean dust when lemon so get
VII Batch → clean dust lemon when so get

33. VI Batch → very say could man on fire
V Batch → very on could man say fire
IV Batch → on could very fire man say
III Batch → say could very fire man on

34. VII Batch → from door no leaf glass but
VI Batch → from door leaf no glass but
V Batch → from glass leaf no door but
IV Batch → glass leaf from but no door
III Batch → door leaf from but no glass

●●●

20

Non-Verbal

SERIES-I

In this form of non-verbal series, which are the most common, four or five consecutive problem figures form a definite sequence and one is required to select the one figure from the given set of Answer Figures that will continue the same sequence.

One has to try different set of moves, changes, replacements, rotations, repetitions and a lot more variations to arrive at the logical pattern making the series. Practising alone will sharpen one's skill of solving such sequences.

MULTIPLE CHOICE QUESTIONS

1. Problem Figures

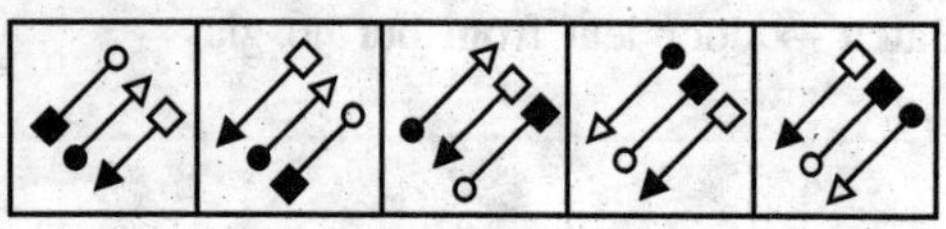

Answer Figures

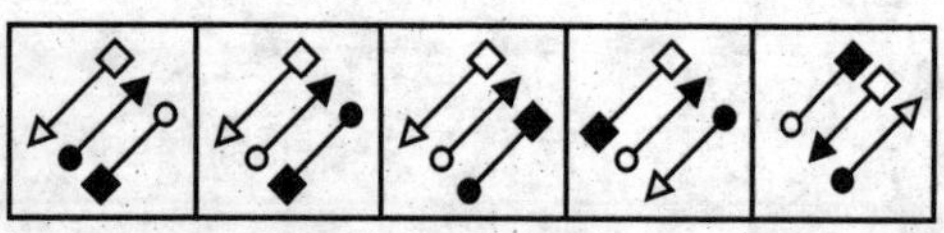

A B C D E

2. Problem Figures

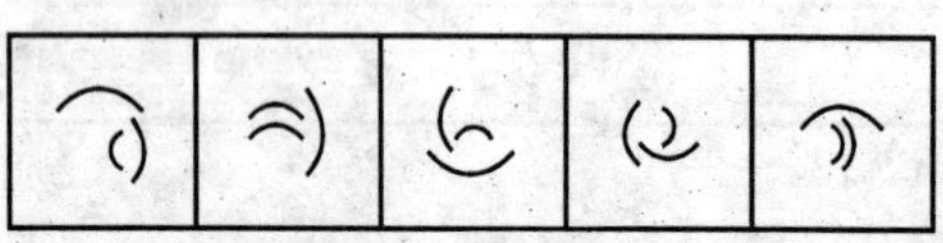

Answer Figures

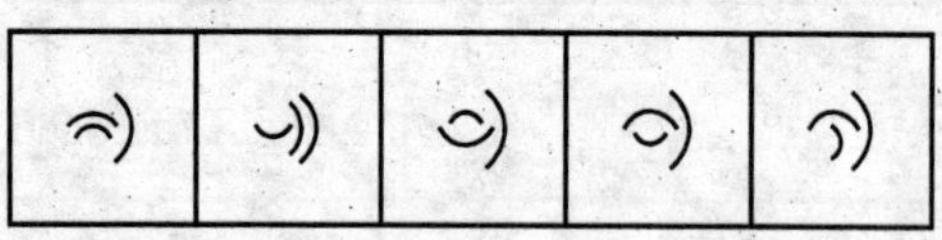

A B C D E

3. Problem Figures

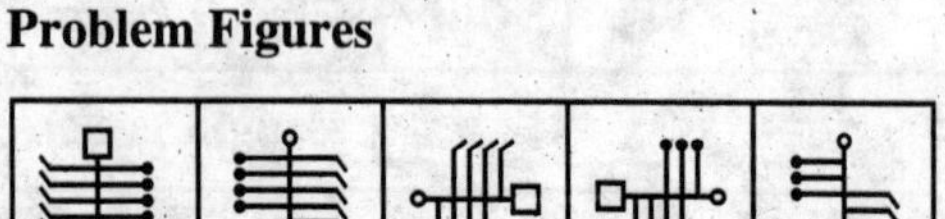

Answer Figures

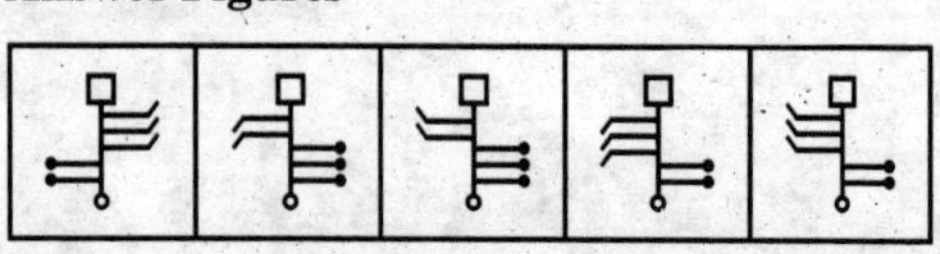

A B C D E

4. Problem Figures

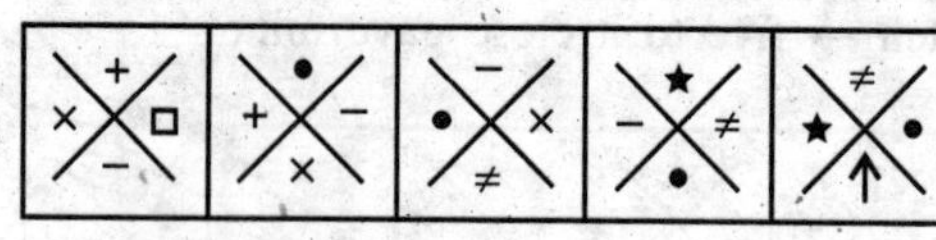

Answer Figures

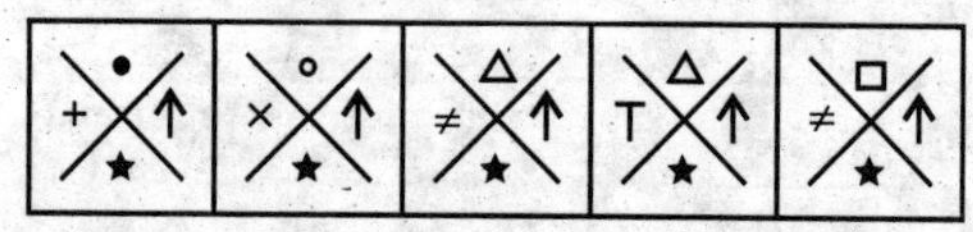

A B C D E

5. Problem Figures

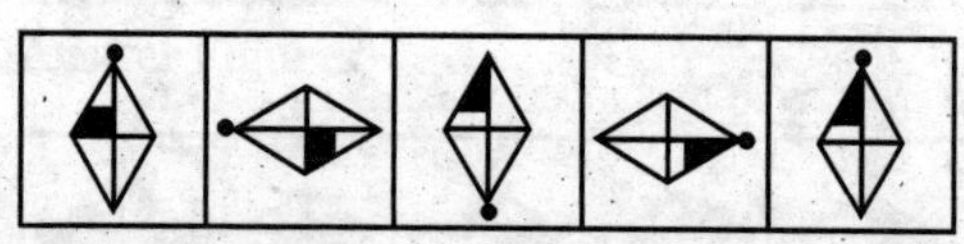

Answer Figures

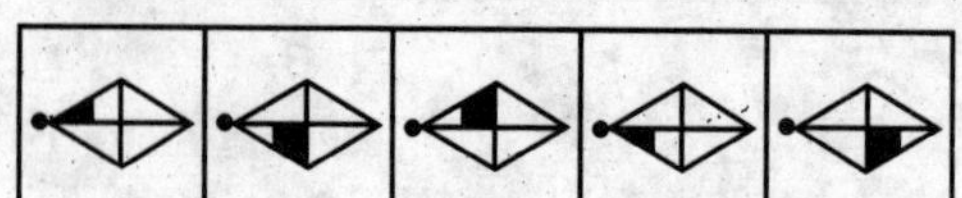

A B C D E

6. Problem Figures

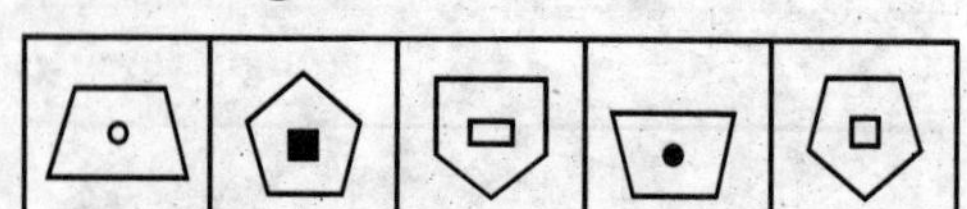

Answer Figures

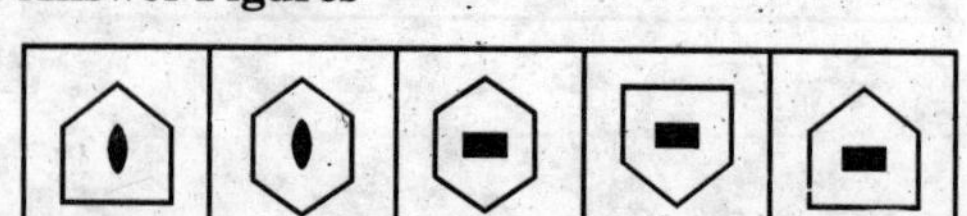

A B C D E

7. Problem Figures

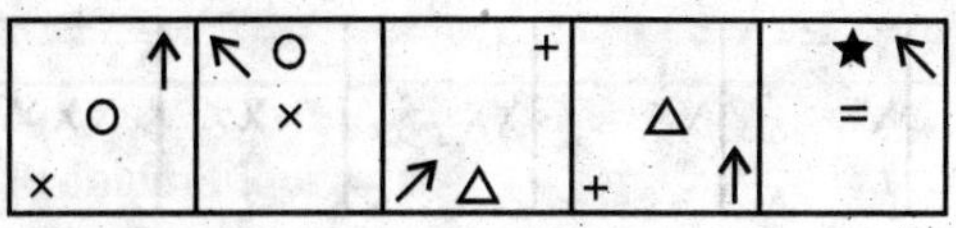

Answer Figures

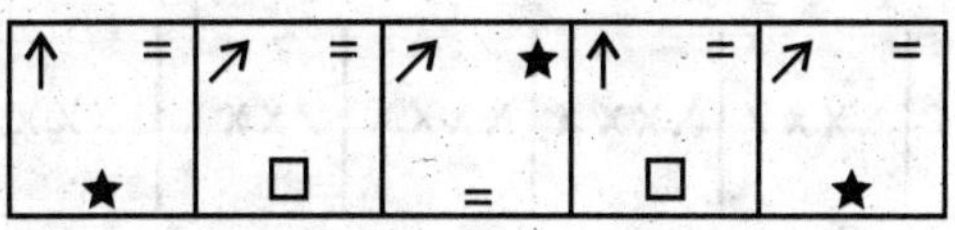

A B C D E

8. Problem Figures

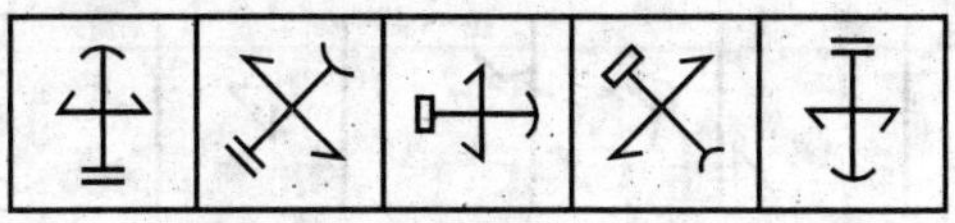

Answer Figures

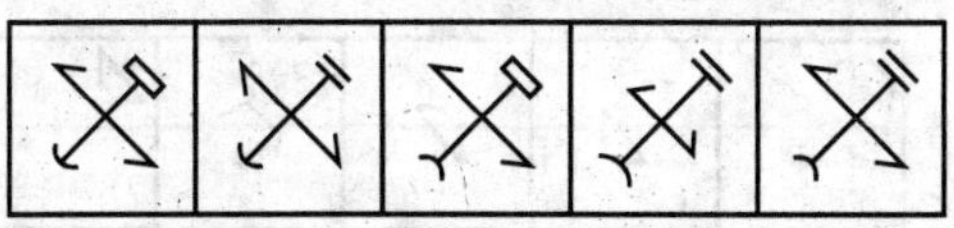

A B C D E

9. Problem Figures

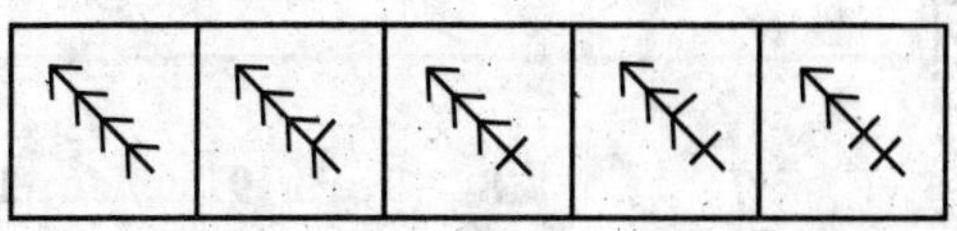

Answer Figures

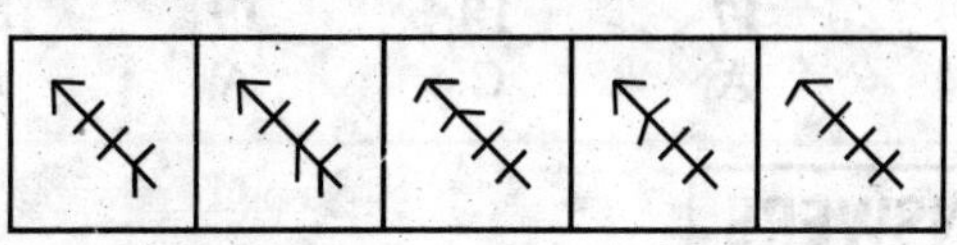

A B C D E

10. Problem Figures

Answer Figures

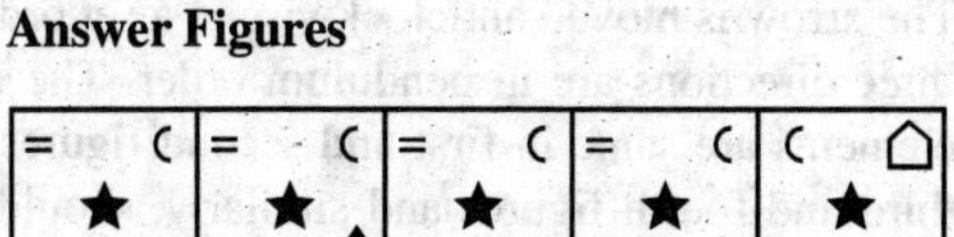

A B C D E

11. Problem Figures

Answer Figures

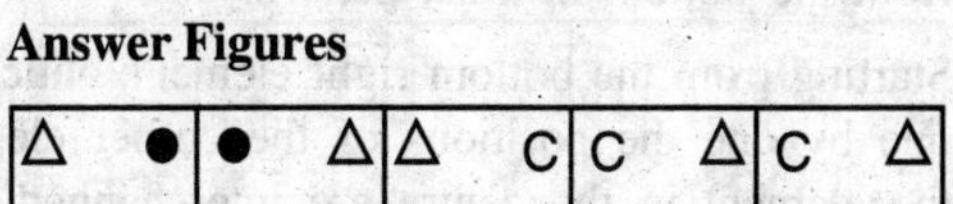

A B C D E

12. Problem Figures

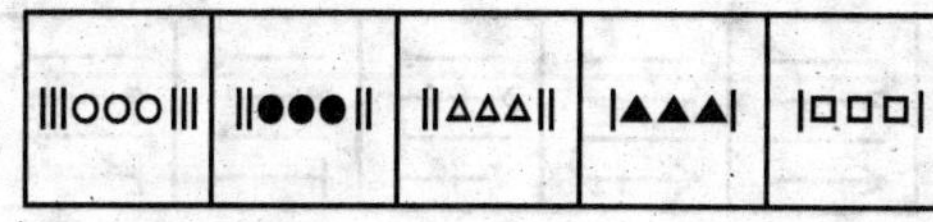

Answer Figures

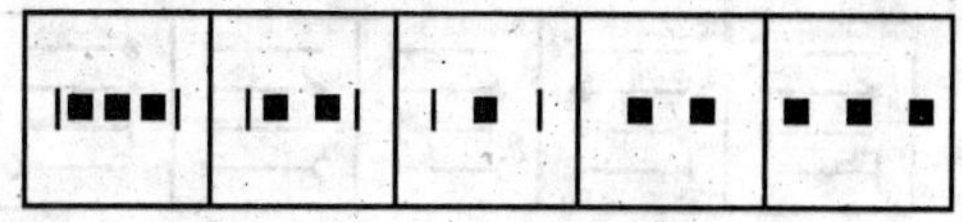

A B C D E

13. Problem Figures

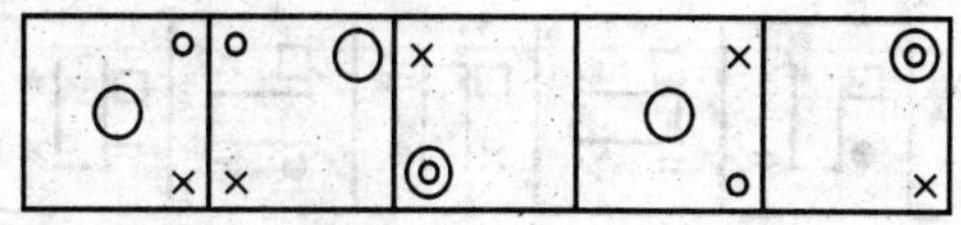

Answer Figures

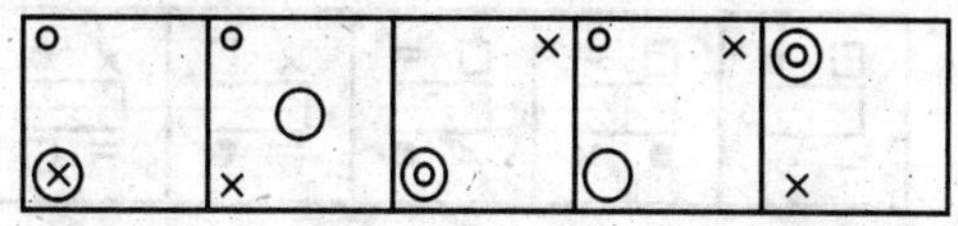

A B C D E

14. Problem Figures

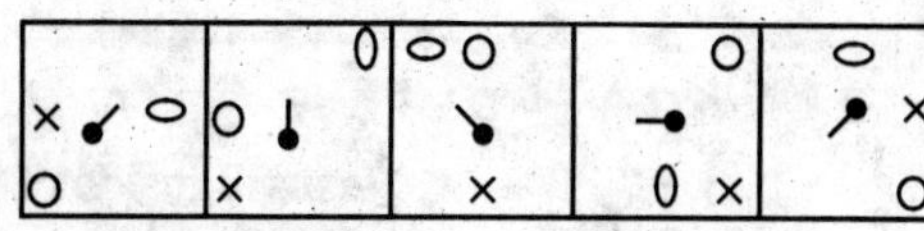

Answer Figures

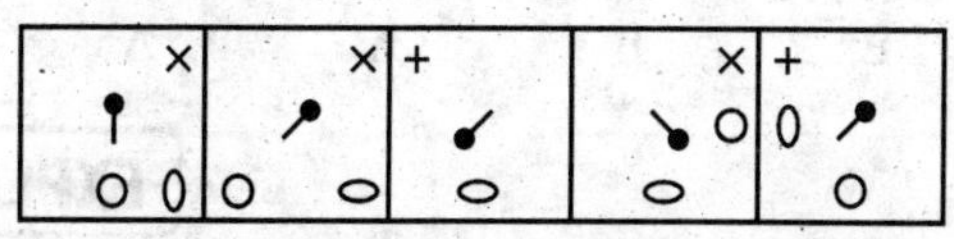

A B C D E

15. Problem Figures

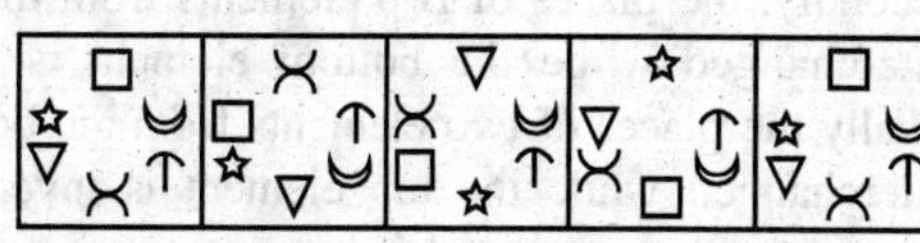

Answer Figures

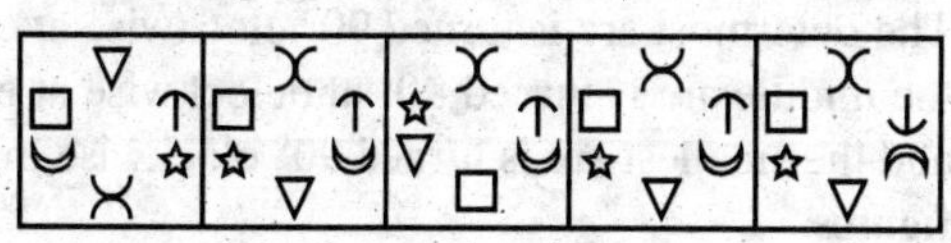

A B C D E

16. Problem Figures

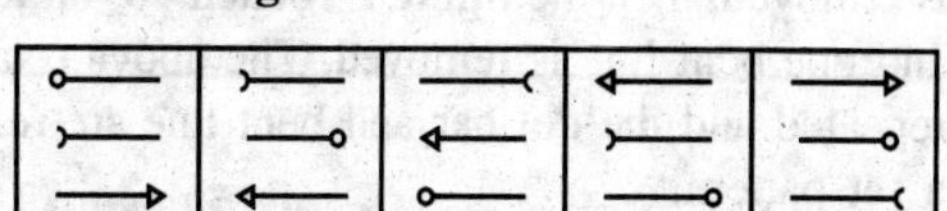

Answer Figures

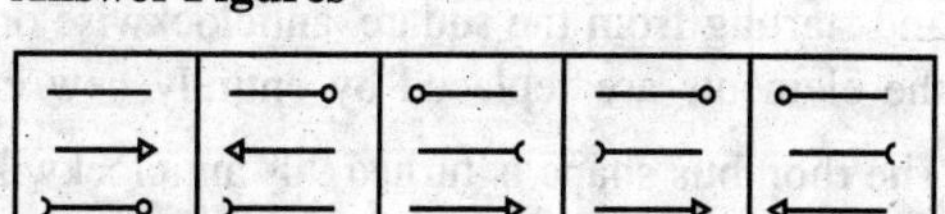

A B C D E

17. Problem Figures

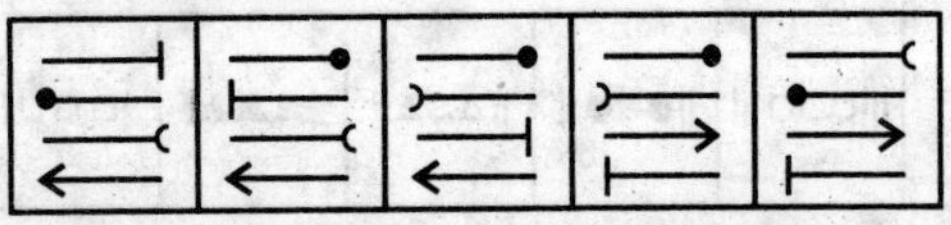

Answer Figures

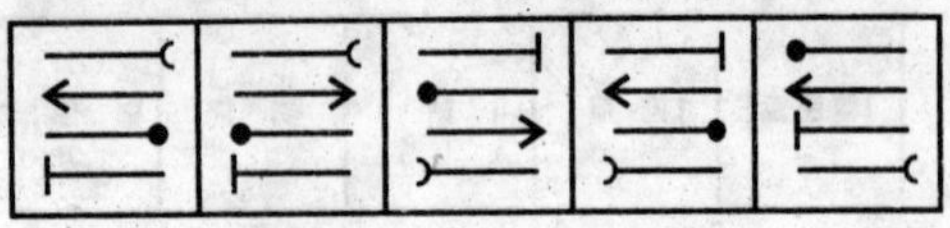

A B C D E

18. Problem Figures

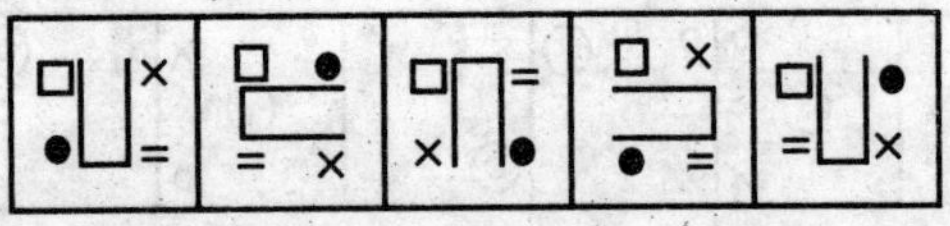

Answer Figures

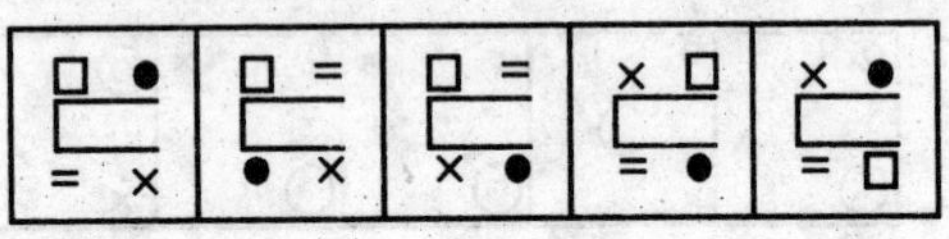

A B C D E

19. Problem Figures

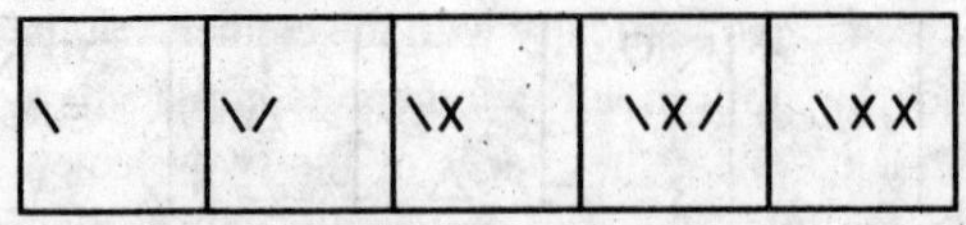

Answer Figures

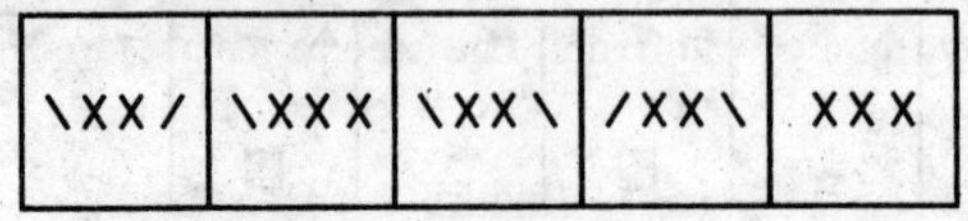

A B C D E

20. Problem Figures

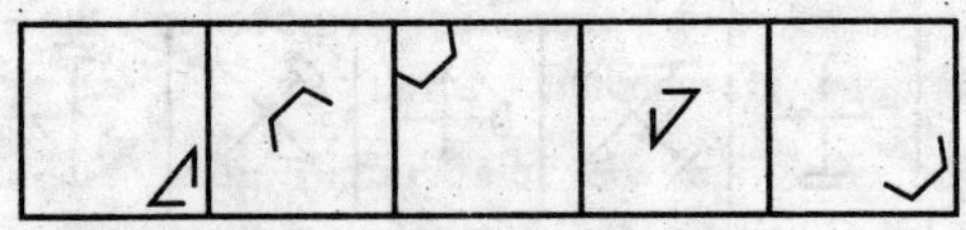

Answer Figures

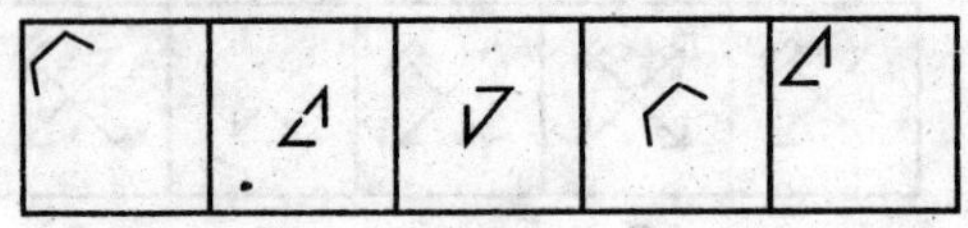

A B C D E

ANSWERS

1	2	3	4	5	6	7	8	9	10
E	D	E	C	E	E	E	E	D	B
11	12	13	14	15	16	17	18	19	20
E	E	A	A	D	B	A	C	A	D

EXPLANATORY ANSWERS

1. First the places of two corner elements are interchanged; secondly, the places of two elements from the top are interchanged while the bottom element is inverted; finally the places of two elements from the bottom are interchanged while the top element is inverted. The above steps are repeated.

2. The outermost arc is turned 90° clockwise at each step; the middle arc is turned 90° anticlockwise at each step; and the smallest arc is turned 90° clockwise in alternate figures.

3. The figure is rotated by 180° degrees and one dot bar is removed, then the figure is rotated 90° anticlockwise and one bent line is removed. The above rotations are repeated and the dot bar and bent line are removed in a set pattern.

4. All the four elements are moved one step anticlockwise and starting from the square, anticlockwise one by one the elements are replaced by entirely new elements.

5. The rhombus shape is turned 90° anticlockwise at each step, and the shade is moved one segment anticlockwise.

6. Figure one is inverted in figure four and the unshaded circle is shaded. Figure two is inverted in figure five and the shaded square is unshaded. Similarly, figure three should be inverted in answer figure and the unshaded triangle should be shaded.

7. The arrow is moved anticlockwise in a set order and its three directions are in pendulum order. The other two elements are same in first and second figures, same in third and fourth figures and similarly, should be same in fifth and answer figures. One of them is moved vertically and the other is moved diagonally.

8. Observe the series. Figure five is an inverted image of figure one. To continue, the answer figure should be an inverted image of figure two.

9. The bent line segments are straightened one by one from the bottom in a set pattern.

10. Starting from the bottom right element, anticlockwise, one by one the positions of the corner element and the element in the centre are interchanged and then the element in the corner is replaced by a new element.

11. First the places of the two elements on the top are interchanged vertically with the elements at the bottom, and the bottom left element is replaced by a new element. Then, the places of the two elements on the top are inter changed diagonally with the elements at the bottom, and the bottom right element is replaced by a new element. The above two steps are then repeated.

12. Observe the series. Figure 1 corresponds to figure 2, figure 3 to figure 4 and similarly figure 5 should correspond to the answer figure in the manner that one line segment on either side is removed and the unshaded elements are shaded.

13. The cross and the small circle are moved one step clockwise and anticlockwise respectively at each step; while the bigger circle is moved diagonally from centre to top right corner to bottom left corner and so on.

14. The circle is moved half step and one step clockwise in alternate figures. The cross is moved half step anticlockwise in each figure. The oval is turned by 90° in each figure and is moved in increasing steps-half, one, one and a half, two and so on The dot bar in the centre is rotated 45° anticlockwise in each figure.

15. Observe the series. The movement of the element is completed in the first four figures and the series is repeated from the fifth figure which is identical to the first figure. So, answer figure should be identical to the second figure.

16. First, the places of two elements from the top are interchanged and then the two elements from the bottom are laterally inverted. Secondly, the two element from the top are laterally inverted and then the places of two elements from the bottom are interchanged. The above steps are then repeated.

17. First, the top two elements are laterally inverted and their places interchanged. Secondly, the middle two elements are laterally inverted and their places interchanged. Finally, the bottom two elements are laterally inverted and their places interchanged. The above three steps are then repeated.

18. The 'U' shape in the middle is rotated 90° clockwise at each step. First the places of two elements to on the left of 'U' are interchanged; then the places of two elements at the base of 'U' are interchanged; further the places of two elements on the right of 'U' are interchanged; and finally the places of two elements on the top side of 'U' are interchanged. To continue the series the places of two elements on the left of the 'U' shape must be interchanged. Also, note that the positioning of the two parallel line segments is same in alternate figures.

19. Watch the series closely. Each time one line segment is added in a set manner where in the '\' line forms the cross over the '/' line.

20. Watch the first three figures. From the fourth figure these figures are moved along the diagonal and rotated by 180°. Figure 'D' is the right answer to complete this series.

SERIES-II

This form of series is almost identical to the one mentioned earlier. Here too are given two sets of figures, the Problem Figures and the Answer Figures. The problem figures follow a particular pattern of movement which constitute the series. The only difference from the earlier mentioned set of series is that instead of depicting the last figure that continues the pattern here one of the middle figures needs to be depicted from the answer figures. This type needs a little more concentration and brain work as the continuity is broken and has to be set right. Understand the set up of elements, pattern and figures in each set and try different styles and rules to find the answer.

MULTIPLE CHOICE QUESTIONS

1. Problem Figures

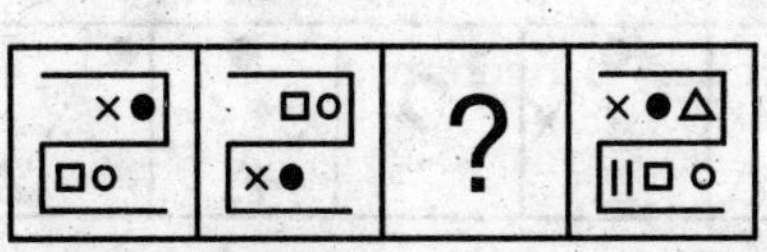

Answer Figures

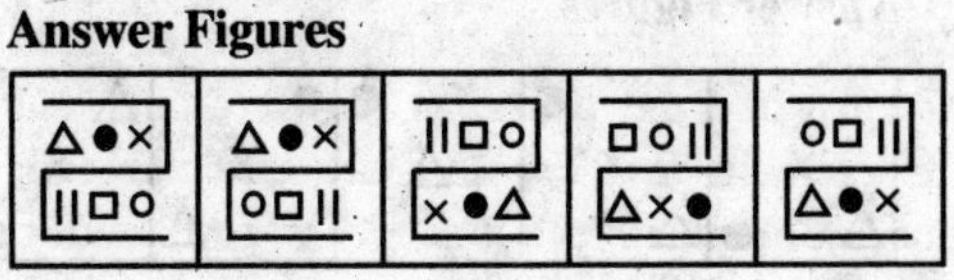

A B C D E

2. Problem Figures

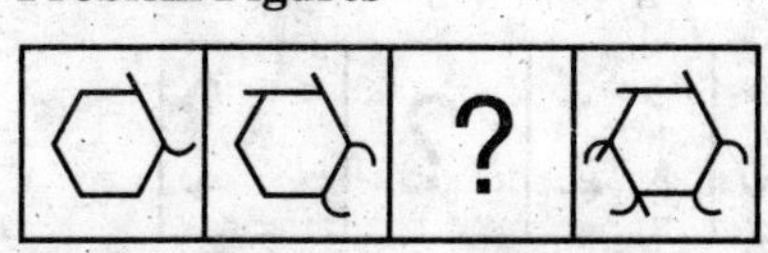

Answer Figures

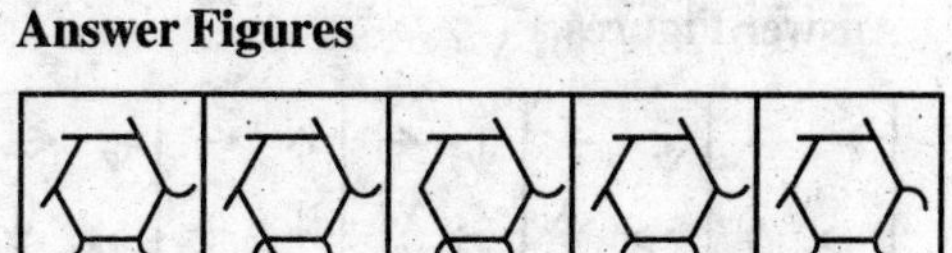

A B C D E

3. Problem Figures

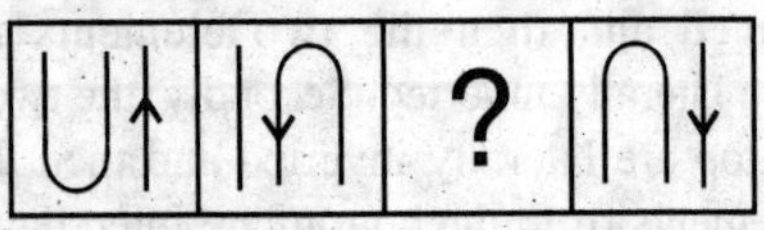

Answer Figures

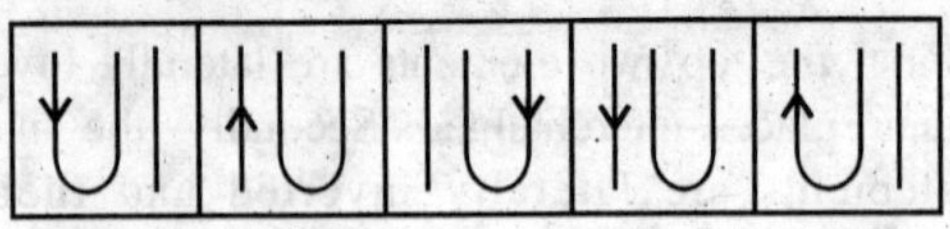

A B C D E

4. Problem Figures

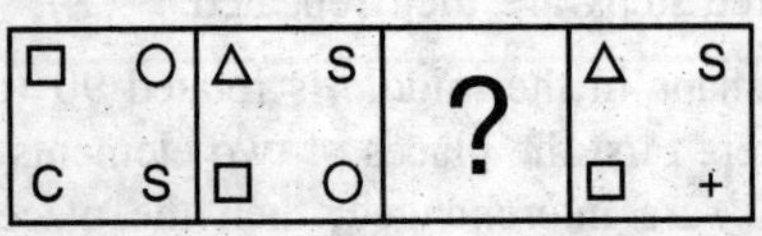

Answer Figures

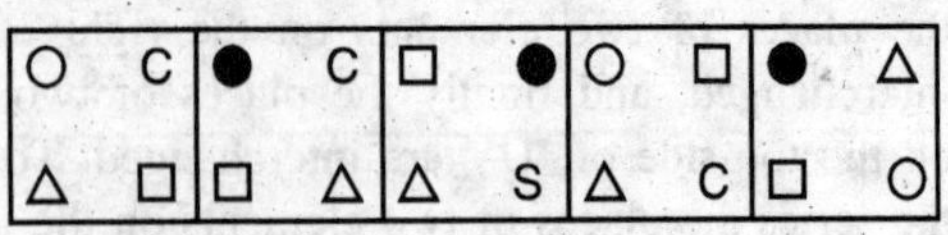

A B C D E

5. Problem Figures

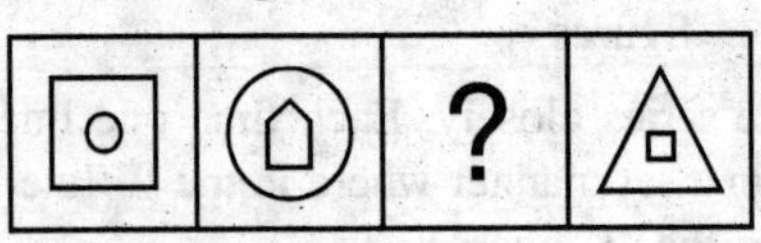

Answer Figures

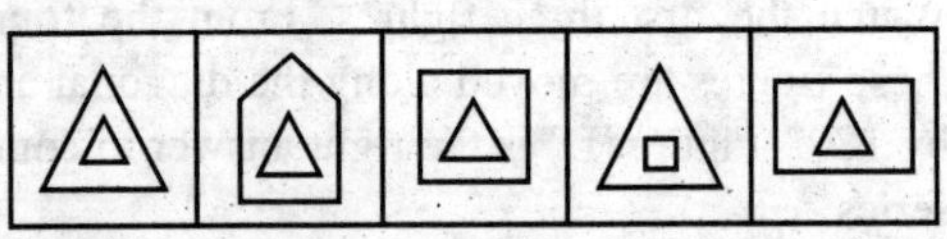

A B C D E

6. Problem Figures

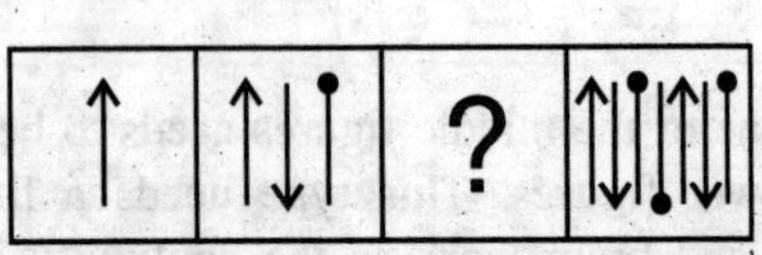

Answer Figures

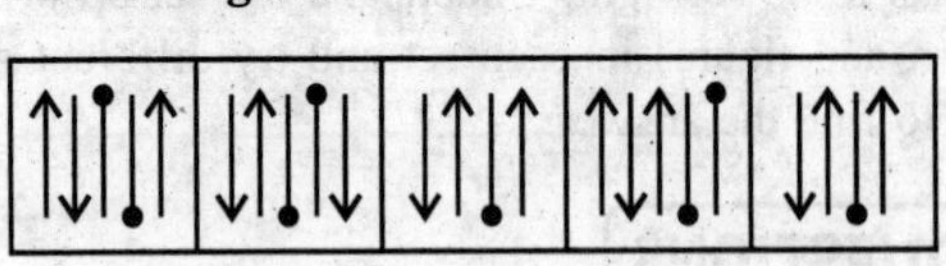

A B C D E

7. Problem Figures

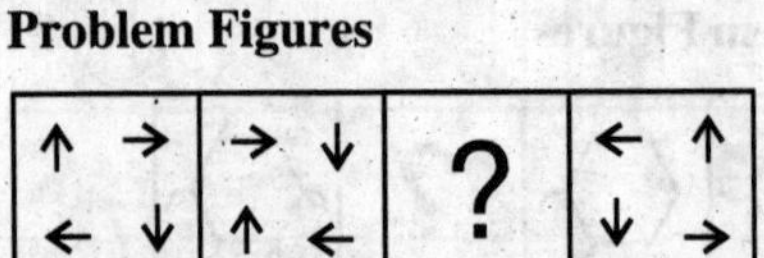

Answer Figures

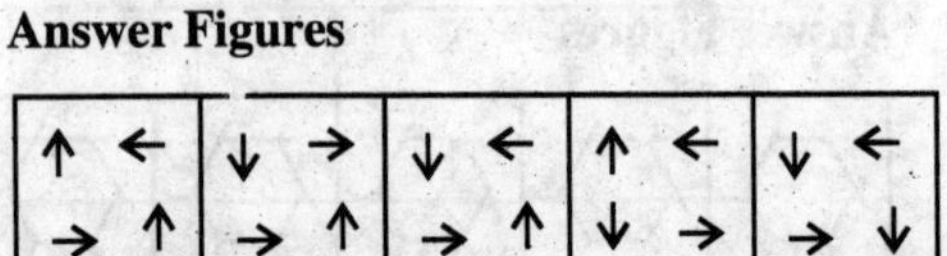

A B C D E

8. Problem Figures

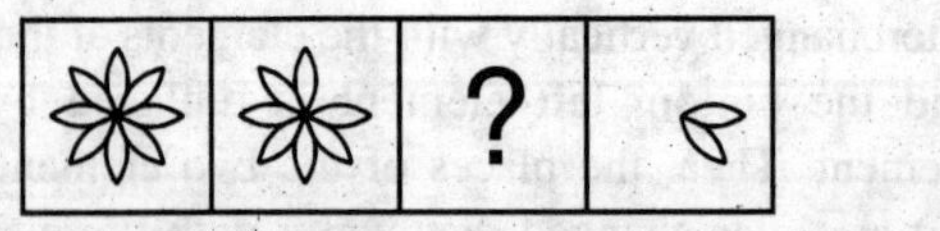

Answer Figures

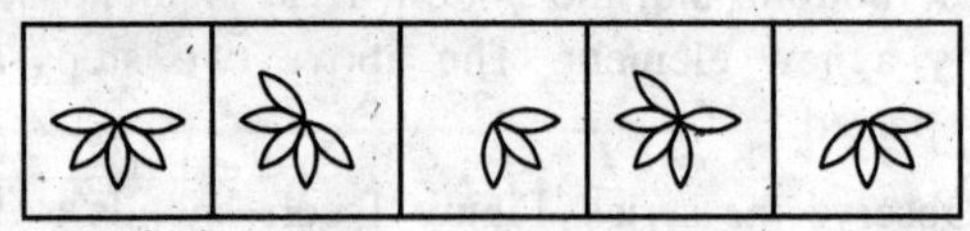

A B C D E

9. Problem Figures

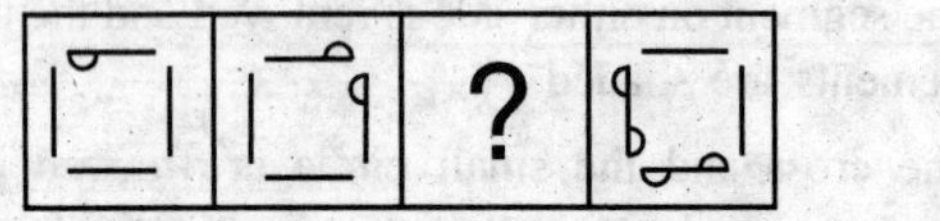

Answer Figures

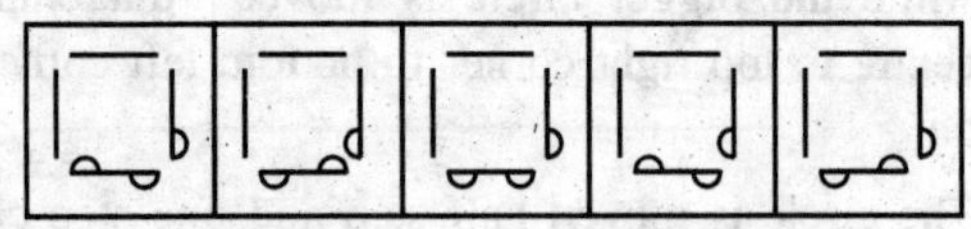

A B C D E

10. Problem Figures

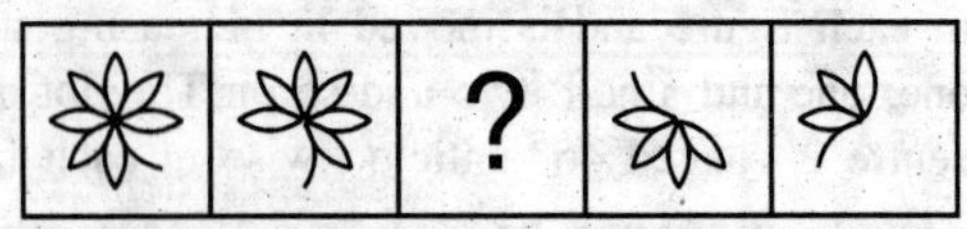

Answer Figures

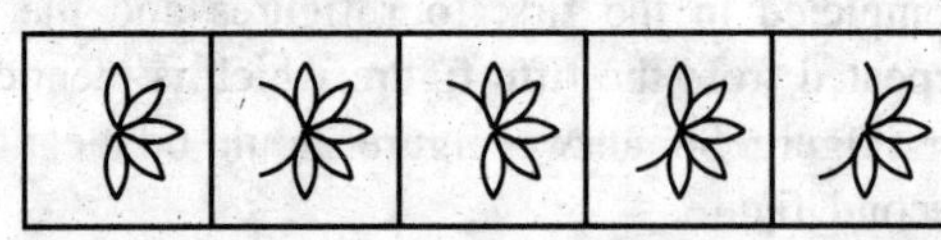

A B C D E

11. Problem Figures

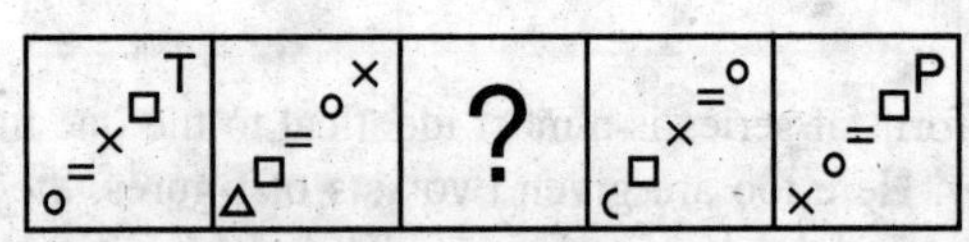

Answer Figures

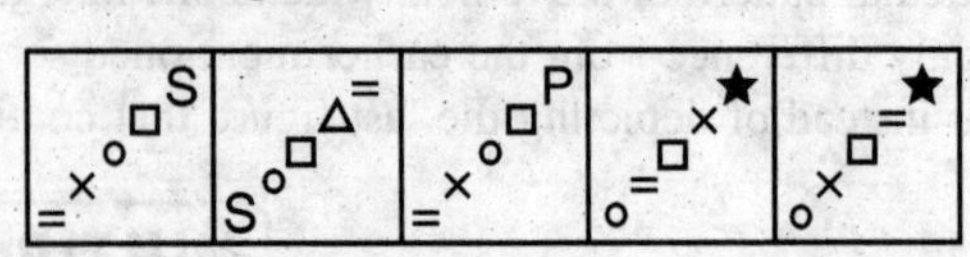

A B C D E

12. Problem Figures

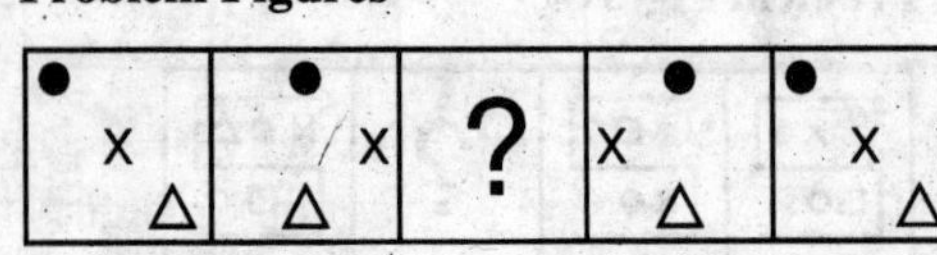

Answer Figures

A B C D E

13. Problem Figures

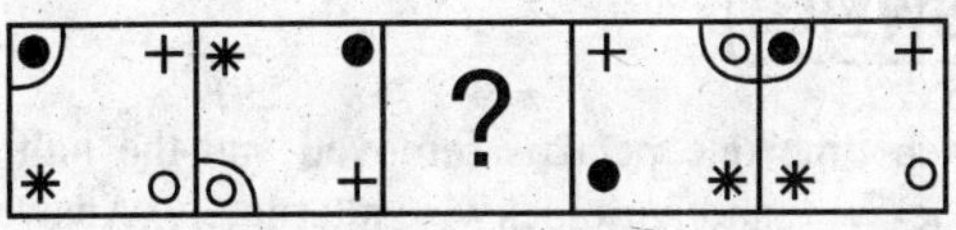

Answer Figures

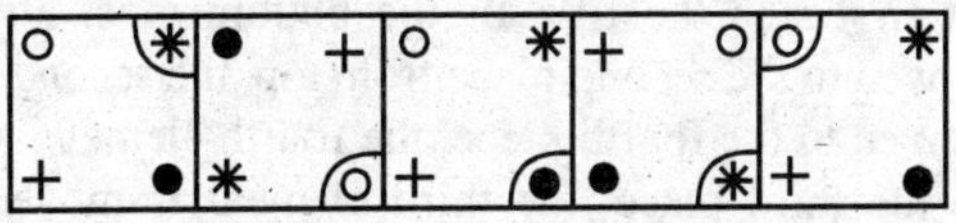

A B C D E

14. Problem Figures

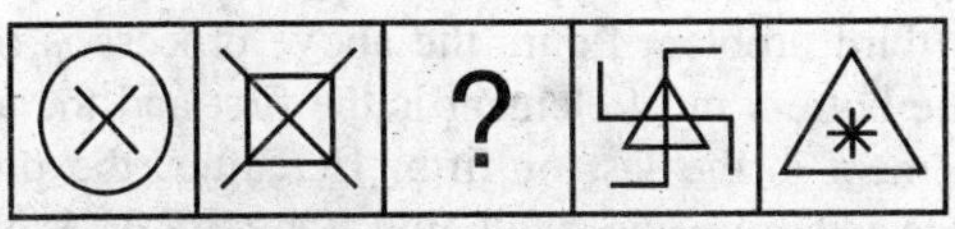

Answer Figures

A B C D E

15. Problem Figures

Answer Figures

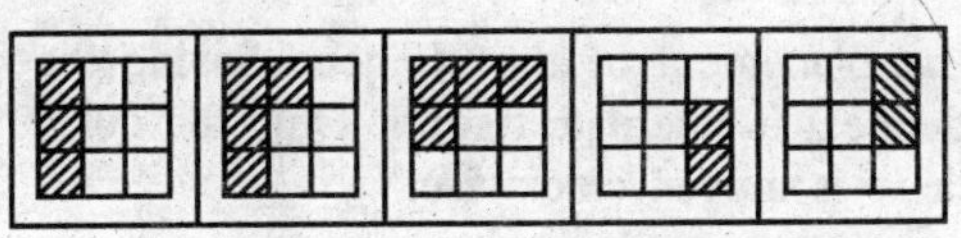

A B C D E

16. Problem Figures

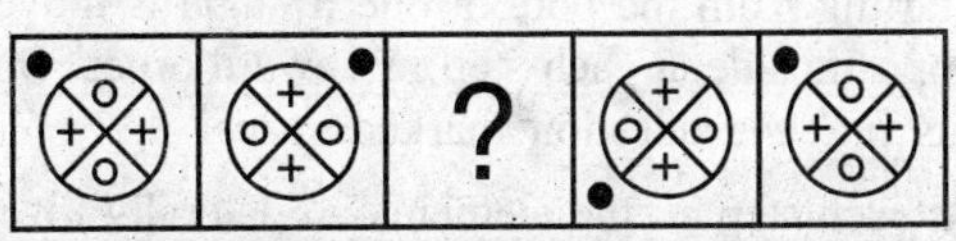

Answer Figures

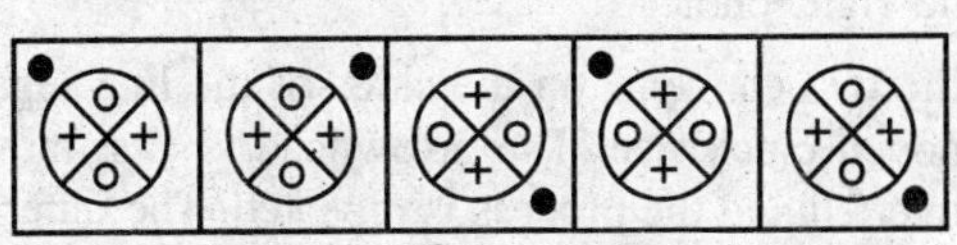

A B C D E

17. Problem Figures

Answer Figures

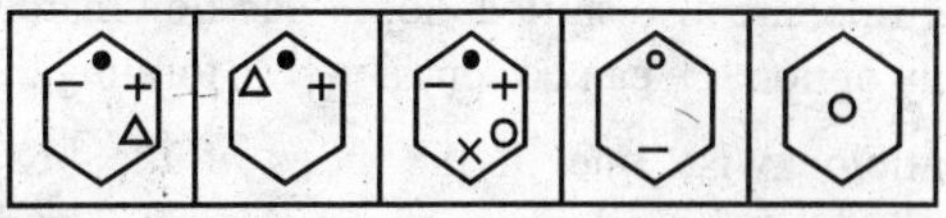

A B C D E

18. Problem Figures

Answer Figures

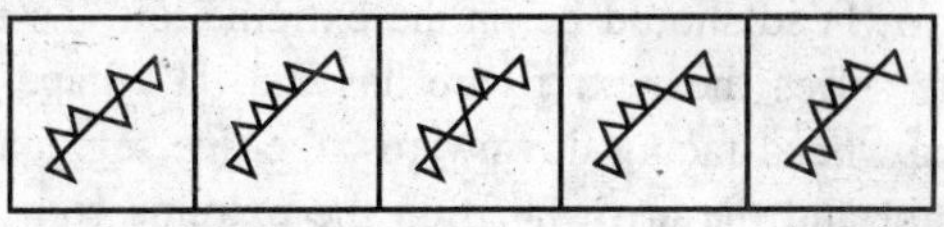

A B C D E

19. Problem Figures

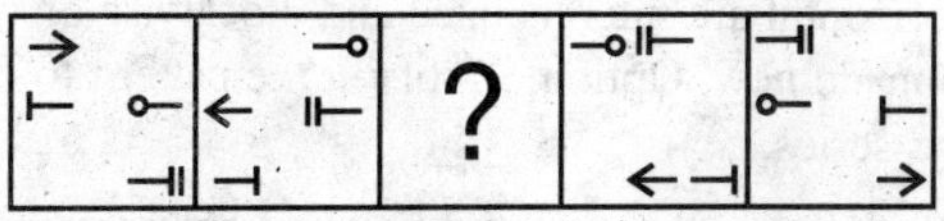

Answer Figures

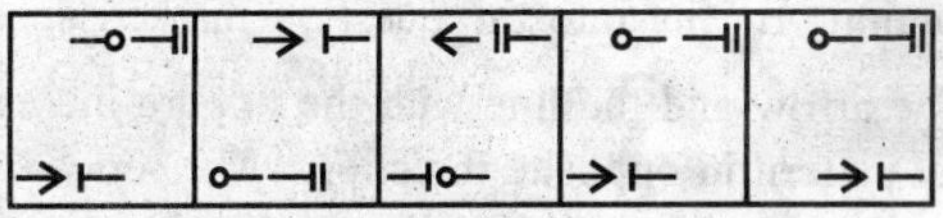

A B C D E

20. Problem Figures

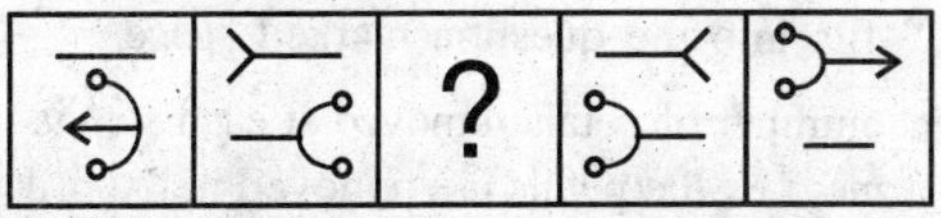

Answer Figures

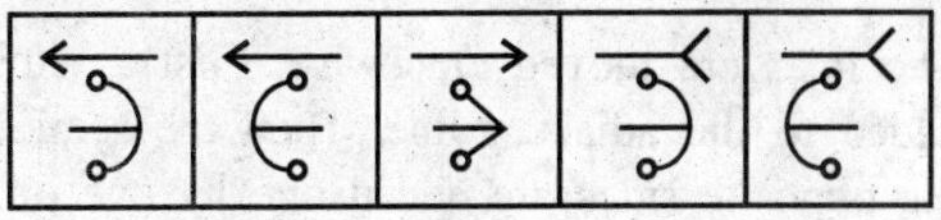

A B C D E

ANSWERS

1	2	3	4	5	6	7	8	9	10
C	D	E	C	B	A	C	A	E	C
11	**12**	**13**	**14**	**15**	**16**	**17**	**18**	**19**	**20**
A	B	C	B	D	E	A	C	D	B

EXPLANATORY ANSWERS

1. From first problem figure to the second the elements on the top are shifted down and vice versa. In fourth problem figure there are three elements which, as per rule, are also shifted. So, in question marked space only option 'C' can be considered as forming the series.

2. Anticlockwise one of the sides of the hexagon is extended and clockwise one arc is added. The direction of the arc is changed at each step. Answer figure 'D' is the right answer.

3. Both the elements are turned upside down, their places interchanged and the arrow head moved left from one element to the other. In the question marked space the 'U' shape and the arrowhead should be facing upwards, the line segment should be on the right and the arrowhead should be on the extreme left. To continue the series the next figure has the 'U' shape and the arrowhead facing downwards, the line segment on the right and the arrowhead on the extreme right. Option 'E' fits into the question marked space.

4. At each step the places of two elements on the horizontal are interchanged and clockwise one element is made new. Option 'C' fits in the pattern to complete the series.

5. At each step the enclosed figure is enlarged in the next and a new figure is placed inside the enlarged figure. Option 'B' fits into the question marked space.

6. The arrow and the line with the dot are increased in a set pattern in opposite directions. The series they form is two arrows and two lines with the dot which is repeated. Answer figure 'A' is the right choice.

7. Each arrow is turned 90° clockwise at each step. Option 'C' fits into the question marked space.

8. The number of petals removed at each step is increased by one, i.e., the petals are removed in the order of one, two and three, leaving only two petals in the last figure option 'A' is the right answer.

9. The lines are moved clockwise. First a semicircle is added to the adjacent line. Then the semicircles on the opposite sides are added one by one on the two lines. Answer figure 'E' fits into the question-marked space.

10. Each time one petal is removed and the half petal is clockwise and anticlockwise alternately. Answer figure 'C' completes the series.

11. At first step the fifth or the bottom most element is moved to the second place from top, the second element moved to the fourth place, the fourth element is moved to the third place, the third element is moved to the first or the topmost place and the element on the top which is made new is moved to the last or the fifth place. At second step i.e., from second problem figure to third problem figure the above process is reversed. The bottom most element is the first and the top most element is the last or fifth. Hereafter, the process is repeated from the beginning. Option 'A' is the right answer.

12. The three elements are moved half step everytime-first till they reach the extreme right position and then back to the left. Answer figure 'B' fits into the question-marked space.

13. The four elements are moved one step clockwise and the arc one step anticlockwise. Option 'C' is the right answer.

14. The smaller design is enlarged in the next and a new smaller design is placed in its centre. Option 'B' fits into the question-marked space to continue the series.

15. The shaded portion is moved one step anticlockwise at each step and one extra portion is shaded alternately.

16. The placement of the elements inside the circle is identical in alternate figures. Only the dot outside the circle is moved clockwise.

17. At every step one element is added to the hexagon. Answer figure 'A' fits into the question-marked space.

18. Starting from the bottom one triangle is moved to the opposite side at each step in upward order. Option 'C' fits into the question marked space.

19. At each step all the elements are laterally inverted and shifted half a side anticlockwise. Answer figure 'D' is the right choice.

20. The two elements on the sides of the line segment are moved clockwise. The arrowhead is first moved then inverted and the process is repeated. The other element is first inverted then moved and the process is repeated. By this process option 'B' is the right answer.

ANALOGIES OR RELATIONSHIPS

Analogy is a process of reasoning between two parallel cases. It relates to agreement or correspondence in certain respects between two things. It is a process whereby the underlying relationship that exists between two figures, designs or patterns is determined. Under the process, one has to discover the features common to the two figures or designs. This common feature is a model or base. The question seeks solution on the basis of this model or base.

MULTIPLE CHOICE QUESTIONS

1. Problem Figures

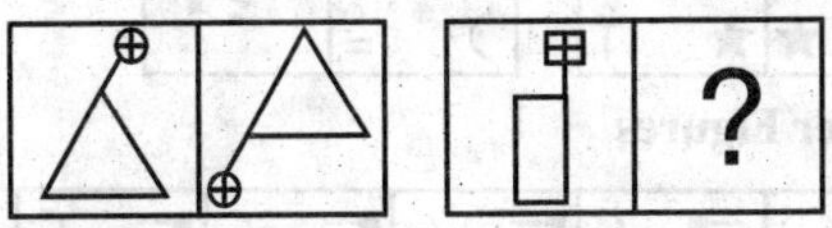

Answer Figures

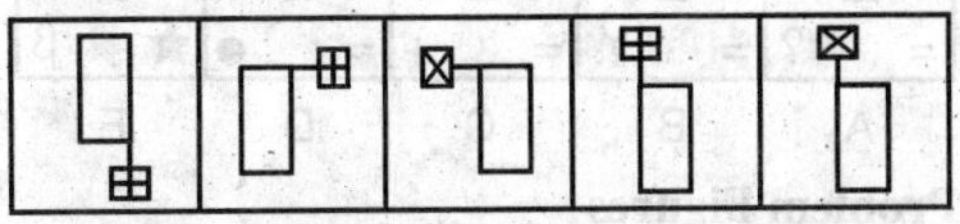

A B C D E

2. Problem Figures

Answer Figures

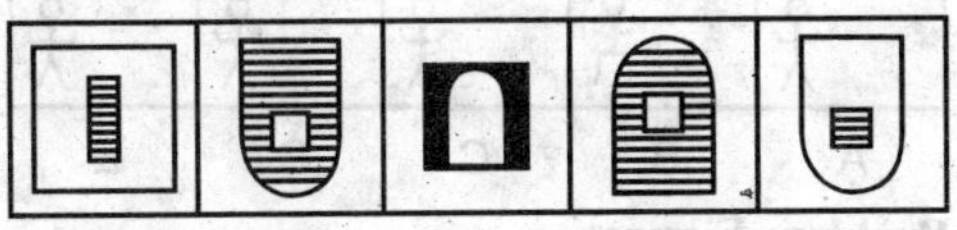

A B C D E

3. Problem Figures

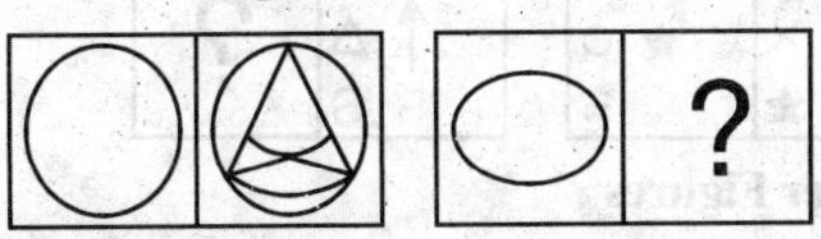

Answer Figures

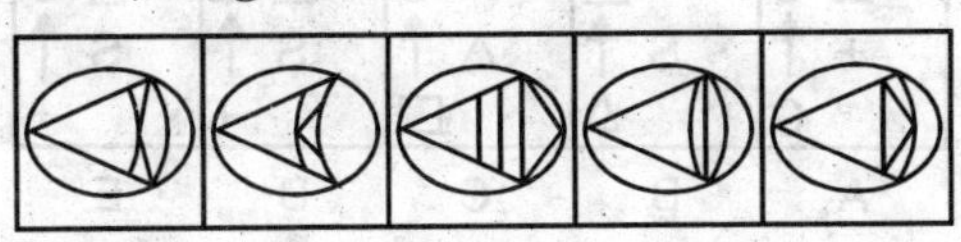

A B C D E

4. Problem Figures

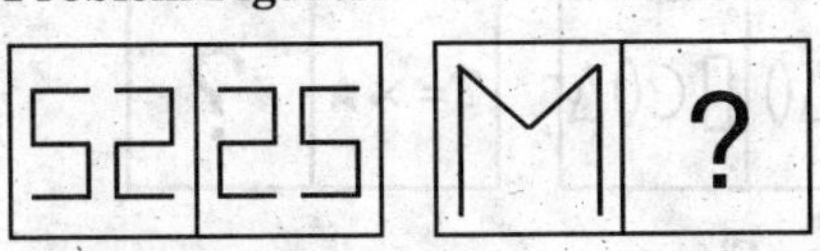

Answer Figures

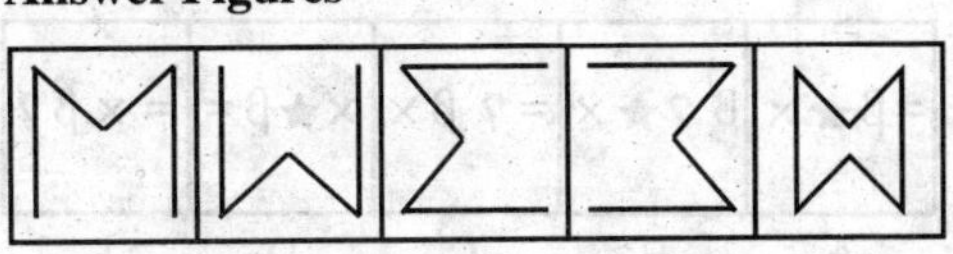

A B C D E

5. Problem Figures

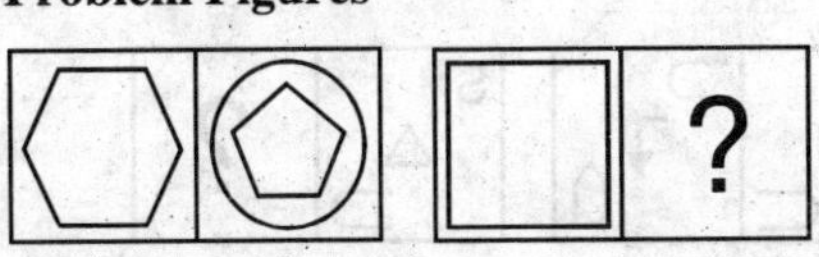

Answer Figures

A B C D E

6. Problem Figures

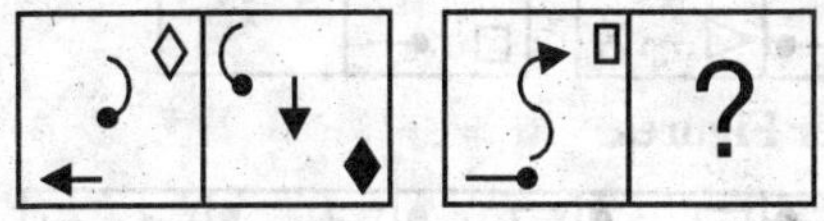

Answer Figures

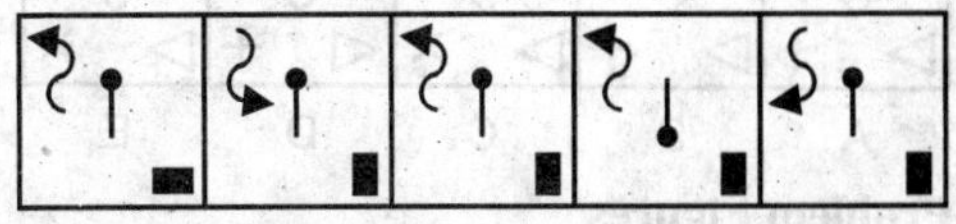

A B C D E

7. Problem Figures

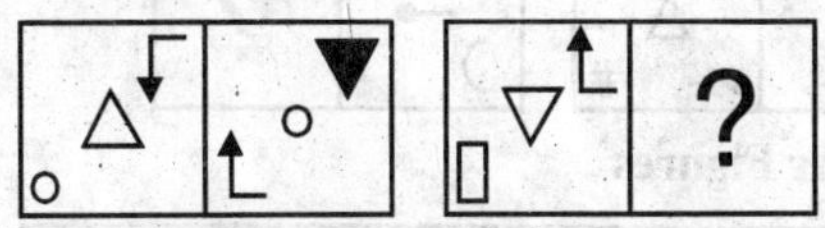

Answer Figures

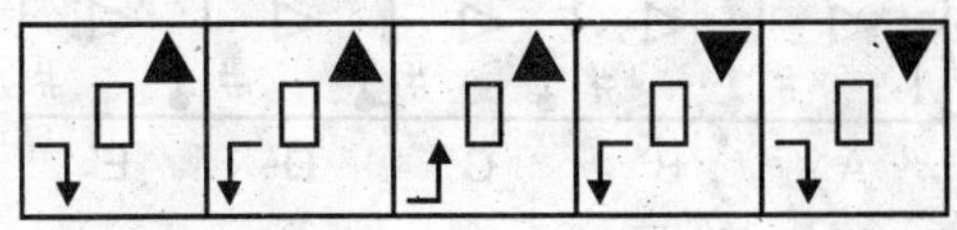

A B C D E

8. Problem Figures

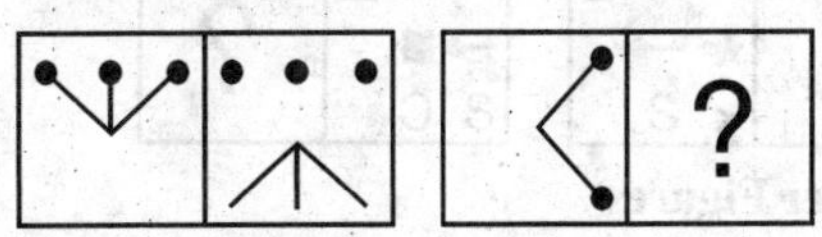

Answer Figures

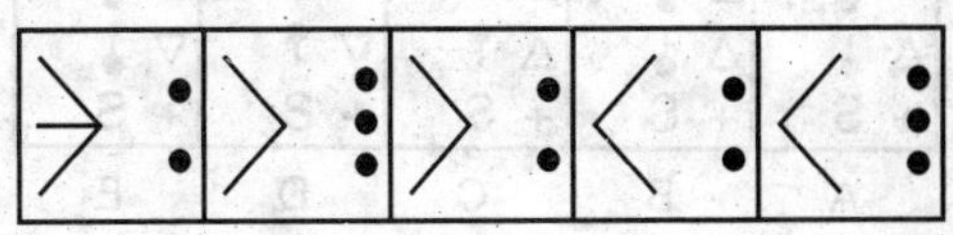

A B C D E

9. Problem Figures

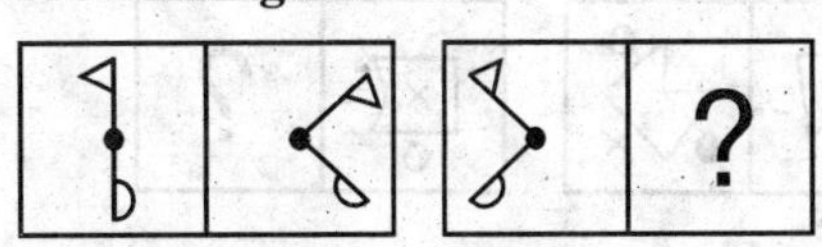

Answer Figures

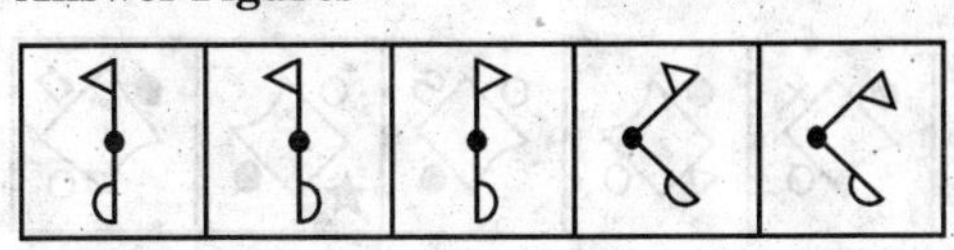

A B C D E

10. Problem Figures

Answer Figures

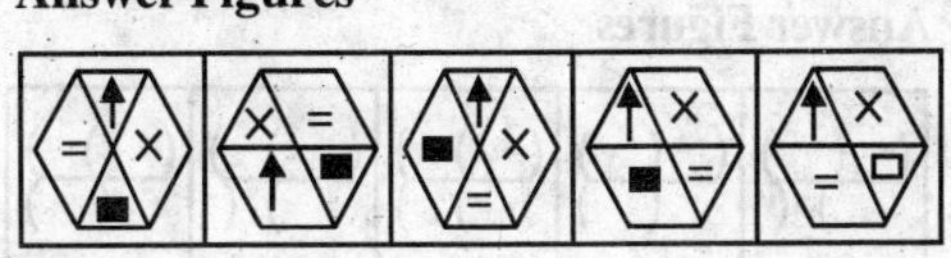

A B C D E

11. Problem Figures

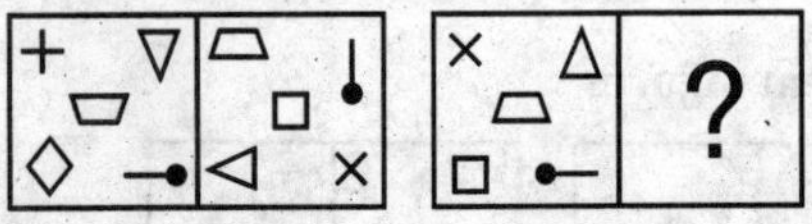

Answer Figures

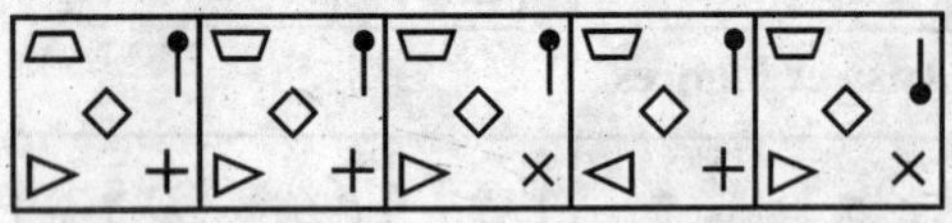

A B C D E

12. Problem Figures

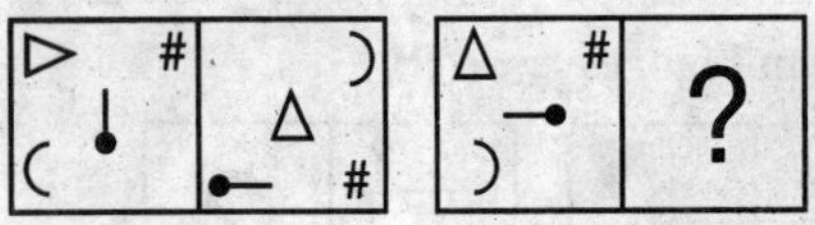

Answer Figures

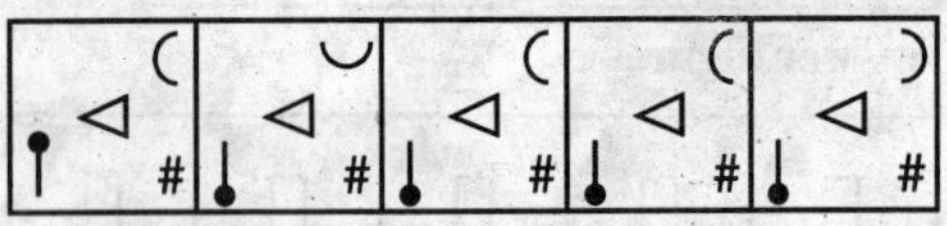

A B C D E

13. Problem Figures

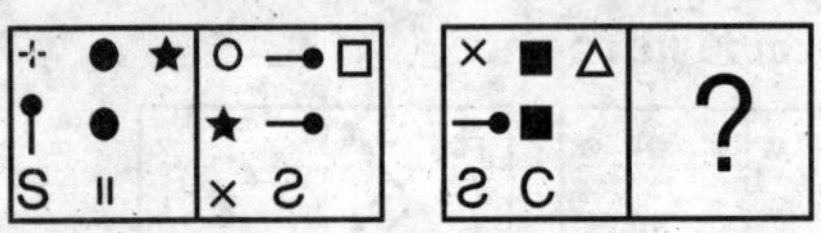

Answer Figures

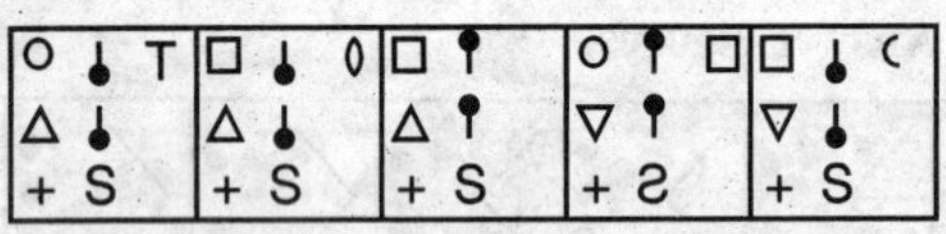

A B C D E

14. Problem Figures

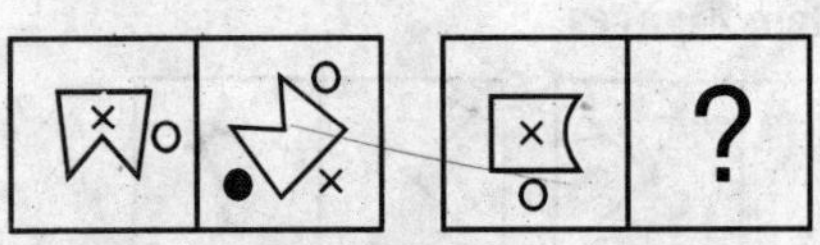

Answer Figures

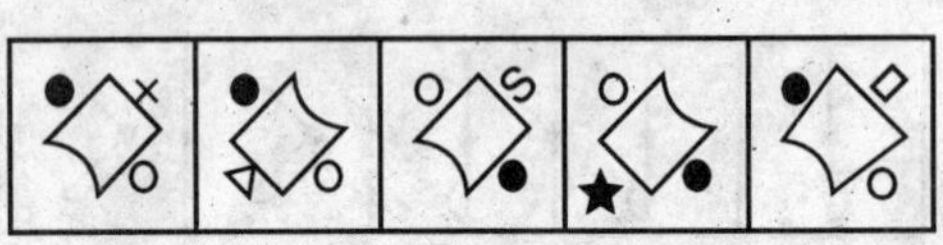

A B C D E

15. Problem Figures

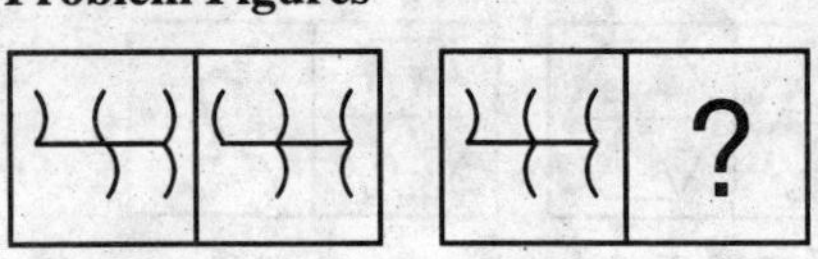

Answer Figures

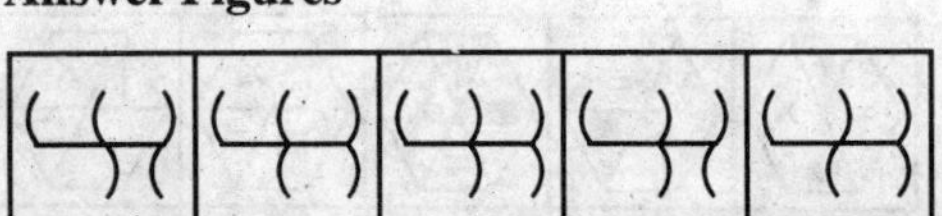

A B C D E

16. Problem Figures

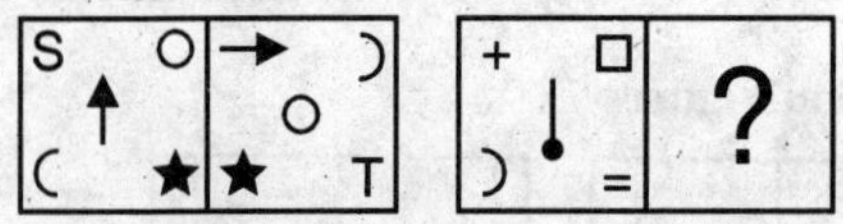

Answer Figures

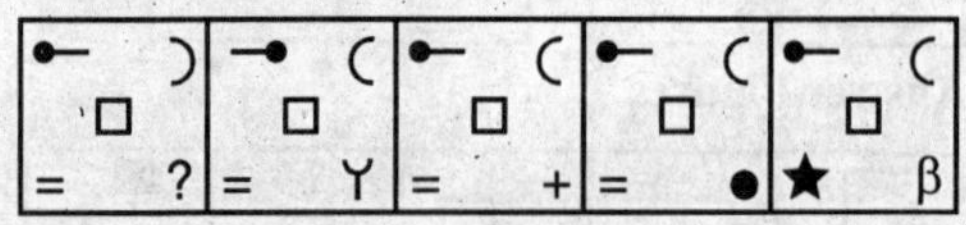

A B C D E

17. Problem Figures

Answer Figures

A B C D E

18. Problem Figures

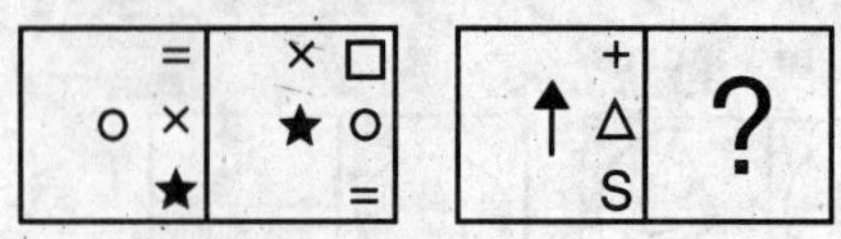

Answer Figures

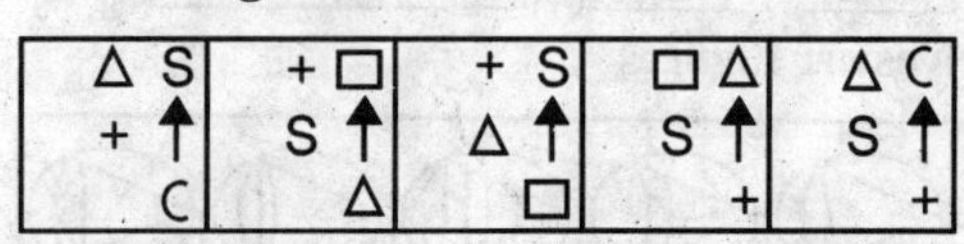

A B C D E

19. Problem Figures

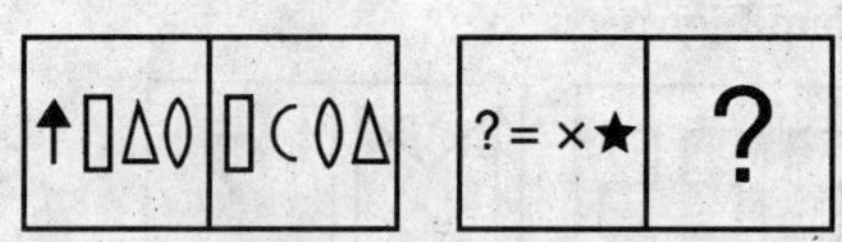

Answer Figures

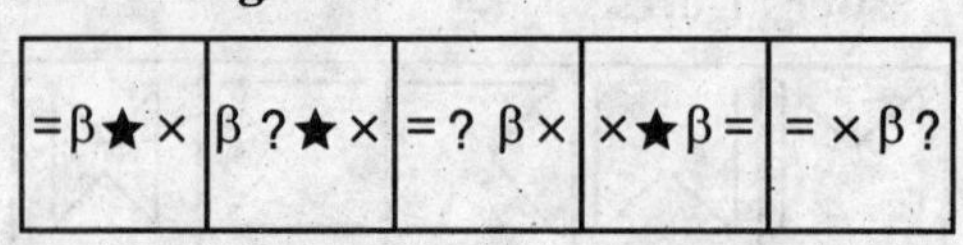

A B C D E

20. Problem Figures

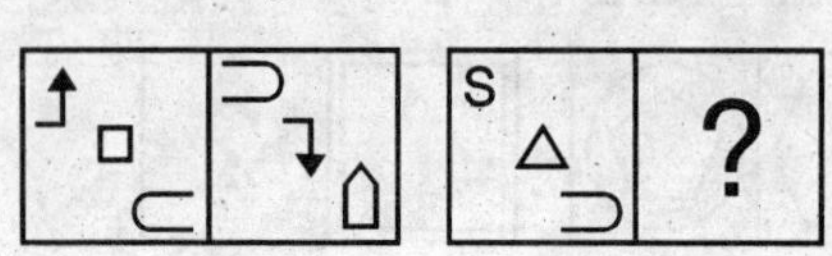

Answer Figures

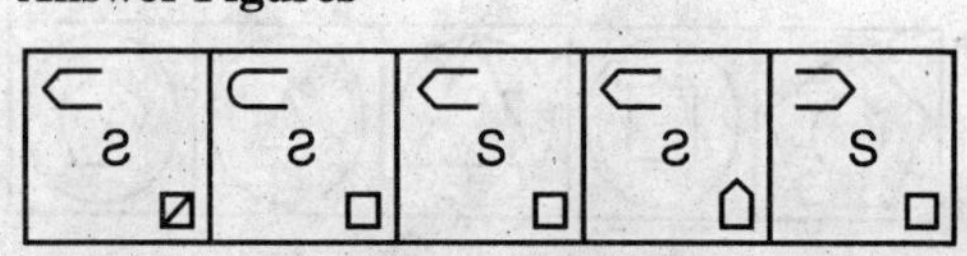

A B C D E

ANSWERS

1	2	3	4	5	6	7	8	9	10
A	B	A	B	D	C	B	C	A	D
11	**12**	**13**	**14**	**15**	**16**	**17**	**18**	**19**	**20**
B	C	B	A	E	D	A	E	A	B

EXPLANATORY ANSWERS

1. The extended line segment is moved to the next corner.
2. The size and place of both the designs in first figure are swapped and the outes figure turned upside-down in the second figure.
3. The blank first figure is filled by a particular pattern in second figure. The answer figure shall contain the same pattern inside the eclipse.
4. The first figure is turned upside down to get the second figure.
5. One of the lines making the first figure is reduced and the new formed figure is enclosed within a circle.
6. The element in the top right corner is moved down vertically and shaded, the element in the centre is laterally inverted and moved to the top left corner position, and the element in the bottom left corner is turned 90° anticlockwise and moved to the centre.
7. The element in the top right corner is turned upside down and moved to the bottom left corner position, the element in the centre is turned upside down, shaded and moved to the top right corner, and the third element in the bottom left corner is moved to the centre.
8. The line segments in first figure are turned upside down in second figure.
9. The elements attached to the line segments are moved to the other side and the top and bottom line segments are turned 45° clock-wise and 45° anticlockwise respectively.
10. The first figure is turned 120° anticlockwise to get the second figure.
11. The element in the top left corner is turned by 45° and moved to the bottom right corner position the element in the bottom right corner is turned 90° clockwise and moved up to top right corner position, the element in top right corner is turned 90° clockwise and moved to bottom left corner position, the element in bottom left corner is turned by 45° and moved to the centre; and the element in the centre is turned upside down and moved to the top left corner position.
12. The element in the top left corner is turned 90° anticlockwise and moved to the centre, the element in the centre is turned 90° clockwise and moved to the bottom left corner position, the element in the bottom left corner is laterally inverted and moved to the top right corner position, and the element in the top right corner is laterally inverted and moved to the bottom right corner position.
13. The element in the top right corner is moved to the left middle position, the element in the left middle position is turned 90° clockwise and moved to the centre, the element in the centre is replaced by the earlier element and moved to the top middle position, the element in the top middle position is made blank and moved to the top left corner position, the element in the top left corner is turned by 45° and moved to the bottom left corner position, the element in the bottom left corner is laterally inverted and moved to the bottom middle position, and a new element is placed at the top right corner position.
14. The first figure is turned 135° clockwise, the inner element is moved out towards the base, the blank circle is shaded and a circle is added on its opposite side to get the second figure.
15. All arcs in the first figure except the left are below the line segment are turned to the other side to get the second figure.
16. The element in the top left corner is made new and moved to the bottom right corner position, the element in the bottom right corner is moved to the bottom left corner position, the element in the bottom left corner is laterally inverted and moved to the top right corner position, the element in the top right corner is moved to the centre, and the element in the centre is turned 90° clockwise and moved to the top left corner position.
17. The human sketch is moved to the right side and its hands and legs are extended and shortened respectively in a particular manner. The other two elements are turned upside down, the smaller one is enclosed within the larger one and then the two together are moved to the left and rotated 45° anticlockwise.
18. The element in the top right corner is moved to the bottom right corner position, the element in the bottom right corner is moved to the centre, the element in the centre is moved to the right middle position, the element in the right middle position is moved to the top middle position, and a new element is placed in the top right corner position.

19. The left most element is made new and then the two corner elements are moved inbetween the two middle elements.

20. The element in the bottom right corner is laterally inverted and moved to the top left corner position, the element in the top left corner is turned upside down and moved to the centre, and the element in the centre is made new by adding one more straight line to its formation and moved to the bottom right corner position.

CLASSIFICATION OR ODD-ONE OUT

Classification means arranging the given content in groups or classes having qualities of same kind. In classification type questions, the figures or items are sorted out in groups on the basis of their similarities in qualities in shapes, size, pattern, structure, genus, order, species, grade, style, constituents and other specifications, and thus the answer is found out.

MULTIPLE CHOICE QUESTIONS

1. 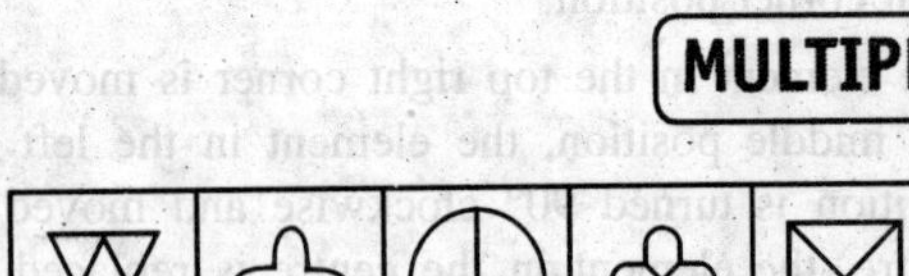

A B C D E

2. 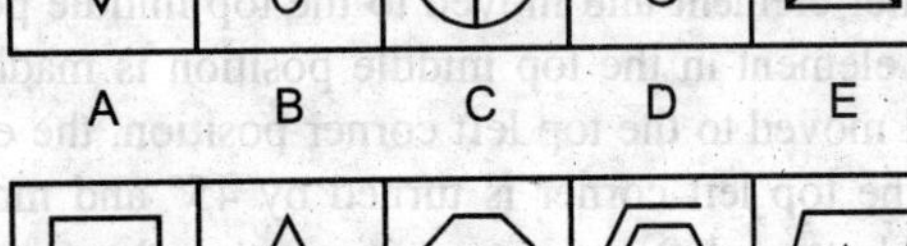

A B C D E

3. 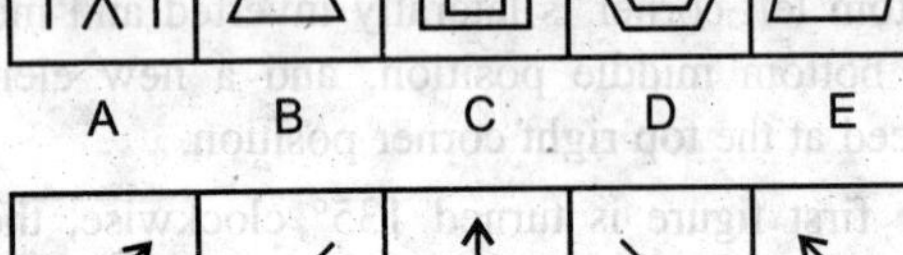

A B C D E

4. 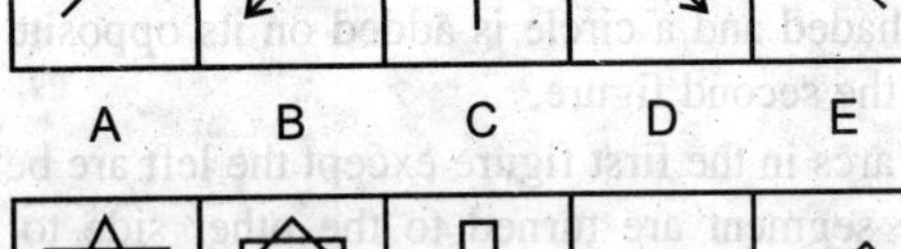

A B C D E

5. 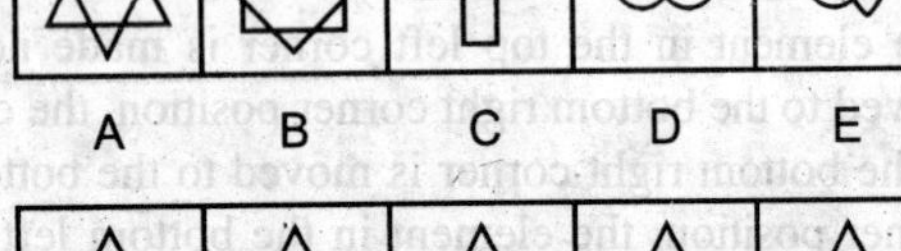

A B C D E

6. 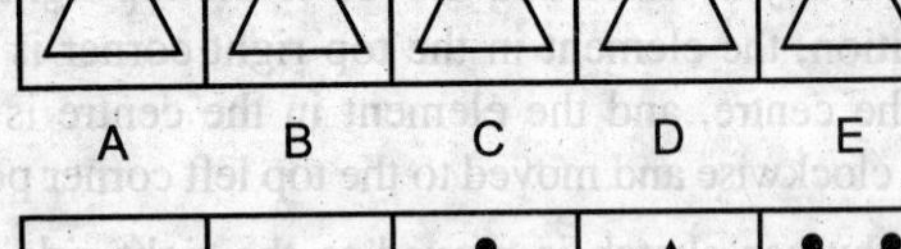

A B C D E

7. 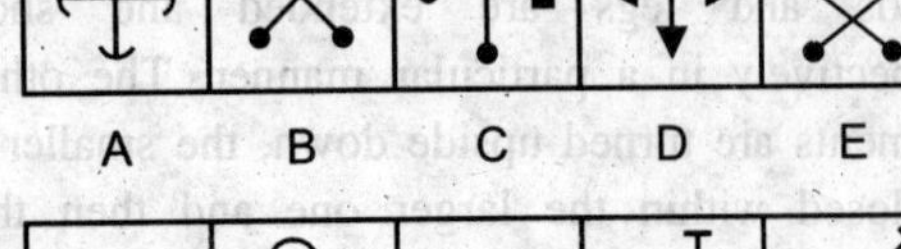

A B C D E

8. 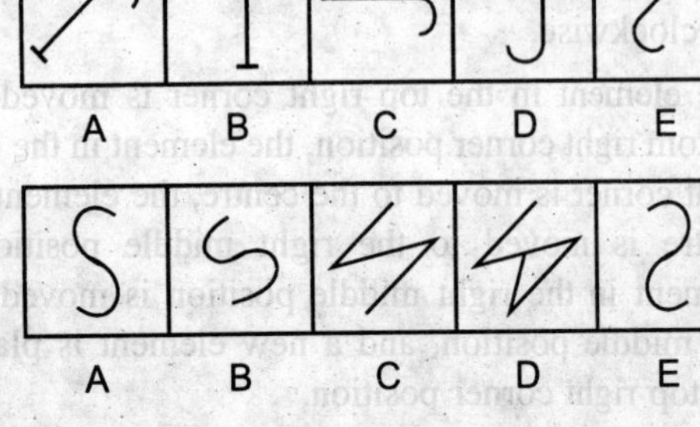

A B C D E

9. 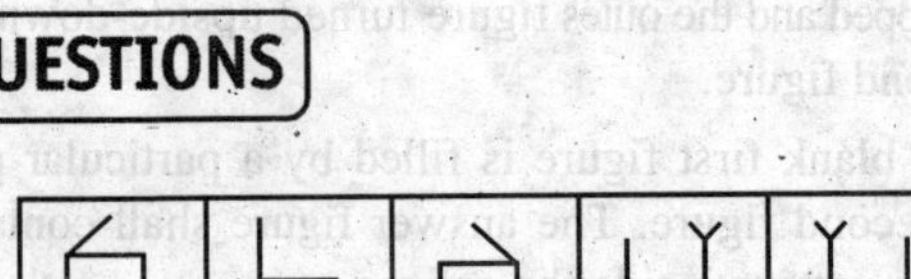

A B C D E

10. 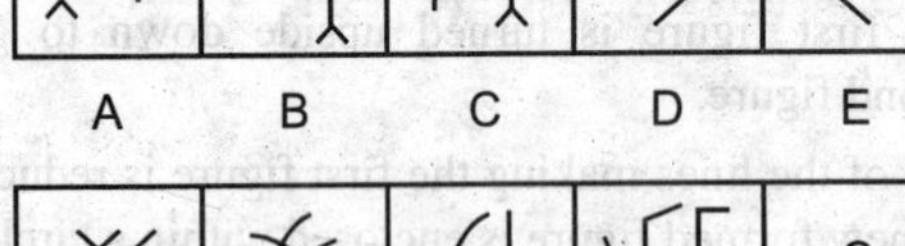

A B C D E

11. 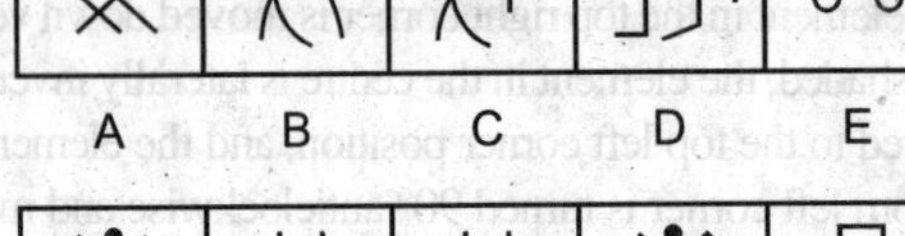

A B C D E

12. 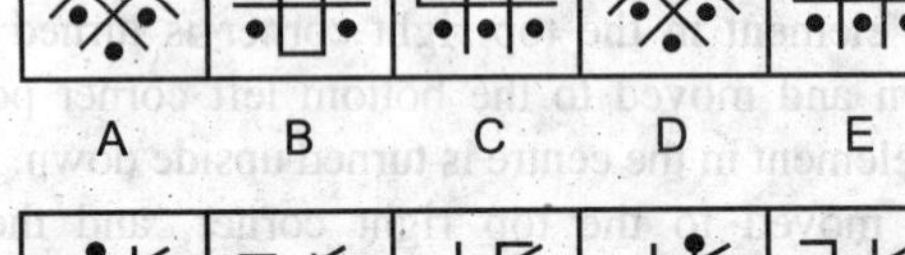

A B C D E

13. 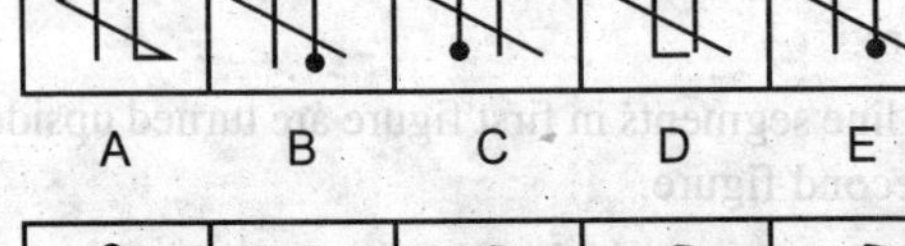

A B C D E

14. 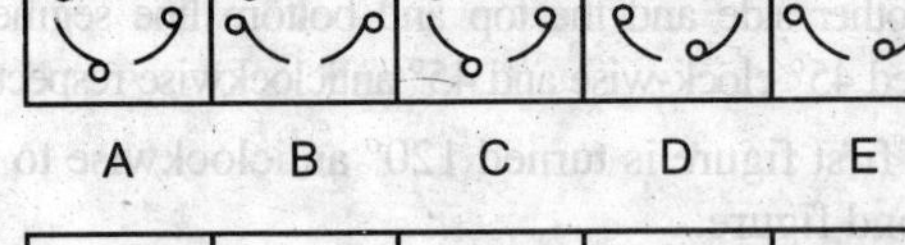

A B C D E

15. 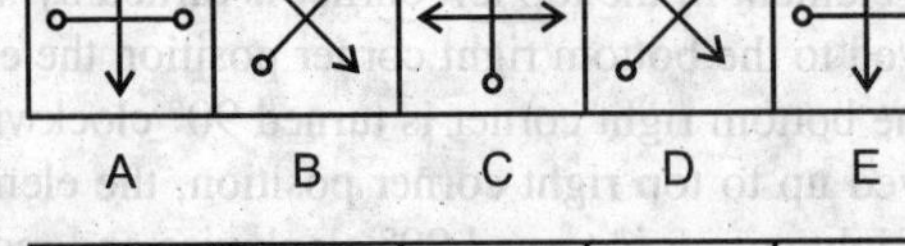

A B C D E

16. 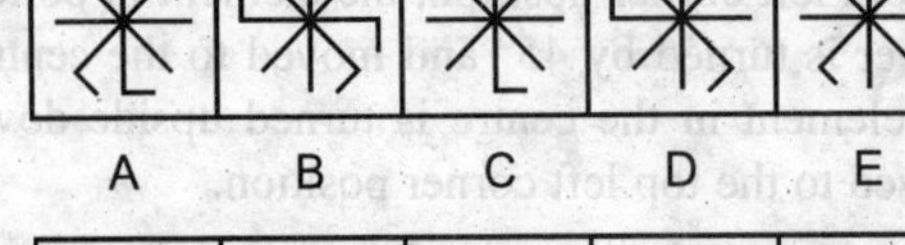

A B C D E

17. 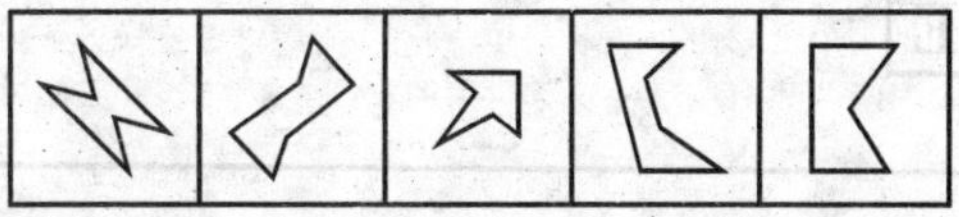

A B C D E

18. 

A B C D E

19. 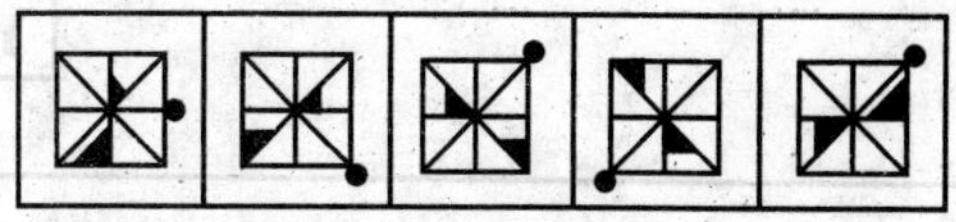

A B C D E

20. 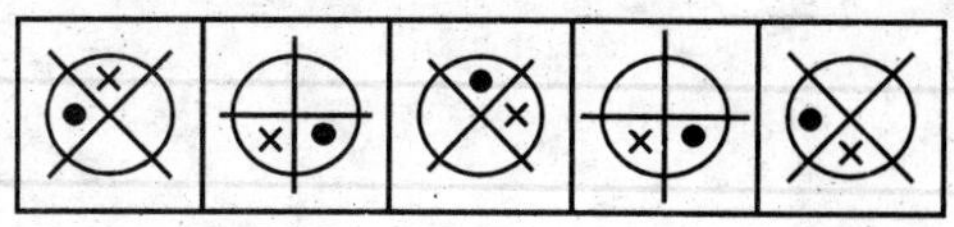

A B C D E

ANSWERS

1	2	3	4	5	6	7	8	9	10
B	D	C	A	D	C	C	D	B	C
11	**12**	**13**	**14**	**15**	**16**	**17**	**18**	**19**	**20**
C	C	D	D	B	C	E	B	E	E

EXPLANATORY ANSWERS

1. Each of the other figures is divided into four equal parts.

2. In all other figures the number of lines making the larger design in one more than the number of lines making the smaller design.

3. In all other figures the arrows are slanted.

4. In all other figures two identical designs are overlapping each other.

5. Only in this figure the triangle is empty.

6. Only in this figure one of the elements held at an end is different from the other three elements.

7. Only in this figure the base of the loop is one-sided.

8. Only in this figure a closed pattern is formed.

9. In all other figures the slant line is on the other side of the forked line.

10. In each of the other figures the three elements are identical.

11. Only in this figure one dot is enclosed within a square section.

12. In all other figures the straight vertical line is drawn and turned on its left.

13. Only in this figure all the small circles are drawn inwards.

14. In all other figures the straight lines have identical elements on both ends.

15. In all other figures there are two free ends after one bent end and three free ends after two bent ends. In this figure it is opposite.

16. In all other figures the two elements are lateral inversions of each other. In this option one triangle is a right angle triangle at the end of the line.

17. Only this figure is made of 5 straight lines.

18. In all other figures the number of spikes on the top indicate the number of lines used to make the figure.

19. In all other figures the line with a dot end is perpendicular to the line having the shades on both sides.

20. In all other figures the dot and cross are placed clockwise. In this figure they are placed anticlockwise.

●●●

YOUR SPACE

ENGLISH LANGUAGE

1

COMPREHENSION PASSAGES

Comprehension means the act of comprehending or the capacity of the mind to understand. In the examination papers, questions on comprehension test are included to judge your ability to understand the given passages. Practice of solving these questions will greatly help you in the examination.

Directions: *Read the following passages and answer the questions given below each passage. Certain words have been printed in italics to help you locate them while answering some of the questions.*

PASSAGE-1

A struggle for power began with Bimbisara and Ajatshatru of the Kingdom of Magadha. In the 4th century BC, the Nandas came to power, with their capital at Pataliputra. The latter were replaced by the Mauryas at the close of the same century. This came about partly as a result of Alexander's invasion and the decline of Iranian strength in India. Chandragupta Maurya took advantage of the unsettled conditions and with the help of his adviser Kautilya, built the first great empire in India. Under him and his two great successors, Bindusara and Ashoka, almost the whole of India, with the exception of the farthest south, was unified into one empire.

Many important developments took place in the social, economic and cultural life of the Indian people in this period—322 to 184 BC. Particularly important was the spread of Buddhism, which had been introduced earlier.

The decline of the Mauryan Empire after the rule of Ashoka was followed by a long period of new invasions and the formation of small states. Of the foreign invasions, the first was that of the Greeks who were the rulers of Bactria. They conquered the Punjab and parts of Sind and their contact had a lasting influence on the culture of India. Gandhara style of art emerged and flourished. The greatest Greek ruler in India was Menander (Milinda) in the 2nd century BC, who became a Buddhist.

The Greek invasion was followed by that of the Sakas. The Sakas displaced the Greek in Bactria and spread their power in Western India. One of the Saka kings was Rudradaman who, as the name suggests, was a devotee of Siva. He was responsible for important irrigation works in Saurashtra. The Sakas, like other invaders, became a part of Indian life and played an important role in the development of Indian Culture. Another group of invaders from Central Asia was that of the Kushanas early in the first century AD. The greatest of the Kushana rulers was Kanishka who, according to some historians, started the Saka Era in AD 78. Kanishka ruled his vast empire in India and Central Asia from Purushapura (modern Peshawar) for 40 years. Kanishka's empire brought to India the cultural tradition of Iran, Greece and Rome. It also provided a stimulus to trade between India and other parts of the world Kanishka patronised the Mahayan form of Buddhism. It spread to Central Asia during this period and from there to China, Korea and Japan. The Kushana Empire declined in the third century AD.

1. A suitable title for the above passage is.......
A. Alexander's invasion of India
B. Kanishka, the great Kushana ruler
C. Development of India's Culture
D. India—the Period of Empires
E. None of these

2. The Kingdom of Magadha was ruled by the Nandas about.......
A. 2000 years ago
B. 2400 years ago
C. 2800 years ago
D. over 3000 years ago
E. None of these

3. The successors of the Nandas, whose capital was at Pataliputra, were the.......
A. Greeks B. Iranians
C. Mauryas D. Sakas
E. None of these

4. The cultural traditions of Iran, Greece and Rome came to India during the rule of.......

A. Ashoka B. Kanishka
C. Menander D. Rudradaman
E. None of these

5. Who, amongst the following, had their capital at Purushapura (modern Peshawar)?

A. The Mauryans B. The Nandas
C. The Kushanas D. The Sakas
E. None of these

6. The Saka Era is believed to have been established by.......

A. the Kushanas
B. Milinda, the Greek ruler
C. the Nandas
D. The Sakas
E. None of these

7. All of the following were foreign invaders of India, except.......

A. the Greeks B. the Kushanas
C. the Mauryas D. the Sakas
E. None of these

8. The greatest Greek ruler in India was.......

A. Ajatshatru B. Bimbisara
C. Bindusara D. Milinda
E. None of these

9. Who were the founders of the first great unified empire in India?

A. The Mauryans B. The Nandas
C. The Kushanas D. The Sakas
E. None of these

10. Which particularly important development took place in India between 322 to 184 BC?

A. The rulers of Bactria invaded India
B. Buddhism spread far and wide
C. The Sakas displaced the Greeks
D. Gandhara style of art attained its zenith
E. None of these

PASSAGE-2

One could, in theory, conceive of a country "specialising" entirely in agriculture and obtaining all its industrial requirements from abroad. But it could never become a high income country simply because technologically developed agriculture could never absorb more than a fraction of the working population on the available land. Though in all underdeveloped countries the greater part of the working population is "occupied" in agriculture, most of this represents disguised unemployment; a rural community maintains all its members and expects everyone to share in the work. Much of the greater part of this labour could be withdrawn from agriculture if alternative employment opportunities were available without any *adverse* effect, and probably with a beneficial effect, on total agricultural output. For the relief of the pressure of labour on the land is itself a most potent factor in *inducing* improvements in technology which raise yields per acre, as well as the yield per man. These improvements normally require an increase in the capital employed on the land; but the savings necessary for the increase in capital are themselves a by-product of reduced population pressure. The reduction in the agricultural population, and the increased use of capital in agriculture are thus different aspects of the same process. As there are fewer mouths to feed, the "agricultural surplus" rises (the excess of agricultural production over the self-consumption of the farming population). The rise in the "surplus" enables the farmers to plough back a higher proportion of their output—in the form of better tools, improved seeds, fertilisers, etc., and such improvements tend to both "labour saving" and "land saving"; they *diminish* the labour requirements at the same time as they increase the yield of the land.

1. According to the passage, it is theoretically possible to think of country.......

A. advanced both in agriculture and industry
B. specialised in industry but not in agriculture
C. backward both in agriculture and industry
D. specialised in agriculture but not in industry
E. borrowing all its requirements from abroad

2. What, according to the passage, will be the achievement of inducing improvement in technology?

A. Higher specialisation in agriculture
B. Better employment opportunities
C. Beneficial effects on quality of life of people
D. Relieving the pressure of employment in industry
E. None of these

3. What could be done, according to the passage, to induce improvement in agricultural technology?

A. Import of better agricultural technology
B. Providing better weather forecasts
C. To relieve pressure of labour on land
D. Providing irrigation facilities
E. None of these

4. According to the passage, in underdeveloped countries.....

A. agriculture is in a primitive stage
B. per acre yield is very high
C. land is available in plenty
D. alternative employment opportunities will have adverse effect on the lives of people
E. significant proportion of working population works in agriculture

5. Why, according to the passage, a country specialised in agriculture only cannot become a high income country?

A. It simply cannot borrow all its industrial requirements from abroad

B. It can absorb only a fraction of its working population
C. Agriculture needs huge investments and infrastructural facilities
D. Technological advancements in agriculture has limitations
E. None of these

6. Which of the following statements is *true* in the context of the passage?
A. Underdeveloped countries are rapidly growing industrially
B. Technologically developed agriculture solves all the problems of unemployment
C. Relief of the pressure of labour on land raises yields per acre
D. Yield per acre and yield per man are unrelated
E. Surplus in agriculture is spent for domestic purposes

7. Which of the following statements is *not true* in the context of the passage?
A. Theoretically there could be a country specialised entirely in agriculture
B. Capital is required to increase the per acre yield of the land
C. Agriculture surplus will rise if there are fewer mouths to feed
D. Technologically developed agriculture will absorb most of the working population on the available land
E. A rural community maintains all its members and expects everyone to share in the work

8. Which of the following is most *opposite* in meaning of the word *'adverse'* as used in the passage?
A. Negative
B. Facilitating
C. Supplementary
D. Derogative
E. Decorative

9. Which of the following is most nearly the *same* in meaning as the word *'inducing'* as used in the passage?
A. Causing B. Augmenting
C. Reducing D. Developing
E. Increasing

10. Which of the following is most nearly the *same* in meaning as the word *'diminish'* as used in the passage?
A. Reduce B. Shorten
C. Prohibit D. Increase
E. Worsen

PASSAGE-3

Morning and afternoon, all the young girls and maidens used to *gather* around the village well with their water pots. There they exchanged pleasantries, chatted and discussed. Lakshmi was the prettiest girl at the well. But, she was an orphan.

One day, a well-built man came to Lakshmi's house. He brought with him the richest clothes and jewels as presents for her, "I am your dead father's brother," he told the astonished girl. "You have not seen me before because I have been staying abroad. You must come and live with me now." Lakshmi believed his sweet words and in a short time, locked up her little house and set out with the man.

But a terrible surprise was in store for poor Lakshmi when she got to her new-found uncle's home. The man locked her in a room. "I am not your uncle, but a robber. And I am going to marry you," he told her. Lakshmi howled and wept when she heard this. Saying he would be back in a day or two after making arrangements for the wedding, the man went away. Lakshmi continued sobbing for a while and then stopped. "I must think of a plan to escape," she told herself. Lakshmi guessed that the robber would try to enter her room. So she kept near her bed a sharp knife which she could find in the room.

One night the robber did enter her room but Lakshmi did not make any sound. She just kept a tight hold of the knife and pretended to be sound asleep. When the robber was near her bed, she stood up suddenly, brandishing the knife. The robber was taken aback and with a loud cry, he ran out. Lakshmi *gave chase* and he climbed up the nearest tall tree. Lakshmi then gathered some dry twigs and sticks around the foot of the tree and set them on fire. On seeing the rising flames, the robber gave a mighty yell and jumped down. But it was such a long way to the ground that he broke a couple of bones and was unable to move away from the place he fell.

In the meantime, the police was informed by someone about the robber. Very soon they reached the spot and arrested the robber. The people who had gathered at the spot were all praise for Lakshmi's courage and presence of mind.

1. The reason given by the man for his inability to meet Lakshmi was that.....
A. he had not known earlier where she lived
B. he was not in friendly terms with her father
C. he was living in a foreign country
D. he was not sure whether she would recognise him
E. he was staying in another village far away

2. Why did Lakshmi go with the man?
A. She was convinced that the man was her uncle
B. She wanted to get him arrested by the police
C. She intended to teach him a good lesson
D. She wanted the man to marry her
E. She felt it necessary to verify his claim by accompanying him

3. Why did the robber run out of the room?
   A. He was stabbed by Lakshmi
   B. He got scared of the rising flames
   C. Lakshmi told him to go out as fast as possible
   D. He was afraid that Lakshmi would strike him with the knife
   E. He ran out to catch hold of Lakshmi and bring her back
4. How was the robber injured?
   A. Lakshmi stabbed him with the sharp knife
   B. He fell down accidently while climbing the tree
   C. He was beaten by Lakshmi and his bones were broken
   D. He jumped down from the tree to save his life
   E. He got burnt in the rising flames
5. "But a terrible surprise was in store ..... uncle's home." What is the "*terrible surprise*" that is being referred to?
   A. The man told her that her father was dead
   B. The man refused to marry her
   C. The man took away her ornaments and locked her in a room
   D. The man told her that he was her real uncle
   E. The man turned out to be a robber interested in marrying her
6. Where did the robber apparently go after locking up Lakshmi?
   A. He went to her house to loot all the things
   B. He went out to bring a sharp knife
   C. He went away to bring clothes and jewels for her
   D. He went away to make preparations for his marriage
   E. He went out to bring the priest for performing the wedding ceremony
7. Which of the following is most nearly the *same* in meaning as the phrase, '*gave chase*' as used in the passage?
   A. escaped B. continued
   C. followed D. prevented
   E. raced
8. Which of the following is *true* in the context of the passage?
   A. Lakshmi told the robber to climb up the tall tree
   B. At night, the robber entered Lakshmi's room with a knife
   C. Lakshmi had no near relatives and she stayed alone
   D. The robber started running after jumping from the tree
   E. The people who had gathered at the spot set fire to the tree
9. Which of the following is most *opposite* in meaning of the word '*gather*' as used in the passage?
   A. Collect B. Reduce
   C. Distribute D. Break
   E. Disperse
10. Which of the following statements is *not true* in the context of the passage?
   A. The police was summoned by Lakshmi herself
   B. The well-built man was not the real brother of Lakshmi's father
   C. When the robber entered the room at night, Lakshmi was awake
   D. Lakshmi used to go to the village well to collect water
   E. Lakshmi's guess regarding the robber turned out to be correct

PASSAGE-4

Once upon a time there lived a queen in the city of Benaras. Her name was Khema and she was the wife of King Bahuputtaka. One night, the Queen had a dream of a beautiful golden goose that spoke with great wisdom, almost as if he was a sage. She told her husband that she desperately wanted to see a bird just like the one in her dream. So the King asked his ministers to find out all that they could about a bird such as this. He was told that such a bird did exist but was extremely rare and difficult to find. They advised him to build a beautiful lake on the outskirts of Benaras so that he may attract such rare and lovely creatures to reside there. In this way the queen might have her wish fulfilled.

Towards the north, on Mount Citakuta, there lived about ninety thousand wild geese headed by a beautiful golden goose called King Dhataratth. He got to hear of this exquisite lake surrounded by water lilies and lotuses floating on the surface. The King had invited all the birds to come and live on it, promising that none of them would ever be harmed. Corn was scattered on a daily basis in order to attract the birds. So a couple of geese went up to their King, the golden goose and told him that they were quite tired of living up on the mountains and would like to see this wonderful lake where they had been promised food and protection. The King agreed to their request and took the flock down south towards Benaras. Meanwhile, at the lake, King Bahuputtaka had placed hunters all around in order to capture any golden goose that happened to pass by. So the next morning when the headhunter saw this flock of geese approaching, he was very excited to see their golden leader. He immediatey went about setting up a *snare* amongst the water lilies and lotuses, as he knew that the leader would definitely be the first to alight.

The whole flock came flying down in one mighty swoop and as expected it was the King's foot that touched the water first. He was ensnared and could not escape. Seeing this, the other geese flew into a panic. But none had the courage to try to free their king and so flew back to Mount Cittacuta for safety. All except one. He was the chief captain, Sumukha. King Dhataratth entreated him to fly to safety too, as he would surely be captured if he stayed by his side. But Sumukha replied that he would never *desert* his master in the face of danger and would either try to save him or die by his side.

At this point the hunter approached and as Sumukha saw him he decided to appeal to his compassion. The hunter asked the golden goose how come he had not noticed the trap that was set. The golden goose replied that when one's time was up it was no use to struggle against what was fated and one must just accept it. The huntsman was very impressed with his grace and wisdom. He then turned to Sumukha and asked why he had not fled with the other birds even though he was free to do so. Sumukha answered that the golden goose was his King, best friend and master and that he could never desert him even at the cost of his own life. Hearing this, the hunter realised that these were a couple of rare birds of great nobility. He did not much care for his own King's reward and decided to do the right thing and set them free. He told Sumukha that as he was ready to die for his King he would set them both free to fly wherever they wish.

1. Why were the geese keen on visiting the lake in Benaras?
A. They were invited personally by king Bahuputtaka
B. They were tired of their old lake
C. They were amused by the water lilies and lotuses
D. The lake was not very far from the mountains
E. The lake was to be a source of good food and protection

2. Why did the king approach the ministers?
A. In order to find out the best location for the lake
B. In order to find out if a golden goose existed
C. To enquire about his wife's dreams
D. To devise a plan to capture all rare bird species
E. To enquire about the best hunter in the locality

3. Why did the head hunter release the king, the golden goose?
A. He was impressed by his wisdom and nobility
B. The geese were a rare species of birds
C. The golden goose, King Dhataratha promised him a handsome reward
D. The hunter sympathised with the golden goose
E. The hunter did not want the chief captain to lose a friend

4. What was the king's intention behind building a lake?
A. To attract all rare species of living animals and birds
B. To beautify the city of Benaras
C. He did not want to go against the wishes of his wife
D. He wanted to capture the golden goose
E. He enjoyed bird watching and wanted to create a natural habitat for them

5. Why did the flock of geese panic and retreat to Mount Cittacuta?
A. Their king took the wrong route to the lake and they lost their way
B. Their king, the golden goose was captured
C. Their chief captain, Sumukha betrayed the king
D. They spotted many hunters by the lake
E. None of these

6. What advice did the minister give to the king?
A. That no such golden goose existed and he was only wasting his time searching for one
B. To create an artificial golden goose for the queen
C. To build a lake in order to attract the golden goose
D. To open a sanctuary of rare birds for the queen
E. To have a beautiful garden surrounded by flowers and trees

7. Which of the following statements would best describe the qualities of Sumukha?
1. Betrayer of the flock
2. The Selfless Goose
3. Loyal towards the king
4. The naive and ignorant goose
A. Only 1 B. Only 2
C. Only 3 and 4 D. Only 1 and 4
E. Only 2 and 3

PASSAGE-5

Progress in life depends a good deal on crossing one threshold after another. Some time ago, a man watched his little nephew try to write his name. It was hard work, very hard work. The little boy had arrived at an effort threshold. Today he writes his name with comparative ease. No new threshold confronts him. This is the way with all of us. As soon as we cross one threshold, as soon as we conquer one difficulty, a new difficulty appears, or should appear. Some people make the mistake of steering clear of thresholds. Anything that requires genuine thinking and use of energy they avoid. They prefer to stay in a rut where thresholds are not met. Probably, they have been at their job for a number of years. Things are easy for them. They make no effort to seek out new obstacles to overcome. Real progress stops under such circumstances.

Some middle-aged and elderly people greatly enrich their lives by continuing to cross thresholds. One man went into an entirely new business when he was past middle life and made success of it, De Morgan didn't start to write novels until he was past sixty. Psychologists have discovered that man can continue to learn throughout his life. And it is undoubtedly better to try and fail than not to try at all. There one can be placed in the category of the Swiss mountaineer of whom it was said, *"He died climbing"*. When a new difficulty arises to obstruct your path, do not complain. Accept the challenge. Determine to cross this threshold as you have crossed numerous other thresholds in your past. In the words of a poet, *do not rest but strive to pass from dream to grander dream.*

1. What obstructs real progress in life?
A. Remaining at one and the same post
B. Avoiding the thinking and energy
C. Shunning every work
D. Stopping education
E. Worrying about the future

2. What does progress in life depend upon?
A. Good habits
B. Hardwork
C. Overcoming one difficulty after another
D. Spirit of service and cooperation
E. None of these

3. What does '*He died climbing*' signify?
A. He died when he was climbing the hill
B. He died before getting at the top
C. He strove hard till the last moment of life
D. He climbed the hill and then died
E. He found it difficult to climb

4. What does '*to pass from dream to grander dream*' mean?
A. Always having greater and greater aspiration in life
B. Seeing one good dream and then greater aspiration in life
C. Making plan after plan
D. Seeing one dream after the other
E. None of these

5. What did the man entering a new business past middle life do of his business?
A. He miserably failed in it
B. He achieved partial success
C. He dropped the business after sometime
D. He achieved good success in it
E. He started writing novels

6. How can you accomplish the most difficult tasks?
A. By mobilizing all possible resources
B. By avoiding all obstacles
C. By sticking to hardwork
D. By getting other people to do your work for you
E. By doing it bit by bit and persisting in the effort

7. What does De Morgan's life teach?
A. That it is futile to learn many things
B. That one is never old in case he has vigour
C. That it is never too late to learn
D. That creative writing can be made even late in life
E. None of these

8. How do middle-aged and elderly people add brilliance to their lives?
A. By overcoming difficulty one after another
B. By getting sycophants to surround them
C. By making fine speeches
D. By acquiring resourcefulness
E. None of these

9. What should we do when a new difficulty obstructs our path?
A. Run away from it
B. Be bold and face it
C. Manoeuvre to get it removed
D. Enlist other people's help to get it over
E. None of these

10. When did De Morgan start to write novels?
A. When he was sixty years old
B. When he was below sixty
C. When he studied psychology
D. When he was a student
E. None of these

PASSAGE-6

In terms of the total energy consumed by different sectors, the largest consumer is understandably the industrial sector, which accounts for nearly half the total energy used in the country today. This is followed by the transport sector which consumes about 25%, the household sector (about 14%) and the agricultural sector (about 9%). This last sector has shown considerable increase in energy use over the last four decades. Among the primary fuels, the relative proportion of coal has dropped from nearly 80% to 40% and that of oil has gone up from 17% to 44% over the same period.

Total energy consumption in India today is equivalent to 291 million tons of oil of which 26% comes from wood. On a per capita basis it works out to about one litre of oil per day, which is extremely low by international standards. The future energy demand depends upon the level of development envisaged and also on the sections of people to be affected by it.

The energy disparity between the urban and the rural population is at present *as wide as* between nations on a *worldwide scale*. There is apparently a greater need to provide energy in the rural areas and to improve the efficiency of energy use than merely to increase the national figures for energy consumption limiting its use to those who are getting the bulk share already.

With the projected rate of population growth, improving upon the per capita energy consumption is a Herculean task as our coal reserves and the capacity to import oil cannot be increased beyond a point. *There is clearly no escape* from the utilisation of renewable energy sources in a big way if the gap between the desired levels of energy supply and available resources has to be kept at the minimum.

1. The author is laying greater emphasis on which of the following?
1. Efficient use of energy
2. Increasing national indices for energy consumption
3. Controlling population growth

A. Only 1 B. Only 2
C. Only 3 D. All the three
E. Both 2 and 3

2. The author feels that increasing per capita use of energy is
A. rather difficult, but not impossible
B. not easy, but certainly achievable
C. not at all desirable
D. a matter of great difficulty
E. a routine matter

3. According to the passage, the energy requirement of the future will be decided on the basis of which of the following?
1. Total energy already consumed by us in the past
2. Level of development of oil industry
3. Profile of the affected people

A. Only 1 B. Only 2
C. Only 3 D. Both 1 and 2
E. Both 2 and 3

4. Which of the following shows correctly the different sectors consuming energy arranged in ascending order?
A. Agriculture, transport, household, industrial
B. Agriculture, household, transport, industrial
C. Industrial, transport, household, agriculture
D. Industrial, household, agriculture, transport
E. None of these

5. Which of the following has been suggested by the author as the best possible solution to overcome energy crisis?
A. Importing large quantities of coal
B. Exploration of oil reserves
C. Reducing share of bulk users
D. Maximisation of renewable sources
E. Reducing the energy disparity between urban and rural areas

6. Which of the following styles has been adopted by the author?
A. Unsubstantiated arguments and views
B. Data based, but coloured by socialism
C. Highly subjective with bias for rural people
D. Objective, descriptive, lacking clarity
E. Data based, objective, positive, solution oriented

7. Which of the following has been mentioned as a major hurdle in enhancing per capita consumption of energy in India?
A. Present level of development in India
B. Increased use of energy in agriculture sector
C. Disparity in use of energy in rural and urban areas
D. International norm of 1 litre of oil per day per person
E. None of these

8. Which of the following statements is *true*?
A. The household sector has shown considerable increase in energy use
B. Use of oil has increased from 40% to 80%
C. Industrial sector uses 50% of total energy used in India
D. Energy consumption in India is 26% of world consumption
E. Import of oil to the extent required is quite possible

9. The energy disparity ..... as wide as ..... worldwide scale, the first sentence of third paragraph means
A. disparity in urban and rural is observed in all nations
B. in no other nation such disparity is observed
C. developed countries consume more energy than developing countries
D. worldwide scale is different for rural and urban areas
E. None of these

10. There is clearly no escape ..... means.....
A. there is a way out, but it is ambiguous
B. there is a problem, but not without solution
C. there is also no solution to this
D. there is hardly any alternative except
E. there is more than one way

PASSAGE-7

Peace and order are necessary, not just in our own country but also at the international level, if we are to secure national progress and development. The different countries in the world are coming closer today due to faster means of transport and communication. Economically, they are becoming increasingly interdependent. If peace is disturbed in one part of the world, it has adverse effects in other parts of the world as well. Nuclear weapons have already threatened the world with nuclear war. If the conflicts between different nations are not settled in time, they might *culminate* in a nuclear war destroying the whole world. It is therefore, in our own interest that the world is free of conflicts. If at all there are any, they must be settled promptly and peace should be resotred. That is why we have declared the establishment of international peace and understanding as an objective of our foreign policy.

We need the help and cooperation of other countries for our scientific, industrial and economic development, especially in those fields where we have yet to achieve self-sufficiency. We obtain the latest machinery, technology and financial aid from the developed countries. On our part we, too, offer help to the under-developed countries. We are keen on maintaining friendly relations with other countries. Such friendly relations *foster* international understanding.

We have always exerted ourselves to see that the disputes arising between the different nations are settled through peaceful negotiations. We play an active role in the United Nations, the South Asian Association for Regional Cooperation, the Commonwealth Nations and other such international organisations. We make it a point to participate in the international conferences on issues like energy crisis, environmental imbalance, nuclear arms race etc. We always offer a helping hand to other nations affected by natural calamities such as famines, earthquakes, floods and so on. We strive to maintain peaceful and friendly relations with our neighbouring countries. *Why do we do all this!* We sincerely believe that conflicts in today's world should be minimised, making way for better cooperation among the nations. If this is achieved, human resources will no longer be wasted in things like war or aggression. There will be no destruction of wealth. We believe that, in a peaceful world, there will be greater scope for the economic and cultural development of countries.

1. According to the passage, maintaining friendly relations with other countries facilitate ....
A. developing international understanding
B. exchange of scientists and technologists
C. strategic planning in defence matters
D. import and export of several vital commodities
E. None of these

2. If conflicts between nations do not cease ....
A. international bodies will have to take up these issues
B. international understanding will not be fostered
C. nuclear war will destroy the whole world
D. the means of transport and communication will be disrupted
E. None of these

3. Which of the following is obtained by us from the developed countries, according to the passage?
A. Fertilisers B. Foodgrains
C. Leather Products D. Technology
E. Crude Oil

4. Which of the following according to the passage, is facilitating the process of different countries coming together?
A. Emerging world order
B. Asian Association for Regional Cooperation
C. Our participation in international conferences
D. Need for self-sufficiency
E. Faster means of transport and communication

5. Minimising the conflicts and making way for better cooperation among the nations will result in ....
A. useful and purposive utilisation of human resources
B. better utilisation of means of transport and communication
C. culmination of nuclear war destroying the world
D. keenness on maintaining friendly relations with other countries
E. preservation of our national unity and integrity

6. Which of the following statements is *not true* in the context of the passage?
A. International conflicts must be settled promptly
B. We try to maintain friendly relations with our neighbours
C. We participate in many international conferences
D. Friendly relations with other countries foster international understanding
E. Each country can be considered isolated and insulated from the effects of other countries

7. Which of the following words is largely *similar* in meaning of the word '*culminate*' as used in the passage?
A. Reach the highest point
B. Stretch to the maximum
C. Absolute standards
D. Total destruction
E. Coming of age

8. Which of the following words is most *opposite* in meaning of the word '*foster*' as used in the passage?
A. Advocate B. Hinder
C. Obviate D. Facilitate
E. Jettison

9. The question "*Why do we do all this !*" is asked in the passage in which of the following contexts?
A. We always offer a helping hand to other nations in improving their technology
B. We endeavour to maintain peaceful and friendly relations with our neighbours
C. We obtain the latest machinery, technology and financial aid from the developed countries
D. We have shaped our foreign policy in a balanced and purposeful manner
E. None of these

10. Does any of the following sentences contain any idea expressed in the passage?
A. We have to make conscious efforts to preserve our national unity
B. Our country is huge in size and population where many languages are spoken
C. We have adopted the objective of democracy in the interest of overall development of our country
D. Citizens must be well-informed about public issues in order to participate meaningfully in public
E. None of these statements contain any idea expressed in the passage

PASSAGE-8

There is a fairly universal sentiment that the use of nuclear weapon is clearly contrary to morality and that its production does not go far enough. These activities are not only opposed to morality but also to law and if the legal objection can be added to the moral, the argument against the use and the manufacture of these weapons will considerably be reinforced. Now the time is ripe to evaluate the responsibility of scientists who knowingly use their expertise for the construction of such weapons which has *deleterious* effect on mankind.

To this must be added the fact that more than 50 per cent of the skilled scientific manpower in the world is now engaged in the armaments industry. How appropriate it is that all this valuable skill should be *devoted* to the manufacture of weapons of death in a world of poverty is a question that must touch the scientific conscience.

A meeting of biologists on the Long-Term Worldwide Biological Consequences of Nuclear War added frightening dimensions to those forecasts. Its report suggested that the long biological effects resulting from climatic changes may at least be as serious as the immediate ones.

Subfreezing temperatures, low light levels and high dose of ionizing and ultraviolet radiation extending for many months, after a large-scale nuclear war, could destroy the biological support systems of civilization, at least in the Northern Hemisphere. Productivity in natural and agricultural ecosystems could be severaly restricted for a year or more. Post-war survivors would face starvation as well as freezing conditions in the dark and be exposed to near-lethal dose of radiation. If, as now seems possible, the Southern Hemisphere were affected also, global disruption of the biosphere could ensue. In any event, there would be severe consequences, even in the areas not affected directly, because of the interdependence of the world economy. In either case the extinction of a large fraction of the earth's animals, plants, and micro-organism seems possible. The population size of Homo Sapiens conceivably could be reduced to pre-historic levels or below and extinction of the human species itself cannot be excluded.

1. The author's most important objective of writing the above passage seems to
A. highlight the use of nuclear weapons as an effective population control measure
B. illustrate the devastating effects of use of nuclear weapons on mankind
C. duly highlight the supremacy of the nations which possess nuclear weapons
D. summarise the long biological effects of use of nuclear weapons
E. explain scientifically the climatic changes resulting from use of nuclear weapons

2. The scientists possessing expertise in manufacturing destructive weapons are ....
A. very few in number
B. irresponsible and incompetent
C. more than half of the total number
D. engaged in the armaments industry against their desire
E. not conscious of the repercussions of their actions

3. According to the passage, the argument against the use and manufacture of nuclear weapons ....
A. does not stand the test of legality
B. possess legal strength although it does not have moral standing
C. is acceptable only on moral grounds
D. becomes stronger if legal and moral considerations are combined
E. None of these

4. Which of the following is one of the consequences of Nuclear War?
A. Fertility of land will last only for a year or so
B. Post-war survivors being very few will have abundant food
C. Lights would be cooler and more comfortable
D. Southern hemisphere would remain quite safe in the post-war period
E. None of these

5. Choose the word which is most *opposite* in meaning of the word '*deleterious*' as used in the passage.
A. Beneficial
B. Harmful
C. Irreparable
D. Non-cognizable
E. Revolutionary

6. The author of the passage seems to be of the view that ....
A. utilization of scientific skills in manufacture of weapons is appropriate
B. the evaluation of the scientists' expertise show their incompetence
C. manufacture of weapons of death would help eradication of poverty
D. spending money on manufacture of weapons may be justifiable subject to the availability of funds
E. utilization of valuable knowledge for manufacture of lethal weapons is inhuman

7. Which of the following best *explains* the word '*devoted*' as used in the passage?
A. dedicated for a good cause
B. utilized for betterment
C. abused for destruction
D. underutilized
E. overutilized

8. It appears from the passage that the use of nuclear weapons is considered against morality by ....
A. only such of those nations who cannot afford to manufacture weapons
B. almost all the nations of the world
C. only the superpowers who can afford to manufacture and sell weapons
D. a minority group of scientists who have the necessary skill and competence
E. most of the scientists who devote their valuable skills to manufacture nuclear weapons

9. Which of the following statement(s) 1, 2 and/ or 3 is/ are definitely true in the context of the passage?
1. Living organisms in the areas which are not directly affected by the consequences of nuclear war would also suffer
2. There is a likelihood of extinction of the human species as a consequence of nuclear war
3. The post-war survivors would be exposed to the risk of near-lethal radiation

A. Only 1
B. Only 2
C. Only 3
D. Only 1 and 2
E. All the three

10. The biological consequences of nuclear war as given in the passage include all the following except ....
A. fall in temperature below zero degree celsius
B. ultraviolet radiation
C. high dose of ionizing
D. low light levels
E. None of these

PASSAGE-9

An independent, able and upright judiciary is the hallmark of a free democratic country. Therefore, the process of judicial appointments is of vital importance. At present, on account of the Supreme Court's last advisory opinion, the role of the executive and its interference in the appointment of judges is minimal, which, *in the light of our previous experience,* is most welcome. However, there is a strong demand for a National Judicial Commission on the ground of wider participation in the appointment process and for greater transparency. The composition, the role and the procedures of the proposed National Judicial Commission, must be clearly spelt out, *lest* it be a case of *jumping from the frying pan into the fire.*

Recently, there has been a lively debate in England on the subject. A judicial commission has been proposed but there are not many takers for that proposal. In the paper issued this month by the Lord Chancellor's Department on judicial appointments, the Lord Chancellor has said, "I want every vacancy on the Bench to be filled by the best person available. Appointments must and will be made on merit—irrespective of ethnic origin, gender, marital status, political affiliation, sexual orientation, religion or disability. These are not mere words. They are firm principles. I will not tolerate any form of discrimination."

At present, there are hardly any persons from the ethnic minorities manning the higher judiciary and so far not a single woman has made it to the House of Lords. The most significant part of Lord Chancellor's paper is the requirement that "allegations of professional misconduct made in the course of consultations about a candidate for judicial office must be specific and subject to disclosure to the candidate." This should go a long way in ensuring that principles of natural justice and fair play are not *jettisoned* in the appointment process, which is not an uncommon phenomenon.

1. Which of the following could be in the author's mind when he says *'in the light of our previous experience'*?
A. Not having enough judges from backward communities
B. Interference of the executive in the appointment of judges
C. Professional misconduct of judges
D. Delays occurred in the judicial appointment
E. None of these

2. According to the passage, there has been a demand for a National Judicial Commission to ....
A. clear the backing of court cases
B. make judiciary see eye to eye with executive
C. wipe out corruption at the highest places
D. make the appointment process of judges more broad based and clear
E. None of these

3. What, according to the passage should go a long way in judicial appointments?
A. Decision that all sections of the society are represented
B. Candidates' qualifications and seniority are considered
C. Candidate must know the charge of professional misconduct levelled against him
D. There should be strong reason for discrimination
E. None of these

4. The role and procedure of the National Commission must be spelt out clearly
A. because executive wing will depend on it heavily
B. because judges will take judicial decisions on the basis of it
C. as it will be represented by the cross section of the society
D. as it will bring a qualitative change in the interpretation of law
E. None of these

5. Which of the following words is *similar* in meaning as the word *'jettison'* as used in the passage?
A. Sacrifice B. Accept
C. Modify D. Destroy
E. None of these

6. Which of the following group of words is *similar* in meaning as the word *'lest'* as used in the passage?
A. In spite of B. For fear that
C. For want of D. In order to
E. With regard to

7. What does the expression *"jumping from the frying pan into the fire"* mean?
A. Seeing one dream after the other
B. Making plan after plan
C. Crossing one hurdle after the other
D. Jumping from one high place to another
E. None of these

8. What, according to the author, is the typical characteristic of an independent democratic country?
A. Objective process of judicial appointments
B. Supreme Court's advisory opinion on legal matters
C. Responsible, free and fair judiciary
D. Lively and frank debate in the society on the role of judiciary
E. None of these

9. What has been the subject of lively debate in England?
A. Role of judiciary in free and democratic nations
B. Appointment of judicial commisison
C. Seniority as the basis of appointment of judges
D. Appointment of judicial posts
E. None of these

10. Which, according to the passage, is not an uncommon phenomenon?
A. An independent and upright judiciary
B. Delays taking place in legal pronouncements
C. Justice begin denied to poor people
D. Partiality and subjectivity in judicial appointments
E. None of these

11. Which one of the following forms part of what the Lord Chancellor has said?
A. Appointments to judicial posts must take into consideration the aspirations of the weaker sections of the society
B. Vacancies in the judiciary must not remain unfilled
C. Merit should be the sole criterion for judicial appointments
D. Selective discrimination may be preached and also practised
E. None of these

12. Which of the following, according to the author, is the most welcome thing?
A. The negligible role played by the executive in the appointment of judges
B. Coordinating role played by the executive in the appointment of judges
C. The appointment of judges from the ethnic minority classes
D. Appointment of judges purely on the basis of merit
E. None of these

PASSAGE-10

India has come a long way since the Bengal Famine of 1943. The food situation in India, once characterised by *chronic* shortages and the spectre of famines, has changed dramatically over the years. From being the biggest recipient of PL-480 and during the 1950s and 1960s, India today is relatively self-sufficient in foodgrain at the given level of incomes and prices; in fact, it has marginal surpluses. The General Agreement on Tariffs and Trade (GATT) has been signed, with India as one of the signatories, under which all countries will have to gradually open up their agricultural sectors.

It is, therefore, neither feasible nor desirable to keep India's foodgrain sector insulated from world markets. In fact, this is an appropriate opportunity for India to *integrate* its agriculture with global agriculture and make use of private trade (both domestic and foreign) as an important instrument for efficiently allocating her resources as well as providing food security to her people at the lowest economic cost. The time to change gears in food policy has come.

Food security, in a broader context, means that people have physical and economic access to food. Since foodgrains have the largest share in the food basket of the poor in a developing country like India, it is the availability of foodgrains that lies at the heart of the concept of food security. The first step in this direction, therefore, is to make foodgrains physically available to the people. This can be done by augmenting production, or through imports and transportation of grain to people wherever they are.

There are several ways of achieving these targets. One may rely on private entrepreneurship by *letting* the individual farmers produce, traders trade/import and make it available to consumers far and wide; or the Government may directly intervene in the production and/or the trade process. In the former case, the Government follows policies that provide appropriate market signals while in the latter, it acts as producer, importer and trader itself. Indian policy-makers have followed a mix of both these options. For production, they have *relied* on the farmers while the Government has retained control over imports. For distribution, it created public agencies to do the job along with private trade, thus creating a dual market structure.

Providing economic access to food is the second part of the concept of food security. This can be best *obtained* by adopting a cost effective technology in production so that the real price of foodgrains come down and more people have access to it. In case it still fails to reach the larger sections of the population, the Government can directly subsidise food for the poor, *launch* a drive to augment their incomes, or try a combination of the two strategies. India has followed both these policies.

1. India has come a long way means ....
A. many years have passed after the Bengal famine
B. the food position is now largely improved
C. India now handled such problems under PL-480 Scheme
D. India has advanced in science and technology
E. India is no more isolated from the world

2. According to the author, why is it necessary to make available food security to people?
A. To sustain economic growth
B. As per PL-480 guideline
C. To enable us to export foodgrains
D. Not given in the passage
E. None of these

3. The author seems to be advocating which of the following views regarding GATT?
A. India should seize the chance and make efforts to fulfill its objectives

B. India should not have signed it to insulated our foodgrains sector
C. India should handover issue of food security to only private sector
D. India should have signed GATT excluding the agricultural sector
E. None of these

4. Which of the following forms the most essential part of the concept of food security in India?
A. Availability of effective technology of food production to poor farmers
B. Availability of all food items in the market for urban poor
C. Easy access of foodgrains to the weaker sections at the affordable price
D. Providing subsidy on all food items for rural poor
E. None of these

5. If the private agencies are entrusted the work of making foodgrains available to people, what facilitative role Government should undertake?
A. Nationalise all distribution system
B. Take those decisions that give appropriate message to the market
C. Should undertake responsibilities of production and distribution
D. Make efforts to increase the income of the farmers
E. None of these

6. According to the author, food at affordable price could be made available to the poor by which of the following measures?
1. Reducing the cost of production of foodgrains by using appropriate technology
2. Offering foodgrains at lower cost and offering economic support for maintaining lower cost
3. Raising the earning of the poor

A. Only 1
B. Only 1 and 2
C. India is now poised for globalisation and privatisation
D. India is now technologically advanced country
E. None of these

7. According to the author, why have India's policy makers created mixed market structure?
A. This is a practice followed by many developing countries
B. This is a natural fallout of GATT agreement
C. India is now poised for globalisation and privatisation
D. India is now a technologically advanced country
E. None of these

8. Which of the following can be inferred about the general view of the author in the context of the passage?
A. Full advocate of liberalisation and privatisation
B. State controlled, socialistic but closed economy
C. A very practical and pragmatic approach to guard our economy in view
D. A staunch supporter of stable international relations
E. Theoretical view not concerned with ground realities

Directions (Qs. 9 to 11): *Choose the word which is* ***most opposite*** *in meaning to the word printed in bold as used in the passage.*

9. LETTING
A. demanding B. permitting
C. disallowing D. refusing
E. rejecting

10. INTEGRATE
A. isolate B. analyse
C. distinguish D. mark
E. distribute

11. CHRONIC
A. acute B. fleeting
C. irregular D. temporary
E. recurring

Directions (Qs. 12 to 14) : *Choose the word which is* ***most similar*** *in meaning to the word printed in bold as used in the passage.*

12. OBTAINED
A. combined B. procured
C. acquired D. conquered
E. attained

13. RELIED
A. Emphasised B. Depended
C. Convinced D. Followed
E. Referred

14. LAUNCH
A. Review B. Begin
C. Propel D. Push
E. Force

PASSAGE-11

In the town of Agra there lived a rich businessman. But he was also quite a miser. Various people used to flock outside his house everyday hoping for some kind of generosity, but they always had to return home disappointed. He used to ward them off with false promises and then never lived up to his word. Then one day, a poet named Raidas arrived at his house and said that he wanted to read out his poems to the rich man. As the rich man was very fond of poetry, he welcomed him in with open arms.

Raidas started to recite all his poems one by one. The rich man was very pleased and especially so when he heard the poem that Raidas had written on him. In those days it was a custom for rich men and kings to show their appreciation through a reward or a gift, as that was the only *means* of earning that a poor poet possessed. So, the rich man promised Raidas some gifts and asked him to come and collect them the next day. Raidas was *pleased*.

The next morning when he arrived at the house, the rich man pretended that he had never laid eyes on him before. When Raidas reminded him of his promise, he said that although Raidas was a good poet he liked the poem which was written on him and the rest of the poems were very ordinary. He also said that he had earlier promised a reward to Raidas not because he was really pleased or impressed, but to simply encourage him. Raidas was extremely upset, but as there was nothing that he could do, he quietly left the house. On his way home he saw his brother Kuber riding a horse. So, he stopped him and asked for his help after *narrating* the whole incident. Kuber took him to his own house in order to come up with a plan. After giving it some thought he asked Raidas to go to a friend's house with five gold coins and request the friend to plan a dinner where the rich man would also be invited. He then narrated his plan to him.

Raidas had One *trustworthy* friend whose name was Mayadas. So, he went up to him and told him the plan. The next day, Mayadas went to the rich man's house and invited him for dinner. He said that he *intended* to serve his guests in vessels of gold, which the guests would get to take home after the meal. The rich man was thrilled to hear this and jumped at the offer. After the rich man arrived at Mayadas' house, he was surprised to see no other guests there but Raidas. Anyhow, they welcomed him in and started a polite conversation. The rich man had come on an empty stomach and so was getting hungrier by the minute.

Finally at midnight the rich man could bear his hunger no longer and asked Mayadas to serve the food. Mayadas sounded extremely surprised when he asked him what food was he talking about. The rich man tried to remind him that he had been invited for dinner. At this point Raidas asked him for proof of the invitation. The rich man had no answer. At that point Raidas reminded the rich man of the same treatment that he had meted out to him. The rich man realised his mistake and begged for forgiveness. He said that Raidas was a good poet and had not asked him for any reward. He himself had promised to give him some gifts and then cheated him out of them. To make up for his mistake he took out the necklace that he was wearing and gifted it to Raidas. Then they all sat down to eat a happy meal.

1. Why was the rich businessman thrilled on being invited over to dinner by Mayadas?

A. He was thrilled to have dinner for free
B. No one had ever invited him over for dinner since he was very miserly
C. Mayadas had promised to serve in gold dishes which the guests were allowed to take home with them
D. Mayadas had promised many delicacies in the dinner
E. None of these

2. Which of the following is *true* in context of the passage?

A. It was Raidas' brother Kuber's plan to teach the rich businessman a lesson
B. The rich businessman had to return empty stomach from Mayadas' house
C. Mayadas was a trustworthy friend of the rich businessman
D. None is true
E. All A, B and C are true

3. What did Raidas and Mayadas do when the rich businessman came over for dinner?

A. They were thrilled to have a rich businessman as their guest and served him well
B. They served him in gold utensils which he later took with himself
C. They did not serve him any food until he learnt a lesson on what he had done with Raidas
D. They forced him to give away his necklace to Raidas in return of the dinner which they had served
E. None of these

4. What did the rich businessman do when Raidas went to collect his reward from him the next day?

1. The businessman refused to award him even though he had promised so earlier
2. He said that he had promised a reward only to encourage him not because he was pleased with him
3. He said that most of the poems written by Riadas were ordinary

A. Only 2 B. Only 1 and 3
C. Only 2 and 3 D. None of these
E. All of these

5. Why did people flock outside the rich businessman's house everyday?

A. The businessman was very kind-hearted and generous
B. They sought an explanation from him on not keeping the promises made to them
C. All of them wanted to recite poem to him as he was fond of poems
D. They would hope for some generosity from the businessman since he was rich
E. None of these

6. Why did the people always return home disappointed from the rich businessman's house?

A. He would donate less than what he had promised to them
B. He made promises to them but never kept his words
C. The rich man would only reward those who had written poetry on him
D. Both B and C
E. None of these

7. How did the rich businessman react when he realized his mistake of not keeping his promise which he had made to Raidas?
A. He asked Raidas to come to his house the next day to take his reward
B. He left Mayadas' house immediately without having dinner
C. He justified that Raidas did not deserve an award since his poems were very ordinary
D. He said that Raidas was lying and that he had already awarded him with a necklace
E. None of these

8. Which of the following is the moral of the story?
A. A house divided against itself cannot stand
B. A bird in hand is worth two in the bush
C. Never make a promise
D. Never go back on your promises

9. Why was the rich businessman pleased with Raidas?
A. Raidas had recited poems to him but had not asked for any gifts in return
B. Raidas was also as miserly as him
C. Raidas had invited him over for dinner
D. The businessman liked his poetry, especially the one written on him
E. None of these

10. Which of the following best describes Kuber ?
A. Manipulative B. Clever
C. Miserly D. Influential
E. None of these

Directions (Qs. 11 to 13) : *Choose the word which is most* ***similar*** *in meaning to the word printed in bold as used in the passage.*

11. NARRATING
A. Talking B. Performing
C. Departed D. Executing
E. Describing

12. MEANS
A. Expression B. Idea
C. Intention D. Way
E. Purpose

13. INTENDED
A. Presumed B. Wanted
C. Promised D. Confirmed
E. Expected

Directions (Qs. 14 to 15): *Choose the word which is most* ***opposite*** *in meaning to the word printed in bold as used in the passage.*

14. TRUST WORTHY
A. Worthless B. Unfair
C. Unreliable D. Discriminating
E. Awful

15. PLEASED
A. Disappointed B. Stunned
C. Hostile D. Jealous
E. Pensive

PASSAGE-12

All cultures, even the simplest, seem to be in a continuous state of change. The earlier anthropologists, as opposed to the moderns, assumed that cultures with relatively simple technology and political structure represented only slightly modified survivors of the ancient conditions of our own ancestors and for that reason dubbed them primitive. Also, largely as a device for simplifying their own theoretical studies, they assumed that such cultures were static or nearly so, persisting unchanged over long time periods. Actually, we have plenty of evidence that this is not the case. Not only do all archaeological records, fragmentary as they are, show change through time, but wherever explorers have visited a primitive tribe at intervals of a generation or more, their reports show that changes have taken place. Since there is always the possibility that these changes have been set in motion by the first explorer's visit or by contacts with other Europeans during the intervals, the archaeological evidence is more reliable. From this it appears that changes in technology are the only part of culture on which it provides conclusive evidence, were exceedingly slow during the first nine-tenths of human existence. Thousands of years have gone without the introduction of any new tool or appliance. However, during the last twenty-five or thirty thousand years, there has been a progressive speeding up of cultural change. In their operation, the process of cultural change falls into a definite sequence. The first step is the presentation to the society of a potential addition to its culture. This is followed by the new elements' acceptance or rejection. If accepted there are further processes of modification and integration by which the new elements and the pre-existing culture are brought into adjustment. Lastly, there is usually, but not always, the elimination of an older culture element, or elements where functions have been taken over by the new elements.

A potential element of culture may be invented or borrowed. In either case, the new idea or appliance originates with some individual or at work with a small series of individuals who have either pooled their ingenuity to solve a problem or contributed to improving details during the developments of the invention. There can be no invention or cultural change without an inventor. The main difference between invention and borrowing is that if the new thing originates within the setting provided by the society and its culture, we refer to it as culture borrowing, The processes of acceptance or rejection or integration will be the same, although the attitude of the receiving society towards the one in which the potential element originated may influence acceptance.

1. According to the passage ....
A. modern anthropologists are more systematic and accurate than earlier ones
B. a relatively simple society will see progress as spasmodic, resulting from the borrowing of cultural elements
C. the last twenty years have seen societies rapidly becoming cultured
D. cultural interaction is necessary for the cultural progress of primitive societies
E. None of the above

2. According to the passage ....
A. foreign cultural elements are never assimilated in their original form
B. assimilation of a cultural element is partly dependent on the attitude of the borrower society to the source society
C. the process of cultural change is usually random
D. self-sufficient societies rely on inventions rather than cultural borrowings
E. None of the above

3. According to the author, earlier anthropologists assumed some cultures to be static because ....
A. of insufficient interaction with them
B. of poor or unreliable analysis
C. it made their task of studying these cultures more simple
D. of fragmentary archaeological evidence
E. None of the above

4. According to the passage ....
A. a culture with simple technologies and political structure is likely to be static
B. explorers seem to have begun a process of change in many societies
C. much of the culture seen today is the result of changes in the recent past
D. all cultures seem to have continuous rates of change
E. None of the above

5. All the following are essential to the process of borrowing cultural elements, except ....
A. the projection of a particular cultural element as attractive to and suitable for the recipient society
B. the displacement of the cultural element performing the same task in the recipient society
C. the modification of cultural elements to suit the recipient society
D. the widespread acceptance of the new element within the recipient society
E. None of the above

6. According to the passage ....
A. "cultural borrowing" is primarily dependent on the relationship between the donor and recipient societies
B. the process of assimilation of a new element, whether borrowed or indigenous, will be the same once the society becomes receptive to it.
C. borrowing a new element carries the risk of conflict between the new element and the original element that performed the same task
D. a technologically more complex society will always be a donor to a technologically simpler society
E. None of the above

7. No cultural change is really possible without ....
A. a willingness to learn and imbibe from alien cultures
B. a process of integration, which brings the culture and the innovation into a state of adjustment
C. the human element which acts as a source of all innovation
D. a society's receptivity to change
E. None of the above

8. From the passage, we can infer that ....
A. a society takes much longer to integrate a "culture borrowing" than an "invention"
B. altering the sequence of cultural assimilation will result in unintegrated cultural elements in a society
C. a society with a simpler political and technological structure is more likely to be receptive to new cultural elements
D. as the political and technological structure of a society becomes complex, cultural change becomes faster
E. None of the above

PASSAGE-13

One of the most critical demographic events in the world today is population ageing i.e. the process by which the share of older individuals in the total population starts becoming larger. The ageing phenomenon, which has been initially experienced by developed countries, is now steadily approaching the developing world. Projections show that over the next five decades, world median age will continue to increase, resulting in enhanced old age dependency ratios in all parts of the world. Thus, population ageing would be a major global public policy *concern* in the twenty-first century posing unprecedented challenges for fiscal, monetary and overall macro-economic management.

There is a general *consensus* that ageing population reduces output growth, limits economic welfare and lowers employment. One direct effect of population ageing is labour shortages that are caused by declining birth rates and increasing life *spans*. This translates itself into a higher old-age dependency ratio (i.e. proportion of population aged 65 and older to population aged 15 to 64). Consequently, with ageing, the economy's capacity to *sustain* the elderly population would decline. An important consequence of this development is reflected in increasing fiscal pressures through higher government spending on social security, health care and other welfare programmes for the elderly accompanied by lower tax buoyancy consequent to falling proportions of the productive labour force.

Given the hard budget constraint for many developing countries, this could mean lower government spending for programmes that primarily benefit the young. With public pension schemes coming under increasing pressure to raise contribution levels or cut the size of social safety benefits, the issue of fiscal sustainability is one of the principal challenges facing policymakers worldwide, particularly in the context of intergenerational equity.

The experience of US, Western Europe and other Organization for Economic Cooperation and Development (OECD) countries suggests that substantial demographic changes have occurred in the past few decades. Improvements in life standards, health care and nutrition have increased life expectancy. As a result, the old-age dependency ratio in OECD countries is projected to reach nearly 50 per cent by 2050. This is going to pose a huge fiscal burden in terms of social security, health care, pension and other related expenditures. In this regard, an OECD exercise reveals a rise in old age pension spending, on an average, by about 3-4 percentage points of GDP over the period till 2050. Expenditure relating to health and long term medical care is estimated to increase by more than 3 percentage points of GDP over the same period. Overall, total age-related expenditures relative to GDP could rise on average by about 7 percentage points over the period 2000-2050. In turn, this would imply an average decline of 6-7 percentage points in the primary balance to GDP ratio.

1. Which of the following is definitely *true* of population ageing?

A. It was almost simultaneously experienced by all the countries of the globe

B. The underdeveloped countries cannot experience the phenomenon

C. Developing and developed countries experienced the phenomenon respectively in succession

D. The challenges posed by population ageing had been witnessed in the past also

E. None of these

2. On which of the following points related to population ageing, there is no dispute among thinkers?

A. The direct effect of population ageing is abundance of labourers

B. Economic welfare will be enhanced due to availability of experienced people

C. Employment will be lowered significantly due to population ageing

D. Old age dependency ratio will be lowered significantly

E. None of these

3. The term "*population ageing*" refers to ....

A. the proportion of senior citizens in a developed country

B. the percentage of older people in a developing nation

C. increase in the overall population of a developed country

D. enhancement in the proportion of older people in the population

E. None of these

4. Which of the following factors is responsible for increase in longevity?

1. Substantial raise in living status
2. Adequate and timely health care
3. Nourishing and healthy diet

A. 1 and 2 only B. 2 and 3 only

C. 1 and 3 only D. All the three

E. None of these

5. Which of the following is most likely to happen by middle of the 21st century?

1. In countries like US and Western Europe, the old-age dependency ratio is likely to touch 50%
2. Six to seven points increase in primary balance to GDP ratio in OECD countries
3. Raise to the extent of three to four percentage points of GDP in age old pension spending.

A. 1 and 2 only B. 1 and 3 only

C. 2 and 3 only D. All the three

E. None of these

6. What is most likely to happen if the dependency ratio is higher?

A. It would lower the economist's capacity to sustain the elderly population

B. Government spending on social security would significantly decline

C. Productive labour force will increase significantly

D. Due to increased longevity expenditure on health care will reduce

E. None of these

Directions (Qs. 7 to 8): *Choose the word which is most nearly the* ***same*** *in meaning as the word given in bold as given in the passage.*

7. CONSENSUS

A. agreement B. consent

C. harmony D. compromise

E. interaction

8. SPAN

A. width
B. gap
C. duration
D. distance
E. extent

Directions (Qs. 9 to 10): *Choose the word which is most* ***opposite*** *in meaning of the word given in bold as given in the passage.*

9. CONCERN

A. reassurance
B. comfort
C. anxiety
D. indifference
E. neglect

10. SUSTAIN

A. prolong
B. uphold
C. protract
D. diminish
E. quit

PASSAGE-14

Seeking a competitive advantage, some professional service firms (for example, firms providing advertising, accounting, or health care services) have considered offering unconditional guarantees of satisfaction. Such guarantees specify what clients can expect and what the firm will do if it fails to fulfil these expectations. Particularly with first-time clients, an unconditional guarantee can be an effective marketing tool if the client is very cautious, the firm's fees are high, the negative consequences of bad service are grave, or business is difficult to obtain through referrals and word-of-mouth.

However, an unconditional guarantee can sometime hinder marketing efforts. With its implication that failure is possible, the guarantee may, paradoxically, cause clients to doubt the service firm's ability to deliver the promised level of service. It may conflict with a firm's desire to appear sophisticated, or may even suggest that firm is begging for business. In legal and health care services, it may mislead clients by suggesting that lawsuits or medical procedures will have guaranteed outcomes. Indeed, *professional service firms* with outstanding reputations and performance to match have little to gain from offering unconditional guarantees. And any firm that implements an unconditional guarantee without undertaking a commensurate commitment to quality of service is merely employing a potentially costly marketing gimmick.

1. The primary function of the passage as a whole is to ....
   A. account for the popularity of practice
   B. evaluate the utility of a practice
   C. demonstrate how to institute a practice
   D. weigh the ethics of using a strategy
   E. explain the reasons for pursuing a strategy
2. Which of the following hypothetical situation best exemplifies the potential problem noted in the second sentence of the second paragraph?
   A. A physician's unconditional guarantee of satisfaction encourages patients to sue for malpractice if they are unhappy with the treatment they receive
   B. A lawyer's unconditional guarantee of satisfaction makes clients suspect that the lawyer needs to find new clients quickly to increase the firm's income
   C. A business consultant's unconditional guarantee of satisfaction is undermined when the consultant fails to please clients
   D. An accountant's unconditional guarantee of satisfaction leads clients to believe the tax returns prepared by the accountant are certain to be accurate
   E. None of these
3. The passage most clearly implies which of the following about the 'professional service firms' mentioned in the second paragraph?
   A. They are unlikely to have offered unconditional guarantees of satisfaction in the past
   B. They are usually profitable enough to be able to compensate clients according to the terms of an unconditional guarantee
   C. They usually practice in fields in which the outcomes are predictable
   D. Their fees are usually more affordable than those charged by other professional service firms
   E. Their clients are usually already satisfied with the quality of service that is delivered
4. The passage's description of the issue raised unconditional guarantees for health care or legal services most clearly implies that which of the following is *true*?
   A. The legal medical professions have standards of practice that would be violated by attempts to fulfil such unconditional guarantees
   B. The result of a lawsuit or medical procedure cannot necessarily be determined in advance by the professionals handling a client's case
   C. The dignity of the legal and medical professions is undermined by any attempts at marketing of professional services, including unconditional guarantees
   D. Clients whose lawsuits or medical procedures have unsatisfactory outcomes cannot be adequately compensated by financial settlements alone
   E. Predicting the monetary cost of legal or health care services is more difficult than predicting the monetary cost of other types of professional services
5. All of the following are mentioned in the passage are circumstances in which professional service firm can be benefited from offering an unconditional guarantee, except ....
   A. the firm is having difficulty in retaining its clients of long standing

B. the firm is having difficulty getting business through client recommendation
C. the firm charges substantial fees for its services
D. The adverse effects of poor performance by the firm are significant for the client
E. None of these

6. Which of the following is cited in the passage as a goal of some professional service firms in offering unconditional guarantees of satisfaction?
A. A limit on the firm's liability
B. Successful competition against other firms
C. Ability to justify fee increases
D. Attainment of an outstanding reputation in a field
E. Improvement in the quality of the firm's service

PASSAGE-15

The goal of our present system of primary and secondary schooling is to prepare students for the examination system which will take them to the best technical institutions in the country. While the teaching of science and mathematics has over the years been upgraded, the teaching of the humanities and social sciences continues to be straight-jacketed in grotesque ways. Those areas of the Indian reality, which ought to form the proper subject, like caste, poverty and environmental degradation do not form part of the syllabus.

The capacity to think independently and critically about problems that plague modern Indian society, which ought really to be a prominent part of a humanities curriculum, is perceived to be intractable from the point of view of the examiner. Lest the evaluation become subjective, every effort is made to reduce both history and economics to a series of facts; a one-to-one correlation between facts ensures proper systems of grading.

1. According to the author, the present educational system ultimately helps the students in which of the following?
1. Understanding the real problems of people
2. Acquiring various techniques to face the challenges of the future
3. Getting admission to renowned technical institutions

A. Only 1 B. Only 2
C. Only 3 D. Only 1 and 2
E. Either 1 or 2

2. According to the author, the teaching of science and mathematics develops capacity of the students in which of the following?
1. Considering pros and cons of each decision
2. Examining the problem minutely with proper analysis

A. Only 1 B. Only 2
C. Either 1 or 2 D. Both 1 and 2
E. Not mentioned in the passage

3. What seems to be the purpose of the author in writing this passage?
A. To critically look into the methods of teaching of science and mathematics
B. To point out the deficiencies in the curriculum and examination system
C. To reduce importance of science and mathematics in our system of education
D. To put up a case for proper objective system of grading
E. To appreciate the present educational system

4. According to the author which of the following is the main reason leading to upgradation of teaching of science and mathematics?
A. Science and mathematics can solve our problems
B. It inculcates proper values for becoming an ideal citizen
C. The evaluation of these subjects is objective and critical
D. The syllabus of science and mathematics have been modified from time to time
E. None of these

5. The author seems to believe in which of the following?
1. The capacity to think can be developed by a properly designed curriculum of humanities and social sciences
2. Objective evaluation is necessary for social sciences
3. Proper education can help a person to become a responsible and responsive citizen

A. Only 1 B. Only 2
C. Only 3 D. Either 1 or 2
E. Both 1 & 3

6. What problems does the author see in the improvement of the teaching of humanities and social sciences?
1. The present syllabus of these subjects
2. The difficulties of the examiners
3. The present system of evaluation

A. Only 1 B. Only 2
C. Only 3 D. Either 1 or 2
E. Not mentioned in the passage

PASSAGE-16

What is the future that awaits our children? The underlying assumption of the question, that Indian children have a common future is itself dubious. It can legitimately be asked whether a student who is well-fed, attending a boarding school in the salubrious climate of the hills and learning to use computers has any future in common with a malnourished child who goes to a school with no blackboards, if indeed he does go to school. The latter may have no worthwhile future at all. And it might be worthwhile to analyse the significance of this marginalisation of more than 75 per cent of the children of this country.

The failure to provide an infrastructure for primary education in the villages of India more than 40 years after independence is in sharp contrast with the sophisticated institutions, for technical institutes of higher education are funded by the government, which essentially means that the money to support them comes from taxes. And, since indirect taxation forms a substantial part of the taxes collected by the government, the financial burden is borne by all the people. L.K. Jha put it graphically when he observed that 25 paise of every rupee spent on educating an IIT student comes from the pockets of men and women whose children may never enter a proper classroom.

1. The author is trying to highlight which of the following?
A. Faulty system of direct taxes
B. The greatness of L.K. Jha
C. Need of sophisticated education for rural poor
D. Need to have common future for Indian children
E. None of these

2. Which of the following pairs have been termed as 'sharp contrast' by the author?
1. Infrastructure for technical education
2. Lack of infrastructure for rural primary schools
3. 25 paise of every rupee earned by Government is spent on education
4. The financial burden of higher technical education is borne by all people
5. 75% of children have limited opportunities

A. 2 and 4 B. 2 and 3
C. 3 and 4 D. 1 and 2
E. 4 and 5

3. Which of the following statements is *not true*?
1. The author welcomes Govt.'s initiative on primary education
2. 75% of the children have a bright future
3. 25% cost of educating a technocrat comes from poor people

A. Only 1 B. Only 2
C. Only 3 D. Only 1 and 2
E. Only 1 and 3

4. According to the author, who among the following does not have a hopeful and prosperous future?
1. All students from technical institutes
2. All students financially supported by the Government

A. Only 1
B. Only 2
C. Both 1 and 2
D. Neither 1 nor 2
E. Not mentioned in the passage

5. What seems to be the likely answer of the author to the question posed by him in the first sentence of the passage?
1. There is no common future for the Indian children
2. The future is worthwhile for majority of Indian children
3. The majority may never enter a proper classroom

A. Only 1 B. Only 2
C. Only 3 D. Both 1 and 2
E. Both 2 and 3

6. What seems to be the purpose of the author in writing this passage?
A. Setting goals for children of upper middle class
B. Questioning the legitimacy of public schools
C. Highlighting lack of infrastructural facilities for primary education
D. Focusing on inequality in educational opportunities
E. None of these

PASSAGE-17

The Indian scenario can be described very briefly. The apparatus of the state has become an integral part of what Americans term the iron triangle : a collusion *of* (*a*) those who benefit from the subsidies: the industry, urban populations, rich farmers; (*b*) those who decide on who is to be subsidised at whose cost: the politicians; and (*c*) those who administer the subsidies : the bureaucracy.

Let me explain what I mean. Take the example of bamboo. Bamboo has been made available to paper mills at rates as low as one to two rupees per tonne, when the basket weavers were buying it in the market at a *high* price—several thousand rupees per tonne. Cement factories receive power and raw materials at subsidised rates and pass on the costs of pollution to the society at large; the cement thus subsidised flows to metropolises. These metropolises also attract *large* quantities of bricks made from the previous topsoil of farms and baked with old banyan trees now being liquidated for kilns.

When *a giant* hydel project on a river in one State was concluded, the *bulk* of its power was given over to a single aluminium industry at a few paise per unit, well below the cost of production. Later, the State government decided to charge only a nominal flat rate per irrigation pump, ensuring that the farmers kept the pumps running whether they needed the water or not. Villagers who lose their lands and *small* homes under irrigation projects have always been inadequately compensated, thereby keeping the cost of projects low. But the beneficiaries in the command areas never have to pay for water to take care of even these artificially depressed costs.

1. Which of the following industries have been referred to in the passage?
A. Aluminium B. Brick
C. Paper D. Iron
E. Cement

2. According to the author, who decides the beneficiaries of various subsidies?
   A. The bureaucrats B. The Industrialists
   C. Rich farmers D. Villagers
   E. None of these
3. Which of the following describes correctly the approach of the author?
   A. Positive criticism followed by suggestions for improvement
   B. Prove how government has handled the situation effectively
   C. One sided, negative and highly critical
   D. Indifference to both government and welfare of people
   E. Instigate people to revolt against the government
4. Which of the following is the main reason which helps the authorities to keep cost of irrigation projects low?
   1. The beneficiaries contribute money to the project
   2. The government keeps nominal rates for the supply of water
   3. Low compensation is provided to the affected villagers
   A. Only 1 B. Only 2
   C. Only 3 D. Either 1 or 2
   E. Both 1 and 2
5. The author has given sufficient examples which make us feel that
   1. proper costing of the projects is not being done by the government
   2. the government is protecting interests of rich and urban people
   3. the present practice of subsidy should be reviewed
   A. Only 1 and 2
   B. Only 1 and 3
   C. Only 2 and 3
   D. All the three 1, 2 and 3
   E. Only 1
6. Four of the five words used in the passage form one group, the fifth one does not belong to that group. Find out the word that does to belong to the group.
   A. Giant B. Bulk
   C. High D. Small
   E. Large
7. Which of the following statements is *true* in the context of the passage?
   A. Paper mills and basket weavers both get bamboo at very low rates
   B. Wood from banyan trees is used by the cement industries
   C. The government machinery is taking a balanced view about development
   D. The cement industry is responsible for polluting the atmosphere
   E. The government is influenced by American terms

PASSAGE-18

Economic growth involves both benefits and costs. The desirablity of increasing production has frequently been challenged in recent years and some have even maintained that economic growth is merely a quantitative enlargement that has no human meaning or value. However, economic growth is an increase in the capacity to produce goods and services that people want. Since the product of economic growth can be measured by its value to someone, it is important to ask whose standard of valuation counts.

In the United States, the value of a product is what purchasers pay for it. This is determined by the purchasers' preferences combined with conditions of supply, which in turn reflect various other factors, such as natural and technological circumstances at any given time and the preferences of those who supply capital and labour. The value by which we measure a product synthesizes all these factors. Gross National Product (GNP) is the market value of the nation's total output of goods and services.

Gross National Product is not a perfect measure of all the activities involved in economic output. It does not account for deterioration or improvements in the environment, even when they are incidental results of the production process. On the other hand, it does not take into account many benefits provided as side effects of the economic process; it does not include 'productive but unpaid work' (such as that done by a housewife); and it does not reckon with such other factors as the burdensomeness of work, the length of the work, week and so forth.

Nonetheles, the GNP concept makes an important contribution to our understanding of how the economy is working. While it is not a complete measure of economic productivity and even less so of "*welfare*" the level and rate of increase of the GNP are clearly and positively associated with what most people throughout the world see as an improvement in the quality of life.

Although there has been much soul searching about the role of increasing material affluence in the good life, it seems quite certain that most Americans prefer a rapidly growing GNP and its consequences. This does not mean that growth of the GNP is an absolute requirement that must be furthered at all costs, and beyond a certain point they are not worth paying. Moreover people wants thing that are not measured in the GNP. Still, while human values and conditions of the life change and might conceivably make the social cost of a rising GNP seems too high, it is likely that we would still be concerned about the growth of our nation's GNP.

In any case, since there is little evidence of decline in the value assigned to economic output as a whole, the factors that influence our capacity to produce remain of great importance. In the long run, the same factors result in a growing GNP and in other social benefits. They are size and competence of population, state of knowledge, amount of capital and the effectiveness with which these are combined and utilized.

1. Those who decide the value of a product are ....
A. the GNP
B. economic theorist
C. its advertisers
D. its patent holders
E. its purchasers

2. The rhetorical purpose of the third paragraph of the passage is to ....
1. anticipate objection to what the GNP fails to take into account
2. cite examples of "products" the GNP ought to include
3. develop the definition of paragraph two with specific details

A. 1 only
B. 2 only
C. 3 only
D. 1 and 2 only
E. 1, 2 and 3

3. The main purpose of the passage is to ....
A. define the limitation of using GNP to measure the nation's well-being
B. contrast the American and the European GNPs
C. argue for the value of increased economic output
D. explain the disadvantages of measuring the quality of life using a scale of material affluence
E. define Gross National Product

4. A critic of the limitations of the measurement of the GNP might cite its failure to consider all the following except ....
A. the steady increase in American worker's leisure then
B. cooperative baby-sitting projects among parents with young children
C. the widespread existence of chemicals in American rivers
D. the value of the time a salaried stock broker spends on research
E. the valuation of family household management

5. We might assume that the authour favours the continuing growth of the GNP because ....
A. although he mentions that the GNP has its costs, he doesn't examine those costs
B. it does not include such factors as the burdensomeness of work
C. he wishes to represent a minority opinion
D. he does not believe in perfect measure of economic growth
E. he believes that human values and the conditions of life are subject to change

6. We can infer from the passage the factor that does not influence the growth of the GNP is ....
A. the condition of the population
B. a dependence on spiritual values
C. the capital available in the country
D. knowledge related to production of goods and services
E. the efficiency of the production process

7. As it is used in the fourth paragraph of the passage, the word "*welfare*" can be best defined as ....
A. a measure of economic productivity
B. the quality of life of the public as a whole
C. government-supported payments to the indigent
D. public payments for unpaid production work such as child care
E. state-supported income supplements

ANSWERS

PASSAGE-1

1	2	3	4	5	6	7
C	D	C	B	C	A	C
8	**9**	**10**				
D	A	B				

PASSAGE-2

1	2	3	4	5	6	7
D	E	C	E	B	C	D
8	**9**	**10**				
B	B	A				

PASSAGE-3

1	2	3	4	5	6	7
C	A	D	D	E	D	C
8	**9**	**10**				
C	E	A				

PASSAGE-4

1	2	3	4	5	6	7
E	B	A	A	B	C	E

PASSAGE-5

1	2	3	4	5	6	7
A	C	C	A	D	E	B
8	**9**	**10**				
A	B	E				

PASSAGE-6

1	2	3	4	5	6	7
A	D	E	B	D	E	E
8	**9**	**10**				
C	C	D				

PASSAGE-7

1	2	3	4	5	6	7
A	C	D	E	A	E	A
8	**9**	**10**				
B	B	E				

PASSAGE-8

1	2	3	4	5	6	7
B	C	D	A	A	E	C
8	**9**	**10**				
B	E	E				

PASSAGE-9

1	2	3	4	5	6	7
B	D	A	C	A	B	C
8	**9**	**10**	**11**	**12**		
A	D	C	B	D		

PASSAGE-10

1	2	3	4	5	6	7
B	D	C	C	C	C	C
8	**9**	**10**	**11**	**12**	**13**	**14**
A	C	A	D	E	B	B

PASSAGE-11

1	2	3	4	5	6	7	
C	A	C	D	D	E	E	
8	**9**	**10**	**12**	**13**	**13**	**14**	**15**
E	D	B	E	D	B	C	E

PASSAGE-12

1	2	3	4	5	6	7
A	B	C	A	B	B	B
8						
C						

PASSAGE-13

1	2	3	4	5	6	7
E	C	D	D	B	A	A
8	**9**	**10**				
C	D	D				

PASSAGE-14

1	2	3	4	5	6
B	D	E	A	B	B

PASSAGE-15

1	2	3	4	5	6
C	E	B	E	E	D

PASSAGE-16

1	2	3	4	5	6
D	A	D	A	A	E

PASSAGE-17

1	2	3	4	5	6	7
D	E	C	C	B	D	D

PASSAGE-18

1	2	3	4	5	6	7
E	A	A	A	A	B	D

2

CLOZE TESTS

A cloze test is a test in which you are asked to supply words which have been removed from a passage. It is meant to test your ability to comprehend text. Try and practise it in this chapter to master it.

Directions: *In the following passages, there are some blanks, each of which has been numbered. These numbers are printed below the passage and against each, five words are suggested, one of which fits the blank appropriately. Find out the appropriate word in each case.*

Passage-1

Women have ... 1 ... made ... 2 ... the corporate work-place but certainly not as much as they had ... 3 ... . We have new laws, rules and ... 4 ... relating to women in the workplace, but what we have not changed much is male ... 5 ... . Women have fallen short in their goals because we ... 6 ... the potency of the male need to ... 7 ... their power. We can abide ... 8 ... by the laws and rules we create in order to ... 9 ... women an equal opportunity in the corporate workplace and still not ... 10 ... the problems that afflicted and eventually capsized the women's raft.

1. A. seldom B. not C. optimistically D. undoubtedly E. perhaps
2. A. attempts B. progress C. decisions D. efforts E. automation
3. A. prescribed B. informed C. encompassed D. predisposed E. expected
4. A. problems B. revolutions C. policies D. cases E. activities
5. A. behaviour B. population C. achievements D. patterns E. hatred
6. A. risk B. minimize C. respect D. retaliate E. underestimate
7. A. know B. maintain C. evolve D. absolve E. diminish
8. A. them B. partially C. occasionally D. scrupulously E. excessively
9. A. deprive B. donate C. assure D. deny E. share
10. A. emphasize B. explore C. judge D. mentioned E. overcome

Passage-2

To the curious and the ... 1 ... , the sea still presents the challenge of the unknown, for ignorance is still the ... 2 ... characteristic of men's relation to the sea. But now, more than ever, necessity ... 3 ... us onward in our exploration of the sea. We now have submarines capable of ... 4 ... submergence for many months ... 5 ... missiles capable of ... 6 ... many times greater than that ... 7 ... by World War II. For ... 8 ... reasons, therefore, we need ... 9 ... to learn more about the ... 10 ... of ocean bottom, about deep ocean currents, temperature, density and so on.

Another necessity ... 11 ... us to learn to master the sea. That necessity is food. The lives of two-third of the world's people are wholly ... 12 ... by that basic necessity; they are ... 13 ... by hunger and by the weakness and disease which hunger generates.

1. A. outgoing B. courageous C. formidable D. watchful E. intelligent
2. A. outstanding B. remarkable C. valuable D. critical E. distinguishing

3. A. projects B. excites C. goads D. propels E. makes

4. A. provocative B. turbulant C. deadly D. durable E. steady

5. A. guiding B. subjecting C. providing D. holding E. directing

6. A. expansion B. destruction C. projection D. domination E. aggression

7. A. forced B. witnessed C. experienced D. conceived E. wrought

8. A. traditional B. academic C. deliberate D. strategic E. historical

9. A. urgently B. drastically C. judiciously D. cautiously E. wilfully

10. A. tenacity B. distribution C. topography D. resources E. velocity

11. A. involves B. threatens C. presses D. wants E. provides

12. A. projected B. galvanised C. dictated D. developed E. challenged

13. A. oppressed B. salvaged C. controlled D. governed E. perturbed

Passage-3

The world economy is in recession — the deepest and the most widespread ... 1 ... the 1930s. There are ... 2 ... of ... 3 ... in the industrial countries, but most serious economic ... 4 ... anticipate that rates of growth and levels of economic activity will remain low.

In all that has been written about world ... 5 ..., the ... 6 ... have been overwhelmingly and narrowly economic. Few have ... 7 ... the human consequences in more than a superficial manner. Not a single international study has ... 8 ... the recession's ... 9 ... on the most vulnerable half of the world's population — the children.

The need for ... 10 ... clearly the ... 11 ... between world economic conditions and child welfare has thus become even more urgent in the last few years. The worldscale of current child distress also makes it artificial to restrict the analysis of causes to the ... 12 ... level.

1. A. in B. for C. by D. before E. since

2. A. risks B. glimmers C. studies D. tips E. histories

3. A. development B. downfall C. recovery D. slackness E. impact

4. A. analysts B. journalists C. surveys D. findings E. students

5. A. development B. economy C. wars D. recession E. conflicts

6. A. emphasis B. aims C. glimpses D. suppositions E. preoccupations

7. A. delved B. taught C. propagated D. investigated E. manifested

8. A. understood B. analysed C. highlighted D. prepared E. planned

9. A. analysis B. undercurrents C. impact D. overtures E. study

10. A. chalking out B. curbing C. bringing out D. implementing E. propagating

11. A. linkages B. fallouts C. dependence D. contrasts E. similarities

12. A. international B. political C. low D. national E. highest

Passage-4

Countries which do not have a very well-developed machine tool industry can never ... 1 ... to be even a first grade ... 2 ... and economic power, much less a global industrial power. This is known from the ... 3 ... of countries like Germany, USA, Japan, Switzerland and so on. When at the end of the Second World War, Japan wanted to become an industrial power, the ... 4 ... step she took was to ... 5 ... a machine tool industry. She decided to be ... 6 ... and not depend on ... 7 ... industrial nations. This was ... 8 ... in the long-term rather than going in for ... 9 ... advantage of import of machine tools. Similarly, India also established a machine tool industry ... 10 ... after independnece to foster its fledging industries.

1. A. aspire B. manifest
C. agree D. prosper
E. pursue

2. A. political B. industrial
C. military D. progressive
E. rich

3. A. feelings B. perceptions
C. plans D. experience
E. establishment

4. A. important B. useful
C. economic D. wise
E. first

5. A. develop B. nurture
C. introduce D. admit
E. establish

6. A. revolutionary B. industrious
C. self-sufficient D. systematic
E. progressive

7. A. European B. developed
C. neighbouring D. technical
E. foreign

8. A. planned B. decided
C. tried D. beneficial
E. achieved

9. A. temporary B. exceptional
C. easy D. fast
E. financial

10. A. days B. months
C. immediately D. years
E. much

Passage-5

Conventional medical wisdom does not advise taking ... 1 ... vitamins as pills and capsules. On the contrary there was a strong lobby which ... 2 ... the supplementary intake of vitamins. This used to leave the ... 3 ... person confused. However, modern research is ... 4 ... a surprise. More and more scientists are beginning to ... 5 ... that ... 6 ... medical views on vitamins has been ... 7 ... . Evidence shows that ... 8 ... extra vitamins plays a role in assuring vitality and ... 9 ... health than was ... 10 ... thought.

1. A. some B. extra
C. insoluble D. strong
E. all

2. A. facilitate B. criticised
C. communicate D. projected
E. advocated

3. A. medical B. stick
C. scientific D. average
E. educated

4. A. trying B. manufacturing
C. practising D. holding
E. inventing

5. A. trust B. consider
C. refute D. forget
E. suspect

6. A. indigent B. all
C. traditional D. modern
E. allopathic

7. A. practical B. limited
C. feasible D. correct
E. confusing

8. A. marketing B. manufacturing
C. swallowing D. taking
E. buying

9. A. pleasurable B. manly
C. optimal D. stronger
E. useful

10. A. previously B. occasionally
C. seriously D. even
E. now

Passage-6

Fundamentally, all human ... 1 ... possess combinations of fixed inherited traits. All men possess the ... 2 ... highly developed nervous system, back-bones, erect posture, hair, etc. Therefore, ... 3 ... among men arise only ... 4 ... changes of this ... 5 ... pattern. Racial ... 6 ... represent one of the finest distinctions and are based on certain ... 7 ... differences. Two races may be ... 8 ... in hair colour, in eye colour but ... 9 ... in stature while two others may be ... 10 ... in stature but differ in the colour of eyes and hair.

1. A. animal B. beings
C. mind D. society
E. thinking

2. A. large B. different
C. same D. natural
E. biological

3. A. sameness B. naturalness
C. growth D. substance
E. variations

4. A. no B. large
C. fundamental D. minor
E. artificial

5. A. fluctuating B. mad
C. picturesque D. basic
E. maddening

6. A. differences B. clashes
C. hatred D. tolerance
E. sameness

7. A. clearcut B. minor
C. unnoticeable D. massive
E. neat

8. A. alike B. different
C. mismatched D. beautiful
E. untouched

9. A. matched B. same
C. different D. close
E. tall

10. A. tall B. short
C. uncouth D. ugly
E. same

Passage-7

Operation Flood Scheme was ... 1 ... with the primary objective of ... 2 ... rural milk producers with urban milk consumers, by ... 3 ... viable producers' cooperatives in the milk sheds, and thus ... 4 ... rural milk producers earn higher income from milk. The programme ... 5 ... some 72 lakh members in nearly 61,600 village societies ... 6 ... over diverse ecologies in 174 milk sheds. These cooperatives procure an average of 90 lakh litres of milk a day to ... 7 ... the evergrowing urban demand for fresh milk of the country.

1. A. visualised B. created
C. launched D. devoted
E. recognised

2. A. joining B. linking
C. bringing D. identifying
E. locating

3. A. exposing B. generating
C. bringing D. providing
E. creating

4. A. offering B. activating
C. justifying D. enabling
E. providing

5. A. covers B. relates
C. motivates D. follows
E. leads

6. A. distributed B. assembled
C. situated D. spread
E. divided

7. A. control B. meet
C. satisfy D. contain
E. respond

Passage-8

Nowadays, under the ... 1 ... system of education, however good it may be, when a young man comes out of the University, there seems to be this ... 2 ... in him that the higher the standard of living rises, the less should a man work. Thus, mathematically higher the standard of living, according to this misconceived notion, the less the ... 3 ... . Ultimately, what should be the highest standard of living then? ... 4 ... work! This leads to an unhealthy ... 5 ... among the workers. A typist who types over twenty letters a day asks his ... 6 ... how many letters he had typed that day. The latter ... 7 ... "fifteen". The former thinks, "Tomorrow I should type only fifteen or even ... 8 ..." . This tendency is quite ... 9 ... , and may ultimately lead to ... 10 ... . Even one's family life may be affected adversely due to such tendency.

1. A. developed B. extinct
C. outdated D. proposed
E. modern

2. A. anxiety B. misconception
C. realisation D. worry
E. apprehension

3. A. salary B. comfort
C. work D. energy
E. time

4. A. Minimum B. Maximum
C. Less D. No
E. Ample

5. A. competition B. dispute
C. delay D. jealousy
E. ambition

6. A. employee B. subordinate
C. boss D. client
E. colleague

7. A. suggests B. remembers
C. replies D. types
E. all

8. A. less B. all
C. more D. few
E. some

9. A. discouraging B. heartening
C. healthy D. unfortunate
E. unnatural

10. A. evil B. retardation
C. progress D. denial
E. complexity

Passage-9

Mobile banking (M-banking) involves the use of a mobile phone or any other mobile device to ...1... financial transactions linked to a client's account. M-banking is new in most countries and most mobile payment models even in developed countries, to date operate on a ...2... scale. A mobile network offers a ...3... available technology platform onto which other services can be provided at low cost with effective results. For example, M-banking services which use ...4... such as SMS can be carried at a cost of less than one US cent per message. The low cost of using existing infrastructure makes such services more ...5... to use by customers with lower purchasing power and opens up access to services which did not reach them earlier due to ...6... cost of service delivery. Although M-banking is one aspect in the wider ...7... of e-banking there are reasons to single it out for focus—especially because there are a lot more people with mobile phones than bank accounts in India.

M-banking could provide a ...8... solution to bring more "unbanked" people to the financial mainstream. Without traditional credit, individuals are ...9... to exploitation by abusive lenders offering very high interest rates on short term loans. Also of considerable importance are public safety implications for the unbanked—they are often victims of crime because many operate on a cash only basis and end up carrying significant amounts of cash on their ...10... or store cash in their homes.

1. A. Disburse B. Undertake C. Subscribe D. Lure E. Amass
2. A. Full B. Voluminous C. Substantial D. Limited E. Rapid
3. A. Readily B. Tangible C. Routinely D. Securely E. Unique
4. A. Process B. Waves C. Deliveries D. Connection E. Channels
5. A. Valuable B. Answerable C. Amenable D. Exposed E. Responsible
6. A. Waning B. Stable C. Proportionate D. Marginal E. High
7. A. Archive B. Domain C. Purpose D. Component E. Aspect
8. A. Law abiding B. Tried C. Reassuring D. Cost effective E. Stopgap
9. A. Inclined B. Immune C. Vulnerable D. Surrendered E. Pressured
10. A. Person B. Own C. Relatives D. Purses E. Self

Passage-10

... 1 ... change is the ... 2 ... of the day, a proper orientation to ... 3 ... with the change becomes a natural necessity ... 4 ... assured organisational stability. In this ... 5 ... of organisational change and survival, the author brings in the concept of 'praxis', ... 6 ... it as the dynamo of change and uses it for ... 7 ... a conceptual and methodological ... 8 ... for the identification of training needs. Training, ... 9 ... perceived as only one of the many elements in the organisational reflection process, is believed to stand ... 10 ... as the means for relevant learning.

1. A. Few B. Many C. No D. If E. Why
2. A. order B. scope C. large D. direction E. result
3. A. assist B. renew C. become D. try E. cope
4. A. in B. for C. from D. which E. but
5. A. end B. decision C. context D. scope E. focus
6. A. describes B. throws C. rejects D. leaves E. derives
7. A. neglecting B. developing C. calculating D. experiencing E. diluting
8. A. routine B. idea C. book D. follow up E. framework
9. A. be B. may C. though D. gets E. as
10. A. in B. against C. through D. out E. with

Passage-11

I think ... 1 ... a successful old age is easiest for ... 2 ... who have strong ... 3 ... interests involving ... 4 ... activities. It is in this sphere that long ... 5 ... is really fruitful, and it is in this sphere that the ... 6 ... born of experience can be exercised without being oppressive. It is no ... 7 ... telling ... 8 ... children not to make mistakes, ... 9 ... because they will not believe you, and because mistakes are an ... 10 ... part of education.

1. A. because B. as C. really D. that E. certainly
2. A. them B. those C. they D. boys E. girls
3. A. impersonal B. personal C. good D. happy E. proper

4. A. good B. joyful
C. appropriate D. happy
E. strong

5. A. knowledge B. expertise
C. experience D. thoughtfulness
E. hobby

6. A. joy B. wisdom
C. greatness D. love
E. strength

7. A. benefit B. use
C. point D. sense
E. justice

8. A. grown up B. happy
C. little D. young
E. small

9. A. as B. since
C. after all D. actually
E. both

10. A. essential B. unavoidable
C. agreeable D. appropriate
E. admitted

Passage-12

It is not this that we have to break ... 1 ..., but with all the dust and dirt of ages that have covered her ... 2 ... and hidden her inner beauty and significance, the excrescences and abortions that ... 3 ... twisted and petrified ... 4 ... spirit, set it in rigid frames, and stunted her growth. We have to cut away these excrescences and remember afresh the core of that ... 5 ... and adapt it to our present circumstances. We have to get out of ... 6 ... ways of thought and living which for all the good in them—have ceased to have significance today. We have to make our own all the achievements of the human ... 7 ... and join up with others in the exciting adventure of man, more exciting today perhaps than in earlier ages, ... 8 ... that this has ceased to be governed by national boundaries or old divisions and is common to the race of man everywhere. We have to revive the ... 9 ... for truth and beauty and freedom which gives meaning to life, and develop afresh that dynamic outlook and spirit of adventure which distinguished those of our race who, in ages past, built our house on these strong and enduring foundations. Old ... 10 ... we are, with memories stretching back to the early dawns of human history and endeavour, we have to grow young again, in tune with our present time, with the irrepressible spirit and joy of youth in the present and its faith in the future.

1. A. in B. out
C. with D. up
E. into

2. A. up B. with
C. at D. over
E. for

3. A. has B. is
C. have D. had
E. was

4. A. her B. its
C. it's D. their
E. our

5. A. present spirit B. ancient wisdom
C. old philosophy D. modern life
E. ancient love

6. A. outdated B. useless
C. traditional D. irrational
E. superstitions

7. A. race B. life
C. kind D. efforts
E. experiments

8. A. feeling B. hoping
C. realizing D. thinking
E. loving

9. A. desire B. lust
C. longing D. passion
E. aspiration

10. A. because B. since
C. however D. though
E. as

Passage-13

Clay tablets uncovered in southern Egypt from the tomb of a king ... 1 ... Scorpion may ... 2 ... the earliest known writing by humans. If confirmed, the discovery ... 3 ... rank among the greatest ... 4 ... in the search ... 5 ... the origins of the ... 6 .... Gunter Dreyer, head of the German Archaeological Institute, said the tablets record linen and oil ... 7 ... made about 5,300 years ago as taxes paid to King Scorpion-I reports Seattle Post-Intelligencer, USA. He said the tablets have been carbon-dated with ... 8 ... to between 3300 BC and 3200 BC. The discovery opens for ... 9 ... a widely held belief ... 10 ... historians that the first people to write were the Sumerians of the Mesopotamian civilisation sometime before 3000 BC. The exact date of Sumerian writing remains in doubt.

1. A. mentioned B. named
C. designated D. nominated
E. characterized

2. A. show B. present
C. represent D. point
E. mention

3. A. would B. might
C. may D. will
E. can

4. A. also B. even
C. certainly D. ever
E. truly

5. A. for B. of
C. at D. into
E. in

6. A. printed matter B. carbon copies
C. written word D. deciphered matter
E. computerized composition

7. A. discoveries B. inventions
C. experiments D. paintings
E. sculpture

8. A. surety B. assurance
C. certainty D. definiteness
E. perfection

9. A. debate B. application
C. practice D. acceptance
E. regulations

10. A. between B. among
C. in D. by
E. for

Passage-14

Babies use a ... **1** ... undiscovered ... **2** ... for rules to master the building ... **3** ... of language, according to scientists at New York University. The discovery is ... **4** ... that the ability to think in terms of ... **5** ... and rules is not just something that must be learned through schooling, as some scholars have argued, but is also a fundamental ... **6** ... of every human mind. Working with seven month-old infants, NYU researchers determined that even the ... **7** ... young can make ... **8** ... of speech by figuring out on their own simple rules about the ... **9** ... of language structure and grammar. Babies appear to deduce these formal rules well before they can understand what words mean or how to say them. The research, published in "Science," broadens the understanding to what may be built into every human brain ... **10** ... birth.

1. A. outwardly B. anciently
C. formerly D. previously
E. finally

2. A. desire B. instinct
C. longing D. hope
E. expectation

3. A. qualities B. structures
C. blocks D. nuances
E. powers

4. A. persuasive evidence B. true proof
C. desirable virtue D. right instinct
E. happy intuition

5. A. formulas B. formulae
C. laws D. acts
E. regulations

6. A. virtue B. instinct
C. desire D. habit
E. characteristic

7. A. very B. much
C. quite D. enough
E. sufficiently

8. A. urge B. sense
C. a lot D. much
E. realization

9. A. kinds B. structures
C. designs D. patterns
E. formulas

10. A. at B. after
C. during D. before
E. in

Passage-15

Vocationalising education after high school (even before) is a ... **1** ... more sensible approach to face the job problem than ... **2** ... every Tom, Dick or Harry to go up to the gradaute level, irrespective of suitability.

... **3** ... from scholdays most students could be branched ... **4** ... to different professions. This way higher education would become ... **5** ... purposeful and also help save a fat budget spent on it.

The ... **6** ... of education also needs to be improved and teachers who are paid ... **7** ... should pay back society appropriately. Unfortunately, the standard of education with the rise in the salary of a teacher has been ... **8** ... declining. This trend should be checked and institutions should ensure that teachers do their job honestly and to the satisfaction of students and society.

This would help obtain suitable ... **9** ... from the existing system of education where the average student's education is ... **10** ... subsidised.

1. A. truly B. certainly
C. actually D. desirably
E. far

2. A. allow B. let
C. allowing D. inviting
E. allure

3. A. right B. truly
C. properly D. definitely
E. quickly

4. A. up B. out
C. away D. at
E. in

5. A. quite B. much
C. very D. more
E. truly

6. A. quality B. quantity
C. amount D. load
E. quantum

7. A. sufficiently B. satisfactorily
C. handsomely D. heavily
E. unduly

8. A. quickly B. slowly
C. rapidly D. often
E. steadily

9. A. return B. gain
C. income D. remuneration
E. compensation

10. A. strongly B. unduly
C. improperly D. certainly
E. heavily

Passage-16

September 13, 1993 ... **1** ... go ... **2** ... in world history as a fateful day. On this day Israel and the Palestine Liberation Organisation (PLO) signed a peace agreement. The agreement ... **3** ... to an end a 45 years old war or a war-like situation. Israel and the PLO recognised each other and agreed ... **4** ... a plan for Palestinian self-rule in the occupied territories. The pact was signed in Washington by the Israeli Foreign Minister and a senior PLO official. It was signed in the presence of the Israeli Prime Minister Yitzhak Robin and PLO Chairman Yasser Arafat. The US President and the Russian Foreign Miniser were also present on the ... **5** ..... A senior Israeli official listed five classes of the pact. The pact ... **6** ... as a historic act. Mr. Clinton called it "this great occasion of history" and "an extraordinary art in one of history's defining dramas." The pact granted the Palestinians limited self-rule in the occupied West Bank and Gaza Strip. It enjoined ... **7** ... the Israeli troops to begin withdrawing from Gaza and the West Bank town of Jericho within three months. The credit for bringing Mr. Ralim and Mr. Arafat closer ... **8** ... the Norweigian Foreign Minister Mr. Holst. He acted ... **9** ... a mediator and facilitated secret talks between Israeli and PLO leaders. The decks were ... **10** ... when Mr. Robin received a letter from Mr. Arafat which recognised the right of Israelis to exist.

1. A. would B. shall
C. will D. can
E. may

2. A. up B. down
C. away D. out
E. for

3. A. brought B. led
C. resulted D. caused
E. fructified

4. A. with B. for
C. to D. on
E. against

5. A. opportunity B. function
C. meeting D. agreement
E. occasion

6. A. was hailed B. was recognised
C. was accepted D. was declared
E. was announced

7. A. at B. to
C. for D. upon
E. in

8. A. rests with B. falls upon
C. belongs to D. revolves round
E. goes to

9. A. as B. for
C. upto D. against
E. in lieu of

10. A. set right B. erected
C. allowed D. cleared
E. set up

Passage-17

Compassion must be ... **1** ... at the heart of human life, in a world ... **2** ... far too ... **3** ... by principles of power and destructive control. Compassion is no longer merely an eraser of human mistakes, it is a force of prayer and action — the expression of God's love for us and our love for Him and one another. Compassion should ... **4** ... the spirit and spur us towards the constructive ... **5** ... of mankind. Compassion is ... **6** ... close to our ... **7** ... disposition as any of the other ... **8** ..... The challenge lies in not ... **9** ... animosity and prejudice to stunt its natural growth. And to keep the divisive 'isms' — racism, sexism, and chauvinism etc. — ... **10** .... .

1. A. considered B. believed
C. decided D. placed
E. accepted

2. A. governed B. controlled
C. decided D. checked
E. applied

3. A. large B. big
C. long D. powerfully
E. briefly

4. A. rule over B. control
C. sway over D. pervade
E. prevail over

5. A. freedom B. good
C. happiness D. love
E. cooperation

6. A. undoubtedly B. certainly
C. as D. quite
E. greatly

7. A. natural B. physical
C. spiritual D. actual
E. human

8. A. virtue B. virtues
C. qualities D. activities
E. characteristic

9. A. letting B. allow
C. allowing D. germinating
E. bearing

10. A. at tenterhooks B. at bay
C. in dilemma D. in a fix
E. at sixes and sevens

Passage-18

Population education is a recent ... 1 ... in the area of school curriculum. The need for population education ... 2 ... from the fact that there is an urgency ... 3 ... controlling and arresting the population growth in our country and the youth should be educated on the hazards of population ... 4 ..... .

Today's student will be tomorrow's parent and they need to be made ... 5 ... population problems and importance of small family. Similarly, a UNESCO report also urges educational institutions in all countries to ... 6 ... their curricula to include a study of population dynamics and policies, including where appropriate responsible parenthood and the role of population dynamics to ... 7 ... development and international relations.

Population education deals ... 8 ... present-day population problems and its demographic consequences. It aims at making children aware of the causes and consequences of uncontrolled fertility with stress on developing ... 9 ... towards planned parenthood among them. Mr. D.R. Ganesan defines population education as an attempt to engender in the mind of students ... 10 ... of their demographic predicament.

1. A. discovery B. addition
C. innovation D. example
E. idea

2. A. results B. stems
C. takes place D. occurs
E. comes into account

3. A. for B. of
C. in D. with
E. against

4. A. holocaust B. catastrophe
C. devastation D. trap
E. explosion

5. A. acquainted with B. familiarized with
C. aware of D. attuned to
E. inured to

6. A. increase B. relax
C. decide D. embark upon
E. expand

7. A. socio-economic B. politico-economic
C. sociolistic D. humanistic
E. economic

8. A. out B. in
C. off D. at
E. with

9. A. positive attitudes B. healthy atmosphere
C. healthy competition D. appropriate methods
E. right instincts

10. A. knowledge B. danger
C. future D. awareness
E. area

ANSWERS

PASSAGE-1

1	2	3	4	5	6	7	8	9	10
D	B	E	C	A	E	B	E	C	E

PASSAGE-2

1	2	3	4	5	6	7	8	9	10
D	B	C	E	D	B	B	D	A	C
11	12	13							
C	C	A							

PASSAGE-3

1	2	3	4	5	6	7	8	9	10
E	A	D	A	B	B	A	B	C	C
11	12								
D	D								

PASSAGE-4

1	2	3	4	5	6	7	8	9	10
A	B	D	E	E	C	B	D	A	C

PASSAGE-5

1	2	3	4	5	6	7	8	9	10
B	E	B	D	A	D	D	D	C	A

PASSAGE-6

1	2	3	4	5	6	7	8	9	10
B	C	E	C	D	D	C	A	C	E

PASSAGE-7

1	2	3	4	5	6	7
C	B	E	D	A	A	B

PASSAGE-8

1	2	3	4	5	6	7	8	9	10
E	B	C	D	E	C	C	A	A	B

PASSAGE-9

1	2	3	4	5	6	7	8	9	10
B	D	D	A	D	E	B	D	C	A

PASSAGE-10

1	2	3	4	5	6	7	8	9	10
D	A	E	B	C	A	B	E	C	D

PASSAGE-11

1	2	3	4	5	6	7	8	9	10
D	B	A	C	C	B	B	A	E	A

PASSAGE-12

1	2	3	4	5	6	7	8	9	10
C	A	C	A	B	C	A	C	A	A

PASSAGE-13

1	2	3	4	5	6	7	8	9	10
B	C	A	D	A	C	A	C	A	B

PASSAGE-14

1	2	3	4	5	6	7	8	9	10
D	B	C	A	A	E	A	B	D	A

PASSAGE-15

1	2	3	4	5	6	7	8	9	10
A	C	A	B	D	A	C	E	B	E

PASSAGE-16

1	2	3	4	5	6	7	8	9	10
C	B	A	C	E	A	D	E	A	D

PASSAGE-17

1	2	3	4	5	6	7	8	9	10
D	A	C	D	B	C	A	B	C	B

PASSAGE-18

1	2	3	4	5	6	7	8	9	10
C	B	A	C	C	E	A	E	A	D

3

SPOTTING ERRORS

The most common errors in English are of grammar and usage of words and phrases. By regular practice, the errors can be minimised. Try and practise it in this chapter to master it.

Directions: *Read each sentence to find out whether there is any error in it. The error, if any, will be in one part of the sentence. The letter of that part is the answer. If there is no error, the answer will be 'E'. (Avoid the errors of punctuation, if any).*

1. (A) Neither of the three/(B) tables/(C) is/(D) worth purchasing./(E) No error.

2. (A) The patient/(B) died/(C) before/(D) the doctor came./(E) No error.

3. (A) The jury/(B) is/(C) divided on/(D) the issue./(E) No error.

4. (A) Has/(B) both/(C) of you/(D) been to London?/(E) No error.

5. (A) It takes/(B) five days/(C) to a letter/(D) to go from Delhi to Oslo./(E) No error.

6. (A) Half of us/(B) are free on Tuesday/(C) and other half/(D) on Thursday./(E) No error.

7. (A) If I was rich/(B) I would/(C) spend all my time travelling/(D) throughout the country./(E) No error.

8. (A) Rosy admits that/(B) she's no more/(C) a great singer/(D) than me./(E) No error.

9. (A) I ought have/(B) phoned Meena/(C) this morning/(D) but I forgot./(E) No error.

10. (A) He has been undergoing/(B) the special training course/(C) which each of the employees/(D) is required to./(E) No error.

11. (A) You must had/(B) a kind and gentle heart/(C) if you want/(D) to be a successful doctor./(E) No error.

12. (A) If you cannot/(B) sympathy with the poor,/(C) how will you be/(D) able to do social work?/(E) No error.

13. (A) He loosened his temper/(B) whenever he knows/(C) things do not take place/(D) as per his planning./(E) No error.

14. (A) They wanted money/(B) to purchase certain things/(C) for themselves and/(D) for donated to their colleagues./(E) No error.

15. (A) The children/(B) were playing/(C) besides the road/(D) in the afternoon./(E) No error.

16. (A) I could not see her face as/(B) it was covered/(C) with a vale/(D) of silken cloth./(E) No error.

17. (A) The thief was/(B) caught red handedly/(C) by the police/(D) in the crowded market./(E) No error.

18. (A) A clerk/(B) cannot make/(C) his both ends meet/(D) nowadays./(E) No error.

19. (A) The news of/(B) his father's death/(C) came as a/(D) bolt form the sky./(E) No error.

20. (A) Mohan has collected/(B) assembled on the ground/(C) and are waiting for/(D) the Principal to come./(E) No error.

21. (A) The book is making/(B) waves and the sale/(C) is quite brisk in/(D) all major cities./(E) No error.

22. (A) Well, I spend six or seven years/(B) after high school/(C) trying to find a job for me/(D) but could not succeed in it./(E) No error.

23. (A) I used to go/(B) to France/(C) seven times/(D) during the last seven years./(E) No error.

24. (A) He presented/(B) a glass venetian ashtray/(C) to his father/(D) on his birthday./(E) No error.

25. (A) He placed/(B) his books/(C) on the glass round table/(D) when he went to the library./(E) No error.

26. (A) Motivating employees with/(B) traditional authority and financial/(C) incentives have become/(D) increasingly difficult./(E) No error.

27. (A) Several issues raising/(B) in the meeting could/(C) be amicably resolved/(D) due to his tactful handling./(E) No error.

28. (A) The health workers are/(B) being tried their best/(C) to popularise/(D) preventive measures./(E) No error.
29. (A) Of the two/(B) sisters/(C) Meena is/(D) the elder./(E) No error.
30. (A) Bible/(B) can be/(C) regarded as/(D) a great./(E) No error.
31. (A) Such/(B) rules do not/(C) apply to/(D) you and I./(E) No error.
32. (A) If it will rain/(B) I shall/(C) not go/(D) to college./(E) No error.
33. (A) I am quite sorry/(B) to hear/(C) of/(D) your failure./(E) No error.
34. (A) Please wait for me/(B) until/(C) I do not/(D) come back./(E) No error.
35. (A) I, you and he/(B) should be able/(C) to manage/(D) our affairs./(E) No error.
36. (A) Shyam neither/(B) respects his father/(C) nor does not/(D) helps him financially./(E) No error.
37. (A) He is/(B) not only/(C) an honest man/(D) yet also a gentleman./(E) No error.
38. (A) All the members/(B) of his family opposed him/(C) nevertheless he stuck to/(D) his decision to go abroad./(E) No error.
39. (A) An honest man sticks/(B) to his words/(C) whereas a dishonest man/(D) violates it./(E) No error.
40. (A) If your son/(B) is not regular/(C) then he will be/(D) dismissed from service./(E) No error.
41. (A) It rained/(B) during the/(C) night for two/(D) for three hours./(E) No error.
42. (A) I'll call in/(B) and see you for/(C) a few minutes/(D) during the afternoon./(E) No error.
43. (A) I write to/(B) every of my/(C) children once/(D) a week./(E) No error.
44. (A) If the teacher/(B) is good the students/(C) will respond/(D) positively to them./(E) No error.
45. (A) I will put on/(B) a note in this regard/(C) for your consideration/(D) and necessary decision./(E) No error.
46. (A) The mission provides/(B) able service to all/(C) the needy people in this area/(D) during last few years./(E) No error.
47. (A) I am pleased to sanction/(B) one special increment/(C) to all the employees/(D) with this month./(E) No error.
48. (A) The English defeated/(B) Germans/(C) in the/(D) last world war./(E) No error.
49. (A) Newly acquired freedom/(B) is sometimes/(C) liable/(D) for abuse./(E) No error.
50. (A) Neither of the/(B) two boys/(C) were successful/(D) in the examination./(E) No error.
51. (A) Many a man/(B) were/(C) drowned/(D) in the sea./(E) No error.
52. (A) They would not/(B) have able to plan/(C) the details of the job,/(D) if you had not cooperated./(E) No error.
53. (A) In the absence of/(B) clear instructions/(C) one cannot be expected/(D) to be functioned effectively./(E) No error.
54. (A) They could have/(B) helped him/(C) had they approached by him,/(D) for help well in advance./(E) No error.
55. (A) He has in/(B) his possession a/(C) price collection of very old coins/(D) and some ancient paintings./(E) No error.
56. (A) Rakesh recommended for me/(B) to the officer/(C) for a/(D) promotion./(E) No error.
57. (A) The child/(B) begged pardon/(C) from his father/(D) for his coming late./(E) No error.
58. (A) Though you have/(B) a strong body/(C) but you are/(D) a coward./(E) No error.
59. (A) Do keep us/(B) informed/(C) as mother is anxious/(D) for your welfare./(E) No error.
60. (A) I am writing/(B) a letter/(C) with green ink/(D) to my brother./(E) No error.
61. (A) They went/(B) to Faizabad/(C) in bus/(D) yesterday./(E) No error.
62. (A) She congratulated/(B) me for/(C) my promotion/(D) in the office./(E) No error.
63. (A) Everyone agrees/(B) that Kalidas/(C) is Shakespeare/(D) of India./(E) No error.
64. (A) I have been/(B) writing/(C) this book/(D) from Monday./(E) No error.
65. (A) I am suffering/(B) from fever/(C) for/(D) the past three days./(E) No error.
66. (A) The English/(B) is the mother tongue/(C) of the/(D) English./(E) No error.
67. (A) I have not eaten/(B) bananas/(C) since/(D) I have been a child./(E) No error.
68. (A) Foolishly Rajani opened/(B) the cooker when/(C) it was full steam/(D) and burnt her hands./(E) No error.
69. (A) From a tiny room in/(B) the slums, they have/(C) managed to move to a good/(D) house in a better locality./(E) No error.
70. (A) Even if the doctor/(B) put in his best efforts, he/(C) could not succeed in/(D) saving the patient./(E) No error.
71. (A) Yesterday, a visitor to/(B) the part was attacked/(C) by a tiger and/(D) had to hospitalise./(E) No error.
72. (A) You, he and I/(B) should/(C) beat/(D) him./(E) No error.

73. (A) Somnathan/(B) and Bhushan's books/(C) are/(D) worth praising./(E) No error.

74. (A) This house is/(B) built of/(C) bricks/(D) and not of stones./(E) No error.

75. (A) I do not/(B) remember/(C) the date of him/(D) leaving India./(E) No error.

76. (A) I could not find/(B) it anywhere/(C) Where is/(D) my letter's envelope?/(E) No error.

77. (A) Even at/(B) this age/(C) his hair is/(D) not grey./(E) No error.

78. (A) He has/(B) bought/(C) new furnitures/(D) for his flat./(E) No error.

79. (A) It's very/(B) kind of you/(C) to help Surinder/(D) in such a manner./(E) No error.

80. (A) His father was/(B) angry with/(C) his leaving/(D) the house in the night./(E) No error.

81. (A) We think that/(B) it is no use/(C) to go there/(D) at this late hour./(E) No error.

82. (A) The aim and the object/(B) of his association/(C) is to help/(D) the poor./(E) No error.

83. (A) This factory/(B) is not worth/(C) buying for/(D) ninety five thousand rupees./(E) No error.

84. (A) Each cigarette/(B) a person smoke/(C) does some harm and eventually/(D) it may cause a serious disease./(E) No error.

85. (A) This is one of/(B) the most interesting book/(C) I have/(D) ever read./(E) No error.

86. (A) In my opinion/(B) the balance sheet exhibits/(C) a true and fair/(D) view of the state of affairs of the bank./(E) No error.

87. (A) He neglects/(B) attending lectures/(C) regularly/(D) though college was only a few yards away from his house./(E) No error.

88. (A) We have helped them not only/(B) with money but also/(C) with new machinery/(D) and raw material./(E) No error.

89. (A) Sudha wished/(B) to thoroughly revise/(C) her plan/(D) to construct a new house./(E) No error.

90. (A) Neither he came/(B) nor did he/(C) send the money/(D) through his brother./(E) No error.

91. (A) See these words/(B) in the dictionary/(C) and write down/(D) their meanings./(E) No error.

92. (A) Two of those/(B) dreaded dacoits/(C) were hung/(D) by the neck./(E) No error.

93. (A) The school/(B) is too much small/(C) to accommodate/(D) all the students./(E) No error.

94. (A) I am/(B) quite sorry/(C) to learn about/(D) the death of your father./(E) No error.

95. (A) I went to see/(B) the film because/(C) he had told me/(D) that it was too good./(E) No error.

96. (A) Everybody says that/(B) Lucy resembles with/(C) her mother/(D) a lot./(E) No error.

97. (A) For hours/(B) I discussed on/(C) this point with him/(D) but he could not decide anything./(E) No error.

98. (A) The last year proved/(B) quite bad/(C) as major industries/(D) witness lot of problems./(E) No error.

99. (A) I offered him part-time work/(B) but he turned it over/(C) saying that he would/(D) rather wait for a full-time job./(E) No error.

100. (A) The foremost criterion of selection we adopted/(B) were the number of years of training/(C) a dancer had received/(D) under a particular guru./(E) No error.

101. (A) He fixed a metal ladder/(B) for the wall below his window/(C) so as to be able to/(D) escape if there was a fire./(E) No error.

102. (A) Scarcely had I/(B) finished washing the car/(C) than the master came/(D) and asked me to clean the floor of the house./(E) No error.

103. (A) Students/(B) as well as the teacher/(C) was/(D) playing./(E) No error.

104. (A) Neither Ram/(B) nor Shyam/(C) are/(D) at fault./(E) No error.

105. (A) Neither women/(B) nor/(C) children/(D) was admitted./(E) No error.

106. (A) If I shall /(B) go to Calcutta/(C) I shall bring/(D) a beautiful watch for you./(E) No error.

107. (A) I told him that/(B) he could/(C) go home/(D) by all mean./(E) No error.

108. (A) After the death/(B) of their father/(C) the two brothers are/(D) having their hand at the daggers./(E) No error.

109. (A) He added insult/(B) to his wounds/(C) by making/(D) sarcastic comments./(E) No error.

110. (A) He has achieved/(B) success in life/(C) from dint of/(D) hard work./(E) No error.

111. (A) He burnt a fire/(B) and started/(C) roasting/(D) the chicken./(E) No error.

112. (A) I have written/(B) a letter/(C) at him to his Delhi address/(D) today./(E) No error.

113. (A) His favourite maxim/(B) is — cut your shirt/(C) according/(D) to the cloth./(E) No error.

114. (A) His brother/(B) Dharmender is/(C) an excellent cook/(D) is it not?/(E) No error.

115. (A) I have/(B) brought a/(C) he-duck and a she-duck/(D) for my friend./(E) No error.

116. (A) Later on he/(B) became a monk/(C) and she became/(D) a monkess./(E) No error.

117. (A) By arresting the local criminals/(B) and encouraging good people/(C) we can end/(D) hostilities of that area./(E) No error.

118. (A) The apparently obvious solutions/(B) to most of his problems/(C) were overlook by/(D) many of his friends./(E) No error.

119. (A) We decided not tell to/(B) the patient about/(C) the disease he was/(D) suffering from./(E) No error.

120. (A) The principals of equal justice/(B) for all is one of/(C) the cornerstones of our/(D) democratic way of life./(E) No error.

121. (A) The Trust has succeeded/(B) admirably in raising/ (C) money for/(D) its future programmes./(E) No error.

122. (A) Honesty, integrity and being intelligent/(B) are the qualities which/(C) we look for when/(D) we interview applicants./(E) No error.

123. (A) In order to save petrol,/(B) motorists must have to/(C) be very cautious/(D) while driving along the highways./(E) No error.

124. (A) The war of/(B) Panipat was/(C) won by/(D) Babar in 1526./(E) No error.

125. (A) He applied the break/(B) to stop the scooter/(C) and averted/(D) the accident./(E) No error.

126. (A) He has recruited/(B) many persons/(C) to canvas for him/(D) during the forthcoming elections./(E) No error.

127. (A) His father is/(B) suffering from/(C) a serious heart attack/(D) and his death is eminent./(E) No error.

128. (A) Ram and Ramesh are/(B) fast friends/(C) the farmer is a merchant/(D) and the latter is an officer./(E) No error.

129. (A) It is a fact/(B) that Ferozepore is/(C) further than/ (D) Faridkot from Delhi./(E) No error,

130. (A) I feel that/(B) I have given you/(C) very trouble/ (D) in this matter./(E) No error.

131. (A) These two brothers/(B) cannot live without/(C) one another/(D) for a long time./(E) No error.

132. (A) I shall/(B) do your work/(C) in these holidays/(D) without fail./(E) No error.

133. (A) Hindustan Times/(B) of Delhi/(C) is the best/(D) newspaper in India./(E) No error.

134. (A) Gold of South Africa/(B) is exported to/(C) many/ (D) countries./(E) No error.

135. (A) The chairman/(B) as well as six other/(C) members of the committee/(D) were present./(E) No error.

136. (A) Whether he will be/(B) able to come/(C) or may not/(D) depends on the train service./(E) No error.

137. (A) He requested/(B) the director/(C) to admit his son/ (D) in his institution./(E) No error.

138. (A) On his way back/(B) he was absorbed with/(C) his own/(D) thoughts./(E) No error.

139. (A) She had no sooner/(B) arrived than/(C) she was asked/(D) to leave again./(E) No error.

140. (A) He counted the books/(B) to make sure that/(C) none of them/(D) were missing./(E) No error.

141. (A) Buses run along this road/(B) but today/(C) they didn't run/(D) because of a strike./(E) No error.

142. (A) This book is/(B) well printed and attractively bound/ (C) making altogether/(D) an attractive volume./(E) No error.

143. (A) I/(B) am thinking/(C) you are/(D) over reacting./ (E) No error.

144. (A) Tushar was trying for admission/(B) in the Medical College/(C) even though his parents wanted him/(D) to take up computers./(E) No error.

145. (A) The weather being cold and stormy/(B) we decided not to go out/(C) for the whole day and/(D) stayed indoors./(E) No error.

146. (A) The old man was leading/(B) a happy and leisurely/ (C) life after his retirement/(D) from service./(E) No error.

147. (A) Normally I don't wear spectacles/(B) but today/(C) I wear one /(D) because of the sun./(E) No error.

148. (A) A little elder/(B) to myself me,/(C) both were devoted /(D) to tennis and football./(E) No error.

149. (A) You can get/(B) all the informations/(C) you want/ (D) in this book./(E) No error.

150. (A) He was/(B) such a fast writer that/(C) he used to write a story/(D) during two hours./(E) No error.

151. (A) He took/(B) computer/(C) coaching for three full/ (D) academic years./(E) No error.

152. (A) The government has shown /(B) a lukewarm attitude/ (C) to the sufferings of /(D) the aged./(E) No error.

153. (A) It is the duty of the government /(B) of taking up measures/(C) for providing social care welfare/(D) to the old people./(E) No error.

154. (A) He is possessing/(B) this apartment/(C) for the last/ (D) five years./(E) No error.

155. (A) This company/(B) manufactures/(C) many/ (D) cold drinks./(E) No error.

156. (A) Next summer/(B) there is a chance/(C) of my visiting /(D) a hill station./(E) No error.

157. (A) The boy sitting /(B)at the corner of the classroom /(C) is constantly/(D) watching at the window./(E) No error.

158. (A) Our laxity/(B) in duty increases /(C) with our dislike/ (D) for work./(E) No error.

159. (A) His /(B) knowledge /(C) of English are /(D) very limited./(E) No error.

160. (A) How to solve the financial crisis /(B) is the main concern/(C) of the government/(D) at the moment./(E) No error.

161. (A) Everyone of the survivors /(B) of the train accident/ (C) have told/(D) the same story./(E) No error.

162. (A) Each cigarette/(B) which /(C) a person smokes/(D) does some harm to him./(E) No error.

163. (A) As soon as the Managing Director/(B) entered the factory/(C) all the workers approached him and /(D) report the matter./(E) No error.

164. (A) He studied /(B) at /(C) the Medical College/(D) during three years./(E) No error.

165. (A) This is /(B) the painting/(C) I was /(D) telling you./ (E) No error.

166. (A) The mother as well as /(B) the daughters were/(C) mysteriously missing /(D) from the house./(E) No error.

167. (A) It is/(B) extremely important /(C) for an engineer / (D) to know to use a computer./(E) No error.

168. (A) The Director has asked that/(B) each clerk and supervisor/(C) sign their name on the attendance register/(D) before leaving the office./(E) No error.

169. (A) In India/(B) as early as the nineteenth century, /(C) young boys enjoyed/(D) to play cricket./(E) No error.

170. (A) She is /(B) more clever /(C) than/(D) I thought she was./(E) No error.

171. (A) A body of volunteers/(B) have been/(C) organised to assist the committee/(D) in their attempt to collect funds./(E) No error.

172. (A) The blue curtain/(B) on the window/(C) provides an appropriate contrast/(D) with the pink wall./(E) No error.

173. (A) Her ability to/(B) interact and communicate with strangers/(C) is one of her/(D) stronger points./(E) No error.

174. (A) If he will follow/(B) his teacher's instructions/ (C) he will secure good marks/(D) in his examination./(E) No error.

175. (A) Sooner than she had arrived /(B) her friends arranged a dinner /(C) in her honour in the/(D) best restaurant in town./(E) No error.

176. (A) Ever since this child/(B) was taught by/(C) its new tutor/(D) it has done in exams./(E) No error.

177. (A) Children ran/(B) into the school building/(C) when/(D) the bell started ringing./(E) No error.

178. (A) To the volunteers/(B) who worked so hard/ (C) on campaigning, the election result was profound/(D) disappointing./(E) No error.

179. (A) It is essential that/(B) AIDS is diagnosed and treated/ (C) as early as possible in order/(D) to achieve a successful cure./(E) No error.

180. (A) There has been/(B) little change in the patient's condition /(C) until he was/(D) shifted to the intensive care unit./(E) No error.

181. (A) We have heard his speech/(B) many a time/(C) but today he was/(D) best./(E) No error.

182. (A) The people gathered there /(B) were very much surprised /(C) at hearing the news of a child surviving/ (D) under the debris./(E) No error.

183. (A) Each of the candidates whom/(B) I have chosen to contest election /(C) have indicated that/(D) he will be happy to do so./(E) No error.

184. (A) The alarmed report of/(B) earthquake in Ahmedabad /(C) frightened everyone of /(D) the adjoining region./(E) No error.

185. (A) While interrogating, he disclosed/(B) that he used to snatch chains/(C) along with his accomplice/(D) who was recently killed in a road accident./(E) No error.

186. (A) The burning of leaves/(B) have been/(C) declared illegal in Delhi /(D) due to the pollution it causes./(E) No error.

187. (A) The decomposed body of a 13-year old boy /(B) who was /(C) suspected to have been kidnapped,/(D) was find lying./(E) No error.

188. (A) On hearing/(B) Gurmeet's screams, Surjeet/(C) came rushing /(D) and he too was stabbed./(E) No error.

189. (A) The value of the rupee/(B) declines/(C) as the rate of inflation /(D) raises./(E) No error.

190. (A) Before T.V., the common man haven't got/ (B) the opportunity /(C) to see his leaders /(D) express their views./(E) No error.

191. (A) The new model of the washing machine/(B) costs/ (C) twice as much as/(D) last year's model./(E) No error.

192. (A) He hoped to finish/(B) the assignment /(C) in the last month/(D) but in fact he could not./(E) No error.

193. (A) Everybody/(B) was in the lawn/(C) enjoying/ (D) themselves./(E) No error.

194. (A) Nobody offered to give up /(B) their seat /(C) to the blind man /(D) holding his stick in his palm./(E) No error.

195. (A) Subhash Chandra Bose/(B) was a great nationalist/ (C) and a/(D) great scholar./(E) No error.

196. (A) If you would have seen/(B) yesterday's cultural programme,/(C) I am sure you /(D) would have enjoyed watching the little ones dance./(E) No error.

197. (A) In evaluating your progress/(B) I have taken/(C) into account your classroom performance, your attendance, your sincerity and /(D) how you have improved./(E) No error.

198. (A) Although the marks/(B) obtained in written examination by both the candidates/(C) are same yet the/(D) differences among them are considerable in the marks obtained in interview./(E) No error.

199. (A) Aristotle systematically /(B) set out the various forms of the syllogism/(C) that has remained /(D) an essential reference for logic./(E) No error.

200. (A) The lucky number will be announced/(B) just one time; therefore,/(C) you must listen /(D) very careful in order to tally your own number./(E) No error.

Answers

1	2	3	4	5	6	7	8	9	10
A	B	B	A	C	C	A	D	A	D
11	12	13	14	15	16	17	18	19	20
A	B	A	D	C	C	B	C	E	C
21	22	23	24	25	26	27	28	29	30
C	A	A	B	C	C	A	B	D	A
31	32	33	34	35	36	37	38	39	40
D	A	A	C	A	C	D	E	E	C
41	42	43	44	45	46	47	48	49	50
E	E	B	D	A	A	D	B	D	A
51	52	53	54	55	56	57	58	59	60
B	B	D	C	C	A	C	C	D	C
61	62	63	64	65	66	67	68	69	70
C	B	C	D	A	C	D	C	C	A
71	72	73	74	75	76	77	78	79	80
D	A	A	C	C	D	E	C	E	B
81	82	83	84	85	86	87	88	89	90
C	A	E	B	B	E	D	E	D	A
91	92	93	94	95	96	97	98	99	100
A	C	B	B	D	B	B	D	B	B
101	102	103	104	105	106	107	108	109	110
B	C	C	A	D	A	D	D	B	C
111	112	113	114	115	116	117	118	119	120
A	C	B	D	C	C	C	C	A	A
121	122	123	124	125	126	127	128	129	130
E	A	B	A	A	D	D	C	C	E
131	132	133	134	135	136	137	138	139	140
C	C	A	A	D	C	D	B	A	D
141	142	143	144	145	146	147	148	149	150
C	C	B	B	D	A	C	B	D	D
151	152	153	154	155	156	157	158	159	160
A	E	B	A	C	E	D	D	C	E
161	162	163	164	165	166	167	168	169	170
C	B	D	D	D	B	D	C	D	C
171	172	173	174	175	176	177	178	179	180
B	D	D	A	A	B	E	D	B	C
181	182	183	184	185	186	187	188	189	190
D	C	C	A	A	B	D	A	D	A
191	192	193	194	195	196	197	198	199	200
E	A	D	B	D	A	D	D	C	D

4

SENTENCE CORRECTIONS

One may use the same words in many ways but the best way is only one that makes the perfect usage of the words and conveys the proper meaning of the expression. Try it yourself in the following questions.

Directions: *Which of the phrases A, B, C and D given below each sentence should replace the phrase printed in bold type to make the sentence gramatically correct? If the sentence is correct as it is then mark 'E' as the answer.*

1. If Indian people are united, this nation **can become a source of** strength for the entire world.
A. could become a resource of
B. can become resourceful for
C. would be a source in
D. can become a source with
E. No correction required

2. All their efforts **were direct to** promote harmony among various groups of people.
A. were directing to B. were directed at
C. have directed for D. were directed to
E. No correction required

3. What did happen there in the first place is not a matter of our concern.
A. What happens
B. What would have happened
C. What happened
D. What should have happened
E. No correction required

4. The speaker highlighted the contribution of women **for bringing about** social changes.
A. for bringing in B. in bringing of
C. for the brought over D. in bringing about
E. No correction required

5. Such inequalities **can be founded** enshrined in the constitutions of other countries also.
A. could have been founded
B. can be found
C. could be founded
D. could have found
E. No correction required

6. The local authorities **were never bothering to** care about the unfortunate happenings.
A. were never bothered to
B. never bothered to
C. never were bothering to
D. were never bothering to
E. No correction required

7. India's outlook on the world **is composing of** these various elements.
A. is composed of
B. is composed by
C. is composing with
D. has been composing at
E. No correction required

8. How religious intolerance can blight social peace and harmony can be gauged from events **take place around** the globe.
A. taken place over B. taking place around
C. took place around D. taken place in
E. No correction required

9. This exploitation of the helpless tribals **need to be condemned.**
A. need to be condemned
B. needs condemnation
C. needs to be condemned
D. need to condemnation
E. No correction required

10. The fact finding team **which had been to** the area found villagers giving information to police.
A. which had been for B. that led to
C. which led to D. that has been to
E. No correction required

11. **Despite being tried his best** to persuade people to give up smoking, he could not attain success.
A. Despite his best trialing
B. Despite of his best
C. Inspite of being tried his best
D. Despite trying his best
E. No correction required

12. His suggestion were so **trivial and hence** nobody took any cognizance of them.
A. so trivial that and have
B. very trivial and hence to
C. too trivial to and hence
D. very trivial and hence
E. No correction required

13. Even on most critical moments, he is calm, but today he **appears very much disturbed.**
A. appeared very much disturb
B. appears very much to disturb
C. appeared to be very much disturbing
D. is appearing very much disturbing
E. No correction required

14. He failed in his attempt to disperse the mob before the miscreants **sets the fire on the bus**.
A. set the bus on fire
B. setting fire on the bus
C. set fire to the bus
D. set the fire on to the bus
E. No correction required

15. **But for your time of helping,** we could not have accomplished our goal in such a small time span.
A. But for your timely help
B. Because of your timely helping
C. Despite your time of helping
D. But your time for helping
E. No correction required

16. In our country women **have opportunities to rise** to the top in every walk of life.
A. have been having opportunities
B. have has opportunities for a raise
C. have opportunities to rise
D. having opportunities to rise
E. No correction required

17. Any one **who known to India's villages knows** the meaning of scarcity.
A. knowing India's villages knows
B. is known to India's villages knows
C. knows India's villages knows
D. knew India's villages knowing
E. No correction required

18. For every citizen it is mandatory to help the civic administration **for keep us the city clean.**
A. for upkeep clean the city
B. for clean and keep the city
C. for keeping of the city cleanliness
D. to keep the city clean
E. No correction required

19. How can one mobilize support from colleagues without **being cordially to** them?
A. being cordially for
B. been cordially to
C. being cordial to
D. cordially being to
E. No correction required

20. Their attempt of rioting was foiled because **of the police squad arrived** on time.
A. of the police squad being arrived
B. of the arrival of the police squad
C. the police squad arrival
D. of the police squad had arrived
E. No correction required

21. Though we **have kept in mind to try and maintain** most facilities, we would like to request you to kindly bear with us any inconvenience that may be caused.
A. must keep in mind to try and maintain
B. have kept in mind trying and maintain
C. would keep in mind to try and maintain
D. should have kept in mind to try and to maintain
E. No correction required

22. The tea-estate administration is **in such mess there** is not leader to set the things right.
A. in such a mess here
B. in a such mess that here
C. in such a mess that there
D. with such a mess that there
E. No correction required

23. We met him immediately after the session in which he **had been given** a nice speech.
A. would be giving
B. has been given
C. will have given
D. had given
E. No correction required

24. The moment the manager came to know of the fraudulent action of his assistant, he **order immediately dismissed him.**
A. immediately ordered his dismissed
B. ordered his immediate dismissal
C. immediately order dismissal of his
D. ordered for immediately dismissal him
E. No correction required

25. The drama had many scenes which were so humorous that it was **hardly possible to keep** a straight face.
A. hardly possible for keeping
B. hardly impossible keeping
C. hardly impossible to keep
D. hardly possible keeping
E. No correction required

26. He confidently asked the crowd if they thought he was right and the crowd shouted **that they did.**
A. that he did B. that they had
C. that they had D. that he didn't
E. No correction required

27. Acquisition of certain specific skills **can be facilitated from** general awareness, education and exposures to novel situations.
A. can be facilitated by
B. may facilitate through
C. can be felicitated with
D. may be felicitated with
E. No correction required

28. The man who has committed such a serious crime must **get the mostly severe** punishment.
A. be getting the mostly severely
B. get the most severe
C. have got the most severely
D. have been getting the severemost
E. No correction required

29. The research study is an eye-opener and **attempts to acquaint** us with the problems of the poor nations.
A. attempted to acquaint
B. attempts at acquainting
C. attempt to acquaint
D. attempting to acquaint
E. No correction required

30. **If I would have** realised the nature of the job earlier, I would not have accepted it.
A. If I have had B. In case I would have
C. Had I been D. had I
E. No correction required

31. He could not give a **good explanation for** his extra-ordinary behaviour.
A. account for B. be satisfied with
C. provide evidence D. count on
E. No correction required

32. **Those who pass through this gate without permission** will be prosecuted.
A. bypassers B. absconders
C. thoroughfares D. trespassers
E. No correction required

33. **A careful preservation and protection** of wild life is the need of the hour.
A. management B. embarkment
C. enhancement D. conservation
E. No correction required

34. I could achieve success through **conscious efforts.**
A. efforts made with critical awareness
B. tremendous efforts
C. efforts done after gaining consciousness
D. efforts done after being awakened
E. No correction required

35. We are **looking forward to** a good winter this year
A. predicting B. getting
C. expecting D. visualising
E. No correction required

36. **Supposing if he fails** again, will he be able to hold his head high?
A. Suppose he fails B. Suppose if he fails
C. Supposing he will fail D. Supposing if he fail
E. No correction required

37. **I have been knocking** at the door five times; I don't think anybody is in.
A. I am knocking B. I had been knocking
C. I have knocked D. I knocked
E. No correction required

38. Unless you stop **to interfere** in the matter, I'll go away.
A. by interfering B. from interfering
C. interfering D. in interfering
E. No correction required

39. A man's modesty is **in inverse proportion with** his ignorance.
A. with inverse proportion to
B. in inverse proportion to
C. at inverse proportion with
D. on inverse proportion at
E. No correction required

40. They will come if you **will invite** them.
A. would invite B. invite
C. did invite D. should
E. No correction required

41. The jury could not arrive at any decision **in the strength of** scanty evidence.
A. with the strength of
B. on the strength of
C. on strength with
D. upon the strength of
E. No correction required

42. We have read that book, **haven't we?**
A. isn't it? B. didn't we?
C. have we? D. don't we
E. No correction required

43. If only **I knew earlier** I would have sent a telegram
A. I had known earlier
B. I know earlier
C. I had been knowing earlier
D. I was knowing earlier
E. No correction required

44. **I never in all my life have heard** such nonsense!
A. I have never heard in all my life
B. Never in all my life have I heard
C. Never I have heard in all my life
D. I have never in all my life heard
E. No correction required

45. Scarcely had the people retired **than** the earthquake shook the whole area.

A. that B. when
C. while D. then
E. No correction required

46. The river **has overflown** its banks on account of the flood.

A. has overflowed B. overflew
C. had overflown D. have overflown
E. No correction required

47. Susheela **availed herself of** all the leave to her credit.

A. availed of B. availed
C. availed for D. availed her
E. No correction required

48. By the time the programme gets under way you **would know** the joy of having planned it.

A. will have known B. had known
C. could know D. have known
E. No correction required

49. He asked me **what I am doing.**

A. that what I was doing
B. what I was doing
C. what was I doing
D. what am I doing
E. No correction required

50. The doctor is not sure whether the patient died **from cholera or of over-eating.**

A. of cholera or of over-eating
B. of cholera or because of over-eating
C. from cholera or from over-eating
D. with cholera or with over-eating
E. No correction required

51. You can make **alternate** arrangements if you are going to be on leave.

A. alternating B. altering
C. alternative D. alteration
E. No correction required

52. Everything **depend upon them coming** on time.

A. depends upon them coming
B. depends upon them come
C. depends upon their coming
D. depending upon their coming
E. No correction required

53. Primitive man **believing that a crime created** an imbalance which could be rectified only by punishing the wrong-doer.

A. believes that a crime created
B. believed that a crime created
C. believed that a criminal created
D. believed that a crime creates
E. No correction required

54. The more we look at these carvings, **the more life we perceive hidden** within them.

A. the life we perceive more hidden
B. we perceive life more hidden
C. more than life we perceive hidden
D. we perceive life more than hidden
E. No correction required

55. In 1996, India exported twice as much of its national output of sugar **as that had** in 1986.

A. than it had B. than it did
C. as that had D. as it did
E. No correction required

56. We should realise that the chance of an accident **may be as great or greater in our homes than** in a train or on the road.

A. may be at least as great in our home as
B. was at least as great as in our homes
C. can be as great or greater in our homes than
D. may be at least as great or greater in our homes than
E. No correction required

57. It is difficult to prevent assault against environment as those **that are against** animals.

A. those against
B. it is against
C. preventing those against
D. it is to prevent those against
E. No correction required

58. By failing to keep his promise the candidate will earn the distrust of all the voters.

A. Because the candidate failed, he
B. If the candidate has failed, he
C. Since the candidate failed, he
D. If the candidate fails, he
E. No correction required

59. Because of scientific progress, we **expect to life better than our parents have.**

A. should expect to live better than our parents
B. expect to live as good as our parents lived
C. expect to live better than our parents did
D. expected to live better than our parents
E. No correction required

60. Most of the boys and girls like to **see these kind of movies.**

A. this kind of movies
B. this kinds of movies
C. these kind of movie
D. this kind of movie
E. No correction required

61. Calamities and indigence in the past **was afflicting more** than at present.

A. were more afflicting
B. was afflicted more
C. we more afflict
D. was afflict more
E. No correction required

62. As there was no time, the remaining items **were deferred into** the next meeting.
A. are deferred till
B. were deferred till
C. were deferred to
D. had deferred with
E. No correction required

63. **Leaving aside little room for** misinterpretation, the senior politician offered clarification about his role in the party elections.
A. Leaving little room for
B. Leaving for little room to
C. Leaving less room for
D. Having left less room for
E. No correction required

64. The principal lamented that though a detailed report was submitted to the management a month ago **no action is being took** so far.
A. no action had taken
B. no action was being taken
C. no action has been taken
D. any action had been taken
E. No correction required

65. We **must make for** our foreign policy on the basis of guarding national interest alone.
A. have made for
B. must be making to
C. must make
D. must make to
E. No correction required

66. I am **absolute confident what** we are going to move forward strongly.
A. absolutely confidence that
B. absolutely confident what
C. absolute confidential what
D. absolutely confident that
E. No correction required

67. One of the men gave first aid to Nitesh **who is injured** in a road accident.
A. which was injured
B. who had injured
C. as he was to injure
D. who was injured
E. No correction required

68. The quality of food served in this hotel is so poor that no respectable person **would want to eat** over here.
A. will want to eat
B. will have wanted to eat
C. will be wanting to eat
D. will want to have eaten
E. No correction required

69. Shilpa was going to the temple **then Jyoti came on** meet her.
A. when Jyoti was coming on to
B. when Jyoti came to
C. before Jyoti was coming to
D. after Jyoti was coming to
E. No correction required

70. The more we look at these carvings, **the more life we perceive hidden** within them.
A. the life we perceive more hidden
B. we perceive life more hidden
C. more than life we perceive hidden
D. we perceive life more than hidden
E. No correction required

ANSWERS

1	2	3	4	5	6	7	8	9	10
E	D	C	D	B	A	A	B	B	E
11	**12**	**13**	**14**	**15**	**16**	**17**	**18**	**19**	**20**
D	D	E	A	A	E	C	D	C	B
21	**22**	**23**	**24**	**25**	**26**	**27**	**28**	**29**	**30**
E	C	D	B	E	E	A	B	B	D
31	**32**	**33**	**34**	**35**	**36**	**37**	**38**	**39**	**40**
A	D	D	A	C	A	C	C	B	B
41	**42**	**43**	**44**	**45**	**46**	**47**	**48**	**49**	**50**
B	E	A	B	B	A	E	A	B	A
51	**52**	**53**	**54**	**55**	**56**	**57**	**58**	**59**	**60**
C	C	C	E	D	A	D	E	C	A
61	**62**	**63**	**64**	**65**	**66**	**67**	**68**	**69**	**70**
A	B	A	C	C	D	D	E	B	E

5

SENTENCE REARRANGEMENT

A paragraph is formed from sentences, it will convey its true meaning and purpose only when the sentences are arranged in a proper manner. Try and practise it.

Directions: *In these questions, each passage consists of six sentences. The first and the sixth sentences are given in the beginning as S_1 and S_6 respectively. The middle four sentences in each passage have been removed and jumbled up. These are labelled P, Q, R and S. Choose the proper sequence of the four sentences P, Q, R, and S from the alternatives A, B, C, D and E.*

1. S_1 : She said on the phone that she would report for duty next day.

S_6 : Eventually we reported to the police.

P : We waited for a few days, then we decided to go to her place.

Q : But she did not.

R : We found it locked.

S : Even after that we waited for her for quite a few days.

The proper sequence should be:

A. P R S Q B. Q P S R

C. Q P R S D. S Q P R

E. R P S Q

2. S_1 : A force of attraction exists between everybody in the universe.

S_6 : The greater the mass, the greater is the earth's force of attraction on it—we call this force of attraction gravity.

P : Normally it is very small but when one of the bodies is a planet, like the earth, the force is considerable.

Q : It has been investigated by many scientists including Galileo and Newton.

R : Everything on or near the surface of the earth is attracted by the mass of the earth.

S : This gravitational force depends on the mass of the bodies involved.

The proper sequence should be:

A. P R Q S B. P R S Q

C. Q S R P D. Q S P R

E. R P S Q

3. S_1 : Metals are today being replaced by polymers in many applications.

S_6 : Many Indian Institutes of Science and Technology run special programmes on polymer science.

P : Above all, they are cheaper and easier to process, making them a viable alternative to metals.

Q : Polymers are essentially long chains of hydrocarbon molecules.

R : Today polymers as strong as metals have been developed.

S : These have replaced the traditional chromium-plated metallic bumpers in cars.

The proper sequence should be:

A. Q R S P B. R S Q P

C. R Q S P D. Q R P S

E. P Q R S

4. S_1 : It is regrettable that there is widespread corruption in the country at all levels.

S_6 : This is indeed a tragedy of great magnitude.

P : So there is hardly anything that the government can do about it now.

Q : And there are graft and other malpractices too.

R : The impression that corruption is a universal phenomenon persists and the people do not cooperate in checking this evil.

S : Recently several offenders were brought to book, but they were not given deterrent punishment.

The proper sequence should be:

A. Q S R P B. S Q R P

C. R S Q P D. P Q S R

E. P Q R S

5. S_1 : It was a dark moonless night.
S_6 : They all seemed to him to be poor and ordinary—mere childish words.
P : He turned over the pages, reading passages here and there.
Q : He heard them on the floor.
R : The poet took down his books of poems from his shelves.
S : Some of them contained his earliest writings which he had almost forgotten.
The proper sequence should be:
A. R P Q S B. R Q S P
C. R S P Q D. R P S Q
E. P Q R S

6. S_1 : A noise started above their heads.
S_6 : Nearly two hundred lives were lost on the fateful day.
P : But people did not take it seriously.
Q : That was to show everyone that there was something wrong.
R : It was a dangerous thing to do.
S : For, within minutes the ship began to sink.
The proper sequence should be:
A. P Q S R B. P R Q S
C. Q P R S D. Q P S R
E. P Q R S

7. S_1 : The cooperative system of doing business is a good way of encouraging ordinary workers to work hard.
S_6 : The main object is to maintain the interest of every member of the society and to ensure that the members participate actively in the projects of the society.
P : If the society is to be well run, it is necessary to prevent insincere officials being elected to the committee which is solely responsible for the running of the business.
Q : They get this from experienced and professional workers who are not only familiar with the cooperative system, but also with efficient methods of doing business.
R : To a large extent, many cooperative societies need advice and guidance.
S : The capital necessary to start a business venture is obtained by the workers' contributions.
The proper sequence should be:
A. S Q P R B. P Q S R
C. S R Q P D. P S R Q
E. R S P Q

8. S_1 : American private lives may seem shallow.
S_6 : This would not happen in China, he said.
P : Students would walk away with books they had not paid for.
Q : A Chinese journalist commented on a curious institution: the library.
R : Their public morality, however, impressed visitors.
S : But in general they returned them.
The proper sequence should be:
A. P S Q R B. Q P S R
C. R Q P S D. R P S Q
E. S R P Q

9. S_1 : The *Bhagavadgita* recognises the nature of man and the needs of man.
S_6 : A man who does not harmonise them, is not truly human.
P : All these three aspects constitute the nature of man.
Q : It shows how the human being is a rational one, an ethical one and a spiritual one.
R : More than all, it must be a spiritual experience.
S : Nothing can give him fulfilment unless it satisfies his reason, his ethical conscience.
The proper sequence should be:
A. P S R Q B. R S P Q
C. Q P S R D. P S Q R
E. S R P Q

10. S_1 : I usually sleep quite well in the train, but this time I slept only a little.
S_6 : It was shut all night, as usual.
P : Most people wanted it shut and I wanted it open.
Q : As usual, I got angry about the window.
R : The quarrel left me completely upset.
S : There were too many people and too much luggage all around.
The proper sequence should be:
A. R S Q P B. S Q P R
C. S Q R P D. R S P Q
E. P Q R S

11. S_1 : For decades, American society has been called a melting pot.
S_6 : In recent years, such differences—accentuated by the arrival of immigrants from Asia and other parts of the world in the United States—have become something to celebrate and to nurture.
P : Differences remained—in appearance, mannerisms, customs, speech, religion and more.
Q : The term has long been a cliche, and a half-truth.
R : But homogenisation was never achieved.
S : Yes, immigrants from diverse cultures and traditions did cast off vestiges of their native lands and become almost imperceptibly woven into the American fabric.

The proper sequence should be:

A. Q R S P B. S Q R P

C. S Q P R D. Q S R P

E. P Q R S

12. S_1 : While talking to a group, one should feel self-confident and courageous.

S_6 : Any man can develop his capacity if he has the desire to do so.

P : Nor is it a gift bestowed by Providence on only a few.

Q : One should also learn how to think calmly and clearly.

R : It is like the ability to play golf.

S : It is not as difficult as most men imagine.

The proper sequence should be:

A. S Q P R B. Q S P R

C. Q R S P D. R S Q P

E. P Q R S

13. S_1 : In 1934, William Golding published a small volume of poems.

S_6 : But *Lord of the Flies* which came out in 1954 was welcomed as "a most absorbing and instructive tale".

P : During the World War II (1939-45) he joined the Royal Navy and was present at the sinking of the *Bismarck.*

Q : He returned to teaching in 1945 and gave it up in 1962, and is now a full-time writer.

R : In 1939, he married and started teaching at Bishop Wordsworth's School in Salisbury.

S : At first his novels were not accepted.

The proper sequence should be:

A. R P Q S B. R P S Q

C. S R P Q D. S Q P R

E. Q R P S

14. S_1 : Our ancestors thought that anything which moved itself was alive.

S_6 : Therefore some scientists think that life is just a very complicated mechanism.

P : The philosopher Descartes thought that both men and animals were machines.

Q : But a machine such as a motorcar or a steamship moves itself, and as soon as machines which moved themselves had been made, people asked, "Is man a machine?"

R : And before the days of machinery that was a good definition.

S : He also thought that the human machine was partly controlled by the soul action on a certain part of the brain, while animals had no souls.

The proper sequence should be:

A. P R S Q B. R P Q S

C. P S Q R D. R Q P S

E. S R P Q

15. S_1 : But how does a new word get into the dictionary?

S_6 : He sorts them according to their grammatical function, and carefully writes a definition.

P : When a new dictionary is being edited, a lexicographer collects all the alphabetically arranged citation slips for a particular word.

Q : The dictionary makers notice it and make a note of it on a citation slip.

R : The moment a new word is coined, it usually enters the spoken language.

S : The word then passes from the realm of hearing to the realm of writing.

The proper sequence should be:

A. P Q R S B. P R S Q

C. R Q P S D. R S Q P

E. S R P Q

16. S_1 : The heart is the pump of life.

S_6 : All this was made possible by the invention of the heart-lung machine.

P : They have even succeeded in heart transplants.

Q : Nowadays surgeons are able to stop a patient's heart and carry out complicated operations.

R : A few years ago it was impossible to operate on a patient whose heart was not working properly.

S : If the heart stops we die in about five minutes.

The proper sequence should be:

A. S R Q P B. S P R Q

C. S Q P R D. S R P Q

E. P Q R S

17. S_1 : Throughout history man has used energy from the sun.

S_6 : This energy comes from inside atoms.

P : Today, when we burn wood or use electric current we are drawing on energy.

Q : However, we now have a new supply of energy.

R : All our ordinary life depends on the sun.

S : This has come from the sun.

The proper sequence should be:

A. S Q P R B. R Q P S

C. Q S R P D. P S R Q

E. P Q R S

18. S_1 : In India marriages are usually arranged by parents.

S_6 : She felt she was a modern girl and not a subject for bargaining.

P : Sometimes girls and boys do not like the idea of arranged marriages.

Q : Most young people accept this state of affairs.

R : Rosy was like that.

S : They assume their parents can make good choices.

The proper sequence should be:

A. S P R Q B. P S R Q
C. Q S P R D. R Q P S
E. P Q R S

19. S_1 : I had halted on the road.
S_6 : I decided to watch him for a while and then go home.
P : As soon as I saw the elephant I knew I should not shoot him.
Q : It is a serious matter to shoot a working elephant.
R : I knew that his 'mast' was already passing off.
S : The elephant was standing eighty yards from the road.

The proper sequence should be:

A. S P Q R B. P Q S R
C. R Q P S D. S R P Q
E. P Q R S

20. S_1 : A man can be physically confined within stone walls.
S_6 : No tyranny can intimidate a lover of liberty.
P : But his mind and spirit will still be free.
Q : Thus his freedom of action may be restricted.
R : His hopes and aspirations still remain with him.
S : Hence, he will be free spiritually if not physically.

The proper sequence should be:

A. P Q R S B. S R Q P
C. Q P R S D. Q P S R
E. R S P Q

21. S_1 : The dictionary is the best friend for your task.
S_6 : Soon you will realize that this is an exciting task.
P : That may not be possible always.
Q : It is wise to look it up immediately.
R : Then it must be firmly written on the memory and traced at the first opportunity.
S : Never allow a strange word to pass unchallenged.

The proper sequence should be:

A. P Q R S B. S P Q R
C. Q R P S D. S Q P R
E. R S P Q

22. S_1 : Far away in a little street there is a poor house.
S_6 : His mother has nothing to give but water, so he is crying.
P : Her face is thin and worn and her hands are coarse, pricked by a needle, for she is a seam-stress.
Q : One of the windows is open and through it I can see a poor woman.
R : He has fever and he is asking for oranges.
S : In a bed in a corner of the room her little boy is lying ill.

The proper sequence should be:

A. S R Q P B. P Q S R
C. Q P S R D. R S P Q
E. P Q R S

23. S_1 : Kolkata unlike other cities, has kept its trams.
S_6 : The foundation stone was laid in 1972.
P : As a result, there is horrendous congestion.
Q : It was going to be the first in South Asia.
R : They run down the centre of the road.
S : To ease congestion in the city it was decided to build an underground railway line.

The proper sequence should be:

A. P R S Q B. P S Q R
C. S Q R P D. R P S Q
E. Q P R S

24. S_1 : We now know that oceans are very deep.
S_6 : This reaches from India to the Antarctica.
P : For example, the Indian Ocean has a range called the Indian Ridge.
Q : Much of it is fairly flat.
R : However, there are great mountain ranges as well.
S : On average the bottom is two and a half to three and a half miles down.

The proper sequence should be:

A. S Q P R B. P Q S R
C. R S Q P D. Q P R S
E. P Q R S

25. S_1 : As he passed beneath her he heard the swish of her wings.
S_6 : The next moment he felt her wings spread outwards.
P : He was not falling head long now.
Q : Then monstrous terror seized him.
R : But it only lasted a minute.
S : He could hear nothing.

The proper sequence should be:

A. P S Q R B. Q S P R
C. Q S R P D. P R Q S
E. S R P Q

26. S_1 : When a satellite is launched, the rocket begins by going slowly upwards through the air.
S_6 : Consequently, the rocket still does not become too hot.
P : However, the higher it goes, the less air it meets.
Q : As the rocket goes higher, it travels faster.
R : For the atmosphere becomes thinner.
S : As a result there is less friction.

The proper sequence should be:

A. Q P R S B. Q S P R
C. P Q R S D. P Q S R
E. R S P Q

27. S_1 : Sunbirds are among the smallest of Indian birds.
S_6 : Our common sunbirds are the purple sunbird, the glossy black species and purple-rumped sunbird, the yellow and maroon species.
P : Though they are functionally similar to the hummingbirds of the New World, they are totally unrelated.
Q : They do eat small insects too.
R : They are also some of the most brilliantly-coloured birds.
S : Sunbirds feed on nectar mostly and help in pollination.
The proper sequence should be:
A. S Q P R B. R P S Q
C. Q P R S D. P S R Q
E. P Q R S

28. S_1 : Venice is a strange and beautiful city in the north of Italy.
S_6 : This is because Venice has no streets.
P : There are about four hundred old stone bridges joining the island of Venice.
Q : In this city there are no motor cars, no horses and no buses.
R : These small islands are near one another.
S : It is not an island but a hundred and seventeen islands.
The proper sequence should be:
A. P Q R S B. P R Q S
C. S R P Q D. P Q S R
E. Q P R S

29. S_1 : A ceiling on urban property.
S_6 : Since their value would exceed the ceiling fixed by the Government.
P : No mill-owner could own factories or mills or plants.
Q : And mass circulation papers.
R : Would mean that.
S : No press magnate could own printing presses.
The proper sequence should be:
A. Q S R P B. R P S Q
C. S R P Q D. Q P S R
E. P Q R S

30. S_1 : The weather-vane often tops a church spire, tower or high building.
S_6 : The weather-vane can, however, give us some indication of the weather.
P : They are only wind-vanes.
Q : Neither alone can tell us what the weather will be.
R : They are designed to point to the direction from which the wind is coming.
S : Just as the barometer only tells us the pressure of the air, the weather-vane tells us the direction of the wind.
The proper sequence should be:
A. P Q R S B. P S R Q
C. P R S Q D. S P Q R
E. R P S Q

31. S_1 : Most of the universities in the country are now facing financial crisis.
S_6 : The Government should realise this before it is too late.
P : Cost benefit yardstick thus should not be applied in the case of the universities.
Q : The current state of affairs cannot be allowed to continue for long.
R : Universities cannot be equated with commercial enterprises.
S : Proper development of universities and colleges must be ensured.
The proper sequence should be:
A. Q R P S B. Q S P R
C. Q R S P D. Q P R S
E. P Q R S

32. S_1 : I keep on flapping my big ears all day.
S_6 : Am I not a smart, intelligent elephant?
P : They also fear that I will flap them all away.
Q : But children wonder why I flap them so.
R : I flap them so to make sure they are safely there on either side of my head.
S : But I know what I am doing.
The proper sequence should be:
A. S R Q P B. Q P S R
C. Q P R S D. P S R Q
E. R P S Q

33. S_1 : Urban problems differ from State to State and city to city.
S_6 : There is no underground drainage system in most cities, and the narrow historical roads are already congested.
P : Most of the cities have neither water nor the required pipelines.
Q : The population in these cities has grown beyond the planners' imagination.
R : However, certain basic problems are common to all cities.
S : Only broad macro-planning was done for such cities, without envisaging the future growth, and this has failed to meet the requirements.
The proper sequence should be:
A. P Q S R B. Q P S R
C. R Q P S D. R S Q P
E. S R P Q

34. S_1 : A gentleman who lived alone always had two plates placed on the table at dinner time.

S_6 : In this way the cat showed her gratitude to her master.

P : One day just as he sat down to dine, the cat rushed into the room.

Q : One plate was for himself and the other was for his cat.

R : She dropped a mouse into her own plate and another into her master's plate.

S : He used to give the cat a piece of meat from his own plate.

The proper sequence should be:

A. Q S P R　　B. P S R Q
C. Q R S P　　D. R P Q S
E. S R Q P

35. S_1 : I took cigarettes from my case.

S_6 : Then he continued to draw on it.

P : But when the fit of coughing was over, he replaced it between his lips.

Q : I lit one of them and placed it between the lips.

R : Then with a feeble hand he removed the cigarette.

S : Slowly he took a pull at it and coughed violently.

The proper sequence should be:

A. P S Q R　　B. Q P S R
C. Q S R P　　D. S R P Q
E. R S Q P

36. S_1 : Forcasting the weather has always been a difficult business.

S_6 : He made his forecasts by watching flights of the birds or the way smoke rose from fire.

P : During a period of drought, streams and rivers dried up, the cattle died from thirst and the crops were ruined.

Q : Many different things affect the weather and we have to study them carefully to make an accurate forecast.

R : Ancient Egyptians had no need of this weather in the Nile valley hardly ever changes.

S : In early times, when there were no instruments, such as thermometer or the barometer, man looked for tell-tale signs in the sky.

The proper sequence should be:

A. P R Q S　　B. Q P R S
C. Q R P S　　D. S P Q R
E. R P Q S

37. S_1 : Once upon a time there lived three young men in a certain town of Bharat.

S_6 : All of them set out in search of their foe called Death.

P : All the people of the neighbourhood were mortally afraid of them.

Q : They were so powerful that they could catch growling lions and tear them to pieces.

R : Someone told them that they would become immortal if they killed Death.

S : The young men believed themselves to be very good friends.

The proper sequence should be:

A. Q P R S　　B. S Q P R
C. R S Q P　　D. S R P Q
E. P S R Q

38. S_1 : Duryodhana was a wicked prince.

S_6 : This enraged Duryodhana so much that he began to think of removing Bhima from his way.

P : One day Bhima made Duryodhana fall from a tree from which Duryodhana was stealing fruits.

Q : He did not like that Pandavas should be loved and respected by the people of Hastinapur.

R : Duryodhana specially hated Bhima.

S : Among the Pandavas, Bhima was extraordinarily strong and powerful.

The proper sequence should be:

A. P S Q R　　B. Q P R S
C. Q S R P　　D. P S R Q
E. R S P Q

39. S_1 : You know my wife, Maggi, always urged me to give up smoking.

S_6 : Poor girl!

P : I really gave it up.

Q : And so when I went to jail I said to myself I really must give it up, if for no other reason than of being self-reliant.

R : When I emerged from jail, I wanted to tell her of my great triumph!

S : But when I met her, there she was with a packet of cigarettes.

The proper sequence should be:

A. P S R Q　　B. S P Q R
C. Q P R S　　D. R S P Q
E. P Q R S

40. S_1 : A black-haired, young woman came tripping along.

S_6 : Both disappeared from view.

P : She was leading a young man wearing a hat.

Q : The woman swept it off and tossed it in the air.

R : The child jumped up to catch the hat.

S : The young man tossed his head to shake the hat back.

The proper sequence should be:

A. P S Q R　　B. R P S Q
C. Q R P S　　D. S Q R P
E. P Q R S

41. S_1 : Jawaharlal Nehru was born in Allahabad on 14 November, 1889.

S_6 : He died on 27 May, 1964.
P : Nehru met Mahatma Gandhi in February, 1920.
Q : In 1905 he was sent to London to study at a school called Harrow.
R : He became the first Prime Minister of Independent India on 15 August, 1947.
S : He married Kamla Kaul in 1915.

The proper sequence should be:
A. Q R P S B. Q S P R
C. R P Q S D. S Q R P
E. P S R Q

42. S_1 : An elderly lady suddenly became blind.
S_6 : The lady said that she had not been properly cured because she could not see all her furniture.
P : The doctor called daily and every time he took away some of her furniture he liked.
Q : At last, she was cured and the doctor demanded his fee.
R : She agreed to pay a large fee to the doctor who would cure her.
S : On being refused, the doctor wanted to know the reason.

The proper sequence should be:
A. P Q R S B. R P Q S
C. R S P Q D. R Q P S
E. Q P R S

43. S_1 : The path of Venus lies inside the path of the Earth.
S_6 : When at its brightest, it is easily seen with the naked eye in broad daylight.
P : When at its farthest from the Earth, Venus is 160 million miles away.
Q : With such a wide range between its greatest and least distances it is natural that at sometimes Venus appears much brighter than all others.
R : No other body ever comes so near the Earth, with the exception of the Moon and an occasional comet or asteroid.
S : When Venus is at its nearest to the earth it is only 26 million miles away.

The proper sequence should be:
A. S R P Q B. S Q R P
C. P S Q R D. Q P R S
E. R S P Q

44. S_1 : Religion is not a matter of mere dogmatic conformity.
S_6 : A man of that character is free from fear, free from hatred.
P : It is not merely going through the ritual prescribed to us.
Q : It is not a question of ceremonial piety.
R : Unless that kind of transformation occurs, you are not an authentically religious man.
S : It is the remaking of your own self, the transformation of your nature.

The proper sequence should be:
A. S P R Q B. Q P S R
C. P S R Q D. S P Q R
E. R P Q S

45. S_1 : For some time in his youth, Abraham Lincoln was manager of a shop.
S_6 : Never before had Lincoln had so much time for reading as he had then.
P : Then a chance customer would come.
Q : Young Lincoln's way of keeping shop was entirely unlike anyone else's.
R : Lincoln would jump up and attend to his needs and then revert to his reading.
S : He used to lie full length on the counter of the shop eagerly reading a book.

The proper sequence should be:
A. S R Q P B. Q S P R
C. S Q R P D. Q P S R
E. R S P Q

46. S_1 : Binnie went shopping one morning.
S_6 : She drove home with an empty shopping basket.
P : Disappointed she turned around and returned to the parking lot.
Q : She got out and walked to the nearest shop.
R : She drove her car into the parking lot and stopped.
S : It was there that she realised that she'd forgotten her purse at home.

The proper sequence should be:
A. R S Q P B. R Q S P
C. P Q R S D. Q P R S
E. P R Q S

47. S_1 : Several sub-cities have been planned around the capital.
S_6 : Hopefully the housing problem will not be as acute as at present after these sub-cities are built.
P : Dwarka is the first among them.
Q : They are expected to alleviate the problem of housing.
R : It is coming up in the south-west of the capital.
S : It will cater to over one million people when completed.

The proper sequence should be:
A. Q P R S B. P R S Q
C. P Q R S D. Q R S P
E. R S Q P

48. S_1 : Just as some men like to play football or tennis, so some men like to climb mountains.

S_6 : You look down and see the whole country below you.

P : This is often very difficult to do, for mountains are not just big hills.

Q : Paths are usually very steep, and some mountain-sides are straight up and down, so that it may take many hours to climb as little as one hundred feet.

R : There is always the danger that you may fall off and be killed or injured.

S : Men talk about conquering a mountain, and the wonderful feeling it is to reach the top of a mountain after climbing for hours and may be, even for days.

The proper sequence should be:

A. P Q R S B. Q P S R
C. R Q P S D. S R Q P
E. P R S Q

49. S_1 : Ms. Singh started a petrol pump in Madras.

S_6 : Thus she has shown the way for many others.

P : A total of twelve girls now work at the pump.

Q : She advertised in newspapers for women staff.

R : They operate in two shifts.

S : The response was good.

The proper sequence should be:

A. P Q S R B. S Q P R
C. Q S P R D. P Q R S
E. Q R P S

50. S_1 : Your letter was a big relief.

S_6 : But don't forget to bring chocolate for Reeta.

P : How did your exams go?

Q : After your result, you must come here for a week.

R : You hadn't written for over a month.

S : I am sure you will come out with flying colours.

The proper sequence should be:

A. P S R Q B. Q R P S
C. R P S Q D. R S P Q
E. S R P Q

ANSWERS

1	2	3	4	5	6	7	8	9	10
C	D	A	A	D	C	A	B	B	B
11	**12**	**13**	**14**	**15**	**16**	**17**	**18**	**19**	**20**
B	B	A	C	A	A	D	C	B	A
21	**22**	**23**	**24**	**25**	**26**	**27**	**28**	**29**	**30**
D	C	D	A	C	A	A	C	B	D
31	**32**	**33**	**34**	**35**	**36**	**37**	**38**	**39**	**40**
A	B	D	A	C	B	B	C	C	A
41	**42**	**43**	**44**	**45**	**46**	**47**	**48**	**49**	**50**
B	B	A	B	B	B	A	A	C	C

6

FILL IN THE BLANKS

Fill in the blanks is such an exercise that begins with the primary schools and continues at the highest level of competitive examinations. One must practise it regularly to score well.

Directions: *In each of the following sentences, there are one or two blank spaces. Below each sentence there are five words/pair of words denoted by letters A, B, C, D and E. Find out which word/pair of words can be filled up in the blanks in the sentence in the same sequence to make the sentence meaningfully complete.*

1. Leadership defines what the future should look like and ...... people with that vision.
A. aligns B. develops
C. trains D. encourages
E. transforms

2. We upset ourselves by responding in an ...... manner to someone else's actions.
A. unabashed B. irrational
C. arduous D. arguable
E. invalid

3. All the people involved in that issue feel a great ...... to his suggestion.
A. contradiction B. adherence
C. indifference D. objection
E. repugnance

4. These elections will be remembered as much for its anti-incumbency mood as for its ...... mandate.
A. invincible B. rational
C. unprecedented D. deliberate
E. pervasive

5. How do you expect us to stay in such a ...... building even if it can be hired on a nominal rent?
A. scruffy B. disparate
C. fragmented D. robust
E. damaging

6. ...... efforts from all concerned are required to raise the social and economic conditions of our countrymen.
A. Perpetual B. Dynamic
C. Massive D. Exploring
E. Penetrative

7. Many companies see technology as a ...... for a whole host of business problems.
A. consideration B. preference
C. linking D. panacea
E. craving

8. Known as devout and serious person, she also has ...... sense of humour.
A. better B. plentiful
C. quick D. beautiful
E. good

9. The matter would have become serious if ...... action had not been taken.
A. hasty B. fast
C. timely D. unusual
E. deliberate

10. The ...... with which he is able to yield the paint-brush is really remarkable.
A. ease B. practice
C. majesty D. sweep
E. energy

11. The speaker did not properly use the time as he went on ...... on one point alone.
A. devoting B. deliberating
C. diluting D. distributing
E. dilating

12. They decided to ...... down their original plans for the bigger house and make it smaller.
A. climb B. turn
C. scale D. play
E. change

13. Esha was badly ...... by the news which she got in the letter.
A. electrified B. petrified
C. deranged D. shaken
E. frozen

14. In spite of her other ......, Madhuri still managed to find time for her hobbies.
A. occupations B. preoccupations
C. predilections D. business
E. promises

15. Success comes to those who are vigilant not to permit ...... from the chosen path.
A. distraction B. deviation
C. alienation D. diversion
E. obstruction

16. It is advisable to ...... on this issue rather than create unnecessary problem by taking a rigid stand.
A. lose B. promise
C. evade D. compromise
E. forfeit

17. After a short holiday we came back totally ....
A. rejuvenated B. reborn
C. refurbished D. revamped
E. restored

18. The victim tried to tell us what had happened but his ...... were not audible.
A. assailants B. sounds
C. letters D. proofs
E. words

19. The ...... between the twins is so slight that it is very difficult to identify one from the other.
A. similarity B. distance
C. resemblance D. difference
E. rift

20. The members were ...... of the date of the meeting well in advance.
A. communicated B. conveyed
C. ignorant D. informed
E. known

21. A ...... of ships was kept ready to scour the sea in case of an emergency.
A. group B. pack
C. unit D. fleet
E. battalion

22. I had not expected to meet him; it was quite an ...... meeting.
A. organised B. intentional
C. undesirable D. auspicious
E. accidental

23. The window of our room ...... the rear.
A. overlooks B. opens
C. opposes D. adjoins
E. precedes

24. I could ...... see the sight since it was dark.
A. clearly B. barely
C. obviously D. aptly
E. abruptly

25. The top-ranking manager ...... his success in the profession to his Managing Director's guidance.
A. account B. agrees
C. attributes D. claims
E. refers

26. Does your pride keep you ...... making the decision you know you should?
A. away B. alert
C. from D. quiet
E. intact

27. Their ...... to scale the mountain peak was an absolute failure.
A. attempt B. desire
C. anxiety D. proposal
E. dedication

28. The writer, like a spider ...... a web; the creatures caught in the web have no substance, no reality.
A. spins B. catches
C. writes D. compiles
E. finds

29. In a ...... move the Chief Minister today dropped two ministers from the cabinet.
A. secret B. delicate
C. continuous D. consistent
E. surprise

30. In his address to the teachers, the Vice-Chancellor ...... certain measures being taken for improving the quality of college education.
A. declined B. directed
C. advised D. highlighted
E. demanded

31. Changes in the legal system are inevitable for we are not working for a ...... society.
A. backward B. dynamic
C. stagnant D. modern
E. ruthless

32. Modern science began ...... the influence of Copernicus, Kepler, Galileo and Newton.
A. by B. under
C. from D. upon
E. with

33. A meeting of senior police officers was held to ...... the law and order situation of the town.
A. review B. curb
C. cover D. support
E. criticise

34. The problems that India's economic development faces are ....

A. myopic B. dubious
C. enormous D. strong
E. morbid

35. In our zeal for progress we should not ...... the executive with more powers.

A. avoid B. arm
C. give D. enhance
E. improve

36. At present, all over the world, moral standards ...... to have fallen.

A. look B. wish
C. started D. appear
E. intend

37. He was one of the ...... spirits behind the successful agitation of the citizens for keeping the city clean.

A. revolving B. moving
C. evolving D. amazing
E. rising

38. The employees were unhappy because their salary was not increased ....

A. marginally B. abruptly
C. substantially D. superfluously
E. negligibly

39. ...... the being a handicapped person, he is very co-operative and self-reliant.

A. Because B. Although
C. Since D. Basically
E. Despite

40. The child broke ...... from his mother and ran towards the painting.

A. away B. after
C. down D. with
E. heavily

41. With his ...... income, he finds it difficult to live a comfortable life.

A. brief B. sufficient
C. meagre D. huge
E. adequate

42. He could ...... a lot of money in such a short time by using his intelligence and working hard.

A. spend B. spoil
C. exchange D. accumulate
E. pay

43. Though the brothers are twins, they look ......

A. alike B. handsome
C. indifferent D. identical
E. different

44. Unfavourable weather conditions can ..... illness.

A. cure B. detect
C. treat D. enhance
E. diagnose

45. No sooner did the bell ring ...... the actor started singing.

A. when B. than
C. after D. before
E. through

46. If I ...... realised it, I would not have acted on his advice.

A. was B. had
C. were D. have
E. being

47. Why don't you ...... your work in advance before commencing it.

A. start B. complete
C. finish D. plan
E. execute

48. Contemporary economic development differs ...... from the Industrial Revolution of the 19th century.

A. usually B. specially
C. literally D. markedly
E. naturally

49. Mounting unemployment is the most serious and ...... problem faced by India today.

A. profound B. intractable
C. unpopular D. dubious
E. unattainable

50. Unemployment is not only ...... throughout the emerging world, but is growing worse, especially in urban areas.

A. endemic B. peripheral
C. absorbing D. prolific
E. endangering

51. Manpower is the ...... means of converting other resources to mankind's use and benefit.

A. inimitable B. indivisible
C. indispensable D. inequitable
E. insuperable

52. This article tries to ...... us with problems of poor nations so that we help them more effectively.

A. enable B. convince
C. allow D. deny
E. acquaint

53. Among human beings, language is the principal ...... of communication.

A. methodology B. instrument
C. accomplishment D. theory
E. appreciation

54. These essays are intellectually ...... and represent various levels of complexity.

A. persistent B. superior
C. modern D. demanding
E. revealing

55. ...... the doctor's advice my father started taking some daily exercise.
A. In B. To
C. On D. Towards
E. At

56. Do you ...... giving that book to me for a few days?
A. desires B. mind
C. call D. observe
E. thought

57. Our volunteers will ...... your donations either in cash or kind and give you a receipt.
A. lend B. borrow
C. return D. give
E. collect

58. If you need some money, I will ...... the amount from my bank and give you.
A. deposit B. return
C. withdraw D. require
E. took

59. ...... Ajay wanted to attend his friend's party, he could not attend it.
A. As B. But
C. Since D. Although
E. Because

60. The boss considered the situation and ...... only three days leave to Ashok.
A. granted B. submitted
C. sanction D. asked
E. took

61. If you want to do well, you must follow a strict ...... in your studies.
A. discipline B. belief
C. view D. report
E. ambition

62. It was very difficult to dig as the ground was very ..... .
A. thin B. soft
C. rigid D. volatile
E. hard

63. As a general rule, politicians do not ...... centre stage.
A. forward B. forbid
C. forgive D. forsake
E. foster

64. Shivam ...... classical music. He always prefers Bhimsen Joshi to Asha Bhonsale, and Pandit Jasraj to Kumar Sanu.
A. adores B. apprehends
C. encompasses D. cultivates
E. cares

65. Indications are that the Government is ...... to the prospect of granting bonus to the striking employees.
A. aligned B. obliged
C. reconciled D. relieved
E. authorised

66. The ...... study on import of natural gas from Iran through a pipeline would be completed shortly.
A. natural B. calculated
C. economic D. reallocation
E. feasibility

67. His party is solely to be blamed for the political ...... in the country.
A. devaluation B. revival
C. advocacy D. stalemate
E. degradation

68. We still have not given our ...... to conduct the survey of natural resources in our State.
A. projection B. consent
C. request D. compliance
E. provision

69. He is the best man for this job. He has mental ...... to carry it out.
A. predilection B. durability
C. adroitness D. persuasion
E. assimilation

70. Man is ......; however, he is more in need of mental companionship than of physical companionship.
A. egoistic B. biological
C. emotional D. democratic
E. gregarious

71. We cannot go on strike every year. Now that we have gone on strike we must ...... this issue.
A. clinch B. culminate
C. cross D. canvass
E. coordinate

72. I was totally ...... by his line of thinking and could not put forth any argument.
A. demolished B. nonplussed
C. exhausted D. refuted
E. degraded

73. Any problem to be ...... needs to be broken down to small pieces.
A. chosen B. taught
C. tackled D. posed
E. invented

74. He has ...... people visiting him at his house because he fears it will cause discomfort to neighbours.
A. forbidden B. warned
C. stopped D. request
E. curtailed

75. Nowadays, why ...... people so scared of each other?
A. were B. have
C. had D. are
E. do

76. If the perceptions of two individuals do not ...... there is bound to be problems.
A. reflect B. differ
C. match D. express
E. change

77. There are ...... educational theories that try to explain this fact.
A. one B. differing
C. entertaining D. theoretical
E. defending

78. ...... by people's perception it seems that democracy has succeeded in India.
A. Making B. Planned
C. Going D. Liked
E. Following

79. This year the number of candidates appearing for the examination has ....
A. disturbed B. crushed
C. broken D. dwindled
E. disintegrated

80. We must try to ...... new active workers to strengthen this organisation.
A. change B. bring
C. talk D. close
E. stop

81. ...... folded hands I request you to observe peace during the prayer.
A. Despite B. For
C. With D. At
E. Since

82. I cannot ...... it to you right now, tomorrow we will discuss about it.
A. demand B. disturb
C. worry D. expect
E. explain

83. Lata's programmes ...... taking place throughout the state since last week.
A. has been B. have been
C. is D. will be
E. would be

84. The pilot of the aircraft accepted a gift ...... the passengers who were happy about his skill.
A. from B. by
C. to D. about
E. with

85. Finally, the prizes were ...... to all successful participants at the hands of the Chief Guest.
A. divided B. shared
C. honoured D. distributed
E. handed

86. Can you please drop ...... ? I want to discuss some important matter.
A. for B. to
C. on D. out
E. in

87. As the Principal adopts a ...... approach towards the running of the school, the school is losing its prestige.
A. casual B. proper
C. strict D. cumulative
E. dilute

88. The account of the crime given by the accused was ..... and ..... .
A. dependable, uncognizable
B. fictitious, unreliable
C. false, appreciable
D. complete, imaginary
E. exaggerated, unpardonable

89. Problems of the country can only be aggravated by ..... and ..... citizens.
A. careful, unscrupulous
B. extraordinary, uncompromising
C. dedicated, patriotic
D. selfish, irresponsible
E. independent, practical

90. If you kindly bear ..... me for some time, I shall ..... the whole issue.
A. out, understand B. on, solve
C. for, know D. with, clarify
E. at, inform

91. The WHO has ..... the government for taking prompt ..... action.
A. lauded, preventive
B. criticise, obligatory
C. blamed, ineffective
D. appreciated, hectic
E. admired, unreasonable

92. Though the hospital is extremely rich, the conditions there are .....
A. equally, rich
B. apallingly, poor
C. admirably, comfortable
D. extremely, conducive
E. frequently, tolerable

93. Nine members have ..... about the decision, but the tenth one views it .....
A. solution, critically
B. consensus, similarly
C. disagreement, collectively
D. grievance, grudgingly
E. agreement, differently

94. Vision is usually ..... most effectively when many different ..... are used.
A. developed, manifestations
B. adapted, organisations
C. communicated, vehicles
D. exhibited, forms
E. described, thought

95. People who have been through difficult, painful and not very ..... change efforts often end up ..... both pessimistic and angry conclusions.
A. successful, drawing
B. meaningful, projecting
C. reliable, evolving
D. strong, following
E. challenging, lamenting

96. If misery is the effect of ill-fortune, it ought to be pitied; if of ..... to be ..... .
A. virtue, criticised
B. calamity, reverenced
C. virtue, protected
D. vice, reverenced
E. virtue, reverenced

97. It is the ..... of selfishness for men, who fully ..... in their own case the great advantages of good education, to deny these advantages to women.
A. parody, demand
B. height, appreciate
C. height, assimilate
D. degree, appreciate
E. level, advance

98. His death ..... many tributes than have been paid at the ..... of any other human being in history.
A. brought, passing
B. directed, helm
C. delivered, description
D. invited, living
E. acknowledged, perpetuation

99. All the performances of human art, at which we look with praise or wonder, are ..... of the restless ..... of perseverence.
A. manifestations, pronouncement
B. projections, component
C. instances, force
D. proofs, humanity
E. visions, future

100. The issues could be ..... amicably only because of his ..... handling of the situation.
A. dropped, haphazard
B. raised, careful
C. discussed, enthusiastic
D. suppressed, emphatic
E. resolved, tactful

101. The only way to ensure best output from your vehicle is to provide it a ..... and ..... maintenance.
A. nurturing, expensive
B. proper, timely
C. careful, costly
D. trouble-free, everlasting
E. resolved, tactful

102. ..... your colleagues for important decision making activities ensures their ..... cooperation.
A. Counselling, wholehearted
B. Helping, occasional
C. Guiding, meagre
D. Neglecting, enthusiastic
E. Dominating, unstinted

103. The recent ..... in oil-prices has given an unexpected additional ..... to the cost-spiral.
A. slump, drawback
B. cut, blow
C. rise, twist
D. development, cut
E. deterioration, impetus

104. People ..... to work hard if you ..... certain conditions on them.
A. decide, negotiate
B. try, thrust
C. plan, invoke
D. hesitate, impose
E. volunteer, place

105. Our latest battle plan ..... some projects ..... at saving the earth's biological diversity.
A. destroys, stirring
B. covers, aimed
C. finances, looking
D. encompasses, looked
E. excludes, arriving

106. Unless the authorities adopt the principle ..... the strategies cannot become .....
A. wholeheartedly, successful
B. fully, defunct
C. mechanically, obsolete
D. legitimately, noteworthy
E. forcefully, trivial

107. Trying to ..... a team without a good and simple ..... system is like trying to drive a car without a steering wheel.
A. form, working
B. lead, exploratory
C. organise, empowering
D. run, guidance
E. achieve, developmental

108. ..... members of a group often ..... influence the outcome of a consensus forecast.
A. Permanent, exert
B. Majority, rightly
C. Vocal, legitimately
D. Minority, inadvertently
E. Dominant, unduly

109. Transforming ..... bureaucracies into dynamic, customer-driven organisations is ..... under any circumstances.
A. ideal, essential
B. lazy, undesirable
C. inefficient, challenging
D. civilized, ineffective
E. customer, unsurmountable

110. He was initially ..... at the suggestion but was soon ..... it himself.
A. frowning, rejecting
B. thrilled, propagating
C. shocked, advocating
D. impressed, negating
E. suspicious, trusting

111. The Minister felt that the ..... made by the Committee was ..... even though similar schemes had worked earlier.
A. election, acceptable
B. choice, profitable
C. decision, gainful
D. recommendation, infeasible
E. acceptance, approved

112. The officer was not ..... by the criticism and paid no ..... even when her best friend talked against her.
A. threatened, warning
B. troubled, mind
C. deterred, heed
D. bothered, attention
E. shaken, indication

113. The activities of the association have ..... from the ..... objectives set for it in the initial years.
A. emerged, total
B. deviated, original
C. grown, simple
D. details, grand
E. increased, perverse

114. The ..... imposed for non-payment was too ..... for it to bring in improvement in collection.
A. penalty, low
B. fine, severe
C. punishment, harsh
D. toll, simple
E. damage, cruel

115. Although his first few attempts were ....., ultimately he ..... .
A. fruitful, won
B. futile, succeeded
C. laborious, gave up
D. appreciable, retarded
E. thwarted, lost

116. The glaring success of the Indian Cricket team was the ..... of the ..... efforts.
A. reason, untiring
B. cause, painstaking
C. result, persistent
D. outcome, negligible
E. extent, indomitable

117. His face gave us a clear ..... that he was free from all his ..... .
A. indication, worries
B. picture, comforts
C. message, relations
D. notice, obstacles
E. impression, opportunities

118. None of the passengers was ..... of ..... was going to happen in the next two hours.
A. beware, incidence
B. knowing, that
C. anticipating, fact
D. expecting, anything
E. aware, what

119. We had to face a lot of ..... due to their ..... act which was avoidable.
A. problems, desirable
B. consequences, immeasurable
C. worries, kind
D. humiliation, disgraceful
E. disaster, merciful

120. Having accumulated enough ....., they are now thinking of ..... a bigger bungalow.
A. trouble, selling
B. patience, leaving
C. hardships, repairing
D. courage, building
E. wealth, buying

121. He was scarcely in his teens when he became completely ..... by German ..... and writing of Shakespeare.
A. harassed, army
B. engrossed, people
C. captivated, literature
D. seized, soldiers
E. broken, rules

122. As he was the century's ..... man of Science, his ..... was universally mourned.
A. wealthiest, experiment
B. greatest, death
C. happiest, accepted
D. oldest, invention
E. saddest, grief

123. In case you have ..... his feelings, though unintentionally, you must ..... to him now.
A. hurt, apologise
B. tendered, pardon
C. cajoled, appease
D. evoked, surrender
E. passioned, excuse

124. Being an incorrigible ....., he will never tell the ..... .
A. liar, truth
B. idiot, story
C. criminal, message
D. person, reason
E. offender, details

125. Your ..... will ..... all the benefits you derived from your hard work.
A. patience, delete
B. possessiveness, enhance
C. carelessness, nullify
D. apathy, increase
E. sluggishness, accumulate

126. To succeed in any ..... task, ... is needed.
A. challenging, impatience B. critical, approach
C. appropriate, strategy D. difficult, preseverance
E. competitive, anxiety

127. There are ..... instances to prove that the leader ..... courteously with everyone.
A. no, major B. treats, works
C. various, demands D. absolute, helps
E. several, behaves

128. Being a cruel task-master, he always ..... too ..... work on his servants.
A. does, much B. entrusts, difficult
C. performs, little D. imposes, much
E. assigns, little

129. If the government firms ..... to earn profits, they ought to get rid of ..... measures.
A. fail, healthy B. decide, populist
C. have, proper D. plan, planning
E. achieve, far-reaching

130. The sack was so ..... that I could ..... carry it.
A. full, hardly B. hardly, full
C. heavy, hardly D. light, easy
E. large, precisely

131. The demand to ..... the ancient monument of the town was long ..... with the state administration.
A. excavate, extinct B. maintain, maintained
C. dispose, clear D. preserve, pending
E. demolish, considered

132. Four of the ..... were hanged against whom, the Judge had ..... the verdict.
A. criminals, passed
B. thieves, entered
C. accomplices, declared
D. murderers, declared
E. murders, entered

133. Students have ..... using wrong procedures in the examinations because they are aware that these could be ..... .
A. started, false B. stopped, detected
C. detected, stopped D. tried, detected
E. detected, proved

134. Some animals can live comfortably both ..... water and ..... land.
A. into, at B. on, in
C. inside, over D. in, on
E. over, on

135. Although the ceremony was ..... scheduled for three days, yet it was ..... later to one day.
A. originally, curtailed
B. formerly, declared
C. timely, decide
D. decided, curtailed
E. therefore, curtailed

136. His ..... at work is the outcome of his ..... .
A. commitments, honesty
B. loss, commitments
C. diligence, sincerity
D. concentration, honesty
E. sincerity, diligence

137. The victory of Indian hockey team was the ..... of the ..... efforts.
A. outcome, hard B. persuation, strict
C. result, persistent D. cause, persistent
E. persistence, poor

138. None of the travellers was ..... of ..... was going to happen in the next two days.
A. beware, something B. aware, what
C. expectant, there D. aware, that
E. aware, something

139. We had to face a lot of ..... due to their ..... action that could have been avoided.
A. humiliation, disgraceful
B. disgrace, humiliate
C. pressures, poor
D. difficulties, difficult
E. difficulties, disgraceful

140. Your ..... would ..... all the benefits that you derived from your toil
A. empathy, decrease B. apathy, increase
C. carelessness, nullify D. attitude, decline
E. virtues, kill

141. There are ..... examples to prove that the PM ..... warmly with the masses.
A. various, meeting B. several, behaves
C. illustrious, charms D. many, interact
E. some, listens

142. He was scarcely an adult when he became completely ..... by the English ....., especially, by the plays of Shakespeare.
A. bewitched, poetry
B. caught, theatre
C. captivated, theatre
D. overwhelmed, poems
E. overpowered, literature

143. In order to succeed in any ..... assignment, ... is required.
A. difficult, perseverance
B. competitive, anxiety
C. critical, viewpoint
D. challenging, standpoint
E. difficult, power

144. In case you have ..... his feelings, you must ..... to him.
A. hurt, apologise B. evoked, surrender
C. touched, talk D. offended, appeal
E. mauled, apologise

145. Having accumulated enough ....., they are now planning to ..... a bigger office.
A. courage, sell B. space, buy
C. wealth, purchase D. wealth, sell
E. money, renovate

146. ..... your subordinates for vital activities ensures their ..... support.
A. Guiding, uncomplete
B. Guiding, wholehearted
C. Persuading, heartfelt
D. Pressurising, controlled
E. Coaxing, willful

147. The servants ..... to work hard if we ..... certain conditions upon them.
A. hesitate, impose B. prefer, force
C. volunteer, impose D. hesitate, try
E. try, revoke

148. As he was the ..... man in the field of arts, his ..... was mourned universally.
A. happiest, joy
B. finest, death
C. clever, death
D. greatest, birthday
E. greatest, wisdom

ANSWERS

1	2	3	4	5	6	7	8	9	10
A	A	E	C	A	A	D	E	C	A
11	**12**	**13**	**14**	**15**	**16**	**17**	**18**	**19**	**20**
E	C	D	B	A	D	A	E	D	D
21	**22**	**23**	**24**	**25**	**26**	**27**	**28**	**29**	**30**
D	E	A	B	C	C	A	A	E	D
31	**32**	**33**	**34**	**35**	**36**	**37**	**38**	**39**	**40**
C	B	A	C	B	D	B	C	E	A
41	**42**	**43**	**44**	**45**	**46**	**47**	**48**	**49**	**50**
C	D	E	D	B	B	D	D	B	A
51	**52**	**53**	**54**	**55**	**56**	**57**	**58**	**59**	**60**
C	E	B	D	C	B	E	C	D	A
61	**62**	**63**	**64**	**65**	**66**	**67**	**68**	**69**	**70**
A	E	D	A	C	E	D	B	C	E
71	**72**	**73**	**74**	**75**	**76**	**77**	**78**	**79**	**80**
A	B	C	D	D	C	B	C	D	B
81	**82**	**83**	**84**	**85**	**86**	**87**	**88**	**89**	**90**
C	E	B	A	D	E	A	B	C	D
91	**92**	**93**	**94**	**95**	**96**	**97**	**98**	**99**	**100**
A	B	E	A	B	C	C	A	C	E
101	**102**	**103**	**104**	**105**	**106**	**107**	**108**	**109**	**110**
B	A	C	D	B	A	A	E	C	C
111	**112**	**113**	**114**	**115**	**116**	**117**	**118**	**119**	**120**
D	C	B	A	B	C	A	E	D	E
121	**122**	**123**	**124**	**125**	**126**	**127**	**128**	**129**	**130**
C	D	A	A	C	D	E	D	B	C
131	**132**	**133**	**134**	**135**	**136**	**137**	**138**	**139**	**140**
D	A	B	D	A	C	C	B	A	C
141	**142**	**143**	**144**	**145**	**146**	**147**	**148**		
B	C	A	A	C	B	A	B		

7

SYNONYMS

English is the most popular language in the world. It comprises thousands of words. No one can remember all the words and their meanings but everyone must try to read and learn maximum number of words and their meanings. One must keep and use a dictionary religiously.

Directions: *In the following questions, each word is followed by four options A, B, C and D. Select the option that best expresses the meaning of the given word. If no option seems correct, select 'E' as answer.*

1. USURP
A. Seize B. Precede
C. Custom D. Repress
E. None of these

2. INSCRIBE
A. Distant B. Crazy
C. Greedy D. Mark
E. None of these

3. ASTUTE
A. Cognizant B. Hostile
C. Provoke D. Shrewd
E. None of these

4. FOMENT
A. Provoke B. Abrasion
C. Extirpate D. Isolation
E. None of these

5. INSIPID
A. Delicate B. Solve
C. Stupid D. Gentle
E. None of these

6. CAJOLE
A. Doubtful B. Lure
C. Warm D. Suggest
E. None of these

7. WONT
A. Clam B. Exception
C. Rigid D. Habit
E. None of these

8. GUILE
A. Sense B. Candour
C. Deceit D. Wander
E. None of these

9. ARID
A. Accuse B. Apprehend
C. Dry D. Charge
E. None of these

10. DEXTERITY
A. Eloquent B. Rueful
C. Adroitness D. Shameful
E. None of these

11. BIZZARE
A. Eccentric B. Fair
C. Normal D. Young
E. None of these

12. FULMINATE
A. Barren B. Prodigal
C. Clamour D. Misfire
E. None of these

13. METEORIC
A. Sudden B. Cowardice
C. Mean D. False
E. None of these

14. JOCUND
A. Puzzle B. Barren
C. Gay D. Calm
E. None of these

15. YEARN
A. Release B. Crave
C. Timid D. Taunt
E. None of these

16. DON
A. Pine B. Doff
C. Blithe D. Wear
E. None of these

17. VERTIGO
A. Midst B. Uniform
C. Steadiness D. Dizziness
E. None of these

18. DECOY
A. Lead B. Escape
C. Gather D. Mislead
E. None of these

19. IMP
A. Demon B. Fair
C. Fairy D. Angel
E. None of these

20. APPELLATION
A. Pertinent B. Anonymity
C. Respect D. Designation
E. None of these

21. JARGON
A. Clear B. Biased
C. Youth D. Terminology
E. None of these

22. SPENDTHRIFT
A. Extravagant B. Fallacious
C. Liberal D. Waste
E. None of these

23. ABSONANT
A. Unnatural B. Objectionable
C. Discordant D. Absurd
E. None of these

24. UNLAWFUL
A. Scant B. Elicit
C. Illicit D. Draw
E. None of these

25. INCLINATION
A. Attitude B. Applause
C. Aptitude D. Aspiration
E. None of these

26. INDICT
A. Allege B. Reprimand
C. Condemn D. Accuse
E. None of these

27. CANNY
A. Handsome B. Stout
C. Obstinate D. Clever
E. None of these

28. BENEVOLENCE
A. Illness B. Vision
C. Kindness D. Ill-will
E. None of these

29. EXTRICATE
A. Complicate B. Tie
C. Pull D. Free
E. None of these

30. LUCRATIVE
A. Profitable B. Attractive
C. Tempting D. Amusement
E. None of these

31. TACITURNITY
A. Hesitation B. Dumbness
C. Reserve D. Creation
E. None of these

32. LAMENTABLE
A. Deplorable B. Terrible
C. Upgraded D. Unpardonable
E. None of these

33. RESTRAINT
A. Restriction B. Hindrance
C. Repression D. Obstacle
E. None of these

34. INCENSED
A. Enthused B. Excited
C. Inflamed D. Enraged
E. None of these

35. LUCID
A. Complex B. Noble
C. Elaborated D. Clear
E. None of these

36. STRINGENT
A. Stringy B. Strict
C. Shrink D. Vivid
E. None of these

37. DEIFY
A. Face B. Flatter
C. Challenge D. Worship
E. None of these

38. RUPTURE
A. Damage B. Gap
C. Break D. Distortion
E. None of these

39. DILIGENT
A. Hard-working B. Introvert
C. Prospective D. Progressive
E. None of these

40. LUDICROUS
A. Serious B. Recall
C. Comic D. Dissolve
E. None of these

41. FORAY
A. Ranger B. Contest
C. Excursion D. Intuition
E. None of these

42. SYCOPHANT
A. Submissive B. Proud
C. Foppish D. Flatterer
E. None of these

43. REFECTORY
A. Parlour B. Living Room
C. Dining Room D. Restaurant
E. None of these

44. LYNCHED
A. Killed B. Mutilated
C. Captured D. Harden
E. None of these

45. SHALLOW
A. Artificial B. Stupid
C. Worthless D. Superficial
E. None of these

46. PROPENSITY
A. Aptitude B. Quality
C. Natural tendency D. Charm
E. None of these

47. BAFFLED
A. Foiled B. Defeated
C. Thwarted D. Circumvented
E. None of these

48. RETAIN
A. Preserve B. Recall
C. Conserve D. Keep
E. None of these

49. CONNOISSEUR
A. Interpreter B. Delinquent
C. Ignorant D. Lover of art
E. None of these

50. SCANDAL
A. Disgraceful action B. Talk
C. Rumour D. Silly notion
E. None of these

51. VIGILANT
A. Ambitious B. Smart
C. Intelligent D. Watchful
E. None of these

52. VORACIOUS
A. Angry B. Insane
C. Hungry D. Quick
E. None of these

53. IMPROMPTU
A. Effective B. Impressive
C. Glamour D. Off hand
E. None of these

54. ANNIHILATED
A. Split B. Miracle
C. Secured D. Destroyed
E. None of these

55. PRECARIOUS
A. Brittle B. Cautious
C. Perilous D. Critical
E. None of these

56. GARRULOUS
A. Laughs a lot B. Talks a lot
C. Silence D. Gossip
E. None of these

57. GERMANE
A. Logic B. Relevant
C. Responsible D. Possible
E. None of these

58. GULLIBLE
A. Unrealistic B. Fallible
C. Enthusiastic D. Unsuspecting
E. None of these

59. ALLEVIATED
A. Moderated B. Removed
C. Mitigated D. Lightened
E. None of these

60. CONSEQUENCES
A. Difficulties B. Results
C. Applications D. Conclusions
E. None of these

61. FICTITIOUS
A. Unreal B. Uncamped
C. Unreliable D. Unbelievable
E. None of these

62. APPROBATION
A. Admiration B. Understanding
C. Appreciation D. Approval
E. None of these

63. TEPID
A. Cold B. Hot
C. Warm D. Frozen
E. None of these

64. SUBSEQUENT
A. Few B. Earlier
C. Many D. Later
E. None of these

65. INEBRIATE
A. Unsteady B. Dreamy
C. Drunken D. Stupefied
E. None of these

66. COMMENSURATE
A. Beginning B. Appropriate
C. Measurable D. Proportionate
E. None of these

67. OUTWITTED
A. Cheated B. Befooled
C. Defeated D. Out-manoeuvred
E. None of these

68. TIMID
A. Slow B. Medium
C. Fast D. Shy
E. None of these

69. GARNISH
A. Garner B. Abuse
C. Adorn D. Paint
E. None of these

70. CHASTE
A. Virtuous B. Dignified
C. Noble D. Honest
E. None of these

71. OBJECT
A. Disapprove B. Disobey
C. Deny D. Challenge
E. None of these

72. INDUSTRIOUS
A. Diligent B. Excellent
C. Energetic D. Prompt
E. None of these

73. CANDID
A. Explicit B. Bright
C. Apparent D. Frank
E. None of these

74. IRONIC
A. Bitter B. Inflexible
C. Disguisedly Sarcastic D. Normal
E. None of these

75. TRANSPARENT
A. Witty B. Verbose
C. Lucid D. Blocked
E. None of these

76. SCOLD
A. Repress B. Reprieve
C. Reprisal D. Reprimand
E. None of these

77. SKETCH
A. Paint B. Draw
C. Portray D. Draft
E. None of these

78. PROTOTYPE
A. Duplicate B. Triplicate
C. Substitute D. Original
E. None of these

79. SUBMISSION
A. Humility B. Surrender
C. Politeness D. Carnivorous
E. None of these

80. ERADICATE
A. Resolve B. Remove
C. Report D. Uproot
E. None of these

81. SHORT-LIVED
A. Mortal B. Tempting
C. Transient D. Truant
E. None of these

82. MELANCHOLY
A. Happy B. Malice
C. Cruelty D. Sad
E. None of these

83. OBESE
A. Officious
B. Lean and thin
C. Fat and dull-looking
D. Soft
E. None of these

84. SHREW
A. Woman of violent temper
B. A person who is dull
C. Man of violent temper
D. Rude person
E. None of these

85. FEROCIOUS
A. Angry B. Dangerous
C. Fierce D. Monstrous
E. None of these

86. VENERATION
A. Modesty B. Exhalation
C. Brave D. Adoration
E. None of these

87. NONCHALANT
A. Natural B. Hot
C. Excited D. Cool
E. None of these

88. SAGACITY
A. Swell B. Surrender
C. Wisdom D. Resolve
E. None of these

89. ATOM
A. Placid B. Whole
C. Mass D. Iota
E. None of these

90. GRATUITOUS
A. Shear B. Justified
C. Amass D. Voluntary
E. None of these

91. WAIVE
A. Silent B. Relinquish
C. Press D. Bore
E. None of these

92. WARBLING
A. Dormant B. Vigilant
C. Inert D. Active
E. None of these

93. MILD
A. Loud B. Pass
C. Discuss D. Balmy
E. None of these

94. DUBIOUS
A. Trust
B. Obligatory
C. Unreliable
D. Worthy
E. None of these

95. TRIVIAL
A. Peculiar
B. Candid
C. Frivolous
D. Serious
E. None of these

96. BEMOAN
A. Lament
B. Acclaim
C. Defect
D. Perfect
E. None of these

97. FRUGAL
A. Thrifty
B. Prolific
C. Clamour
D. Efficacious
E. None of these

98. HIDEOUS
A. Concealed
B. Charming
C. Ugly
D. Embarrass
E. None of these

99. INVIDIOUS
A. Placate
B. Alluring
C. Unfair
D. Normal
E. None of these

100. CHAGRIN
A. Solemnity
B. Brave
C. Joy
D. Annoyance
E. None of these

101. OSCILLATORY
A. Dancing
B. Swinging
C. Running
D. Kissing
E. None of these

102. SCHOOLING
A. Instruction
B. Going to school
C. Coming from school
D. Reading
E. None of these

103. TORTUOUS
A. Gathering
B. Binding
C. Winding
D. Sending
E. None of these

104. SCARCELY
A. Rigid
B. Closely
C. Deficiency
D. Scantily
E. None of these

105. DESIST
A. Discontinue
B. Dreary
C. Desertion
D. Ripeness
E. None of these

106. RENUNCIATION
A. Relinquishment
B. Periodical
C. Correspondence
D. Arbitration
E. None of these

ANSWERS

1	2	3	4	5	6	7	8	9	10
A	D	D	A	C	B	A	C	C	C
11	12	13	14	15	16	17	18	19	20
A	C	A	C	B	D	D	D	C	D
21	22	23	24	25	26	27	28	29	30
D	A	D	C	C	D	D	C	C	A
31	32	33	34	35	36	37	38	39	40
C	A	D	D	D	B	D	C	A	C
41	42	43	44	45	46	47	48	49	50
C	D	C	A	D	C	A	D	D	A
51	52	53	54	55	56	57	58	59	60
D	C	D	D	D	B	B	D	C	B
61	62	63	64	65	66	67	68	69	70
A	D	C	D	C	C	C	D	C	A
71	72	73	74	75	76	77	78	79	80
A	A	D	C	C	D	C	D	B	D
81	82	83	84	85	86	87	88	89	90
C	D	C	A	C	D	D	C	D	D
91	92	93	94	95	96	97	98	99	100
B	A	D	C	C	A	A	C	C	D
101	102	103	104	105	106				
B	A	C	D	A	A				

8

ANTONYMS

In English, while learning the meanings of words, learning their opposite words is also equally important for a good learner. One must learn as many as one can to score well in the exam.

Directions: *In the following questions, each word is followed by four options A, B, C and D. Select the option which looks like the antonym of the given word. If no option seems correct, select 'E' as answer.*

1. THEIST
   A. Frail B. Obscure
   C. Alienate D. Atheist
   E. None of these
2. JOYOUS
   A. Pathetic B. Cruel
   C. Native D. Gay
   E. None of these
3. TRANSIENT
   A. Discredit B. Vague
   C. Eternal D. Meek
   E. None of these
4. GAIETY
   A. Pleasure B. Melancholy
   C. Dull D. Warm
   E. None of these
5. STALE
   A. Fresh B. Massive
   C. Dirty D. Amiable
   E. None of these
6. THRIVE
   A. Decline B. Ruin
   C. Favour D. Link
   E. None of these
7. LUSCIOUS
   A. Insipid B. Fickle
   C. Retrograde D. Relish
   E. None of these
8. AMATEUR
   A. Amiable B. Staunch
   C. Timid D. Veteran
   E. None of these
9. YIELD
   A. Resist B. Tasteful
   C. Cheerful D. Brimful
   E. None of these
10. FRAIL
   A. Weak B. Delicate
   C. Healthy D. Unicorn
   E. None of these
11. SUBLIME
   A. Unholy B. Ridiculous
   C. Yielding D. Submitting
   E. None of these
12. WEAN
   A. Resign B. Artlessness
   C. Guile D. Art
   E. None of these
13. PLENTY
   A. Enough B. Much
   C. Less D. Lack
   E. None of these
14. RELISH
   A. Sublimity B. Relevant
   C. Dislike D. Love
   E. None of these
15. SYNTHESIS
   A. Thesis B. Diagnosis
   C. Analysis D. Prognosis
   E. None of these
16. MEAGRE
   A. Fabulous B. Hard
   C. Continuous D. Small
   E. None of these

17. PERENNIAL
A. Rare B. Regular
C. Frequent D. Lasting
E. None of these

18. REBUKED
A. Invited B. Awarded
C. Praised D. Received
E. None of these

19. BALANCE
A. Disbalance B. Debalance
C. Imbalance D. Misbalance
E. None of these

20. ALIEN
A. Resident B. Domiciled
C. Native D. Foreign
E. None of these

21. EXPEDITE
A. Defer B. Delay
C. Postpone D. Adjourn
E. None of these

22. STEADFAST
A. Humble B. Sincere
C. Fickle D. Brave
E. None of these

23. MAGNANIMITY
A. Meanness B. Jealousy
C. Poverty D. Enmity
E. None of these

24. EXTRAVAGANCE
A. Poverty B. Alike
C. Luxury D. Economy
E. None of these

25. MORBID
A. Cheerful B. Insipid
C. Healthy D. Applying
E. None of these

26. CELESTIAL
A. Spiritual B. Psychic
C. Internal D. Material
E. None of these

27. MALICIOUS
A. Boastful B. Kind
C. Indifferent D. Generous
E. None of these

28. HOLLOW
A. Strong B. Weak
C. Solid D. Perfect
E. None of these

29. ABHOR
A. Applaud B. Respect
C. Dislike D. Admire
E. None of these

30. IMPERTINENT
A. Smooth B. Healthy
C. Inadequate D. Respectful
E. None of these

31. PRUDENT
A. Injudicious B. Inconsiderate
C. Reckless D. Weak
E. None of these

32. CULPABLE
A. Blameless B. Careless
C. Defendable D. Restoration
E. None of these

33. MASSIVE
A. Heavy B. Short
C. Meagre D. Complete
E. None of these

34. POSSESS
A. Deny B. Agree
C. Approval D. Relinquish
E. None of these

35. SUBTRACTION
A. Multiplication B. Division
C. Addition D. Contraction
E. None of these

36. OBSESS
A. Divert B. Haunt
C. Notice D. Harass
E. None of these

37. EXTENUATE
A. Quality B. Enhance
C. Offhand D. Palliate
E. None of these

38. CORRIGIBLE
A. Covetous B. Obverse
C. Docile D. Incorrigible
E. None of these

39. ONEROUS
A. Visitor B. Feed
C. Irresistible D. Easy
E. None of these

40. WANTON
A. Total B. Revolve
C. Entire D. Discreet
E. None of these

41. JARGON
A. Slang B. Silly
C. Language D. Terminology
E. None of these

42. ABSURD
A. Adorn B. Flourish
C. Scarcity D. Rational
E. None of these

43. OSTENTATIOUS
A. Centre
B. Height
C. Boastful
D. Modest
E. None of these

44. MACABRE
A. Attractive
B. Trash
C. Gruesome
D. Splendour
E. None of these

45. FALLACY
A. Error
B. Truth
C. Blunder
D. Abandon
E. None of these

46. IMBECILE
A. Heretic
B. Idiotic
C. Bewitched
D. Clever
E. None of these

47. PALLIATE
A. Aggravate
B. Extenuate
C. Miraculous
D. Purchase
E. None of these

48. LOATH
A. Reluctant
B. Haste
C. Willing
D. Brisk
E. None of these

49. FRAGILE
A. Abrasion
B. Horrid
C. Strong
D. Brittle
E. None of these

50. BLOOMING
A. Mild
B. Flowering
C. Fading
D. Bright
E. None of these

51. PROGRESSIVE
A. Unprogressive
B. Disprogressive
C. Non-progressive
D. Retrograde
E. None of these

52. LASTING
A. Everlasting
B. Elastic
C. Transient
D. Non-elastic
E. None of these

53. FUTILITY
A. Utility
B. Fertility
C. Unfertility
D. Keenness
E. None of these

54. SENTIMENTAL
A. Callous
B. Romantic
C. Prosaic
D. Emotional
E. None of these

55. OMINOUS
A. Auspicious
B. Favourable
C. Horrible
D. Encouraging
E. None of these

56. VIRTUOUS
A. Corrupt
B. Scandalous
C. Cunning
D. Vicious
E. None of these

57. IMPASSE
A. Continuation
B. Combination
C. Resurgence
D. Breakthrough
E. None of these

58. EPILOGUE
A. Epigram
B. Dialogue
C. Prelude
D. Postscript
E. None of these

59. SQUANDERING
A. Saving
B. Boarding
C. Discarding
D. Caring
E. None of these

60. FLAGITIOUS
A. Vapid
B. Frivolous
C. Innocent
D. Ignorant
E. None of these

61. LEND
A. Borrow
B. Hire
C. Pawn
D. Cheat
E. None of these

62. BENIGN
A. Friendly
B. Malevolent
C. Wise
D. Unwise
E. None of these

63. GUILE
A. Bubble
B. Growl
C. Candour
D. Deceit
E. None of these

64. CONCORD
A. Bestow
B. Discord
C. Consolidate
D. Outline
E. None of these

65. BUCOLIC
A. Urbane
B. Rustic
C. Vindictive
D. Pastoral
E. None of these

66. JOVIAL
A. Sagacity
B. Fixed
C. General
D. Gloomy
E. None of these

67. DIDACTIC
A. Leading
B. Misleading
C. Unfair
D. Warbling
E. None of these

68. OFFICIOUS
A. Aloof
B. Intrusive
C. Alight
D. Blunt
E. None of these

69. ZEALOT
A. Moderate
B. Devotee
C. Plaint
D. Bigot
E. None of these

70. HOOT
A. Jostle
B. Tint
C. Uproar
D. Honour
E. None of these

71. CARICATURE
A. Glory
B. Fidelity
C. Prim
D. Painting
E. None of these

72. MENIAL
A. Noble
B. Notion
C. Humble
D. Servile
E. None of these

73. GLIB
A. Fluent
B. Misty
C. Ready
D. Hesitating
E. None of these

74. AXIOM
A. Angle
B. Height
C. Maxim
D. Absurdity
E. None of these

75. VIVACIOUS
A. Quickness
B. Lively
C. Nice
D. Dull
E. None of these

76. PRODIGAL
A. Preface
B. Hasty
C. Frugal
D. Reckless
E. None of these

77. IRK
A. Amuse
B. Exodus
C. Iota
D. Annoy
E. None of these

78. FABLE
A. Peevish
B. Forge
C. Fact
D. Devil
E. None of these

79. FLUX
A. Swerve
B. Motion
C. Wince
D. Stillness
E. None of these

80. SPURIOUS
A. Barren
B. Dissipate
C. Genuine
D. Weak
E. None of these

81. IMPLICATE
A. Extricate
B. Hinted
C. Involve
D. Lazy
E. None of these

82. GRUESOME
A. Grisly
B. Stern
C. Disgusting
D. Attractive
E. None of these

83. CAPRICIOUS
A. Yielding
B. Concentrate
C. Unchanging
D. Volume
E. None of these

84. ABJURE
A. Deny
B. Hate
C. Acknowledge
D. Disown
E. None of these

85. COMIC
A. Tragic
B. Fearful
C. Emotional
D. Horrible
E. None of these

86. MORTAL
A. Eternal
B. Divine
C. Immortal
D. Spiritual
E. None of these

87. DENSITY
A. Clarity
B. Intelligence
C. Rarity
D. Brightness
E. None of these

88. CERTAIN
A. Important
B. Famous
C. Fixed
D. Doubtful
E. None of these

89. DEAR
A. Worthless
B. Priceless
C. Free
D. Cheap
E. None of these

90. ENCOURAGE
A. Discourage
B. Disapprove
C. Warn
D. Dampen
E. None of these

91. MITIGATE
A. Exclusion
B. Appease
C. Aggravate
D. Innate
E. None of these

92. LUSTRE
A. Hide
B. Splendour
C. Lie
D. Gloom
E. None of these

93. OBSCURE
A. Lucid
B. Glory
C. Distinct
D. Noisy
E. None of these

94. PROFANE
A. Holy
B. Dupe
C. Divine
D. Hoary
E. None of these

95. PRESAGE
A. Rash B. Indication
C. Benefit D. Fulfilment
E. None of these

96. CATACLYSM
A. Quibble B. Deluge
C. Peace D. Conjecture
E. None of these

97. USURP
A. Custom B. Assume
C. Inherit D. Origin
E. None of these

98. TACITURN
A. Loquacious B. Unbound
C. Chattering D. Stunted
E. None of these

99. RECKLESS
A. Cautious B. Careless
C. Deprave D. Headless
E. None of these

100. ENNOBLE
A. Degrade B. Loud
C. Dignity D. Void
E. None of these

101. AID
A. Agreement B. Persuasion
C. Hindrance D. Support
E. None of these

102. TRANSPARENT
A. Vivid B. Ominous
C. Opaque D. Shaggy
E. None of these

103. CONCEALED
A. Revealed B. Secret
C. Denied D. Quiet
E. None of these

104. ADORN
A. Deform B. Decorated
C. Attraction D. Numbness
E. None of these

105. POIGNANT
A. Scarce B. Scanty
C. Frugal D. Blissful
E. None of these

106. MEEK
A. Disabuse B. Arrogant
C. Disregard D. Sharp
E. None of these

107. QUEER
A. Usual B. Chaos
C. Sage D. Admire
E. None of these

ANSWERS

1	2	3	4	5	6	7	8	9	10
D	A	C	B	A	A	A	D	A	C
11	12	13	14	15	16	17	18	19	20
A	B	D	C	C	D	A	C	C	C
21	22	23	24	25	26	27	28	29	30
B	C	A	D	A	D	D	C	D	D
31	32	33	34	35	36	37	38	39	40
C	C	C	D	C	A	B	D	D	D
41	42	43	44	45	46	47	48	49	50
C	D	D	A	B	B	A	C	C	C
51	52	53	54	55	56	57	58	59	60
D	C	A	C	A	D	D	C	A	C
61	62	63	64	65	66	67	68	69	70
A	B	C	B	A	D	B	A	D	D
71	72	73	74	75	76	77	78	79	80
B	A	D	D	D	C	A	C	D	C
81	82	83	84	85	86	87	88	89	90
A	D	C	C	A	C	C	D	D	A
91	92	93	94	95	96	97	98	99	100
C	D	A	A	D	C	C	A	A	A
101	102	103	104	105	106	107			
C	C	A	A	D	B	A			